In God's Country

In God's Country

The Patriot Movement and the Pacific Northwest

David A. Neiwert

WSU
PRESS

Washington State University Press
Pullman, Washington

Washington State University Press
PO Box 645910
Pullman, WA 99164-5910
Phone 800-354-7360; FAX 509-335-8568
Copyright 1999 by the Board of Regents of Washington State University
All rights reserved
First printing 1999

Library of Congress Cataloging-in-Publication Data

Neiwert, David, 1956-
    In God's country : the patriot movement and the Pacific Northwest / by David A. Neiwert.
      p. cm.
    Includes bibliographical references and index.
    ISBN 0-87422-175-7 (pbk. : alk. paper)
    1. Militia movements—Northwest, Pacific. 2. Government, Resistance to—United States. 3. Right-wing extremists—Northwest, Pacific. 4. Radicalism—Northwest, Pacific. 5. Militia movements—Montana. 6. Radicalism—Montana. 7. Right-wing extremists—Montana. I. Title.
HN79.A19N45   1999
322.4'2'0973—dc21
                                               98-50203
                            HN   CIP
                            79
                            A19
                            N45
Cover image: A farm near Roundup, Montana.   1999

Sleep comes like a drug
In God's country
Sad eyes, crooked crosses
In God's country

—U2

Contents

Acknowledgments

THIS PROJECT WOULD NOT HAVE BEEN possible without assistance from many people—from researchers, law-enforcement officials, and academics who provided important factual and conceptual information, to family and friends who provided support of a more personal nature.

I especially wish to thank my friends and colleagues in journalism—Bill Morlin of the Spokane *Spokesman-Review*; Clair Johnson of the *Billings Gazette*; Jane Kramer of *The New Yorker*; Scott North of the *Everett Herald*; Cathy Logg of the *Bellingham Herald*; David Johnson of the *Lewiston Tribune*; Frank Lockwood of the *Idaho Statesman*; and free-lance writer David Newman of Seattle—for doing much of the legwork that let me compile the factual grounding on which I built my own reportage. This book could not have happened without them.

I also relied on the excellent research work of a wide range of non-profit human-rights organizers and academics who have focused their attention on the problems posed by the Patriot movement. I am especially indebted to Daniel Junas, a Seattle political researcher (and longtime friend) who in 1994 first alerted me to the building militia movement; Susan DeCamp of the Montana Association of Churches; Ken Toole of the Montana Human Rights Network; Bill Wassmuth and Eric Ward of the Northwest Coalition Against Malicious Harassment; Robert Crawford of the Coalition for Human Dignity; Devin Burghardt of the Center for New Community; Chip Berlet of Political Research Associates; Michael Reynolds of Klanwatch; economist Alexander Khan of Princeton University; and Dr. James Aho, professor of sociology at Idaho State University. I am also deeply grateful to Calvin Greenup's attorney, John Smith of Missoula, for his insight and help.

I also owe a debt of personal gratitude to the many friends and family members around the Northwest who provided me with lodging and companionship during my travels collecting material: my brothers, Eric Neiwert of Portland, Oregon, and Barry Neiwert of Hailey, Idaho; my sister, Becky Spiker of Boise, Idaho; my parents, Leonard and Delone Neiwert of Boise; my siblings-in-law, Anne and Kurt Keith of Bozeman, Montana, and Denise and Chris Dowling Johnson of Spokane, Washington; friends Jim and Joan Hinds of Bend, Oregon; Tom and Lori Webster of Missoula, Montana; Gary and Shannon Jahrig of Missoula; Monica Vandermars of Noxon, Montana; Brian and Val Beesley of Lewiston, Idaho; and Randy Fife of Moscow, Idaho. I owe a special debt to my parents-in-law, Tom and Diana Dowling of Helena, Montana, not only for food and lodging, but also for their editing and proofing help and being there as invaluable sounding boards.

And most of all, this project would never have gotten off the ground, let alone completed, without the moral and material support—as well as the diligent editing and editorial help—of my precious wife, Lisa J. Dowling.

This book is dedicated to my grandparents: Rose and Mel Aslett, and Ruth and Alex Neiwert.

Foreword / Notes of a Native Son

THE MORNING AFTER the world exploded in Oklahoma City, I telephoned John Trochmann.

Trochmann, the leader of the Militia of Montana, had rambled at length to me the previous November about the significance of April 19 throughout history—so much so that I had circled the date in red in my calendar book. Now, as I watched the smoking rubble of the Murrah Building and the gory terror unfolding on my television screen, I wanted to know what he meant.

"It's the track record of the federal government, the British government," he told me. "In 1993 Waco burned. In 1992 they tried to raid Randy Weaver the first time. In '43, Warsaw burned. In 1775, Lexington burned. That's when they tried to take our guns the first time."

Right. I remembered that much from our first interview.

That's not all, he said. "It is also the beginning day of the Satanic preparations for the grand climax, according to the Satanic calendar. And I got this from a witch, a former witch out of a coven in St. Cloud, Minnesota. Their preparation for the sacrifice is April 19th to 26th.

"The grand climax, which is what they're preparing for, is the 26th through the 31st, in which they have oral, anal or vaginal sex with females ages 1 to 25. They don't take infants."

OK. Um . . . What do you think happened yesterday?

"Well, with the information that's rolling in, it becomes very interesting. We've got a seismographic machine that's recorded 15 miles from the site: two separate blasts, eight seconds apart. One was the vehicle outside and one was the technical blast inside. High-tech blast, high, high, high-tech."

"We got a call at 11:30 last night from Special Forces, being questioned, 'Where were you?' It continues today."

You guys are suspects?

"Oh, I think they're going to try to use it. First off, they say that there's three olive-skinned people from the Middle East that were doing it with the rig parked outside. Then we find out that that same morning NORAD was under Level 2 Alert, which is lockdown, nobody comes or goes.

"Then we find out the Kitty Hawk, the carrier fleet [with] the Kitty Hawk, is heading into the Indian Ocean. And another carrier fleet, is heading into the eastern Mediterranean. What is all this connected to?

"We have two witnesses now that say there was a black helicopter hovering over that building earlier in the day, earlier in the morning.

"I think the most significant thing is the seismographic machine measuring two blasts, and it does not measure echoes, as the FBI is trying to defend. We full well believe that it's an inside job to justify their future deeds here, to give them justification for coming after—whoever."

Trochmann, of course, was suggesting it was a setup to justify a crackdown on militias. I tried to suggest the more plausible explanation: Wasn't it possible that someone from the militia movement actually carried it out in retaliation for Waco?

Trochmann was offended: "Well, don't you find that kind of strange? We the people are extremely upset for them killing all those babies, and here we go kill more babies? Does that make sense to you?

"But look at the April 19 track record. It's not us that has it, or anyone else that has it. It's these shadow governments that has that track record of April 19. And it's all British involved."

I chatted John up a little more—talked about his pending case in the wake of his arrest outside the county jail in Roundup, Montana. I ask for a few more new fliers and books. (As always, he sent them promptly.) He offered some parting advice: "Keep an eye out." Good old John. He has a way of making even non-believers paranoid.

If it was a setup to pin a disaster on the militias, though, it took several days for the media co-conspirators to catch on. Over the next day or so, most of the speculation over who drove a Ryder truck into the heart of Oklahoma City and set off a massive bomb centered on Middle Easterners. A few unfortunate Muslims had to put up with having their homes searched and privacy violated as the accidental spotlight wrought by the search for a suspect—any suspect—played out in various locales. But by noon on Friday, the early word started to come over the wire: the bombing might have been connected to militias.

By mid-afternoon, it was official. Police were searching for two Caucasian males, identified only as John Doe 1 and John Doe 2, and Attorney General Janet Reno was refusing to comment on speculation that the militia was involved. Then, word came that police had arrested a suspect matching the description of John Doe No. 1.

His name: Timothy McVeigh. He was a hard-core follower of the militia movement, and he had rented the yellow Ryder truck that had carried the bomb that destroyed the Murrah Building. The same afternoon, a friend of McVeigh's, Terry Nichols, also turned himself in to police as word of McVeigh's arrest spread. Nichols didn't match the description of John Doe 2 (who has never been found), but his long-term connection with McVeigh and the militia movement was self-admitted. A third player in the plan, Michael Fortier of Kingman, Arizona, eventually pleaded guilty to federal weapons charges. In exchange for not being charged in the conspiracy, Fortier agreed to be a government witness in the case against McVeigh and Nichols.

As the story unfolded over the next weeks and months, partly with Fortier's help, it became clear that the trio had hatched the plan to bomb a federal building as an outgrowth of their ideology: to strike back at what they saw as a tyrannical government bent on destroying the U.S. Constitution. McVeigh in particular had become obsessed with the FBI's fatal raid on the Waco, Texas, Branch Davidian compound on April 19, 1993, in which 75 people died, fully convinced the agents had actually murdered the people inside. The conspirators' beliefs mirrored those commonly expressed at militia meetings; these three merely had acted on them.[1]

If there was a shock in all this, it was at the surprising competence of these mass killers. The standard media portrayal of the people who had been forming militias was of a scruffy, amateurish collection of beer-bellied louts and loudmouths who liked to bellyache about everything in sight—especially the government. They liked to shoot their guns in the woods and grunt around on military-style obstacle courses. And they had ties to racist hate groups.

Every stereotype, of course, has its foundation in reality, and this movement seems to attract plenty of people who fit the description. But the typecasting also creates a dangerously shallow perception of what the militias represent, the danger they signal.

It is often called (by a breathless press, usually) the militia movement, but that is something of a misnomer. For starters, this is not a movement about armed units organizing in the woods and practicing military maneuvers—such activities are among the things some of its followers engage in, but not many of them, really, and these only reflect secondarily what the movement is really all about.

Rather, the work of organizing militias is only one of several strategies the movement employs to achieve its end, which is nothing less than a complete political transformation of the United States. It intends to achieve this revolution through the creation of its own alternative legal, political and economic system, which it promotes largely through so-called "common law" schemes. The militias are merely intended to enforce and defend the system.

I prefer the name used by followers: the Patriot movement. As it gained momentum in the Pacific Northwest in the early 1990s, the movement's followers called themselves "Christian Patriots," reflecting the essentially fundamentalist outlook of its believers.[2] But as the movement shifted its recruiting efforts to more secular segments of aggrieved society—particularly among gun-rights partisans and military personnel—the "Christian" phraseology dropped to the background, though the fundamentalist strain did not; most of them like to argue from the original text of the Constitution as though it were Biblically inerrant. By 1995, all of these followers were content to refer to themselves as being part of "the Patriot movement."

(This is not to suggest that these believers are in fact patriotic Americans, other than in their own minds—rather the contrary is the case if one examines their essentially anti-democratic agenda. Using a capital P, I hope, will sufficiently differentiate Patriots from people of a more genuinely patriotic mold.)

The term is in some respects broad because the people who could be said to be involved in the Patriot movement are quite diverse in their beliefs and activities. They range from the cross-burning Christian Identity followers of the Hayden Lake variety to the buttoned-down advocates of "constitutionalism," from the bomb-flinging robbers of the Phineas Priesthood to the seemingly mild-mannered "sovereign citizens" who quietly form "common law" courts.

It is not so broad a term, however, that it cannot be usefully defined. The Patriot movement is an American political ideology based on an ultranationalistic and selective populism which seeks to return the nation to its "constitutional" roots—that is, a system based on white Christian male rule. Its core myth is that such a reactionary revolution will bring about a great national rebirth, ending years of encroaching moral and political decadence wrought by a gigantic world conspiracy of probably Satanic origins.

Patriot movement beliefs are deeply held with religious fervor. They promote a fearful, paranoid worldview that isolates believers from the mainstream of society. The movement is expressly antagonistic to democracy, promoting a political agenda that would end most of the institutions and constitutional protections that, for the mainstream at least, effect social justice in America, replacing them with a theocratic hierarchy founded on racist, ostensibly Old Testament-based beliefs. Its violent rhetoric and threatening demeanor poison the well of public discourse and inspire some of its less stable followers to commit acts of extreme violence. The movement's leaders, however, are adept at obfuscating their role in these violent acts by diversionary tactics, the use of Orwellian Newspeak, and endless conspiratorial theorizing. The public only becomes more unsure about whose story to trust.

Moreover, outside of the occasional armed standoff and terrorist plot, most Americans see the movement as hardly an important threat. It seems to have become manifest only in distant parts of the country and attracts a less-than-threatening following.

Boston *Globe* columnist Jeff Jacoby, with whom I occasionally correspond, put it this way to me once. "To a Bostonian, they are a remote irritation with no visible impact on mainstream media, culture, or politics," he wrote. "To the extent that I think of hate groups in [the Northwest] at all, I probably think: If the worst problem we have is a bunch of survivalist anti-Semites hiding out in the Idaho woods, we're doing okay. It's hard—from where I sit—to view them as a problem worth taking seriously."

Jacoby neatly voices the mainstream world's common-sensical, but problematic, attitudes about the significance of the Patriot movement in their own lives. American culture is so thoroughly geared to a white-collar urban perspective that the goings-on in the blue-collar, working-class rural world seem hardly to be worth our time. The reality is that while the Patriot movement is relatively small yet in numbers, it is significantly widespread, manifesting itself in virtually every rural county in the country.

The movement itself represents a real challenge to the nation's identity. Patriots don't simply want to escape society; they want to "save" it. And their plan to save it probably would destroy everything people in the mainstream think of as the basis of a just society: equal opportunity free of racial discrimination; equal protection under the law; and equal political power.

Their agenda has been around for a long time, lurking before in the backwaters of fringe hate groups that over the years have come to make their home in the Pacific Northwest. But the overtly racist features of these groups ensured their long-term marginalization and limited influence. The Patriot movement, on the other hand, represents a mutation of the belief system to one that disguises the racial and anti-democratic implications of its agenda and emphasizes, instead, its populist appeal across a broad range of issues, all wrapped in the bright colors of American nationalism. In the Patriot movement, just about any national malady—unemployment, crime, welfare abuse, drugs, abortion, even natural disasters—can be blamed on the "un-American" federal government or the New World Order. If you don't like gun control, or the way your kids are being taught in school, or even the way the weather has affected your crops this year, the Patriot movement can tell you who's to blame.

The movement's recruits are not gullible in the usual sense. Indeed, many of them are deeply suspicious people whose fear and distrust is focused on the modern urbanized world. The Patriots attract these people precisely because they claim to be able to peel back the curtain and reveal to the select few what is really going on behind the Wizard of Oz's facade. The idea of possessing such knowledge is very appealing to anyone, particularly people who feel the world has disenfranchised them, because it offers special empowerment that few others possess.

Behind the curtain, of course, is a nefarious scheme to enslave all of mankind. What is the New World Order? In the Patriots' world, it is simply the same dirty conspirators (the Council on Foreign Relations and the Trilateral Commission) who have been in cahoots with World Communism all these years, and now they're creating pretexts for moving in with military equipment and instituting a police state. As proof, the Patriots offer a mind-boggling blizzard of blurry photographs of military equipment loaded onto rail cars and obscure government documents with "revealing language"—the shreds of the real world out of which the Patriots have woven a gigantic tapestry of impending apocalypse.

Don't ask why these stories go unreported in the mainstream press, because to the Patriots, it's self-obvious the media are part of the conspiracy, covering up the "real story." The Patriots, as with most purveyors of conspiracy theories (from UFO abductions to Elvis sightings), rely on people's skepticism—particularly the widespread belief in a "liberal bias" in the journalism business—as an inroad for their claims in this regard. The media's failure (outside of the tabloids) to report on these goings-on is taken as proof of the cover-up itself.

The opening into which the Patriot movement and other conspiracists have leapt is the gap between public perceptions of what journalists do and what they really do. Over my 20 years of newspaper work, I've tried to track down my share of unbelievable tales to see if there was any truth to them—everything from stories of nighttime demonic rituals to alien abductions to lake-dwelling monsters to bizarre kidney removals. There never is anything credible to report when you investigate the factual grounding of these stories—people always hear the tales from "a friend of a friend," and if you try to track down the source, you proceed into a series of blind alleys. No one in the business of doing responsible reporting will even bother to print that there is nothing to a story beyond a rumor—unless, of course, the rumors start growing wildly out of hand, which is sometimes known to happen. Journalists as a rule believe that reporting crazy stories without any evidence they're real is nothing but irresponsible rumor-mongering, and they're right. But conspiracists turn the media's responsibility against them; what in fact is constraint is widely believed to be a cover-up.

And so the movement operates at will in that nether world, where suspicions run so deep they breed a kind of selective credulousness. People who are skeptical of any legitimate and reasonable explanation of anything that might be construed as unusual are seemingly willing, in a perverse sort of way, to believe virtually any concoction that might reinforce their growing new worldview—the "alternative" universe of the Patriots—even if it comes from people who to a mainstream observer are clearly raving, racist lunatics. The extreme skeptics become extremely gullible.

The people who are drawn into the Patriot belief system are often Joe and Mary Smith from next door, or their son and daughter-in-law, or maybe John down the street who just got out of the Army: decent, caring, upright, otherwise seemingly normal people. Many of them live in rural areas. And they're not the least bit racist, or at least don't believe they are. They may have told a Polish joke or two, and might have laughed at a "Rastus n' Liza" joke in their time. If they are racist at all, it may be in a predilection to believe they can presume some kind of personal characteristics—be it superior skills at math among Asians or superior athleticism among blacks—but they probably don't dislike or fear people because they're black or Jewish and probably don't blame the problems of the world on an entire race or religion.

At the same time, they are people who feel disenfranchised. In the agrarian Pacific Northwest—Washington, Oregon, Idaho and Montana—where the economic cruelties of living off the land have hit hard in recent years, the anger level is rising. The ground is fertile for finding a scapegoat.

The region's national image as the last pristine, unspoiled corner of the country draws people who want to escape the same big-city problems that are the scourge of the Patriot movement. When Patriot believers living in cities around the rest of the country make their move to get out, to get back to the land, they most often move to the Northwest. This is not merely by coincidence. In fact, the Northwest was specifically targeted in the 1980s by the Patriots' antecedents in the radical right as the place to form a new "white homeland," an image that continues to resonate through the movement today.

One of the Northwest's peculiarities is that, in terms of sheer geographic size, the bulk of the region is dominated by blue-collar rural dwellers. Urban, suburban and semi-urban places are relegated to a few concentrated locations. Yet, in terms of population concentration (and thus political power), the region is dominated by these pockets. So the vast portion of the Northwest's landscape is occupied by people whose ability to control that land, which is a function of the political process, is limited and sometimes nonexistent, and often instead in the hands of people in those few urban patches.

These rural areas are resource-driven economies—crops, timber, grazing, mining—subject to all of nature's vagaries. Most of all, their economies are dependent on what their goods can fetch on the market—a factor set by distant forces in places like Chicago and New York, operating mostly out of the general view and often mysteriously. When the market's not paying, and people are having a hard time making a living, the situation breeds mistrust and an accusatory environment. In the past 15 years, as the United States has shifted to a service economy, the people left behind in the manufacturing and resource sectors have suffered.

Further deepening their disenfranchisement is the suspicion that, not only is their way of life viewed with deep contempt, but there is an active campaign to eradicate it. Rural dwellers feel acutely the sneering ridicule that lies behind the "hayseed" stereotype, and can be defensive about it when conversing with city folk. When, at the same time, they see millworkers and loggers being laid off, longtime grazing lands being locked up, and mining operations being shut down, it is not a far leap for them to conclude that they have become expendable in the eyes of the urbanites who are deciding their fates.

This ancient tension between rural and urban—as old, at least, as the fable of "The Country Mouse and the Town Mouse"—becomes a central factor in the way the region's defining issues, the ones that really stir people's passions, are played out, affecting every political race from local to national, and similarly every policy decision. At stake is the quality of life, particularly the interwoven web of land-use, property-rights, game-management and environmental issues, vital to nearly every person who lives in the region. At the same time, matters of deeply held personal belief—abortion, gun control, education, taxes and gay rights—stir the political pot with the same passion. In either case, the sides tend to divide along rural and urban lines.

All of this builds a widening anger in the Northwest that focuses on a government carrying out urban-based policy decisions. The radical right, which has always thrived in the land of the disempowered—promising its dwellers a national rebirth that will return them to power—correctly saw the region as a potential future power base. After the Aryan Nations was established at Hayden Lake, Idaho, in the 1970s, the concept of a "Northwest homeland" gained wide circulation among the hardcore racists of the old Ku Klux Klan and Posse Comitatus. These people, as well as believers in the racist Christian Identity movement, began moving to the region in the 1980s. By the 1990s, they began making their mark on the region, especially as their emphasis shifted and their agenda was more carefully disguised.

Thus the Pacific Northwest became the cradle of the Patriot movement. Not only is there an avid following here, but possibly its most significant leaders reside here as well. The Militia of Montana is the top distributor of Patriot literature and materials in the nation. Colonel James "Bo" Gritz, founder of an Idaho Patriot enclave and a onetime presidential candidate on the Populist Party ticket, is perhaps the movement's most charismatic figure.

And then there is a claque of radical racist Patriots calling themselves the Freemen, who engaged in a long standoff with police authorities in the plains of eastern Montana. Not only did they successfully defy authorities for nearly two years leading up to the standoff, they also spread their belief system in the months before and during the standoff to most states in the Union. Common-law courts and phony liens, threats against public officials and phony checks suddenly became not just a Northwest problem, but a national one.

Most of the movement's leaders arrived from elsewhere, but they found a notable recruitment base in the small towns, the forested hillsides and the big, open plains, among people who are desperate for answers to their problems. These are people I know. I am a fourth-generation Idahoan, with deep roots in the state's southern half. Most members of my family are typical Idahoans, largely blue-collar construction workers and farmers. Not terribly well educated, but decent and hard-working, genuinely patriotic, and usually conservative. They're like people elsewhere: in Oklahoma, Michigan, Pennsylvania, California, Texas. In those places, too, the Patriot movement is thriving.

So the activity of the Patriot movement here, by virtue of its intensity, may serve as a precursor for the rest of the nation—where many of the same conditions that made the Northwest such fertile ground for the movement also fester and worsen. Likewise, efforts to confront the movement here may provide a model for people elsewhere.

In the past, the challenge posed by so-called hate groups was successfully met merely by marginalizing them, excluding them. They were often painted as an enemy of normal people, and their popular appeal vanished. There is, however, a dilemma inherent in this approach. Racists and hate groups are a problem for society because they engage in demonizing the select objects of their wrath, their scapegoats of the moment. When opposing groups combat the haters by demonizing them, this simply perpetuates their presence, because it participates in the same enemy-naming that began the vicious cycle.[3]

In the instance of the Patriot movement, marginalization is not a viable option. For one thing, it's difficult to label the Patriots a hate group in the fine tradition of the Aryan Nations and the Ku Klux Klan, because the movement's leaders disguise the racial implications of their agenda, and indeed go to great lengths to repudiate imputations of racism or anti-Semitism. Moreover, the movement enjoys too broad a base, drawing its strength by attracting many followers from the mainstream who cannot, and should not, be accused of harboring racist intent.

For communities to successfully confront the Patriot movement, they will need first to resist the impulse to exclude, to marginalize, to dismiss its followers contemptuously. Meeting the challenge will require a simple recognition:

They are not the enemy. They are us.

— Seattle, March 1999

Chapter 1 / Land of the Freemen

THE REPORTER'S FACE is as gray and grim as the winter Montana sky. Having a run-in with the Freemen will do that to you.

The members of his TV crew, parked in the frozen, muddy lot of Jordan's only gas station, are pulling out equipment from the trunk of their car, taking a quick inventory. The reporter watches them pensively. He's screwed and he knows it.

"What's going on?" I ask him.

"We've just been robbed," he says.

I've seen the reporter around town the last couple of days. His name is Tom Cheatham; he's a free-lancer from Los Angeles filing reports for NBC. He says his crew and equipment just flew in from California about a half-hour before at the little Jordan airstrip. They promptly crammed themselves and all their equipment into a rental sedan and headed up the road to the Freemen's compound.

It's still the first week of the standoff, and the perimeter of the compound where the heavily armed Freemen are holed up is being patrolled rather loosely by the FBI and Montana State Patrol officers. You can drive practically right up to and past the ranch on a county road, if you choose.

The Freemen, however, have posted a large sign on this road about a quarter-mile from the ranch, announcing that you are entering "Justus Township," the name they gave their little community. Tacked onto the sign is a piece of poster board with more details, printed in large red letters: "Warning! No Trespass! This means YOU!!!" A drawing of a noose appears with it.

In a land where common sense is a prerequisite to survival, you take such signs at their word and stop there. This is especially so if you're talking about property claimed by adherents of the right-wing "Patriot" movement. And the Freemen are among the most radical of all the Patriots.

Still, there's no gate, and in fact this is a public county road, so it's possible to just keep driving. Which, in this case, is what the NBC crew decided to do.

Big mistake.

"Next thing we know, there's this big white truck that's pulled up behind us," Cheatham tells me. "We get out to talk to them and they tell us to get the hell out of there. So we all get back in the car and head down the road.

"We just stay on the road, because it looks like it will take us out of there. We get far enough away that it looks like we're off their land, so we get out the cameras to try and get a shot of the ranch, because it's still visible.

"All of a sudden, the big white truck is back, and this time they get out with their guns and make a lot of noise. There's a lot of yelling. They take our cameras and some of our other equipment and tell us to leave now. So we did."

He's shaken and wan. We're all shivering a little because of the icy wind driving across the winter-slate landscape, but the reporter's chills run deeper. Not only has he come close to being shot, but now he is without $50,000 worth of uninsured equipment. He can't file stories now or in the near future. He'll have to fold up shop and head back to L.A., hoping to recoup his losses.

"Next time," he says, "I'll pay attention to signs that say 'No Trespassing.'"

Welcome to Montana. Welcome to the Wild West.

The other reporters in town are not surprised, nor are the locals. Everyone knew an ABC camera crew the previous fall had pulled the same stunt as Cheatham's crew and likewise had their cameras confiscated by armed Freemen. In fact, the Freemen now faced a felony robbery charge from that incident in addition to all of their other crimes. A Polish reporter had some potshots taken at him a couple of weeks before that when he tried to approach the ranch. And an Associated Press reporter and photographer had their cameras confiscated and got roughed up a little only a few weeks before the big standoff started.

The Freemen first raised a ruckus in neighboring Musselshell County, where the standoff with law-enforcement officials actually began in 1994. Wanted on a variety of charges involving guns, taxes and money scams, some of their group also had been arrested in an incident in which they purportedly threatened the lives of a local judge and prosecutor. The Freemen leaders—LeRoy Schweitzer, Dan Petersen, Rodney Skurdal and Dale Jacobi—holed up on Skurdal's ranch near Roundup, refusing to surrender to authorities. The local sheriff and prosecutor, knowing the men were heavily armed and likely to resist, tried talking them down, but it was like spitting into the wind.

Among the Freemen's followers were Ralph and Emmett Clark, who meanwhile also began to hide out at their ranch near Brusett, a little post office of a town 120 miles to the northeast, after tax authorities foreclosed on it in 1994. They also had been part of a second incident in which the Freemen tried to take over the Garfield County Courthouse in Jordan. And they too refused to surrender to authorities.

In September 1995, the Freemen in Roundup loaded up a caravan of vehicles in the middle of the night and drove north to Brusett as federal agents stood by and watched. Their forces combined, the Freemen set about creating their own government: "Justus Township," a state separate from the United States, and not under its laws. And they began using the ranch as a center for spreading their beliefs.

★★★

Every weekend for five months after the Freemen made their move north, a stream of cars traversed the gravel roads across the desolate Big Sky plains leading out to the Clark ranch, full of would-be students from all over the country: license plates were from California, Oklahoma, Ohio and Florida. The vans were full of people who paid $300 each to come hear how they, too, could form their own government. Over those five months, the local sheriff says, about 800 people came out to the ranch.

The Freemen also made video tapes of their lessons that they sold for a nominal donation. The videos mostly featured LeRoy Schweitzer, handgun strapped to his hip, standing at the head of a table, showing the class how to attack and undermine the nation's current government.

The first lesson: America is not a democracy. "This is a Republic," says Schweitzer. A corrupt clique of conspirators, he claims, has created a government by corporation, what he calls a false, "de facto" government. The government the Freemen wish to establish is a "theocratic republic," designed specifically to be run only by white male property owners, under what the Freemen call the "organic Constitution." This would be a "de jure" (by right) government of the people.

These beliefs are made explicit in some of the stacks of pseudo-legal liens, edicts and "true bills" the Freemen filed over the previous two years with various local and state elected officials. "We do not submit to foreigners nor aliens to rule over us nor are We the People subject to the laws of man nor the constitutions, for these only apply to their own corporations and their officers, agents, servants and employees," says an "Edict" issued in 1994 by Rodney Skurdal. "We the People must follow our one and only Almighty God; or, you can go on worshipping your new false Baal's and de facto master, i.e., congress and legislators, etc., under their 'color of law,' for you are now their 'slave'; which is contrary to the Word of our Almighty God."

The only Constitution the Freemen recognize is the "organic" one: the main text of the document, and the Bill of Rights, or the first 10 amendments. They believe subsequent amendments perverted the intent of the Founding Fathers and took the nation away from its Christian roots. Topping their list is the 14th Amendment, which they believe creates a separate class of citizenship: federal citizens (minorities and women) and "state" citizens (white males). The Freemen also say the separation of church and state is a myth.

If all this sounds like it has a religious tone, it does. For that matter, religion is the key to the Freemen's beliefs, and they spell out the details in their legal documents:

—There are two "seed lines" within Genesis: one from Adam and Eve, descended through their son Seth, and one from Satan and Eve. "Simply put, Eve had sex with Satan and then Adam," writes Skurdal. Cain, their offspring, went into exile after killing Abel, mating with the "beasts," or mud people created before Adam. "It is the colored people, or the jews, who are the descendants of Cain," says the "Edict."

—Events recorded in II Kings show that the children of Israel were scattered after a war with the Assyrians, or Edomites, and all the tribes but Judah went into exile. These became the northern Europeans, or Aryans.

—Thus, white people are the true children of Israel; black people and other races are merely soulless "pre-Adamic" races. The satanically descended Edomites now call themselves the Jews.[1]

This system of beliefs is called Christian Identity, and adherence to it is probably the single greatest common denominator among all the various fragmented factions of the radical right wing in America. It is practiced by the neo-Nazis of the Aryan Nations, by the leaders of the Militia of Montana, and by remnants of the Ku Klux Klan in the South.

Its foremost preacher is the Reverend Pete Peters, a Colorado-based minister whose 1992 gathering in Estes Park—drawing such luminaries as John Trochmann, Ku Klux Klan leader Louis Beam, and onetime Pat Buchanan adviser Larry Pratt—is often credited with being the chief formative event behind the militia movement.

The core beliefs of Christian Identity are so far astray from those of mainstream Christianity—and so repellent to average Americans—that they induce in the religion's followers a cult-like closed mindset: a sense of persecution coupled with self-righteousness that is supported by the group's social peers. True believers—often drawn from the ranks of the disenfranchised—will not be dissuaded by any amount of logic and reason.[2]

They live in a kind of alternative universe, complex and wholly unlike anything in mainstream life. It is populated by soulless non-humans, satanic conspirators and a handful of true Christians who abide by "God's law." By closing off the other world, they reinforce each other's beliefs in the confines of their tight social circle.

At the stark, isolated setting of the Clark ranch, this cycle reached intense proportions, especially as the Freemen's leaders scoured a library full of law books for documents, rulings and obscure citations that would reinforce their beliefs. Coupled with a siege mentality, the beliefs spun a web that fully ensnared those inclined to join it, putting them outside the reach of longtime neighbors and friends, even family members. Forget about law-enforcement officials.

In the Freemen's world, not only are law enforcement authorities out of control, but the Federal Reserve is a Jewish hoax, money is merely counterfeit currency printed by the conspirators, taxes are an illegal form of blackmail by a renegade corporation that calls itself the United States, and the courts have placed themselves above God's law, thereby issuing a series of satanic and perverted rulings that are destroying the nation. Their solutions:

—Declare yourself a "sovereign citizen" outside the reach of the federal government. Only white male property owners need apply.

—Create "common law" courts comprised solely of "sovereign citizens." These courts are the only really legal courts in the land, they believe. The body of law they hearken to includes not only the "organic" Constitution but also other laws "common" to Western civilization, especially the Magna Carta, and a bevy of outdated codes and federal rulings.

—File liens against the "phony" public officials who may interfere with the functioning of the "common law" courts. If they continue to interfere, the courts may convene trials and, if these officials are found guilty of treason, they may be hung.

—Freemen are free to use those liens as collateral to back up phony money orders printed at the ranch. These money orders are then cashed for Federal Reserve notes or used to purchase items, often for much less than the amount of the money order, and the company filling the orders then reimburses the Freemen for the remaining amount with cash of its own.

Such procedures, of course, are blatantly illegal, and the "common law" courts have no legal standing whatsoever, according to mainstream legal scholars and law-enforcement officials. Moreover, the victims not only are the banks and politicians the Freemen target, but also their neighbors and local businessmen, who have to deal with the consequences of the bad checks and the threat of the phony liens.

Nonetheless, not only do the Freemen promote these schemes as legitimate, they pass their systems along to their students. Streaming out of that ranch in their cars, they return to their homes across the nation and proceed to employ these tactics there. The Freemen's common-law courts have popped up in Ohio, Pennsylvania, California, Texas—indeed, in just about every state in the nation. And with them have appeared the phony liens and bogus checks.

"We're going to make the common law here the law of the land," said Schweitzer in one lesson. "Under the organic states, not the compact party state or the contract state or the shadow state. We're going to do this real. We'll set the tenor of the agreement, and then, let's see what happens."

Schweitzer soon enough had a chance to test his legal theories.

An undercover agent posing as a radio-antenna installer began attending the Freemen's weekend sessions early in 1996, and soon gained the confidence of the group's leaders, including Schweitzer and his star pupil, Dan Petersen, a Winnett car mechanic. When the Freemen expressed an interest in obtaining a more powerful ham radio antenna, the agent offered to set one up on their property. On March 25, an installation crew arrived and spread out the materials on a ridge near the ranch.

The agent asked Schweitzer and Petersen to make a final check of the antenna site, and they readily agreed. They found a phalanx of federal agents waiting for them with guns drawn. Petersen tried to struggle and was knocked down.

The two men were handcuffed and whisked off to the Yellowstone County jail in Billings, 180 miles away to the southwest. A contingent of law-enforcement officials from around the state, both federal and local, immediately surrounded the ranch.

The standoff had begun.

★★★

The next day, the two worlds—the Freemen's and mainstream society's—collided in the federal courtroom in Billings.

LeRoy Schweitzer had the look of a caged tiger: ferocious but not fearful, even defiant. Everything he believed, everything he had been teaching others to believe for the past two years, was about to face its first real test.

Schweitzer, a square-jawed man with piercing blue eyes, is graying and burly, but he clearly keeps himself fit. On his first day before U.S. Magistrate Judge Richard Anderson, he only wore a V-necked white undershirt with his jeans, and his hair was rumpled. His eyes were watery and there was a red mark just below his right eye, possibly the remnant of a struggle at the ranch.

Both he and Dan Petersen, seated to Schweitzer's right, were bound with waist chains and shackles. Petersen is almost the physical opposite of Schweitzer: small, thin and dark, with hawkish black eyes. Both, though, share an intense laser beam of a baleful stare that they turned, respectively, on the judge, the federal prosecutors, the public defenders summoned to assist them, and the press gathered in the gallery.

Their eyes lit up, though, when they got a look at the front row nearest them.

Seated along the long bench was a collection of about a half-dozen friends and fellow Patriots, all gathered to check on the condition of the prisoners, and to offer them moral support. Among them was Petersen's stepson, Keven Entzel. Entzel's mother, Cherlyn Petersen, remained holed up at the Clark ranch.

Before the proceedings had begun, I chatted up a few of the men in the front row. Now I asked a man in a SPIKE hat, seated directly in front of me—Steve McNeil, a tall, thin middle-aged man with a mostly bald head—what he thought the captured Freemen's strategy would be. Would they accept a court-appointed lawyer?

"They'll be their own counsel," he said. "There isn't anybody knows the law better than LeRoy."

He looked darkly around. "Unless . . ." he said. "Unless they've got 'em drugged."

Sure enough, the condition of Schweitzer and Petersen was the chief object of the Patriots' interest when the two prisoners were led to their courtroom seats. "How's he look?" McNeil murmured to the man seated next to him. They noticed the red mark beneath Schweitzer's eye. They noted the red eyes of both men. Drugged? Maybe. Abused? Maybe.

Schweitzer waved with his shackled hands and smiled at his friends. There was a measured sigh of relief.

Assistant U.S. Attorney James Seykora stepped to the dais to open up the arraignment proceedings. Judge Anderson, a steel-haired and steel-eyed man with a sturdy but quiet baritone voice, began to read from the case document. Schweitzer and Petersen immediately jumped in.

"Before any further proceedings, I haven't had a chance to read this so-called indictment," Petersen proclaimed loudly. "I haven't had the chance to read the charge."

The judge looked at him over his glasses: "Would you identify yourself?"

"Dan Petersen."

"You are the defendant, Daniel E. Petersen, Jr.?"

"No, I'm not. I haven't read the charges. I don't know what the charges are. You handed—"

"We're going to get to that," interrupted the judge, "but are you Daniel E. Petersen, Jr.?"

"Yes, sir, I am."

"All right."

"But I am not the defendant, because I haven't read the papers. I was just now served and I was brought in in chains. This isn't due process of law."

Judge Anderson asked Seykora if the two men had been served copies of the indictment, and the prosecutor explained that they had.

"Well, that is a kangaroo court," shouted Petersen. "This was supposed to have been done at the time of the arrest and they have taken my glasses and I can't read this. I can't follow along. I am not sure that you people know how to read."

"We'll read it to you," Anderson retorted. "You won't need your glasses."

Now Schweitzer swung into action. "I'd like to object," he said, standing up and looking about the room. "Is Mr. Schweitzer in the courtroom?" No one answered, but the judge duly noted Schweitzer's query.

"I object to the word Schweitzer, if you are looking at me," he continued. "My Christian name is LeRoy Michael, and that is the only way I'll be referred to."

The judge looked Schweitzer over. "Do you also go by LeRoy Schweitzer?"

"I do not. I will not go by M or all caps. I do not want the non-demur name. That is a legal fiction. I won't take it."

So it went throughout the arraignment. Court officials tried to proceed as they might normally, but could scarcely finish a sentence without being interrupted by either Schweitzer or Petersen.

"I will not be denied common law venue," proclaimed Schweitzer. "I want a jury of my peers. It will be—I'm in the wrong venue. I live in Justus Township."

"Sir," growled the judge, "if you do not restrain yourself, I'll see that you are restrained."

Anderson's warnings seemed to have little effect. Schweitzer and Petersen both kept objecting and haranguing the judge and prosecutor at every turn. The Freemen's disruptive tactics ensured that none of the usual procedures in the courtroom could be observed. When Anderson tried to appoint public defenders to the pair, they shouted out objections ("This is an invasion of my privacy," said Petersen); the judge responded by placing the hapless lawyers on "standby" status. Petersen announced a "writ of prohibition" against the lawyers and the judge. "This man will not represent me," said Schweitzer.

At several points in the hearing, Schweitzer would look to his friends in the front row and then stand up to launch into another tirade, citing verse and chapter of obscure codes. It became clear he believed he was taking effective control of the courtroom, somehow transforming it to a venue for his own common-law court. For a moment, he tried to bring the district court into his world.

"Is there anyone who would deny me my 11th Amendment due process?" he cried. A couple of the men in the front row murmured a response: "None."

Judge Anderson, growing tired of Schweitzer's charade, jumped in, glaring at the gallery. "Did I hear some comment from the back of the room just now?" he demanded to know.

"That will be my justices," said Schweitzer. "They are—"

The judge interrupted. "If there is any further comment from the gallery in the back of the courtroom from anyone back there during these proceedings, other than perhaps whispering just between yourselves, I'll ask the Marshal's service to exclude you." The Patriots in the front row looked at each other knowingly but fell silent.

It did not last long. Petersen protested questions about his own mental competence: "I object and take exception to your libel and slander of my character. I am not a 14th Amendment person as stated in the code book. I go under common law rules." He turned to the gallery. "Any objections?"

"None," came the murmurs in the front row again.

The judge signaled to the rows of marshals lining the courtroom, and they descended on the front row. Three of the Patriots were told they had to leave. Dave Sullivan, seated next to Steve McNeil, objected. "There ain't no ifs," said the marshal. "You're gone."

Sullivan staggered into the aisle, claiming he had an injury, and tried to don his cowboy hat. The marshal forced him to remove it until he had left the courtroom. "Yes, your highness," he responded. The trio were marched out, and the marshals returned. Only Steve McNeil, his son, and Keven Entzel remained in the front row.

"This is a sham proceeding," protested Schweitzer. "My justices have left." He and Petersen began exclaiming loudly, declaring a "writ of mandamus" against the court, citing more verses and chapters of more obscure laws.

Anderson called for a brief recess and consulted with the assembled lawyers how best to proceed, since video-camera equipment which would allow them to place the two men in a sealed room had not yet arrived from Denver. Anderson decided to try bringing them in separately, warning the men that they'd be held in contempt and, if the disruptions continued, to continue the proceedings on a day when the sealed rooms would be an option.

When he returned, Schweitzer again launched into his citations, accusing the judge of being out of order. "You're without power to move forward," he told Anderson. He called for protection of his rights. "Would anyone in the courtroom say that they are going to deny me my 11th Amendment protections?" he asked, looking about the room.

Anderson tried to warn Schweitzer he'd be found in contempt of court. But the Freeman continued his banter. Finally, Anderson gave up. He ordered Schweitzer's arraignment postponed to a later date, and the Freeman leader was led out of the courtroom. Petersen was brought back and, when he too continued his protests, the judge likewise postponed his arraignment.

As Petersen was led from the courtroom, he shouted: "You are in violation of the Constitution. It has been totally suspended. That's justice, folks."

The audience filed out of the courtroom. I walked into the cloakroom to retrieve my recorder. As I was signing the form for its release, Steve McNeil came into the small room with three of the law-enforcement men who had been in the courtroom.

"What do you want?" he asked as they backed him into a corner of the room.

"We're placing you under arrest," one of them said. Suddenly, the door to the cloakroom was closed, and I found myself three feet away from a physical confrontation.

"What for?" McNeil shouted, starting to struggle. The three lawmen began wrestling with him. "For breaking the conditions of your release," said one, struggling to bring one of McNeil's arms behind him.

McNeil began flailing, and the three officers wrestled him face down onto a desk, pulling his arms back and clacking handcuffs onto his wrist. "Ow! Ow!" he shouted, kicking and twisting his torso.

I had backed into a corner to avoid the wrestling match. Another officer finally opened the door and shoved me out. A cluster of reporters stood outside. I joined them and told them what had happened.

Then the door to the cloakroom opened and McNeil, now cuffed and surrounded by lawmen, was carted to the elevator and away. His teenage son bolted down the stairs in pursuit.

The next day, we learned that McNeil had been arrested the month before for paying a batch of traffic fines (failure to carry a license) with one of Schweitzer's bogus money orders. A resident of nearby Gallatin County, he'd been ordered by a judge not to leave town. Gallatin County deputies had read that he planned to attend the arraignment, and showed up to arrest McNeil if he came. He did, and they were there to greet him.

In case there was any question, law-enforcement officials were taking a hard line on the Patriots' antics. Two days later, when Judge Anderson reconvened the court and Dan Petersen again tried to disrupt the proceedings, marshals hauled him off to a soundproof cell with a two-way video-audio feed. When Petersen tried shouting from his cell, the sound blared from the courtroom speakers, and marshals simply switched him off. LeRoy Schweitzer registered his usual long list of complaints and obscure citations, but remained mostly civil throughout the hearing, and the men's arraignment proceeded as usual.

Matters ran more or less the same the next day at the detention hearing: Petersen was escorted out and Schweitzer remained behind, and the proceedings were more or less civil—enough so that Schweitzer persuaded Anderson to allow Petersen to return. As they were led from the courtroom, Petersen made a final stand, shouting out to the gathering: "Give me liberty or give me death." "We won't eat your food or drink your water from the corporation. It's a joke. You've already murdered us. It's going to be worse than Waco."

Schweitzer, too, chimed in. "We will not touch food nor water while held under unlawful detainer," he proclaimed to the gallery. "And that is a common-law right and it is going to start and end here. Where two or more are gathered in the eyes of Almighty Yahweh, we shall prevail."

Then the door closed behind the two Patriots.

The next day, Schweitzer was transferred to a federal prison in Missouri. Petersen remained in Montana. Shortly thereafter, both men ended their hunger strikes, and settled in for the long road to their trial.

★★★

The upside of all this brouhaha, for Montanans at least, was that it helped resurrect the state's image as the home of the Wild West.

Of course, the average daily life in the West, the Pacific Northwest in particular, is more like that of a typical suburbanite in the Midwest than like the cowboy movies whose images are embedded in the American mythos. But the wildness has always been a part of the perception of Montana—the home of Custer's Last Stand, cattle drives, standoffs at high noon and dry gulches. And people from elsewhere still clutch these images as though they were relevant to the present day; some tourists to the state half expect to yet find Indians with bows and arrows lurking behind trees in ambush.

Still, in 1996, long after the demise of the Old West, Montana started to go really wild. First the state removed its speed limits altogether for daytime driving on highways. Then the Freemen's standoff with law enforcement—which actually had been going on for well over a year by that time—escalated into a major media event. The real watershed, though, came a week or so after that, when Unabomber Ted Kaczynski was caught hiding out in a cabin in the western Montana woods.

It's hard to tell if all this wildness and wooliness will hurt or help the state. Will vacationers and the romanticists who think Montana is a wonderful place now stay away, frightened off by all these violent yahoos? To many Montanans—maybe not to the Chamber of Commerce or the Tourism Council, but to just about everyone else—such a development actually would be a blessing.

Personally, I'm rather fond of the nonexistent speed limit. When I drove out here the previous month, the roads were clear and dry—locals were speculating that they were going to get an early spring—and I got to sample the wide-open speedways. It's especially appropriate to drive all-out in the vast scrublands and plains of eastern Montana, because they go on so interminably and the curves in the roadways are few and far between. I found it pretty comfortable to hit about 80. The fun part came when I crossed a rise and zoomed past a county sheriff doing 84. Seeing him in his patrol car, sitting there watching me fly by, gave me one of those flush-faced adrenaline rushes that always accompanies a speeding ticket. But he didn't even blink at me. I drove on and thought: Yeehaw. Welcome to Montana.

About the same time the Jordan standoff erupted, though, winter returned with a vengeance. An ice storm dropped down out of Canada and blasted the state with a layer of snow. It's no fun to drive in. Nobody in their right mind tries to push beyond about 50 or 60 mph, and on many curves you have to drop down to about 35 mph to keep from spinning off the road and into a ditch. I wonder about all these media folk from California and other places where these kinds of conditions are reckoned as something from Neptune. Most of them, I figure, will be so frightened they'll crawl out here doing about 25 mph with the whites of their knuckles showing—which will, after all, get them there safely.

This is especially true of the road between Jordan and Brusett. Brusett is technically the town where the Freemen's ranch is located, but it's really just a meeting hall and a post office in a mobile home at a four-way junction. The gravel on the road out there is thick and heavy, and driving in it has the feel of mashed potatoes. Mixed with ice and snow, it's easy to lose control on it. A couple of weeks later, an FBI agent would be killed in a flipped four-wheel rig on this road. If you want to stay safe this time of year, you learn to slow down.

The only real sign of the federal presence is at the county fairgrounds on the way out of town, where the agencies' coordinating center is located. There are rows of vehicles, some with lights on them and some without, lined up in the big yard. A couple of marshals get out of their jeep and wade through the mud to greet anyone who comes up to the gate. No, they tell me, no one's allowed inside. The only spokesmen who can speak to the media officially are in Billings, they say.

Out at the four-way junction that marks the town of Brusett—comprised of a single-wide trailer that serves as the local post office—the assembled media types have set up a temporary camp, waiting for something to happen. Nothing is happening at all. Word is getting around that there will be a gathering of local ranchers at the nearby Fairview Hall, so now the story has turned into a waiting game. The wind is blowing that steady and insistent way it does on the open plains, like one of those steady headaches that just sits and pushes on your skull all day. It's cold and gloomy and everyone is wondering what the hell they are doing out here. Is this some surrealist joke?

One of the television trucks is providing a pool feed for other crews, and it is hooked up by satellite to New York. The crews hover around outside it, trying to ward off the cold, but still talking, speculating whether there would be an assault soon. Rumors have flown about, but no one's heard anything.

FBI agents approach each newly arrived vehicle and take down information about the occupants. They don't want anyone bringing arms in to the Freemen, so they're stopping and talking to everyone who drives out. After this morning's incident with the NBC crew, they warn everyone sternly to stay away from the ranch—and certainly don't go past that "No Trespass" sign.

Some of the NBC free-lance crew are at the media camp. They're still fuming, but now the shock has had time to sink in. One of them describes the weapons that were brandished on them: a couple of deer rifles, a quick-action shotgun, an assault-style gun. He thinks. "I don't know, hell," he says, "they were guns and they looked big. That's all you see at a time like that."

Most of the media types are staying in Miles City, a mere 90-mile drive away; Billings is a good three hours if you can avoid a wreck. The two motels in Jordan filled up instantly, so only a handful are staying on the scene.

The only people in Jordan who are happy about the sudden media horde are the owners of the motels, the two bars, the one gas station and the three cafes in the little town of about 500. Just about everyone else is disgusted and annoyed by what they see as a plague of locusts, and they blame the Freemen for it.

Worse yet, they hear through the grapevine that militias from around the region, perhaps the country, are planning to march into Jordan soon. Which is why the locals are gathering that morning at Fairview Hall. They start arriving a little before 11 o'clock, and pretty soon there are about 15 or so people, not counting the reporters.

Cecil Weeding, a onetime state legislator and the Clarks' brother-in-law, has called the meeting to prepare for their biggest concern—namely, the arrival of armed outsiders in their back yards. The day before, some Patriots from Bozeman had told television reporters in Billings they planned to proceed to Jordan the next day to "monitor" the situation.

As it happens, no one shows up today. Maybe the roads are too bad. Just as likely, perhaps Steve McNeil's arrest the day before in Billings has dissuaded his fellow Bozeman Patriots from continuing further. So the gathered ranchers start talking about how to deal with the Freemen themselves. Weeding tells the audience he wants the community united in a front against the Patriots—militias, Freemen, common-law advocates—whatever form they take.

Just about everyone in the room agrees. These are all hard-working people. The weather and the years line their faces, and they wear western shirts with snaps on them and woolen hats with flaps, though baseball caps are still the most common headgear. They are concerned about how the fabric of their lives has been ripped up by people who stand against everything they've worked their whole lives being a part of: a whole community.

"We're not a bunch of anti-government hillbillies up here," says Frank Phipps, standing in the front. The audience murmurs its approval.

There now are about 25 ranchers at the meeting. They want the issue resolved soon. They've been pushing to get it resolved for months. They don't like having law-breakers for neighbors.

"We've lived here all our lives and we love it here," said Phipps. "I obey the laws of the land. I pay my taxes."

Cecil Weeding knows from personal experience that getting the Freemen out won't be easy. He was among the community leaders who, last fall, began encouraging the federal agents keeping watch on the ranch to make the needed arrests. Neighbors adjacent to the ranch weren't able to harvest winter wheat or plant spring crops, and they too were being threatened with guns and gunfire. And the purchaser of the Clark ranch in the 1995 foreclosure sale faced the potential loss of his own ranch if he wasn't able to plant this spring. Somebody needed to get these guys out of there.

When the feds continued to wait, some of the ranchers were rumored to be readying their own expedition into the Clark ranch to root them out. Around town, it is widely believed that the rumor was what finally spurred the FBI to action this week.

"This isn't the first time the community has pleaded on its hands and knees to get them out of there," says Weeding.

Some of the folks at these meetings express their cynical views of the Freemen. The Clarks' problems, they tell me quietly, began with just plain, old, poor manage-ment of their ranch and farm operations. Ralph Clark, they say, took thousands of dollars in federal subsidies every year, but he'd blow them on things like a Lincoln Continental, and then he'd get hit with a hailstorm that wiped out his barley crop. Another of the Freemen—Bill Stanton, who's now in jail for threatening a federal judge—would take his subsidies and buy things like big motor homes and trips to Ve-gas.[3]

"These guys are just professional bellyachers who have to blame somebody else for their own damned problems," says one rancher.

"It's nobody's fault but their own they got foreclosed on," says Brett Dailey, a lo-cal rancher. "There's no reason to blame the government. Everybody who has a ranch out here has worked hard to keep it."

Everyone has their say, the reporters pick up some video tape, and the militiamen from Bozeman never show up. Eventually the meeting dissipates; everyone has to get back to work.

The sentiments heard in the meeting hall are echoed back in Jordan, especially at the Hell Creek Bar, one of two local watering holes, owned and operated by Joe Herbold. Herbold's wife is the Garfield County clerk, and she has had to deal with personal threats and bizarre behavior from the Freemen. Joe has no use for them.

The Hell Creek Bar has become Media Central in Jordan. Every journalist in town feels obligated to make a stop there, if not for a beer, then at least for a few interviews. The ability to find a new angle for the next day's news stories is wearing thin. After in-terviewing townspeople, interviewing visitors, and anyone else they can get their hands on, some of the reporters have resorted to journalistic cannibalism: interview-ing each other.

"I don't believe we've got enough people in Jordan for everyone to interview," says Nick Murnion, the sardonic county prosecutor, whose office is a half-block away.

The Hell Creek Bar has a grill, wide-screen TV and pool table—more accommodations than most places in the little town. Joe Herbold—wiry, dark-haired with quick eyes and a drooping mustache—makes a roaring welcome of sorts for most of the visitors. He's getting a kick out of the boost to his business, and the craziness of it all.

"This is an opportunity if you look at it the right way, a chance to show off our little community," says Herbold. "If this were different circumstances, this would be more fun than you could shake a stick at."

Joe is a live wire of a bar owner, chatting up his guests and reveling in the excitement. It puts a lot of the out-of-towners at ease, and helps break the ice between them and the locals.

Charlotte, his wife, is in the same energetic mold. She's an attractive personality, bright and sharp and funny, and makes sure the newbies feel welcome.

Charlotte asks every newcomer if they're a member of the media contingent. If they are, she asks them to sign a register, a yellow legal pad. Then, up on the beautiful old cherry-wood bar, she keeps a jarful of pink tickets. Buy a ticket for a buck, write your name on it, and guess the number of media people signed up on the register on the day the standoff ends. The winner gets the pot. Everyone gets a laugh out of the contest.

Joe and Charlotte's low opinion of the Freemen is widely shared at the bar. Bill, a native Montanan who works as a trapper for the county, says he tried attending a few of Schweitzer's classes. He sympathizes with their concerns, but he couldn't swallow their beliefs: "It's just crazy, if you ask me. And when they start threatening people, well, you have to do something."

Just about everyone in town knows everyone else. Or they're related. Everyone knows someone at the ranch.

One man says his cousin, just a year younger than him, and his best friend all his life, is holed up at Brusett. He says he went out hunting near there last year and was chased off, somewhat politely, by his cousin. He tried hunting in the same area a couple of weeks later and was outright threatened by his old friend, who clacked a gun at him.

"I looked in his eyes," he says, "and I just didn't recognize him. That was nobody I knew anymore." He shakes his head sadly.

This was, I was beginning to find, a common complaint from people whose loved ones had become Patriot believers.

Chapter 2 / Parallel Universe

T HE PATRIOT MOVEMENT appears to operate in the mainstream world, but truthfully, it does not. Rather, its believers reside in a different universe—one dominated by an evil government and a conspiracy to destroy America. Agents of the dark side lurk at every corner; every disbeliever is a pawn. Proof of this hidden reality can be found in everyday news stories and ordinary documents, if only seen with the right eyes.

The alternative reality that is the essence of the Patriot movement is like a big quilt, a patchwork of factual items—United Nations reports, government documents, news stories—that are pieced together with other less credible information—black helicopter sightings, suggestions of troop movements, and the like. The thread that weaves them all together is a paranoid belief in the existence of a vast conspiracy; even if elements of the patchwork don't appear to fit together, the irrational fear driving the movement will overlook inconsistencies. Everyone is free to make a contribution: a military-vehicle sighting here, an obscure document there. Believers are free to ignore some elements of the patchwork if they happen to disagree, so long as the quilt itself hangs together as an all-encompassing blanket.

The dwellers in this otherworld can be found not just among the most radical believers residing in the wilds of Montana, like the Freemen. They can be found seemingly everywhere in the Northwest: in suburban conference centers, in rural town halls, in Bible study groups.

Step into one of the militias' organizing meetings—typically held in small community halls in rural areas and in towns outlying urban centers—and you will have walked into this world.

★★★

It's Sunday, January 14, 1996, in Mount Vernon, a Skagit Valley town of about 30,000 people in western Washington. At the local Best Western's convention room, the Washington State Militia is holding a meeting.

It seems like any other typical community gathering—the Kiwanis or the Lion's Club, say—except the attire might be a bit more informal: lots of flannel shirts and jeans and big belt buckles. I'm just wearing my winter coat, a T-shirt and jeans, so I'm not likely to stand out. The crowd is all ages and sizes and kinds, but middle-aged rural males seem to dominate.

Out in the foyer is a table covered with stacks of fliers. I mill through them. Here's a good one, illustrated with an assault-style weapon: "The Patriot's Prayer: God grant me the serenity to accept the things I cannot change, the courage to change the things I can, and THE WEAPONRY to make the difference! Never Surrender Your Firearms!"

There's a copy of "Sighting In: The Militiaman's Newsletter," house organ of John Pitner's Deming-based Washington State Militia; a copy of a report from the Center for National Security Studies decrying anti-terror legislation; and a copy of a story by retired Arizona sheriff Jack McLamb titled "Now Is the Time For Militias," from McLamb's own "Aid and Abet," a Patriot newsletter aimed at recruiting law-enforcement officers.

One of the fliers is comprised of several sheets stapled together, each one a full-page blowup of a famous or patriotic quote: from Thomas Jefferson, Abraham Lincoln, and Edmund Burke. And this one from Henry Ford: "It is well enough that people of the nation do not understand our banking and monetary system, for if they did I believe there would be a revolution before tomorrow morning."[1]

Revolution is on the minds of this meeting's organizers; this becomes even more evident in the main conference room. At the back of the room, the Militia of Montana (MOM) has set up its standard table setting: books, video tapes, audio tapes, caps and shirts. All are geared to overthrowing the "New World Order."

The crowd mills back and forth, looking over the wares.

Want to find out about the New World Order? Pick up a videotaped copy of "Invasion and Betrayal," MOM's exposé treatment of the conspiracy they claim is trying to overthrow the U.S. Constitution. It features Bob Fletcher, a onetime "researcher" who until just a few months before was the chief speaker at most of MOM's gatherings.

Want to know how to prepare for urban guerrilla warfare? Pick up a copy of *The Road Back to America*. This is William Potter Gale's right-wing classic, now sold by a Kentucky ex-Klansman named Robert Pummer, and once a favorite of people like Robert Mathews, leader of The Order.[2] It contains recipes for pipe bombs, industrial sabotage, and tactical formations in warfare. There's a recipe for ammonium nitrate bombs on page 135. Then, on page 208, you can read some good reasons why public buildings should be targeted: "Sabotage is the art of destruction. Destruction of anything of use to the enemy is a blow for victory."[3]

There's a whole rack devoted to Department of Defense manuals: "Boobytraps," "Guerrilla Warfare," "Hand to Hand Fighting," "Sniper Training and Employment." They're only $5 each and a popular purchase. Most of the video tapes are about $20. There's Congresswoman Helen Chenoweth's "America in Crisis." A video from former Posse Comitatus leader James Wickstrom, a virulent anti-Semite, titled "The Pestilence (AIDS)," about the disease's role in an insidious plan to exterminate millions of people. Or you can get Mark Koernke's militia classic, "America in Peril." Among the other people Koernke has inspired: Timothy McVeigh.

Books range in price from $8 for *Survival Bartering* to $25 for *Primitive Wilderness Living and Survival Skills*. One of the most popular is *Blueprint for Survival*, a $20 manual that covers everything from "Caching Out" to "Retaking America."

You can pick up back copies of "Taking Aim," the MOM newsletter, for a buck apiece. Or there's documentation, like the stapled report on "Weather Modification." The prize piece of all this is "Enemies: Foreign and Domestic," a 200-page montage of MOM's collected evidence of the conspiracy, with an accompanying video tape.

At the end of the table are the fun items: T-shirts ("Had enough? MILITIA"), camouflage baseball caps ("Enough is Enough—Militia"), gas masks and even chemical/biological suits ("Desert Storm issue") at about $40 apiece. The big bearded man behind the row of tables on which all these are arrayed stays pretty busy. MOM only takes cash: no checks or credit cards.

A customer asks: "Are you guys on the Internet?"

"No," the bearded man answers. "We were on the Internet for about five days and it made all of our computers crash. They shut us down pretty quick. So we decided it wasn't worth the risk."[4]

The crowd, numbering about 400 and starting to settle into the seats, is largely nondescript middle Americans. Most of the younger men look very fit, with close-cropped hair, like guys just out of the military or still serving in the National Guard. There's only one obvious skinhead.

The crowd's attention turns to the front of the room as John Pitner steps up to the podium and taps on the microphone. Pitner is in his late 40s, a bit shorter than six feet, balding and thickly built. His gray mustache accentuates his serious demeanor.

Pitner opens with a prayer. When it ends, a man in the crowd says loudly, "Praise Yahweh." Others murmur the same phrase. The Identity folks, it appears, are out in force today.[5]

Pitner welcomes the audience, and notes that there are protesters outside. "We welcome them in too," he says. "And I see our friends in the media are here. All we ask is that you report on us fairly. Some of what's been reported has been fair. Some of it has not."

The crowd applauds.

"As for this," he says, holding up a copy of the *Bellingham Herald* with a story about the militias, including information about MOM's links to racist organizations, "well . . ." Pitner crumples the paper with both hands and tosses it on the floor, in the direction of the reporter who wrote the story, *Herald* staffer Cathy Logg—a fiftysomething grandmother who simply pretends not to notice and keeps scribbling in her notebook.

More applause, and louder. "We know there are some folks from law enforcement out there, from the FBI and ATF," Pitner says. "We welcome them, too, and we hope you learn something from this."

There's a rustling in the audience. People make sideways glances, hoping to detect the undercover agents in their midst. Everyone checks everybody else out. The fear level in the room rises.

The mainstream media, says Pitner, has made the militias out to be terrorists. "Quite the contrary," he says. "We are people who actually love our great nation, love our children, and are quite concerned for their future.

"We are defensive by nature with offensive capabilities *if attacked.* We are now currently engaged in trying to educate our fellow Americans as to the very real threat of the collapse of the American Way that we have come to love and cherish—not only for ourselves, but for our children, and ultimately, to the rest of the world, as many see us as the last hope for freedom and liberty in their own land.

"The Washington State Militia first came into being on April 28, 1993, as I and a few friends were still reeling from the disaster at Waco. We pledged to one another at that time that such a thing would never occur again, if it meant forfeiture of our own lives to prevent it. Thus, the Washington State Militia was born."

Pitner looks down from the sheet he's been reading from, somewhat statically. Public speaking is a new role for him.

"I wanted to basically do a little bit of damage control." He brushes his hand across the remaining strands atop his head. "You don't see any tattoos on my forehead, do you? I am losing my hair, so if that makes me a skinhead, well, I don't know." The crowd chortles.

Pitner turns serious: "Basically, this country is in deep doo-doo. We all know that." He holds up a finger. "Number one. Fact: The federal reserve and everything else with it, we are five trillion dollars in debt. That means every one of our children are $190,000 in debt at birth. Now if that's not something to be afraid of, I don't know what there is to be afraid of.

"It's really bringing an end to the country. Basically, there's a lot of things happening in America today, such as detention facilities being made, such as this heinous law H.R. 666, the counterterrorism bill, a lot of this stuff happening, and it's not whether we're fear-mongers, we're just trying to bring these to the light, public light, let people know what this stuff is.

"I don't call that fear-mongering. But basically, *they* do," he says, pointing outside. The protesters today—about 70 of them are parked outside the front door with signs decrying the goings-on inside—probably represent the first demonstration of any kind against a militia meeting in the Northwest, maybe anywhere. The militiamen are clearly not accustomed to this, and it has them rattled.

Pitner then begins to launch into a smorgasbord of Patriot beliefs, patches on the local quiltwork: detention centers are being built in the state to house large numbers of criminals; your votes aren't really being counted on election night, and all elections are rigged; the drug war is a front for a conspiracy to abrogate people's constitutional rights; that unconstitutional laws, especially gun-control laws, are being foisted upon the public.

"As far as I'm concerned, the sheriff is the supreme law of his county," says Pitner, echoing Posse Comitatus credo. "He's an elected official, and therefore bound by the Constitution of the United States. He doesn't have to listen to the federal government when they tell him, 'You've got to go in there and bust down these people's doors, and take away their weapons.' And I hope they don't. And as long as they don't we'll support them, we'll support them and protect them against the federal government to the best that we can."

Pitner also sounds an anti-democratic note frequently heard at Patriot gatherings: "The other thing that really catches in my craw is when I see one of our elected officials going up there and calling it, 'Our great democracy.' That's a crock of baloney. This is a republic." Loud applause follows.

But Pitner denounces the notion that any part of his group is racist: "The only people we will refuse in the militias are those based on hate and fall into the hate groups, or those who are attempting to wreak personal gain from the troubles that are troubling America today under the guise of the militia."

Pitner reads from a mission statement for the Washington State Militia: "We will fight to the last breath to preserve our great nation. If we fail and we fall, the rest of the free world will fall with us, and tyranny shall certainly reign.

"God bless America, long live the Republic."

That said, Pitner brings on the main attraction: "We have a lot of problems that plague our great nation and I can sit here for 9,000 hours and go through them all for you, but I'm not going to do that because we have a really good speaker today, somebody that's really on top of things."

Up walks another balding man, fiftyish, with a wiry gray beard and piercing eyes peering out from a sharp brow. "John Trochmann, ladies and gentlemen," says Pitner.

The crowd stands and applauds.

The leader of the Militia of Montana clears his throat and waits for the applause to die down. He smiles and acknowledges the crowd. He shuffles the transparencies he has stacked next to the overhead projector, and switches on the projector.

Trochmann has done this many times. He's become much more polished as time has gone on; early on in his public-speaking career, as recently as a year before, his delivery was still halting, frequently muffled, almost always rambling. Trochmann has a way of spitting out some of his oft-delivered lines in a rat-a-tat fashion that sometimes loses his listeners. Some of that is still there—his presentation runs in fits and starts—but he's developed better enunciation and he's learned to make his points quickly and succinctly, then move on.

That afternoon's presentation, he tells the crowd, comes from material gathered from all over the country. "Our fellow Americans have been sharing things with us, and that's what we bring to you now," Trochmann says. "We could never do this without your help, and I appreciate it very much.

"All across our country, from Capitol Hill to law enforcement to military, and of course the public is participating in the Great Awakening. This is the best time of all to be living in our country. It's a wonderful time. America truly is coming alive."

It's responding, Trochmann says, to a threat to the American way of life that's been building for years and is coming to a head now. "Remember that oath we took in the military?" Trochmann asks. "To protect this great nation from enemies foreign and domestic?"

There are many nodding heads in the room, a few "Yeps."

"Well, even today we face a grave threat from enemies both foreign and domestic. And the best way of combating them is by exposing them and their dirty ways. That's what we're going to do here today."

Trochmann then turns on the overhead projector and puts on the cover page. It reads: "Enemies: Foreign and Domestic: Part I—The Problem." A few words: "You'll have to excuse me, I'm going to fly right through this, because it takes about an hour and a half." He flips to the next sheet. It's the cover of a military journal with a story about international armed forces cooperating under United Nations auspices, and the cover illustration shows a number of national flags, including the Stars and Stripes, all subordinately positioned beneath a U.N. flag.

So begins a sojourn for the audience that comes closer to two hours in length, as Trochmann treads through 190 pages of "documentation"—each page a strand in a web the bearded man spins, all pieces of a puzzle Trochmann claims proves there's a conspiracy to destroy the United States.

The New World Order, he says, is a shadowy one-world-government group that conspires to put an end to the U.S. Constitution by subsuming it under the "Communist" United Nations. Conspirators include the President, the Speaker of the House, and most financial and political leaders around the world.

The new world government Trochmann envisions would be a population-controlling totalitarian regime. Guns will be confiscated. Urban gangs like the Bloods and the Crips will be deployed to conduct house-to-house searches and round up resisters. Thousands of citizens will be shipped off to concentration camps and liquidated, all in the name of reducing the population.[6]

The conspirators' evil designs, he says, already have surfaced in numerous key ways, including:

—Gun control. "What is it about the word 'infringe' they don't understand?" Trochmann asks, referring to the Second Amendment, which he believes completely protects people's gun rights.

—The botched police raids at Ruby Ridge, Idaho, and Waco, Texas. "These things prove our government is out of control," he says. Moreover, Trochmann claims they are harbingers of a future government crackdown on law-abiding citizens.

—Troop and equipment movements throughout the country. Trochmann flashes pictures of armored vehicles, tanks, missiles, all kinds of military hardware—some marked with U.N. symbols or lettering, some with red Russian stars. These pictures are sent in from all over the country, Trochmann says, and the government can't explain them.

—Black helicopters. They're being used for training now, says Trochmann. What they're training for: rounding up citizens to put them in concentration camps.

—"Unconstitutional" executive orders. These range from the inclusion of U.S. troops among U.N. forces in Somalia, Haiti and Bosnia under Presidents Bush and Clinton to seemingly innocent preparations for disaster under the Federal Emergency Management Administration. All, says Trochmann, are meant to undermine the U.S. Constitution.

—Floods, hurricanes and other natural disasters. Government conspirators are manipulating the world's weather (using, Trochmann claims, technology at an Alaska project called HAARP), causing all these horrible weather patterns that affect crop production around the world. The intent, he says, is to induce food shortages, which will become a pretext for imposing martial law. Then, he says, they'll start rounding people up.

"It's going to end up like this—the most mild and calm of scenarios will be: 'Would you like to eat today? Give me your guns. Would you like your children back from school today? Give me your guns.' That's the mildest of versions you'll see."

The "evidence" in all this is a dizzying array of newspaper and magazine clippings, copies of government documents, reproductions of other Patriots' work, and, of course, the requisite tank-transport shots from around the nation.

"Here's the documentation, folks," boasts Trochmann, holding up the sheaf of pages. "We'll prove you wrong. You're welcome to copy this, and the tape, there's no copyright on any of it. Get it out to the people of America, and prove the media wrong."

In truth, most of the material Trochmann flashes across the projector screen would not be considered admissible under most rules of evidence. The bulk of the documentation in "Enemies: Foreign and Domestic" falls into one of two categories: fully explicable and normal activity cast in a sinister light, a kind of innuendo; and material obtained from dubious sources, usually other conspiracy-mongers' theories (which is both hearsay and factually inadequate evidence).[7] Neither kind of evidence supports the wild and damning charges of a grave nature, amounting to treason, that Trochmann levels against nearly every government official in sight.

Nonetheless, Trochmann's audience seems not to care. The evidence is more than enough for them. Most of them appear intent on gathering in every word he utters.

When another proof of government perfidy—say, photos of tanks being unloaded on the end of a wharf, or a seismographic chart that Trochmann says proves the Oklahoma City bombing was a government setup—comes up on the screen, they shake their heads and mutter. Murmurs ripple through the crowd regularly, punctuating Trochmann's pregnant pauses. And, with almost every murmur, Trochmann has a firm, or patriotic response: "We're not going to let them!" Or: "We'll have something to say about that!" From the audience comes a scattering of responses: "That's right!" "You bet!" "Amen!"

Trochmann elicits many of these responses most often by these little verbal interludes between items as they're flashed on the screen. His favorite: "Wow," delivered in flat, ironic manner, kind of like someone saying sarcastically, "Gee, no kidding." Trochmann, just with the tone of his voice, implies: "*Of course, you and I aren't going to fall for that line.*" It's a remarkably effective way of drawing people in. It draws an us-them line between those who see the world one way, and those who see it the "right" way: full of danger, conspiracy, looming satanic evil, apocalypse.

Once his listeners feel they have an exclusive window on the world, they know simultaneously what they're supposed to fear, just how great the threat is, and feel ready to help solve the problem. Then Trochmann tells them how they can: the militias.

"The militia movement is springing up everywhere," he intones early in the second half of his presentation. "Why?"

"You know, if they want the militias to go away, all they have to do is stop breaking the law they swore an oath to uphold," he says, flashing an angry glare. "Our public servants have broken the law and are out of control."

By forming militias, Trochmann says, average citizens can prepare themselves to resist the New World Order when it comes cracking down. Eventually, he believes the armed resistance of the general populace will be able to outgun the enemy's superior weaponry, if they're prepared.

He describes for them the cell structure, the kind of "leaderless resistance" first outlined by ex-KKK Grand Dragon (and Aryan Nations leader-in-waiting) Louis Beam and implemented by The Order's Robert Mathews (though Trochmann, naturally, does not mention these sources to the audience). Under such a design, militias form as groups of four to seven people; when the group recruits enough new followers and it reaches eight, it splits up, back into groups of four, and the process starts over.

The structure not only reduces the effect of spying by the enemy, it also prevents the organization from faltering if any single leader is arrested or "taken out." "So if there's any corruption within the cell structure, it's not going to take the whole thing down," Trochmann says. "If there's any infiltration, it's not going to take the whole thing down."

Trochmann wraps the package up with a poem, "The Final Hours," by Connie Benson of Trout Creek, Montana, with the verse:

> *Why no mention of insidious intention;*
> *To trash our trusty Constitution?*
> *Would the truth unveiled of government betrayal;*
> *Spark a civil revolution?*

Trochmann reads the poem aloud, somewhat haltingly. It's meant to be a bang-up, rousing end to the presentation, but today, he's a little flat.

> *"Will we heed the signs? Will we halt their designs?*
> *"Our opposition bravely tender?*
> *"In the final hours, will we resist wrong powers?*
> *"Or will we meekly surrender?"*

Trochmann looks up at the audience, which has fallen mostly silent, and pauses briefly: "Thanks for coming out today, folks."

The crowd stands and applauds for several minutes.

★★★

The Mount Vernon meeting is like hundreds of others held across the Northwest since 1994. They range in locale from modern suburbs like Bellevue, Washington, to dusty little ranching towns like Roundup, Montana. They attract everyone from black men in business suits (though these are a distinct minority) to aging cowboys with three days' stubble.

The meetings are always a town hall-style forum. They attract usually about a hundred participants, depending on the size of the town and the numbers of times the militias have held organizing meetings. On more than a few occasions, audience numbers have dropped sharply on the militias' second or third swing through town.[8]

Trochmann is the most visible speaker at these events, but the 1990s have produced a whole array of Patriot leaders who travel through the region, leading these meetings, and rallying believers and recruiting new ones. Their backgrounds widely differ, but all of them are colorful:

—Samuel Sherwood, erstwhile president of the United States Militia Association. Sherwood considers himself a mainstream political operative, and generally only attends rallies prepared by others. Sherwood espouses the militias as a way to counter political trends he says are leading to an imminent "civil war."

—Richard Mack, an Arizona sheriff who gained notoriety for refusing to enforce the Brady gun-control law in his county. Mack is a disciple of W. Cleon Skousen, a Mormon conspiracy theorist and John Birch Society pillar. Mack travels the nation giving seminars on how to resist the New World Order and its gun-control measures, and he recommends militias as an effective step. The National Rifle Association named him the organization's "Law Enforcement Officer of the Year" for 1995.[9] Mack's drawing card is gun control, but often a point of emphasis is what he calls the "myth of the separation of church and state."

—Mark Koernke, known for awhile by his radio moniker: "Mark From Michigan." Koernke, a University of Michigan janitor, toured the Northwest on a MOM-sponsored tour from Spokane, to Kalispell, to Great Falls, to Hamilton, and which finally wrapped up in Noxon, Trochmann's hometown. Koernke espouses theories essentially identical to Trochmann's, and his delivery, straight out of Rush Limbaugh's style of mannerisms on radio, is downright engaging in the often dry, unpolished world of Patriot public speakers. Koernke's best-known association, however, is his now-denied friendship with Timothy McVeigh.

—Colonel James "Bo" Gritz, the gruff, charismatic ex-Green Beret. He doesn't do the town-hall circuit much, though he's still one of the best speakers of the lot. Gritz prefers to concentrate on his traveling "SPIKE" (Specially Prepared Individuals for Key Events) training sessions, which impart his knowledge of Special Forces techniques to average Patriots. Gritz is a former Populist Party presidential candidate who achieved his greatest fame as the mediator who talked Randy Weaver down from his cabin. His base of operations is at his "Almost Heaven" community, a trio of tracts for homes atop a high ridge overlooking the isolated logging town of Kamiah, in north-central Idaho.

—Jack McLamb, a former Arizona policeman whose anti-New World Order "Operation Vampire Killer 2000" campaign has brought him national notoriety. McLamb tours the country giving talks on why law-enforcement officers should join the Patriot movement. He has a long association with Gritz (McLamb also had a role in the Weaver incident), and he's one of the chief co-investors in "Almost Heaven" and even advertised the "covenant community" in his police newsletter, "Aid and Abet."

—Gary DeMott, a constitutionalist from Boise, Idaho. As the president of the Idaho Sovereignty Association, he is a one-man show who tours the region tirelessly, spreading the gospel of "common law" courts. "We are the law," he tells his audiences. "We are the law enforcers." He predicts an economic crash in the near future, and recommends that people obtain as much gold and silver as they can.

—Gene Schroder, based in Campo, Colorado. Schroder tours the country explaining to people how to set up "common law" courts. His United Sovereigns of America is a leading Patriot group that specializes in the pseudo-legal activities of these courts, which are an outgrowth of Posse Comitatus beliefs. Militias are a basic ingredient of Schroder's model of a proper government, and of the solution for ending "unconstitutional" government intrusions.[10]

—Johnny Liberty, longtime resident of Eugene, Oregon. Liberty (his real name is John Van Hove) attracts followers from the remnant hippie subculture of the '60s that still thrives in Eugene. Liberty promotes "common law" courts, "sovereign citizenship" and "jury nullification" at town-hall meetings around the state. While his constituency derives from the hippies' barter-fair ethos, his legal theories are virtually identical to those promoted by the far-right Posse Comitatus. Liberty denies he has a racist agenda; he contends he is merely trying to help solve the nation's problems, and if that means associating with racists, then he can live with that, so long as the information they promote is the truth.[11]

—Carl Klang, a singer-songwriter from rural Oregon. Klang livens up the usually somber settings of Patriot gatherings with his voice and guitar. Among the selections he sings: "Watch Out for Martial Law," "Wheresoever Eagles Gather (The Ballad of Randy Weaver)," "Hang'um High," "Seventeen Little Children (Waco)" and his recent Patriot hit, "Evil, Filthy, Rotten Conspiracy."

—Edwin Pund, a longtime figure in western Washington's far right. Pund appears at Patriot gatherings to discuss the evils of the modern education system. He urges parents to remove their children from public schools as soon as possible, lest they be forever contaminated by the godless schooling offered by "secular humanists."

—Bill Tinsley, a regular semi-fringe candidate for Congress, and actually the Republican nominee for Washington's 4th District House race in 1996, which he lost handily to incumbent Representative Norm Dick. Tinsley is a World War II veteran who heads up an organization called the "Eagle Alliance," "dedicated to restoring the Constitution to a free and independent America." Tinsley argues that treaties with Indian tribes and federal efforts to preserve endangered species, such as the spotted owl, are part of a government "land grab" with sinister motives.

—Don Kehoe, a landscape contractor from Monroe, Washington. Kehoe takes Tinsley's arguments a step further. He suggests that ecosystem-management efforts, like the international plan proposed by local environmental groups for the North Cascades in Washington and British Columbia, are part of a government plan to drive people out of those areas altogether. The New World Order, Kehoe says, plans to implement population control by installing concentration camps in the Cascades to house and liquidate the masses.[12]

—Last, but not least: Bob Fletcher. Fletcher is a self-described "congressional researcher" who came to work for the Militia of Montana in the fall of 1994. Within a short span of time, Fletcher became the prime speaker at MOM events, delivering the militias' message with a little more deftness than the often-erratic Trochmann. For the better part of the next year, especially during the uproar that followed the Oklahoma City tragedy, Fletcher was the point man for the militia movement. When there was a televised Town Hall meeting on the militias in Seattle, Fletcher— backed by an audience stacked with Patriots—was the spokesman. When informal congressional hearings were held on the militias, Fletcher and Trochmann sat together and answered questions.

Trochmann liked to tell reporters that "they had tried to kill Bob twice." The first time, Trochmann says, someone tried to drive a truck right into his office and run him over.

The second time, he said, "somebody put some type of CIA chemical on his neck that gave him a heart attack. He didn't realize it until after it had happened to him, and he was sitting down at a table talking to somebody else that had the same thing, how both of them were survivors of this attempt, with high accumulations of this poison in their bodies. They later determined that was what it was."[13]

Fletcher ran the militia meetings very smoothly. He was adept at saying things that were simultaneously pessimistic and empowering. "My personal feeling is that it's too late to stop this," he would tell crowds. As for surviving, he'd say, "I recommend a year's worth of food and plenty of ammo."

Listeners feared for their future and their well-being. But at the same time, Fletcher was arming them with advance knowledge. An alert Patriot could prepare for the coming doomsday, and perhaps his family might survive, all thanks to the Militia of Montana.

Fletcher abruptly ended his association with the Militia of Montana in the fall of 1995 and moved south to California, where he set up shop operating a new Patriot organization. Trochmann at first said he didn't know where Fletcher was or how to get ahold of him. He said he'd returned to "the South, somewhere, maybe Georgia."

Why the split? "We just couldn't afford him any more," Trochmann curtly answered most who asked. He told one reporter, though, that a lot of quarters appeared to be flowing out of Fletcher's paychecks and into the poker and keno machines at the Noxon-area bars Fletcher liked to haunt.[14]

★★★

The focus at Patriot meetings varies, but usually revolves around the subject presented by a keynote speaker. At Richard Mack meetings, the emphasis is on gun control and recruiting law-enforcement officers to the Patriot cause. Gene Schroder and Gary DeMott sessions accent "constitutional law" and the "common law" courts.

And, at MOM meetings and others like them, the attention is on confronting the New World Order by forming militias.

In all of them, though, the message remains essentially the same: The world is rotting at the seams. The American way of life, embodied in the Constitution, is threatened by forces conspiring to enslave the world. Only by forming an armed Patriotic resistance can the plan be thwarted.

By challenging the mainstream view—that the world is essentially a safe place, that the nation is, in general, functional, even if it has problems—the Patriots persuade their followers to place themselves outside of the rest of society. Simultaneously, they offer a social structure of their own, drawn together by a Patriot sensibility that informs every aspect of the followers' lives: legal, religious, even business behavior becomes an expression of their beliefs.

This is how people are drawn into the alternative universe of the Patriots—a world in which the same events occur as those that befall the rest of us, but the events are seen through a different lens. Anything that makes it into the newspapers or the evening broadcasts—say, flooding in the Cascades, or the arrival of U.S. troops in Bosnia—may be just another story for most of us, but to a Patriot, these widely disparate events all are connected to the conspiracy. Believers tend to organize in small local groups. They all have similar-sounding names—Concerned Citizens for Constitutional Law, Alliance for America, and the like. They play host to touring Patriot leaders, with local leaders nervously introducing their admired guests. These groups operate out of the public limelight, connected by a low-level communications system: a combination of mailings, faxes and Internet postings which advertise meetings, locally and regionally. Rarely does an announcement make the local mainstream press.

Most of the Patriots' real recruiting, however, takes place before the meetings, by word of mouth. It usually works like this:

John, a Patriot, tells Joe, a co-worker at his plant who's going through a divorce, that he can find out "what's really going on" by attending a militia meeting. The Patriots, Joe is told, have answers to the moral decay that's behind the way men get skewered in divorce cases.

Joe attends. He thinks the New World Order theories might be possible. He buys a video tape, maybe a book. It all starts to fit together. So this is why he hasn't been able to get ahead in the world financially, he tells himself. He attends another meeting. Pretty soon he's getting "Taking Aim" in the mail.

Joe tells his neighbor Sam about the Patriots. Sam is dubious, but he's been having a difficult time paying his taxes, and Joe passes on what he knows about the Internal Revenue Service and the Federal Reserve from the Patriot literature he's read. Sam is intrigued. He reads some of Joe's material. He goes to the next meeting with Joe. A month or two later, Sam starts drawing up papers to declare himself a "sovereign citizen."

Sam goes to a picnic outing at his parents' house. His older brother Jeff, an engineer at Boeing, asks Sam about the "sovereign citizen" stuff. Sam explains. Jeff, too, is dubious, but he also happens to be a gun collector and sometime hunter, and he's received mailings from the National Rifle Association that lead him to wonder if there isn't something to this whole militia thing. When Sam starts talking about how the government is out of control, passing unconstitutional laws like the Brady Bill, Jeff tunes in. A month later, he, too, sits in on a Patriot town-hall meeting.

One by one it builds. Any of a number of issues—land use, property rights, banking, economics, politics, gun control, abortion, education, welfare—can serve as a drawing card. In many cases, they are deeply divisive and polarizing social, legal and economic matters that the mainstream fails to adequately address.

Once recruits pass through any of these gateways into the Patriot universe, they are inexorably drawn along further. What once seemed like simply a screwed-up government has become monstrously, palpably evil. Then they learn about Patriot legal theories from people like the Freemen or from Schroder and DeMott:

—The Federal Reserve is bankrupt. It is a front for a phony system, run by private corporations, which prints money that really only helps keep rich bankers awash in cash.

—The Internal Revenue Service is illegal. Paying federal taxes actually is strictly voluntary.

—You can exempt yourself from paying federal taxes by filing a statement declaring yourself a "sovereign citizen." This ostensibly frees you from obligation to the United States, which Patriots say is just an illegal corporation based in Washington, D.C. This is done by nullifying your participation in federal citizenship status as established by the 14th Amendment. This distinction, arguing that only the 14th Amendment extends federal citizenship to minorities, forms the basis for the Patriots' contention that just white male Christian property owners enjoy full citizenship under the "organic Constitution."

—The only valid U.S. Constitution is the "organic Constitution," which is the main body of the Constitution and the first 10 amendments, or the Bill of Rights. Patriots believe the remaining amendments either should be repealed or were approved illegally. In any case, they would end the prohibition of slavery (13th Amendment); equal protection under the law (14th Amendment); prohibitions against racial or ethnic discrimination (15th Amendment); the income tax (16th Amendment); direct election of Senators (17th Amendment); the vote for women (19th Amendment); and a host of other constitutional protections passed since the time of the Founders.

—Establishing "sovereign citizenship," or "Quiet Title" (which similarly declares a person a "freeman"), exempts a person from the rules of "equity courts," which means you don't have to pay for licenses, building permits, or traffic citations, not to mention taxes.

—The only real courts with power are the "common law" courts comprised of sovereign citizens, which have the authority to issue rulings and liens against public officials they deem to have overstepped their bounds. If these officials fail to uphold the directives of common-law courts, they can be found guilty of treason, and threatened with the appropriate penalty: hanging.[15]

It is at this end of the Patriot belief spectrum that much of its deeper agenda is revealed. When Patriots talk about "restoring the Constitution," what they often have in mind is rolling back protections embodied in a wide range of amendments, as well as establishing a reading of the Second Amendment radically different from the one traditionally accepted by the U.S. court system.[16]

It is here that the charges of divisiveness and racism often leveled at the Patriots take on weight. Plainly, the constitutional rollbacks would return racial injustice. Not surprisingly, this is where Patriot beliefs most closely resemble, and arguably are directly descended from, the openly racist and anti-Semitic belief systems of the Ku Klux Klan, the Aryan Nations, and the Posse Comitatus.

Most of these views are often dismissed by the mainstream legal profession as simple nonsense promoted by crackpots. And, for the most part, the Patriots' legal theories completely disintegrate when the facts are examined in the cold light of day. Nonetheless, the movement's ranks continue to grow, and the mainstream courts, particularly in rural jurisdictions, now are faced with a sudden deluge of "common law" documents that throw an already overburdened system into a tangle.[17]

All the same, there is no law against being a crackpot. Otherwise, hundreds of Elvis sighters and UFO abductees would be sitting in prison cells alongside the Patriots. They are quite free to spread their conspiracy theories among themselves. The concern, of course, is what happens when the agenda of the Patriots, constructed out of an insular, paranoiac world view, is asserted in the American legal and social system. The believers' attempts to institute their "republic" is certain to come into conflict with mainstream America. Moreover, when Patriots begin to threaten public officials with hanging and other kinds of bodily harm, the potential for violence enters into the picture.

"What is going on in our society when somebody can come up with an idea like this, and a package of materials like this, and attract 200 people to a community meeting?" wonders Ken Toole, director of the Montana Human Rights Network. Toole has attended many of the sessions.

"To me, it's almost like a canary in a coal mine, and it's very indicative of how negative and hostile we've become about ourselves—that somehow these people have managed to objectify the government at all levels, blame it for all kinds of things, and look for a way to kind of focus that anger."

This is where the sense of community, a central facet of life in the rural Northwest, becomes important. Toole's human-rights group and other similar anti-hate organizations, as well as political researchers who monitor the Patriots, have targeted this sense of ignored grievances in the community and its alienation towards much of America's government, social and economic system. This is the key to understanding and dealing with the challenge the movement represents.

"You wouldn't have people following these kinds of leaders if there wasn't discontent in the U.S. over the way the government works," observes Chip Berlet, an analyst with Political Research Associates, a Cambridge, Massachusetts, think tank. Berlet has tracked the growth of the militias since the early 1990s.

"It's really important not to make fun of the premise that there's something wrong that needs to be changed," he says. "I think a lot of people feel that way, and they're very justified in that feeling. The problem is, when people sense that there's widespread discontent among the population and channel that discontent toward scapegoats, rather than channel that discontent toward what I would hope would be a very vibrant dialogue about how to change things."

The popular scapegoats of the Patriot movement are usually government officials, especially Bill and Hillary Clinton (a Richard Mack remark—"Hitler was more moral than Clinton; he had fewer girlfriends"[18]—is typical of the animus directed toward the president) and Attorney General Janet Reno, nicknamed "Butch," or sometimes called "Nero." But on a broader scale, welfare mothers, immigrants, environmentalists, and liberals also become targets of Patriot rhetoric. Virtually anyone who disagrees with them is the enemy, and thus becomes essentially disposable. For many in the alternative universe, this also includes (and focuses upon) homosexuals, minorities, immigrants and Jews. For some of the most determined believers, they take action.

Berlet further elaborates on the problem. "Your average rancher, or your average person who works in an extractive industry, they solve complex problems every day of their lives," he says. "It may not be the ones that people in an urban, white-collar environment solve. If these people had access to information, and if people took their complaints seriously and decided to spend the time to educate them about these questions so they can take part in a serious discussion, then we would not have the problem of scapegoating. Scapegoating and conspiracy theories flourish when the only group reaching out to a discontented population is a group peddling the theories. If in fact the leaders—whether they're business, or political, or religious or social leaders of our country—actually decided to talk to the people in the country about some of these complex problems, outside of this kind of demagoguery that passes for politicking these days, you've got to trust in the ultimate outcome of democracy.

"If the premise is that people are incapable of understanding these issues, then we're all in big trouble. My premise is that these people are very capable of understanding these issues, if people ever had the respect and courtesy to talk to them about them.

"Anybody who can keep a 1958 John Deere tractor running can understand the budget deficit. I mean, the complexity of a carburetor, the complexity of planning your seed sources and delivery for the season, your irrigation systems—there's a lot of arrogance in the body politic right now that thinks that common people can't understand complex situations.

"And that's ridiculous. The dilemma is that Bo Gritz and his friends are the only ones out there respecting the grievance of these populations, and talking to these populations as if they were intelligent. And that's a real problem for democracy.

"My formula for democracy is a simple one: Given enough information, the majority of people over time reach the right decision. But if you cut out any of those sectors, you're in trouble."

Seeing so many average, ordinarily mainstream people attracted to the Patriots' beliefs is what worries many.

"This really speaks to me," says Ken Toole, whose family dates back to Montana's origins; his great-grandfather's brother was the state's first governor, and his father was a revered University of Montana history professor. "The amount and the number of people that are going to these meetings is something that I think everybody ought to be sitting up and taking note of."

★★★

Before the militia meeting in Mount Vernon, some other people in Skagit County took note. Now about 70 of them show up outside with protest signs:

"No private armies"

"Say no to hate"

"Not in our town"

Most of them say they were contacted by friends, or read local newspaper reports about the upcoming meeting. Some say the planned protest was announced that morning from pulpits in local churches—one Unitarian, one Presbyterian—and they decided to join in. (A month or so later, the subsequent issue of "Taking Aim" identified the organizers behind the Mount Vernon protest as the Freedom Socialist Party, "a communist front." There was no truth to the report; most of the picketers came from mainstream churches.)

Alec McDougall is a history teacher at one of the local high schools. The lanky redhead came out to hold a sign because he wanted to provide a counterweight to the militias' message.

"With what has gone on in the last year, which has really publicized the militia movement in the country, we didn't feel we could let it go ignored," says McDougall. "Too many things and too many situations in the past have been ignored, and as a result, tremendous bad has occurred. So we figured we ought to stand up, speak up, even if speaking up means that, possibly, we're giving them more publicity."

The crowd of protesters starts singing: "America the Beautiful." Loudly. Repeatedly.

Maybe because of the way that the group outside steals one of the Patriots' own favorite tactics—openly displaying their American patriotism—or, more likely, because they're being protested against, the Patriots inside the conference hall are clearly on edge about it.

People milling in the hallways mutter about "that bunch outside." Rumors—as is their wont at Patriot gatherings—circulate freely. One man comes up to a group of friends: "Hey, did you hear what they're saying about us out there? That if you're Jewish, you can't get in? That's bullshit!"

Ben Hinkle, head of Citizens for Liberty—one of the local groups that has organized today's gathering—takes the microphone at the end of an intermission.

"Those people out front," he fumes—jingling the change in his pocket furiously—"they're so ignorant, they don't even know they're ignorant!" The crowd applauds.

When Trochmann is in the early stages of his presentation, John Pitner decides to step outside and just straighten things out with the protest group. Two worlds head for a collision course.

Pitner walks up to the knot of people closest to the door and asks them why they are protesting.

"Because you're only interested in tearing down the government and creating fear," one of the protesters replies.

"No, it's not tearing down the government," Pitner responds. "We're not anti-government, we're anti-bad politicians. We're trying to educate the public to get these bad politicians out of government. That fact is that we're $5 trillion in debt. That's scary.

"It's about money, it's about the New World Order, it's about those who would attempt to overthrow the Constitution and replace it with a new Constitution. It's all kinds of things. So that's where we're coming from."

One of the picketers, an elderly man, wants to know more: "I understand that there are ties to hate groups."

"There is no hate in the Washington State Militia," replies Pitner, shaking his head. "There isn't. None. None whatsoever."

Alec McDougall steps up. "I'm very positive about your being here," he says. "Because I'm glad we got the opportunity to talk."

"That's what makes our country great," Pitner says. Now everyone's smiling for a moment. It seems as if the two planes—the mainstream and the Patriot universes—might not be all that distant.

"There are a lot of individuals here who are very concerned," McDougall says.

Pitner nods. "And we're going to belay those myths. We're going to try and belay those concerns. We're going to put action where words are. We're going to speak through our actions. You'll not find any hate or anti-Semitism in our unit.

"And if we do, we're going to put it right on out. We don't have any patience with that kind of situation. None whatsoever. We need to join together, and not let people pull us apart. This country's in trouble. We're in big trouble."

McDougall is in a raincoat, like most of the protesters. He's been wearing it a lot the past few days. The Skagit River has risen to flood stage the previous two days, and brigades of volunteers have been staving off the floodwaters with constant sandbagging. Pitner claims his group has been involved in the effort. McDougall has in fact been there, and he spots the common ground, observing to Pitner that they've all been pitching in to fight the river. Pitner is eager to join him. "We're doing the same thing, and yet, we're looked at as adversaries, and that's not true," he says. "Let's focus on the good things."

An elderly man steps up to Pitner and eyes him warily. "Are you affiliated with the Montana group?" he asks, cocking an eyebrow.

"I'm not affiliated with any other group than the Washington State Militia," Pitner says.

The man is persistent. "Is the Washington State Militia affiliated with the Montana group?"

"We share information and things of that nature—but we're not affiliated with them, no."

"Do you believe in everything they believe in?"

"No, I don't. Of course I don't. No."

Alec McDougall is not persuaded. "Regardless of what you say," he says, "people who support the militias in other areas of the country are racist, are anti-Semitic, do have fears that government is secretly plotting against us as individuals, and act those things out in violence and intimidation."

Pitner: "We don't do that."

McDougall stresses the point. "In many other cities, in this country, we could point to situations where militia members and people who are associated with militia members act that way."

"Yes, yes," Pitner agrees, "and there is bad apples in the barrel. And I will not ever try to tell you that there isn't. And I tell you something, if you ever hear of a Washington State Militiaman doing that, then I want to hear about it. Because we're going to give those guys the boot. Because that's not where we're at."

Pitner seeks desperately for common ground in the conversation again. "Like I said, there's a lot of factions that are trying to pull us apart here in America. We need to draw together, just like we joined together in sandbagging, to help individuals, the same thing we need to do to bring the country back to a viable economic structure, to something we can be proud of, something where we're not sending troops to Bosnia to herd people—something where we're not taking away guns, our Second Amendment rights—from the Haitians, things of that nature."

By now, the schoolteacher is pressing Pitner about his ideas. "In the militia," he says, "people affiliated with the militia are people who arm themselves, train themselves, organize systems related to the U.S. government. In opposition to the federal government, on the theory that the U.S. government is against the people of the United States."

Pitner realizes he's going to have to defend some of the Patriots' beliefs, and tries: "Well, OK, there's one thing that I'd like to point out about the federal government—There wouldn't be any federal government without some of the heinous legislation that came up. Also, the very fact that—"

McDougall shakes his head: "I didn't understand what you just said."

Pitner recovers. "OK, basically, what I'm getting at is the federal government—the IRS. Basically, they're taking away our hard-earned money, OK? You know where that money's going? It doesn't go to the roads. You know where your federal income tax goes? It goes into a private banker's pocket."

McDougall knows where this is heading: "And who is that?"

"That's whoever happens to be a private banker."

The teacher shakes his head. "You guys have developed a very sophisticated way of transmitting your message with code words."

Pitner protests. "No! It's the truth! It's the truth! Not one penny you pay in federal income tax goes into the U.S. Treasury. Not one penny!"

"Those are the militias' code words for armed resistance to the U.S. government," says McDougall. "And bankers are a code word for anti-Semitism."

Pitner shakes his head. "No. We're a defensive organization."

"Yes, I understand that."

Now Pitner decides a mild offense is a good defense: "Tell me this, wasn't the government at fault for Waco?"

McDougall has to agree. "Yes, the government made a terrible mistake at Waco. They made a terrible mistake at Ruby Ridge."

"And you don't think we should be fearful of our government when things like that happen?"

"I think we have to chide our government when it makes mistakes, yes," says the schoolteacher. "But I don't think we have to harm ourselves to protect ourselves. I don't think we have to scapegoat minorities."

"All right, would it be right for me to say, to try to pass legislation that you had to have a gun in your house?"

"Of course not."

"Well, would it be right for you to pass legislation telling me I can't have a gun in my house?"

"No, but in most other civilized countries, people enjoy a greater degree of personal security when they walk the streets at night because they're disarmed countries—"

Suddenly, Pitner realizes he's talking to someone who actually thinks gun control might be acceptable. A switch goes off and his face turns blank. He reddens a little, and replies forcefully, finger wagging: "Yeah, and a heck of a lot less freedom. That's where it comes from—a heck of a lot less freedom."

Pitner looks around briefly, then turns to go inside. He waves farewell at the knot of protesters and smiles: "God bless you people."

Then he returns to his own universe.

A mere six months later, it would collapse around John Pitner in a clattering heap of pipe bombs, guns and FBI agents. And all of Alec McDougall's suspicions—almost every word—would prove uncannily accurate.

Chapter 3 / God's Country

I T WAS SUPPOSED to be a pleasant evening dinner, though I wasn't really sure why the businessman had invited me into his home. I'd only met him briefly at a local Chamber of Commerce gathering, but he said he had something he wanted to show me. He was known to be active in Republican Party politics, and I was the editor of a newspaper (owned by a staunch Democrat) widely considered by conservatives to be a liberal rag. I wasn't sure what we might have to share; still, the offer stirred my curiosity, and I accepted.

We enjoyed a nice summer barbecue meal of hamburgers and chips with the man's wife and children. Then his wife cleared off the table, the children went to the TV room, and the businessman and I retired to his den. He remained coy about what he wanted to discuss.

By then, my curiosity was in high gear. What was this, an Amway pitch? I'd gone through that before, by someone who also said he had "something he had to show me." But I remained quiet while the man set up his projector. It was one of those filmstrip devices, the kind schools still used then to show history lessons in accompaniment to a record that narrated the script and beeped when it was time to advance to the next frame.

The lights out and the shades drawn, the businessman put the needle on the record and turned on the projector. Then I proceeded to watch another history lesson of sorts: an explanation that America as designed by its Founding Fathers was a republic, not a democracy;[1] how, over the past half-century, the republic had been subverted by a Communist plot, using the ruse of "democracy," that extended to the highest levels of government; that the conspirators' intent was to place America, and the whole planet, in slavery under a totalitarian "one world government"; that the core of the conspiracy revolved around a cadre of "international bankers"; and that you could find evidence of the conspiracy in everyday headlines if you knew how to interpret their *real* meanings. Finally, of course, came the solution: to join the John Birch Society. The JBS, the filmstrip explained, was the world's leading organization in defending the American way of life against Communism.

The lesson was over, the man turned on the lights and looked knowingly at me. "So, what do you think?" he asked me.

"It's certainly something to think about," I answered, being coy myself. I thanked him for the dinner and the hospitality and assured him I would keep in mind everything he had shown me that night. Then I went home.

It struck me then how conspiratorial the whole thing was, how secretively the Birch Society behaved—precisely the kind of shadowy behavior it liked to accuse "suspected Communists" of undermining America with. At least I understood why the businessman had invited me to his home. I was all of 23, a rather fresh-faced guy who probably looked like someone open to recruitment into the Birch Society. And, as the editor of Sandpoint's local paper in northern Idaho, it might be useful to have someone like me on their side. I later found out he tried recruiting a few members of my reporting staff, too.

What the businessman hadn't known was that I had been exposed to the Birch Society's ideas at an earlier age. It was an inescapable fact of growing up in southern Idaho in the 1960s. All my life, it seemed, I had heard these ideas voiced at family gatherings, among my parents' friends, brought up during debates over school policies and political candidates. They seemed especially to emanate from our neighbors and family members who belonged to the Church of Jesus Christ of Latter Day Saints, which meant just about everyone. Well over half my high-school class was Mormon. My mother's rather sizable side of the family was largely Mormon, too. (My mother left the LDS Church shortly after marrying my father in 1952; our family attended a local Methodist church.)

What was well-known in Idaho then was that there was an overt alliance between the LDS Church and the John Birch Society. The church's then-president and prophet, David O. McKay—whose pronunciations were to Idaho Mormons what the Pope's are to rural Italians, only more so—was an open proponent of the Society and its beliefs. Just about every Mormon family I knew had a copy of the definitive John Bircher opus, a book by Gary Allen titled *None Dare Call It Conspiracy.* It wasn't very long, either, which made it *real* popular.

At an early age, then, the subject of politics and religion became connected. So it seemed logical, as I grew more interested in politics in my teens, that the place to inquire about these troubling ideas—all the swirling stories of conspiracy and looming evil—was with our family's pastor.

Gray-haired and genial, Allan Reesor happened to be a man I admired greatly. We talked after school sometimes over malted milk shakes at a local cafe. I remember, not perfectly but clearly, the answer he gave when I asked him about the John Birch Society and its tales of a Communist conspiracy.

There are two problems with the John Birch beliefs, he told me. For starters, nothing that they offer as evidence of a vast conspiracy among all these international bankers has ever been proven as fact. If you try to track their "facts" down, you wind up in an endless maze of blind alleys. So whether or not they're right—and they could be—the only real fact is that there is no proof at all for the wild charges the Birchers make.

Second, he said, and more important, is that their beliefs, and their solutions, ultimately come down to creating a scapegoat. The Communists, or hippies, or liberals, or Jewish bankers—they tell us that these people are the ones to blame for our problems. But most of our problems are of our own making, and blaming some group of people or another for them does nothing to really solve them. It prevents us from finding real solutions, in fact.

I must have absorbed this perspective, because it became integral to my own world view. I particularly remember something else he told me toward the end of our conversation.

If you choose not to believe in these ideas, he said, it's not easy. They're very common out here. It's almost like you have to believe them to be considered a patriotic American.

Allan Reesor had spent most of his ministerial career in rural churches. He sighed, thinking about the many battles he'd waged within his own parishes.

"Maybe it's something in the air, or in the soil," he said. "It goes back a long way. It's rooted deeply here."

★★★

In the Northwest, the far right has indeed found fertile ground, historically speaking, for its beliefs. It scarcely turns up in the region's early history, though in a few rural locales—notably the Silver Valley in northern Idaho, and scattered pockets of rural western Washington—you could find Confederate states loyalists, escaping economic destruction in the South after the Civil War, who settled and formed insulated communities that remained tight-knit for several generations.[2]

These communities are rumored to have been participants in the sudden rise of the Ku Klux Klan in the Pacific Northwest in the 1920s. They may indeed have been, but their numbers were so small that they could only have made up a tiny fraction of the numbers of people in the Northwest who joined the Klan then.

Truth is, most of the '20s Klansmen who claimed membership in Oregon and Washington were plain old white Protestant farmers and loggers. They were part of a national resurgence in Klan activity that began in 1915. Headquartered in Atlanta, the Ku Klux Klan was revived (it had lapsed into disrepute a few years after its initial rise as a Southern vigilante army in the decade following the Civil War) that year by William Joseph Simmons, who set about creating an organization that would spread throughout much of the United States in the early 1920s.

The new Klan sent a couple of "Kleagles"—political operators who could organize the local entities—out to Portland in 1921. They found an eager audience among the working-class timber workers and farmers and small town businessmen, who liked to consider themselves deeply patriotic Americans. And that was what the Klan was selling: "Americanism," the defense of all things white and Protestant.[3]

First on the Klan's list of evil conspirators, in those days, were Catholics (Jews and blacks played a secondary role, and only years later moved to the top of the far right's list of scapegoats).[4] "Papists," as the Klan's leaders liked to call them, were behind all of the nation's moral decay, because the nation's political machinery was run by people taking their orders from Vatican City. So the Klan proposed an initiative to require children to attend public schools, thereby outlawing parochial schools (i.e., Catholic schools) in the state. Also on the Klan's agenda: driving out bootleggers and other moral reprobates. The Klan was a devoted defender of Prohibition.

For the loggers and blue-collar workers trying to make ends meet in hard times, the Klan sounded a resonant message. In the Northwest, the vast majority of these people were the poorly educated Protestants like those who filled the Klan's ranks elsewhere. Phrases like "pure womanhood" and "just laws" and "Christian values" poured from behind the lecterns of Klan speakers, convincing thousands that the Klan stood for the organized good of the community.[5] Some 25,000 people in Oregon claimed membership in the Klan, fully half of whom were from Portland.[6]

Sometimes, though, enforcing this "good" meant a little extralegal activity here and there. In Medford, a gang of "night riders" in Klan masks chased off a couple of locals they didn't like—one of them a black man accused of bootlegging—by stringing them up over the limb of a tree and then letting the noose go slack at the last second, repeating the threat three times.[7] This worked well enough with the first victim, who seems to have been frightened into silence, but it didn't work very well with the second man, a white piano salesman who was suspected of being overly intimate with a local girl and who had made the mistake of pressing the local Klan leader about an overdue bill. He also had a heart condition, and on the third hoist of the noose, suffered a seizure and nearly died, scattering the nervous Klansmen, who had not bargained on being party to manslaughter. They returned the piano salesman to his home by rolling him out of their car; and when he had sufficiently recovered, he went to the district attorney and pressed charges against the perpetrators.[8]

At the same time, the Klan's rolls began to rise; however, the two Kleagles in Portland soon fell to quarreling over their newfound power. Disgusted, the Oregon locals fired them both and replaced them with one of their own: Fred Gifford, a one-time telegraph operator who had become an administrative honcho at Northwestern Electric Company. Gifford may have been a little surprised to be thrust into the limelight, but he quickly proved able at building a genuine political power.

Indeed, between 1922 and 1924, Oregon could have been called a Klan state. The 1922 Democratic candidate for governor, Walter Pierce, openly courted—and won—the support of the Klan, and it apparently turned the tide for him, giving him a victory over a Republican incumbent in a state that voted sturdily Republican in every other arena. Moreover, Klan-backed candidates took control of the Legislature, and Portland's mayor was believed to be part of the Klan's political machinery.[9]

The passage in 1922 of the Klan's education initiative—which was ruled unconstitutional by the U.S. Supreme Court two years later—turned out to be the Klan's only real political victory, however. Soon, the Klan was being challenged by locals who disagreed with their agenda, and openly questioned some of the Klan's wild charges against Catholics. When the Klan members responded only with threats, their credibility within the community shriveled up.[10]

Meanwhile, Luther I. Powell, one of the Kleagles fired by the Portland group, moved his act northward to more populous Puget Sound. He set up shop in downtown Seattle, publishing an anti-Catholic sheet called "The Watcher on the Tower" and organizing small Klan groups throughout the region. The Klan also operated on a social level, offering fraternal advantages to its members, and one Seattle proprietor even operated "The Klansman's Roost" on Westlake Avenue, "Where Kozy Komfort and Komrade Kare Kill the Grouch with Viands Rare."

However, Powell's activities met stiff opposition from the local media. Both the *Post-Intelligencer* and the *Seattle Times* ran editorials denouncing the Klan. Numbers drawn to Powell's early rallies were decidedly small. Evidently deciding the pastures were greener back in Oregon, he closed shop in October 1923 and returned to Portland.

His move may have been premature; for the next year or so, the forces Powell had set in motion gained momentum. The Klan's membership in Washington blossomed to an estimated 35,000 to 40,000, and as it had in Oregon, the Klan pushed a compulsory public-school bill on the 1924 ballot. A Klan rally organized by the local groups Powell helped set up drew an estimated 30,000 people to a cross-burning and "informational rally in Issaquah" in July 1924. The Klan was hailed as "the return of the Puritans in this corrupt, jazz-mad age."[11] Without the binding presence of the national organization, though, the Klan soon dissolved under the weight of its own inertia. It went through the usual local schisms over financing and control; by 1925, its activities in the Puget Sound region were practically nonexistent.[12]

Back in Oregon, Powell became engaged in an all-out war for control of the Oregon Klan with Gifford, reflecting a larger schism in the national organization between Joseph Simmons and a onetime right-hand man, H.W. Evans, who was attempting to take control of the national Klan. Soon the Oregon Klan itself was deeply divided, as Powell (an Evans supporter) and Gifford (a Simmons backer) became engaged in a public mud-slinging contest in which both sides came away with soiled reputations. Gifford was accused of playing fast and loose with Klan dues, and Powell was accused of carpetbagging. Both claims had considerable basis in fact.[13]

Already losing credibility in the communities, the Klan promptly lost all its political power. Candidates ceased courting the Klan. People stopped turning out to hear its speakers. Crosses were no longer lit in towns like Eugene, Salem and Portland. By 1925, contemporary observers claim, the Klan was no longer a political presence of any note.[14] Powell left Oregon and ultimately went to work for the self-proclaimed fascist mystic William Dudley Pelley, leader of the Silvershirt Legion of America, based in Asheville, North Carolina.

The Klan was hoist on its own petard of civic nastiness in the Northwest, but the region's right-wing populist faction simply shifted like a blob of mercury into new shapes. Foremost among these was the Silvershirts, an overtly Nazi-esque American support group for Adolf Hitler's politics led by Pelley. Following in the footsteps of the Klan in the 1930s, it attracted the same kind of Northwest followers to its ideology, drawing particularly on the economically displaced blue-collar workers of the Depression era.[15]

Not surprisingly, some of the players in the Northwest Klan scene were now involved in the Silvershirts. Fred Gifford joined the Portland chapter of the Silvershirt Legion of America in 1933 and took a prominent role in its activities until he came to the conclusion in 1935 that it wasn't suitable—probably due to Pelley's cult of personality—for his desire to form a revived Klan.

More notably, perhaps, Luther I. Powell was commissioned by Pelley to return to Portland in 1933 to help the Silvershirts set up a statewide shop. When Powell arrived, the group was under the leadership of a local auto-garage mechanic named Anchor Gregor, under whom the group had grown little beyond its original 20 members. Powell promptly attempted to displace Gregor as state leader with his own handpicked chief, Ralph Bowerman. However, Powell neglected to clear the change with Pelley first, who promptly reinstated Gregor. As punishment, he demoted Powell to the rank of field organizer. Powell instead marched off to Texas and announced that he was now the leader of the Anti-Communist Legion of the World. For all its titular magnificence, Powell's group (and his moment on the public stage) rapidly faded into oblivion.[16]

At its height, in 1939, the Portland Silvershirts chapter eventually grew to 250 members, and another 500 or so joined statewide. The city hosted a couple of mass Silvershirt rallies, drawing several hundred attendees to each, but by 1940 the usual local bickering and lack of popular momentum had again taken the life out of the fascists' attempts to organize, and the Legion disbanded.[17]

The Silvershirts had a much more vigorous presence in Washington, partly because the Legion developed into an actual political body. Organizing began as early as 1933, but remained relatively stagnant at about 150 members statewide by 1935. However, that all changed when Pelley's followers—notably, a Seattle organizer named Roy Zachary and a Chehalis Silvershirt named Orville Roundtree—succeeded in landing Pelley's name on the state's 1936 presidential ballot. Organizing as the Christian Party, the Silvershirt Legion cobbled together a slate of candidates for a variety of regional offices, including Roundtree as the party's nominee for the Third Congressional District and Seattle activists Malcolm Moore and Harry Picot as the nominees for governor and lieutenant governor, respectively.[18]

Pelley came to Washington in 1936 for several campaign rallies, pegging his political hopes on his steadily growing Northwest ranks. He spoke in Seattle twice, and appeared at a rally in Tacoma's Boxing Arena that reportedly drew 1,000. But Puget Sound also has a history of leftist labor organization, and Pelley's Boxing Arena speech attracted a crowd of opponents—described later by Pelley as "a mob of 500 Communists, led by diminutive Heinie Huss, radical Jewish labor agitator." The shouting, chanting crowd broke up the Silvershirt gathering.[19]

For all the attention Pelley attracted, his campaign was spectacularly unsuccessful. When Washington's ballots were counted that November, Pelley had garnered a mere 1,598 votes out of 692,340 (Franklin D. Roosevelt handily carried the state with 459,579 votes). Pelley finished behind both the Communist Party and Socialist Party nominees. Likewise, none of the nominees for statewide office collected more than a mere handful of votes.[20]

However, the campaign laid the groundwork for the Silvershirts' continued life, in several regards. Seattle organizer Roy Zachary—a onetime schoolteacher, timber-mill operator and clerical worker—was promoted to lead Pelley's recruitment and organization on a national level at the Asheville headquarters, and his skills are largely credited with keeping the Silvershirt Legion afloat from 1937-40.[21] Orville Roundtree, meanwhile, kept the home fires in Washington burning rather warmly.

Roundtree, an insurance salesman, used his Chehalis home base to lead a broader statewide recruiting drive after the 1936 campaign, and he enjoyed some noteworthy success. From the time of his arrival in 1935 until the Legion's apex in 1939, he increased the rolls from 150 to 1,600 members. He managed the feat by establishing Silvershirt chapters in 26 Washington cities, feeding members and local leaders a steady stream of propaganda and revolving speakers. He also secured a lodge near Redmond—the property of Rubie S. Johnson of Redmond, who had been the Christian Party's nominee for state school superintendent in 1936—as the permanent location for statewide Legion meetings, called Silvershirt Cavalcades.[22]

These gatherings were highly ritualistic and usually adorned with Nazi flags. Everyone was required to wear a uniform: for the men, silver-gray shirts with a scarlet silk "L"—for "Love, Loyalty and Liberation"—emblazoned over the heart, blue corduroy knickers and long socks; for women, a red-and-blue skirt worn with the same silver-gray shirt. All meetings opened with a rendition of the Legion's anthem, "The Battle Hymn of the Republic."[23]

Monthly local meetings were only slightly more relaxed, being simply smaller versions of the Cavalcades. Roundtree's Chehalis chapter of the Legion was the subject of a March 1939 profile by *Life* magazine on "Fascism in America": a two-page spread replete with photos of the uniformed members gathered in a small circle in Roundtree's living room, arms crossed and hands on chins thoughtfully, intently listening as their leader reads weekly instructions from Pelley. The same spread includes photos from a Seattle Swedish Lodge gathering of 300 or so Silvershirts who came to hear a Roy Zachary address—which included the claim that both President Franklin Roosevelt and Labor Secretary Perkins were secretly Jewish, and that "Washington has been turned over to the Jews." The text accompanying the spread notes that the Silvershirt audience was not comprised of "guttural-voiced 'hyphenated Americans' but simple folk of the kind to be found in any American small town. Depression-worried about their jobs and small businesses, groping for something to fight back at in a bewildering, swift-changing world, they were meat for William Dudley Pelley's Silver Shirt organizers and propaganda."[24]

The Christian Party machinery created for the 1936 election proved to be a worthy engine for continued Silvershirt organizing. The Seattle chapter of the Legion grew to 400 by 1937, while Spokane's smaller population drew some 350. Again, as with the Klan a decade before, internal bickering and outside opposition eventually unwound the mainspring; Orville Roundtree engaged in a power struggle with the Seattle Legion leader, Harry Picot, that drained the statewide organization of much of its energy by 1938. Further, the Silvershirts' Naziesque image was attracting unwanted attention.

In Spokane that July, chapter leader Isaac Crow organized a rally featuring Roy Zachary that drew a crowd of 700 or so protesters who far outnumbered the 300 or so attendees; trouble broke out when police moved in to stop the protest, and 11 people—mostly from the local chapter of the Communist Party—were arrested.

Crow began to become concerned about the increasingly anti-Semitic focus that Roundtree brought to the Legion's agenda, particularly in the speeches the Chehalis insurer gave to the Spokane crowds. Crow urged Roundtree to try emphasizing the political agenda, but Roundtree refused. Gradually, Crow cut back on his organizing work—Roundtree's wife later commented that he had simply become "too old for the fight"—and the Spokane Legion dissolved in entropy. So eventually, did the statewide Silvershirts organization—once 1,600 strong—by mid-1939.[25]

This was largely because suddenly Pelley and the Silvershirts were under attack on the national level. The Legion became a focus of the House Un-American Activities Committee's investigation into subversive groups in 1939, about the time that Pelley was attacking the committee as being the tool of Jews. He was called before the committee in 1940 and testified for three days; other legal problems began to catch up with him, and Pelley folded the Silvershirts Legion of America's shop that summer. Pelley tried staying afloat, but when the United States went to war with Hitler's Nazi Germany following the Japanese attack on Pearl Harbor in 1941, the tide turned with finality. Pelley was charged and convicted in June-August 1942 with conspiring to interfere with the success of American armed forces by distributing Nazi propaganda, and was sentenced to 15 years in prison.[26]

Ironically, the same event—Pearl Harbor and World War II—set off one of the greatest convulsions of hysterical scapegoating inspired by rightist conspiracy theories in American history, as white landowners along the entire Pacific Coast demanded the removal of all persons of Japanese descent—citizens and non-citizens alike—under the pretense that they posed a security threat to the people and industries on the coast. For years, a favorite theory of the Pacific Coast's rightists—notably trade-publishing magnate Miller Freeman of Seattle—was that the wave of Japanese immigrants who were increasingly making the West Coast their home were in fact "shock troops" for a planned invasion of America by the Japanese emperor. Faced now with actual war with Japan, Freeman and others who argued that everyone of Japanese descent comprised a potential "fifth column" of Nipponese loyalists moved swiftly, convincing officials in Washington (after the requisite congressional hearings) that their long-sought forced removal was the only appropriate solution. By mid-1942, some 110,000 Japanese-Americans (70,000 of them citizens) were forced out of their homes, rounded up and removed to "internment camps" located in the interior West, at places like Manzanar, California, and Minidoka, Idaho. White landowners moved in on the now-vacant property made habitable and arable by Japanese farmers; and when the relocation camps closed in late 1944, many of the communities in which the Japanese had previously lived organized campaigns (often successful) to discourage their return. The entire episode is considered today by legal experts to represent perhaps the most significant mass denial of basic constitutional guarantees for U.S. citizens in history.[27]

Once the "Japs" were vanquished, America soon found a new enemy: the Soviet Union and Communism. As news stories trumpeted the onset of the Cold War, Senator Joseph McCarthy and his "Red Scare" tactics swept like a tidal wave across the nation, searching for "Commies" in every corner of the country, including the halls of government. The Northwest was far from immune. In Washington in 1948, a Spokane legislator named Albert Canwell held state hearings on Communist activities, concluding that the state was "acrawl" with subversives, a finding that resulted in the dismissal of three faculty members at the University of Washington. Another accused man, philosophy professor Melvin Rader, successfully challenged the findings—in the end bringing ridicule upon Canwell and his eventual defeat at the polls.[28]

Nonetheless, Canwell's smear campaigns persisted. From Spokane, he published a newsletter titled "American Intelligence Report" that named individuals he believed were Communist traitors. In 1962, copies of the newsletter were distributed to every household in rural Okanogan County linking a "local state legislator" to the Communist Party, concluding: "These people are professionals. They are dangerous. They are out to kill us." Everyone in the county knew who the unnamed legislator was: John Goldmark, chairman of the House Ways and Means Committee and a Democrat. He and his wife, Sally, it was darkly rumored, were secret operatives for the Communist Party, and a few weeks later—just before the election—a local newspaper identified Sally as a member of a secret Communist group (all of which turned out to be provably false). Still, when voters turned out the next month for the primary election, John Goldmark finished fourth out of four candidates.[29] John and Sally Goldmark promptly sued their tormentors for libel and won on all counts, securing a $40,000 judgment. But in the minds of their community, they remained forever stained with the label of "Communist."

(The legacy of that stain haunted the family for decades afterward, and ultimately in the most nightmarish way possible. Twenty years later, on Christmas Eve 1985, a transient and devout anti-Communist named David Rice, who'd heard the Goldmarks' name prominently mentioned at local meetings of an anti-Communist group as prime examples of local Seattle subversives, entered the home of David and Annie Goldmark—John and Sally's son—on Queen Anne Hill in Seattle. He chloroformed the Goldmarks and their two young children and then proceeded to stab and beat them to death. Rice, who originally was condemned to death for the murders, won enough appeals regarding his handling at trial and sentencing to eventually plea-bargain his way into a life sentence with no chance of parole.)[30]

McCarthy-style smears, though, had already fallen out of favor on the national scene by the late 1950s, though as the 1962 Goldmark incident suggests, the propensity for them to occur on a local level lingered well after that. By 1954, McCarthy's own smear tactics had eventually resulted in his "condemnation" by his colleagues in the Senate, and he soon found himself out of power. Without his presence as a central charismatic figure on the national scene, the people who believed in fighting Communism had fallen into a kind of leaderless limbo by the late 1950s.[31]

Into the void stepped the John Birch Society.

★★★

The "clean" rightist politics of the John Birch Society—which often trod perilously close to suggesting the hoary myths of the anti-Semites when it scapegoated "international bankers" for America's ills, yet pronounced itself opposed to racism and anti-Semitism—enjoyed wide success in the Northwest in the 1960s. From school-teachers in Darby, Montana, to politicians in Washington and Oregon, the Birch Society's beliefs in a gigantic conspiracy were echoed often and loudly. When the Birch Society, founded in 1958, reached its estimated membership peak of 100,000 in 1964, surprisingly high numbers from the Northwest comprised its rolls. Larger aggregate numbers could be found in states like California, but the Northwest—Washington in particular—led the nation in per-capita enrollment.[32] The trend continued into the 1980s, when Idaho and Montana ranked second and third in per-capita enrollment (South Dakota was first) and Washington ranked sixth.[33]

It was in Idaho, though, mixed with a religious belief that Communism represented the very forces of Satan himself, that Birch beliefs became an especially potent brew that flowed freely throughout the wide-open farmlands. The LDS Church, so dominant on the social landscape, was the key ingredient in this theo-political force. Some of this was the result of the Birch Society's outright recruitment of Mormons to its cause. Robert Welch, the candymaker who founded the Society, stood before a portrait of the Mormon President and Prophet, David O. McKay, in 1966 and told a press conference: "If we are looking for conservative, patriotic Americans of good character, where would you go looking for them any more hopefully than among the Latter-day Saints? The Latter-day Saints are as individuals the kind of people we would like to have in the John Birch Society."[34]

The church/Birch connection was a mutual-admiration society. LDS apostle (and later prophet and president) Ezra Taft Benson appeared as a guest speaker at a 1963 Birch gathering in Los Angeles, touting the society as "the most effective non-church organization in our fight against creeping Socialism and Godless Communism."[35] Benson's sons were the society's Utah and Idaho coordinators. Fliers handed out at LDS gatherings in the 1960s pointed out similarities between the Birch Society's agenda and Mormon beliefs.[36]

The common ground exists on several levels. For Mormons, the U.S. Constitution is considered a sacred document inspired by God, and the church believes itself to be among its most dedicated defenders.[37] Since Communism at the time was widely believed to be the greatest threat to the American way of life, support for the Birch Society seemed only natural to many.

The mindset of the two belief systems is not dissimilar. A central story in *The Book of Mormon,* the seminal work of the LDS faith, tells of the Nephites, a tribe of Israelites who wandered all the way to America. Their efforts to establish a civilization in the wilderness were undermined by the conspiratorial "kingmen," evildoers who sought to place their fellow Nephites under authoritarian rule. Opposing them were the noble "freemen," who struggled mightily to counter the evil but ultimately were undone by treachery.[38] In the end, the "kingmen" conspiracy so weakened Nephite society from within that they were unable to withstand the onslaught of their enemies, the dark-skinned Lamaanites, who overpowered them in a final, apocalyptic battle at Cumorah Hill. At the battle's climax, a Nephite leader named Mormon buried the tribe's tale, inscribed on golden plates. Centuries later, LDS members believe, the angel Moroni revealed these plates to a young farm boy named

Joseph Smith who, though illiterate, was able to translate the plates as *The Book of Mormon.*[39]

The "kingmen" were notably similar to Freemasons in their rituals and titles, but they also bore a strong resemblance to the "conspirators within" who the Birch Society claimed comprised the Communist conspiracy within America's borders—indeed, at the highest level of the U.S. government (at the time, Birchers even claimed that President Dwight Eisenhower was an active Communist).[40] More important, perhaps, is the fact that the Mormons' religious beliefs may inspire acceptance of a conspiratorial worldview, one that neatly coincides with Bircher conspiracy claims.[41]

The Mormons' rapid adoption of the Birch Society in southern Idaho soon translated into political power for the group. When a Pocatello insurance salesman named George Hansen challenged Democratic incumbent Ralph Harding in the 1964 election for Idaho's southern-district House seat, it soon became clear which way the cards were falling. The LDS's Hansen was the Birch Society's man, while Harding, though also Mormon, wasn't tough enough on the Commies.

Harding complained to church authorities about the Birch connections, and some wrote him letters agreeing with his position. But the damage had already been done. Hansen won rather handily, launching a career that would career through a botched run for the Senate in 1968, head-on confrontations with the Internal Revenue Service during a second House term, a self-promotional trip to Iran to meet with the Ayatollah Khomeini during the 1979-80 hostage crisis, close connections with the Reverend Sun Myung Moon, and finally a disgraced departure from the House after he was convicted a second time on tax-evasion charges in 1983.[42] And in that time, regardless of the seemingly annual national embarrassment he brought to the state, George Hansen was perhaps the most unbeatable figure in all of Idaho politics.

By the time Hansen met his political demise, though, he and the John Birch Society had become harmless figures, comparatively speaking, in the Northwest far right. Bigger fish with bigger agendas were on the scene.

★★★

The letters all arrived the same way: neat, clean, carefully typed all in capitals. It was the neatness—and the capitals—that made them distinctive from many of the other letters to the editor that crossed my desk at the Sandpoint *Daily Bee*. After awhile, it was easy to recognize the correspondence from Robert Mathews.

The *Bee* was a small-town paper; we published five days a week and editions sometimes consisted of only 10 or 12 pages. We didn't get all that many letters to the editor, so we treasured the few we received. If someone wrote a letter to us, it was probably going to get published.

Robert Mathews' case, though, was different.

Mathews sent us letters regularly, one about every three or four weeks, from his home in Metaline Falls. This was actually out of the *Bee*'s circulation area, and we knew he sent the same letters to our sister paper, the weekly *Priest River*

Times, and its cross-river competitor, the *Newport Miner.* Since we preferred to publish letters from people who lived among our subscribers, we had an easy excuse not to run them.

There were better reasons, though. Almost inevitably, Mathews' missives were filled with anti-Semitic rants about the "Zionist Occupation Government" and the international banking conspiracy, and at other times were attacks on "shiftless blacks" whose welfare burden was killing the nation with taxes. Yes, we welcomed an open debate on the pages of the *Bee*; but we felt like we had to draw a line when it came to spreading hate and falsehoods.

Most of Mathews' letters went directly to the "round file." Because he wrote so regularly, though, I looked for an opportunity to reward his doggedness, deciding I would run a letter if it appeared to be free of racist or anti-Semitic references. This, however, never did occur.[43]

Robert Mathews' letters were part of a disturbing rising tide of racial hate, and bizarre radical-right belief systems, that we had observed in the Northwest in the 1970s. The phenomenon was a puzzling one, especially for those of us in the newspaper business, because we were uncertain how to respond to it. Were we simply observing a few loud-mouthed ranters wishing to attract attention to themselves? And, would covering them or allowing their hate to spew on our pages just give them the publicity, and the foothold, they sought? Would reporting on them just encourage them?

By this time, the John Birch Society's beliefs had developed something of a mainstream acceptance in Idaho politics, mostly through the continual re-election of such Birch-backed figures as George Hansen and U.S. Representative Steve Symms (later a U.S. Senator) of Idaho's northern House district. Certainly, as strange as the John Birch Society conspiracy theories often sounded, they were downright normal compared to some of the ideas we started to hear about by the late 1960s.

In 1968, a Portland retiree named Henry L. "Mike" Beach, who had been an Oregon state liaison for William Dudley Pelley's Silvershirts in the 1930s, founded a group called the Posse Comitatus that spread like wildfire through the rural areas of the Northwest and into California by the early 1970s, and through much of the rest of the nation by the mid-1970s. Beach taught that the sheriff of each county was the highest law of the land (thus the group's name, Latin for "power of the county"), and that the federal government had usurped citizens' powers. "We're strictly under a dictatorship," he claimed.[44] Beach also argued for a return to the "organic Constitution," which would strip the nation's ruling document back to its basic text and the Bill of Rights. Further, he said, people should form "common law" courts comprised of "sovereign citizens"—that is, those given citizenship under the "organic" law: namely, white male property owners.[45] By 1974, one such "court" had already organized in Eugene.[46]

Then there were the Minutemen. Not only did they preach a more rabid style of anti-Communist paranoia than the Birch Society, their activities also manifested, for the first time, the violent undercurrent of these beliefs.

Led by a Missourian named Robert DePugh, the Minutemen not only believed that the government had been infiltrated at its highest levels by Communists, but that a Communist takeover was virtually inevitable. Therefore, they told their believers, citizens should arm themselves with whatever weaponry would be effective as a counterforce to strike back when the takeover occurred. DePugh, a onetime associate of Robert Welch before DePugh was dropped from the John Birch Society, also told his followers to harass "the enemy," and compiled at his headquarters a list of 1,500 people he identified as members of the "Communist hidden government," with the intent to assassinate them in the event of the Communist coup.[47]

The Minutemen soon became associated with groups like Wesley Swift's Church of Jesus Christ-Christian, a Christian Identity organization located in Hollywood, California. Swift preached the "two-seed" brand of Identity, holding that not only are white people the true Israelites and descendants of Adam, but that blacks, Asians and other non-whites are "pre-Adamic" people without souls, and Jews are either descendants of Satan himself (the offspring of conjugal relations with Eve) or practitioners of a Satanic religion. Among Swift's more notable adherents: retired Colonel William Potter Gale, a former General Douglas MacArthur aide who eventually became a key figure in Posse Comitatus; and a quiet-spoken Lockheed engineer named Richard Girnt Butler.

Likewise in attendance at Swift's Sunday services was Keith Gilbert, a gunshop owner who also was a Minutemen member. Gilbert was arrested in 1965 and convicted for the theft of 1,400 pounds of TNT. He later said this was part of a plot to plant a bomb under the stage of the Hollywood Palladium during an Anti-Defamation League convention, and to detonate it during the keynote speech by the Reverend Martin Luther King Jr.—a plot only disrupted by Gilbert's arrest.[48]

Other Minutemen were getting into trouble around the nation. The group was connected to an October 1966 plot, broken up by the FBI in New York City, to bomb three summer camps operated by liberal East Coast organizations. And, illegal caches of weapons and ammunition linked to the Minutemen kept popping up around the countryside.[49]

By this point, though, DePugh had decided to move into the political arena. Using the Minutemen's agenda as a platform, he formed the Patriotic Party and made public speeches around the country touting its potential in the wake of Barry Goldwater's 1964 presidential election campaign, which he saw as a foothold for ultra-conservatives. Two of those appearances were in Seattle in 1966. A mail-room employee of Seattle City Light named Duane I. Carlson put up $500 of his own money to sponsor the Northwest convention of the Patriotic Party at the Hyatt House. In November, DePugh made a stump speech for a Patriotic Party gathering; some 600 people, paying $1 apiece, were in attendance. DePugh, however, only spoke to the crowd by a telephone hookup.[50] The Minutemen's leader was temporarily indisposed: he and an associate recently had been convicted on a variety of felony firearms violations and sentenced just the week before to four years in prison.[51]

Over the next year, DePugh fought that conviction, and managed to stay out of jail through a string of appeals. But the legal troubles started taking their toll on the organization's finances—and pressure mounted to find alternative sources of revenue.

Soon, Duane Carlson's activities moved well beyond public meetings. He gathered together a group of six other Seattle-area men—a longshoreman, a church sexton, a grocery clerk, a civilian driver at nearby Fort Lewis (U.S. Army), a self-employed draftsman, and an unemployed ship's oiler—and began plotting ways to finance the Minutemen's armaments operations and to strike a blow against the "Communist-controlled" government at the same time. Their plan: Set off a bomb at the city hall of a small Seattle suburb, Redmond, while simultaneously detonating another at the local power station, thereby simultaneously creating a major distraction while taking out police communications. This would enable the gang to strike three Redmond banks they had targeted for a series of successive robberies.

Their downfall, however, came when a federal informant infiltrated the group. On the day the Minutemen planned to strike—January 26, 1967—the FBI swooped down on them in two parking lots, one in Bellevue and another in Lake City, where the conspirators were meeting to carry out their plot, and arrested all seven. DePugh denied they were part of his organization, claiming Carlson had been dropped from his rolls for "non-payment of dues."[52] Federal prosecutors, who found evidence that DePugh actually was party to the plan from its early stages, put out a warrant for his arrest.

DePugh went into hiding but was caught a few months later hiding out in Spokane, where he was charged in the Redmond plot.[53] Five of the seven Seattle plotters were charged, and all five were convicted. DePugh, convicted in September 1970, wound up serving four years out of a ten-year sentence on the original firearms charges, but by then, his career in politics was in the ashheap. He later tried to resuscitate his ambitions by heading up an ultra-conservative organization called the Committee of 10 Million, but the numbers fell well short of those suggested by the group's name. DePugh currently is in prison again, this time on a 1992 conviction for sexual exploitation of a minor.[54]

After Minuteman (and would-be Martin Luther King assassin) Keith Gilbert finished five years of his prison term at Alcatraz in 1970, he moved to northern Idaho, where one of his acquaintances from Wesley Swift's church lived. With his friend's help, he set up a retail shop called AR-YA Electronics. He scandalized the locals by driving about in a swastika-inscribed Volkswagen.[55]

Gilbert's old acquaintance at Wesley Swift's Hollywood church, Richard Butler, had meanwhile taken over the reins of the congregation following Swift's death in 1971. Butler, on a visit to northern Idaho in the early '70s, decided it was time to fulfill his dream of creating an all-white "Aryan Homeland," and the Northwest was where he wanted to do it. In 1974, he purchased a 20-acre tract surrounded by forest near Hayden Lake and proceeded to move the Church of Jesus Christ-Christian from Hollywood to Idaho. Along the gravel roadway leading to the new compound he built, Butler erected a sign bearing the group's crest and the words designating the church's new home: "Aryan Nations."

Gilbert quickly became a high-profile member of the Aryan Nations. But Gilbert apparently always suspected Butler of selling him out on his 1965 arrest.[56] The tension erupted in 1977 with a public falling-out between the two, punctuated by Gilbert accusing Butler of a lack of will in confronting the "Zionist Occupation Government," and Butler accusing Gilbert of being a welfare cheat (correctly; Gilbert had done another short prison stint for welfare fraud since coming to Idaho). Gilbert promptly started up his own organization, the Socialist Nationalist Aryan People's Party, and started handing out flyers. Among them: "Hitler was Elijah," a two-page handout that expounded on the Nazi leader's place in history as a Biblical prophet.

Other flyers exhibited the white supremacists' idea of humor. It seemed as though nearly everyone in the Idaho Panhandle saw these flyers, and they left a vivid impression. I received one in the mail at the Sandpoint *Daily Bee*. It was an "Official Running Nigger Target," a shooting-range-style silhouette of a sprinting black man, replete with huge Afro and monstrous lips. The highest score listed on the target was on its feet, implying that the figure could take a shot in the head and keep going. Eventually, Gilbert confessed to distributing the posters.[57]

Outside of Gilbert—who was a moderately fit middle-aged man—most of the men we heard preaching this racial hatred, frequently rising to a violent call for arms, seemed merely to be impotent, frustrated old screechers who fantasized about violent acts but were completely incapable of carrying them out. Richard Butler of the Aryan Nations was the archetype, and I met more than a few men like him while I worked at the *Bee*. Many of their followers, middle-aged men with well-established beer guts, seemed similarly incapable. These men, some well into their 80s, seemed to be the kind of people from whom I would receive letters detailing vast conspiracy theories and calling for racial separation. Typically the letters were strangled, pompous-sounding prose, grandiose and melodramatic and incompetent all at once, often making scarcely any sense at all. Robert Mathews wrote like that.

So, although I had never met Robert Mathews, I had a mental picture of him: some aging logger or miner who took the radical's path somewhere late in life, bellyaching about taxes and the government and blaming it all on racial politics. The kind, in my work as a reporter, I had met plenty of—living out in the woods, eking out a living, often spreading the word with his buddies at a local backwoods bar.

I couldn't have been more wrong.

★★★

When growing up in Arizona in the 1950s, his parents and friends called him Robbie. Robbie's dad worked for a paper manufacturer, and the family—Johnny and Una and the three boys—all lived a quiet suburban life in the Phoenix suburbs. Except, of course, when Grant, the oldest, was diagnosed as a schizophrenic. Then the two younger boys, Lee and Robbie, seemed to draw closer together, partly because their parents had to spend so much time tending to Grant's needs. Lee and Robbie seemed normal and well-adjusted.

Robbie, on the other hand, did develop peculiar interests that were all his own. He joined the John Birch Society in 1964 at age 11. A lot of the older men in the organization encouraged the young enthusiast, giving him a sense of accomplishment he didn't get from his classmates. Then Robbie joined the Mormon Church. Once he graduated from high school, he decided not to go to college; campuses were too full of Commies, he told his parents. Instead, he went off to work in a mine.

At night, though, the 19-year-old Robbie Mathews was carrying the crusade against Communism to another level. Working with other Mormons and some fellow young Birchers, Mathews organized a group called the Arizona Sons of Liberty. They conducted paramilitary training sessions in the desert, preparing for the day when the Communists would try to take over the country.[58]

The FBI soon came down on Robbie's group for its illegal nighttime weapons training, and he fled to California for awhile to let things cool down. When he returned to Arizona, he promptly got into trouble again, this time for listing 10 dependents on his income-tax form—while claiming "single" status. Robbie was arrested, convicted of tax evasion, and placed on probation. When his probation ran out the summer of 1974, he decided to clear out and make a fresh start somewhere else.[59]

Bob, as he now called himself, had always been fascinated with his Scottish ancestry, and he imagined the Pacific Northwest to be a landscape like the Highlands of his forefathers' country. So, he and a buddy drove up there, hoping to scout out a mining job somewhere. Mathews found one in the northeast corner of Washington, at a lead and zinc mine run by Bunker Hill in the town of Metaline Falls. Later that summer, with help from his father, Johnny, he bought a plot of land a little outside of town.

Bob married a Kansas girl named Debbie McGarrity who he met through a personals ad in 1976. He worked the land hard, hoping to carve out a home for his family. Combined with his mine work, it made him muscular, lean and fit. Three years later, Johnny retired and he and Una moved to Metaline Falls, where Bob had built them a home. Johnny had made Bob promise that there would be no more involvement with radical politics.[60]

However, by 1980, it was clear Bob was falling back on his promise. Still pursuing his interest in the far right, he had been reading books published by William Pierce's National Alliance, including *The Turner Diaries,* a novel detailing the eruption of a race war in America. He began writing voluminous letters to the editors of local papers. And, he began attending Butler's gatherings in Hayden Lake, an hour's drive away. In February 1982, he had his first son baptized at the Church of Jesus Christ-Christian.

By June 1983, Mathews was in the fore of Butler's entourage. He served as a security officer for an Aryan Nations rally in Spokane's Riverside Park, and got into a shouting-and-pointing match with a group of counter-protesters. The next month, Mathews was in the audience listening as Butler hosted that year's Aryan Congress. The main topic of discussion was the martyr's death the month before of Gordon Kahl, a 63-year-old Posse Comitatus leader from North Dakota. Kahl had killed two lawmen in a February standoff near his family farm, went on the lam for five months, and killed another lawman before dying himself when he was finally cornered in rural Arkansas.[61] The gathering at Hayden Lake featured one expression of outrage after another over Kahl's fate.

The crowd also heard ex-Klansman Louis Beam, who had led a vigilante Texas army in its harassment of Vietnamese fishermen in 1981, proclaim: "We are at war! We must pledge our blood for the new nation! There's nothing we won't do to bring about the new kingdom, the new nation!" Michigan racist leader Bob Miles, in his speech, suggested it was time to fight back. Miles expressed admiration for radical Black Liberation Army members who had committed a Brinks armored-car robbery in 1981: "If we were half the men the leftists were, we'd be hitting armored cars too."[62]

All these calls for action apparently had their effect on Bob Mathews. Shortly after that 1983 Congress, he began assembling a group of close friends and fellow believers in a spinoff organization he called the White American Bastion.[63] Their ultimate purpose: igniting a civil war that would liberate the "white race." In late September, he called eight others to his farm and, with the infant daughter of one of the men placed in a circle on the floor of a woodshed, they swore an oath as "Aryan Warriors," concluding with: "We hereby invoke the blood covenant and declare that we are in a full state of war and will not lay down our weapons until we have driven the enemy into the sea and reclaimed the land which was promised to our fathers of old, and through our blood and His will, becomes the land of our children to be."[64] They called themselves the Bruders Schweigen (Silent Brotherhood), or, at other times, a name William Pierce had given the band in *The Turner Diaries:* The Order.

First on the to-do list, the group agreed, was to acquire money to finance their schemes. They tried their hand at a logging contract, but the effort lasted one dismal day of thrashing about in the thick, north Idaho woods. Mathews was fit enough for the job, but not many others were. So, they turned to their second option: robbery.[65]

On October 26, 1983, four men led by Mathews nervously committed a robbery of a Spokane X-rated video shop, making off with a grand total of $396.10. In short order, they graduated to more ambitious heists; Mathews pulled off a solo robbery of a City Bank branch north of Seattle for $25,900 in December; his two right-hand men, Bruce Pierce and Gary Yarbrough, robbed an Idaho truck stop; then the same pair robbed a Spokane bank, creating a distraction by leaving a fake bomb near the video shop they had robbed previously. The trio started to hit their stride when they robbed an armored car at a Seattle Fred Meyer store in March 1984. A month later, they hit another armored car at Seattle's Northgate Mall, making off this time with $250,000.[66]

Nor was robbery their only means of extralegal fund-raising. Yarbrough, a former Arizona prison inmate, had tried making counterfeit bills using the printing press at the Aryan Nations compound, where he was a security officer. But the phonies were badly made; Pierce was arrested for trying to pass them off in Union Gap, Washington, though he later walked on bail and promptly disappeared. After that incident, though, Mathews decided to employ more professional means.

Mathews attended church services that spring at a Christian Identity congregation in LaPorte, Colorado, led by the Reverend Pete Peters. It was there that he met Robert Merki, a former Boeing engineer who was on the lam for counterfeiting. With his robbery money, Mathews set up Merki and his wife with a printing press and a little house in Boise, Idaho, that became The Order's operational center—a meeting place, information locus, and counterfeiting factory. They passed the counterfeit bills using a network of associates that spread all the way to Philadelphia.

All this wealth did not remain in Mathews' hands. The Order distributed it freely to fellow believers in the white supremacist movement. Mathews traveled around the country and dropped off bundles of money to William Pierce, to Richard Butler at the Aryan Nations compound, to a Klan leader in North Carolina, to Tom Metzger of the White Aryan Resistance, and to Bob Miles in Michigan.[67]

Working now from a real power base, Mathews made preparations to move on to the next stage of "the revolution": assassination. Atop the list was Morris Dees, the brilliant lawyer who headed the Southern Poverty Law Center in Alabama, a man whose career was built on making life hell for the radical right. But closer to home, and just a little further down the list, was a man who had gotten truly under Mathews' skin: a Denver radio talk-show host named Alan Berg.

Not only was Berg Jewish, he also liked to roast his right-wing callers on the air, then cut them off. Among his victims had been Colonel Jack Mohr, a speaker Mathews had idolized since his days in the Arizona Sons of Liberty, and David Lane, a member of Mathews' band. So, on a warm June evening, as Berg arrived home from work and stepped from his Volkswagen beetle, a car containing Mathews, Pierce and Lane pulled up. Pierce stepped out, pulled out a MAC-10 automatic assault gun and poured .45-caliber slugs into the radio jockey. Berg died instantly, and the killers made a clean getaway. Police were baffled for months by the assassination.

Mathews then decided it was time to make a hit for big money. On July 12, 1984, with a group of 12 men, The Order staged a mid-highway robbery of a Brinks armored car outside the northern California town of Ukiah, where they made off with $3.8 million. It remains the largest overland bank robbery in American history.[68]

At about the same time, though, the scheme began to unravel for Mathews. His Philadelphia contact, Thomas Martinez, was caught passing phony bills. Faced with jail time, Martinez soon started spilling his guts to the FBI about Mathews' activities. Simultaneously, a gun left behind at the Ukiah robbery put the FBI on the trail of Pierce and Yarbrough. They nearly nabbed Yarbrough in an ambush at his Sandpoint home in mid-October, but Yarbrough escaped. Pierce hid out in Nevada. Mathews and the rest of the group stayed mobile.

Tom Martinez flew out to Portland in late November to meet with Mathews, who had found a "safe house" to rent in a nearby suburb. By then, the FBI had converted Martinez into an informant, and when he met with The Order leaders at a Portland motel November 24, federal agents swooped in on the gang. They captured Yarbrough, but Mathews made a mad dash to escape, wounding one agent in the leg and suffering a hand wound himself.

Two weeks later, an anonymous informant spilled the secret of Mathews' whereabouts to the FBI. Mathews, Ronald Duey and the Merkis were hiding on Whidbey Island, a sizeable strip of land north of Seattle in Puget Sound, accessible by bridge from its northern end and by ferry from the south. Again, the FBI swooped in, successfully capturing the Merkis and Duey on the morning of Friday, December 7.

Bob Mathews, though, refused to leave the cabin where he was holed up, and he stayed there the next day, while the FBI tried to negotiate. When agents tried to storm the cabin on Saturday afternoon, he repelled them with a barrage of automatic fire. Finally, as night approached, the agents lobbed a flare into the cabin to light up the scene. The flare set the building on fire. Still Mathews did not come out. The fire was punctuated by explosions as his weapons cache caught flame, and the building burned to the ground. The next day, sifting through the ashes, they found Bob Mathews' charred body, curled up inside the bathtub.

Over the course of the next year, 24 people would be indicted for The Order's crimes. Twelve pleaded guilty; 10 were convicted in December 1985 by a Seattle jury, while another, Richard Scutari, pleaded guilty after finally being apprehended in 1986. The last, David Tate, was never tried; instead, he was convicted in the 1985 slaying of a Missouri state trooper and is serving a life sentence. The major players—Bruce Pierce, Gary Yarbrough and David Lane—all will be in prison for the rest of their lives. A few months after the trial concluded, the Aryan Nations' security chief, Elden "Bud" Cutler, was convicted of hiring a hit man (who actually was an undercover FBI agent) to behead Tom Martinez; he was given a 12-year sentence.

The Order's legacy was debated among the leaders of the far right for awhile; some suggested Mathews had hurt their cause more than he had helped it. Richard Butler, the aging leader of the Aryan Nations, wasn't among them. The Order, he said, was in the vanguard of the fight for racial purity.

"The future is theirs," he said. "We cannot tell them what to do. It encourages me, because it shows there are still some patriotic young men in this country."[69]

Keith Gilbert agreed. He asked for Mathews' remains to be released to his Post Falls, Idaho, organization, saying the man deserved a hero's burial. "He is a man of honor," Gilbert said. "He is a soldier killed in the line of battle. He's a martyr."[70]

Within his own family, though, Mathews' death was simply tragic. Lee Mathews, speaking from his Metaline Falls home, was critical of his brother's actions. "My brother is the one who joined the Nazi group," he said. "If he hadn't done this he'd be alive today. I'm not so sure he didn't want to die. If there's anybody we hold hatred for, it's the neo-Nazis.

"I love my brother, but I was totally against what he was doing."[71]

Mathews himself had died with an eye on his legacy. Two days before the shootout, he had mailed off a final, four-page letter to his old hometown newspapers. It rambled on about his experiences in Arizona and Metaline Falls, and concluded with a premonition of his onrushing death:

"I am not going into hiding: rather I will press the FBI and let them know what it is like to become the hunted. Doing so it is only logical to assume that my days on this planet are rapidly drawing to a close. Even so, I have no fear. For the reality of life is death, and the worst the enemy can do to me is shorten my tour of duty in this world. I will leave knowing that my family and friends love me and support me. I will leave knowing that I have made the ultimate sacrifice to secure the future of my children."

Four days after he died, his last letter ran in the Sandpoint *Daily Bee.* In full.

★★★

Bob Mathews and The Order weren't the only people from the radical right stirring up trouble. Beginning in 1980, a series of incidents underscored the violence brewing in northern Idaho:

—Some black families in Coeur d'Alene started receiving notes in the mail saying, "Nigger, don't let the sun set on your head in the Aryan Nations."

—A Jewish restaurateur's Hayden Lake steakhouse was spray-painted with swastikas and the words "Jew swine." He promptly put the restaurant up for sale, and a year later was out of business altogether. Swastika graffiti also started popping up around the Coeur d'Alene area, notably on a Baptist church and a printing business.

—A Coeur d'Alene woman whose son was of mixed racial heritage suffered a barrage of hate-filled threats from a neighbor who attended Aryan Nations meetings. Among them: a poster mailed to her warning that "race traitors, those guilty of fratinizing [*sic*] socially or sexually with blacks, now stand warned that their identities are being catalogued . . . Miscegenation is race treason, race treason is a capitol [*sic*] offence; it will be punished by death." When the boy encountered the man in the neighborhood one day, his tormentor asked: "How art thou today? Thou shalt not live very long."[72]

—A group of young white males associated with the Aryan Nations physically and verbally attacked a young mixed-race couple outside of a Coeur d'Alene bowling alley.

—Crosses were burned on the lawns of two different Coeur d'Alene families in 1982 and 1983. In the latter case, the victims were an all-white family living in a mixed-race neighborhood, mistakenly targeted, police say.[73]

The trouble caused the community to reach a boiling point. Trying to counter the venom bubbling out of the Aryan Nations, a group of Coeur d'Alene ministers put together a proclamation denouncing racism and anti-Semitism in late 1980. By the next year, combining the efforts of Kootenai County's newly hired Undersheriff, Larry Broadbent, the Reverend Rick Morse from the ministers' group, community activist Dina Tanners, and several others, the Kootenai County Human Rights Task Force was under way, forming a community front that included business, church and government leaders. The group's efforts were instrumental two years later in passage by the Idaho Legislature of a law making malicious harassment—for racial, ethnic or religious reasons—a felony.[74]

Father Bill Wassmuth, pastor of Coeur d'Alene's St. Pius X Catholic Church, took the reins of the KCHRTF in late 1984, incorporating it in 1985 as a non-profit entity. The group immediately raised its profile, especially by drawing in the participation of the Chamber of Commerce and local business leaders. It began pushing for passage of a bill outlawing paramilitary groups in the state.

It wasn't long before the objects of this campaign struck back. On September 15, 1986, a pipe bomb was left behind the door to a back room of Wassmuth's Coeur d'Alene home while he was asleep. No one was injured, but the blast blew out a part of the house, and would have been lethal had anyone been in the room.[75] (At his trial later, the man who threw the bomb admitted that the original plan was to throw it in Wassmuth's bedroom, but he changed his mind at the last moment.)[76]

Two weeks later, three other bombs went off: at the Coeur d'Alene Federal Building, on the roof of a couple of retail stores, and in a restaurant parking lot. A fourth unexploded bomb was found on the roof of a building kitty-corner from the Federal Building. An anonymous woman phoned offices at North Idaho College, where a human-rights rally had been held the week before, and tried to pin the blame on black revolutionaries: "Three pipe bombs have gone off already. You wanted a nigger uprising, and now you've got one, honey."[77]

Richard Butler similarly tried to pin the blame for the bombings on the Anti-Defamation League, but within a few days the chickens came home to roost in the Aryan Nations' own back yard. Police raided the home of Butler's new security chief, David Dorr, and found explosives and other evidence linking him and three others to the crimes. Two of them, a husband-and-wife team, also were discovered to be operating a counterfeiting scheme.

They called themselves the Bruders Schweigen Strike Force II, or The Order II. The counterfeiting couple pleaded guilty that winter after two days of a jury trial. Dorr was convicted in the spring of conspiracy, firearms charges and counterfeiting after the fourth figure, a former chief henchman named Robert Pires, turned state's evidence on all involved. Furthermore, Pires told authorities he and Dorr had killed another Aryan Nations follower—a onetime pal of Pires'—when they came to feel he could no longer be trusted. Pires pleaded guilty to first-degree murder, then was the chief witness against Dorr, who received a 40-year sentence for the combined crimes.[78]

For every action there is an opposite and equal reaction, and this chain of violence—from The Order and The Order II, to the death threats against minorities—brought down law-enforcement officials on the Aryan Nations compound in a big way. Although Richard Butler himself was charged with sedition in 1987, along with William Pierce, Louis Beam and a host of other national white-supremacist leaders, and acquitted by an all-white Arkansas jury, he was never charged as an accessory or for incitement to any of the crimes. But his compound soon was swarming, it seemed, with federal informants—independent investigators who contract with the federal agencies to work undercover. Just such an informant, Pires, had been the key to cracking The Order II case. But, as a harbinger of the problems the role of informants would pose, Pires also had been a participant in the crimes. Many of the men pulled into this line of work either were unsavory or were just craven racists who gladly squealed on their Aryan brothers if it meant saving their own skins.

Among the undercover investigators was a former professional wrestler named Rico Valentino, a big, blustering guy who claimed he had become a born-again Christian and

Identity follower, and now was a tax protester fleeing the IRS. In truth, the FBI gave him $100,000 for three years' work as an informant, and Valentino put the money to use. He bought the Aryan Nations a new water tank, paid for new flooring and roofing at a compound bunkhouse, and even bought a large new metal "Aryan Nations" sign for the compound gate. The generosity effectively encouraged Butler and most of his followers to trust Valentino as one of their own.[79]

In 1990, a small group that included Valentino began laying out the blueprint for continuing the work of The Order. Their plan: to engage in a series of bombing attacks on the enemy—homosexuals, blacks, Jews and Asians.

Their first target, they decided, would be a large Seattle gay disco called Neighbours in the city's Capitol Hill neighborhood. They tested a pipe bomb in the woods and were impressed by its explosive power, especially if it were to go off in the middle of a crowded room. Neighbours was known to pack in as many as 300 people on a weekend night—the place "would resemble a meat grinder." They worked out a "kill zone" strategy in which the explosives would be placed inside the bar, with other bombs placed outside. Then they would call the bar, give warning that a bomb was about to go off, and set off the charges as the disco cleared out, creating a greater fatality rate.[80]

On Saturday, May 12, the trio of Valentino, Robert John Winslow and Stephen E. Nelson, the Aryan Nations security chief, drove together to Seattle in a van stocked with pipe-bomb makings, a .12-gauge shotgun, a .38-caliber revolver, a stun gun, knives and a pile of hate literature. As they got out of the van to check into a SeaTac motel near the Seattle airport, the FBI moved in and arrested them. In Hayden Lake, they arrested another member of the group at his home: Procter James Baker, 58, an Aryan Nations regular. Winslow, Nelson and Baker went to jail; Valentino went into protective hiding to await the trial as the chief witness in the case. In October, after 10 days of testimony, a Boise jury convicted all three on conspiracy, bomb-possession and firearms charges. They were sentenced to a range of prison terms, with Nelson getting the longest, a 25-year sentence. Baker served two years of his 10-year term before being released on probation.

Another informant, working for the Bureau of Alcohol, Tobacco and Firearms, was also getting close to some of the more radical members of the Aryan Nations. He told everyone he was Gus Magisono, an East Coast arms dealer and biker who had become a white supremacist, and he looked the part—big, burly and bearded. His real name was Ken Fadeley, a private investigator who, unlike the unsavory types who typically comprised the ranks of informants, had turned to undercover work when a friend of his in Spokane, a cop, was killed by a gang of bikers in 1983.

Fadeley had befriended a Bonners Ferry man named Frank Kumnick at the Aryan Nations who talked often about carrying on the work begun by The Order. Kumnick's idea revolved around his workplace, a private school near Sandpoint, Idaho, called the Rocky Mountain Academy, where Kumnick was a maintenance man. It catered to the children of wealthy families; among its students was the daughter of newscaster Barbara Walters. Kumnick, Fadeley said, talked about kidnapping a group of the students, especially Walters' daughter, and holding them for a huge ransom. The money then would be used to finance "the cause."[81]

In January 1987, Fadeley met with Kumnick in Sandpoint to talk about providing the guns needed for his plan. Kumnick was nervous about Fadeley, and brought along a friend of his, someone he trusted, to help check out the "arms dealer."

The friend's name: Randy Weaver.

★★★

The Weaver family moved to the Idaho Panhandle in the summer of 1983 from Iowa, drawn by religious visions of an imminent Armageddon and a belief that God was calling them. Randy and Vicki, married in 1971, had been drawn into a hardcore survivalist belief system based on "Bible prophecy" in the years after their conversion in the early 1970s to fundamentalist Christianity. They simply loaded up a truck one day, put their worldly possessions and their three children—Sara, Sammy and Rachel—in the back, and headed off to Idaho, trusting that God would find them a home. When they first saw a plot of land tucked away in the woods south of Bonners Ferry that September, they knew it was the place God had intended for them; indeed, it matched perfectly the place Vicki had seen in her visions.[82] The locals called it Ruby Ridge.

The family slowly jigsawed together a cabin made from timber cut on the property and scraps from a local lumberyard, straddling it on the rocky ridge. Randy got a job at a local timber mill. By 1986, they were driving the hour or so south to Richard Butler's church for the occasional Aryan Congress, and Randy gradually was drawn into full-blown Christian Identity beliefs, an easy progression from his survivalist views. They frequently went with Frank Kumnick and his wife. But the Weavers never joined the Aryan Nations, mainly because of the large numbers of ex-convicts attracted to the compound.

The Weavers and the Kumnicks were close friends from early on, and the four of them, Randy and Frank especially, would weave many conversations in the local coffee shops and pizza parlors, mostly complaining about Jews and niggers and queers. Randy Weaver was fond of black-leather clothes, and he was known to wear German SS insignias on his jacket around Bonners Ferry. Frank Kumnick met Ken Fadeley, the ATF informant, at the 1986 Aryan Congress. Early the next year, Fadeley drove up to Sandpoint to talk over Kumnick's plans to raise money for "the cause." Weaver accompanied Kumnick, and watched impassively in the car where the three men met as Kumnick pulled out a gun and held it to Fadeley's head until he was satisfied the "arms dealer" wasn't an undercover agent.[83]

After awhile, Fadeley and the ATF agents he was in contact with on the case realized Kumnick was a wild talker but not inclined to, or likely even capable of, taking action. Randy Weaver, though, was a different case. Weaver was much more serious, and in 1989, Fadeley later said, Randy approached him with an offer to sell him some sawed-off shotguns.[84]

Randy had run for Boundary County sheriff, promising only to enforce the laws "the citizens" wanted him to enforce. On the back of fliers touting his candidacy were the words: "Get out of jail free." He told a Sandpoint-based reporter for the Spokane paper that he was opposed to mixed marriages.[85] When the primary election came around, Randy lost by a wide margin. By the next year, he was scraping for work and looking for ways to make money. So when Fadeley visited him that October—the two had run into each other at that year's Aryan Congress—Randy told him he was ready to do business. You want some .12 gauges cut off? he asked Fadeley. I can get you up to five Remingtons a week.

The real object of Fadeley's interest was not a minor player like Randy Weaver, but a couple of men in Montana who the ATF agents believed were engaged in gun-running, perhaps over the Canadian border: Chuck Howarth, a former Ku Klux Klansman who, after serving prison time for illegally possessing explosives, had moved to the Noxon area; and David Trochmann, a Constitutionalist and Identity follower from Minnesota who had moved to Montana in 1984. Trochmann's brother and sister-in-law John and Carolyn had moved out to join him in 1988. David's son Randy lived there with them, too.[86]

Randy Weaver was a friend of the Trochmanns, and Fadeley talked to him that October day about driving to Montana to talk to David Trochmann. Randy put him off, but wanted to deal in sawed-off guns. A couple of weeks later, the pair made the transaction at the Sandpoint City Park.

The two of them never did make it to Montana. Weaver grew increasingly suspicious of "Gus" and kept putting off the trip. The following summer, Fadeley was questioned about his identity by the Aryan Nations security chief Steve Nelson and Procter James Baker—two months before their arrest for the Seattle disco bombing plot—and the informant knew his cover there had been blown. The arms-dealing career of "Gus Magisono" was over.

ATF agents were chagrined at losing such a valuable source of inside information, especially since they felt they were getting somewhere on the Montana gun-running case. But they had an ace in the hole: Randy Weaver had sold Fadeley two sawed-off shotguns. By leaning on Weaver, perhaps, they could get close enough to the Trochmanns to determine whether they were up to something illegal.

One day in the summer of 1990, the Spokane ATF bureau chief and another agent drove up to meet Randy and talk it over with him. Most criminals, placed in the same situation, usually squeal quickly and loudly on their comrades-in-arms. But Randy Weaver backed away from the two agents when they made their offer—no prosecution on the gun charges if he'd help them on surveillance of Trochmann and Howarth—and told them: "You can go to hell."

Six months later, with a warrant out for his arrest, ATF agents arrested Weaver on the road leading to his home. But Weaver only spent one night in jail; a part-time magistrate hearing the case let him go on a $10,000 unsecured bond. He retreated to his Ruby Ridge home and refused to leave the property. When he failed to show for his February 1991 trial in Moscow, Idaho, Randy Weaver officially became a fugitive, and his case was handed over to the U.S. Marshals Service.

The marshals decided to proceed carefully, since they knew Weaver carried weapons and would be likely to resist. They first tried negotiating with him through family friends, but that got them nowhere. Public pressure began to mount, especially as media accounts of Weaver's running feud with authorities started to make headlines.[87] The Weavers remained holed up in their cabin; Vicki gave birth there in October 1991 to their fourth child, a girl they named Elisheba. Meanwhile, a family friend named Kevin Harris joined them on the mountaintop and started making trips into town to get them their supplies. The 24-year-old had been "adopted" by the Weavers nine years before when he was a teenager in trouble with the law, and had eventually become the only old friend the Weavers trusted. He was close pals with Sammy, the Weavers' 13-year-old son.

By the summer of 1992, the marshals had been working the case for a year. They set up monitors around the Weaver cabin and observed the family's movements. They knew Weaver had made a few quiet trips into town and they hoped they could detect when he made such moves, on the chance they'd be able to capture him away from his family.[88] On Friday, August 21, a group of six marshals went in to check the monitors and do a strategic survey of the Weavers' land.

The trip went horribly awry. The Weavers' dog, Striker, detected the men below the cabin and began heading in their direction. Thinking the dog was after a deer, Randy, Sammy and Kevin Harris started following him. The marshals, fearing the dog would give away their presence and the position of the monitors, shot Striker. But by then it was too late; the Weavers were already upon them. One stood up and announced their presence, and Randy turned and fled.

Sammy Weaver was close enough to witness Striker's death, though. He turned to the marshal who had fired the gun and shouted: "You killed my dog, you son of a bitch!" He opened fire on them, and they returned the gunshots. Kevin Harris wheeled and fired his deer rifle into the chest of one of the marshals. Sammy fell dead, shot in the back and in one arm, in the hail of gunfire, but Harris escaped unscathed. Also dead: William Degan, the veteran marshal Harris had fired his gun at.[89]

The Ruby Ridge standoff had begun.[90]

Immediately, the case became the purview of the FBI, who moved in a horde of agents trained in tactical assault, and surrounded the Weaver property with every piece of hardware imaginable—and with a full complement of snipers.

The next day, Randy and Kevin went outside the cabin with their guns, 16-year-old Sara in tow; the dogs were barking again, and they wanted to see why. Unable to spot anything, they headed back to the cabin, but Randy decided to pay a visit to the shed where they had placed Sammy's body. As he reached the door, a sniper fired, hitting him in the side. He ran for the cabin, Kevin Harris close behind him; Sara was already on the stoop when the firing began. The sniper, believing Harris was about to aim at a helicopter containing other agents, fired at the young man as he made a dash for the cabin door. He missed.

Standing behind the door, holding it open for the men, with the baby Elisheba in her arms, was Vicki Weaver. The sniper's shot intended for Harris hit her squarely in the head, killing her instantly. Her skull exploded, and the fragments from it and the bullet pierced Harris' side, wounding him severely. The girls screamed and screamed. The baby was still in Vicki's arms; Randy pried it from her dead grasp a few minutes later.

Vicki's body remained where it had fallen, under the kitchen table. Kevin's and Randy's wounds were bound up, and the family settled into its long wait. They fully expected the "ZOG bastards" to finish them off. Sara prayed that it would come soon, that the agents would set fire to the cabin and end the standoff.[91]

Instead, someone else showed up at their cabin a few days later: Colonel James "Bo" Gritz.

The most decorated Green Beret in the Vietnam War, and a folk hero to many veterans and families of men missing in action in Southeast Asia, Gritz showed up Wednesday at the blockade on the road leading to Ruby Ridge. He was not alone; a crowd of Weaver supporters, including a conclave of Portland skinheads and friends from the Aryan Nations church, had gathered there, harassing police and federal agents who stood guard at the blockade. The Trochmanns also were there; Carolyn Trochmann cooked pancakes in the mornings and gave interviews to visiting reporters.

Gritz tried for two days to talk his way into Weaver's cabin, saying he could negotiate an end to the standoff. The FBI at first refused, but when Weaver indicated he'd be willing to talk with Gritz, the FBI added him to the negotiating team. On Friday, Gritz met with Weaver for the first time. By Sunday, he and his co-negotiator, retired Arizona lawman Jack McLamb, had talked Harris into surrendering and removing Vicki's body. On Monday, Randy surrendered, his two daughters emerging with him into the sunlight and the waiting arms of the FBI.

As Gritz walked past the blockade and announced the surrender, he spoke to the group of skinheads gathered at the road. "Mr. Weaver wanted me to pass this along to those of you out here," he said, and then gave them a stiff-armed Nazi salute.

Randy Weaver and Kevin Harris went to trial in Boise in April 1993. Gerry Spence, the famed defense attorney who had made national headlines in the Karen Silkwood case, was in Weaver's corner. Spence spent the trial trying to convince jurors that Weaver had simply been trying to defend himself and his family against overzealous, arrogant law-enforcement officials. As always, Spence succeeded.

Kevin Harris was acquitted of killing Marshal Degan. Weaver was cleared of conspiracy and all other charges, except for the original one that brought the marshals knocking on his door in the first place: failure to appear in court on the firearms charge. He spent another four months in jail, and then reunited with his surviving children in Iowa.

★★★

The Ruby Ridge case officially ended then, but it was a stone thrown into a pond whose ripples have since grown into a tidal wave.

For FBI officials, the case meant years of self-examination and, ultimately, an internal scandal. The initial Justice Department investigation mostly exonerated the officials atop the agency but left some of the agents, especially those on the scene, on the hook for Vicki Weaver's death. The agent in charge at the Weaver scene, Gene

Glenn, wound up taking the rap for the incident, at least within the bureau. His complaints to the Justice Department led to a second probe in 1995, one which, this time, placed blame for the altered "rules of engagement" at the scene—which many observers said were responsible for the atmosphere in which Vicki Weaver was killed—where it belonged: on the higher-ups who had approved them. They were demoted not only for participating in altering the rules, but in covering up their approval later. At about the same time, the FBI settled a wrongful-death suit with the Weavers for $3.1 million.

Congressional hearings, held for three weeks in the summer of 1995, also tried to get at the heart of the matter, but no easy scapegoats were found. Republicans in charge of the hearings attempted to vilify the FBI and the ATF, and a final report condemned the agencies' actions and called the sniper's shot "unconstitutional," although both the trial and the Senate hearings confirmed the sniper's contention that he was operating under standard rules of engagement, protecting other agents—in this case, the men in the helicopter. Almost unnoticed in the testimony, which included Randy Weaver and Bo Gritz, was that offered by Karen Degan, widow of the murdered marshal:

"What kind of message has the government sent my two boys by paying the Weavers millions of dollars for the events of Ruby Ridge? And what kind of message will these hearings ultimately send these boys? As it stands now, the message is that this is a topsy-turvy world where those who deny the law are somehow transformed into heroes and martyrs and those who work to enforce the law are labeled 'trained killers.' "[92]

★★★

Precisely those upside-down views began growing in the weeks and months immediately after the Ruby Ridge standoff. The Reverend Pete Peters, pastor of the LaPorte Church of Christ in Colorado—the Identity preacher who had ministered to Bob Mathews as he was forming The Order—decided it was time to make hay with the new martyrs of the right wing. A few days after Weaver surrendered, he sent out a batch of letters to like-minded men around the nation, inviting them to a gathering in Estes Park, Colorado, to "confront the injustice and tyranny manifested in the killings of Vicki Weaver and her son Samuel." Some 160 accepted; they ranged from Richard Butler to Larry Pratt, head of the arch-conservative Gun Owners of America.

The Estes Park gathering, October 23-25, 1992—titled "A Gathering of Christian Men"—spent three days rehashing the Weaver case, but it also was a strategy session for countering the government's forces. Keynote speaker Louis Beam—the ex-KKK Grand Dragon who was even then moving into a prominent leadership role at Aryan Nations—spoke at length about his "leaderless resistance" concept. Essentially, Beam argued that resistance is best organized by forming small cells no larger than about six or eight men, bound together by ideas and agendas, but without any overt organizational connections. Thus if one person or one cell were to fall, the whole structure could remain intact.

Bo Gritz, who had been a long-time ally of Pete Peters, was not present. Their friendship had erupted into a feud that spring over Peters' advocacy of the death penalty for homosexuals. But Gritz's prominence was very much felt at Estes Park. Throughout his Populist Party presidential campaign that summer and leading up to the Ruby Ridge standoff, he had called for people to form "citizen militias" that would protect not just the rights of individuals but the Constitution itself. Gritz's idea meshed perfectly with Beam's "leaderless resistance" concept.

Their strategies were later formulated by Peters' church into "A Battle Plan for Future Conflicts," which outlined the strategy evolving from the Estes Park gathering for transforming the nation into "a Christian Civil Body Politic." It was, in essence, a blueprint for patriots to begin a "militia movement."

Among those in attendance at Estes Park was John Trochmann. He listened very carefully.

Chapter 4 / MOM and Apple Pie

I 'M WAITING NEXT TO the steel bridge over the Clark Fork River because John Trochmann is paranoid. He doesn't want anyone coming near the "compound," as locals like to call it, where he and his family operate the Militia of Montana (MOM). At least, not anyone from the media.

So, following his instructions, I phone him from a gas station on the road into Noxon and let him know I'm there, and we agree to meet on the highway side of the bridge. I drive to a gravel turnout at the approach to the bridge and park, waiting for John to show.

It's a clear, sunny day, unusually nice for February, good for leaning on the fender of your car and watching the river flow. The Clark Fork at this point is broad and swift and powerful. Just a few days before, it had ravaged the county with ice floes and floods the likes of which, as they say in these parts, people have not seen for years.

It was a disaster, caused by a sudden warm spell that had broken up the frozen-over river suddenly, and swelled it with runoff from that winter's heavy snows, which carried along what were now giant chunks of ice. These floes floated downstream and collected on bridges and other objects, creating dams that not only backed the floodwaters up even further, but also damaged the structures they built up against. A couple of bridges went floating down the river atop a crust of ice that resembled a swift-moving glacier.

That's the thing about living in places like northwestern Montana. Mother Nature still pretty much runs the show up here, though humans do their best to tidy it up in their own way—highways, clearcuts, dams. But wander into the woods the wrong way at the wrong time and you can wind up dead any number of ways: grizzlies (not likely, actually), missteps that turn into cliff falls, fishing accidents, or hypothermia after you've been lost for awhile.

The winters, though—that's when Nature really has everyone by the throat. People pretty much just bundle up, close the doors and sit through the winter. They slog through the snow, of course, but the normal activities—logging, hunting, fishing—go into hibernation. Saloons are very popular that time of year, especially since in Montana they offer such social amenities as poker tables where you can sit down with your neighbors and blow a whole wad of money. Or maybe win one.

And every now and then Mother Nature really lets loose and reminds everyone who's really in charge. I remember one winter in Montana when an Arctic blast ripped out of the north in record time, dropping the thermometer in Eureka from 40° at noon to -35° twenty-five minutes later. Thousands of trees throughout the region literally exploded at the base and toppled over; their sap, suddenly expanding as it froze in the trunks, weakened the wood fibers enough that they simply burst from the pressure. Entire cherry orchards in the Flathead Valley—a major source of employment there—were wiped out.

This week's floods were another reminder like that, but on winter's opposite end. The sudden thaw had hit the whole Northwest; there were major floods in Oregon, Washington and Idaho that week, too. Hello, federal emergency disaster relief funds.

Floods like this always worry people in Noxon, because the big steel bridge across the river to the highway is their main link to the world, especially in the wintertime. There's a dirt road you can take into Trout Creek or Heron, but if there are floods, they're likely to be blocked, too, and their bridges aren't as sturdy as Noxon's.

The bridge certainly has survived the floods nicely this time. It's about a half-mile across and one lane, built back around the 1940s, but it's all steel and sturdy as they come. Up until a year or so ago, crossing it by car required a slow, steady crawl, because its road surface was comprised of cattle-crossing-style gratework that simulated a nasty washboard: "thumpa thumpa thumpa" went your car (at no faster than about 5 mph) as you crossed it. The local folks put a new, smooth surface on it last year, so you can cross at 15 mph if you like, but it's still so narrow that you have to wait for other drivers on the opposite end if they happen to make it to the bridge first. Thus the wide gravel pullouts like the one at which I'm waiting for John Trochmann.

I've always wondered about this bridge and the Trochmanns. If you're a strategic military thinker—and John Trochmann and his brother David are both in that particular mold—then you love the prospects of defending a town like Noxon. Backed up next to a mountain, easily defended roads to the west and east, a narrow bridge on which you can see anything coming across for a good long way: Hell, you could sit there and knock off anybody coming at you for days, weeks on end if you had the right weaponry. If you were afraid the Commie invaders, or worse, the New World Order's forces, might try to get to Noxon, you could make quite a defense.

I asked John about this once and he admitted there were some advantages to the way his family was situated. But he denied that was why David, who first chose the town as a place to live, picked it. Having natural surroundings was the only criteria, he said. Of course, he said this in that stilted, practiced way that John uses when he's decided what to say in advance when asked certain kinds of questions, so you're not sure if what you're hearing is really the whole truth.

That is what I'm after on this visit: the truth about John Trochmann, at least a little more than I've been able to get from him in the past. Trochmann is an enigma, a man who hides himself in the storefront of the Militia of Montana, behind conspiracy theories and proofs and political theorizing. This persona, the one who gets up on the public stage all the time, is what the public knows of him.

More than a few people expect to find a rattle-eyed, irrational savant when they meet Trochmann, and are surprised by the congenial, white-bearded figure with sharp twinkling eyes. This, indeed, has a lot to do with Trochmann's appeal. Most Montanans are fair-minded people inclined to some skepticism of press accounts, so their first impression of Trochmann often is the mere fact that, contrary to some characterizations of him, he does not have horns growing out of his head nor does he seem like he belongs in a straitjacket. The general image of him doesn't fit the reality. Maybe there's something to what he's saying . . .

Truth is, I kind of like John Trochmann on a gut level. Politics aside, he is an affable and pleasant enough person. He square dances with his neighbors on odd weeknights, and takes his dog for walks every day in the woods around town. I appreciate his seeming straightforwardness and his conviction, but I'm not sure it is real.

The problem is, Trochmann is evasive when confronted about his connections (the ones that are establishable fact) to racist groups and belief systems—for that matter to anything he decides it's wise to distance himself from, like the Freemen. If you ask him about his lengthy ties to the Aryan Nations church, for instance, you get a stream of well-rehearsed denials. Sure, he was a featured speaker at the Aryan Congress of 1990, he says, but he was only there to lecture them about their poor morals and the way they mistreat their women. All of which, of course, begs the fact that you don't get to be a featured speaker at any kind of Aryan Nations gathering by being someone who takes a position contrary to their own. The Rev. Richard Butler invites only his friends and fellow travelers as speakers at his annual bashes.

So I want to get the truth from Trochmann, if I can. Is he a racist or isn't he? Is he a believer in Christian Identity, or not? He denies, angrily, having a racist bone in his body or his agenda. But evidence keeps cropping up: a letter from Butler, for instance, that outlines Trochmann's long and storied activities at Hayden Lake (including having co-authored the Aryan Nations' code-of-conduct manual). Documents Trochmann filed in Sanders County declaring himself a "sovereign citizen" by virtue of being a "free white Christian." Books carried in MOM's catalog that suggest a Jewish conspiracy of "international bankers" is behind the New World Order.

On my own, I'd found other evidence suggesting the whole Trochmann clan was comprised of Identity believers. I'd heard in early 1995 from friends in the Sandpoint area that John Trochmann had at one time organized Identity Bible studies in the Panhandle. So I decided at the next opportunity to ask the Trochmanns about it.

The chance came at a militia meeting in Maltby, Washington, that February. The meeting was at a little barn-red town hall in the semi-rural village, the kind of town where edge dwellers proliferate. Bob Fletcher was the MOM representative that day, but Randy and Dave Trochmann were operating the book-and-video tables where they hawked their wares. They saw me taking pictures of the table and came over and asked who I was. I gave them a card, and we stepped outside for a smoke.

Dave Trochmann has the same kind of intense demeanor as his brother, but there's something vaguely unsettling about him. I've known men like him, that hard-eyed working-class kind of man, and they are not people you want to mess with. If you do, they'll fix you and anybody close to you. It's hard to believe that Randy is his son. Randy, a skinny, dark-haired twentysomething, is doe-eyed and easygoing, a little jittery like all the Trochmanns, but you get the feeling he'd find it possible to like you even if you were a liberal.

I asked Dave about the Identity Bible studies. Any truth to that?

"Well," he said, looking about before answering, "you know, we're not white supremacists. We just think the races should be separate."

I'd heard the distinction made before.

"We just don't believe in race mixing," Trochmann said. "It's the laws of Nature. You don't see robins and sparrows mating, do you? We don't have a bunch of spobbins flying around."

I started explaining the genetic distinction between race and species, but realized it was a useless argument here.

"We don't hate other races," Randy said. "We just don't think they should mix. That's all Identity means to us." I let it go at that, and we wandered off to other topics, and eventually back into the meeting hall.

These are not the kinds of questions you like to pose to people over the phone or in the context of a large meeting hall, which were the only circumstances after the Maltby chat when I encountered any of the Trochmanns. So, about a year later, I finally set up this interview in Noxon.

The question of the Trochmanns' racism isn't all-important in and of itself. I've known neighbors, even family members, who are deep-seated racists but have other qualities that obscure the stain, a sort of internal integrity that at least lessens, on a personal level, the corrosive effect these kinds of beliefs can have on friendships. But this very integrity induces them to be up-front about their beliefs; most of them, in my experience, may not have been admirable for the way they thought, but at least they earned some respect for not trying to blur where they stood.

For John Trochmann, the question of whether or not he is a believer in Christian Identity becomes a matter of trustworthiness. Is he the straight shooter he seems to be on the surface? Or is he the three-dollar phony he likes to accuse Bill Clinton and anyone who disagrees with him of being? Is all of his rhetoric about the militias' purpose being to safeguard the civil rights of everyone simply so much smoke and mirrors?

These are the kind of thoughts that turn over in one's mind while waiting next to the Clark Fork for John Trochmann to show. I'm a little annoyed with him already, for not letting me visit him at the "compound," MOM's operational headquarters: really just a big home and a garage where they keep books and tapes stocked. He's consistently told me over the nearly two years I've been interviewing him that he doesn't let any media onto the place, but during the height of the post-Oklahoma-City hoopla, when TV trucks and print reporters by the hundreds trundled into Noxon for the obligatory Trochmann interview, I saw plenty of photos and stories coming out of his home. I suppose the crush was so bad he needed to make some concessions then, but I'd like to get a feel for his operations. Still, no go. We were talking at a local cafe again.

I'm annoyed, too, because he seems to be taking his time getting to our rendez-vous, but soon enough I see his car coming across the bridge: a plain white Ford sedan, about a 1982 model, I figure. John's not a phony about living a simple life. Some people think he's getting rich off the Militia of Montana, but I doubt that.

He pulls up to my car, gets out, and we shake hands. I can tell he only vaguely remembers who the hell I am. But when you've met as many people in the past year as John Trochmann has, another writer isn't going to matter much. Still, his greeting is warm and cordial, and we chat a bit about the weather and the river. My annoyance melts away.

John shows me the passenger window of his Ford. It has a piece of plastic over it. "That's where those sons-of-bitches in Roundup knocked it out," he says, "and I haven't been able to replace it. I will if our lawsuit goes through, though."

John's friends in Jordan, the Freemen, got him into that mess. But that's another story. I should say former friends, because they had just issued one of their "arrest warrants" for Trochmann. Apparently he wasn't radical enough for them. According to news accounts, LeRoy Schweitzer wrote up a bounty for him after John told a reporter he thought the Freemen should negotiate an end to their standoff with local authorities. It was February, and the FBI had not made their big move yet.

I shake my head sympathetically. I once drove around for a week in a Montana winter with plastic for a window, and it's nearly impossible to get warm if you go faster than about 30 mph. Well, it's a sunny day, but it's getting cold, so we agree to hop in our cars and head up the road to the Hereford Cafe, where we can get a hot cup of coffee and talk.

John leads in his white Ford. He drives like he talks: fast, a little jittery, all over the road, pedal to the metal. It only takes a couple of minutes to complete the two miles or so to the log-cabin lodge alongside the highway.

★★★

The Trochmanns are nowadays linked in popular imagery to Montana as though they came from the land there, but in fact they hail from Wright County, Minnesota, just a little west of Minneapolis. The family patriarch, Ernest Trochmann, was a hellfire-and-brimstone preacher up in Pennington County, in the state's northwestern corner, where the boys were born and raised. They eventually migrated south to Delano, where David and John and a third brother ran a snowmobile business that was a booming concern by the mid-1970s.

According to people still in Delano, John had a bit of a reputation for wild behavior in Delano. He went through four wives, and had three children by two of them, and was fond of a particular drink: apricot brandy and sours. By the early 1980s, though, he had turned his attention to a healthier lifestyle and was soon involved in a health-food cult that believed vitamins and other supplements were being suppressed by a government conspiracy. It was from there that he began pursuing a belief in conspiracy theories that led him to Christian Identity. He also told friends he believed the public-education system was corrupt. He stopped paying child support for Brandi, his teenage daughter by his third wife, who says Trochmann called Brandi a harlot if she showed up for visits wearing lipstick. More ominously, he told Brandi he wanted her out of school after she was 14 years old; it is a tenet of Identity faith that girls can be married and begin bearing children at the same age.

David moved to Noxon in 1984, looking for a place to get away from the creeping urbanism of his home county. John decided to moved out four years later, selling off his interest in the snowmobile business to the remaining brother (who sold it himself a few years later).

That summer, Brandi ran away from home and went to live with her father. She refused to return to her mother, despite a court order, and that fall ran away again, this time to parts unknown. Word around Delano was that John had slipped her off to Montana ahead of his own departure, but local police had no luck substantiating the rumor. Then, in 1991, Brandi showed up at the local Sanders County Fair in Thompson Falls, Montana, with John, who introduced her to Sheriff Bill Alexander, saying: "She doesn't look unhappy, does she?" In the meantime, John had become a married man again, this time (the fifth) a common-law marriage to a woman from Missoula named Carolynn Carter.

A Minnesota deputy swore out a felony warrant for John when he heard about the county fair incident in 1992, and Sheriff Alexander showed up at the Trochmann home the next day and arrested him. John was in jail for a week, and he swears they fed him something during his stay that weakened and numbed the entire left side of his body, probably because of his "political and Biblical convictions." He called the Minnesota deputies and their witnesses liars, and denied he ever had Brandi with him.[1] Brandi was located, though; detectives tracked her down in northern California, and she was returned to her mother that spring.

It became evident later that Brandi had been living in Montana almost the whole time; she had married the son of one of John's associates, and had given birth to a baby girl. John, she says, sent her off to California late in the fall of 1991 when detectives and posters started showing up in Noxon.

Indeed, Brandi's mother says she believes John Trochmann's whole motive in moving to Montana was simply to get Brandi away from her. Brandi's now back in Minnesota, married to a new husband, and raising her young daughter. She says she avoids contact with her father, though he calls her from time to time. In the meantime, Brandi's mother says John still owes her $15,000 in back child-support payments. "He's a deadbeat Dad," she says.[2]

While he was in jail, John filed "sovereign citizen" documents that declared him a "free white Christian man" outside the jurisdiction of the state and the federal government. "I am not a Federal citizen by virtue of the Fourteenth Amendment," the document declared.[3] John got out a week later on bail, and eventually served a total of 40 days in the Sanders County hoosegow after working a plea bargain on the child-custody charges.

Meanwhile, Dave Trochmann had taken up with a former Klansman, Chuck Howarth, and word around the radical-right underground—never proven—was that the two of them were running guns over the Canadian border, where there was a pretty profit to be earned. The ATF got interested, but no charges were ever filed, mainly because the agency's chief hopes for getting information on the Trochmanns was Randy Weaver. After that first meeting at the 1990 Aryan Congress, the Weavers and the Trochmanns had become unusually close; Carolynn Trochmann's son dated young Sara Weaver on occasion, and Carolynn herself served as midwife at Elisheba Weaver's 1992 birth. When the feds came crashing down on Randy Weaver for his refusal to inform on the Trochmanns, John and Carolynn were among the family friends who ferried groceries and supplies up Ruby Ridge.

Indeed, when John discusses the significance of April 19 in the New World Order universe, he points to that date in 1992. He says the feds first tried to attack the Weavers at their cabin that day and were scared off by the arrival of himself, Randy and Carolynn at the Weavers' cabin.

As Randy tells it, Vicki Weaver greeted them at the road with a gun in her hands and waved them off. She'd heard a rumor the Trochmanns were informants, and told them to go back. When they asked why, she pointed to the forest behind them. There, Randy says, was "a whole line of feds. I guess they saw us and decided they couldn't risk the operation with any witnesses."

When the situation erupted four months later into a violent standoff, the Trochmanns were on the front lines of the gathering at the road near Ruby Ridge that shouted obscenities at federal agents and yelled support for the Weavers. Carolynn made pancakes every morning for the crowd. And they all wept when they were told their friend Vicki was dead.

When the standoff ended, John immediately formed an alliance with Chris Temple, a Montana man who wrote for the Identity newspaper *The Jubilee*, to organize United Citizens for Justice. The UCJ's mission, its material stated, was to ensure a fair trial for Weaver and to combat government misbehavior like the Ruby Ridge case. They collected money and contributed to Weaver's defense fund. Temple accompanied Trochmann to Pete Peters' gathering that October of 1992 in Estes Park, Colorado. When Weaver's trial ended in the fall of 1993, Trochmann and Temple reportedly fell to disagreeing over strategy, so with the UCJ's mailing list in hand, John in early 1994 set up the Militia of Montana.

I first encountered Trochmann's material that fall, and decided I wanted to interview him. I called him up and asked if I could visit him in Noxon, because I wanted to find out what MOM's intentions were. Of course, Trochmann was up front about that. "The No. 1 goal," he told me over the phone, "is to inform the people to expose the filthy government that's reigning over us now. We are not against government, we are against government that breaks the law they have sworn to uphold."

We settled on an early November date, and I drove out to nearby Libby, where I stayed with friends, and then drove down to Noxon to meet John. We met that first time at a little cafe in Noxon itself, and drank coffee while the owner watched the news on a big-screen TV behind our booth. There was no one else in the cafe that day.

John laid out for me MOM's agenda: Combat the New World Order, educate people, and help them organize to resist the evil government. He claimed seven million followers of the militia movement was "a conservative estimate."

"It's a grass-roots movement that's been generated because of the government that's out of control," he told me. "It's spontaneous. It's nothing that we had to recruit. They're looking for answers, and we just happened to be in the right place at the right time.

"We're not causing this to happen. Government has disobeyed the law they have sworn to uphold, and is out of order."

He detailed for me the various troop and tank sightings that led him to believe that foreign troops were massing on, or in some cases within, our borders, preparing for a United Nations invasion of the U.S. Their ultimate intent: "A business takeover of America," he said.

What, I asked, like a corporate takeover? Multinational corporations?

"Correct. A financial investment. America has become a multi-trillion-dollar business to these people. And they believe that people like you and I are wasting their natural resources at much too rapid a pace. And we must be culled back.

"The investors, according to the information we have in print from the United Nations, will guarantee them up to 990 percent per year return on their investment, which is a pretty good incentive, especially for the politicians that are voting against the people. It's obvious where their love lies."

You're talking about a military action, aren't you?

"Yes," he said. "A military coup, if you like. Using foreign troops and foreign equipment."

Trochmann told me that Ruby Ridge and Waco were mere harbingers, test runs for what they intended to start doing to average citizens. Street-gang members from the Bloods and Crips, he said, were being trained in Spokane right then in house-to-house search and seizure techniques. When the big crackdown came, they'd round people up, ship them off to concentration camps (which he said were already being built), and then "liquidate" them until the population was stabilized.

The pretext, he said, would be "most likely a food shortage." And they would start with urban dwellers.

"Look at the cities," he said. "Look at them. They're totally captive. Somebody supplies their heat, somebody supplies their light, their transportation, their water, their communications, food. Look how vulnerable they are. They'll obey to the letter, or they'll die, because they're not ready for what's going to happen."

How are they going to organize resistance, I wondered—a few assault rifles against tanks and jets?

"The first thing we're going to do is forget about protecting the cities. If people aren't willing to fight for themselves, there's nobody that in their right mind would try to protect them. I'm not going to help them. Unless they learn to help themselves. They're beyond help, as far as I'm concerned. I've got no time for the cities.

"Here's the best way to say it. I was asked a question at a militia meeting while I was talking in Great Falls. The guy says, what is your M-14 or your AK-47 to an Abrams tank or a T-72 Soviet tank? Well, what is a chow line? What is a barracks? What is a maintenance crew? What is a foot soldier to an AK-47 or an M-14? They can't be in their iron hulls all the time, can they? And they have to eat. Their supply line comes in somehow, doesn't it?"

Okay, I said, let's just play the scenario out. They invade, they hit the cities first, then go after the pockets of resistance out here. What hope do you see for ultimately winning this conflict?

"When those who have been bit by the government, the invading force, wake up and realize they've got to do something. Then we'll have more people in the militia.

"Something's got to happen. I mean look at the things that have been happening. Like the Brady Bill," he says, arguing that gun owners' fears over the gun-control law had sparked a secondary phenomenon—namely, an increase in people's ability to defend themselves: "Suddenly, crime has disappeared in the whole country. There's trillions of rounds of ammo in the hands of private citizens, just overwhelming."

Federal conspirators, he said, had already put the mechanisms in place for the big coup. "Most of this Emergency Powers Act that we've been studying that they put together . . . They have to have a replacement for war to get down to those levels and still retain the legitimacy of power. What might that be? Catastrophes to deal with? We know that electromagnetically, they control our weather now. There's all kinds of documentation of that. We've got documentation right from the United Nations that say that people have to get a permit to change the weather somewhere."

On the big-screen TV behind us, pictures from a national broadcast showed a hurricane slamming into Florida, and an announcer displayed the storm's path on a map.

Trochmann looked at the owner of the cafe, and they exchanged knowing glances. "See the hurricane?" John asked him. "Boy, that's really late, isn't it?" The owner nodded.

You mean, I asked, this is part of the weather-control pattern?

"Sure," Trochmann said. "Naples, Florida, got hit at the same time Naples, Idaho, did."

Coincidence, maybe?

"Yeah, right," he said. "And I have another bridge for sale for you."

Here was a common Patriot irony: John, like just about everyone I'd met in the movement, thought anyone who didn't see the conspiracy as self-evident—who didn't believe the evidence, no matter how thin—was a fool gullible for the government "cover story." Yet the Patriots' stories themselves stretched the limits of credulity, to put it kindly; I mean, who really believes the government is in a position to manipulate weather? Certainly not any legitimate scientists I could contact. Welcome to the Elvis Drives a Pink UFO Chat Room. And every time I looked into one of John's pieces of "evidence," I found there was a legitimate explanation for each one. Believing that any of the items are evidence of a conspiracy requires a leap of faith only people who want to believe in evil plotters are likely to make.

Still, poking at hypocrisies like these is a good way to have an interview end abruptly, especially when you're dealing with True Believers like John Trochmann. So I switched to a related topic: Was John a believer in white supremacy?

He answered by attacking the term itself, one of his main tactics for deflecting questions about his personal views. "What's supreme about the white race?" he said. "They're a supreme race of idiots. All they care about is the dollar and whoever's buying the six-pack.

"Our forefathers said that the price for freedom is eternal vigilance. They haven't even made a down payment on it. They don't deserve any better. If you don't stand for anything, you'll fall for anything and wind up with nothing."

So in other words, I said, you don't consider yourself a racist.

"Here's the way to measure it. Don't measure it by who they are, measure it by what they are. Are they good people or bad people? Don't put a label on it other than that. Do they obey the laws of the land they live in or don't they?"

Well, as you know, I said, some of these skinheads don't.

"They're not the only ones who don't. We've got some public employees who are sworn into leadership positions that don't. What part of the word 'infringe' don't they understand? They swear an oath to uphold and then they stick us in the back. Self-serving, trust-sucking subversives.

"We create terror in their hearts because we know what they're up to, and we're telling the public about it, so they're calling us the terrorists."

This is Trochmann's other favorite tactic for dealing with tough questions: Rather than answer them directly, he sidetracks onto a related matter and then goes on the attack on the suddenly switched subject. He's very artful at redefining the terms of the conversation this way, so that if you try to get a straight answer from him, you wind up feeling after a couple of hours that you've been trying to grasp a shadow on the wall.

What interviews eventually devolve into is a soapbox for John's beliefs, a chance for him to attack his critics and the government.

"There's no question," he said, as we drank the last of our coffee, "they've started a grass-roots movement that cannot be stopped. It's going to swallow them up and spit them out, just like it should. Just like the law commands us to do. To get rid of this tyrannic, evil government.

"It's not our government. Where's our government? What happened to our government?"

Still, for all his fiery rhetoric, John has his moments of reflection. We wandered outside and looked at the river flowing by, and he pondered for me the point of a 51-year-old retiree taking up a cause like this from a remote, peaceful corner of Montana.

"If I had my druthers, I'd rather be out fishing, or hunting, or something," he said. "I came here to retire, not to get involved with this. But when I see what's happening to my country—what kind of future do my children have? We owe to our children at least what we've been bequeathed, don't we?"

At least his motives, as he described them, seemed to be pure. But by that point, I wasn't sure if I could believe anything coming out of John Trochmann's mouth. When a man evades questions as skillfully as he had just done for two hours, his credibility becomes an open question. And it was the way he deflected questions that made me simply not believe John's denials of racist beliefs. Even talking to him on the riverbank, I had the sense he was reciting lines he had devised carefully sometime before.

Perhaps, I thought that night, mulling over the interview and its frustrations, I could do better on a second try. Either get him to come clean, or at least get him to explain himself.

A year and a half later, I found myself waiting next to the Clark Fork to make that second try.

★★★

The cafe is a classic backwoods Montana kind of place—a bar on one half, replete with pool tables and a jukebox, and restaurant on the other, all done in varnished wood, and built about forty years ago, when wooden decor connoted real ruggedness instead of fern-bar veneer.

As we walk in, John explains why he's changed venues for his interviews. The owner of the previous cafe, he says, got tired of the media hordes that came pouring into town after Oklahoma City last year. It was a gigantic headache, and he didn't want to be associated with the militias anymore. The owner here, he says, is much more supportive.

We choose a booth next to a window, and sit down facing each other. It's a family kind of restaurant; everyone else there, besides John and myself, is dining in a group, most of them with children. The waitress smiles, recognizing John, and comes trotting over with a coffee pot. We turn our cups over and let her pour.

It must have been crazy then, I say. I know what media behavior is like at times—utterly ruthless, utterly inconsiderate, absolutely certain that everyone else is eager to be interviewed so they can be on TV. Yes, TV crews are the worst in this regard.

"Right after the bombs went off, for the next three weeks, there were at least 360 different media here," John says. "Out of that 360, about 300 were U.S., and out of that 300, ninety percent of them had the same questions and the same orders, just like the Goebbels of Germany. Who's the propaganda minister here?

"It was asinine. It was absolutely sickening. People would just sit there—reporters would just sit there as I told them what their next question would be."

We talk about business—he says it's been busier than ever, but he's not making a great deal of money. The clothes he wears are hand-me-downs, he says, and his car window is missing.

I ask him about that Freemen arrest warrant. Isn't John a little angry? After all, he had gone to the trouble of getting himself arrested with them the year before, putting his own neck on the line for their cause. Why would they go and turn on him like that?

"Schweitzer told me over the telephone that he was issuing an arrest warrant for me," Trochmann says. "And then he hung up, so I never got to ask why or anything. But from his people that called up and said they wanted to be taken off our mailing list, and no longer wanted to get our newsletter, I asked them, 'What is the problem over there?' And he says, 'You've been tampering with the grand jury.' What does that mean? Tampering with the grand jury? Who is the grand jury? How can I tamper with the grand jury if I don't know who they are?"

What do you think of the common-law courts now?

"We have a real large concern about the common-law courts—who controls them. Much as we do about the courts that are out there now—who controls them? They seem to do as they darn well please. Justice is for sale. Crime's not for everyone; it depends on how much money you have. That's the kind of justice you get nowadays.

"Their common-law courts . . . at least as they have proceeded in eastern Montana, from Schweitzer, is the personal vendetta court. A person who can sit in the position of judging should not have a leaning in any direction, should not be affected personally."

It's February, and the Freemen are still trucking students in to their classes at the Jordan ranch while the FBI stands by and watches. I ask John how he thinks the FBI is doing this time, compared to the Ruby Ridge standoff.

"The FBI is caught between a rock and a hard place with the financial thing Schweitzer is doing over there," Trochmann says. "The issuing of these CMOs, these money orders that they're doing. They're using the same basic steps the Federal Reserve is using. So, one's wrong, is the other wrong? Why are they arresting one and not the other?

"This fraudulent money system goes back to 1913, when it was given away from our Treasury Department of our nation to a bunch of private people called the Federal Reserve.

"The Federal Reserve is just as private as Federal Express. And to pay the national debt, all we have to do, under presidential order, is to have the Treasury Department print thousand-dollar bills at three cents a bill, and pay off the national debt. That's how they made it in the first place. That's how they made it. The cost of the printing. Our Treasury Department prints it for the Federal Reserve, and the Federal Reserve issues it. And all they pay is the cost of the printing."

Well, speaking of the Freemen . . . I fish through my files and find a "True Bill" written by Dale Jacobi the previous summer. Look, John, I say, there are a lot of references to Adam, Israel, people of Israel, Yahweh, the white race, that sort of thing. It's pretty obviously Christian Identity. I wanted to know your views on all that.

John frowns at the question and won't look at the Jacobi document. "Religion doesn't enter into this at all," he says. "Religion has been the curse of this nation. We have one Bible and seven hundred religions that divide us, at least.

"Come on, let's put that away. We have a country at stake. We have a nation full of people that need help. Instead of dividing and separating us from each other, we need to rub shoulders with each other.

"Put away this religious thing. Put away the political thing, the economic thing, the race thing—we're all in this together, dammit. We all share the same enemy. We measure it like this, Dave: Good people, bad people."

Religion can be a problem, I say. I mention a wild rumor I'd heard from a former Delano resident, who suggested the Trochmanns left Minnesota because the local folks wouldn't take their racist beliefs and stopped patronizing their business. I'm about to say that I'd checked the rumor out, found it to be utterly groundless, and that this is an example of how people's beliefs can become fodder for wild gossip. But I'm too late. John is steamed.

"Let me get this straight," he says angrily, his eyes darting. "This stupid ass . . . had no concept of what we had. We didn't have anybody ever stop coming to us. Our religion was no part of why we moved. We sold the business because we got tired of all the little rules those bastards in the federal bureaucracy made us stick to, all the hoops they made us go through just to run a business. It was sickening."

I try to shift gears, calm him down. What was it about Noxon that brought him here in the first place? I ask.

"It was peaceful. Clean water, fresh air, lots of greenery. It was nice. I'd been looking for a lot of years. It just so happened my brother David sold his place first in Minnesota, before I did, and moved out here. I decided to look around here when I came to visit him, and said, 'Yeah, Dave, you chose a good spot here.' I'd been all over the country before, many times."

John's still angry about the rumor. Normally I might enjoy the irony, since Trochmann's conspiracy theories are chock-full of rumor and innuendo, but at this point I'm trying to keep the conversation rational. You understand, I tell him, why I have to ask these questions.

He's not mollified. "The information you're getting is absolutely pathetic," he says. "It's sickening."

Sometimes the best way to defuse these situations is to try a question for which he probably has a rehearsed answer: What about Butler's letter, I ask, the one saying you weren't telling the truth about your association with the Aryan Nations? Trochmann shifts into his standard-response mode.

"Butler's letter said that I had been there twice. That's not true. They got their information out of the *Missoulian*. The gal that printed it in the *Missoulian* didn't print it right. I hadn't told her that I was there only twice. I was there five times, maybe six times total.

"The first time I was there it was to pick my children up that I had sent over with friends. The second time I was there was to preach about morality. The third time I was there was to help them put some ground rules together. And the fourth time I was there was either to attend a wedding, a bagpipe wedding—and I love bagpipes—it's pretty hard to find them in this neck of the woods—I love bagpipes, and so we went there. And the other time was to drop off air-conditioner stuff, or a refrigeration unit, they were taking to Thompson Falls, and I was going that way with my truck anyway. And it was no big deal to drive a couple miles out of my way to drop it off.

"That's the extent of my visits. That was all in 1990—or late '90, early '91, whatever. About a year span.

"But I don't see anybody else going over there. If they think they have a problem with the Butlers, why don't they go over there and try to help straighten them out instead of condemn them all the time? If I think you have a problem and all I do is go out in the countryside and bad-mouth you all the time, how the hell does it help you? Why don't these jerks get off their duffs and go over there and try to help them? That's what I did. But instead, I get condemned for it constantly.

"But these Human Wrongs Task Forces around the country—this ADL that never finds out what the truth is. Instead, they report it six or four times a year to every law enforcement in America as gospel truth, and these fools in law enforcement gobbled it up.

"It's a sick society when it runs on rumor."

What about Bible studies? Did you do that over there?

"No. No more than what they usually have going over there. I went over one night to help them put that together."

I was talking with Dave and Randy in Maltby about the Bible studies and Christian Identity.

"Well, Dave and Randy and I don't get along on it either. We just don't talk about it.

"When people want to bring it up in regards to—I just flat don't talk about it. If you want to burn a friendship, or burn a group, you get religion involved. It'll shut it down every time.

"Religion is the destruction of our country. The truth is in Nature. If it doesn't fit Nature's laws, then don't buy it."

How do you describe Nature's laws?

"For every action there's a reaction. For instance, if you put herbicides and pesticides and all the other suicides into your soil, where do you expect that to lead? You're gonna have unhealthy children. It's the laws of action and reaction—a blessing or a cursing. You treat your land right, it's going to respond to you right. Nature. Nature's laws."

I'm reminded of the "organic" Constitution of Patriot lore, and Trochmann tries to explain it: "The 14th Amendment, I believe, took freedom away from everyone. The papers that I put coming out against the 14th Amendment, and declaring my sovereignty that's filed in the state of Montana here, was totally in regards to authority that may be over me with that amendment. It had nothing to do with any race at all. People misconstrue that."

I don't know how you can misconstrue that, especially since for some people—like the Freemen—it does refer specifically to race.

"It's jurisdiction," Trochmann says. "The whole thing is jurisdiction. As far as I'm concerned, the blacks were under slavery before the 14th Amendment. And all that happened with the 14th Amendment was to put everyone under slavery. It just shifted for the blacks from the plantation owners to the federal government."

Now John goes on the offensive again. He wants to know what my book will be about. He doesn't like the kind of questions I've been asking. He tries convincing me I'd make more money on his side.

"Instead of looking at the nitty-picky shit, like everybody's trying to throw in our faces, to vilify the messenger, instead of getting out the message, why don't you try getting out the message? Because that doesn't sell books.

"You ought to get on the bandwagon of selling books, because those are the books that are selling now—what's really happening to our country, instead of this stupid, stupid stuff like you're trying to put together now. It accomplishes nothing. All it does is divide America even further."

I politely decline; I'm not interested in being anyone's messenger. I admit, though, that there's widespread dissatisfaction with mainstream media in America's heartland. MOM obviously has touched a nerve to which people respond.

"Sure they do, because they're not getting it from mainstream media," he says. "They want to get it somewhere. They know something's wrong, and they're not getting the answers. A lot of mainstream media has already admitted to having lost 53 percent of the information highway, and rightfully so. If they're going to lie, and not tell anything, they deserve to lose it. And that's what's happening. Hallelujah. Wow."

John looks up when the waitress brings us more coffee, then abruptly excuses himself. I ponder his words, since I have some personal experience in this area. As a newspaper editor, you have the power to choose what stories run and which don't, and what information should be in the paper and what should not. And a basic standard of journalism is that all facts must be substantiated. A serious journalist can't just print groundless speculation, wild claims and rumors. Yet such fabric, from almost all my dealings with Trochmann, was Militia of Montana's stock in trade. John, at various times, told me the North Cascades were "ringed with surveillance equipment," but couldn't tell me where it was located, just that someone had told him it was there. He told me someone saw the Spokane police chief sign an order to train street-gang members in search-and-seizure techniques, but couldn't tell me who or when. The Oklahoma City bomb was actually set from the inside, he told me, but couldn't explain why there was no crater where he claimed it would be. My conversations with him, and his speeches before large crowds, were an endless stream of rumor and innuendo. If he thinks that's what the media should be reporting, I think he's mistaken.

He's back in a minute, with Randy, just arrived, in tow. John slides back into his seat and Randy sits down beside him. We exchange pleasantries, but John is still unhappy. He turns to Randy.

"I think Dave here is trying to write about whether or not we're racists," he says. "He's been asking a lot of questions about Identity."

The sudden attack throws me off balance. I've been friendly and even-keeled, but I've never hid the tenor of my questions, and now Trochmann is acting like I'm trying to weasel something out of him. I'm sure my tone is defensive when I try to explain myself. Of course, John, you should expect these questions. It's what we hear most often about you.

"You'll never find it, or you'll find a lie, I'll guarantee you," Trochmann says. "I had good friends in the military that were black. We have good friends in the militia that are black. They share the same enemy that we do. It's about time we forgot differences. I recommend putting away any differences that there are and resolve the situation at hand and put America back together.

"The people that were screwed over first in America were the Native Americans and the blacks. Now it's our turn. So we better line up with them. They know more about it than we do."

These questions are about your credibility, I tell John.

"Bluntly, it pissed me off. You're getting your information from people that don't apparently care about America, like the Human Rights Task Force over there, Ken Toole. He could give a rip less about the American way or the laws of our land that he's advocating breaking every day.

"A lot of the media come back to us and get our side of it, and they'll twist it, they'll put a spin on it. So much worse than if you'd said nothing. When you say nothing, then they'll put their own spin on that. It's a lose-lose situation, dealing with what I call the lying lips of Satan."

His eyes still flash anger. "We're in trouble and we're damn near out of time," he says, and points to a packet he's brought with more MOM evidence. "When you see this and this you'll see why."

Randy dives into the conversation. "We see it again in the paper this morning, where the U.S. Marshals go in and raid Kmart," he says. "We called Senator Burns' office, said, 'We gotta put a muzzle on these guys.' Holy smokes! People wonder why people are joining the militia."

"They're our best recruiters," John says. "Clinton and Janet Nero have been our best recruiters."

The conversation turns back to a normal tone, and I'm grateful for Randy's presence in this regard. He and I have had many chats and I have the feeling that, outside of this conversation, we could probably share a beer and a pool game. I ask him about an interview with him I saw in a Seattle paper, and he snorts. "What a piece of crap," he says. Somehow, I get the feeling he'd offer the same verdict on my stories.

John's curious. He doesn't know what story we're talking about. "Oh, it's that one in that Seattle paper about my Identity beliefs," Randy says.

John shrugs. "What the hell does Identity mean? To identify your ancestry? Blacks can have their 'Roots' on television, and have a whole series about it. But a white man can't find out what his ancestry is? That's all it means to me. It doesn't tie anything with anything.

"I know where I came from, I know my ancestry. That's all it means to me. It shouldn't be Identity anyway. I mean, Jewish people have their identity, everybody has their identity. Yet certain people—it's taken so out of context it's absolutely ridiculous. Including those that claim this word Identity and take it for something that it isn't. It may be that's what they think it means. But it doesn't mean that to us. At least to me."

I'm a little stunned. Trochmann has spent the last hour or so dodging the question of whether or not he's an Identity believer, and now it seems he's just admitted to me that he is one. At the same time, he's told me he doesn't believe Identity is a racist belief system.

John continues his self-defense. He says his critics won't debate him. He complains about their tactics. He tells me the militias and common-law courts are only thriving because of government corruption that inspires them. I listen, but I've heard it all before.

Abruptly, John looks at his watch, then gets up. "Well, you take care. I gotta go." We shake hands, and he heads out the door.

I hang out with Randy for the next hour or so. We chat amiably, as we always do. He tells me he's thinking about running for office. The waitress keeps the coffee warm in my cup, while Randy orders a beer.

I'd like to join him but I have a long ride back to Missoula. After awhile we wrap up our chat, and I head back down the highway along the ice-swollen Clark Fork with a headful of questions.

★★★

The going is slow on Highway 20. The road has only been open a day or so, and the scars from the flood are everywhere. A portion of the road near Paradise was completely washed over and turned to gravel, and homes along the river are still under water in places, as are a number of fields and sloughs. Whole fields are strewn with the glistening ice chunks, giving the countryside a wrecked, chaotic feel.

State and federal disaster officials, who immediately moved in with a phalanx of bulldozers and road graders, have done a remarkable job of returning life to a semblance of normalcy in record time. And people whose homes were wiped out are being promised full packages of federal disaster aid to fix things up. Certainly, I don't hear much grousing about the government from locals along the Clark Fork this week. They're just grateful to have their lives back.

I pull into a roadside gas station to pick up a soda, and the local weekly catches my eye. It's full of pictures from the flooding, some of them remarkable examples of the awesome power of water.

I ask the clerk about how well the rescue efforts went. She tells me the disaster-relief people have done a great job. "I'm amazed how soon they have this highway back open," she says. "I thought it'd be a week. We wouldn't be doing much here without it, either."

I've had some personal experience with flood disasters, too, and I know the flip side of them: from all the chaos and pain and misery emerges an amazing cohesiveness to the human spirit. Mother Nature's rampages remind us to what a great degree we remain at her mercy, but they also give us a chance to demonstrate our resiliency. Whole communities forget their differences; people forget how you voted or what cause you stand for, and pull together to make life right again.

This, the clerk tells me, is what has happened this week along the Clark Fork. "It was incredible," she says. "Everyone was out helping everyone else. We sandbagged all night, we evacuated families together, we made sure everyone was OK, and now we just have to put the pieces back together. I think we all forgot about our petty arguments. All that mattered was beating the flood."

I thank her for the paper and the Coke, and return, strangely happy, to my long slow drive, watching the river flow on and on, washing everything, the ice and the poison, away with it.

Chapter 5 / Roundup

HOW THE WINDOW of John Trochmann's car was broken out: He was sitting in the driver's seat of his Ford sedan, waiting for three companions. It was a snowy day: March 3, 1995. At that time of year, it's always cold in Roundup, and on that day, it was a regular blizzard. The parking lot at the Musselshell County jailhouse was covered with snow and the wind was blowing, and since the sun always sets early in Montana during the winter, it was dark already at 6 p.m.

His three companions, who came in another vehicle, were inside the jailhouse, trying to retrieve some equipment the county deputies had confiscated from one of their friends earlier in the day. Suddenly, from the side door of the jailhouse, two deputies walked out, with a determined look on their faces, guns drawn.

One deputy walked up to John on the driver's side, and the other went to the passenger side, where his companion, Marc Basque, sat talking into a hand-held radio. John locked his door to prevent the officers from getting to them, and Marc followed suit.

"Come on out. You're under arrest," said the thin deputy at John's window. Marc, radio still in hand, started to reach into his jacket.

Suddenly, the air was filled with the sound of shattering glass. John thought the thicker, bigger deputy at Marc's window had shot Marc. But he had only taken his shotgun's stock and bashed the glass out.

The big deputy opened the door and pulled Basque out of the passenger seat. The other deputy asked Trochmann: "You want to come out now?" Trochmann put up his hands and unlocked the door, and the deputy pulled him out to the ground. They were both lying there in the snow as the deputies slapped on handcuffs.

The two lawmen picked them up and led them inside to the jailhouse. There, on the floor of the sheriff's office, with their hands bound behind their backs, were John's three companions.

All of them were in the hands of the law. Which, as far as John Trochmann was concerned, was about the worst place they could be.

★★★

That is the short version of what happened. The full story of how John Trochmann's window came to be broken is much more complicated: a tale involving guns and video cameras, threats to execute public officials by hanging, and a small Western town in the grip of genuine fear. It's the story, also, of how the Freemen came to be.

Trochmann wasn't sitting in a car in that particular parking lot that day by mere happenstance. He was there because the activities of his then-friends, the Freemen, were reaching a fever pitch and threatening to explode in the little town of Roundup. As for whether John was there to make things better or worse—well, it depends on who's talking, and who you believe.

Roundup is about an hour's drive north of Billings and a good nine hours' drive from Noxon. About 1,800 people live there, and they enjoy plenty of elbow room. The town is built around two main streets that intersect at the only stop light. The courthouse is a brick building about the size of a school, and two blocks away sits the jailhouse—which doubles as the sheriff's office—a squat, square brick building with one door and a few barred windows.

Unlike most other eastern Montana towns, Roundup actually is surrounded by a bit of greenery. It is nestled at the foot of the Bull Mountains, one of the only interruptions of the otherwise endless plains that comprise the regional landscape. The Bulls are not exactly verdant, but their limestone bluffs provide a home for the rather sparse pines that are typical of the West's arid mountains.

It was up on a ridge in these mountains that two men, Rodney Skurdal and LeRoy Schweitzer, formed the Freemen in the early 1990s—incubating and nurturing their plans for a new kind of government based on Christian Identity beliefs in a three-bedroom cabin a few miles outside of town, on a winding, dusty trail called Johnny's Coal Road.

While almost all the other leaders in the Northwest's Patriot movement moved here from elsewhere, Skurdal and Schweitzer were native sons, born and bred in eastern Montana. They both led relatively obscure, normal lives in blue-collar work until traumatic events started them on the road to radicalism.

LeRoy Schweitzer was raised in the Bozeman area, attending a local Catholic school, graduating in 1957. He was married at age 27 in Bozeman, and he and his wife, Carol, moved to the Palouse region of eastern Washington and northern Idaho, where LeRoy got a job operating a plane for Fountain Flying in the college town of Moscow, Idaho. A few years later, they moved over the border to Colfax, Washington, where LeRoy operated a crop-dusting business called Farm-Air.

Crop dusting is a dangerous and difficult line of work, in the same league as logging and mining for death and injury. Not only are you in constant danger of exposure to toxic chemicals, but the work itself requires the highest kind of pilot's skill level—namely, the ability to come in low enough over the crops to adequately administer the spray, and then to pull up sharply to avoid potentially fatal obstacles like power lines and trees, which sometimes force banked climbs so steep the G-forces pull your face back into a grimace. Other pilots say LeRoy was one of the best in the business—gutsy and smart and agile.

LeRoy first started quarreling with the government in 1977, when the IRS decided he owed them $700 in unpaid taxes. Following his accountant's advice, Schweitzer refused to pay, and the IRS retaliated by freezing $6,000 in his business

bank account. Schweitzer was furious, not only at the IRS but at his bank for allowing the government to touch his money. "The IRS can steal my money, but nobody
else can," he told friends.[1]

The whole affair drove Schweitzer into the company of other tax protesters in
the area, notably a Whitman County rancher named Ray Smith, who was engaged
in a running duel with the government over his $1 million in unpaid Farmers Home
Administration loans. Smith eventually lost his land, claiming he had been set up by
Jewish bankers.[2]

Schweitzer and Smith attended Posse Comitatus meetings at local town halls. It
was Schweitzer's first foray into the conspiracy-theory-driven world of Constitutionalists and survivalists who were drawn to the region, and it wasn't long before both
men were full-fledged participants in the far-right movement. Smith also employed
a ranch hand named Elden "Bud" Cutler, who spent the rest of his time at Hayden
Lake (an hour-and-a-half's drive away), working as the Aryan Nations security chief.
A few years later, in 1986, Cutler was sent to prison for his plot to behead The
Order's chief snitch, Thomas Martinez.[3]

Schweitzer, like Smith, decided to stop paying taxes on his business, and continued to battle other authorities as well. A state safety inspector dropped in to check
on his operation one day, and wrote Farm-Air up for failing to properly ground a
grinding machine—which, as the inspector explained, was a matter of protecting
Schweitzer's workers.

Schweitzer turned around to his sole employee and fired the man on the spot.
"Now there are no employees who work here, so see how your regulations protected
that man," he told the inspector.[4]

In the mid-1980s, Schweitzer sold Farm-Air and moved to Belgrade, Montana.
He also stopped paying his income taxes and ceased registering for either his driver's
license or pilot's license. Once in Belgrade, he started up a fireworks business, and he
started hanging out at the Road and Ranch Supply, owned by a lifelong local named
Jack Bolls. Schweitzer, Bolls and others would gather in an office and exchange their
Constitutionalist views, sometimes treading into Christian Identity, especially when
the subject of international bankers came up. In this tight circle, the belief in a vast
conspiracy to destroy America spun into an ever-enlarging web that emboldened the
group to take action.

Chief among the group's ideological avatars was a Billings tax protester named
Martin J. "Red" Beckman, who Schweitzer met in 1984 when he first returned to
Montana. Beckman, a Posse Comitatus speaker and leader, had authored a number
of anti-tax tomes with titles like *Do Unto the IRS as They Would Do Unto You, The
IRS and the Black Robed Cover Up,* and *The Born Again Republic.* At the time,
though, his most recent work, *The Church Deceived,* was in wide circulation in
Christian Patriot circles. In it, he described the IRS as "an organization totally controlled by the money changers and the Anti-Christ Church," which the book makes
clear is Judaism. As for the Jews themselves, Beckman wrote:

"They talk about the horrible holocaust of Hitler's Nazi Germany. Was that not
a judgment upon a people who believe Satan is their God? The true almighty God

used the evil Nazi government to perform judgment upon the evil anti-christ religion of those who had crucified the Christ."

Beckman also argued that the current government was illegitimate and unconstitutional, and recommended challenging it through the court system. LeRoy Schweitzer decided to put this plan into action. When a member of the Belgrade group, Bernard Kuennen, was charged in 1988 with allowing his unvaccinated dogs to run free, Schweitzer showed up in court as his lawyer and tried arguing with the judge about whether or not the court had jurisdiction over his client. He queried the judge on whether he knew about the difference between admiralty law and common law. The judge wrote that the arguments were unintelligible and slapped a fine on Kuennen.[5]

Schweitzer also had a few brushes with law officers over his driver's license and vehicle registration. When pulled over for expired tags, he would pepper them with his own view of the law. "He would ask questions," recalled Gallatin County Sheriff Bill Slaughter (who even attempted to speak to the Road and Ranch group once). " 'Do you have a bank account? Do you own your own home?'

"One time he locked me out of the vehicle. When I told him I was going to stick a shotgun butt through the window, he opened up."[6]

Schweitzer and his friends also began a rite common to followers of the Posse Comitatus: filing reams of documents filled with seeming gibberish, a combination of contorted legalisms and Biblical prose.[7] The Gallatin County court clerks say they were terrified of Schweitzer's appearances. "They became demanding. They became belligerent," one told a Billings reporter.

About the same time, a new member started showing up at the Road and Ranch meetings. Rodney Skurdal fit in immediately; like them, he was a Montana native, and he shared their hatred of the federal government and their belief that the system had been corrupted by a massive Jewish conspiracy.

Rodney Skurdal grew up in Yellowstone and Golden Valley counties, on a farm near Lavina, and joined the Marines when he graduated from high school in 1972, staying in the military for nearly ten years. Among his stints: an honor guard at the White House. In 1981 he left the service and returned to the West, finding work in the Wyoming oil fields near Gillette. But in 1983, a drilling rig collapsed and he suffered a severe head injury, permanently disabling him. He began working on a lawsuit against his former employer, Exeter Drilling Company. About the same time, his preoccupation with Constitutionalist beliefs appeared.

His former wife—who had since moved to Texas—told Exeter's lawyers that the injury had definite effects on Skurdal's behavior. Rodney, she said, had trouble remembering friends and family members, and even details of their marriage. Since the injury, "he has an odd personality and refuses to use a Social Security number or driver's license," she said.[8]

Although Skurdal received workers' compensation for his injuries, he still sued the state—because he received payment in checks. Skurdal wanted it in gold and silver, claiming the government lacked the authority to print paper money. He took his case all the way to the Wyoming Supreme Court, which summarily dismissed it in 1985, calling it "perhaps the most frivolous appeal ever filed here."[9]

By the time he moved back to Montana in 1988, he was completely in the thrall of Constitutionalist beliefs. And, meeting with his like-minded friends at the Road and Ranch Supply, he came to believe in Christian Identity too.

By the 1990s, the group was ready to coalesce and take on the feds. Schweitzer was charged in a federal indictment on 48 counts of illegally flying an airplane in Idaho in 1992, and his plane and home were seized. Federal agents at first couldn't find the plane, but eventually located it up in Garfield County, on a ranch belonging to a friend of Schweitzer's. The rancher's name: Ralph Clark.

★★★

Ralph Clark was something of a local legend in Jordan, having once achieved a kind of fame throughout the intermountain West—in Montana, Idaho and Wyoming, as well as parts of Colorado and Alberta—at least among people in the wool industry. Even though he was illiterate and had no formal education beyond elementary school, it was Clark, a handyman and sheep shearer by trade, who invented a device in the 1970s that revolutionized the way people sheared sheep.

Ralph Clark's brother-in-law, Cecil Weeding, witnessed the whole affair. He says Clark and an associate who worked the sheep-shearing routes with him dreamed up the device during their down time. "They were sitting around one winter—they always had plenty of time in the wintertime; there was very little to do, they didn't have much livestock—and they conceived this idea of a shearing rig," Weeding recalls. "Before that point, shearing had always been done on the sheep owner's premises, and [with] whatever they might happen to have. It had all gone to electric shearing by that time, so they had to have power. It took lots of help, and some operators had good facilities and some hardly had any.

"They conceived this idea of a shearing plant, where there would be a mobile plant where five or six or so shearers had their little stations inside, and there would be an alleyway built right through the plant, right up one side of the plant, and they could just back this plant right up to a gate winging and pull the sheep right up into the plant and be pulled out of this alleyway in the plant by the shearers, and sheared, and then dumped out the other side of the plant to be caught and branded and whatnot. And the wool also kicked out there, and the tyer and the stomper would be set up out there to tie the wool and sack it, bag it there.

"So they got hold of an old trailer house somewhere, gutted it out and built this thing. And had it ready by spring, and took it out and used it. My goodness, it was fantastic. It worked like a dream. And Ralph all of a sudden found himself the manager of a shearing rig. He still sheared some himself, too. But they took this thing around, and everybody was taken by it. The shearers loved it, the sheep owners loved it because they didn't have to provide any facility anymore. It had light plants so they weren't even dependent on somebody's power or wiring and that. They could just fire up their own light plant."

Clark's invention was brilliant, but it promptly inspired imitators and competitors. "It was just a matter of a year, practically, that every other shearing rig in the country had one of those plants," Weeding says. "Ralph sold his, I believe, and built another one next winter, or maybe even perfected it the first winter, and the second winter he sold it to some other outfit, and built himself a newer, bigger and better one. But the basic design is still there today, with slight modifications from the first plant that Ralph built. It's my belief that Ralph built the first shearing plant in the country. I had never heard of one before that, and the few queries I have made, that seems to be the case with everybody. Ralph had an up-and-coming business all of a sudden."

Although he was approaching forty then, this was something new to Ralph Clark. Prior to then, he had played the role of the family's ne'er-do-well to the hilt. During his teenage years, Clark—who, like most young eastern Montana boys growing up in the '40s (or anytime prior), had dropped out of school early—spent most of his time playing, and when he married a girl named Kay Nordell from the other side of the county at age eighteen, they set up house at a home directly adjacent to Ralph's strict pioneer parents, Todd and Ethel Clark. Todd Clark ruled his family tightly, and Ralph especially. He doled out money to the young couple and kept Ralph on a tight leash; when he set up all of his sons with farms of their own, the one he designated as Ralph's was his own. It wasn't until Ralph was in his thirties, when his father retired and moved into town, that he even got to sample free adulthood. "Ralph was not developing any management abilities whatever during this period of time," Weeding says. "And suffice it to say that you know he had some wild ideas that would indeed have given one a little uneasiness about turning him loose with any money to spend or any property that he might be able to dispose of."

On their own, the brothers decided to buy a Caterpillar with a bulldozing blade to handle earth-moving chores on their ranches, and Ralph cottoned to it—in fact, he undertook construction of a reservoir on the ranch by digging out the necessary pit with the dozer. He mastered the machine so well that, by the early 1960s, he was doing contract work (people in the industry call it "Cat-skinning") with a local road-building company, operating their machines. And to pick up even more money on the side, he hooked up on the seasonal sheep-shearing circuit. Then came the shearing-rig invention and the all-too-brief small fortune that came with it.

With a little cash in his pocket, Clark also picked up a drinking habit about that time. "He wasn't a town drunk at all, but he nevertheless was developing this tendency to become addicted to things," observes Weeding.

Ada Weeding, Cecil's wife, says her brother developed another significant trait then. "When he was drinking, he could blame his wife or kids when things went wrong—it was never his fault," she says.

When the sheep-shearing business slumped for him, Clark tried making more of a living from his ranch and grew frustrated, since the 960 acres bequeathed to him weren't enough to turn a profit. He turned to the local Farmers Home Administration for help in augmenting his revenues. The local agent saw that Clark had built a reservoir at the place and hit upon an idea: Make the Clark ranch into a game farm for hunters and fishermen to come out and recreate on, as some other ranchers in the region had done successfully. The ranch was adjacent to the Missouri Breaks, which dropped steeply down to the waters of the Fort Peck Reservoir, and there already was a certain amount of native game on the place.

With a $30,000 government loan in hand, Ralph procured all the materials he'd need to build three cabins near the reservoir and erect a tall fence to keep the game in. The cabins were built right away, and Clark officially opened his game farm for business. The fence, however, was never built; the materials lay rusting and rotting out on the back forty for a couple of years until Ralph clandestinely sold them to a friend. The elk and the antelope that were supposed to be the draw for sportsmen never were purchased. For that matter, Ralph's tourist business lacked an even more important element: revenues.

It wasn't so much that no one visited the Clark ranch; plenty of folks arrived as tourists. "People came in droves to the farm and the reservoir, and people came and stayed in the cabins," says Weeding. "The problem was, Ralph fraternized too much with his customers, and all of them become friends, and he would not hear of charging friends to come and stay. The nature of Ralph again—the nature of that community for that matter: They were always willing and generally anxious to take people in and make them feel at home. Ralph forgot he was in business to make money at that. So he'd go fishin' and let the people stay for nothing. Got other people in there that had nothing to do—weren't even fishermen, that just took up the space. These people who were taking space in his cabins weren't recreational people at all, they were just boozin' buddies that happened along or Ralph picked up somewhere along the way. He picked up every stray dog that he found, and every other transient that would follow him home. He wasn't making any money with these cabins at all. I doubt that he ever charged a soul to spend a night in them cabins."

Clark's children all had reached adulthood by that time, and Ralph decided it was his obligation to help provide a living for them. After a family discussion, it was agreed they'd try their hand at farming. They settled on a parcel of land, several thousand acres' worth, called the Hilliard place, which beforehand had been used solely for grazing livestock. This meant that, in addition to having to buy all the necessary equipment (tractors, diggers, trucks and thrashers) the land itself would have to be tilled for the first time—as arduous and difficult a process as exists in farming. But with federal loans in hand, the Clarks proceeded ahead full steam.

The first couple of years, the Clarks did pretty well, and it looked to their neighbors as though the family would make it. But then in 1980, their place was hit by an early-summer hailstorm that wiped out their grain. The next year they had another poor crop. Bad news followed bad: the farm-foreclosure crisis struck, with banks calling in the debts of heavily strung-out farmers and taking their homes away in virtually every rural community. When the Clarks failed to make their loan payment, the sharks began to circle.

The Clarks were simply small cogs in a nationwide crisis. Recognizing that family farmers were endangered by the situation, Congress moved to act. Legislation was quickly passed creating a series of emergency loan programs, whereby delinquent loans could be carried over for a year at a very nominal rate, with the idea that this was simply a one-year anomaly. The programs provided first for paying off delinquent bills, and to provide operating funds for the next crop year. But they were short-term loans with a maximum life of twelve months, at which time they would become just ordinary loans again, subject to the going rate of interest, which was rising drastically into the twenty percent range. So, farmers the following year would be faced with an almost certain double whammy, Ralph Clark among them.

Well before then, reality had begun to sink in for the Ralph Clark family's farm operation. In 1981, they failed to make their farm payment for the first time—and the Clarks never made another payment on the place again. Clark's oat crop that year went into storage, since the going price at the market wasn't adequate. He took out an end-of-harvest loan to compensate for the lack of income from it, using the stored oats as collateral, with the idea that when the market price rose, he'd be able to sell it and pay back the loan. However, Ralph Clark never did that.

Instead, the grain mysteriously disappeared from Clark's bins, and Ralph was charged with illegal disbursement of mortgaged property. It was his first tangle with the court system—and he won. "Ralph was brought into criminal court on that charge, tried and acquitted," Cecil Weeding recalls. "There was considerable sympathy for him then. People knew what a predicament they had been in, and they simply had to have some of that money to live on. They probably had sold some of it, but who could blame them? They had families to feed and necessities that had to be bought somehow, and they were already at the end of their credit. Nobody would have loaned them any more money.

"So they chose that route, and got away with it. Probably a sad commentary on the system at that time. It seemed rather apparent that the government's case against them was pretty cut and dried—they had simply converted mortgaged property. But the jury system being what it was, they had a way."

Weeding says Ralph Clark's acquittal then eventually came back to haunt the community: "It probably emboldened them in the things that were to happen thereafter. The idea that somehow the system wouldn't hold them accountable—that they were victims of some horrendous scheme and that their fellow man wouldn't convict them of anything. After all, it was just the government that they were defrauding."

Geraldo Rivera came to town that year and featured Ralph Clark in a story he was putting together for ABC News on the farm crisis. Rivera did not, however, endear himself to the locals; he tangled with one of them at a local tavern and wound up having his head rammed through a wall, according to local legend.

Other outsiders began circling around Ralph Clark and his family then too. They called themselves the Posse Comitatus, and they told Clark that his problems were rooted in the gigantic conspiracy run by Jewish bankers to enslave all of America, beginning with the farmers. No one else seemed to understand or respect Ralph's problems, but these people did. Ralph not only believed what they told him, he became one of their leading advocates in eastern Montana. Soon, Clark would have his own following. His nephew, Richard, became a Posse believer. A close neighbor, William Stanton, who faced similar financial problems, likewise was converted.

Bill Stanton filed for bankruptcy in 1988, but maintained possession of his ranch through the process. Still, he blamed the government for his problems, and convinced his wife, Agnes, and son, Ebert, that his cause was just. Stanton, like Ralph Clark, was also a recipient of federal subsidies, and likewise was less than adroit in handling the sudden wealth that came with those government checks. Neighbors say that one year he purchased a mobile home and a gambling trip to Las Vegas with the money he received in a land-conservation program intended to replace lost income.[10]

Perhaps Ralph Clark's most important association, though, was with Dan Petersen.

★★★

Dan Petersen didn't ever think much about the government. He was simply an auto mechanic, and a good one. He seemed able to resurrect just about any kind of clunker folks would drag into the garage at the little gas station in Winnett where he worked. And when he fixed them, they ran for a long time.

Then, one day, the government confiscated a batch of his tools and wouldn't give them back. From that day on, he developed an abiding hatred for the authorities.

Petersen grew up in Winnett and the Big Open countryside around the Musselshell River, which is the kind of place that seems unconnected from everywhere else in the world. The town itself, a roadside weed of a village in the middle of the eastern Montana plains, part way between Roundup and Jordan, has a population of less than 200. If you want something other than what they sell at the grocery store, the post office, and the gas station where Dan Petersen worked, you have to drive 45 miles to Roundup, or maybe all the way to Billings.

Petersen, his mother says, was a bright boy. He started working on cars when he was 11 and quickly proved gifted at it. But like others with intelligence living in a town like Winnett, he was a restless teenager. If he cracked a book, it meant an easy A, but he had to be dragged into such chores. Moreover, he started getting into conflicts with the local police. She and her husband sent him off to Miles City for his senior year of high school in hopes it would straighten him out.[11]

After school, he settled into a series of mechanic jobs, often working for himself, but occasionally for garages around Garfield and Petroleum counties. He married and had two children. The marriage eventually broke up, but Petersen stayed steady in his work, though he never made much money at it. He earned some extra cash on the side by supervising a motor-carrier route for the Great Falls newspaper.[12]

Petersen remarried, and treated his stepsons like his own children. He settled into a job at the Reuben Oil Company garage in Winnett as a mechanic. When one of the boys developed financial problems, Dan lent him a truckful of his tools so he could go find mechanic's work and get back on his feet again. Before that could happen, though, government officials came to confiscate the stepson's property as part of a collection procedure, and included Dan Petersen's tools along with everything else. Since they were about the only valuable thing in the stepson's possession, the authorities were loath to release them to their rightful owner. Petersen became infuriated, family members say.[13]

One day in 1989 Petersen came in to work at the gas station and found Ralph Clark perched on a stool in the station lobby, spouting his theories on government to anyone who would listen. The men at the station already knew Clark just from doing business with him, and they knew about his financial troubles on the farm. But Dan Petersen was eager to hear what Clark had to say, and in short order was spouting the same rhetoric himself.

Ralph Clark became a regular at Reuben Oil; he brought video tapes to play on the television set in the gas station's back room, until one day the owner put an end to it. "I came in and they were playing this tape about that KAL Flight 007 and how the government was covering up this gigantic conspiracy," he recalls. "You could hear it clear out here. I told them we can't have any more of that. So from then on, they just watched the tapes at home."

From the vantage point of the crossroads at Winnett, Petersen managed to make connections with the group of Posse activists at the Road and Ranch Supply in Belgrade. Petersen and Clark both became friends with LeRoy Schweitzer and Rodney Skurdal, sharing ideas and strategies through Montana's growing right-wing network. Petersen eventually left his job at Reuben Oil, embarking on a joint venture with Ralph Clark.

The two of them toured the eastern Montana countryside, selling water-filtration systems that eliminated the notoriously sulfuric taste of the region's drinking water. The customers, which included family and neighbors, all say the systems worked well initially but broke down after a few months' use and required frequent repair from Ralph and Dan. Most of the buyers say the water systems weren't the only thing the two men were selling; the visits also provided them with ample opportunities to recruit for the Posse Comitatus.

The discontent boiling among the Posse Comitatus believers started coming to a head in eastern Montana in 1992. Rodney Skurdal finally settled his lawsuit with Exeter Drilling out of court, and bought a ranch outside of Roundup with the money. Before long, LeRoy Schweitzer, recently dispossessed of a home due to an IRS foreclosure for non-payment of taxes, and already a fugitive because of federal indictments over his pilot's license, had moved in with Skurdal at the place near the end of Johnny's Coal Road. Their previous acquaintance with Ralph Clark and his clique of malcontents became an even tighter bond as their proximity grew. Dan Petersen began making regular visits. Soon he became one of LeRoy Schweitzer's prize acolytes, displaying an ability to cite chapter and verse of the obscure codes that provided the framework for the Freemen's legal system.

That September, Skurdal walked into the Musselshell County Courthouse and filed a couple of do-it-yourself court documents that mostly confused the local clerk and recorder. He declared the Internal Revenue Service was an illegal entity which had no standing in its claim that he owed $29,000 in back taxes.

Two days later, Skurdal offered the clerk a more disconcerting document to file: a "Citizens Declaration of War," which proclaimed his separation from the "de facto" government in order to "honor my God and the laws of the Bible," to "regain my rights to acquire private allodial property" and to "regain our Justices Court." He embossed it with a signature, a fingerprint, and a private court seal: Skurdal had purchased a self-designed notary's seal and then declared himself a notary public of "our one supreme Court."

That same year, the Freemen—as they now called themselves—developed an economic system to accompany their political and religious beliefs. A Colorado Constitutionalist, Roy Schwasinger, toured Montana offering "We the People" seminars for $300 that taught students how to cash in on the idea that the federal government was bankrupt and illegally printing money. Moreover, he claimed, the government had tucked away $600 trillion in gold as part of a covert U.S. military operation. Citizens, he said, could file damage claims that would enable them to collect a share of that gold.

Among those attending the Billings session in November were LeRoy Schweitzer, Ralph Clark and Bill Stanton.

With Schwasinger's idea—turning the supposed phoniness of federal money into your own personal gold mine—as a base, Schweitzer and Skurdal came up with their own concoction: a hefty helping of their own practice of filing reams of pseudolegal documents, a dose of Posse Comitatus-style liens commonly used to terrorize local politicians, and several dollops of Christian Identity religious beliefs. The potion that poured out became the Freemen's blueprint for riches through right-wing revolution.

★★★

Armed with state-of-the-art computer equipment that not only let them produce reams of new documents but also let them transmit their ideas through the Internet—not to mention the complete legal libraries they obtained either through CD-ROM or by simply buying the code books—the Freemen began piecing together a complex legal, historical and religious theory that became the basis for their system of economics. They became, in their own minds, "the new Federal Reserve."

The system is based on the concept of "sovereign citizenship," a self-designation they claim is possible by filing the same kind of documents John Trochmann employed in Sanders County, declaring oneself free of the citizenship of the United States. Once someone makes his stance official, he can enjoy "de jure" status under the "organic Constitution"—reserved, that is, for white male property owners, who now were no longer second-class "federal citizens" under the designation they say was created by the 14th Amendment (which they claim was not legally enacted). Doing so, they argue, makes a person a "free man" and not a "freedman," or somebody under slavery.

The next step is to form a "common law" court comprised of other "sovereign citizens." These, the Freemen say, are the only truly legal courts that can operate under the Constitution. The mainstream courts are part of the "de facto" government in Washington, D.C., and mere corporate creations of it. Common-law courts are what should be administering social justice in America, they claim.

Once the court has been established, one can begin filing grievances against "foreign" government agencies (like, say, the federal government). This is done in the form of "True Bills" and "Quiet Titles," documents that essentially are long confessions aimed at officials and citizens deemed to have offended the constitutional foundations of the country. These could range from local county judges to the top leaders of the federal government.

Then-Treasury Secretary Lloyd Bentsen, for instance, was the subject of a 1994 "True Bill" filed by LeRoy Schweitzer. Running four pages long, each paragraph begins: "I, Lloyd Bentsen . . ." and then continues with admissions to a variety of supposed perfidies inflicted upon Schweitzer in the form of the IRS agents who seized his Bozeman home. One says: "I, Lloyd Bentsen, hereby admit our United States Bureau of Internal Revenue agents do not have any supporting implementation regulations which could enforce a regulation process against LeRoy M. Schweitzer in his foreign country of Montana . . ." Another: "I, Lloyd Bentsen, being a foreign agent taking pay for presumed specific performance from the International Monetary Fund, must obey simple contract law, or become liable upon said contract."

As with all the "True Bills," Bentsen was given ten days to respond, either by signing the document or, apparently, by offering a refutation, though that option is never outlined in the bills. Otherwise, by default, he would owe the court a sum of money for his judgment by the common-law court. In the case of Bentsen, it was a mere $100 million. For others, the amount could range from a few thousand to a billion dollars, depending on the severity of the grievance.

According to the Freemen, once an official defaults on the "True Bill," the holder of the judgment is free to file a lien against the individual targeted in the bill—and for the amount of the judgment. Of course, the liens have no merit and could be eventually (sometimes quickly) dismissed, but in the meantime, they could have the effect of clouding the target's title to property and credit record. Moreover, until they were found and registered as worthless, they would pop up on bank computers as assets.

The Freemen's computers provided them with the tools for the final, crucial step in the scheme: creating bogus money orders. Using somewhat sophisticated programs, their laser printers would emit documents that looked like a genuine article issued by a real bank. Some of them used a phony account number from Norwest Bank, while others were simply labeled "Certified Bankers Check." These money orders, listing the liens at the banks where they were registered as assets, then would be filed with another bank. The banks would cash them in as though they were real. A few days later, they'd find to their chagrin that this was not the case.

Banks weren't the only victims of this scheme. Anyone who did business with the Freemen and accepted a "LeRoy check" were soon dismayed to find they had been ripped off. This included car and motor-home dealers, computer salesmen, furniture retailers, even farming supply and machinery dealers. A Freeman would present each of them with a money order that was usually for an amount well over—sometimes double—the amount of the sale. The firm would then not only release the merchandise, but would reimburse the buyer for the difference in cash.

The Freemen justified this with an argument straight out of Roy Schwasinger's seminars: The federal government was bankrupt and illegally printing bogus money anyway, money that no longer had any basis, since the government took the dollar off the gold standard in 1971. So the Freemen were free to create their own money out of equally thin air—not only that, but by basis of the "constitutional" nature of the common-law courts that issued the liens, their system was more legitimate than the federal government's.

The alternative-universe notion that the Federal Reserve system prints "funny money" based on no actual foundation has floated about on the far right for years, and is a key component of some cult belief systems like Lyndon LaRouche's. There's a glimmer of truth in this—today's currency is fiat money, based on nothing but the willing agreement of everybody to use it as a medium of exchange. But it obviously is a genuine store of value; you can buy real things with it. Trying to use a "LeRoy check" based on Freemen liens is another matter.

Those who argue that money must be based on some hard commodity—usually gold and silver—ignore the fact that when a currency is based on gold, the value given to gold is as essentially arbitrary as that assigned to paper currency. And the obvious advantage of fiat currency is that it allows human policymakers to control the monetary supply instead of tying it to a market-vulnerable commodity like gold, chief among the many reasons the United States went off the gold standard in 1971.

In a logical world, it's clear the U.S. Federal Reserve System's dollars are not mere ephemera but the working symbols of a robust, highly productive economy. The only economic activity represented by the Freemen's "monetary" system, on the other hand, was the phony liens they filed against public officials, which allowed them to get their hands on the very money they claimed was pure paper. In reality, the Freemen's claims to equal or superior legitimacy were worth less than the paper they printed their copious documents with.

Still, as with almost all dwellers in the Patriots' alternate reality, reason, fact and logic are not significant components of the Freemen's beliefs, because their foundation is a wall of religious faith—specifically, a belief in the tenets of Christian Identity. For them, revelation is more important than reason, because it is divine, while logic is human and fallible.

The world the Bible reveals to them—at least, through the peculiar brand of fundamentalism Identity represents—is not compatible with modern society. Indeed, its outlook is distinctly Old World in temperament, a universe where only "God's laws" as defined by Old Testament prophets have any value, a world constantly at war with other tribes and willing to commit violence in the name of God—or, in Identity, "Yahweh." In this world, white people are the true descendants of Adam, the inheritors of Israel. Those who call themselves Jews are the deceitful descendants of Satan himself, whose son, Cain, mated with the soulless "pre-Adamic" populace of Earth and gave rise to the hated "Canaanites" who later, after the twelve tribes of Israel were scattered, took on the appearances of the Jewish heritage but who in reality worship Satan. All other races—blacks, Asians, Indians, Native Americans, Middle Easterners—are strictly descended from the "pre-Adamic" peoples. To this day, the Satanic "Jews" conspire to destroy the true children of Israel, who built America into a great Christian nation, but now find it under attack because of the moral decay inspired by Jewish conspirators in the government and banking system and throughout the media and entertainment industries.

Believers in Christian Identity (and especially so-called "two-seed theory" proponents like the Freemen) know well that these views are reviled as "racist" by the mainstream world, but that scarcely matters to them. Rather, they see themselves in a distinctly valiant light: they are trying to save the white race from extinction, to pull white culture back from the brink of annihilation. They know they will be persecuted for their beliefs, as they are warned will happen in the Bible. But for them, it is worth the effort, because in their own hearts they are worthy of being called "heroic," and fully believe that history will cast them in such a light.[14]

Certainly the Freemen see themselves this way. "There has been much said about the 'freemen' [characters] in the papers lately," read a 1995 affidavit authored by Skurdal, "yet one must recognize that you are either 'free' or a 'slave.' As the old saying goes, one can not be a little bit pregnant, either you are pregnant or your not, i.e., either you are 'free' i.e., a 'freeman' or you are a 'slave' . . . Which are you: a 'freeman' or a slave?"[15]

All these religious beliefs came pouring out over the next few years in the prodigious pseudo-legal documents the Freemen concocted up on Johnny's Coal Road. Each was peppered with references to "Yahweh" and "Israel" as well as Biblical quotations. Some, like Skurdal's October 1994 "Edict," were purely extended Identity theological lessons. Of course, they couldn't call them court documents without the requisite legal language, and the convoluted mumbo-jumbo common to the world of modern law practice makes up the bulk of the Freemen's filings. But there is a distinct difference (other than the proliferation of religious references) between the Freemen's work and standard legal documents: the Freemen, unlike mainstream lawyers, feel no compunction about drawing from any laws produced by Western civilization going back to the Magna Carta—as well as, of course, the Bible.

Indeed, much as they do with the Bible, the Freemen in the legal world engage in a kind of illogic which first decides what the truth is, and then finds passages in some obscure authority (frequently misinterpreted) to help justify their idea of the truth. Virtually any law that has ever been written, no matter how outdated or overruled, can be produced as evidence of their legal position. More important, they become in effect calcified, much as Scripture is in their worldview: If a law was written three hundred years ago, then it remains in effect in the body of "common law." Besides the Magna Carta and Biblical law, the available list also includes numerous outdated codes, especially unused portions of the old Uniform Commercial Code. Others cited by Freemen: a 1620 American Colonial law and an 1830 ruling long since overturned.

Many of these laws actually existed at one time, but then, it's important to remember that the nation was, in fact, overtly racist for at least its first hundred years, when it held an entire race in slavery, and innately so for most of the intervening years, when "Jim Crow" laws and active prejudice kept blacks effectively disenfranchised, politically and economically. The arrival of a widespread social sanction against racism is a relatively new phenomenon in America in historical terms. All the Freemen are really doing, when you think about it, is resurrecting laws reflecting that past and asking Americans to return to those times with them.

In the plains of Montana, they began working hard to build the pathway to that past.

★★★

Neighbors and family members say that Dan Petersen and Ralph Clark were like two peas in a pod by 1992, scouring the countryside selling their water systems and Posse Comitatus nostrums. So it was Petersen, naturally, who accompanied Clark in to Garfield County Prosecutor Nick Murnion's office one day in January 1993.

They wanted Murnion to prosecute the Farmers Home Administration for fraud. Clark's long string of luck staving off foreclosure had finally given out; the FHA had just finished up its final foreclosure proceedings on Clark's ranch and was preparing to sell it at auction. Petersen spouted a stream of obscure laws to back up their claims, but Murnion knew gobbledygook when he heard it, and told them he had no intention of pursuing their request. The next day, Clark and Petersen filed a lien against him. It was the first of many Murnion would have directed his way.[16]

Meanwhile, the Freemen were spreading the word to everyone they came in contact with around Roundup. Rodney Skurdal frequented a tavern near Johnny's Coal Road called the Branding Iron, where he liked to hold court with the locals, regaling them with theories and tales of conspiratorial perfidies. Skurdal's reddish mane of hair and beard and his piercing blue eyes gave him a messianic look. Even though his brain injury often prevented him from completing sentences, his innate charisma drew a loyal following.

Sheriff Paul Smith liked to mosey into the Branding Iron after work for a beer, too, and used to listen in. Once, he said, Rodney confronted him at the bar, complaining that as sheriff he was failing to follow his constitutional duties.

"I turned around to him and said, 'Rodney, I came in here for a quiet beer. If you don't leave me the hell alone, I'm going to knock you from here to that corner,'" Smith recalls.

"As soon as I said that, I was sorry, because I thought then for sure I was going to have to fight him. But he just backed off and went back to his little circle of friends.

"I always thought I could talk things out with Rodney on his own. He could be very reasonable then. But if he had an audience it was a different story."[17]

The courts, though, were the main venue for the Freemen's efforts. Between 1992 and 1995, Skurdal and Schweitzer and their friends in Jordan flooded the court systems in Musselshell and Garfield counties with reams of "True Bills," affidavits, claims of "Quiet Title" and liens against both public officials and private businessmen, especially banks, who refused to recognize the legitimacy of their claims.

They also began forming their common-law courts throughout the Great Plains counties, sometimes in dramatic fashion. This is when the Freemen's confrontations with authorities started to take on a violent tinge.

On a frigid day in Jordan—January 27, 1994—a group of 26 Freemen, including Rodney Skurdal, Dan Petersen and Ralph Clark, walked into the little one-story Garfield County Courthouse, some with handguns strapped to their hips, and booted out all the regular county employees. They then proceeded to hold a two-hour session—which they videotaped for posterity's sake—proclaiming the establishment of their own county government and common-law court. Then they issued writs against the judges and lawyers who were handling the divorce case of Richard Clark.

Richard Clark, the son of Ralph's older brother Emmett Clark, and a Posse camp follower, was contesting the amount of alimony and child-support payments that had been ordered by the courts in his case. Clark refused to make the payments, and local authorities in return threatened to take the money out of his forthcoming federal Conservation Reserve Program subsidy check, which totaled about $50,000. To forestall that eventuality, the common-law court announced it was holding the judge and the lawyers in contempt.

Not that it made much difference. The next day, Richard Clark's ex-wife, Gloria, successfully attached his CRP check to collect on his divorce debt.

A month or so later, the Freemen began posting bounties of $1 million for nearly every non-Freeman involved in the case: the judge, the lawyers, a couple of bank officials, even Nick Murnion and Sheriff Charlie Phipps. The bounty listed William Stanton as the constable. The Freemen faxed it worldwide—or at least to the following they had gained through the Internet.

Sheriff Phipps, who grew up in the county and knew the Clarks and the Stantons like family, at first was a little amused. He saw Stanton in town and asked him if he could get the reward if he turned himself in to the common-law court. Yes, Stanton told him, he could, but he wouldn't live long enough to enjoy it. "You'll be tried, convicted and hung," he said.[18] He told Phipps he'd soon be dangling from a local bridge anyway. He also said that Ralph Clark had issued the bounties.

Phipps and County Prosecutor Murnion were no longer amused. Two weeks later, Murnion filed charges against 13 of the Freemen for impersonating a public servant, a misdemeanor, and filed felony charges against Ralph Clark, for threatening to kidnap and hang a federal judge. An April 1 appearance date was set.

When the appointed day came, only two of the accused appeared: the Freemen court's Justice of the Peace, Clay Taylor, and his wife, Karen. They pleaded innocent; Taylor, a longtime local rancher, claimed he didn't know anything about the bounties before they came out and had nothing to do with them. Arrest warrants went out for the rest, including Schweitzer, Skurdal, Stanton, Petersen and Richard and Emmett Clark.

As for Ralph Clark's kidnapping-solicitation charge, his court appearance was scheduled for the same date—April 14—as the sheriff's auction to sell off his ranch. Rumors began flying around Jordan as the day approached: that there were Patriot sharpshooters en route to Montana who were going to pick off seven local officials and then head back to the Clark ranch to hide out; that the Freemen were planning to bomb the courthouse while the auction proceeded. Everyone in town, Murnion and Phipps especially, was on pins and needles.

Phipps decided not to fool around. He organized a sheriff's posse—a legitimate one comprised of local farmers and ranchers—to back him up at the auction. At its first meeting, 150 people attended, and 85 signed up. On the day of the auction in Jordan, several dozen posse members showed up at the courthouse and stood by while local rancher K.L. Bliss bought the 6,000-acre foreclosed farm once known as the Hilliard place. None of the Freemen showed; Ralph Clark simply had announced he was going to hole up at the family ranch where he still lived.

Now Sheriff Phipps faced a dilemma; later that afternoon, in the same courthouse, Clark failed to appear on the kidnapping charge, and a warrant was issued for his arrest. But with Clark holed up on the ranch and heavily armed, Phipps had good reason to believe he and his two-deputy department weren't going to be able to serve the warrant without violent resistance. So he chose to wait him out.

For the next year and a half, both sides more or less stayed put. Around them, though, the drama continued to escalate.

★★★

The next few months, as summer arrived on the plains and temperatures and tempers rose, a flurry of charges and counterclaims, arrests and frequently ignored court hearings stirred up a rising dust storm in the territory the Freemen claimed as the "country of Montana"—namely, Musselshell, Petroleum and Garfield counties.

Edwin Clark, Ralph's son, was arrested at a Jordan gas station and released on $2,500 bond; three days later, he failed to appear for his detention hearing and his bond was forfeited. Rodney Skurdal and Gary Clark (another of Ralph's nephews) were arrested in Roundup, arraigned and released on bond. When his trial date came around August 1, though, Skurdal was securely ensconced in his Roundup ranch. He was tried and convicted in absentia.

Bill Stanton, who was hiding out with Clark, lost his farm that June when it was auctioned off by Sheriff Phipps. One of Charlie's uncles, Tim Phipps, bought the place. Emmett Clark was arrested, too, and like the rest of the Freemen, refused to show for his subsequent court dates. Worse, he paid for his bail with a $10,000 "LeRoy check" that promptly bounced, and a few weeks later, had bad-check charges added to his growing list of criminal counts.

The Freemen fought back in their own way: with a blizzard of court filings. The Garfield County Clerk, JoAnn Stanton, swears she lost 40 pounds trying to deal with all their documents. They issued subpoenas to Max Baucus and Conrad Burns, Montana's U.S. senators, and to a host of other state officials, notably the attorney general and the governor.

Skurdal kept appealing the cases created by his "True Bills" and phony liens by filing documents through surrogates at the various county courthouses, until one of them reached the Montana Supreme Court in July. Chief Justice Jean Turnage decided it was time to cut the Freemen off. The filings, he found, were "not only nonsensical but meritless, frivolous, vexatious and wasteful of the limited time and resources of this court, of the clerk of this court and of the various public officials and counsel that are forced to deal with and respond to Mr. Skurdal's abuse." He slapped a $1,000 sanction on Skurdal and limited his access to the courts to documents filed only by a member of the Montana Bar (who the Freemen frequently referred to as "corporate prostitutes"). Local judges in Garfield and Musselshell counties did the same, announcing that county clerks were instructed to refuse Skurdal's pseudo-legal documents.

While their legal defeats were coming in rapid succession, the Freemen's recruiting was going well. Another key follower showed up at the Freemen ranch that fall: Dale Jacobi. A Canadian businessman who had moved from Calgary in the 1980s south to Thompson Falls, Montana, Jacobi became involved in the radical right while operating a propane-gas business in the little Clark Fork River logging town just a few miles east of Noxon. He fell in with John and Dave Trochmann, and also became acquainted with another local Constitutionalist, John Brush.

Brush decided to move to Musselshell County in 1994, partly to be closer to the Freemen, so he bought a parcel of land out in the distant woods and set about raising and training horses with his wife and daughter. Jacobi, who became a Freemen follower after Trochmann recommended he attend the four-day seminars described in the Militia of Montana newsletter that spring, sold his business and moved onto Brush's land, living in a trailer on the property.

In one afternoon that fall, though, Brush not only disavowed Dale Jacobi but the Freemen as well. He later explained why to John Bohlman, the Musselshell County prosecutor.

One morning, Brush told Bohlman, when he drove into town for supplies, Jacobi took Brush's 8-year-old daughter, with her dog in tow, out to a remote part of their land. He carried with him a stool and a piece of rope. Under a tree, Jacobi set up the stool and placed the little dog on it. Then he made a noose with the rope, placed it over the dog's neck, and slung it over the tree. He pulled the open end of the rope tight and held it at a distance from the dog, then told the girl to come stand in front of him. Call the dog, he told the girl. She did. It jumped off the stool and hung itself as Jacobi held the line taut.

The girl was in hysterics when her father returned home. Enraged, he asked Jacobi why he did it. Jacobi told him he felt the girl needed some toughening up, and that this would help her. Brush screamed at Jacobi to leave and never come back. Jacobi packed his things into his car and left. He found an open room at Skurdal's ranch, and soon was named one of the group's constables. Brush announced he wanted nothing more to do with that bunch—and asked Bohlman to remove the arms cache Jacobi had left behind. Bohlman and a deputy went out to Brush's place and found PVC pipes hidden under some brush, stuffed with a few guns and a massive load of ammunition, reloading tools, powder and bullets, enough to make thousands of rounds. Brush also told Bohlman he knew of similar caches like this in strategic spots throughout the Northwest.

Meanwhile, the circle of law enforcement started to tighten around the Freemen; that October, Bill Stanton was arrested in the parking lot of a Billings grocery store. By then, he too had charges for using "LeRoy checks" to pay his tax bill tacked onto his "criminal syndicalism" case in the county courthouse takeover. His trial date was scheduled for February, but the judge declined to allow his release on bail, considering the Freemen's track record.

The next month, Clay and Karen Taylor were convicted of impersonating a public servant, a misdemeanor, and were given suspended sentences. They retreated to their ranch and tried to piece their lives back together. Taylor remained a devout Constitutionalist, but he had some lingering bitterness over the Freemen as well. "They sent me to a gunfight armed with a ballpoint pen," he later told a Billings reporter. "And I'm not a good enough communicator. I lost."[19]

The Freemen fought back against their tormentors that December by firing off a warning to Jack Shanstrom, the federal judge handling Stanton's case, as well as to Sheriff Phipps and the clerk of the court. It warned of dire consequences if they attempted to come onto the Clark property. "We will not hesitate to use our Lawful deadly force by whatever means necessary to fully support protect, guarantee and defend our law," it read. "Our special Orders . . . is for our special appointed Constables and our Lawful Posse to shoot to kill any public hireling or fourteenth amendment citizen who is caught in any act whatsoever of taking Private property."

As bad as things went in 1994 for the Freemen, in general, 1995 turned into an even worse year. The hammer dropped that February, when Bill Stanton was convicted on both criminal syndicalism and bad-check charges. His trial lasted only two days; sentencing was set for March 2 in Miles City.

Less than two weeks after the verdict, with the Freemen's violent warning in hand, Prosecutor Murnion and the U.S. attorney filed "criminal syndicalism" charges against LeRoy Schweitzer, Rodney Skurdal, Dan Petersen, and Emmett, Richard and Ralph Clark, for threatening a federal judge. Now the Freemen leaders faced an array of both federal and local charges, and were gradually being boxed in at their ranch on Johnny's Coal Road.

An explosion was building. There was a run on guns at the outdoors shops in Musselshell and Garfield counties, and dealers in Billings even noted a rise in business from residents in those parts. Most locals figured something might happen around the time Bill Stanton was sentenced.

They were right.

★★★

In the days before Stanton's sentencing, rumors started to fly like the snow that blanketed Roundup that winter. The principal of the local high school heard that the Freemen planned to invade the school with guns and take over the building, holding the children hostage. He started locking the doors to the school, and a few parents even decided to hold their kids out of class on the day of the sentencing.

John Bohlman, the Musselshell county prosecutor, heard enough death threats directed his way on the rumor circuit that he bought a handgun and started carrying it when he took his dog for a run each day. A neighbor who moved into a home he once owned accused him of selling it to hide from the Freemen, and threatened to put a sign on her lawn announcing that John Bohlman no longer lived there.

Paul Smith, the sheriff, heard some of the rumors and dismissed them as just that. He had enough real worries to deal with. The FBI told him that a Patriot informant in western Montana had learned what the Freemen's counter-strategy was—namely, that they planned to kidnap a judge and prosecutor, try them in their common-law court, convict them, and then hang them. They also planned to videotape the whole affair, including the executions.

A burly, square-jawed man with a bristling black mustache and a fondness for western attire—boots, jeans, and shirts with snaps—Paul Smith looks and talks like a Western sheriff, and acts like one too. He grew up in the town of Dillon, another farm-and-ranch community in western Montana, a little more populous but culturally the same kind of community as Roundup. In small towns, he knew, rumors had a way of taking on lives of their own. But when it came to genuine death threats, Smith knew he had to take steps. And he took it a little personally.

Smith had been dealing with Skurdal's group for two years now, and held them in rather low regard—mostly for the way they used local people in dire straits to foment their "revolution."

"I think basically what they've done is use people's Montana heritage, thinking, the culture of Montana, the free-thinking, independent, agricultural-type person, they've used that to recruit these people," Smith says with a twinge of a Montana drawl. "Sure, there's always a certain amount of discontent with our government, with government regulations. And as time goes on, farmers, everyone sees more and more federal regulations in one way or another.

"These guys, what they are is a bunch of con men—they have no personal interest in seeing some rancher save his ranch out here. They could care less. The only thing they're there for is to use him, convince him to support them financially, and otherwise bleed that rancher dry when he'd be better off to pay his loans with that money and possibly keep that ranch.

"These guys, putting it bluntly, are bloodsuckers on our culture, and have taken advantage of people that are in economically desperate situations."

Smith knew, too, that they were capable of carrying out their threats, so he decided to provide protection for a district judge involved in the case, Roy C. Rodeghiero, and assigned reserve deputies to the detail, as well as an extra reserve on duty at the courthouse to keep an eye out for the clerk and prosecutor. The sheriff himself provided a daily escort for the judge to and from his house.

When the sentencing date arrived in Miles City (where the nearest federal courtroom was located), District Judge Jack Shanstrom threw the book at Bill Stanton. He handed the Freeman ten years in prison and classified him a dangerous offender, not eligible for parole for five years. He also tacked on a $10,000 fine. When he walked out of the courthouse that day, the judge was surrounded by a phalanx of law officers.

But nothing happened that day, neither in Miles City nor in Roundup. The principal kept the Roundup schoolhouse doors locked, but no one approached the building. John Bohlman waited the day out nervously in his office, since he didn't know whether the prosecutor they intended to target was himself or Nick Murnion up in Garfield County. No one from the ranch even came to the clerk's office to file any documents.

The next morning, though, the Freemen were there. Frank Ellena, one of Skurdal's regular acolytes, walked into the clerk's office and tried to file some documents relating to his property. The clerk, following court orders, told him she couldn't accept the documents because they used Skurdal's personal notary seal. When he argued, she sent him down to talk to John Bohlman.

"And I said, no, for several reasons," Bohlman recalls. "One is that there's a court order that Skurdal's stuff has to be approved as to form by a judge or a lawyer before we'll file it. Second, it's not a real notary, it's a de jure notary. And he argued with me about why he thought that was legitimate.

"And I said, third, it's a first and last page. In between it could say anything. It's an incomplete document and she's not going to record it. And fourth, you're not going to record a trust anyway. You record the real property transcripts, you don't record a trust. It was part of one of their stands against the IRS for Quiet Title or hiding title.

"Anyhow, he argued with me and put his arm around me and told me I was treasonous traitor and seditionist, and that I had a lot to learn."

Watching the whole process was one of the reserve officers the sheriff had assigned to watch the courthouse.

"And this reserve officer thought this was suspicious—more than I did. He was standing right behind me while this conversation took place. So that reservist then followed him out of the building to see where he went—walked up the street behind him and saw that he got in a truck at IGA as a passenger. And the reservist is really good friends with the sheriff, and he had seen that truck out at Rodney's that week.

"So he radioed the sheriff and said, this guy's in the courthouse, he acted funny, and he went and got in the truck that we've been seeing at Rodney's house—this white truck, a flatbed. So the sheriff went one direction looking for it, and the other deputy, Buzz Jones, went this direction down Main Street and took a right at Main Street, just to see if this was important."

When Jones caught up to the pickup, he saw that it had no rear license plates. So he hit his lights, and pulled the truck over just past the city limits (by mere yards). In the driver's seat was Dale Jacobi.

Jacobi had no license, no registration, no insurance, and told Jones he didn't need it, and hadn't in five years. Jones told him to get out of the vehicle, and Jacobi did. Jones patted him down and found a gun in his waistband. Ellena got out of the vehicle on the passenger's side, pulled a handgun out of his waistband, and tossed it on the seat of the truck, and then got back in.

Sheriff Smith arrived on the scene, and both men were arrested—Jacobi for the traffic offenses and carrying a concealed weapon with no permit, and Ellena for carrying a concealed weapon with no permit. The arrests and bookings were all completed by 3:30.

As the afternoon wound down, nothing else seemed to be stirring. Paul Smith accompanied the judge to his home. John Bohlman wrapped up his work and went home; it was Friday and the work week was over. He barely had walked through his front door when the phone rang.

"It was Deputy Jones," Bohlman says. "He was real excited. He says, 'You've got to come here—we've got the guys who were going to off the judge—we've got all these weapons and gold and video camera and plastic restraints.' And they were just yelling at me: 'You've got to see this.'"

When Bohlman arrived at the sheriff's office, the deputies had laid out all the materials they found inside Jacobi's truck: an arsenal of guns and rifles, duct tape and plastic hand restraints, a video camera and bandoleers of ammunition. There were some gold bars and hand-held two-way radios as well.

The most chilling discovery, though, was a piece of paper: a hand-drawn map of Jordan, with the location of Garfield County Prosecutor Nick Murnion's home highlighted.

"So I look at all this stuff, and I say, 'Oh my God, these are the men who were going to kidnap the judge'—I buy into the paranoia and say, 'It's too big for me, I need to call the attorney general.' But it's 6 o'clock, and I don't know how to reach Joe Mazurek at home.

"So I call my friend Blair Jones, whose brother is [Deputy] Buzz Jones. Blair's the county attorney in Stillwater County, and I want to know how to reach Joe Mazurek at home. And I'm telling him what's going on, and that's when I hear these two officers—one of them's Dutch Van Syckel, and he's yelling, there's two vehicles pulled into the parking lot, there's five men, they're talking in radios, and they're going to opposite ends."

Dutch Van Syckel is a no-nonsense Marine veteran who thinks tactically, and he could see the two cars had just pulled up in the jailhouse parking lot. He says they immediately raised his suspicion because the cars arrived together, but two men remained in one car in the parking lot while the three occupants of the other got out and headed toward the jailhouse.

"Buzz runs in and grabs a shotgun and pumps shells into it, pumps one into the chamber," says Bohlman. "I'm going, 'Give me a gun, I'm sitting in here, you guys get shot I'm a sitting duck.' He gives me his pistol.

"So that's when I said to Blair, 'You've gotta believe me, Blair, I'm behind this desk with a pistol,' so his dispatcher sends out from the Stillwater County sheriff's office that these men are raiding the courthouse, because that's where he thinks I am. Which caused hell, and made the sheriff really mad at me, because we had phone calls all night about the invasion of the courthouse."

The sheriff's office has a small standing room outside its secure area where the public can talk to deputies through a barred window. The three men came in there, and asked to talk to the sheriff. Van Syckel told them the sheriff wasn't there. They asked if they could recover some of Ellena's property that had been confiscated earlier that day. Van Syckel told them no. They argued. And that's when one of them pulled back his jacket and revealed a handgun strapped to his waist, in the way that people do to let you know they mean business.

However, carrying a gun into the jailhouse is also against the law; a bright red sign on the only door announces that firearms are forbidden in the building. When Van Syckel saw the gun, he pulled out his own and ordered the men onto the floor.

Bohlman heard it all from around the corner, in the sheriff's private office. "Dutch, he's yelling, 'Gun! Gun!' So Buzz steps through the doorway with the shotgun and says, 'You guys are under arrest.' I hear some yelling.

"They arrest those three people. There were only two officers there, and one officer is back behind the jail cells with the prisoners because they think these guys are coming for the prisoners, and they told him to get back there with them. So these guys have three prisoners, and there's two more out in the car, because they think everybody's got radios—they see the guys out in the cars talking into radios. So they decided to go out."

With three prisoners prone on the floor and short of handcuffs, Jones and Van Syckel grabbed some of Ellena's plastic ties from the pile of evidence and tied the three men's feet. Then they walked out into the snowy parking lot, one officer to each side of the car. They saw an older man with a beard in the driver's seat, and a younger man on the other side talking into his radio. Van Syckel went to the driver's side, and Buzz Jones went to the passenger side. Both men locked their doors.

"Come on out, you're under arrest," Van Syckel told the driver. The men refused. Then, Jones noticed the passenger reach into his jacket. With the butt of his shotgun, he smashed out the window, opened the door and pulled the man out onto the ground. Sure enough, inside the jacket where he was reaching was a handgun.

The driver was yelling. Van Syckel asked him if he wanted to come out now; the man opened the door and Van Syckel pulled him out onto the ground, cuffing him with the ties and searching him. The gray-bearded man, too, had a handgun, tucked into the waistband of his pants. They picked the two prisoners up and walked them into the jail.

"They take those guys, bring them in, and they came and told me I could crawl out now," says Bohlman with a wry grin, recalling the scene with five prisoners jammed into the little jailhouse office. "I came out, and Buzz said, 'Here, hold my shotgun,' because they were kneeling on each side of these guys to help them up. So they took each one back there, I gave Buzz back his shotgun, and then, that was that.

"I end up with Joe Mazurek on the phone—the sheriff wasn't there yet. When the sheriff showed up, he was mad. And there was a variety of reasons, and one of them was me.

"Anyway, I talked to the attorney general's office, and the governor calls. Paul's on the phone with different law-enforcement agencies, because he wants some support, because we don't know what's up, because he knew that there were a lot of people at Skurdal's that week." Smith called Chuck Maxwell, the neighboring sheriff from Billings, and tried to get him to come up and help. But Maxwell had heard through his dispatcher that the Freemen had taken over the courthouse, and he was afraid to send his men into a trap.

"Chuck was trying to ascertain whether Paul Smith who was on the phone was really Paul Smith the sheriff or was somebody pretending to be," says Bohlman. "Chuck was asking some question about, 'When I was with you at such-and-such a place, did you smoke a cigarette?' And Paul's going, 'I don't know.' " Finally, Smith persuaded Maxwell he was the real thing.

The FBI showed up. "We try to figure out what to do, and what to do with these guys, and if there's anything happening. People are calling their families, and saying, 'Go hide.' I told my wife to take the kids next door. And it's blizzarding."

The FBI agent told Bohlman he'd been in touch with Jim Seykora, the assistant U.S. attorney in Helena, and Seykora wanted him to have bail set on the seven prisoners as soon as possible. Bohlman went to work. He filled out complaints charging the five with criminal intimidation and criminal syndicalism.

"I had the Highway Patrol go over and pick up Judge Noreen Lehfeldt in Lavina and brought her over because our local JP was gone. And I hand-wrote out the charges, a charge against each person. And she did a courtesy arraignment, or at least an initial appearance so they could be transferred to another county. She told them what they were charged with, and that bail was set at $100,000. And they were taken about 1 in the morning to Yellowstone County."

That's the long version of how John Trochmann's window was broken out.

★★★

Before the weekend was out, the Patriot lines were buzzing with the news of the "Roundup Seven" arrests, especially since John Trochmann was among them. Randy Trochmann fired off faxes to everyone on the Militia of Montana's list, providing bulletins on the situation and urging militia members to "stand by." Word got around on the Internet, too.

When John Bohlman arrived for work Monday morning, the phone started ringing off the hook. Many of the callers criticized both Bohlman and Smith for putting the men in jail. There were death threats if any harm came to any of the Freemen or Trochmann. Some were directed at Bohlman, others even at his secretary when she handled the calls. When she went home from work that night, she packed up her child's belongings and sent the girl to stay with relatives in Minnesota.

The producer at a Billings TV station received an anonymous call, too, telling her that the men arrested in Roundup were part of a common-law jury that intended to kidnap a judge and prosecutor and hang them.

Some of the calls to Bohlman's office were warnings, mostly rumors that local people had heard. "Monday and Tuesday, the phones never quit ringing," says Bohlman. "We're hearing everything, including some guy who calls from some marshals service, supposedly, and tells us that 50 armed men left Medford, Oregon, and they're going to prevent an initial appearance at the jail in Yellowstone County, that armed men are coming to Montana and are going to blow up power substations until we release these guys. That the Militia of Florida is sending ex-Navy SEALs to help them escape, to get Trochmann out of jail."

At that point, Bohlman knew things were getting out of hand, but he was unsure what was real and what was fantasy. He had learned not to put anything crazy past the Freemen and their compatriots. So he decided to move quickly on the prisoners' first court hearing.

"We were going to do this initial appearance, a formal one in Billings, on Wednesday," he says. "At three in the afternoon, I had my paperwork done, and that's about when we were told 50 armed men from Medford, Oregon, were coming, so I asked the sheriff and I asked the attorney general's office if they thought it would be a good idea if I could stop the JP and head to Billings, and just do it with no announcement, and we did.

"The press was pissed, and these guys railed to make a little political hay out of it, because we did it without the public being present. The *Gazette* wrote an editorial against me.

"Later, I stood up in a meeting we had with all law enforcement around the state and with the U.S. attorney's office, and I said, 'I did something I'm embarrassed about, but I did it because I had no reliable information. I had no way of sorting out fact from fantasy and bizarre threats. And so I really hope the next time we would have something in place so we would have some reliable intelligence.' " Bohlman says officials there promised him quick action to develop better communications, but he's heard nothing about it since.

Worse still, Bohlman found that he was being hung out to dry on the charges he had filed against the seven men arrested Friday, including Trochmann. The criminal-syndicalism cases were based on the FBI's information that the Freemen had planned to kidnap a judge and prosecutor. But the FBI decided it couldn't come forward with that information in a court of law yet, since their informant apparently still was on the inside.

"The foundation of the charges I filed—there was a lot of circumstantial evidence I put forward, but it also depended on the FBI," says Bohlman. "It was based on the FBI having alerted us, and having an informant who put this thing together. By the next week, when it was obvious they weren't going to give us diddly, I had to dismiss them all except the two concealed-weapons charges."

So Ellena and Jacobi wound up the only two of the "Roundup Seven" who faced any charges, and those two were released on $10,000 bond. Trochmann was defiant the day he was released; he told the press the only reason he had been in Roundup at all was to try to negotiate a "settlement" between the Freemen and local authorities. He didn't explain why he had a handgun in his waistband.

Months later, he was still angry about the incident.

"What the sheriff should have done, in my humble opinion, is to have invited these people to a dinner, or sit down at a table, at least for coffee, and talk," he said. "But it's divide and conquer now these days. These little Hitlerian bastards come out of the police academies and think that they walk on water, and that we're scum of the earth and that we can be kicked around any way that they like. This is the wrong mentality. They are our public servants, after all.

"We pay them to do a job. This contract is the parameters, in other words, their job description. And they violate it every day. They don't even know the oath they swore. They don't know the Constitution. And then they call us Constitutionalists. What the hell's the matter with this picture? Somebody's gone wacko on us."

John Bohlman agrees that, in retrospect, he was caught up in the fear of the moment when it came to handling the five jailhouse visitors. They only had a few guns on them, after all, and made no direct threats, though the gesture of brushing back the jacket to reveal a handgun could easily be construed as one. Several law-enforcement officers, as well as Bohlman and Nick Murnion, speculate that the group likely was going to be part of the common-law jury, but they have no evidence to prove that.

Jacobi and Ellena, though, were a different story.

"The first two guys, I'm certain, were going to do something," he says. The clincher in his mind was the hand-drawn map pointing to Murnion's home. "For crying out loud, you're going to Jordan, Montana, you can find anything you want. You don't need a map unless you're going in the dark and looking for somebody's house.

"The first two guys had so many guns. They just seemed really ready for something."

Out on bail, the Freemen retreated to Skurdal's cabin, where Paul Smith knew he would be hard-pressed to make any arrests. However, he did catch Frank Ellena early in May during an excursion into town, arresting him on felony charges of threatening and impersonating public officials. The warrant was based on documents Ellena sent Smith and a local justice of the peace, warning the sheriff and the JP that they would be hung if they pursued the concealed-weapons charge.

★★★

The rest of the Freemen remained holed up on Johnny's Coal Road, and when a grand jury handed down federal indictments for the entire gang—Schweitzer, Skurdal, Petersen, Stanton and Emmett and Richard Clark—the stakes were raised even higher. Smith knew the case was too big for him and his six-man department to handle.

The FBI began circling the ranch and watching for a chance to make their move, setting up a couple of observers at a neighboring ranch that overlooked Skurdal's place. The agent in charge advised Sheriff Smith to lay low and not to make any arrests—though the sheriff knew he could probably walk in on any number of nights to the Branding Iron and put Rodney in handcuffs if he wanted to. But he followed the feds' advice and let them handle it.

Certainly, if there was any local ardor in Roundup for the Freemen beyond Skurdal's circle, it withered and blew away in a single blast that spring: on April 19, when the Oklahoma City federal building went up in smoke and a couple of Patriot believers were arrested for the crime. Now, no one wanted anything to do with the Freemen, and locals started pressuring Smith to get them out.

"Almost overnight the attitude changed a whole lot against them," Smith recalls. "We were getting a lot of pressure to just go in and arrest them."

In the Freemen's early days, Smith says, there was a lot of sympathy for their cause, mainly because they were taking on the government. "But finally people realized that it was costing them. It was costing the taxpayers of this county a lot of money. And these people out here, they earn their money hard, and when they finally realized what money they were taking away from them in the way of the resources they were draining from the county government, and particularly through the courts, through the county attorney's office, this law-enforcement office, it started getting them pretty upset."

Still, Smith heeded the FBI's counsel and kept his eye out. If any of them showed their faces in town, he decided, he'd put them in jail, but he'd leave any attempt to serve the federal warrants up to the federal agents. And so it dragged on through most of the summer.

One evening in September, Dale Jacobi was out on the county road leading up to the ranch and shooting the breeze with a couple of neighbors who lived in one of the houses nestled atop the ridge near the Freemen's place. He told them the Freemen were going to pack up and move—the next day, in fact.

The neighbors were surprised. How come? they asked. Because we think the FBI is getting too close, Jacobi said.

As it happened, Jacobi was more right than he knew. The two neighbors themselves were FBI agents. They reported the plan to move to their superiors. The intended destination: the Clark ranch near Jordan. The FBI contacted the local sheriffs, Smith and Charlie Phipps and the Petroleum County sheriff, and warned them of the impending move. Don't do anything, they said; just let them go on by unmolested.

"We were made aware that the move was gonna be made, it was confirmed and the bottom-line decision was to sit back and let them go, and not try to stop them or anything like that, that they would be observed wherever they went," Smith says. "I took all my people off the street during that period of time when they traveled. There were no cops on the street in Roundup when they came through."

It was dark, and a caravan formed: three vehicles loaded up with all the Freemen's computers and law books and equipment. FBI agents watched the preparations from a nearby hill and kept watching until the vans and trucks headed down Johnny's Coal Road for the last time and toward the highway that would take them to Jordan.

Sheriff Smith had to swallow hard when the Freemen paraded through Roundup. He and Charlie Phipps were good friends, and when Phipps heard what was about to happen, he called Smith on the phone and pleaded with him not to let the caravan cross into his county. Smith had to turn him down.

"It was hard to let them go mainly because all they were going to do was relocate their problem on a neighbor of mine," Smith says. "A sheriff that I respect a whole lot. As far as I was concerned, it appears he has less resources than I had, with his smaller department—a two-man department. I felt real bad letting the problem get out of here and go to him."

Like two drops of mercury combining to form a big blob, the Freemen's move to Jordan made them more substantial—a larger army, more men, more weapons. And the Clark ranch, besides offering a lot more room, also was an easier place from which to monitor encroaching movement. In Roundup, the ranch had been surrounded by trees, and an artful tactical unit could have approached undetected until just before they knocked the doors down; in Jordan, conversely, the Freemen could see a single vehicle coming for miles.

They gave the ranch and its surroundings a name: Justus Township. It was separate from the "corporate" United States, they said. This was the place, they proclaimed, where American freedom would be reborn.

After a few weeks, the Freemen's operation was up and running again—sending out their "Free[Man] Newsletter" over faxes and the Internet, attracting students from around the country. Nick Murnion, forced to watch and wait just as John Bohlman had, figures he saw 40 vehicles a week going out to the ranch for classes. Over the course of the next six months, he tallied somewhere between 600 and 800 students attending LeRoy's lessons. And the license plates he saw going in and out were from all over the country: Florida, California, Pennsylvania, Arizona, Texas.

Schweitzer by now wasn't merely advocating a money scheme. He started talking about an actual takeover of the local county government. On one video tape lesson, he talked about what lay ahead, perhaps that coming summer:

"Let's say a road grader came by here today, a county road grader. Now we go out there and say, 'Step off, walk to town; we want to take that road grader. See, we got a $50 million lien on the probation state here.

"That's coming, in the future. We haven't done it yet. We will. We're working in another way. First we're going to the banks, taking it from the banks, teach our people, then we will go out and specifically pick up a county pickup, a cop car, you name it. We're gonna take it to the Township. There's gonna be a sale the next day. And we'll put out a warning and say, 'Any public hireling that wants to mess around with this lawful writ of execution, one year solitary confinement, first offense.' "

Before any of this could come about, though, the Freemen wanted to upgrade their communication equipment. One of their regular students told them he knew how to install an effective short-wave radio antenna—a favorite means of broadcasting and receiving information and propaganda among Patriots. In late March, LeRoy Schweitzer and Dan Petersen took a walk outside with the student to check out the site for the new antenna. To their surprise, they found themselves surrounded, thrown to the ground, and handcuffed by federal agents.

Class was over.

Chapter 6 / A Destroying Wind

Thus says Yahweh: Behold, I will raise up against Babylon and against them that dwell in the midst of them that rise up against me, a destroying wind . . .
——Jeremiah 51:1, quoted in notes accompanying a pair of bombs set off April 1, 1996, in Spokane.

I

T WAS APRIL FOOL'S DAY, but this was no joke.

The two men wore masks and obviously wanted money. One clacked a round into the shotgun as they entered the bank, while the other held up a handgun and announced that this was a stickup. But these weren't ordinary bank robbers. They had a message they wanted to send, too.

"Tell the cops to free the people of Justus or we'll be back," one yelled, as they herded the bank's employees into a corner and started grabbing cash out of tellers' drawers. As the robbery progressed, they shouted more slogans:

"Tell your government and its people not to mess with the Freemen!"

"It's free the people in Justus!"

"Justice for the people in Justus!"

Then they shouted at everyone to get out of the bank, and the employees quickly complied. One of the men set a pipe bomb atop the head teller's counter. As the pair ran out of the bank and into a waiting white-and-maroon Chevy van, the bomb went off, blowing a hole in the bank's ceiling and ripping apart six teller's stations.

The Phineas Priesthood had struck. The ghosts of The Order had returned to haunt Spokane.

The assault actually had begun 11 minutes earlier and 30 blocks away, at a suburban satellite office of the Spokane *Spokesman-Review*. A circulation worker at the newspaper plant's rear delivery door saw the van come roaring up. Peering through a window, he saw a man behind the steering wheel with a long white beard, while a second man in a ski mask jumped out of the passenger's seat and came running up to the plant's rear door. He bent down and set something near the door, looked up and saw the man looking at him, then returned to the van, which screeched off.

Curious, the circulation man poked his head out the door to see what they had left behind. His blood froze when he saw it: a pipe bomb, fuse lit and sizzling toward its end.

For a second, he thought about being a hero and pulling the fuse out. But in the same flash, he thought about his two young sons, both just behind him, visiting him after they had finished school that day.

He ran back in and yelled at everyone to take cover and call the police.

"Then, boom!" he later told a reporter. "It was pretty unreal."

Windows in the plant shattered. Upstairs, an editor was knocked out of his seat, and the cover of his phone was blown off. But no one was hurt. Another worker, outside in the parking lot, thought the rear end of his car had blown off. "The next thing I saw was smoke coming out of the back of the building," he said.

Everyone in the plant, about 12 people, came running out to the parking lot, afraid that perhaps another bomb was about to blow up. Then someone called the police.

Brief moments later, the two men burst through the doors of the Spokane Valley branch of U.S. Bank; this time, both wore masks. When they left less than 10 minutes later, the stunned and scared employees were milling in the parking lot, the sound of the bomb and the slogans for the Freemen ringing in their ears.

The robbers also were $50,000 richer. As the FBI agents who quickly swooped onto the scenes of the attacks discovered, this operation had been very well planned. The robbery occurred at the beginning of the month—days on which most banks are flush with cash in order to convert payroll and government checks. And, it had taken place in the unincorporated Spokane Valley, which is patrolled by the more thinly spread county sheriff's deputies.

Just about the time the bombs went off, a woman's voice was broadcast over the deputies' radios claiming that an officer had been shot. The transmission may have been the first diversion.

Then, the bomb went off at the *Spokesman-Review* plant. Officers were responding to the call about that attack when they got word of the bank robbery, too. By the time the police arrived at the bank, the robbers were long gone.

Investigators found the getaway van about two hours later, parked in a lot outside of a Spokane Valley home-and-garden store. Afraid the van had been booby-trapped, they evacuated the store and surroundings, and sent a robot to open the door and peer inside with a video camera. Nothing went off. Inside, there was a jar filled with gasoline, which also had been splashed around the van's interior.

Apparently, that was the robbers' only mistake. The jar had been intended to detonate, setting the van on fire and destroying its contents. Instead, federal agents and the police were able to comb the van for clues. They came up with some important pieces of evidence, including fingerprints and "items of interest."

The most revealing item, though, had been left intentionally by the robbers. At both the newspaper plant and the bank, near where the bombs went off, they had left copies of the same two-page note sealed in plastic.

It was a typed, a two-page rendition of Biblical verse—mostly Jeremiah 51, and a portion quoting Revelation 18—apparently intended to announce the coming fall of "Babylon." Some of the language was peculiar: it referred to "Yahweh" rather than "the Lord," and changed "man" to "Adam-man." The passages attacked the immorality of secular society, and ended with a warning apparently directed at bankers: "Flee you usurer from the face of our land, and all that would not that the Master should reign over them, for the end of Babylon is come. Praise Yahweh!"

Judging from the language, it seemed clear the note's authors were believers in Christian Identity, and it was evident they were sympathizers of the men in Jordan whose standoff was then only a week old. And the symbol at the bottom of the second page clarified the picture even further.

It was a combination of a P and a cross: the logo of the Phineas Priesthood.[1]

★★★

Of all the permutations of the Patriot movement's Christian Identity factions, the Phineas Priesthood is perhaps the most insidious and frightening. A clear threat of violence lies at the heart of the group's agenda, and as the Spokane bombings suggest, its members are prepared to carry it out—on a national scale. The sect's tendrils extend to some of the most notorious crimes of recent history, to Oklahoma City and, possibly, to the burning embers of black churches in the South.

The Phineas Priesthood wants to force the country to adhere to "God's Laws." And its adherents plan to punish people who violate them. Their blueprint:

—"Executing" interracial couples and homosexuals.

—Bombing abortion clinics and "executing" abortion providers.

—Bombing civil-rights centers and "executing" civil-rights leaders and other "race mixers."

—Robbing banks to finance their activities, purchase arms, and help fund the work of other radical Patriots and white supremacists.

Each of these crimes, adherents of the sect believe, is justified because it represents enforcement of God's laws—specifically, Old Testament laws regarding homosexuality, abortion, race mixing, and money lending. These laws—inspired, evidently, by verses from the Old Testament and the Apocrypha—supersede secular society's rules, they believe, and only when Americans adhere to them will God bless the nation again. They see themselves as real Christian heroes.

The work of carrying out their agenda, conducted within small, secretive, leaderless cells that are connected only by belief and occasional communication, already is being conducted in a flurry of seemingly isolated incidents across the country. The Spokane robbery/bombing is only one of the most recent such cases.

FBI officials in Spokane at first were skeptical that the radical right was behind the attacks. Although there was plenty of evidence to make the link—especially the shouted slogans and the note, featuring the Phineas Priesthood symbol, which in the small amount of literature available on the sect appears as a mark to be left behind, a kind of calling card—the investigators believed the note and other clues were a ruse by some sophisticated robbers hoping to throw them off the track. Three weeks later, they finally became convinced of the connection to the far right, and issued a series of composite sketches of the four known suspects.

Besides the man with the gray beard, there was a thin, smaller, bearded man believed to be the second gunman. A portly, dark-haired man believed to have been seen the day before the robbery in the getaway van wore a beard on that day, but was thought to be the same man, minus the beard and dressed in a shirt and tie, who visited the bank moments before it was robbed and then exited, making a signal that looked like a pump-action shotgun being loaded, according to eyewitnesses.

The van, they discovered, had been stolen the day before in Ellensburg, midway across the state to the west, from a used-car lot. That suggested the criminals might have come from western Washington, and investigators intensified their search there. But months later, they were still frustrated. No sign of the self-proclaimed Phineas Priests had emerged.

What was immediately clear was that precious little actually was known about the Priesthood. Its movements and activities are extremely secretive and not prone to being infiltrated by informants. They follow the strategy of "leaderless resistance" promoted at the Estes Park meeting by Louis Beam, the former Ku Klux Klan Grand Dragon—i.e., forming in small groups of six to eight men dedicated to the cause.

The Spokane incident, though, was far from the first violent act in which the Phineas Priesthood has played a known role. Since the mid-1980s, there has been a series of hate crimes believed to be the acts of the Priesthood. In most cases, the sect's role was identified by the criminals themselves or from those within the movement:

Three masked men walked into a gay bookstore in Shelby, North Carolina, late one night in 1984 armed with guns. They rounded up three people in the store, shot them to death at point-blank range, and then set fire to the store, killing a fourth man inside. Two North Carolina white supremacists, Robert "Jack" Jackson and Doug Sheets, were accused in the slayings. An all-white jury acquitted Sheets, after which prosecutors dropped the murder charges against Jackson.

Eventually, Jackson wound up serving time for plotting to bomb the Southern Poverty Law Center, the headquarters of an Alabama civil-rights activist organization that long has been a thorn in the side of the radical right. In 1991, while campaigning for Jackson's release, an Ohio Posse Comitatus group indicated Jackson was a member of the Phineas Priesthood.

A pamphlet produced a few years later by a Florida Christian Identity group promoting the Phineas Priesthood heralded the North Carolina killings as an example of what awaits people who break God's laws. Titled "Whose Law Will You Follow?" it was apparently written by someone with an inside knowledge of the perpetrators' operations:

> "Oh God," was the cry from one of the male prostitutes, as he gazed from silenced barrels to the zeal-filled eyes of the executioners. Maybe he was calling for God to come down from the Heavens and save him and his fellow temple prostitutes, but more likely he knew it was God who had sent these masked men and, out of desperation, he was preparing to meet the maker face to face!
> Everything went as planned and the building was secured with dispatch. Two weeks of surveillance had paid off. While one man kept the sodomites at gunpoint,

another checked the closets, restrooms and "peep show" booths which were frequently used for committing crimes against nature. The other placed flammable and explosive devices in strategic areas. All was ready!

The trial was simple and to the point. One of the masked men asked the accused what they were doing at a known homosexual gathering place after midnight on the Sabbath, but none chose to answer. Then they were asked to produce wedding bands, a picture of a wife, or a female companion. None could comply. Shortly before the fuses were lit on the explosives, Civil Rights were violated!

The pamphlet goes on to warn: "In cities and towns all over America, names and addresses of law violators are being compiled. Six-man teams are forming across the nation. Soon the fog that comes from Heaven will be accompanied by the destroying wind of a righteous God." The account is signed: "The Phineas Priesthood."[2]

—In 1991, when prosecutors re-filed charges against Mississippi businessman Byron de la Beckwith in the 1963 assassination of civil-rights leader Medgar Evers, they introduced evidence that Beckwith was a member of the Phineas Priesthood and carried out the "execution" as part of his "ordained duty." One potential witness, a former Klan member, declined to testify for fear of retribution by the Priesthood. "You don't know when they're going to strike," he told a Mississippi newspaper. "There is nothing quite so dangerous as a religious fanatic who thinks he's doing the Lord's will." A jury nonetheless eventually convicted Beckwith.[3]

Beckwith's nephew, Reed Massengill, wrote a book on the case afterward. "The Phineas Priesthood is really shadowy—I hate to even call it a group, because we know so little about it," he told a National Public Radio interviewer. "Some people believe it doesn't exist. Those who do believe it exists believe it to be a vigilante band of individuals who take God's law, as they perceive it, into their own hands and commit acts of murder and mayhem—against race mixers in particular."[4]

—Two Oklahoma men, Walter Eliyah Thody and Richard Scott McIntosh, were sentenced in January 1992 to more than 30 years each in prison for twice robbing the same Muskogee savings and loan. Thody, just before his sentencing, told a Tulsa newspaper the stolen money went to support the activities of the Phineas Priesthood.

Thody, a onetime tax protester who believes a "Jewish conspiracy" is out to destroy America, had previously spent six years in prison for passing counterfeit currency. He tried to convince a jury that he was justified in doing so, since the Federal Reserve printed phony currency. While in prison, he made connections that enabled him to form his own cell of the Phineas Priesthood. When he got out, he immediately began robbing banks to finance its work.

He and McIntosh were caught, shortly after robbing a Muskogee bank, as they attempted to switch vehicles with police in pursuit. They commandeered another car from a housewife who had just pulled into a nearby parking lot, but police rammed the car after a short chase and arrested the pair.

"After years of trying to defeat the conspiracy by all legal means, I came to the conclusion that this was an all-out war," Thody told the reporter. He claimed he and his colleagues had robbed up to 50 banks around the country, all to "plunder the enemy."

Thody said cells of the Phineas Priesthood exist throughout the nation, peopled by average-seeming men with families and jobs. The Priesthood, he said, is a "silent brotherhood."[5]

—When anti-abortion activist Reverend Paul Hill gunned down a doctor and his escort outside a Pensacola, Florida, clinic in July 1994, the event was given major play in the August issue of *The Jubilee,* a Christian Identity newspaper, with a story headlined "Phineas Priesthood Emerges to Combat Aborticide?" It concluded: "Perhaps Hill, knowledgeable in scripture, relied on the example of Phineas who saved Israel from the wrath of God by punishing those who broke His law!"[6]

In Hill's own writings, including an anti-abortion tract popular at Patriot gatherings, he envisioned an underground enclave of assassins who commit murders as punishment for "disobeying God's laws"—i.e., abortion, homosexuality, and a host of other crimes, including interracial mixing. He cited the Old Testament story of Phineas as inspiration and justification.[7]

Sometimes just the name of the Phineas Priesthood can be used to suggest a threat. Jonathan Mozzochi, then director of Portland's Coalition for Human Dignity, a hate-group monitoring organization, was approached by an anonymous man after one of his speaking appearances in Oregon. "You ever hear of the Phineas Priesthood?" the man asked with a knowing look, then simply turned around and walked off. Mozzochi says the remark was clearly intended to intimidate him.

When a Unitarian church in Idaho Falls, Idaho, scheduled a speech in April 1996 by sociologist James Aho, an Idaho State University professor who has written two books on the Christian Patriots, an anonymous person or group left pamphlets on cars outside the church—namely, the "Whose Law Will You Follow?" flyers that described the murders of the gay men in North Carolina. Since there are no X-rated bookstores in Idaho Falls, the implied threat appeared to be directed at Aho (who had canceled earlier due to an illness) and others who oppose the radical right.

"This wasn't an anti-gay-rights thing," said Kay Snyder, president of the local chapter of Parents and Friends of Lesbians and Gays, who was at the meeting that night. "It was anti-everything."

★★★

As the Kamikazee is to the Japanese/As the Shiite is to Islam/As the Zionist is to the Jew/ So the Phineas Priest is to Christendom.
    —Inscription on the cover of *Vigilantes of Christendom.*

The nominal inspiration for all these deeds is Phineas (or Phinehas in the King James spelling), an Old Testament "man of God" whose story is related in Numbers 25. Ignoring a commandment from Moses, who blames a plague from God on the "whoredom" of his straying flocks, an Israelite man takes up with a woman of another race—a Midianite. Hearing of this, Phineas rises up from the congregation, takes a spear in hand and stalks outside:

And he went after the man of Israel into the tent, and thrust both of them through, the man of Israel, and the woman through her belly. So the plague was stayed from the children of Israel.

The Biblical verse is cited not only by Hill and *The Jubilee* (and is carried on anti-abortion demonstrators' pickets when they stage rallies at clinics—"Nos. 25"[8]), it is the heart of the chief work about the Phineas Priesthood, a 1990 book titled *Vigilantes of Christendom* by a Lynchburg, Virginia, white supremacist named Richard Kelly Hoskins. At 450 pages, the text is the seminal inspiration for the sect—a blueprint for the group's violent agenda in the same manner that William Pierce's *The Turner Diaries* inspired both The Order's Robert Mathews and accused Oklahoma City bomber Timothy McVeigh.

Hoskins, who first elucidated the concept of a Phineas Priesthood in his 1984 book *War Cycles/Peace Cycles* (which called for the death penalty for homosexuals), sells the black-bound *Vigilantes of Christendom* through Christian Patriot groups, and it can be found on the tables at some militia meetings. Richard Flowers, who sells the book through the Christian Patriot Association, based out of Boring, Oregon, is an associate of militia promoter/trainer Colonel James "Bo" Gritz. Gritz appeared with Hoskins at a July 1991 Christian Identity gathering in Reidsville, North Carolina.[9] That same month, Hoskins traveled to the Northwest to speak as the featured guest at the "First Annual Great Northwest Conference" in Spokane, organized by Identity preacher Dave Barley of Sandpoint.[10]

In his book, Hoskins details the concept of a "never-ending priesthood" dating back to Phineas and continuing down through the ages, enforcing racial purity and the rest of "God's laws." Beowulf, Saint George, King Arthur, Robin Hood, Scottish folk hero William Wallace, even Jesse James—these were all Phineas priests, Hoskins claims. So was John Wilkes Booth, Lincoln's assassin, and the originators of the Ku Klux Klan, particularly the former Confederate general Nathan Bedford Forrest.[11]

The common trait of all these men, according to Hoskins: the zealous pursuit of enforcing God's laws. They were opposed to race mixing, the rape of their daughters, sodomy, and most of all, "usury," the lending of money for interest, a sin forbidden by Old Testament law. But "strangers," as Hoskins calls Jews, blacks and other non-whites, have gradually seduced Western civilization with an international banking system based on usury (he calls it "the establishment"), reaching the depths of perdition in post-Civil War industrial American society.

Adolf Hitler, too, is an object of Hoskins' admiration, though he stops short of conferring Priesthood status on the Führer (Roman Catholics like Hitler, Hoskins notes, "often instinctively know the right thing to do but lack the scriptural training to 'prove' their conclusions by scripture and verse"). However, he says Hitler was on the right track, especially since he "had become a danger to the establishment." Still, he writes, "Germany made a fatal error in assuming that because some of the countries she was fighting were composed of Christians, that she was fighting Christian nations. Nothing was further from the truth. She was not fighting Christian nations, she was fighting nations inhabited by Christians who had been conquered." Hoskins decries U.S. involvement in World War II as Americans "fighting their own kind," and proclaims the Holocaust a "manufactured" hoax.[12]

The modern role model he recommends for the Priesthood, however, is straight out of the Northwest: The Order. For 25 pages, he examines the activities of Robert Mathews' gang of 30 or so "Aryan warriors." From the murder of Alan Berg to bank robberies using bombs at other locales as a diversion, Hoskins extols the way The Order organized itself. He especially appreciates the cell structure of the group, and the financial gains Mathews made through his various crimes against "the establishment."

However, Hoskins says Mathews went astray only in falling away from Christianity (which in Hoskins' case means Christian Identity)[13] and adopting Odinism as his religion. Had Mathews followed Scripture, Hoskins says, he would have known not to make the group any larger than six. As it was, The Order's larger numbers made it inevitable that it would be infiltrated and destroyed.

Hoskins appears to have corresponded with Mathews' right-hand man, Bruce Carroll Pierce, the trigger-man in Alan Berg's murder who now is locked away for life in a federal penitentiary. Pierce buttressed Hoskins' case by enumerating Mathews' mistakes:

> 1) Bob recruited some he shouldn't have. He mistook quantity for quality, incorrectly assuming numbers were a key ingredient to success.
>
> 2) Improper organizational structure from the beginning. Only small cells of 5-6 men, autonomous from the other cells, yet uniting when the situation demands it.
>
> 3) The pistol being left should have been just a temporary setback, with proper planning.
>
> 4) Bob was too kind. He should have excluded T. Martinez for refusing to take the voice stress analyzer test, instead of continuing to coax and coddle him. This led to Bob's death, and the capture of the men in the Washington Whidby Isle [*sic*] area.
>
> 5) Law abiding Christian should not work with pagans. Committed Christians who follow God's Law should not work with those who are not equally committed.[14]

Pierce reiterated the last point when Hoskins queried him whether he would ever work with non-Christians again: "The answer is an unequivocal NO! Not only would they have to be Christians, but they would have to identify with God's Law and believe the Law-commands of God, and their life would have to manifest these beliefs."

Hoskins also corresponded with another Order member, Richard Scutari, who read his manuscript for *Vigilantes of Christendom* and told the author "it will help others to understand what motivates someone to live under God's Laws at all costs." Scutari also reflected on what went wrong: "In answer to your question 'would I do it again'—In a heartbeat! But without the stupid mistakes."[15]

Order members appear not to be the only criminals with whom Hoskins communicated in preparing his book. Another was an unnamed man who had killed a mixed-race couple in Tennessee, and who during the course of his trial claimed that interracial marriage contravened God's law. Hoskins writes of the exchange:

> Later, I was told that the man is believed to have shot perhaps a score, and perhaps many scores of interracial couples. Such statements are difficult to confirm because these executions of mixed-race couples are generally believed to be taking place all the time in all parts of the country, but are censored out of the media so as not to discourage the activity.
> When later talking to this man by phone I found him to be a Bible student presently taking Bible courses by mail. He has a wife and a seven year old daughter that he has seen once. He is sorry that he can't see his family, and wishes that they had the money to visit him, but is content that he has done what God put him on earth to do and has no remorse or regrets.
> He is believed by some to be only one of a large number doing their thing across the country.[16]

Vigilantes of Christendom also extols the virtues of other crimes and seems to credit them as acts of the Phineas Priesthood: the widespread practice of lynching blacks in the South in the years prior to 1970; the bombing deaths of a "race-mixing" federal judge in Texas and a black civil-rights lawyer; the assassination (blamed on the Red Brigades) of German banker Alfred Herrhausen in 1989; and of course, the 1984 North Carolina gay bookstore shootings.[17]

Whether there are any real links between the Phineas Priesthood and these events is unproved. Hoskins' claims that historical figures were Phineas Priests seem fantastic and inflated, and as with most Patriot-movement claims, more hyperbolic than factual; certainly, they lack any hard historical evidence. What's more, among the other crimes Hoskins credits to the Priesthood is the mother of all conspiracy theories: the assassination of President John Kennedy in 1963.[18]

Hoskins himself declines to shed any public light on the Phineas Priesthood. An elderly, soft-spoken man with a gentle Dixie drawl who takes his dog for walks each day to get away from his publishing business, the author declines to offer public explanations of his book. He refuses interviews. "I know you're just doing your job," he told me, "but I'm no meat on a chopping block for your job. I have better things to do, and I have fish to fry."

In private, he is far more forthcoming, but equally genteel in his demeanor. Hoskins occasionally embarks on tours around the country, addressing small gatherings of Christian Identity believers in unpublicized locations. In one such meeting, Hoskins was avuncular and guru-like, first delivering a formal speech and then conducting a small, less formal workshop on identifying God's laws and the appropriate enforcement of them. While Hoskins spoke mostly about evildoers who violate God's law, broadly suggesting that killing such violators was acceptable, he avoided naming individuals or the ultimate penalty that might await them. Audience members could be heard chiming in after a "law-breaker" was mentioned: "He should die," and "Kill them."[19]

When confronted in public, though, Hoskins told an *Atlanta Constitution* reporter in 1991, when asked about the Phineas Priesthood: "Oh, go on. There's no such organization in the world." His defense recalled William Pierce's claim that *The Turner Diaries* was a mere work of fiction. "That's just a biblical story, like Noah and the ark," is Pierce's stock answer. "All I did was write a story—a Biblical story."[20]

★★★

Even if it is merely a story—and *Vigilantes of Christendom* is far more than that—it is one being told around many Patriot and white-supremacist campfires. Copies of Hoskins' book appear on tables at militia meetings throughout the country, and through a variety of Patriot and Christian Identity catalogs.

It is a story that clearly has an effect on its readers, because a number of them are taking the course Hoskins prescribes. As the book suggests, there is in fact no public organization called the Phineas Priesthood. It is more of a belief system—an idea, like the militias, to form units of leaderless resistance, in this case the six-man groups of shadow "Saxon warriors" who enforce God's laws.

Hoskins' disclaimer is particularly disingenuous in light of the hundreds of pages of ostensibly factual history he presents in his book. In writing, at least, Hoskins affirms the facticity of the sect. "It makes little difference whether you agree or disagree with the Phineas Priesthood. It is important that you know that it exists, is active, and in the near future may become a central fact in your life," he writes in the first page of the book's foreword.

Hoskins himself is closely connected to at least one known Phineas Priesthood figure: Byron de la Beckwith, the man convicted of assassinating Medgar Evers. Beckwith's wife, Thelma, said she and her husband knew Hoskins and received his newsletter, "The Hoskins Report." She and her husband also attended gatherings in Hayden Lake at the Aryan Nations accompanied by Hoskins, she said.[21]

And at least one self-proclaimed Phineas Priest, Walter Thody, credits Hoskins' book with catalyzing his own ambitions and providing them a focus, though he was already working in that direction. "We didn't have a name for it," he said. "It was just an organization doing the job. That book for all practical purposes describes very actively what we are."[22]

The Aryan Republican Army, a gang of Midwestern bank robbers, also appears to have been inspired by Hoskins. The ARA was comprised of at least four men who committed some 18 stick-ups before two of their leaders were arrested in January 1996 in Ohio (a third, Jim Thompson of Pittsburg, Kansas, is still at large). Law-enforcement officials believe the group was funneling its ill-gotten gains to other white-supremacist groups, much as The Order did. In a recruitment video, one of the leaders, Peter Kevin Langan, declares that the ARA's goal is to "exterminate Hymie," to "repatriate all non-whites to their homes," and to "return the country to the Bible—these laws." The video also recommends *Vigilantes of Christendom*—

as well as *The Turner Diaries*—as blueprints for conducting war against the government. Langan and his cohort, Richard Guthrie, were also said to have attended Aryan World Congress sessions in Hayden Lake.[23] Guthrie, reportedly about to turn state's evidence after pleading guilty to his crimes, hung himself in his jail cell in Cincinnati on July 12.[24]

Beyond even the obvious claims of affiliation with and inspiration from the Phineas Priesthood, a rising national tide of hate-related crime and violence is an ominous sign that the sect's agenda is being carried out. Some crimes committed by radical-right adherents are consistent with the blueprint:

—An Oklahoma militia leader, Willie Ray Lampley, 65, his 49-year-old wife and another man were convicted in April 1996 of conspiracy to manufacture and possess a bomb. Their targets, prosecutors claimed: civil-rights groups, welfare offices, abortion clinics and gay bars. Like Thody's group convicted in 1992, Lampley operated out of Muskogee.

Lampley was armed with 210 pounds of fertilizer, a gallon of nitromethane, and a triggering device made from a toaster. He and his comrades planned to target the Houston offices of the Anti-Defamation League of B'nai B'rith and the Montgomery, Alabama, offices of the Southern Poverty Law Center. His group had an even longer list of future targets. Fortunately, an informant leaked word of the plans to law-enforcement officials, and the FBI arrested them in November 1995 before any bombs went off.

—James Oswald, a 51-year-old Wisconsin man, was convicted in late 1995, along with his 20-year-old son, for an array of charges on 20 felonies ranging from bank robbery to the slaying of a Waukesha police officer. Oswald refused to answer questions about the anti-Semitic tone of the diaries he kept that were used as evidence in the case, referring to "blood oaths" he took as a "Teutonic warrior." Oswald's diaries outlined a plan of robberies, police shootings and hostage-taking similar to The Order's, and were so incendiary that the judge hearing his case slapped a court seal on them, ordering all who had read them, including a Milwaukee *Sentinel-Journal* reporter, to remain silent.

Oswald was reportedly linked to Oklahoma City bombing suspect Timothy McVeigh by photographs showing the two men together at a shooting range. What really piqued FBI agents' interest, though, was the similarity between Oswald's robbery plans and a series of 13 unsolved stickups throughout the Midwest by two men who resembled McVeigh and John Doe No. 2, the as-yet-unapprehended third suspect in the Murrah Building bombing. The robbers' calling card was a pipe bomb left behind at the scene of each crime; Oswald and his son, likewise, used pipe bombs as diversionary tactics in their robberies (a tactic echoed by the Spokane bank robberies).

While Oswald denied he had any connection to the Oklahoma City bombing or any connection to white supremacists, he refused to say whether he'd distributed any money from the robberies to such groups, saying the question was too broad. "There are many groups that are raising in the country that are concerned about fascism going on," he said. "There is an elite that governs the country and uses charges of racism to keep the country down."[25]

Other seemingly random acts of violence around the country appear consistent with the agenda of the Phineas Priesthood, and sometimes their perpetrators even indicate a familiarity with the sect's precepts. One, a 23-year-old skinhead living in Spokane, walked up to an interracial couple, a black man and a white woman, at the city's Greyhound bus station in 1992 and shot them both to death. After his conviction, he pointed to the Bible tale of Phineas as justification for the act when interviewed by *Spokesman-Review* reporter Bill Morlin. "I wasn't mad at them or anything," Chris Alan Lindholm, now in state prison, told him. "I just knew they should die for what they had done. I think he put his arm around her or something."[26]

Bill Morlin has just about seen and heard it all. A veteran cops-and-courts reporter, he has been covering the radical right in the Inland Northwest since 1982. Indeed, his coverage of the Randy Weaver affair well preceded the fatal standoff (and in fact is blamed unfairly in some circles of the Patriot movement for the escalation of the conflict). He has made numerous contacts over the years with white supremacists, partly by covering a succession of Aryan Congress events and by covering the trials of The Order members.

In the fall of 1995, Morlin was invited by a secretive militia group that offered to let him and a photographer tag along on a training session in the northern Idaho woods. Morlin and *Spokesman-Review* photographer Dan McComb were both blindfolded by their contacts and then taken to the training area, a remote spot somewhere deep in the Idaho Panhandle woods. When the blindfolds were removed, Morlin and McComb found themselves surrounded by a group of armed men with ski masks, who proceeded to conduct military-style exercises and plunk at silhouette targets in the shape of Hillary Clinton and federal agents.

They were well-equipped, with expensive scopes on their rifles, electronic sensing devices and high-tech guns. They told Morlin that they were being financed by a millionaire businessman who supported their work, and said they knew of at least three other militia units in the area, including one comprised solely of teenage boys. Getting caught with the gear was one of their biggest fears; they told Morlin that if a cop pulled them over while traveling with it, they might be inclined to open fire.

"We call it 'traveling hot,'" said one of the masked men. "If we get stopped for a routine traffic incident, we've got to decide up front if we're going to tolerate that. If we've got a fully automatic rifle or something like that, you have to be thinking, 'If he stops me, I'm going on the offensive.'"[27]

On the same day in December that Morlin's story was published in the *Spokesman-Review*, Morlin also ran an interview with a Sandpoint-area man who had made some minor waves with his own weapons. Charles Barbee, who operated a Ponderay body shop, and a traveling companion named Robert Berry had been pulled over in May in western Washington, near Longview, with a large arsenal: guns, silencers, night-vision goggles, stolen license plates, a high-tech global listening device, and a wealth of ammunition. The pair refused to identify themselves and stayed in jail for a month before eventually being released after federal officials decided not to file charges. Their story intrigued Morlin, who called up Barbee and asked for an interview; Barbee agreed, saying he'd "already been compromised" by the arrest.

Barbee, it turned out, was a regular at Dave Barley's America's Promise Ministries church in Sandpoint, having become an adherent of Christian Identity while he was still an AT&T employee in Florida. He told Morlin he was building an arsenal to help erect a defense against the New World Order. "We have to be ready to conduct guerrilla warfare. That's how it will be won," he said. "If there's another Ruby Ridge or Waco, we're not going to tolerate it again. If the federal government sends in their armies to put women and children to death again, we will respond and put as many federal agents to death as possible."

Such a scenario did not strike Barbee as bloodthirsty. "Slaying people is not always wrong if it's justified by God's law," he told Morlin.[28] It all sounded like a page out of *Vigilantes of Christendom.*

In the months before the bombing, Morlin says he began spotting further signs that more people on the fringes of the radical right in the Northwest were picking up the Phineas Priesthood concept and adopting it. At an Aryan Nations gathering, he spotted an Aryan security officer wearing a belt buckle inscribed with the insignia of the Priesthood. Morlin and his photographer convinced the man to pose for a portrait, though all Morlin really wanted was the belt buckle. When he wrote a story about the Priesthood in the wake of the April Fool's Day attacks, he had the belt buckle blown up from the negative and illustrated the article with it.

Fearless journalism doesn't come without its drawbacks, however. Morlin has been threatened on occasion. And, he suspected that the December stories had something to do with why the *Spokesman*'s plant was targeted by the bombers.

As events turned out, he was—once again—right on the money.

★★★

The tide of significant hate crimes in America since 1994 alone has been rising steadily: arson attacks on black churches, bombings at abortion clinics and gay nightclubs (as well as the 1996 Olympic Games), murderous attacks on abortion doctors, beatings and murders of homosexuals, racially motivated assaults on blacks, Hispanics and other minorities, as well as against interracial couples—not to mention Freemen-style armed standoffs, right-wing bank robberies of the Phineas Priesthood kind, and horrendous acts of terrorism such as the one befalling Oklahoma City.

There is nothing, however, to seemingly connect all these acts—in large part because many of them go unsolved, but also because if someone is caught, that person at the most only implicates the three or four other participants in his or her own cell. The floodwaters of hate and violence keep rising, and no one seems to understand what is feeding them.

That, in a nutshell, is how leaderless resistance is supposed to work. And, the fact that the tide is indeed rising is a sign of the strategy's success. The Phineas Priesthood is the ultimate distillation of the logic behind leaderless resistance, yet no one can possibly blame all of these crimes on any single group like the Priesthood—although the fact that so many of them match the agenda of the Priesthood is almost certainly more than a mere coincidence. More likely, it stands as testimony to the effectiveness of leaderless resistance in spreading its ideology widely.

Hate crimes in general are monitored somewhat haphazardly on a national scale. Statistics have only been gathered since 1990, so the database needed for a sense of whether or not a problem is growing is limited at best. But the FBI's number-crunching arm, the Uniform Crime Reporting Program, dutifully stocks up figures showing a general rise in hate crimes in the past few years. No one's sure if that doesn't just reflect an increase in the reporting of those crimes, as hate-crimes laws are more vigorously enforced and victims have become more emboldened.

Crimes against homosexuals are tracked by the National Gay and Lesbian Task Force, though most of its studies are based on statistics strictly from urban areas. Gay-bashing in rural areas is less well-documented, but anecdotally at least is considered by many who monitor hate groups to occur at a far higher rate than in cities. Some states—Idaho and Montana included—don't even rate crimes against homosexuals as belonging in a "hate" category. In general, NGLTF researchers have observed a rising trend in attacks on homosexuals or people with AIDS, though the figures sometimes conflict. The FBI noted an actual decline in reported hate crimes aimed at homosexuals in 1996 from the year previous (from 1,019 to 1,016), but a 1996 national report from the National Coalition of Anti-Violence Projects showed a six percent increase in hate crimes against gays and lesbians. NGLTF executive director Kerry Lobel pointed to a number of factors for the discrepancy: Gays and lesbians, she said, "often do not report hate crimes based on their sexual orientation because of their fear of discrimination by police, lack of interest or diligence on the part of the police, and lack of training in many police departments in working with members of the . . . community."[29]

Attacks on abortion clinics and their workers are perhaps less common but often command more attention, especially when they entail horrifying murders like Paul Hill's fatal shotgun attack on Dr. John Britton and his escort, James Barrett. Hill is only one of several anti-abortionists who have used lethal force against clinics and their employees: John Salvi III killed two women in two gun attacks on abortion clinics in Brookline, Massachusetts, in 1994; Michael Griffin, a onetime associate of Hill, fatally shot abortion doctor David Gunn in 1993; and a still-anonymous assailant known as the "Remembrance Day" sniper (so named for the autumnal holiday around which many of the shootings occur), has now wounded a series of abortion providers by sniper fire, beginning with a Vancouver, British Columbia, abortion doctor as he sat in his home in 1994, continuing through two more shootings in Canada, and culminating with the fatal October 1998 shooting of Dr. Bernard Slepian at his home in Amherst, New York.[30] A Grants Pass, Oregon, woman named Shelley Shannon shot and wounded a Wichita, Kansas, abortion doctor in 1993; from prison, her correspondence to other anti-abortionists has indicated a nationwide underground network of like-minded activists inclined to commit violence against abortion workers.[31] One of these groups linked to Shannon, the Army of

God, later claimed credit for setting off pipe bombs at an abortion clinic and a gay nightclub in Atlanta.[32]

There is, however, one kind of hate crime that law-enforcement people are well aware has been increasing: the burning of black churches. Since 1995, more than 40 black churches have been the target of arson attacks, focused in the South but popping up elsewhere in the country, even in the Northwest. The growing list of arson attacks caught the attention of President Clinton, Attorney General Janet Reno, and officials of various civil-rights groups who testified at congressional hearings that they were convinced the arson attacks had an underlying connection. Not all of the attacks have been hate crimes specifically; in one case, a not-all-there teenager who just liked to start fires was charged. But in other cases, Ku Klux Klan members have been arrested, crosses have been burned on lawns, and white-supremacist graffiti has appeared.[33]

Not surprisingly, the Phineas Priesthood's name has not appeared in connection with any of these crimes. But then, given the sect's general secretiveness, it seems unlikely its members will begin claiming credit for any of its crimes, other than through the occasional robbery note. Some researchers believe that Priesthood status is only conferred upon someone after he has "proven his place."[34] If that is indeed the case, such crimes of initiation would be relatively low-level matters—big enough to warrant an item in the newspapers that can be clipped out and produced as proof, but not big enough to draw attention to the group.[35]

Leaderless resistance ensures that the larger movement can never be concretely linked to these individual acts. The important connection, though, can easily be found on a broader scale. The Priesthood itself is a manifestation of the swelling tide of racial and religious hatred that everyone concerned with these crimes—especially investigators looking into the wave of church arsons—has become most alarmed about. The Phineas Priesthood is merely the expected outcome of combining leaderless resistance with the principles of Christian Identity's hate-filled religious beliefs, but it is not necessarily the only permutation. Other groups, like the Aryan Republican Army, take different names, but the pattern is virtually identical.

"There's a problem talking about 'a conspiracy' or 'a national conspiracy,' " says Michael Reynolds, director of the Southern Poverty Law Center's Klanwatch arm. "What we may have, looking at the overall pattern, are several conspiracies."

The arsonists rely on leaderless resistance: "It's a guerrilla strategy. Instead of a top-down structure, you have cells of two to six individuals going out and committing whatever acts they choose, whether it's assassination, robberies, arson or bombings—all aimed at bringing on the race war that white supremacists, whoever they belong to, all want. The idea is to intimidate and provoke."[36]

The most effective part of the strategy is that its very diffuseness lets it continue on. Even when a cell is arrested and broken up for crimes its members have committed, law-enforcement officials are baffled about what steps to take afterward. The crimes themselves become a way of communicating, especially among the believers dedicated to taking action.

"The real twist to leaderless resistance is that there doesn't have to be a coherent network for the action cells," observes Paul deArmond of Public Good Research in Bellingham, Washington. "The use of the term 'phantom cell' is very revealing, since one of the premises of leaderless resistance is the creation of a 'virtual' network of terrorists who communicate with each other by their actions and the reports of those actions through the media. Every report of a church arson carries the message: Here I am, you do likewise. After a certain threshold is reached, the motives of an individual arsonist—copycat, psycho, white supremacist, whatever—are less important than the fact that churches are burning, and away we go with an epidemic of church arsons."

Reynolds hasn't seen the Phineas Priests' hand appearing overtly in the church arsons, but they fit his profile of the suspects. "They're violent, they organize in cells, and black churches would be natural targets for them," he says. "And we know they exist."

Others who monitor the radical right's activities around the nation agree. Some of the crimes linked to the Phineas Priesthood so far may simply be cases of opportunists and wannabes seeking to inflate their own importance by calling themselves Phineas Priests, says Chip Berlet, an analyst with the Cambridge, Massachusetts, think tank, Political Research Associates. But some are no doubt the work of hardcore believers following Hoskins' prescription of "scriptural dictates."

"There are people using the name, and it's not a name you would pick off the Saturday morning TV," says Berlet. "It's a little bit like walking in the woods. You often don't see the fox, but you see what the fox left behind."

And, Berlet says these people could well be the most dangerous elements of the radical right, future Oklahoma City bombers waiting to happen.

"The level of paranoia is still very high, and it tends to spin off these underground groups that, once they go underground, of course, their world view is so internalized that there really is no reaching them with any kind of discourse. They simply go off.

"They're a lit fuse, and the only question is, how long is it?"

★★★

A bomb went off again in Spokane on July 12, 1996, just a little more than a hundred days after the first explosion. It was a duplicate of the first crime: set off a pipe bomb, then rob a bank. In fact, it was even the same bank.

The bomb, however, went off at a new target this time, one nearly as logical as the newspaper plant: the Planned Parenthood clinic out in the Spokane Valley. What didn't make it quite logical is that, unlike other Planned Parenthood facilities, only birth control advice and items were dispensed there—no abortions were performed. And, the clinic was closed at the time.

Still, two men wearing black ski masks and camouflage ponchos drove up in a white Chevy van at about 1:30 in the afternoon, broke out a glass door, tossed in a pipe bomb, ran to the van and sped away. A witness saw a driver with a white beard, as in the first attack. Moments later, the blast rocked the neighborhood. It blew out the clinic's windows and ripped up its interior. A piece of the pipe from the device flew out of the clinic, over a two-story building and four busy lanes of traffic, and finally landed harmlessly in a restaurant parking lot.[37]

Within minutes the bombers were in familiar territory: back at the U.S. Bank on East Sprague Street, a few miles away from the clinic. This time, three men with masks and ponchos walked in with automatic weapons raised and demanded money. One of them carried what appeared to be a propane tank with some wires rigged to its top, perhaps a large bomb, and set it down on the floor while the other two collected cash.

Bank employees knew the drill. They kept their hands up and handed over the money. Even the customers were familiar with the scene. One of them, Dale McElliott, had been at the bank when it was robbed the first time, and when he pulled into the space at the drive-up window and looked inside and saw arms raised in the air, he knew what was happening. He crept out of his car on his hands and knees and crawled to the other drivers waiting in line behind him, asking for a cellular phone to call the police. One of them had a phone. Another witness, meanwhile, dialed 911 from a nearby pay telephone.[38]

It was too late. Shortly, the bandits emerged from the bank, cool as cucumbers, and jumped into the car. One witness saw a second car pull up behind the van and follow it down the arterial, its driver speaking into a cellular phone. The van was found later, abandoned in the parking garage of a mall. Again, it was loaded with a device that appeared to be meant to detonate and destroy the van, but which the Spokane bomb squad, thanks to a robot, soon found was not functioning. When police moved inside the bank, they found the propane device the men had carried in.

The initial target, a women's clinic the bombers apparently believed was committing abortions, was a new twist. There were other differences: Three men instead of two rushed the bank, there was no bomb set off at the bank this time, and, it appeared, there was no note left behind at either location.

Or so it seemed. As they scoured through the rubble of the Planned Parenthood clinic's doorway—where a two-foot crater had been blasted into the concrete, sheetrock was scattered like paper, and beebees from the bomb itself rolled around on the floor—investigators found a matchbook with some words scrawled on it in pen, adapted from Psalms 139: "Surely thou wilt slay the wicked, O God: depart from me therefore, ye bloody men. For they speak against thee wickedly, and thine enemies take thy name in vain. Do not I hate them, O Lord, that hate thee? And am not I grieved with those that rise up against thee?"[39]

Workers and managers at the clinic were shaken, but immediately put up a temporary clinic in a mobile trailer unit and resumed operations. At U.S. Bank, the company offered to reassign workers who felt too traumatized by events. Eventually, some three-quarters of them took the company up on its offer.

"The mood clearly is different than after the first robbery," one bank official said. "People are frightened. It's going to take longer to rebound from this."

The bank put up a $100,000 reward in August for any information leading to arrests. This in turn spurred correspondence from the Phineas gang itself. They sent a letter to U.S. Bank (and a copy of it to Bill Morlin), declaring, "Your gods are paper" and "no match for Yahweh," warning them to withdraw the reward.

"Publicly rescind your bounty and declare your gods powerless or those who worship at your alter [*sic*] will suffer his wrath," it read. U.S. Bank remained firm in offering a $100,000 reward. A few weeks later, it added $15,000 more to the pot for good measure.

About the same time, Planned Parenthood received a note, too. "So sorry to have missed you July 12, and you missed the note about Psalm 139. Will do better next time. (Praise Ye Yah.)" The return address on the envelope was signed, "Phinehas."

"The note was so chilling, my blood ran cold," said Susan Edgar, Planned Parenthood's interim Spokane director.

"I can't even begin to tell the impact it had," said Gail Elkins, the organization's board president. "I wanted to go in the bathroom and throw up."

The trailer unit in the Valley was closed down immediately, and all workers were called in to the main downtown clinic. Terrified officials at Planned Parenthood kept publicly mum about the note.

The tables were about to turn. By September, the reward money had done its work: two informers had contacted the FBI, eager to collect what by then had become $130,000. One of them had been recruited by the Phineas Priests, who told him banks were "temples of Satan" and that they had come close to killing a guard in the April Fool's Day robbery. A second informer contacted them and corroborated the first man's information. The main informer continued to meet with the gang even after he had officially become a snitch.

The suspects: Charles Barbee, the man Bill Morlin had interviewed the previous October, and his traveling buddy, Robert Berry, as well as a third man, Verne Jay Merrell, who fit the description of the white-bearded man. All three had met at Dave Barley's Identity church in Sandpoint. Two undercover agents, following through on the tip, bought a used 1991 Chevy Suburban from Barbee and discovered that it had bulletproof lead in the doors and remotely opened machine-gun trapdoors in the rear panel.[40]

In his meetings with the men, the informer learned they were planning their next bank hit for October 8. This time, federal agents would be ready for them.

When the trio left their homes early that Tuesday, and drove out of Sandpoint in two Chevy Suburbans, they were already being trailed on the highway to Spokane and being observed from a surveillance airplane. This time, though, they drove through Spokane and kept traveling west on Interstate 90. At Ellensburg, they headed south toward Yakima and then on toward Portland, Oregon. A stolen Ford Aerostar joined them in Hood River, about 50 miles east of the large metropolis. They moved a little closer to the city, setting up a center of operations at a Troutdale truck stop.

By then, a procession of nearly 50 FBI agents had joined in the surveillance, including a change of planes. They watched the men drive their three vehicles back and forth into Portland, where they cased a U.S. Bank branch in the southeast part of the city. They pulled in and out of driveways in an attempt to avoid being observed. Finally, ready to make their move, all three men drove in the Aerostar to the bank.

The FBI was one step ahead of them. They hastily phoned the bank's manager while the men were en route and told them the bank was about to be robbed. They instructed the bankers to lock their doors and for all employees to get down on the floor. Everyone hastily complied.

When the three men pulled up and walked up to the bank, masks on and guns raised, they found the doors locked. Confused and surprised, they jumped back in the van and sped away. Back at the truck stop, two jumped out and climbed into the Suburbans, and the three vehicles sped off up the freeway together.[41]

They finally pulled over in the town of Union Gap, just south of Yakima, to gas up at a convenience store. Two got out and went into the store, while the third pulled around to the side to use the restroom. They'd been drinking. A fellow customer, 71-year-old Pearl O'Dell, snapped at the two inside the store for their bad breath when she encountered them at the beverage cooler. "I asked them to please step back. I said their alcohol breath was more than I could stomach," she later told a reporter.

Suddenly, the place was filled with federal agents, guns raised, running up and down the aisles and into the walk-in cooler, and throwing the suspects to the ground. Some of the customers thought it was an armed robbery. Outside, another agent used his gun butt to smash the driver's side window of one of the Suburbans. Soon, all three men were on the ground in handcuffs. FBI jackets started to swarm the gas station, and the startled customers finally breathed a sigh of relief. Obviously, this was a bust.

"Those guys didn't even know what hit them," store owner Diane Butler later said. The FBI told her they had simply been waiting for a relaxed moment when the suspects were out of their cars, and her roadside stop provided that opportunity.[42]

The next day in court in Spokane, the three men were sullen and uncooperative. They refused to rise for U.S. Magistrate Cynthia Imbrogno, refused to sign cards acknowledging they understood their constitutional rights, and declined to accept court-appointed counsel. "Yahweh is my defense," Merrell told the judge. "I will ask for nothing from the state."[43]

Agents also swooped onto the three men's property, finding a large cache of guns, ammunition, bomb-making supplies, and other weapons, as well as computers, ballistic shields of the type used by riot police and a key-making kit. There were detonators in Jay Merrell's house. And, amid a large cache of guns at Robert Berry's house were seven Bibles.[44]

Merrell, it seemed, like Barbee had come to Sandpoint in large part because of Barley's America's Promise church. He had been a featured speaker at church gatherings on a couple of occasions, testifying of his hatred for the government, and had written for the Identity newspaper, *The Jubilee*. A native of Delaware County, Pennsylvania, where he graduated from high school in 1963, he joined the Navy and became an engineer on nuclear submarines for the next 12 years, before he left to go to work as an engineer at the Peach Bottom nuclear plant in Delta, Pennsylvania. He moved around to different jobs in the nuclear industry, working in Ohio, Florida,

Texas and even Brazil, ultimately winding up with the Bechtel Corporation where he helped construct the Palo Verde nuclear plant near Phoenix.

It was while he was living there that Merrell encountered Dave Barley's church, and he eventually became a regular member. Then, Merrell summarily quit his career as a nuclear engineer and moved up to property he had purchased near Snowflake, Arizona. He became involved with the Arizona Patriots, Robert Mathews' old gang of anti-Semites who partook in paramilitary activities at night in the desert. Then, when Barley packed his bags and moved from Phoenix to Sandpoint in 1989, Merrell followed shortly thereafter.[45]

Merrell, Barbee and Berry finally broke down and accepted court-appointed lawyers to represent them. They were ordered held without bail, though Barbee's lawyer noted that they had strong ties to Idaho and they had not resisted arrest, even though they had weapons within reach. "That also indicates their respect for authority," Berry's lawyer suggested.[46] A few weeks later, citing the complexity of the evidence and the fact that it had become a domestic terrorism case, federal prosecutors asked for, and received, a two-month delay in the men's trial.

With the arrests, it was as though a six-month-old cloud had finally dissipated from over Spokane, especially for the Phineas Priests' victims. U.S. Bank provided counselors for their workers, but several people still quit, and others transferred to other branches. Customers at the bank offered words of encouragement.

At the federal courthouse, located downtown, security guards began checking every bag and purse that came through the doors, and workers installed a protective coating on the windows designed to keep the glass from shattering in a bomb blast. At the *Spokesman-Review*'s downtown and Valley plants, security was heightened— video cameras installed, doors and entryways closed off, trees and bushes pulled out.

Bill Morlin found out that his suspicions about the bombing of the newspaper plant were correct. The informers told the FBI that the April 1, 1996, bombing was intended to send Morlin a message, apparently for his stories of December 3. Morlin discovered this chilling information when he finally got a look at federal documents released in December 1996 containing details of the informers' stories.

At Planned Parenthood, officials began raising funds for a $250,000 security upgrade, and by December had $70,000 in pledges. They also made plans to reopen the Valley clinic, this time at a new location. "They're not going to win," said the nurse practitioner who ran the clinic. "If I was afraid, that would mean that they did win."[47]

However, on their first go-around in the court system, the Phineas Priests did enjoy a kind of victory. The March 1997 trial of Barbee, Merrell and Berry took a month, during which time federal prosecutors presented an array of damning evidence—ranging from computer files and documents found in the men's homes to the arsenal the men had with them when they were arrested in Union Gap—that left little doubt the trio were indeed the bombers.[48] Jay Merrell took the stand and, in three hours of rambling testimony, denied that he and the others committed the bombings and the robberies—but that whoever did was justified, because banks were immoral "usurers" whose crime was punishable by death. He also said he couldn't follow the nation's laws. "The system of laws in the United States are at a direct variance with the laws of my Creator," he testified, keeping a Bible at his fingertips. The Bible also justified his fondness for weaponry. "The words of my King tell me that He expects me to be armed in this world," he said.[49]

There was, however, a problem inside the jury chambers. No sooner had both sides rested their cases than a single juror, known as No. 2, announced early in deliberations: "I could hang this jury right now." Other jurors said the man, a wood-products worker from Yakima, had decided perhaps even before the trial began that he was going to vote to acquit. Initially in the jury's discussion he had a few allies, but they too were persuaded by the weight of the evidence that the trio was guilty; and as they changed sides, the holdout became louder and more aggressive—and more cemented in his position. Finally, with the jury voting 11-1 to convict, the judge was forced to declare a mistrial. Everyone went home and prepared for a second trial.[50]

The imbalance in the jury's vote notwithstanding, the Phineas Priests saw the temporary victory as a sign of divine vindication. Charles Barbee granted an interview in May to a Spokane radio newscaster in which he decried the government's decision to seek a new trial as unconstitutional "double jeopardy," charging that prosecutors were "just usurping power by force of arms again." Barbee claimed the trio's religious beliefs were the cause of their persecution: "It's obvious our religious views were on trial. As to how much impact it had with the jury, I don't know; that'd be speculation." And, he predicted vindication yet again: "They didn't have any concrete evidence that any of us were involved in these crimes. What they got are inferences of guilt."[51]

Barbee's confidence couldn't have been helped by the arrest of the fourth, and potentially most lethal, member of the band: Brian Ratigan, a former Army sniper who had also attended Dave Barley's Identity church in Sandpoint and lived in the wooded countryside near the town. Ratigan had been caught in March, while the first trial was in progress. FBI agents, tipped off by the informants to Ratigan's role as the fourth participant in the earlier robberies, had been searching for the wiry 38-year-old, but he had eluded capture by moving around and staying with various friends in the northern Idaho woods. He was finally caught when he tried to leave by train, and agents, following yet another tip, surprised him at the station by posing as baggage handlers—a ruse that let them put him in handcuffs without incident.[52] At his hearing, he was defiant, earning a rebuke from the judge for shouting at the prosecutor: "You've said enough, Pharisee! Sit down!"[53]

Maledictions notwithstanding, the tide had turned against the Phineas Priests. Barbee, Merrell and Berry went on trial again in July, with the prosecution taking a route identical to that of the previous trial—but this time, it was more careful during the jury-selection process to screen for potential believers in Patriot ideology. So, it was perhaps not surprising that this time around, the jury voted unanimously to convict each of the trio with eight counts of robbery and bomb-making. "After awhile, it was clear that the government's evidence was overwhelming," said one juror. "There were just too many coincidences." All three men were sentenced to life terms.[54]

It went no better for Brian Ratigan, whose trial came in September and brought the same result—guilty of five counts of bombing and robbery, again accompanied by a mandatory life sentence. When he was sentenced in December, though, Ratigan made a last stand of sorts in the courtroom. Calling the judge a representative of the "prince of darkness," he claimed that bank robbery is not a crime because banks participate in "usury"—a violation of God's laws. "For our Creator, there's no such thing as a bank, so there's no such thing as a bank robbery," he said.

Before he was led away, he sounded a warning: "I don't recognize your system. Your Babylon is going to fall. It doesn't need a militia. It doesn't need Phineas priests. It's going to fall by its own evilness.

"People of Spokane, you have been warned. You have been sent four witnesses. Babylon is about to fall. The Messiah, Yashua, is on his way, so repent."[55]

Chapter 7 / Almost Heaven

THE MEDIA HORDE was ready and waiting for Colonel James "Bo" Gritz when he flew into Jordan. Which, as far as Gritz seemed to be concerned, was just fine. For that matter, possibly the most dangerous place to be that day in Montana was between Bo Gritz and a television camera. Scarcely had his light plane touched down at the Jordan airstrip before Gritz climbed out and walked out to meet the waiting newsmen. Right behind him was the man responsible for Gritz's chief claim to fame: Randy Weaver, the martyred widower of Ruby Ridge.

It had been nearly a month since the FBI's standoff with the Freemen had begun, and the situation seemingly was going nowhere, although negotiators said they were making progress. Gritz and Weaver, following through on a promise Gritz made earlier that week on his short-wave radio program, had arrived to try to broker an end to the confrontation.

It was a nasty, windblown Thursday, with gusts hitting 60 miles an hour, and Gritz's entourage seemed intent on getting out of the wind and on with the mission. Gritz held the cameras at bay, chatting briefly with the newsmen, while Weaver and Gritz's two right-hand men, Jack McLamb and Jerry Gillespie, got out of the light plane and into a large pickup. Then, saying he'd make a statement later, the onetime Green Beret colonel climbed into the truck and headed off to meet with the Freemen—or at least try to.

Gritz was far from the first person from the Patriot movement to show up on the scene. Only two days after the standoff started, a Kansas militia activist named Stewart Waterhouse and a cohort, Barry Nelson, took advantage of the loose perimeter around the compound and sneaked onto the Clark ranch, bolstering the Freemen's numbers in the process. The FBI clamped down on activity in the area and set up a checkpoint at the four-corner intersection near the Brusett post office. The media were confined to a hill that overlooked the Clark ranch from a considerable distance.

Over the next few weeks, Jordan saw a steady trickle of militia folks come in and out of town. A small group of supporters from Medford, Oregon, took the long drive out with food supplies and a few guns, but they were stopped at the perimeter by the FBI, their guns confiscated, and turned back. Kamala Webb, a Bozeman woman who headed up a Militia of Montana group in Gallatin County, drove up with another small group, including Dan Petersen's stepson, Keven Entzel. They too had food supplies for the Freemen; they too were turned back. And then there was the occasional solitary supporter, like Bill Goehler of Marysville, California, who drove out on his Honda 750 motorcycle and demonstrated in front of the FBI checkpoint by leaning against his bike and holding an American flag upside down.

The most colorful of all the arrivals so far had been "Stormin' " Norman Olson, the onetime commander of the Michigan Militia, who visited Jordan during the third week of the standoff with his longtime sidekick, Ray Southwell. He was there to support the Freemen, he said, and to make sure the FBI didn't try to pull any fast ones.

"I don't think they should surrender," Olson said. "I think they are doing the right thing, and they ought to stay where they are."

Tension was building around the compound at that point. It was April 16, 1996, only three days away from the Oklahoma City anniversary, and many townsfolk in Jordan were growing fearful that the Patriots would descend on their town and violence would erupt. Olson only made matters worse, saying he was there to organize a "national response team" that would "meet Janet Reno and the FBI, wherever they attack in the future. Waco, Ruby Ridge, now Montana. Where is it going to end?"

Olson tried several times to enter the compound, but was rebuffed by the FBI, even when he carried a stuffed animal and a Bible and claimed he wanted to go in to "minister" to the group. Finally, on April 19, Olson gave up in disgust. As he departed, he issued a warning that the FBI would face "swift and severe retribution" if any of the Freemen were harmed. Agents around the country, he said, would be selectively assassinated for each Freeman death. Only agents who were minorities, women and over age 40 would be exempt.

"I think we're going to go back and prepare for war," he proclaimed in his stentorian way.

An FBI agent watching Olson spout smirked; it's well known among Patriots, and those who observe their activities, that Olson has little following nowadays, his credibility (and his Michigan Militia) blown apart by his wild-eyed remarks about Japanese spies' involvement in the Oklahoma City bombing. Olson's threat to gather an army didn't carry much weight. Olson caught the agent's expression, and pointed his finger at the man, his countenance filled with rage. "You come up to northern Michigan, mister, and I'll see you in my crosshairs!" he shouted.

Four days later, Bo Gritz, always more affable and media-savvy, flew into the Jordan airstrip on his own mission: to negotiate an end to the standoff, much as he did on Ruby Ridge. After his initial bow to reporters, he and his entourage headed up the gravel road to Brusett to see if they could talk their way onto the Clark ranch.

They couldn't. At the checkpoint, a grim-faced Montana Highway Patrolman told Gritz he'd have to get clearance from the FBI. A little nonplussed, Gritz turned to the waiting news cameras and did what comes most naturally to him—he held a press conference.

"We are going to try to do for the Freemen and FBI and the American people what we did at Ruby Ridge," he told the gathered reporters. "We don't want any more Wacos and I don't want to wait for Janet Reno to have a bad hair day to have one."

While Gritz held forth, Randy Weaver and Jerry Gillespie waited inside the pickup. Jack McLamb, on the other hand, stood outside the cluster of newspeople encircling Gritz, looking over the various lawmen who stood nearby. McLamb's specialty in the Patriot movement is recruiting policemen to the belief system. His staredown with the officers at the checkpoint had the look of someone sizing up potential believers.

Gritz spent about 20 minutes with the reporters. He told them he was unsure what standing, if any, he had with the people inside the compound. "I don't think I have any rapport at all, but I got probably the only plan.

"If the Freemen throw me out, then it gives a message to America: they don't care. If the FBI stopped me, isn't it kind of stupid? If we do bring them out, then the FBI can go home where they belong."

When he was done, Gritz got into the pickup with McLamb and headed back up the gravel road to the FBI headquarters, at the Garfield County Fairgrounds just outside of Jordan. Gritz walked in alone to talk things over with officials. His three friends waited outside in the pickup, munching on apples and listening to Garth Brooks tapes. About an hour later, Gritz emerged, got into the pickup without a word, and drove back to the Jordan airstrip, where he had a motor home parked next to his Cessna. Evidently the FBI had said no, at least for the day.

Gritz and his entourage stayed inside the vehicle the rest of the day, evidently talking strategy. Gritz emerged later and told reporters the FBI had given him several suggestions, including writing a letter to the leaders inside the ranch to see if they wanted his help. He said he'd stay in town a few days to pursue those options.

A big gathering was planned for that next day at Fairview Hall, the community meeting place a little outside of Jordan. It was the kickoff for a ballot initiative drive by a collection of local grass-roots organizations calling itself the Montana Anti-Extremist Coalition. Their petition would call for laws allowing people threatened with violence by extremists to sue their tormentors for cash damages, and would outlaw the Patriots' bogus liens and make them easier to remove legally.

The head of the coalition, a onetime labor organizer from Butte named Evan Barrett, was joined at the front of the room by prosecutors John Bohlman and Nick Murnion (both victims of liens and threats) and the various local activists who formed the group. Two were from the Montana Association of Churches. Then there was Tammy Schnitzer.

Schnitzer is a slender, sharp Billings woman who once was married to LeRoy Schweitzer's brother-in-law. When she remarried, it was to a Jewish man; Schnitzer herself converted to Judaism. One December, her son put a paper menorah in his bedroom window for Hanukkah. A few nights later, someone threw a brick through the window and left some anti-Semitic graffiti. The incident received wide play in the Billings media, and out of the resulting outrage, local church officials organized by MAC's Margie McDonald put together an inspired response: Christian families, too, would hang paper menorahs in the windows of their homes. Hundreds of them appeared on display in Billings homes. Since then, Schnitzer has played a prominent role in monitoring the radical right in eastern Montana. She stood next to Barrett through most of the presentation, in front of a sign that read: "Not in our town—Not in our Montana—Not in our America!"

"When one Montanan is threatened by extremists, then all Montanans are threatened," said Barrett. "Mainstream Montana cannot remain silent in the face of extremist activity. We have to stand together and let the extremists and the hate groups know that their tactics are not welcome in our state."

The press was there, having been provided something interesting to do that day other than sit outside the Freemen's compound watching and waiting. Perhaps it was not a great surprise when Bo Gritz and his entourage showed up, too.

Gritz, Randy Weaver and Jack McLamb, with a flag-draped Bill Goehler (the visiting motorcyclist from California) in tow, strolled in a little after the meeting started and stood in the back of the room, listening. They said nothing, but wandered outside after the conference was over and lingered there. Gritz struck up a conversation with Evan Barrett when he came out into the sunshine.

The gruff militia leader wondered if a menorah was going to be the campaign's symbol this time around, too. Barrett said religious concerns weren't part of the initiative. The intent was simply to provide tools to counter the real threats.

"Everything I heard there sounded good to me," said Gritz. "I just wanted to ask you personally, for God's sake, don't limit the First Amendment for where people have a right to stand up to the face of the politicians to give them hell."

Tammy Schnitzer, standing nearby, knows something about standing up in politicians' faces. She was in Gritz's right away.

"Sir, that's not the issue here at all," she said, loudly, firmly. Gritz ignored her and kept talking with Barrett.

The rest of Gritz's group mingled out in the windblown parking lot. Randy Weaver talked with a few reporters. Weaver is generally subdued and quiet-spoken in public, and when he told reporters what he thought he could bring to the negotiations, it reinforced the impression that the Ruby Ridge incident left him with more deep, personal grief than he ever expected in the days when he was making a stand.

"You force them to come in on you like they did with my family and you live through it," Weaver said. "It's going to be worse than dying because the heartache is with you, you have it every day. And that's about all I can say."

Weaver said the deaths of his wife and son still haunt him. "When it comes on TV, right away they're saying, well, this is like having Ruby Ridge and all that. Well, I don't want it to be another Ruby Ridge."

Gritz, meanwhile, told reporters the FBI had delivered their letters to the Freemen. They were waiting to get a response.

The next day, Saturday, they received one: Gritz and McLamb could go in. But not Weaver, whose presence was deemed too potentially volatile.

That morning, Gritz's group traveled to the FBI checkpoint. Weaver and Gillespie got out and waited there; the FBI didn't want Weaver in there either. Gritz and McLamb drove on together up to the Justus Township "No Trespassing" sign and stopped, got out, walking further up the road. A van came down from the

Freemen's watchpost and picked them up and took them back to the main ranchhouse. They remained there for seven hours.

As the day wore on, Weaver mingled with a few reporters at the checkpoint. He saw the duration of the talks as a good sign: "I figure the longer he stays in there, the better the chances are."

When Gritz and McLamb finally returned, Gritz conferred with FBI officials, then turned to the waiting cameras again, and with his usual self-assurance, told the nation that the negotiations would work.

"I think this thing is bridgeable," he said.

Until Gritz's visit, little was known about what life was like inside the Clark ranch. Indeed, no one in the press even knew how many people were in there; most estimates had been between 15 and 18 people. Gritz and McLamb, though, kept count—in keeping with Gritz's reconnaissance days—and had an accurate figure: 21.

The number, Gritz said, included three youngsters: the two young children of Gloria Ward, a follower who had come to the ranch fleeing child-custody charges in Utah, and the teenage daughter of Dana Dudley, a hard-core believer from Colorado. Her husband, Russell Landers, had been the featured speaker on a rambling videotaped presentation the Freemen passed to reporters earlier that month.

Gritz said he thought the Freemen were rationing food, because one of the girls expressed a hankering for a taste of urban living. "Jiminy, if I could just have a Taco Bell," Gritz said she told him.

The Freemen, he told the reporters, were getting a bum rap in the press about their beliefs. "They have no white supremacy, separatist tendencies that I saw. None at all . . . They brought up the fact and said, where is the media getting this idea we have any prejudice or bias?" Gritz either had not read enough of Skurdal's edicts to know better, or was using tactics of disingenuity straight out of John Trochmann's book.

The talks lingered for four more days. The sessions usually lasted for seven hours. And each day, you could sense Gritz's frustration growing. Negotiations, he reported, were comprised of "verbal judo" all day, and he called the Freemen's theories "legal mumbo jumbo." But they had made an offer to surrender.

"Every man, woman and child agreed they will walk out, right now, if the United States government can prove that the documents which I'm going to give you are not the law," Gritz said. "To me, that sounds like quite a challenge." He then proceeded to hand out a 26-page Freemen document that cited the usual array of legal cases and common-law rulings that questioned the FBI's legal right to exist. For most of his tenure as a negotiator, Gritz continued to send out such maddeningly mixed signals—on the one hand seeming to sympathize and concur with Freemen doctrine and legal theory, and on the other hand dismissing it as nonsense. Mostly, he gave the impression of playing both sides against the other, but without any kind of resolution in view.

During the negotiations, Randy Weaver hung out at the hill where the media were encamped, then spent the afternoons and evenings in Jordan. Joe Herbold kicked him out of the Hell Creek Bar after Weaver started attracting a crowd and spinning out his theories on government oppression. Herbold, whose family had weathered threats and liens from the Freemen, confronted the Ruby Ridge martyr and told him to leave. "Take your philosophy and shove it out that door," he said. Weaver, pointing to a tableful of bottles, complained that eight people had just bought him beers, and Herbold replied that the buyers could drink the beers themselves. Weaver left and didn't return.

On the fourth day, Gritz gave up, evidently in disgust. After only three hours, he and Jack McLamb left the Clark ranch no closer to a surrender agreement than when they first entered. The Freemen, he said, believed Yahweh had erected an "invisible barrier" around the compound that made them invulnerable. If the feds wanted to negotiate, they said, perhaps onetime U.S. Supreme Court nominee Robert Bork could come out to Jordan and take up residence while talks progressed. Failing that, they'd accept Chief Justice William Rehnquist. Or better yet, Colorado State Senator Charles Duke, who they said understood their beliefs.

Gritz and his entourage, wearing baffled scowls, packed up and flew out of town that afternoon. The standoff had reached 38 days with no end in sight.[1]

Two weeks later, Gritz described the negotiations in his newsletter. He said that at one point, the success of the talks almost hinged on the Freemen's addiction to cigarettes. "I wish they would have expressed the tone of sincerity in coming out that was used in requesting more tobacco," he wrote.

Gritz said he built a rapport with Ralph Clark's son Edwin, a Vietnam vet like himself, but it soon became evident that the hard-core ideologues among the Freemen—Rodney Skurdal, Dale Jacobi and Colorado fugitives Russell Landers and Dana Dudley—knew their fates depended on keeping their followers on the ranch. Gritz began to feel that the others, especially the three children, were being used as shields.

"I beseeched Edwin to release the non-Freemen," Gritz said. "His pained reply made it clear that they knew the value of placing children between themselves and the FBI." Clark told him, "But Bo, if the others left, what would happen to the Freemen?"

Gritz observed that the Freemen crucially believed their cause would be backed by a nationwide uprising of fellow Patriots. "Skurdal announced in a loud voice that their forceful capture would ignite a multimillion-man militia revolution that would sweep ZOG out of America," he said.

Gritz himself urged Patriots not to support the Freemen. His term for them: "Scam artists."[2]

★★★

The failure in Jordan must have been doubly aggravating for Gritz, because he is so accustomed to success. For all of his life—for nearly every endeavor he has undertaken—James Gritz has been a success.

He is, for that matter, the embodiment of a host of American heroic archetypes: a small-town boy who grew up to be a decorated war hero and run for president (though that was not one of his successes). His steely gaze, gravelly baritone and straightforward manner make him a man's man, the classic picture of masculinity.

Gritz, too, is the source of another archetype: Rambo, the mercenary soldier who combats overwhelming odds to rescue his former comrades from a Vietnamese POW camp. Not only did Gritz's exploits inspire Sylvester Stallone's Rambo movies, but the colonel himself was the model for the cigar-chomping leader of television's "The A Team" played by George Peppard.

Gritz the man is not terribly distant from the myth. He was in fact the most decorated Green Beret commander in Vietnam, and continued to serve the country well afterward as a top-flight training instructor for the Army's Special Forces. Then, in the early 1980s, he launched what was at the time his chief claim to fame: the attempted rescue of American POWs reputed to be still held in Vietnamese prison camps deep in the jungle. Assembling a group of mercenaries and financed by H. Ross Perot and families of missing soldiers, Gritz spent three years traipsing in and out of the jungles of Southeast Asia trying to find the rumored camps. He never did. But the adventure still caught the public's fancy, and the inevitable Hollywood versions provided the happy endings real life could not (both Rambo and the A Team not only found the camps and rescued their buddies, but they blasted the crap out of the bad guys, too).

Gritz did, however, manage to discover something he thought was even bigger: evidence of the U.S. government's complicity in drug dealing in Southeast Asia. The conspiracy, he decided, wove all the way to the highest levels of power in Washington, D.C., and these same conspirators were responsible for covering the trail of the missing POWs. He returned to the States and tried making noise to expose the alleged cover-up, but found little interest among a public already gorged on CIA corruption tales.[3]

There was, however, an audience receptive to Gritz's message, people already inclined to believe in massive government conspiracies: the radical right. Gritz's claims began receiving play in the far-right newspaper *The Spotlight,* and the retired Green Beret found crowds turning out to hear him speak on the Christian Patriot circuit. Soon he was friends with people like Identity minister Pete Peters, speaking regularly at Peters' Family Bible Camp in LaPorte, Colorado. Peters reciprocated by helping finance the publication of Gritz's tell-all autobiography, *Called To Serve.*

Gritz spoke in glowing terms of Identity beliefs and Pete Peters at the Bible camps. "Do you think you're lucky to be an Identity Christian today?" he said in one talk. "I believe that the Identity Christian movement will continue to grow in this nation until it is able to stand self-sufficient in spite of the government . . . I am telling you that He has given us all that we need. He's given us the likes of Pete Peters, he's given us the likes of the Identity Christian movement."[4]

Gritz also made friends with Willis Carto, the publisher of *The Spotlight,* who was the leader of the Populist Party of America, and a renowned anti-Semite. When the Populists' 1988 national convention was held, Bo Gritz was there, and before he knew it, he was on the party's ticket as the vice-presidential candidate and running mate to former Ku Klux Klansman David Duke.

Gritz says now that his nomination was a mistake. "The only reason I agreed to be on the ballot was that Jim Traficant, a conservative and still-sitting congressional representative from Cincinnati, was going to be that choice. They offered up Traficant, and some nut from Texas got up and rejected it.

"Everybody got on the bandwagon for David Duke. When Duke was put on the ballot as president, I didn't really know Duke at that time, I was a soldier. But it took me about a week to find out who he was, and I rejected it. I would not vote, I cannot support anybody who has got so much cowardice as to hide behind a sheet for any reason."[5]

Still, Gritz's political ambitions were whetted, and in 1992 he gladly accepted the Populists' nomination for the presidency. He launched a national campaign of sorts, but found his efforts limited to the standard fate of fringe candidates: hoping to pull off a few key votes in pockets of the country where their voices could be heard. One of those for Gritz, it turned out, was in Idaho. His pollsters revealed as much as 10 percent support in a few counties in southeastern Idaho, which might be enough to gain a foothold.

In the process of broadening his appeal, Gritz wound up parting ways with Peters. Their friendship erupted into an internecine feud in the spring of 1992 when Gritz was interviewed by a writer for the Identity newspaper *The Jubilee*. When questioned about whether he favored the death penalty for homosexuals, Gritz answered: "I'm personally not for it. The reason I am not for it is while I personally abhor these perversions, I'm not certain we are to judge on those things. I think God will judge these individuals."[6] Peters answered Gritz in the form of a full-fledged pamphlet titled *Intolerance of, Discrimination Against and the Death Penalty for Homosexuals is Prescribed in the Bible*, dedicated to his "special Colonel friend" and concluding: "If we as a society refuse to repent and acquire righteous government to punish this crime with the death penalty, then even more will die." Gritz severed his ties with Peters over the dispute, and referred to him afterward as "a true bigot" who "continues to debase me for defending a homosexual's right to life during the campaign."[7]

Then, in August, the standoff on Ruby Ridge presented him with exactly the kind of high-profile opportunity he needed to make a splash. Figuring he might have some credibility with Randy Weaver, by virtue of his far-right credentials and their shared Green Beret backgrounds, he headed north to Naples, Idaho. His entourage in vehicles festooned with "Bo for President" signs joined the crowd of Weaver supporters gathered at the police roadblock.

At first, Gritz had to resort to stunts like demanding to see the FBI agent in charge and then, when refused, threatened him with a "citizen's arrest." But because Weaver indicated he'd be willing to talk to Gritz, two days later the colonel, with Jack McLamb at his side, was at the Weavers' cabin, gradually talking the surviving family members down off the rugged mountainside.

This was Gritz's shining moment. When Randy Weaver surrendered after days of talks, Gritz and McLamb walked down to meet the crowd gathered outside. The colonel was in his element, and he spoke briefly to Weaver's supporters and the press, telling them Weaver and the children would be fine.

Then he relayed a message from Weaver to the skinheads at the back of the crowd. "By the way, he told me to give you guys a salute," he said as he put up his arm in a Naziesque gesture: "He said you knew what that is." The skinheads responded with their own salutes and thumbs-up gestures.

The moment was briefly noted in the press, but was washed aside in the news that Weaver had surrendered. And Gritz was the hero who had talked him down. Still, the glory was fleeting: Gritz's candidacy dropped out of sight again, mostly because he was the nominee of the party of David Duke. He collected a nice chunk of votes that November in southeastern Idaho's Madison County, but he only garnered 46 in Randy Weaver's home county in the Idaho Panhandle.

It was from this campaign experience, though, that Gritz found the inspiration for his next venture: training people to prepare for the coming "New World Order."

"When I finished the presidential campaign," Gritz recalls, "I traveled to 49 states, and people throughout this population had continually said, 'Bo, we don't think you can beat the Republicrats, what do we do? We gotta do more than just talk, we gotta do more than just vote.'

"Well, I catch just one rabbit at a time. So I thought, in my own mind, what I'm gonna do is, I'm gonna write a book called, 'S.' 'S' is the designator for Special Forces once you're qualified. And in that book I would give any who read it all of the knowledge that they would need to become like Special Forces where, basically, you could live anywhere at any time under any conditions, and feel safe. So that was my idea.

"Then, as I finished the campaign, people said, 'Bo, what are we going to do? What do we do now?' And there was an immediate requirement—it would have taken me a year to punch this book out. So I pulled my team in, Gary Goldman, and Scott Weekly, a Navy SEAL who's a real-life Macgyver, and some other people, and I said, in the interim, what I'll do is I'll start training them to be self-reliant, to be secure."

He called the training SPIKE: Specially Prepared Individuals for Key Events. The training sessions, first announced in 1993, filled quickly. The colonel's entourage traveled with him around the country, helping him put on the sessions in a variety of cities from Portland to Miami.

Gritz says graduates will have the skills to survive any kind of situation. "My promise is, if you stick with us, you're going to be as prepared and you can be as equipped and as organized as Delta Force. And it's a promise I'm going to keep, because I'm going to keep the Delta Force curriculum, which I helped make up, and we are completing every requirement.

"Now, there is a difference. For example, in Phase 7, which is what we're doing now, there are in each phase four parts of education that go on. And one of these four parts in Phase 7 is stick-fighting. Rather than teaching people how to take the esophagus out of an opponent, the way that Special Forces and Delta is taught, we are teaching people how to repair esophaguses if they are accidentally or inadvertently extracted, and we're teaching people rather than using violent attack, assault methods, we're teaching them defense.

"For example, every one of the SPIKE phases has had a self-defense side. We've taught basic self-defense—how to use pepper gas, how to use coup batons, how to use things for self-defense against opponents. In Phase 2, we taught how to defend yourself against edged weapons—not by using edged weapons, but by using things like a cane—or your unarmed combat. In Phase 3, we taught how to defend yourself against armed assailants that have guns when you don't.

"Now, in Phase 7, we're teaching people how to use a cane, or a crutch, a broom, a mop, or a stick in self-defense; it's called stick-fighting. So our SPIKE training consists usually of a self-defense class; it consists of an emergency medicine class; we've taught people, for example, in Phase 4, how to give birth in the home without the help of the AMA and Caesaerianism and all of the drugs.

"It's working. People all over the country now are having kids in their home. They report to me all the time. It's a little bit scary, but so far so good. Dads are with their moms the way they're supposed to be at the time of Mom's greatest need. Plus I think it provides a bonding you're not gonna get anyplace else, and the feeling of shared responsibility there."

Gritz touts other details of the SPIKE training, but he never mentions a skill taught at Phase Three: "Defense Against Restrictive Entry." In simpler language, this is known as burglary. Gritz teaches enrollees how to pick locks and enter secure buildings. You can buy a set of lockpicks through his catalog.

The training sessions neatly dovetailed into the concept Gritz had touted in the 1992 presidential campaign, which had formed the inspiration for Pete Peters' Estes Park gathering that same year (which Gritz, because of his feud with Peters, had refused to attend): forming citizen militias to prepare a defense against the New World Order. Gritz himself declined to form any militia units: "I support the unorganized militia. But I see a potential for great failings, because, being unorganized, they don't have the availability of professionals to help them in direction. Training—what should they be doing? Unless all of them want to run out there and act like Rambo, and again, it's the amateurs trying to play like professionals."

Gritz believes the sessions move beyond mere survivalism: "It's not survival, it's preparedness. There's a difference, I believe, while the word is often interchanged by people who don't fully appreciate the meanings. Preparedness means an ark in a time of Noah, and that's what I think the covenant communities and SPIKE training provide. Survival means try to take the high ground and hang in there until the water is up to your nose, and then grab onto something floating by—that's survival.

"Preparedness means that you have already taken the measures to meet the adversities and to provide for yourself, your family, your neighborhood, your church group. I'm training not individuals, I'm training trainers. It's like lighting one candle. What we teach in SPIKE, we ask people, I exhort them, we make videos available to them, so that they can take that training, and go out and light as many other fires as they can. So I can touch about 3,000 people across the United States."

Seeking his own vision of an ark, Gritz decided in 1994 to move to the next step: establishing a community where like-minded Christian Patriots could gather to escape the rising floodwaters. It would have to be somewhere away from the cities, preferably atop a hill that could be easily defended.

He found it in Idaho, in a place he called Almost Heaven.

★★★

There is nothing particularly heavenly about the road up to Bo Gritz's covenant community, except perhaps the views you get as you snake your way along the steep hillside above the Clearwater River valley. Certainly, if you make a mistake on these roads you'll meet your maker in short order. You can see for miles up and down the somewhat narrow, v-shaped river canyon, and at places on the road, you can easily imagine yourself in an airplane, because the blue roiling river and the little town along it, Kamiah, appear so far below that everything seems antlike. The hillside itself drops steeply away to near-invisibility.

This, of course, is exactly what Bo Gritz has in mind. He and Jack McLamb have bought three large parcels of land, about 280 acres in all, atop this mountain-like ridge above the Clearwater, in a position that's inaccessible except by this single road. As Gritz described it for an ABC reporter: "We have an excellent position right here. There's only one road up here, and I get a chance to watch you coming up that road most of the way."

There may be only one road, but it is a loop with two entrances; the road takes off uphill from the river bottom near Kamiah and then returns to the river farther downstream. The Kamiah entrance is the main road, the one on which Gritz can watch everything coming up. The downstream one is a harrowing back route that is only a single car's width in many spots and is a long, torturous grind. If two cars approach in opposite directions, one of them usually has to back up until the driver can find a wide enough spot in the road for both vehicles to pass.

Gritz likes to think strategically, and this is a perfect setup for him. Almost Heaven sits atop a narrow ridge running east and west. To the north is a dense, impenetrable wilderness with no roads. As already mentioned, the only routes to the community come in from below. The place is easy to defend militarily, and it has the potential to be self-sufficient. All this to escape the floodwaters of social decay he sees washing over America.

"I see this tide certainly rising, and I think the high ground is in Idaho," he told me the year before, shortly after setting up the community.

"What I've done is a very careful study," Gritz says. "I did not make my choice of Idaho based on any single reason. First of all, I wanted to know the area that had a climate where you could grow crops assured every year. You cannot do that in St. Anthony in eastern Idaho. You can't do that in Boise, you can't do that in Coeur d'Alene. But where the Nez Perce used to winter over, that little banana belt, that little, tiny belt where Chief Joseph said, 'From where the sun stands today I will fight no more forever,'[8] that area is a mild climate.

"The press didn't believe me. We were up there two weeks ago Saturday, it was pouring down rain, it was horrible, it was ugly, at the Clearwater River at Kamiah.

We drove up through the clouds, popped out, and there, and I said, now do you see why we call this Almost Heaven? Because below us was brilliant clouds illuminated by clear sky and a bright sun and a warm environment. That's the first criteria.

"Secondly, you've got to have soil that will support that kind of growth. That is all volcanic soil almost all over Idaho and it will grow anything.

"Third is water. I've had a geologist check this thing, a geologist at BYU, a good friend of mine, and he has assured me that Idaho has an aquifer under it the size of probably nothing else in the United States, not even Minnesota, with its 10,000 lakes, can equal.[9]

"The next reason is, I looked for things like floods and earthquakes and tornadoes and hurricanes. And you don't find them. This area up here is devoid. I looked for targets, like military targets, that might later be a problem. The nuclear facilities, the power plants, et cetera. There are none of them up there.

"The only thing that could possibly jeopardize Kamiah and that area up there is Mount Hood. St. Helens was just up the street, but you've got Rainier, and they've got Hood, and they've got Shasta. All of these are volcanic, and if it lit up, we'd be downrange.

"And then look at it from a social point of view. Idaho County is the third-largest county in America. It's the largest county in Idaho. There's one stop light, and it doesn't work all the time. Long before I got there, people had already wrested government back from the bureaucrats. For example, there's no building codes in Idaho County. You're not paying all of these fees. The people have done a damned good job of taking the government back.

"So when you look at it from literally every aspect, from political, social, from a natural phenomena point of view, climate, the physiology, the demography, of all places in America, every place from Florida to Maine to Washington to San Diego, California, the best place is Kamiah. That's my conclusion, that's why I'm out there."

The fog seems to be the only thing Gritz didn't take into consideration in formulating his strategy, though. Today, he couldn't see me coming from across the gully like he could on a normal day. On the other hand, any assault force coming up here would be likely to drive off the road in this soup. Or at least get lost.

Which is what happens to me, sort of. Finally, as I pass a gate, I see a sign saying "Almost Heaven" tipped over onto the ground, and I know I'm in the right place. Now the going is especially rough. The roadbeds for the routes into the development have been made out of cobblestone and not yet graveled, so the ride is like something from one of those pickup commercials that shows the sturdy truck navigating a boulder field with ease. My car doesn't seem keen on imitating a Dodge Ram, so I creep along the cobblestones. It's obvious that if I dare tread off the stones I'll be axle-deep in Almost Heaven.

On top of all this, the fog is still so thick I can't even see any residences yet. I turn at the first right, hopeful that this will lead me to Jerry Gillespie's home, which is serving right now as headquarters for the development. But only a few hundred yards up, it dead-ends at a tiny trailer home with a makeshift addition built on, and a pickup at the door. This doesn't look like the Center for Action. It looks like I've stumbled up someone's private driveway.

There's a turnaround there, and it looks semi-solid, so I veer rightward onto it, and immediately discover this was a mistake. As I feared, my car's front-wheel drive is stuck in mud. For that matter, the rear wheels are stuck now too. From the front door of the little addition emerges a short, gray-haired man with a beard, obviously coming out to see what's going on in his front yard. I'm red-faced.

"Hi there," I say. "I'm afraid I'm stuck in your driveway here."

The man walks gingerly through the mud around the car and nods. "Yep, you're stuck. I can pull you out easy, though."

I explain to him that I was looking for Gillespie's place. "Oh, that's the next entrance down," he says. "Be sure and stay on the stones. Otherwise you'll end up like this."

City slicker.

I'm grateful for his help. The man backs up his big pickup, pulls out a hefty chain that obviously has been used this winter for similar purposes, and I attach it to my car's rear. Moments later, I'm back up safely on the rock roadbed.

After we disattach the chain and he parks his pickup back in its accustomed spot, I thank my benefactor for his kindness and we introduce ourselves. His name is Pat, and he's been up here about a year now. He moved here from California. It's ironic: an Idaho native (since moved to the city) has to be rescued from the mud and his own lack of common sense by a guy from California (since moved to Idaho). The joke is on me.

Pat is a pleasant, somewhat soft-spoken man, not very tall but dignified, who escaped the Fresno area the year before. "It's become a real police state. More and more restrictive," he says. "When I left there they had federal troops on the street with automatic weapons, body gear, and black garb, to deal with the gang problem, which they imported—the Vietnamese, the Hmong, the boat people." He tells me federal immigration policies created the problem intentionally with the intent to take away people's guns.

"The New World Order," he says. "That's what it comes back to, the Rockefellers and the Rothschilds."

Pat tells me there are about four or five families living at Almost Heaven now, with more on the way. He and his wife heard about the community by listening to Gritz and McLamb on a short-wave radio program. They had planned to get out of California anyway, and this seemed like the perfect place for them. So far, he says, it has been.

"There's good folks up here," he says. "The media's done a real job on them."

What has irked him, and most of Almost Heaven's residents, is reportage they considered biased against their beliefs—stories that link Gritz with racists, or describe the politics of some of his Identity associates. Bo's not racist, they say; the media is engaging in guilt by association. The stories have often been carried nationally. An ABC crew visited in 1995, and Gritz wound up threatening the reporter when it was suggested the colonel had given the skinheads up at Ruby Ridge a Nazi salute.[10]

I remember Gritz's own response to these charges when I asked him about them. "They're full of shit," he growled. "As a soldier, I have never had any generic tendencies to label Americans as good or bad. I've served with black, white, yellow, brown, red—all religions. Nobody ever asked you about your religion, your blood bleeds red the same as everyone else. I've had Gary Goldman as a member of my closest team for 15 years; Goldman, obviously, is Jewish. And I'm sick and tired of it.

"But what I do find is because my name has some national recognition, people like Morris Dees, who probably wouldn't qualify as a pimple on a militiaman's ass, will make such statements as touting me, along with the FBI's most-wanted Aryan Nations, Posse Comitatus, whatever that is, guerrilla army, passing counterfeit bills, he mentions me: 'A notorious anti-Semite.' Where's he getting this crap? And so it shows me that these groups like Morris Dees' and these other coalitions, they're small squeaky wheels, they do anything to try to buff their image."

The associations with far-right figures and beliefs became the main point of contention in Kamiah when Gritz announced his plans for Almost Heaven in 1994. The town only has about 1,200 residents, and there was an immediate feeling that the presence of someone like Gritz could overwhelm them. A community meeting was called in August that attracted about 700 people, and the colonel came to talk and allay some of their fears. When someone asked him if there would be frequent gunfire from the development, he answered: "The only gunfire that you can expect will be any that comes our way."

Some locals continue to dread his presence. "I think that sooner or later Almost Heaven will become another Waco, Texas," says Rosemarie Thibault, manager of a Kamiah motel. "He calls it a covenant community. That's what they called Waco—a covenant community."

Gritz sees the criticism as a fear of the freedom his plans for creating Christian societies represents. "The reason that we were catching all the flak—if this concept of covenant communities catches on—you can have a covenant community in a borough of New York, where people basically get to know each other, they know that they're not going to stand for any criminal activity on anyone's part, and they'll stand in defense of their neighbors," he says. "You couldn't have abuses by the government, you couldn't have abuses by criminals and hooligans and robbers and thieves. So that's what we're doing."

The communities, he says, are not designed to be hideouts for white supremacists. "We will not hate; we haven't got any time for that. We don't fear anyone as far as I know. There may be those that do, but I don't. We are going to form our covenant communities, we are not going to hate, we are not going to attack, but we're going to be prepared if we have to, to defend against predators, whether they be wearing German-style helmets carrying MP-5 German machine guns with SS— now the Dallas street police are wearing SS on their uniforms, for God's sake—or whether they be hoodlums, any kind of predator will be rejected from the covenant community.

"And yet we're going to police these covenant communities—I won't be doing it, but there will be a 13-person committee in each community that I have anything

Top: Morning mist hangs over the Almost Heaven housing tract, situated on a high plateau above the Clearwater River, near Kamiah, Idaho.

Bottom: Entrance to Almost Heaven, Bo Gritz's "covenant community."

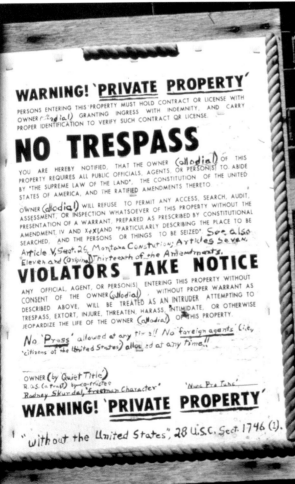

Above: Paul Smith, sheriff of Musselshell County during the Freemen standoff near Roundup, Montana.

Left: Obscure codes and terms utilized in the Patriot's "legal system" are evident in this posted document at the Freeman cabin near Roundup, Montana.

Top right: Another one of Rodney Skurdal's warning signs at the Freeman cabin.

Right: Freemen cabin near Roundup, Montana.

No 'Press' nor 'foreign agents' allowed!!

POSTED NOTICE
ENTRY TO
ALL PROPERTY
DENIED

SIGNED BY- Rod Skurdal, co trustee
for R.O.S. (a common Law Trust)

Top left: Bo Gritz burns a U.N. flag during a Patriot meeting at Puyallup, Washington, August 1998.

Bottom left: Calvin and Lynda Greenup, with son Shad (right) and attorney John Smith (center right); Bitterroot Valley, Montana.

Left: John Trochman and the bridge into Noxon, Montana.

Below: The Clark ranch near Jordan, site of the Freemen/FBI standoff on the eastern Montana plains.

Left: A "Y" (for "Yahweh") posted next to the watch station.

Above: The Freeman watch station on the hill overlooking the Clark ranch.

Below: FBI vehicles parked at the Garfield County fairgrounds at Jordan, Montana, March 1996.

Top left: Cecil and Ada Weeding on their ranch in Garfield County, Montana. Patriot beliefs frequently disrupt interfamily relationships. Two of Ada's brothers, Emmett and Ralph Clark, are Freemen, but the Weedings spearheaded a local movement against their activities.

Above: U.S. Militia Association organizer Sam Sherwood in his well-curtained home, Blackfoot, Idaho.

Far left: As a prosecutor in Owyhee County, Idaho, Lois Hart experienced the full brunt of Patriot threats, liens and nuisance legal filings.

Left: John Bohlman, prosecutor in Musselshell County, Montana, heard enough rumors about death threats originating from Patriots that he bought a handgun and started carrying it when taking his dog out each day.

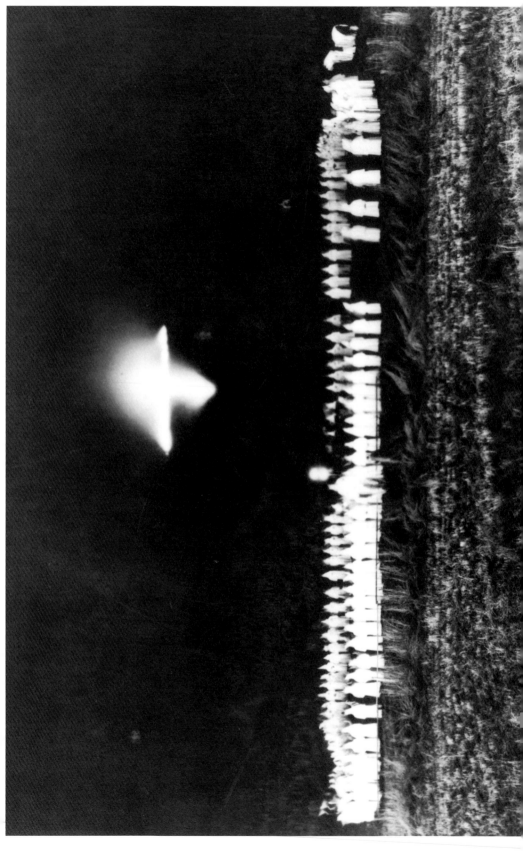

Above: In 1949, the Washington legislature's Un-American Activities committee headed by representative Albert Canwell of Spokane claimed the state was "acrawl with trained and iron-disciplined Communists." Canwell failed in a reelection bid, but his zealous anti-Communism helped set a pattern followed by other believers in fringe conspiratorial theories. Photo: Whitman County Republican Committee, October 27, 1952. *(Washington State University Libraries)*

Left: When a revived Ku Klux Klan spread across the nation in the early 1920s, thousands of white, Protestant men in the Pacific Northwest joined the fraternal organization. However, the Klan's feuding leadership, unfair anti-Catholic stance and occasional clandestine activities sent the regional organization into a nadir by 1925. Some of the leaders and members later reappeared in other right-wing populist groups, such as the fascist-mimicking Silvershirts of the late 1930s. Photo: A rare Pacific Northwest outdoor Klan rally at Spring Flat, near Colfax, Washington. The burning cross on the hillside consists of flammable material in trenches. *(Washington State University Libraries)*

A typical assortment of Patriot pamphlets, posters, flyers, bumper stickers, etc., are depicted here and on the following pages.

ENEMIES:
FOREIGN and DOMESTIC
PART I "THE PROBLEM"

THE DOCUMENTATION
IN SUPPORT OF THE VIDEO

FOR MORE INFORMATION CONTACT:

MILITIA OF MONTANA
P.O. BOX 1486, NOXON, MT. 59853
TEL: 406-847-2735
FAX: 406-847-2246

NEW WORLD ORDER

The Patriot's Prayer

God grant me the serenity to accept the things I cannot change, the courage to change the things I can, and THE WEAPONRY to make the difference!

Never Surrender Your Firearms!

Militia Member Patriot & Proud of It!

PATRIOTIC CONFERENCE
PART II

PRESENTED BY
OLYMPIC
SPORTSMAN'S ALLIANCE

OLYMPIC SPORTSMAN'S ALLIANCE

WHEN: Sunday February 26, 1995
TIME: 5 P.M. - 10 P.M.
WHERE: Givens Community Center
1026 Sydney Avenue
Port Orchard, WA
(See map on reverse side)

Featuring Bob Fletcher, The Militia of Montana

- U.N./Russian troops in America
- Executive orders, rule by decree
- The Police State, American Gestapo
- What can you do?

Tickets: $10.00 per person or $15.00 per couple
GET YOUR TICKETS EARLY AS SPACE IS LIMITED!
For more info call Rick Reitmeyer at (360) 779-5374

❀CITIZENS❀
RULE BOOK

A Palladium of Liberty

"WHERE THE SPIRIT OF THE LORD IS,

...TY." II ...ORINTHIANS...

OF RIGHTS

HANDBOOK

...e in the Document itself:
...CONSTITUTION!

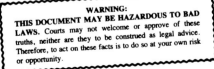

PROCLAIM LIBERTY!

Inscribed on our hallowed LIBERTY BELL are these words "PROCLAIM LIBERTY THROUGHOUT ALL THE LAND UNTO ALL THE INHABITANTS THEREOF."

LEV. XXV X

"Government is not reason; it is not eloquence; it is force! Like fire, it is a dangerous servant and a fearful master."

George Washington

"Woe to those who decree unjust statutes and to those who continually record unjust decisions, to deprive the needy of justice, and to rob the poor of My people of their rights. . . ."

Isaiah 10:1,2

TAKING THE PLUNGE!

"My people are destroyed for lack of knowledge . . .!"

Hosea 4:6

"The only thing necessary for evil to triumph is for good men to do nothing."

Edmund Burke 1729-1797

"If My people which are called by My name, shall humble themselves, and pray, and seek My face, and turn from their wicked ways; then will I hear from Heaven, and will forgive their sin, and will heal their land."

II Chron. 7:14

"We must obey GOD rather than men."

Acts 5:29

to do with forming—and there will be 13 persons so we'll always have the odd man out, there won't be any tie votes—a 13-person committee in each community that will determine if a person is suitable or unsuitable in accordance with their covenant. The only covenant is that they be willing to stand in the defense of the lawful and rightful, the rights of others and their neighbors.

"There's probably a better way to run it, but you're not gonna drink Kool-Aid up there, and if you want to go to church, you gotta go to your own church. But you're going to have the right to home-school your children, regardless of what the Senate decides with the United Nations. And you're going to have the right to use alternative medicine, regardless of what Hillary decides with the health-club business. And you're going to have your rights as an American, that's all."

So simple and wholesome. Certainly, the picture of a tight-knit family of neighbors at Almost Heaven has played true so far, and one of them has just pulled my car out of the mud. After awhile, though, Pat makes it clear that he's uncomfortable talking to a journalist. "I know you've just got a job to do, but we've just learned not to trust anyone," he says. So I thank Pat for his help, and head back through the fog to Jerry Gillespie's place, careful this time to stay on the cobblestones.

There's no one home, besides two friendly dogs who come out to greet me when I knock. The view from the porch, as I stand there pondering where to go next, begins suddenly to transform. The air grows lighter and the fog thinner. In the distance, I begin to make out the forms of trees down the hillside from the house, emerging like a row of giant dark soldiers from the misty shroud. I step down from the porch and around to the front of the house that overlooks the hillside to get a better view, the dogs still wagging their tails and hanging with me.

As I watch, the fog literally lifts from the high ridge. In a matter of moments, the brilliant sun emerges from the west, and the gray blanket disappears down the hillside, chased by the golden light. A small pond emerges into view a hundred yards or so downhill, and behind it a line of trees arcing across the top of the lower ridge.

It is a revelation. Clusters of nimbus cotton drift in the glacial blue sky, while down below the rest of the valley clears away, except for a thick cloud bank that hangs stubbornly just above the river, obscuring the town. The thickets of trees seem to grasp the last wisps of the fog shroud around their shoulders, giving them an unearthly appearance, while the dusky light makes the steep hillside, covered with golden grasslands, glow. Almost Heaven sounds about right.

I walk back around the house and find that I now can see the whole tract. Patrick's little trailer is up in the distance a bit, and another house, medium-sized with its siding still unfinished, is in the middle of the development. A small yellow school bus is parked outside, and children are playing around the house. Signs of construction are visible at a few more sites. A tractor sits idle in the middle of a hayfield adjacent to the land.

There is indeed a sense of peacefulness that fits its occupants' self-description of Almost Heaven as a kindly, old-fashioned community. Some of this feeling, though, comes from a peculiar fact: For all of Gritz's success in selling off the lots—at about

$20,000 apiece—very few people have actually moved here in the year and a half the community has existed.

Foremost among them: Bo Gritz himself.

★★★

It is early 1996. The colonel has for several years now run his operations out of his home in the countryside near Las Vegas, and for some time has been promising, "soon," to build his house at Almost Heaven. The presumption has been that he prefers the warm Nevada winters to the cold muck that awaits him in Kamiah. His absence, though, has become a problem. The leadership void at the community has created a few rumblings from within. Only the week before, a couple of residents created a stir, on the front page of the region's daily paper, the *Lewiston Morning Tribune*, no less. The issue: Where was Bo Gritz?

A trio of Gritz followers had, in his absence, decided to form their own group, calling themselves the "Freemen Patriots," and announced themselves to an old acquaintance of mine, *Tribune* reporter Dave Johnson. The three men—Michael Cain, who had purchased one of the Woodland Acres lots; Ed LeStage, a friend of Cain's who lived on the property; and Chad Erickson, a follower who had bought property adjacent to Gritz's—posed for a big color photo, standing in the snow, hands on hips with mad-as-hell and we're-not-going-to-take-it-anymore glares. They told Johnson, a roving reporter who's covered the region for many years, that they hoped to provide some leadership for the community, since Gritz hadn't.[11]

"We're basically trying to set a course and a direction, since no one else has," said LeStage. "Bo talked the talk and walked the walk. But he has changed the talk and the walk."

The trio told Johnson there were about eight people in their group. Cain and Erickson had spent the month before their announcement getting worked up because they feared an imminent invasion by federal agents, with Gritz nowhere in sight. The Freemen Patriots was their solution.

They wrote letters to the sympathetic editor of Kamiah's weekly paper, the *Clearwater Progress*, warning of an impending attack. "Through a conference with patriots in Montana, one being an ex-government agent with ties intact, we have learned that federal agencies are planning a strike against the patriots in the Kamiah, Idaho, area," Erickson wrote. "Reportedly it will involve helicopter-borne microwave weapons that fry households without photogenic smoke and flame."

"God is with us. He will not forsake us. Be strong and courageous, muster your faith and let us once again restore our Constitution, our liberty and our dignity," said a letter signed by Cain, LeStage and four others. "Brothers . . . to arms!" At Cain's home, an American flag flew upside-down.

The Freemen told Johnson that they took their name from the Freemen of Book of Mormon fame, not from the Montana clan—who they nonetheless supported. They, too, said the only law they recognize is the county sheriff, while federal agencies are illegal. "I've come here to live by constitutional law, and it shouldn't get any more complicated than that," said Cain.

"I suppose if Bo had been here, this wouldn't have happened," said Erickson.

Gritz was warmly ensconced at his Nevada home, and the temperature rose a few degrees more when Johnson called and asked him about the trouble the malcontents were stirring up in his community. "I am directly opposed to what they're apparently doing," he said. "They've invented their own dragon."

He promised to move to Almost Heaven in June, and when he did, the malcontents would be out. "There's no question I will move out of their way, but they're going to be moving off of Almost Heaven."

Gritz, though, had no influence over whether Erickson stayed, since the self-employed land surveyor had bought his own parcel outside of Gritz's tract. And besides, Gritz indicated an affection for his neighbor. "I'm disappointed that Chad would not have better sense," Gritz said. "And the other guy [LeStage] is probably a bum who should be sent packing. And as for the property owner [Cain], I'm sorry he's come under that kind of influence."

The story, and a scathing editorial the following day, stirred up a storm at Gritz's community, where residents already had hard feelings about the *Lewiston Morning Tribune*. Gritz and Gillespie had engaged in a sort of running feud with the paper's editorial-page editor, Jim Fisher, and at various times said they wouldn't talk to the paper anymore. This latest incident inspired a letter of protest from Gillespie, who called Fisher's latest offering "slanderous half-truth comments" and said the paper was turning neighbor against neighbor.

"Jim Fisher, [columnist] Bill Hall and others (except David Johnson) to my knowledge have never visited these communities first-hand, thus demonstrating their ignorance of who we are," Gillespie wrote. "At least the *Spokesman-Review* admitted that rather than being an armed camp it is more like 'little house on the prairie.' "

I have to agree somewhat with Gillespie today. The sunlight playing across the golden grasslands, the children playing outside their home, the helpfulness the people here have shown suggest a rather more pastoral picture than that drawn in the media of a survivalist bunker where everyone's armed to the teeth.

It is this latter image that most seems to upset the people who have moved to Almost Heaven. "All this paramilitary stuff is really a crock," Jan Astwood, a former New Yorker, told Dave Johnson. "Everybody is looking for a bunker."

A British Broadcasting Corporation crew visiting the place even asked Dan and Barbara Fuller, a couple formerly from Utah, where their bunker was. The survivalist stereotypes become fodder for local gossip too; a neighbor saw Ed LeStage drilling a well by hand in a camouflage raincoat and spread the tale that a militiaman was digging a bunker on Gritz's property.[12] "Our news media has been controlled for years and years," Barbara Fuller says. "That's because our government wants people to know only certain things. The government wants people to write things detrimental about this subdivision because then, when the U.N. troops come in to wipe us out, they'll have public opinion on their side."

It seems that nearly everyone here has the same apocalyptic fears. Gene Nelson came up from Dallas to check out the property last summer. "The handwriting is on the wall," he told Johnson. "You're going to have to get out of the big cities. The rest of the country has lost the Constitution."

"There is not a place on God's green acres that is going to be safe," says Barbara Fuller.

I consider these voices as I survey the sunlit hills of Almost Heaven. Underneath the wholesomeness, the peaceful setting, is a layer of fear that is disquieting to any visitor. When there is that much fear, it becomes easy for events to tumble into violence, especially if what you see is a world conspiring to destroy your family, to steal your very soul. As with Randy Weaver, it starts out as simply attempting to get away from the rest of the world. But eventually, these beliefs, and this fear, bump up against the real world and an explosion results: Someone refuses to pay his taxes, agents arrive to arrest him, there's gunfire. I have seen this played out many times on the high ridges of the radical right. I wonder what shape the Freemen Patriots' preparations for the coming federal assault has taken.

The sunlight that has finally come out today is warming and gratifying, but around the edges of the community, lying in the ridges above and behind it, linger the black thick clouds that had formed the fog bank. They have that deep, impenetrable look, the kind that carry lightning and hail.

I do not know if it will come my way. But I decide it is time to take the winding gravel road back down to the river.

★★★

Like many people in the Patriot movement, especially its leaders, Bo Gritz's worldview is straight out of the Old Testament—with a heavy dose of Revelation-based apocalypticism. And like virtually everyone within the movement, Gritz envisions a Phoenix-style rebirth for the nation made possible through a return to those ancient values.

"What I see is, every time you have a birth, anytime you have a metamorphosis, anytime you have a—oh, like the Bible says, be transformed, a transfiguration—you have a struggle," Gritz explained to me the first time I interviewed him, by telephone in November 1994. "Before the caterpillar can become the butterfly, there has to be this struggle. Before the babe is born, there is this struggle. In America, we are struggling to resurface. And I don't know whether we're going to change from a butterfly back into a cocoon, or whether we're going to get out of our cocoon and become something beautiful. I think the next couple of years will tell."

Gritz is a charismatic fellow and an engaging speaker. He has a nice rumbling baritone voice that can electrify audiences and charm the most skeptical interviewer (let alone the naive ones). When he starts talking about the coming high tide, it is hard not to be dazzled.

"I'm not a prophet," he says, sounding like one anyway. "I wish I had the eyes of Elijah, that I could see the angels and chariots of fire. I even wish I had the message of Gideon. I've never asked God, prove to me God, by turning the floor wet when everything else is dry, or vice versa, that I have a message, that I am the Gideon of the 20th Century. That's never happened to me.

"But when I read Revelations 13, I only have to read one page. And it tells me there will be global government. It tells me there will be a world religion. It tells me there will be an economic system that has no cash, but rather you have to have a mark or a name or a number. And when I take that—it's like Rabbi Spivak said the other day—he started out a program I did with him by saying, 'If you read the *New York Times*, you are reading the Bible. You are reading prophecy fulfilled.' Because today, like at no other time, we have a global government. Consciously. Before us. Overtly. We are moving rapidly toward this unification of a one-government system.

"And everywhere you see the banks, you see Petey Wilson here in California, you see the computer technology is there, the GATT is there, we're moving toward a global economic system that will probably, to win the war on crime and drugs, will do away with cash, if you can call Federal Reserve notes that, and other currencies of other nations the same—it will probably go to an electronic system. Everybody's trying to push you that way. I think you'll have to have a name, number to be able to transact. And you can see we have a movement in that direction."

For all his religious beliefs, Gritz says he's a defender of the separation of church and state—in a backhanded way. "We have a state religion today," he says. "The state religion is atheism. The state religion is pro-abortion. The state religion is everything that Christianity and Islam and Judaism are against. So I don't think there's any question we're supposed to have a separation between church and state. And we don't. We now have government fully taking over corporate churches all over America, and probably the world."

Gritz, however, scoffs at rumors of troops massing on the U.S. border and black helicopters performing secretive missions. "Well, to me, that is Patriot paranoia," he says. "I'm an intelligence operative. Not anymore for the government, but I was up until 1987. I've been in intelligence all throughout my career, but not a staff officer. I've been an intelligence commander, where I've been required to go out and get intelligence.

"You get a lot of people like Linda Thompson. Linda Thompson made a statement, I was right there when she did it, that said there were like 50,000 or 80,000 Chinese in Montana. Now when I was at Weaver's, in Idaho up north, they said there were 30,000 Cambodians, U.N. Cambodians wearing blue helmets that were charging toward Weaver's. I sent Jerry Gillespie to go find them. And he did. He went into Montana, and he came back and said, 'I found them, Bo. There are thousands of Orientals—they're not wearing blue helmets, they're not Cambodians— they're from New York, they're from San Francisco, they're from L.A.'—they're all up here picking mushrooms as the forest fires had ravaged Montana, as they do every summer, and that was August that we were up there. The mushrooms pop up everywhere. And all the Oriental grocery representatives flood the area with Orientals to pluck these damned mushrooms. So this is where these kind of rumors come from.

"Stalin said it best. He said, 'We will not ever have to attack America. America will fall inwardly in two generations like an overripe piece of fruit.' I wish there were 5,000 North Korean tanks; I wish that there were 80,000 Chinese. Linda Thompson said that there were U.N. tanks and APCs rumbling down the streets of Portland, Oregon. Horseshit. I wish this were true because it would galvanize Americans against globalism just like it galvanized the Vietnamese when we went to Vietnam.

"But that's not how it's going to happen. You're going to find this subtle, velvet hammer approach where they're going to make it look like it's all wonderful and then they just steal your birthright. One day you wake up and it's USA Inc. And that's what I'm fighting against."

Gritz may be skeptical about Trochmannesque conspiracy theories, but he nonetheless adheres to basic Patriot beliefs about the Constitution and the 14th Amendment, as well as "sovereign citizenship" and the relative position of non-whites within the system. He defends Freeman-style talk of "organic citizens" as opposed to "14th Amendment citizens."

Gritz recognizes that such talk—as well as his references to "international bankers" and his flirtations with white supremacists—causes grave concerns among civil-rights groups and the Jewish community, since the 14th Amendment also guarantees equal protection under the law for all citizens. He says they needn't be fearful.

"Certainly, the Jews are concerned, and they should be, about what their security is," Gritz says. "It's not just white supremacists. But I imagine there are KKK; I imagine there are white—whatever you would call them, supremacists, separatists—that would join a militia.

"I think you're going to find them standing side-by-side beside black men, red men and women, Orientals that have come to America, Spanish-Americans, you're going to find all of them—Catholics, Buddhists—you're going to find Americans. That's a mixed family standing together in the militia."

Gritz growls the loudest when he's accused of being anti-Semitic or racist or homophobic. When *Lewiston Morning Tribune* editorial writer Jim Fisher took Gritz to task over his tax resistance and his gay-baiting rhetoric, Gritz wrote a long response, which the *Tribune* published in full. The colonel was in prime form—issuing, in essence, a plea to let him settle into his new home in peace:

"I've been honest, up front and complete in answering your many charges," he wrote. "Anticipating further allegations, let me reveal all now. I kissed my first girl at 11 (she was Jewish); had a heterosexual experience at 17; haven't tried homosexuality, pedophilia or bestiality, even though I have pondered hippies mating with goats when I see who is running the media. I'm a baptized born-again, Catholic, Mormon. I have zero interest in porn; don't drink, smoke, nor take dope, but I like oldies and riding my Harley with C.J. I spend far too much money keeping my 1955 Cessna flying, but I just can't let her go yet.

"I've never been at a cross burning, but I have burned the U.N. flag. I've never stood by while Old Glory was desecrated, nor while another American was viciously berated, or abused. I no longer shoot at anything that doesn't shoot back; I love small animals and my family. I find myself crying sometimes; I never did before. I want and need God in my life, but I haven't found organized religion the answer. I need to watch my cuss'n; I've noticed that my temper is shorter; I don't carouse.

"Have I left anything out?"[13]

★ ★ ★

Bo Gritz finally moved up to Almost Heaven in July 1996. He sold his place in Sandy Valley, Nevada, and made the leap, shifting his entire base of operations to Idaho. He had already built a modular home on the lot adjacent to Jerry Gillespie's along the plateau's rim, with the grand view overlooking the valley below him. His 38-year-old son, Jim, also moved up from Nevada with his wife, Vicki.

When I visited in early July, Gritz begged off the prearranged interview, saying he was too busy right then to talk to anyone. It was a credible excuse; the road into his new place was worn with all the traffic in and out. A cement truck was backed up to the house, pouring cement for the foundation. Gritz was trying to juggle all of the construction and all of the details of moving, both for his home and his business.

Gritz was not the only one who had moved in. All around Almost Heaven, there were signs of new residents. All the lots at Almost Heaven had been sold, as were the lots at the adjacent "covenant community" of Shenandoah, though a few lots still remained at the two Woodland communities. It was clear Gritz's dream was becoming a reality and, if Gritz himself were to be believed, all the trappings of a quiet retirement atop the Clearwater plateau were falling into place.

A couple of weeks later, with the work finally easing up, David Johnson caught up with Gritz and interviewed him at the new home. Gritz showed off his view to Johnson, especially the one from his office over the garage, from which you can literally see for miles.

"It will be awesome," he said, pointing across the horizon. "There's Grangeville right there. At night, it lights up and you can see the city."

Gritz was elated with the progress of the whole community that summer. "As you can see, the skyline is changing," he told Johnson. "I'm really pleased. People are moving in."

Not everything was hunky-dory; at the Woodland Acres community, the American flag continued flying upside-down at Michael Cain's place. The little enclave of Freemen in his community was still something of an aggravation. "I intend to go over there and talk to them," Gritz said. "It bothers me. If this nation is in distress, let Congress fly the flag upside-down over the Capitol. This is the safest place in the world. I mean, they need to get a damn job."

The picture Gritz painted was of someone anxious to settle into a quiet retirement, building a community that would be prepared for the spiritual floodwaters he believed were coming. "Right over there, I'm going to build a boat dock," Gritz said, pointing to a spot that, like everything at Almost Heaven, was a thousand feet or so above the river. Gritz said he'd attach a sign to the dock: "Bo Knows!"

Gritz, whose life since he joined the Army has mostly been a succession of moves, from Texas to Vietnam to North Carolina to Cambodia to Nevada, said he's looking forward to settling down. "The road ends for me here," he said. "I'm not going anywhere but here."[14]

A few months later, though, he went somewhere: Suffield, Connecticut. On September 30, Gritz and his son, Jim, were arrested outside of a middle school and charged with attempting to kidnap two boys. They were held overnight on a million dollars' bail each, and then were released the next day on $50,000 bond. So much for Gritz's desire to settle into a quiet retirement.

It appeared Gritz's compulsion to get involved in other people's battles had once again thrown him into the fire. A Gritz follower, Linda Wiegand, had been involved in a custody dispute over her two young sons, Jon and Ben, since 1993 and had asked Gritz to help her. Wiegand, a Vermont housewife, had fled with the boys, ages 4 and 7, to Nevada after a judge had awarded custody of the boys to her ex-husband despite child-rape charges (ultimately dismissed) pending against him. She was arrested by the FBI in 1996 and the boys were returned to their father.

Wiegand hired Joe Holland's and John Trochmann's attorney, John DeCamp, to represent her, and she appeared on Gritz's radio talk show on September 16. Wiegand told Gritz she suspected the police in Suffield, where her boys now lived with their father, were part of a Satanic child-abuse ring. Gritz met with Wiegand on September 20 on a trip to Boston, and decided to stay out East to help her.

When the police arrested Gritz on the morning of the 30th, he and Jim were sitting in a car near the middle school where the older of the two boys was enrolled. Officers found pictures of the boys, their school schedule, and letters belonging to Wiegand in the car, which was registered under a Wiegand pseudonym. They also found two-way radios, some of the lockpicking tools Gritz sells for "defense against restrictive entry," and a modified switchblade on Jim.

Bo protested that he and Jim really weren't there to grab the boys and run; rather, they had merely agreed to meet someone selling a 1956 Chevrolet at the school parking lot. He claimed there were no photos, the lockpicks were legal instruments, as was the knife, and the radios were rentals they had used at a parachute event.

"I intend to file a false arrest suit," Gritz said in a prepared statement. "I will continue doing all I can until Linda Wiegand has her custody case heard in the courts. I am not a kidnapper!"

Still, Gritz had come to believe Linda Wiegand's suspicions about a Satanic cult in play at the Suffield Police Department. "I must conclude from my short but intense investigation, including a conversation with the Suffield Chief of Police," Gritz said, "that Linda's misgivings are more than paranoid disillusions."[15]

Gritz returned home to Kamiah, where he tried to return to a retirement mode. As part of his pledge to blend in with the community, he filed for enrollment in the Kamiah School District as a substitute teacher. Gritz has no teaching certificate, but in Kamiah, substitutes are required only to have a high-school diploma. And school officials saw nothing wrong with including Gritz on their list, except of course for those criminal charges in Connecticut. "Once his felony charge is cleared up on the East Coast, then we will have a look at it," said the Kamiah superintendent.[16] In November, the district officially cleared Gritz to teach as soon as he resolved the criminal case.

However, that would take awhile. The case finally got around to pretrial hearings in March 1997, and it appeared as though the case could well drag on into the next year—which it did.

At Almost Heaven, the vision of bucolic retirement for Gritz and his family seemed more distant than ever before. "It's gone the opposite, if anything," said Vicki Gritz, Jim's wife, from their home atop the Clearwater plateau, with a little sigh.

★★★

The Linda Wiegand case was bound to be trouble from the start. One of the great drawing-cards of the Patriot movement is its belief that fathers are the victims of the "liberal" state: first, because of government restrictions on their ability to raise their children as they see fit without interference (an argument heard sometimes from Patriots with molestation convictions in their past); and second, by a judiciary that favors mothers in child-custody cases. When questions arose about Linda Wiegand's tale of paternal abuse, Gritz fell victim to the crossfire.

Criticism first came from John Trochmann, who himself had a history of run-ins with the law stemming from his apparent abduction of his teen-age daughter from her mother in Minnesota. The Militia of Montana began circulating accurate, factual information that countered Wiegand's claims, both on the Web and through e-mails and faxes. Clayton Douglas, the editor of a New Mexico-based Patriot magazine called *Free American* (Douglas, too, had a nasty child-custody dispute in his past), picked up on the charges and began publishing them—depicting Gritz as the well-intentioned victim of a desperate liar's scam. "You Be the Judge," shouted the cover of the magazine's July 1998 edition. It asked readers to decide if Trochmann was a "Critic or Cad," Gritz a "Defender or Dupe," and Wiegand a "Victim or Con." The article left little doubt about which were the correct answers—critic, dupe and con.

Not only was Gritz being abandoned by Patriot colleagues, but Wiegand was distancing herself from Gritz. She told a news reporter that she had only allied herself with Gritz to gain attention for her cause, calling him "simply a well-placed distraction from the real issue." According to Douglas, Wiegand also called up Gritz's wife, Claudia, and demanded money from the defense fund that Gritz had organized for the both of them after his arrest. Claudia reportedly refused, telling Wiegand that the money was intended for both Gritz and Wiegand—so Wiegand simply created her own "Save Jon and Ben" fund. Douglas also hinted that Wiegand had threatened to turn state's evidence against Gritz if he didn't come up with money for her from the fund. Gritz himself appeared to want to sever ties with her, but held back.

The trial in Connecticut finally was set for the fall of 1998, and the feud was rising to a boil when the warring parties—Gritz, Trochmann and Douglas—all found themselves together in a convention hall that summer. The event was Preparedness Expo '98, an Identity-affiliated gathering in August at the state fairgrounds in Puyallup, Washington. Gritz and Trochmann were both featured speakers (as was Jack McLamb), but the relations between the two were fairly chilly.

Preparedness Expos—operated by a group in Midvale, Utah—are fascinating demonstrations of the way the Patriot movement's agenda is camouflaged by its more mainstream affiliations. As you entered the hall in Puyallup, the first booth that was visible belonged to the decidedly mainstream (if somewhat disreputable) Wade Cook Financial Seminars. Other booths promoted solutions to the "Year 2000 Bug," a "Light Energy" treatment to promote wellness, and various food-preparation kits for survivalist purposes.

But as you walked back farther down the convention hall and toward the seminar area, the displays became more militant—conspiracy theorist Terry Reed, the Militia of Montana, and Clayton Douglas were all grouped closely together. A little farther down, Randy Weaver and his daughter, Sara, signed copies of their book, *Incident at Ruby Ridge*, frequently posing for snapshots with proud Patriots. Bo Gritz sold copies of *Called to Serve* at the adjacent booth, talking to admirers. And next door, at the very end of the displays, Gritz's longtime associate, Richard Flowers, sold the usual array of tomes from his Christian Patriot Association booth: *Protocols of the Seven Elders of Zion, Secrets of the Federal Reserve,* Richard Hoskins' *Vigilantes of Christendom,* Holocaust revisionist Arthur Butz's *The Hoax of the Twentieth Century,* and the renowned anti-Semite Eustace Mullins' *New World Order: The Secret Rulers.*

Gritz, as he always does, shrugged off Flowers' collection by saying that he "disagrees" with his friend but believes in his right to free speech. And he politely avoided discussing his "disagreement" with Trochmann and Douglas. What he was eager to talk about instead was his latest rescue mission: an effort to bring fugitive bombing suspect Eric Rudolph out of the North Carolina woods where he had been in hiding since March.

Rudolph was the object of a major manhunt by the FBI because he was believed to be the man behind the January 1998 bombing of an abortion clinic in Birmingham, Alabama, that killed a policeman and maimed a nurse. As they gathered evidence, the FBI also came to believe Rudolph was the man behind the 1997 bombings of an abortion clinic and a gay nightclub in Atlanta, and possibly the pipe bombing during the 1996 Atlanta Olympics. As the "Army of God" letters left behind at the bombings suggested, Rudolph had a history of involvement with Christian Identity—particularly the late Nord Davis' white-supremacist enclave in North Carolina, the same neck of the woods where Rudolph, himself intimately familiar with the terrain, vanished with scarcely a trace.[17] Now a virtual army of 200 agents combed the hills near Andrews, North Carolina, looking for him, a million-dollar reward on his head. Still, the Army veteran proved adept at eluding his hunters indefinitely—he was spotted only once, and that time by a neighbor from whom he mooched some food.

Gritz announced his plan to the media ahead of time: If Rudolph voluntarily surrendered himself to Gritz, the erstwhile colonel would hand the reward money over to Rudolph's mother, who would then mount a legal defense for her son with the million bucks. Gritz also noted that he had already retained the services of "a Patriot Gerry Spence"—John DeCamp, the Nebraska constitutionalist who'd previously handled the defenses, such as they were, of John Holland and Gordon Sellner in Montana . . . both of whom are currently serving long prison terms.[18]

At the Expo in Puyallup, three days before he was due to arrive in North Carolina, Gritz used his bully pulpit to drum up recruits for the expedition to save Eric

Rudolph. He devoted most of the speech—titled "The Heart of the Monster"—to the approaching tyranny of the New World Order, which he foresaw in decidedly Biblical terms. "You are involved in a war," he told the crowd of about 150. "You may not know it, and as far as I know, there are no decorations to be given out. But it will literally mean your eternal life.

"This is a spiritual war, and it is all-deadly as anything any of you have ever faced—and me too—in combat. And very soon, you are gonna get a choice and you cannot sit on the fence."

In the end, he urged his audience to get off the fence by joining him in North Carolina. He was trying to raise an army of a hundred people, he said, to conduct the search. And he noted that he was jumping ahead with the plan even in the face of a fresh obstacle—his marriage.

"I have been blessed by Almighty God to fear nothing on this earth. I was put on this earth to be a warrior," he explained. "But now, like Br'er Rabbit, I'm in the briar patch most of the time, and my bride's not here today because she's mad at me, because I'm goin' down and see if I can't help Eric Rudolph out of the woods. And she sees it as me getting back in the briar patch, when I've already got one leg still stuck in there from what happened in Connecticut."

It had seemed like just another of Gritz's frequent tales about defying the one person whose wrath he feared: Claudia Gritz. And he seemed to be facing it with the usual bravado. He explained how the Rudolph rescue would proceed, and his speech culminated with a last act of defiance. Picking up a paper United Nations flag he'd used throughout the talk as a prop, he set it on fire, holding it up as it burned, and urged his audience to symbolically follow suit in their lives.

However, the Rudolph rescue turned out to be a fiasco. Only 40 or so Patriots joined Gritz the following Thursday in North Carolina, well short of the 100 he'd hoped for. And the search party turned out to be considerably less skilled than the FBI's teams. While Gritz tried communicating with Rudolph by a loudspeaker, his squad managed only to stumble upon a nest of hornets, which required a couple of searchers to be treated at the clinic in Andrews. Pretty soon, the locals had taken to calling them "Bo's Hornet Hunters." Gritz gave up on the enterprise after a week without catching a glimpse of their would-be rescuee and headed home for Idaho.

His greatest disaster yet awaited him there. Claudia had warned Gritz that if he went through with the Rudolph search, she would leave him—and this time, she meant it. She had divorce papers waiting when he came home to Kamiah, ending a 24-year marriage. Everyone who knew Gritz said that Claudia was the key to his durability, and they began to worry about how well he'd hold up now—with good cause, as it turned out.

Gritz spoke on his shortwave radio program about facing the shock of divorce. He told his listeners shortly after the papers were filed that he'd begun seeing a psychological counselor, who told him his compulsion to rescue others—from MIAs in Vietnam to Randy Weaver at Ruby Ridge to the Freemen in Montana—was an expression of a subconscious effort to find and rescue his own father, who had died in combat in World War II. He said he planned to check himself into a Nevada veterans hospital for psychotherapy, adding: "I am sick."

He also spoke about his problems at length with a presumably less sympathetic audience—a researcher for the Southern Poverty Law Center's "Intelligence Report." Indeed, he talked frankly about suicide. "I've thought about looking at the other end of my pistol a few times," he told the researcher. "Because what kind of life do I have without my bride?"

Three days later, he took a look and pulled the trigger.

A local resident driving up the grade out of Orofino on Sunday, September 20, happened upon a bleeding Gritz, lying by the side of a gravel road near his pickup. He had been shot once in the chest, but he was alive and breathing. An ambulance whisked him to the nearby hospital in Orofino. The local sheriff told reporters the wound had been self-inflicted—but it was not life-threatening. Family members rushed to his side.

Naturally, as word spread of the incident, speculation began circulating on the Patriot Internet lines that he had been attacked by government agents. The family quickly stamped out such talk, posting a message on Gritz's Web site assuring his followers: "Please help quell the rumors already abounding that this was not done by Bo's own hand, it was—Claudia and others were at the scene within minutes of the sad event. People need to expend their energy praying for Bo—not spreading rumors."

Strangely, Gritz's shot—from his own .45-caliber handgun—had passed cleanly through his chest without piercing either the lung cavity or any of the major vessels around his heart. He spent the next three days in the hospital and then went home, accompanied by Claudia. However, she returned to the RV park where she had moved, and Gritz decided to head to Nevada for awhile to recuperate. He vowed to return to his nationally broadcast radio program within a few weeks. And sure enough, he did.

No one, after all, had ever accused Bo Gritz of not being tough.

Chapter 8 / A Hard Land

Tᴴᴇʀᴇ'ꜱ ꜱᴏᴍᴇᴛʜɪɴɢ ᴀ ʟɪᴛᴛʟᴇ ɢʀᴀɴᴅɪᴏꜱᴇ about Tim Nettleton's habit of calling Owyhee County *his* county.

It is, after all, Idaho's second-largest geographical entity, totaling some 7,666 square miles, larger than the states of Rhode Island and Connecticut combined. A drive through its vast sagebrush plains underscores the land's immensity; the gently rolling landscape seems to go on endlessly, and the distant Bruneau Range of granite peaks on its southern border with Nevada appears permanently distant on the horizon, no matter how long, it seems, you drive toward it.

On the other hand, hardly anyone lives there: only 9,600 people, most of them concentrated along the borders of the more populous neighboring counties to the north. Owyhee County's population density is the third-lowest in a state already thin in such numbers. Only two paved roads run north and south through its scrublands, and a sparse network of dirt roads connects the widely separated ranches and farms that form the basis of its human community.

The truth is, hardly anyone wants to live in Owyhee County because it is dusty, marginally habitable, and not very appealing aesthetically. Mostly anyone who lives there does so because it is where they eke out a living from the land—which is not an easy proposition.

Tim Nettleton knows almost all of these people. He's been Owyhee County's sheriff 26 years, and has lived here all his life. His great-grandfather established a ranch near Silver City in 1861, and Nettleton himself grew up there, spending most of his formative years astride a horse. "I thought you were born that way," he says.[1]

Nettleton is something of a legend among local residents, a lawman who is irrevocably one of them. And he does take something of a proprietary view. It's not that he actually sees himself as chief dictator of the desert; rather, in his talk and attitude, it is plain he sees himself as a product of the land itself, and he's been given the job of taking care of everything in it as far as the law goes.

He is a smallish, wiry bit of whipped rawhide, and his well-earned reputation for getting the drop on any cowboy who wants to mix it up, regardless of size or strength, is part of why he's been re-elected every year as a Democrat in a staunchly Republican county. He also refuses to play the standard cop bit. "I have a uniform, but I don't wear it," he says. "Out here, a uniform loses the confidence of the people." It also, however, earns him disdain among other law-enforcement people—but it's perfect for the hard-working, unpretentious people who make their living on the harsh Owyhee desert.[2]

Most of these folk are ranchers, and not the kind who live amid the verdant pastures of popular myth. They range their cattle on large tracts of open brushland—allotments from the federal Bureau of Land Management they usually treat as their own. The cattle feed on the sparse grass that grows between the sagebrush and lichen-covered lava rock, and use either the water holes that pockmark the mesas or, when those run dry, the rivers and creeks that trickle through the landscape. The ranchers use pickups and Jeeps that fall apart after a few years' beatings on the rocky trails that sometimes pass for roads, but the horse is still their best way to get around, and saddle skills are as highly prized as shooting accuracy.

Of course, cattle and sheep are hardly the only animal life on the desert. Coyotes abound, and ranchers (the sheep variety especially) make hunting them a regular pursuit. For that matter, the Owyhee country, despite its seemingly barren appearance, has a real wealth of otherwise vanishing wildlife—lynx and cougars, foxes and weasels, a bevy of rare birds, plus large numbers of deer, antelope, rabbits, raccoons and rattlesnakes. Everyone leaves the snakes alone unless one crosses their path, but the other creatures are all, at various seasons, objects of hunters' and trappers' pursuits.

Not everyone observes these seasons, however, usually out of a "mountain man" ethos not uncommon in the desert: a total belief in self-sufficiency, including the view that the government has no business telling a man what he can or can't do to survive—trapping and hunting especially. This makes them poachers, a status generally despised among the rest of Idaho society. But the countryside is so vast and evading the law so simple that state and federal fish-and-game wardens, understaffed and underfunded anyway, feel fortunate if they can apprehend a few of the more blatant violators and ticket or arrest them, temporarily putting them out of business and harassing them in the faint hope it will encourage them to find other lines of work.

Over the years, though, a subculture of poachers has taken root in this desert milieu, checked only by the conservative nature of the ranchers themselves. It's a shadowy, vaguely scary world. If you wander into some of the backroads taverns where the poachers do their trade—they all seem to be dingy, slightly dilapidated and cluttered drinking holes, where the regulars talking in low tones amid the gloom at the end of the bar all turn and stare for a moment at any stranger who enters—the hair on the back of your neck stands at attention, your beer drains quickly, and you feel fortunate to leave unnoticed.

Claude Dallas, the man who cast Tim Nettleton's legend in stone, was one of these people, but with a twist. He actually was a classic outsider, a white-trash kid from Ohio evading the draft. He had a romantic, Marlboroesque notion that the West was a place where a man could still be a man, the kind of pretentious doofus the native ranchhands liked to make fun of when he was out of earshot, which they often did when he first arrived in the Nevada portion of the Owyhee country in 1968. But he soon made up for it by working harder than anyone else, and developing horsemanship and trapping skills no one expected him ever to possess. After awhile, everyone forgot that Claude Dallas was an outsider.

By the mid-1970s, Dallas not only blended in with everyone else, he had become a full-fledged member of the poaching fraternity. He brought in everything—

mountain lions, antelope, deer, raccoons, sage hens, you name it—and sold them through some friends who ran a bar in Paradise Valley, Nevada, and who had black-market contacts. Dallas would spend weeks at a time in the mountains on his trapping excursions. He paid no attention to trapping and hunting laws or seasons. He did manage to have a few brushes with the law, and once came close to being arrested in Nevada. He told his friends he'd never be caught again.[3]

Dallas was camped at a tree-lined gully called Bull Basin, just inside the Idaho border, on January 10, 1981, when a couple of Idaho game wardens, Bill Pogue and Conley Elms, found him while investigating a report of a poaching camp in the area. Dallas got the drop on both of them and gunned them down, blazing away with his rifle from the hip. While the two men lay wounded on the ground, he walked up to each of them and shot them in the head.

A yearlong nationwide manhunt ensued. Dallas' face was plastered on FBI "wanted" posters around the country. Disguising himself, he traveled around the nation while on the lam, and was known to have visited family and friends in California, Texas and Michigan. He seemed to stay constantly on the move, but all along, Tim Nettleton figured he'd come back to the Owyhee desert. Nettleton was ready for him when he did.

The two murders haunted Nettleton; he had known both men, and the killings had taken place in his county. He kept his ear to the ground, hanging out in bars where he knew Dallas' friends frequented, developing a sense for when his man was back within his reach. When the time came, working with FBI agents, Nettleton and a couple of Nevada deputies raided a trailer in Paradise Valley on April 18, 1982, where Dallas was hiding with a friend. After 16 months on the run, he gave up after a brief attempt to flee in a four-wheeler.[4]

Dallas was convicted that October of manslaughter in the two killings, a verdict that disgusted everyone involved with the case, Nettleton especially—he felt it was a cut-and-dried case of first-degree murder. He stood outside the courtroom and fumed: "Bill Pogue was a personal friend of mine. He was an officer doing his job, and he was killed in the line of duty. And that's the support he gets. When we go up to someone to arrest them, and they say, 'Go to hell,' are we supposed to say we're sorry and walk off?"

Dallas eventually was sentenced to 30 years, which helped mollify the feelings somewhat. But that wasn't the last Idaho had heard of Claude Dallas. A year later, he escaped from the Idaho penitentiary in Boise, and again led law-enforcement officials on a merry nationwide chase before finally being caught in California.

Tim Nettleton hasn't seen anything quite so exciting in Owyhee County in the years since, which is just fine with him. He did plow his airplane into a low hillside a while back, in late 1995; he and his passenger just had time to clamber out before it burst into flames. They lit their cigarettes with the resulting grass fire while they stood and watched the plane burn. But the accident broke his ankle, so he walks these days with a hitch, slightly hunched over.

After 26 years as sheriff, Nettleton is ready to retire at the age of 56. He's sore and he's tired. He managed to persuade the Owyhee County taxpayers, notoriously a conservative lot, to buy a new jail and operations center for his sheriff's department, and now that it's built, Nettleton feels he's reached the pinnacle of his accomplishments. It's time to settle in with his wife, Charlene, and enjoy a quieter life.

Not that all is well in Owyhee County. Nettleton is disturbed about a steadily increasing contingent of what he calls "true believers" joining ranks in the desert country. They've been filing common-law liens and harassing court clerks, claiming themselves to be "sovereign citizens" and making vague threats directed at government officials—Nettleton included. He hears echoes of Claude Dallas in these voices, and he knows that ultimately it is law enforcement—the sheriff and his deputies—who are the first in such people's line of fire.

"We've had a few run-ins with these folks," Nettleton says. "Fortunately, they've turned out OK for us so far. But you never know when one is going to turn haywire."

Nettleton has known most of them for some time. One of the leaders, an occasional ranchhand named David Dean Hawks, he considers a con artist. Hawks, he says, squatted on a piece of property near Poison Creek in the northern half of the county, living in a dilapidated old stagecoach stop out in the middle of the sagebrush. He dug a deep hole out in the road and put sharp rocks in it, so that anyone driving out that way would break their axles or blow a tire, and then Hawks would charge them a rich fee to tow them out. On another occasion, he erected a barrier across the road and started charging a toll for anyone wishing to cross it.

Finally, enough of the ranchers and farmers who used the road complained that the county commissioners decided to send a road crew out to repair it and clear away the barrier. Nettleton accompanied the crew as they arrived, and Hawks was there to greet them, but he just glared and kept his distance. The hole was filled in, and the road has remained open since.

In October 1995, a state trooper pulled Hawks over for a minor traffic violation and found he was driving without insurance, so he wrote out one of the state's $100 tickets for breaking that particular law. The next month, at a court hearing to determine whether or not to suspend Hawks' license in the case, Hawks refused to show. Instead, a friend of his named Daniel Carlson arrived with an armful of documents he delivered to the various officials in the case—the trooper, the county prosecutor, the judge and the clerks.

The papers all had a legalistic appearance, but to the lawyers, court officials and police officers, they were gobbledygook that made no sense. One declared the state's action dismissed "with prejudice" because the courts had failed to establish jurisdiction over Hawks, a "Self-Governing, Free, Sovereign and Independent State Free Man Character."[5] Another claimed the no-insurance citation was invalid, because the trooper had "failed to obtain proper due process" and had engaged in an "irregular and abusive process."[6] Many of the documents included several pages of signatures of local residents who had signed their names with a comma between their middle and last names and had their thumbprints next to their signatures.[7]

It was the first time Owyhee County Prosecutor Lois Hart had encountered these kinds of documents. "I hadn't really run into these folks very much," she says. "I hadn't heard about them. Apparently some of the state troopers had run into this a little bit before." As it turned out, so had some of Tim Nettleton's deputies.

The next encounter came a couple of weeks later in Murphy, when heavy winter snow common to the high plateau had fallen. "It had gotten real snowy and slick out here," Hart recalls. "At the corner of Clark and Highway 78, there's a lady at a stop sign and she sees this car just coming way too fast. He's signaling to go up Clark Road, and of course he misses and wipes her out. He gets out of the car and says, 'Please don't call the cops. I'm suspended. I'll have my uncle pay the damages.' And she's like, 'No, no, no. I'm calling the sheriff. I'm calling the sheriff.'

"So, by the time Deputy Taggart shows up, [the driver] is not around, but he's taking a report from the lady and then Klin Hawks, who's David Dean [Hawk]'s son, comes back. And Dennis Taggart says, 'Were you driving the car?' And he says, 'No.' "

Taggart, though, wasn't fooled; he knew the Hawkses. "He says, 'OK, were you sitting in the driver's seat operating either the gas or the brakes?' And Klin says, 'Well, I was traveling, it's my constitutional right.'

"They kind of go the rounds with that and then Dennis finds out he's suspended and it's going to be a felony driving while suspended and he tells him, 'I'm going to take you in for this.' So Klin tears off one of these—it's their version of the Miranda ruling. So he serves Dennis with this thing and rips off the bottom and gives Dennis the main body of it."

The document was entitled, "Notice To Arresting Officer With Miranda Warning." The opening paragraph read:

"NOTICE IS HEREBY GIVEN: The individual you have placed under arrest and have in your custody is working in the capacity of a Civil Rights Investigator. He demands his rights at all times and does not waive any of his rights, including the right to personal time and property, at any time.

"You are hereby Noticed and Warned that from the time you detained him your actions have been scrutinized. Every illegal and/or unlawful action you take will be documented for civil and criminal prosecution forthcoming under USC Title 18, Title 28 and Title 42 1983 . . ."

The document went on to warn the arresting officer that he would need a warrant complete with affidavit and probable-cause statement in order to take the subject—Klin Hawks—under arrest, and that failure to do so would make him liable for false-arrest charges. It also told him he couldn't take fingerprints or photographs.

"If you ignore these warnings," it read, "it will show bad faith on your part and prima facie evidence of your deliberate indifference to Constitutionally mandated rights . . . You are a Public Servant, and as such you are expected to treat me with due respect."

Deputy Taggart looked the document over briefly, then handcuffed Hawks, put him in the car, and drove him to the jail. Hawks was released on bail later that day.

"So the next thing I know, I'm getting more papers," Lois Hart says. "I'm getting served with all kinds of stuff from Klin": abatement notices, an "affidavit of default," and papers identical in content to his father's. Unlike his father, however, Klin at least appeared in court later that month to present his papers and make his arguments.

At about the same time, more "sovereign citizenship" papers were filed in Owyhee County courts, this time on behalf of a 61-year-old Marsing-area woman named Hyla Marie Clapier. "She was arrested for trespassing," says Hart. "She just decided to move into her sister's house, which had been given to the sister by her mother. [The sister] wanted it back and they fought over the mother; it's a bizarre situation."

Clapier's papers—signed throughout with a comma after her middle name, in the classic Patriot style—argued that any attempts to remove her from the home were illegal and unconstitutional. Before her December 13 trial date, she filed a "Non-Statutory Abatement" claiming that the trial papers she had been served with were invalid because they had failed to establish jurisdiction over a "sovereign citizen" like herself. Accompanying this filing were a "Verification" document and an "Asservation of Invalid Nom de Guerre," similarly claiming that the court papers lacked jurisdiction over her. It was signed by 25 people, including Clapier herself, and Daniel Carlson, too. A smudgy series of thumbprints accompanied the signatures.

Clapier's trial date came, and to no one's great surprise, she was a no-show that day. She did come to the courthouse a few days later, bearing more documents—this time, another "Non-Statutory Abatement" claiming the court had no right to try her. These courts, she said, operated without proper authority, and besides, their papers used improper language:

"Whereas, returned papers contain the extraneous dates, October 25, 1995, 12/13/95, etc. etc., which terminology to Me, is confusing; for the reason, I reckon time in years of Our Lord Jesus, The Christ; and

"Whereas, conflicting provisions of the peoples moral law forbids Me use of said foreign way of reckoning time; and

"Therefore, returned papers contain scandalous matter all to My harm.

"Now, therefore:

"I am returning all of your papers, and shall, henceforth, exercise My Right of Avoidance; for the reason; they are irregular, unauthorized, misnomered, defective upon their face and utterly void, and are, herewith, abated as a public nuisance."

In other words, Clapier simply refused to recognize the validity of the courts and the charges against her, as though she could make her trespassing case go away by telling everyone it didn't exist. Hart filled out a warrant for her arrest, but chose not to push for action on it. Clapier stayed ensconced in her home, venturing out only to go shopping or to file some more papers.

Hart grew concerned about the rhetoric the common-law court believers used, particularly the way they applied the word "treason" to public officials conducting jobs they were hired to do. There was a threat lying beneath such talk; she knew the Montana Freemen had spoken explicitly about hanging those found guilty of treason. And, she knew that it wouldn't be hard to carry out those kind of threats here.

Murphy, a town of about 50 people, is the seat of Owyhee County, which means almost all of its residents work for the local government. For that matter, Murphy is essentially just a courthouse and jail, a small grocery/gas shop, a school, and a few houses. It sits on a bench overlooking the Owyhee River, tucked away beneath the lip of a plateau that shelters it from the wind. A winding, narrow two-lane highway connects it to the nearest town, Nampa, about 30 miles north; on some wintery days, this can entail a drive of up to an hour's time.

It's isolated, and there usually are hardly any law-enforcement officers in sight, since Nettleton's five-man sheriff's office is spread out daily across the big Owyhee landscape. If someone wanted to cause trouble, the kind Lois Hart had seen brewing in Montana and northern Idaho, they could do it very easily in Murphy.

"There are days when the sheriff isn't here," she says. "And the only people left are the jailers and it's just us, and you can see our security is not the best. I had somebody come do a walk-through security check and he pointed out that there are a couple of grants available through the Department of Law Enforcement. I talked to them yesterday; they're gonna send a grant form for at least something like a metal detector.

"I don't want to get really paranoid about it. On the other hand, a little bit of awareness would help. For what it's worth, I caught myself the other day forgetting to lock my back door. All those little slips."

The fear in Murphy is distinctly tangible, the kind that comes from the banal and familiar, because the objects of the threats know only too well the people making them. Small communities being what they are, most of the people who work for Owyhee County have some kind of personal connection to the Patriots. Daniel Carlson, one of the key organizers of the county's common-law court, has lived for years at the family home in the northern end of the county near Marsing, and is well known and, at one time at least, generally liked.

"He has been a friend of our clerk, Jim Huntley, for a long time," says Lois Hart. "Seven years ago he lost a daughter under rather tragic circumstances and Jim was a pallbearer at the funeral. And now he's kind of caught up with this common-law thing and he'll call up Jim at night and go, 'Well, you know, we're gonna have to get out some subpoenas and warrants for you pretty soon. Sure you don't want to come to our court and do this and that?' And Jim's a court guy. He has to say, 'No, I can't show up.'"

Hart is plain-spoken and direct, which has not endeared her to the Patriots in Owyhee County. To gather more information about their activities, she attended a seminar in Nampa offered by the Idaho Attorney General's office to educate people working in the courts and law enforcement on how to deal with the pseudo-legal mumbo-jumbo they were being confronted with. As she emerged from the session, a TV reporter caught up with Hart and asked for her impressions of the common-law courts and the Freemen. "These aren't Freemen," she said into the camera. "They're freeloaders." It was the kind of line that plays well on the evening news—which it did, several times.

"Carlson called up Jim the next night and said, 'What you're saying isn't true, it's not true. We're gonna file liens on you and we're going to do this and do that.' And I'm like, please, file a lien on me. Come in here."

Hart's fearlessness is impressive, but it doesn't always make for an easy home life—and especially not that evening, as her smart-aleck remark about "freeloaders" was played several times on the Boise TV stations. "My husband started looking at me weird. We were over at a friend's house. And we went home, he goes into the bedroom and pulls out a rifle and loads it up and racks it back and lays it down and goes, 'Now you've really done it.'

"Dammit, you know, I don't want them doing what they did in Montana. The sheriff ain't gonna put up with it either, which is good. Still, somebody . . . This would be an excellent place to make a statement. It's real scary."

Tim Nettleton didn't exactly welcome Hart to her job the year before. She was appointed when the previous prosecutor quit mid-term, and she definitely wasn't a local. She was raised in Connecticut, and moved out to Idaho just out of high school with a head full of romantic notions about the West, which she managed to survive. A winding path that led through the law school in Moscow brought Hart to Owyhee County. She and her husband live near Nampa in the county's northern end—just the kind of outsiders Nettleton typically doesn't much cotton to.

However, shortly after she took the job, Hart and Nettleton found themselves working together—ironically, battling the federal government. Bureau of Land Management officials, overseeing the lion's share of land in Owyhee County, announced that not only would their rangers begin carrying arms in the field, but they would begin executing law-enforcement duties on BLM land, ranging from arresting poachers to dishing out speeding tickets. Nettleton hit the roof. He fired off a letter to the BLM's regional director warning her that any BLM officers in "his county" would be stripped of their authority to enforce the law. He forced one BLM officer to apologize for threatening a motorist with a ticket.

A short political brouhaha erupted. Bo Gritz sent Nettleton a letter of support, offering help if he needed it. Nettleton snorts about that one still. The feud ended with a truce between Nettleton and the BLM in which the federal agents backed down on the extent of their enforcement activity, but kept their guns. "They got one manager I think they'll send out here that's always been good to work with," Nettleton says. "If they send the other one, I'll kill him." He's only sort of kidding.

Hart backed Nettleton against the BLM, telling him she'd prosecute if he wanted to take the blue lights off their rigs. So far, he hasn't. "You know, I can sympathize with feelings of wanting the feds off your back," Hart says, "and when you see them acting out and when you see them taking people's livelihood, I start to see why they're so down on environmentalists. It has gone too far. I used to be a tree hugger. I mean, my background is in forestry and range management, you know. I've worked in wilderness areas—and I've gotten a whole new twist."

The U.S. military also has invaded Owyhee County. The Mountain Home Air Force Base is located in the desert to the east and large numbers of military jets regularly exercise over Bruneau. Recently, Air Force officials have been trying to expand the bombing range in Owyhee County, which takes up a large portion of potential grazing land. They made their case at hearings with the public—hearings which always seemed to have that inevitable it's-going-to-be-done-this-way feel.

"I was out here last Saturday at the Owyhee Cattlemen's Association winter meeting and these captains or whatever they are get up there and tell us how to be patriotic, hand over your land because we need this range of this many acres because, gawd, when our planes come in, they need practice and we don't want to have to take tight turns. And I'm thinking, that's what war planes are supposed to do. Those things can turn on a dime. What are you talking about?

"But what really broke my heart was seeing some of these ranchers go, 'Well, when can you tell us? When can we negotiate?' They got all this legal stuff to go through and they couldn't really say, but these people were willing to work with them and I thought: 'To your detriment. They're taking your livelihood away.'"

Hart knows the government well enough to understand that it sometimes can take advantage of a local rancher's generally good nature until he unexpectedly finds himself boxed into a corner, and his very livelihood is at risk, by which time it's usually too late to do anything but become angry. "I was talking to the commissioner, Dick Basque, the other day," Hart says, "and he's saying, you know, it's getting to the point where I can see myself up on my land with a shovel in one hand for my water and my ditch and my rifle in the other, you know, because of those kind of inroads."

Still, while Hart can understand the desire to give the feds a swift kick, she draws the line on making threats and forming common-law courts and refusing to pay your taxes. "That's just crazy," she says.

What worries her is how many people are willing to cross that line—and how many of them are straight-up, hard-working people who have been in the community all their lives. "Commissioner Basque was telling me how he ran into a guy he's known for years at the cattle fair," she says. "They're talking and he says, does your Idaho flag have that gold fringe on it? And Dick says, 'Yeah.' 'In the courtroom?' 'Yeah,' he says. And he goes, 'Do you know what that means?' And off he goes—I mean, into the whole spiel. And Dick was just flabbergasted. He didn't know what to say.

"That was a real barometer for him of what is going on. That stuff is really getting popular. I hear that kind of thinking all over the place. This is really fertile ground right here in Owyhee County. Especially with those really independent sorts who live up in our hills."

Nettleton hears more than a little of Claude Dallas in these people. "They say some of the kind of things he used to talk about," he says. "But I don't think many of them have Claude's gumption. Mostly, I think it's kind of a scam. All of the ones who are really involved trying to get away with *something*."

He figures the real hard-core, paper-filing Patriots who are going to be a problem for his deputies number about 20, maybe 30. "But I figure for every twenty of them that's active, there's another two hundred here who support them. Maybe they won't sign the court papers with a thumbprint, but they'll listen to their ideas and say they agree with them. And those are the folks who worry me."

Some of the constitutionalists' rhetoric really galls Nettleton, especially the Posse Comitatus-style theories about the sheriff being the supreme law of the land. "And then they tell me that because I'm part of the system, that I've disqualified myself as sheriff," he says. "Well, tell that to the voters. They're the ones who decide. They've put me in here for twenty-six years."

It would be nice, Nettleton knows, to be able to forget about all this, all the hassles and the threats the Patriots are bringing to his community in a few weeks, when he's really retired, when it will be someone else's problem.

"Thing is," he says, "it's everybody's problem. It'll still be my problem even when I'm out of here. Just like it'll be everyone else's, too. It's not going to just go away. Though I sure wish it would."

★★★

The desert country of Owyhee County is sparsely populated, but its immediate neighborhood includes Idaho's largest city, Boise, and the well-populated suburban/semi-rural crescent to its west. The cadre of Patriots active in Owyhee County were part of a larger group who began organizing in the mid-'90s in these communities—the cities of Caldwell and Nampa and the mostly rural areas around them. Foremost among the Patriots were a couple of Nampa residents, Steve Pallesen and Francis Rife Miller, who kicked up dust with threats that sounded remarkably like the ones their Owyhee neighbors made.

Shortly after the Oklahoma City disaster, Pallesen wrote an op-ed piece for the Idaho *Press-Tribune* warning that the bombing was a mere symptom of the populace's rising anger. Its title: "Innocent blood of many will fall."

Pallesen described his previous attempts to warn the newspaper: "I called you a coward for being nothing more than a sounding board for what the national press wanted people to know; which is very little and certainly not the facts. Your response was that I was the only one who felt this way.

"I warned you of the pending need for violence if the government did not show signs of listening and acting in the interests of the people. If the government is the parent, then we are the abused children. Sooner or later the abuse must stop.

"Like yourself, I do not wish for violence. I predict that if your paper would take on the causes of the people and place our government in check, then violence would not be needed. Unfortunately, the innocent blood of many will fall upon your heads if you do not change your policies . . .

"Where are the men and women of courage, integrity and truth who esteem freedom and liberty over life itself? Where are the Freedom Fighters? It is time to come forward and make peace with yourself and with God Almighty."

Later that summer, Pallesen, too, had a run-in with law officers over his failure to carry a driver's license. Responding to the charges he faced, he filed a "Letter Granting Remedy" in which he claimed he had been "railroaded" because "in fact I was in possession of a Restricted Permit. These acts are acts of TREASON, for which you will be tried in a court of Common Law now in formation within this Judicial District."

Sure enough, a month later a paid legal notice ran in the *Press-Tribune*, announcing "Courts of Justice: Common Law Venue—Supreme Court." Identical to Daniel Carlson's filing of the week before in Owyhee County, it was an announcement of "our special Rules of our Supreme Court in common law venue original and exclusive jurisdiction." Among the rules: the Supreme Court would be formed of 12 justices, "in purview of Chapter 45 of Magna Charta," which the rules explained was "our organic law and our original common law of England." It also observed that the court "explicitly reserves our right to amend our Rules from time to time of necessity; and in relation to the character of the parties, especially in purview of second class citizens subject to the District of Columbia"—that is, blacks and other minorities, anyone not a white Christian. The notice was signed by Francis Rife Miller, "Justice in and for Canyon county, country of Idaho, U.S. of A."[8]

The uniformity of the language of the filings was noteworthy—both "Supreme Court" documents were essentially identical, and the same wording appeared throughout the abatement claims. The language was strikingly similar to that of the Montana Freemen, but slightly different in certain key areas. Whoever was behind the documents, it seemed, was drawing from the same sources as LeRoy Schweitzer and Rodney Skurdal, but was putting his own spin on the ideas.

The description fits Gary DeMott perfectly. DeMott, a Boise landlord and one-time organizer for Ross Perot's presidential campaign, is the leader of the Idaho Sovereignty Association. The Patriots active in Murphy and Nampa appear to have received most of their inspiration—and information, such as it was—from the ISA. Their documents are identical to those proffered by DeMott's group, which provides legal forms to its followers and tells them they can simply insert their own names and local county names to make them work for themselves. They claim they can show nearly anyone how to solve serious legal problems, especially tax-related ones, through the magic of sovereign citizenship.

"We are the law," declares DeMott. "We are the law enforcers."[9]

DeMott is a little dynamo of a man, a chain smoker with deep lines on his face but piercing steel-blue eyes and a shock of gray hair. He likes to spout anti-conventional one-liners—"There are no federal public lands in the West"; "The judiciary system: A closed union shop is all that is"—and tours the state telling anyone who will listen, usually "patriotic" gatherings at local town halls, that the government is a sham, the only real currency is gold or silver, and that the federal income tax is illegal. Most of all, he tells them that the American court system is illegitimate.[10]

"Our goal is to have an alternative to the present court system," DeMott says. "In a Court of Justice you have due process. The individual's rights would not be impaired."[11]

The focus of his talks is the process of setting up common-law courts. In addition to the stacks of pseudo-legal documents he provides followers, he also offers instruction in the concepts behind the system: a manual titled "On Common Law Procedure," divided into two parts, "The Abatement" and "Why Call A Constitutional Common Law Jury." Following arguments proposed by Nebraska constitutionalist Eugene Schroeder, the manual argues that the United States has been under a declared state of emergency since 1933, making all court rulings and procedures since then illegitimate proceedings occurring under military, or admiralty, law. It describes how to file abatements of the kind employed by David Dean Hawks and Hyla Clapier. It prescribes the common-law court system as the ultimate solution to end the usurpation of Americans' rights, which it says have been stolen by the government through "fraud, deception, usurpation, coercion, treason, bribery, extortion and other crimes."[12]

Blacks, Asians, Hispanics or Jews, however, need not apply. The manual explicitly offers the definition of "citizen" eligible for duty on a common-law jury: "One of the Sovereign people. A constituent member of the sovereignty, synonymous with the people. From *Scott v. Sanford* 19 How. (U.S.) 404, 15 L.Ed. 691. This case was pre-14th Amendment pertaining to the white race only." The manual observes, however, that "since this was based on Biblical principles, it should not be a problem."[13]

DeMott himself is, in the Patriot tradition, a model of disingenuousness when it comes to these aspects of his doctrine. When an *Idaho Statesman* reporter asked him about charges that the system is racist at its core, he denied it, saying people of color are welcome to declare themselves American nationals and therefore become subject to the jurisdiction of the common-law court. What he left out of this explanation, of course, is the fact that those people would have no rights—either to vote or participate in the court system as a juror or citizen. White Christians are the only people who enjoy such rights.

Instead, he changed the subject: "We're not Italian Americans, Polish-Americans, Afro-Americans. We're Americans. Not hyphenated stuff. What's affirmative action? That's racist."

Jurors, DeMott says, will be instructed to carry Bibles into the courtroom. Judges will be selected from the "most learned" of the sovereign citizens comprising the court. If someone is found guilty of harming another person, he'll be ordered to make restitution or face outlaw status as punishment.

The same month his followers were establishing court systems in Owyhee and Canyon counties, DeMott himself was setting one up in Boise. The ad he ran in the *Statesman* was notarized by Terry Simmons, a former Boise city employee who served jail time for failing to file state income-tax returns. (Simmons also had identified himself as the "notary public" on a protest filed against Key Bank by a Nampa resident, homemaker Joyce M. Robertson, who had tried passing a $6,372 check based on a common-law court lien and was refused.) And, in mid-December, DeMott held a workshop in Boise, drawing common-law court delegates from across the state, to talk strategy for making the system effective in all 44 counties.[14]

Not surprisingly, DeMott himself got into a scrape with the law. He was arrested for trespassing on his rental property, but claimed he was "flagged" for his political beliefs. But he announced he had no intention of showing up in court. "I'm an American national," he told the *Statesman*. "They have no jurisdiction over me."

DeMott's work, and the resulting uproar his followers created in communities throughout southern Idaho's arid landscape, did not go unopposed, however. Local clerks, sheriffs and prosecutors like Lois Hart and Tim Nettleton did their best to handle the deluge of phony paperwork and threats against judges and court officials. The ISA found its most formidable opposition, however, from a Twin Falls High School and University of Idaho graduate employed in the state attorney general's office: a deputy attorney general named Lawrence Wasden.

Wasden had first encountered constitutionalists when performing work for the state tax commission, trying to collect back taxes through the courts. The toughest cases usually involved the tax protesters Wasden found scattered across southern Idaho: "There was one in Custer County that I can recall specifically, one in Jerome County. I was doing one here in Boise, two over in Rexburg, one in Idaho Falls, one someplace else, all at the same time."

These people were difficult to deal with: "They were, for lack of a better word, pretty mouthy—they filed a lot of garbage documents. The usual sort of thing—they aren't subject to taxes, pretty antagonistic, pretty vocal, pretty acrid attacks."

Most of the time, Wasden says, when push came to shove, most of the constitutionalists would back down and pay their taxes rather than serve jail time. But occasionally, there were those who would go to jail rather than submit to a system they believed was illegal. Sometimes they made verbal threats against their accusers, but Wasden says it hardly ever went beyond that. Wasden himself, along with Attorney General Alan Lance and a host of others, was the subject of one form of Patriot harassment: a lien filed against them and published in the *Statesman* claiming they all owed Terry Simmons, DeMott's "notary public," $100 million apiece.[15]

It was in Madison County, in the heart of southeast Idaho's Famous Potato country, that Wasden first encountered the common-law court threats that quickly became the constitutionalists' tools for fighting back. The farmlands around Rexburg and St. Anthony had long been home to a certain amount of Posse Comitatus activity, dating back to the early 1970s. Also, a number of conservative Mormon farmers there gradually had adopted the similar Constitutionalist philosophy well through the 1980s, and several tax protesters in the county already had had brushes with the law.[16]

When Wasden took Rexburg residents Detsel Parkinson and Gail Mason to court in 1995 over their respective failures to file income-tax returns, the threats suddenly began to fly. In November, Parkinson and Mason each filed common-law "felony" complaints demanding the arrest of Wasden and the judges handling their respective tax cases, Magistrate Mark Rammel and District Judge Brent Moss, as well as the county sheriff's office, the Rexburg Police Department, and members of the Ricks College security force. The complaints indicated the officials named were guilty of treason—"punishable by death"—for crimes ranging from perjury to violating their oaths of office.

Sheriff Greg Moffat announced he was "absolutely" taking the threats seriously, and asked for a new ordinance to ban guns from the courthouse. Moffat also said he planned to make use of metal detectors and to post notices telling visitors to the courthouse they'd be subject to search when they entered.

"All these threats have been sent to the attorney general's office for possible investigation or the filing of felony charges against those who have filed felony charges of threatening or intimidating judiciary officials," Moffat told the press.[17]

A common-law court already had been established in Rexburg in November, headed by Emerson J. Mason, Gail Mason's father. Its establishing papers were the same ISA documents filed the same month in Murphy, Canyon and Ada counties. A copy was published in the Rexburg newspaper as well.

The attorney general's office decided to devise a strategy to confront the common-law courts directly. Wasden, by now deputy chief of staff, went to work that January drafting a bill that would allow residents of Idaho, public officials especially, to easily dismiss or invalidate liens filed against them by common-law court followers. It also made it a simple matter for clerks to refuse to file such claims.

When the State Affairs Committee held a hearing on the bill in February, Gary DeMott and Francis Rife Miller showed up to testify against it, arguing that the legislators had no say in this matter, and that the bill was an attempt to deny citizens their constitutional rights. When it became apparent their arguments carried no weight, DeMott threatened the committee, telling its members that they were next in line to have liens filed against them if they approved the bill. They did unanimously, and sent it out to the House for immediate approval. The next day, they returned the bill to the committee to add an emergency clause which would make its enactment immediate as well—a preemptive action to deal with DeMott's threat. It passed in the House and Senate a couple of days later, with only a few dissenting votes in both chambers.

"That was very satisfying," Wasden says. "It sent a very plain message to these folks."

DeMott retreated for the time being, but the seeds he had sown kept flowering.

★★★

On the surface, at least, Twin Falls does not seem like a hotbed for radical extremists. It seems so *normal*—a pastoral, medium-sized town, with tree-lined streets and neighborhoods where the residents still all know one another. It almost seems like a throwback to the simple, Father-Knows-Best kind of community that your parents grew up in.

Actually, my parents *did* grow up here, and I spent many a summer day in the 1960s as a boy roaming Twin Falls' streets. I would visit my grandparents for weeks at a time when school was out; Mel Aslett, my mother's father, lived on the edge of town, in a big house he had built next to the Aslett Construction equipment yard. We had a horse pasture and, beyond that, a gulch with a river running through it that was great for exploring and being a kid. When those amusements ran out, I liked to ride a bike into town and hang out in the parks, or maybe go to the local drugstore, the one with the soda fountain and counter, and read comic books. In the evenings sometimes, you could catch a baseball game when the Twin Falls' Pioneer League team played at the local stadium, a wooden-bench affair that was torn down years later.

Somehow, Twin Falls has changed relatively little in the ensuing years. I lived here in the summer when I was 19 doing roadwork for my mother's brother, Tom, and again for a year in the 1980s, when I worked for the *Times-News*. A few things had changed irrevocably, but they were all personal; my Grandpa Mel was killed in a car accident in 1971 en route from a job site he was overseeing, and Aslett Construction had become a thing of the past. Mel was the middle brother of a pack of Jack-Mormon siblings who had pooled their equipment back in the '40s to form the company, which became the largest road-building outfit in the state; in fact, they built much of the still-existing freeway system. Through the years, he had kept the drinking, gambling and quarreling brothers together in their venture, and when he died, it all splintered apart. There were only a few scattered successes to come out of the whole thing. One of Mel's nephews now owns a major trucking outfit in Twin Falls, and my uncle Tom ran a reasonably successful seal-coating outfit for a few years. He also was a very successful race-plane pilot, taking the silver cup at the Reno Air Races for several years before he moved up to the gold-cup level—where he took second place in his first few tries. But then he too was killed one day: it was in his race plane, caught in a wind shear at the bottom of performing a loop. Like my grandfather, he died doing what he loved.

I continue to visit my surviving grandparents and other relatives who still live here. Despite the transformation in the world around it, Twin Falls has grown at a relatively gentle pace. Its downtown is still its main retail district, though it is starting to feel the pressure from the standard malls and mini-malls that have set up on the town's outskirts. It is easy to get around in, and generally clean and well-scrubbed; its few run-down districts are relegated to a handful of trailer courts and semi-industrial areas.

The politics here, of course, are conservative to the extreme; John Birch Society membership is still rather popular around the county. Twin Falls voters frequently used to put Republican Representative George Hansen over the top when he was in the midst of his tax-convictions-be-damned tenure in Congress, and the county's contingent in the state legislature not only is staunchly and uniformly Republican, but also occasionally the source of embarrassingly reactionary policy proposals that border on the crackpot. Perhaps, then, it should have been no great surprise to see Patriots organizing in Twin Falls well before the Oklahoma City bombing.

At a dark and smoky tavern on the Kimberly Highway, the monthly meetings of the Twin Falls chapter of the U.S. Militia Association were held through most of 1995. The bar's then-owner, Bill Peters, is a believing Patriot and president of the local USMA group. One of his friends, Bill Tuttle, is president of the state chapter. Peters provided a meeting room at the back of the bar where other Patriots could gather and discuss their plans for opposing the encroaching one-world government. Most of the time it was a discussion held among the like-minded.

When they met in late April 1995, though, the meeting room was packed with non-believers as well—mostly the news media, including a TV crew from CNN, hot on that week's breaking story: the bombing in Oklahoma City and the militia movement that appeared to have inspired it. USMA President Samuel Sherwood was there, having made the two-hour trek from his home in Blackfoot.

Sherwood was animated that night, rather a different figure from the one he presents at his so-reasonable press conferences. He urged the audience to prepare for an apocalyptic future, which included, he said, a star prophesied to crash into the Earth. He said America was falling apart at its seams, calling homosexuals "the dung of perversion" and urging women to stay in their proper Biblical place: the home. Most important, he said, the legal formation of citizens' militias could help all of them survive the turmoil about to descend on the nation.

"Why are we here?" he asked. "We are here for the unforeseen. We are here to prepare for those things which we do not know of, but have been warned about."[18]

Sherwood's audience that night, about 40 people beside the media, was mostly a group of older citizens—people like Bill Steward, a 51-year-old carpenter who had a beef with the federal government's heavy hand in his life. "I don't need the federal government to tell me how to run my life—from seat belts to speeding—or how to raise my kid," he said. The crowd applauded.

Bill and Helen Trowbridge were there. Bill Trowbridge, a toothless 59-year-old, had lived in Twin Falls all his life, making a living as an explosives contractor. He once did some dynamiting work for my Grandpa Mel's road-building company. Now, living in a ramshackle house on the edge of town, he and his wife have grown to fear and ultimately resist the federal government—they haven't paid a cent in taxes since 1977—and hope militias are the answer.

"I don't want no more rights of mine taken away," Trowbridge said.[19] This was not an irrational fear for Trowbridge, since he was shortly thereafter convicted of felony tax evasion.

As the summer and fall wore on, the energy to organize militias, especially in the wake of the Oklahoma City bombing, waned in Twin Falls, so Bill and Helen Trowbridge tried to pick up the pace by organizing a local common-law court. They became involved in Gary DeMott's Idaho Sovereignty Association, and set about to establish a Twin Falls County common-law court. Helen and Bill both became well-known in this circle, and signed as jurors for several of the Nampa and Murphy common-law documents filed by Hyla Clapier and David Dean Hawks.

In January, Bill Trowbridge crashed his car into a pickup driven by a pair of newlyweds. Of course, he had no insurance to cover the damages—not to mention the usual driver's license and plates. He also injured the couple. However, by February, the Trowbridges had formed the Twin Falls common-law court, organizing weekly meetings—which began drawing as many as 70 people, though usually about 30—and filing the ISA forms with the county clerk, which came in handy for Bill's traffic citation. Rather than face the charges from the case, Trowbridge filed an ISA "writ of abatement" with the regular court and said he'd respond in a common-law session.

Helen told Liz Wright, a Twin Falls *Times-News* reporter, that she and her husband considered themselves exempt from the traffic system and its courts. Even though both of them faced sentencing that spring on their tax-evasion convictions, they intended to pay the medical expenses of the injured couple themselves, she said—after all, personal responsibility "is the whole premise behind common-law court."

One of their "court clerks," Linda Smith of nearby Wendell, said the whole thrust of the movement is to return the nation to a time when people "volunteered their time to take care of their needs." "There is a revolution that is going on across the country, and they don't want to admit it," Smith told Wright. The current system, she added, is "a house of cards. And that house of cards is going to fall. When it does, the people who rely on the system will fall with it."[20]

Outside of the circle of fellow believers, though, few people took the Trowbridges and other Patriots seriously—until that spring, when their seeds began bearing fruit.

One of the group, a 68-year-old Hansen man named Joseph Michael Brazier, walked into the town's television station, KMVT, packing a .22-caliber pistol and wearing an old Navy enlisted man's uniform. On its back were the words "United Nations Militia," and the words "U.N. Judge" were emblazoned on the front.

He asked at the front desk for reporter Charles Lemmon and station manager Lee Wagner, saying he wanted to make a "citizen's arrest" on the basis of a common-law court complaint. Instead, Twin Falls police arrived, guns drawn, wrestled with Brazier and hauled him away to face charges of aggravated assault, disorderly conduct and trespassing.[21]

The Trowbridges fared not much better that May when they were finally sentenced in a Boise courtroom for tax evasion. Bill and Helen took turns arguing in court that they were not subject to the court's jurisdiction, pointing to the gold-fringed "Maritime law" flag as proof the government was waging war on its citizens. Judge Lynn Winmill quickly dismissed their pleas and handed them federal prison terms—18 months for Bill, 15 months for Helen. The judge gave Helen 30 days to get the family's affairs in order, but ordered Bill immediately taken into custody, in part because he had been arrested the week before for speeding and improperly transporting explosives.

As they left the courtroom, Bill was led away in shackles by U.S. marshals, while Helen remained with the family. "Wait a minute. Wait a minute," Helen called out. "Do I get a hug before he leaves?"

Bill turned and asked the bailiff. "He said, 'no,'" Bill answered, shrugging.

"Bye, Bill," another family member called out. "I love you."

"See you guys," he answered in a gruff voice, and with a wave was gone.

The Trowbridges' children and grandkids were all there. Some cried. Most of them were confused, and couldn't understand why their aging grandparents were going to jail. Their 17-year-old granddaughter, Renae Rice, said she and other family members "are just curious about how they got into this."

Her mom, Susie Rice of Twin Falls, was wistful. "I think it would make it a better place if they were at home," she said.

Still, she said, "I feel that if they believe in it well enough to go through this, then I support them even though I don't really understand what it is they're doing."[22]

★★★

They say in Idaho that the land shapes the person, and this is often true. But when it is true, it is not always a good thing.

The land in southern Idaho is harsh and unforgiving. There is little room for compromise. The people who come from the land often possess similar characteristics, because they reflect its toughness: the expanses of sagebrush and lava rock, a desert plateau transformed in large patches into productive farmland, a place where the sun bakes you mercilessly in the summer, and the winter simply encases everything in ice and snow, and the wind blows in harsh gusts through all the seasons. One doesn't simply live there; one survives. This affects a person's outlook in a direct, fundamental way. When your success or failure at growing crops, or herding cattle or whatever it is you do, decides whether or not you'll make it through the winter, you take a hard view of anything that stands in your way. The idea of an anonymous deskbound bureaucrat back East who has never looked crossways at a cow telling you how to run things is, well, downright contemptible.

The land's harshness especially shaped the generation that nowadays we call our senior citizens, the people who became adults here during the Depression, before the insulating conveniences of modernity made the matter of sheer survival something to be taken for granted. In their time, the wolves of the southern Idaho landscape were much closer on their heels. People of this age—people like my paternal grandfather Alex, or my maternal grandmother Rosella—grew as hard as they needed to be, and often in completely different ways. The landscape, like the winds that chiseled the desert rock, had a way of molding a person's innate character into sharp relief.

There is a photo in one of our family albums—of a gathering of farming folk smiling for the camera—that looks like it could be of a Sunday outing or a community building project. At the center of the picture is a heap around which the menfolk are standing, their shovels and pitchforks at their sides. At first glance it appears to be a dirt mound, but then you realize that it is comprised of rabbits—thousands of jackrabbits, all clubbed to death and tossed together in a mountain of soon-to-be-rotting fur.

Jackrabbits were the natural enemies of the pioneer farmers of southern Idaho, especially after the appearance of projects like the Minidoka irrigation works that attracted a wave of immigrant Germans who promptly chased off or trapped the coyotes, bobcats and other predators. The result was a regular cycle of heavy rabbit populations, about every five or seven years apart, when the scrawny, tough, rather rodentlike and generally inedible species native to the sagebrush plains exploded across the farmlands and ate nearly everything in sight.

So the farmers held community rabbit drives in those years, sort of in the same spirit as barn building and similar acts of neighborliness. The men set out nets in the targeted areas, and then the kids would all drive the rabbits into them. Once the critters were trapped, everyone would wade in with a club, pick the bunnies up by the ears and whack them across the back of the skull, which would kill them instantly.

It all seems rather brutal now, but it was a mere fact of survival and the source of no anguish whatever for the farmers, outside of the amount of work it cost them. Poisoning was out of the question, since it had the nasty effect of getting into the water and into the food chain. No one dreamed of using guns in these situations; they were more likely to cause suffering, since misses were inevitable, and the clubs didn't miss; and besides, it would have been a good way for someone to get shot, since many of these farmers were only marginally skilled with a gun. No, the whole system was the best the farmers could devise, and proved reasonably effective over the years. Eventually, jackrabbit populations came under a greater degree of control as more of the Idaho desert was converted to farmland and better means of control came into being.

Nonetheless, in the early 1980s, farmers in the Mud Lake area north of Idaho Falls encountered just such a jackrabbit explosion and decided to use the time-honored tactics of their forefathers by organizing a rabbit drive. But this time around, the drive was taking place in the context of a modernized world incapable of comprehending the Idaho landscape's harsh code of survival. When word of the planned mass clubbing got out, a horde of media descended on the drive—not just local and state reporters, but TV crews from the national networks, all of whom seemed intent on portraying the hick farmers of Idaho as a collection of brutal louts. Watching the broadcasts that night, as the drive went on and a small passel of squealing jackrabbits were clubbed to death on national TV, I thought the portrayal succeeded rather well.

I was always fascinated as a child by the shot of the jackrabbit mound, but my favorite old photo from this family album, in truth, was a portrait of my father's parents, Alex and Ruth. Actually, it is their wedding photo, though you could not tell by looking at it, since there are none of the trousseaus and rows of groomsmen that comprise such portraits now. It is just the two of them, standing in front of a farmhouse, she in a long, dark, fancy flapper-style dress, crowned with a rhinestone tiara, he with a simple, short-sleeved white shirt buttoned at the collar—the closest thing they could afford, I suppose, to formalwear. Still, they look rather dashing and high-spirited—Alex was a handsome man, with sexy curls that hung down his forehead, while Ruth had dark good looks that suggested a fieriness before it gave way to severity.

This photo was so fascinating to me because it was a window not merely to another time, but to completely different people, it seemed, than the ones I knew. The Ruth and Alex who were my grandparents always seemed to me to be rather tough, sharp and often dour Germans, serious-minded and yet suspicious of the modern world to the point almost of superstition. The idea of them kicking up their heels, to be honest, astonished me.

In the years since I became an adult, I have had many long talks with Alex—mostly one-sided remembrance sessions as he recounted stories from his youth, stories that helped fill in gaps of what I already knew of our family history. Alex and Ruth, it seems, married in defiance of their respective parents because, even though they both were Germans, they came from different Protestant sects. They didn't care, though. They were in love and full of life. They liked to head down on Friday nights to a roadhouse a few miles from their farms and drink a few beers and dance and smoke cigarettes, Ruth especially. Life was full of promise and dreams then.

After they were married, Alex approached his father, David Neiwert, about farming a piece of land out on an unused portion of the family property. The old man had a well-earned reputation for being hard-nosed. As a young German farmer living in the Ukraine at the turn of the century, he had been conscripted into three years' service in the Russian army, manning a cannon brigade near Vladivostok during the Russo-Japanese war. When he finished up his service, during which time his family had no idea whether he was alive or dead, he showed up at the farm one day and announced they'd be moving to America. Within the year, the Neuwerths now Neiwerts (their name transmutated by Customs officials), had settled into a tract farming the newly irrigated lands of southern Idaho. He built up a steady living through hard-fisted thriftiness and hard work.

So perhaps it was no surprise when the old man turned Alex down flat, and never gave a good reason why. Maybe he thought he'd teach his wild young son a lesson. Alex went to work on the railroad, employed on crews repairing and building track. He was earning about 25 cents a day. Ruth lived with him in the tents in the middle of the sagebrush for a few months, but when she became pregnant, he sent her back to her father's farm near Rupert to live while he stayed on the road. My father was born that September in a little one-room building my great-grandfather David Schorzman, Ruth's father, had built out behind the main farmhouse.

Eventually Alex, who was handy with tools and could make just about any kind of engine run, found a job as a Ford mechanic at the dealership in the nearby town of Rupert, and it was there that his young family first set up a home of their own. A girl, my aunt Ruby, was born two years after my father. A few years later, Alex moved to Twin Falls and a job at the Ford garage there, where he remained for the next 20 years; so it was in the "big town" that my father and his sister grew up and graduated from high school.

The relationship with Alex's father was never fully repaired; Alex and Ruth rarely visited the Neiwert family farm, where they were often treated as hopelessly citified. My father says Ruth just didn't care for Alex's family in general. Alex and David were still mostly unreconciled when the old man died in 1950, and Alex's relationship (and by extension, my father's) with much of the rest of his family remained uneasy. Indeed, I can't recall having met anyone from Alex's side of the family in all my years growing up in southern Idaho, outside of my great-aunt Dolly Pendrey. But she was another story.

Compared to the gregarious and fun-loving Aslett family on my mother's side, Alex and Ruth and their side of the family always seemed to me so much more sober and serious and tense. Somewhere in their lives, their dreams had been crushed—all the fire and spark visible in that old wedding-day photo was snuffed out, seemingly by the hardness and cruelty of the land itself. Perhaps it happened sometime back when the old man turned Alex away. Most likely, it was in that canvas rail-camp tent out in the middle of the desert, when they realized Ruth was pregnant and they were dirt-poor and their love wouldn't be enough to sustain them. Who knows? All I know is that by the time my father was a young man, fresh out of the service with a first child, his own high hopes—he wanted to go to college on the G.I. Bill and become a forest ranger or game warden—were shot down with as little mercy by his own parents, who told him he had to give the idea up and go to work right away to support his new child, which he did. This family tradition—the snuffing of dreams—fortunately ended there.

I still try to visit my maternal grandmother when I pass through Twin Falls. My grandmother Rose lives in a somewhat upscale mobile-home park south of town now. The old family house was sold off after Tom, her only son, was killed in the plane crash. She dated a local farmer and longtime John Bircher, Mel Sackett, for over 15 years after my grandfather Mel's death. However, she eventually married a former merchant mariner named Virgil who lived in Arizona but met Rose while visiting his sister in Twin Falls. Virgil is a good old boy very unlike my grandfather Mel in many of his views and his manner of expressing them, which caused some tension among the daughters for a few years, but he is very much like Mel in his generosity and kindness, so acceptance has come gradually if grudgingly.

When I visit Rose, it's always a congenial time. The toughness she inherited from the land has become a rock-solidness in her later years; well into her 80s, she still likes to fish and boat and get outdoors a lot, though she had to sell her snowmobile a few years back because her hips couldn't take it anymore. Virgil has become a fundamentalist Christian and spends a lot of time listening to Christian radio shows and audio tapes, and Rose has become very religious now too, though she insists on their continuing attendance at a non-fundamentalist church where the pastor is actually rather liberal. She tells me she prayed about it and God told her they should stay with that church.

Alex, too, has become religious, but not in the same way. When I visit him, he seems to be obsessed now with visions he has of the end of the world, the end of creation. To be honest, I am a little worried about him.

Ruth died in 1991 after a long battle with emphysema—she never did quit the cigarette habit she picked up at those old roadhouses—and he still lives in their house in a modern Twin Falls subdivision, where they moved in the 1980s. Unlike Rose, he seems never to get out of the house, except perhaps to visit his daughter Ruby, who lives about a mile and a half away in another new subdivision, or to putter about in his garden in the summer. He does get out now and then for funerals of family members and old friends. All of his brothers but one have died, and most of Ruth's siblings have passed on now too. It is clear that he is at something of a loss now that Ruth is no longer there. She always was the agenda-setter, and now that she's gone, he simply has no agenda. My brother Barry and his family, who live an hour and a half north in Hailey, drop in sometimes to see him too, and I know Ruby and her husband, Emery Pedersen, try to keep him from becoming too lonely.

Still, the tone of our talks, when we have them, is worrisome. Alex was always a little prone to conspiracy theories; back in the 1980s, he was an avid supporter of Lyndon LaRouche, the purveyor of many far-right legends about international bankers who control the economy. It seems possible, even probable, to me that Alex, as a worker in Ford auto shops where the book *The International Jew* circulated back in the 1930s, was exposed to Henry Ford's seminal anti-Semitic tome, whose ideas were much the same as LaRouche's. However, I have never asked him about it. I have been taken aback from time to time by his attitudes about race. Once, when I asked him about some football game or another in an attempt to engage him in some "guy talk," he instead launched into a tirade about professional sports, which he said he despised because they all were nothing but a bunch of "drug-taking nigrahs." I changed the subject.

For all of that, I have always appreciated many of the things Alex has talked to me about. He believes what happened to the Indians was outrageous genocide, and he mourns the loss of Indian cultural values, though he is just as likely to pronounce scorn for the drunken Indians he sees as the chief product of the reservation system. Mostly, I enjoy the pioneer lore and stories he passes along, always leavened with a lesson of some sort or another. My latest visits, though, have grown increasingly dark. I try to ask him about life in the old days again, and he remembers a railroading story or two, but soon the conversation turns to a tirade against the modern world.

"It's all just a big damn mess now," he tells me. "The whole stinking world." People don't understand what's important anymore, he says; they're all in a big race for money and power. I agree with him.

"Someday," he says, "not too far away, the Man in Heaven who made it all is just going to come down and clean house. This will all be swept away in a great wrathful fire. There will be nothing left. It'll all be gone. That's what's coming."

I say nothing. I don't know what to say. My grandfather has been peering into the abyss for so long now, waiting for his own death to overtake him as it did Ruth, that he seems unable to turn away from it. I have no wish to join him. Though I have always tried to listen to my grandfather, I am not ready to start staring over that edge.

As I leave that evening, it strikes me that this is how it happens: how the land can damage people when it hardens them, how their outlook becomes so thick with disappointment that they come to believe the whole world is rotten at its core—indeed, the world conspires against them at every turn. Alex has not joined Bill and Helen Trowbridge's common-law court and I doubt that he ever would. But their paths are not very dissimilar. When your dreams are crushed early, and all that is left is surviving and living a raw existence afterward, the world takes on a different appearance. Eventually, any of its good—the families we raise, the friends we make, the good times in our memories—seems to fade, so that all that is left to contemplate is the exposed greed and venality and meanness: the abyss. Some, like my grandfather, merely gape in despair, while others, like Bill and Helen Trowbridge, fling themselves headlong into it.

I'm thankful I wasn't damaged this way, but I am a little ashamed, too, because I have said nothing to him to counter this, just as I have fallen silent in the past when confronted with this dark side. I love my grandfather, and I cherish the short times we are able to spend together. So I say nothing, because I don't want to get into an argument with him. I tell myself we are just going to disagree on this subject, and I find something else to talk about.

And I know that this is how it happens too: As the people we love wander toward the abyss, we do nothing to stop them, because it's easier that way—better to avoid their anger and hope they don't get any worse. And, when they finally teeter over the edge, we wonder in anguish how it could have happened.

★★★

The house Samuel Sherwood lives in is not very far from the place I rented when I lived in Blackfoot in the early 1980s, a lower-middle-class neighborhood in a town that is not exactly upscale to begin with. Blackfoot is in the heart of potato-farming country and nestles up to the border of the Shoshone-Bannock Indian Reservation. It has a split personality, wavering between being a spud-farming town and a reservation town (appropriate, I suppose, since it is also home to the state mental hospital). Mostly, it leans to the farming side of things.

The sidewalks in this neighborhood are sporadic at best, and there are none in front of the old, white two-story house where Sherwood lives. There are children's toys scattered around the yard, and a beater car sits in the driveway, apparently defunct. I wend through boxes on the porch and knock on the door. A pretty, dark-haired young girl, about 12 years old, answers the door and peers out through a crack. I explain to her who I am. She says she'll be right back and closes the door.

Soon it reopens, and Sam Sherwood's wife opens the door and lets me in. She says Sam will be right in, and invites me to a seat on the couch, then leaves to return to her work in the kitchen. It is the middle of a bright winter day, but the house is dark because all the curtains on the smallish windows are drawn shut.

There are a few books and papers lying about. On the wall above the fireplace mantle is a huge framed print of a painting known well to most Mormons, a depiction of George Washington kneeling, receiving divine inspiration at Valley Forge: a testament to the inexorable twining of Mormon faith and the American mythos, expressed in their belief that the Constitution is a divinely inspired document. The house has the musty smell of cooked potatoes. I turn on a lamp and go over my notes before Sam Sherwood arrives downstairs.

In press accounts, Sherwood is mercurial. On one occasion he's the classic Bible-thumping rabble-rouser churning up the crowds, while on others he's reasonable, pleasant and surprisingly knowledgeable about a wide range of subjects. Perhaps Sherwood's most notorious moment came in March 1995 when, ranting to a Boise audience about how public servants in the federal and state government were plotting treasonous acts, he reportedly urged the audience: "Go up and look your legislators in the face, because some day you may have to blow it off." The state press picked up the comment, and Sherwood became the subject of wide-ranging public denunciations. Before the outrage reached a crescendo, Sherwood confirmed to Twin Falls *Times-News* reporter Frank Lockwood and city editor Mark Kind that he had made the remark, but within a week he began claiming he had been misquoted. One eyewitness suggested that Sherwood was actually making the remark as a way of arguing against the use of violence.

Whether or not he said it or meant it the way it was construed, it's clear Sherwood likes to fire off attention-getting one-liners that someone less prone to speculation and more prone to action might just act upon. That same winter, Sherwood appeared at a militia-organizing meeting in Challis, a mining town on the edge of the Salmon River wilderness, and made wildly inflammatory remarks. A judge's ruling the month before had raised the prospect that biologists' plans to help the once-magnificent runs of salmon that passed through Challis en route to and from their spawning grounds could also shut down mining and logging operations on the surrounding lands, and thereby throw thousands of people out of work.

"We're ready to look the federal government in the eye," he told the gathering. "We want a bloodless revolution, but if the bureaucrats won't listen, we'll give them a civil war to think about . . . All it's going to take is this crazy judge to close down central Idaho, and there'll be blood in the streets."[23]

At another winter meeting in Boise, Sherwood launched into the visiting lieutenant governor, Butch Otter, who tried to explain to an audience of Patriot believers that, no, a planned "Conference of the States" scheduled for that September did not intend to transform into a constitutional convention that would do away with the current system of government. Sherwood had suggested this was the case in his earlier remarks to the crowd. The convention in question, in fact, was designed to bolster states' rights, and Otter hoped to persuade his audience that this was the case.

"You've been tricked, Butch," Sherwood shouted. "You've been tricked. A lot of you have been tricked." Otter ultimately fended off the angry crowd by reminding them that regardless of how strong their feelings were, they had to continue obeying the law.[24] After the ordeal was over, Otter thenceforth politely declined any further invitations to Patriot gatherings.

Like his Militia of Montana counterpart John Trochmann, Sam Sherwood is something of an enigma—if for no other reason than that, unlike Trochmann and most of the Patriots, he does not reject the legitimacy of the current system of courts and legislatures. Even as he's urging his followers on with visions of blood in the streets, he counsels them to stay within the law and change the system through legitimate means. The meeting with Otter was part of Sherwood's overt attempt at winning over mainstream politicians to his agenda, even though it had rather the opposite effect.

How he came to this philosophical juncture is unclear. He first appeared in Patriot circles in 1992, when he was involved in helping a group of Patriots in Madison County, Idaho, organize one of the first militias in the nation, the Constitutional Militia Association. Eventually he pulled out and the fledgling group folded its tent, ostensibly because of what Sherwood called "loose cannons" in Madison County. The next year, 1993, he moved his family from Utah to Idaho and set up shop with the U.S. Militia Association.

Certainly, there's nothing extraordinary about Sherwood's appearance, when he finally makes his way downstairs. He's a medium-built man of average height, with thinning brown hair and a ruddy complexion, and he wears a nice white turtleneck shirt and Dockers, relaxing into the big chair in front of the Washington painting. If there was any question, it is clear in the first minute of the interview that the face Sherwood is presenting this morning is the reasonable, mainstream one—not the rabble-rousing visionary of USMA gatherings.

The USMA's current agenda, he says, is to persuade lawmakers to make the militias part of a legitimate, state-approved armed force. "We have statewide, have tried to push the leadership towards the state people, and make them move toward the legislative agenda more," he says. "So that's our business right now—just trying to build that kind of leadership.

"Title 32 of U.S. Code has the provision for each state to have other defense forces. In the original language of the 1960 National Defense Act, it called that a militia. Still within states, state language, over 17 states have state militias in the form of state militias, state guard, or state defense forces. Washington, Oregon, California, Utah, New Mexico—just in the western states, all have those in place. We have encouraged every one of our people who belongs to the United States Militia Association to go join their state guard, join their state defense forces.

"We are a political awareness organization, with the idea of bringing to pass the furtherance of these things and making them grow. Instead of being 50 or 60 or a hundred guys, they should be 5,000, 50,000 guys. There should be 50,000 people in the Utah State Guard, or state defense forces as they call them.

"And in fact the militia movement has hurt what we're doing because it is viewed as the shadow, vigilante type of thing, what I call the angry guys—you know, guys with guns and green grousing about the government."

Indeed, Sherwood stresses the distance between his organization and traditional Patriot groups, especially those in the Gritz and Trochmann style: "They haven't got a picture. They don't understand that all that is is anarchy. The moment you assume you're above the law, the moment you assume you're beyond the civil government which you formulate constitutionally, you're no better or worse than the Panthers or the ADL."

Sherwood laughs at MOM-style conspiracy theories, especially tales of troop movements and black helicopters. He says his organization has checked out many of the claims and found nothing there: "You don't find any of this stuff. I cannot find 500,000 U.N. troops hiding in America let alone the toilets being shipped to run their outhouses for them or the water pipes going in there.

"It's absolutely ridiculous. Every single rumor that has come up that we've checked out—every single one, every single one of these conspiratorial-type things has proved negative. Haven't found one of them to be true. The enemy is not invading us. The enemy is in Washington writing legislation.

"Fortunately, there's enough good guys there to block it, OK? And even if they pass it, we still don't have any worries about that because we still have a court system, we still have a Supreme Court. OK? We still have an electoral process, we still have a system that works. So what are we pushing the button on?"

Sherwood sees creating these individual state militias as a way of decentralizing Big Government and returning power to the states. "The solution at the state level is for the states to have something," he says, pointing to floods that in February 1996 ravaged much of the Northwest. "Why were so many people caught unawares and their homes washed away? Because the state had no mechanism to respond to dike or sandbags or moves, et cetera. So they couldn't. They put it out over the news—'By the way, people, it's going to rain heavy. If you're near the river you're probably gonna get washed away.' That's about all they could say.

"Why? Because they didn't have the manpower to deal all of the sudden with 100,000 fleeing people. They couldn't set up a camp. They couldn't do this. So they simply threw on the altar a sacrifice to the god Weather those people who lived in those areas, knowing that they would get federal relief disaster funds. As opposed to saying, 'Wait a minute here. Call out the state militia. We have 100,000 people enrolled. Get them over here. We're going to move these people. We're going to get their stuff out of their homes. These 10,000 will start banking this river. Those 10,000 will start dredging it so that we move more water.'

"You see—you mobilize that and protect your citizens. Now you say to the federal government, 'We don't need federal emergency management agents, we don't need FEMA. We do it ourselves. We don't need your money now to clean up after the disaster. What we need is less taxes and less bureaucracy at the federal level because we had 100,000 guys show up and we've had equipment costs and other things that we the state are going to take care of. Well, how are we gonna pay that? Well, we're gonna tax our citizens to pay for that and instead of passing the money to you and then you come back and clean up the disaster, which never works.'"

All this sounds well and reasonable, but when I start probing further about the uses of these individual state armies, I find that Sherwood has thought through their utility in a variety of other areas—the drug war, for instance. Sherwood says the militias could end the drug wars overnight if they were put to work patrolling the nation's borders: "Honest to goodness, guys, we can stop the drugs from coming in from Mexico or anywhere else. You really can. I mean, give me some surplus E2 Hawkeyes and P3 Orions that we can watch every single plane and every single boat coming and going from this country. We really have that technology. We got enough satellites up there that we can do it.

"It takes long enough for boats and planes to get here, that you give Alabama, the Alabama State Guard, a couple of used F100s—'cuz that's all you need, you don't need anything fancy—just F100s and F86s sitting out in mothballs out in the desert in Arizona. Give them to them. Say, 'Now look, here's the deal. When you get within 100 miles within the coast of Florida or Alabama or something you tell us who and what you are and if not we sink you or shoot you down.' And drugs will stop overnight because the good guys will tell you who they are real quick. 'Oh yeah, this is us and here's our flight plan.' You bet. There, now we have secure borders."

Sherwood also sees the militias conducting military actions in America's inner cities as another aspect of their role in the drug war: taking neighborhoods under the control of urban gangs like the Bloods and the Crips back by military force. "Well, we don't have 1,250,000 combat personnel to go get the gangs in Chicago," Sherwood says, speculating on the logistics of such an operation. "Not without looking out your back door in Los Angeles or Cleveland or Washington, D.C. Could the state solve the problem?

"Could the state of Illinois, interestingly enough, solve the problem? They have an 11 million population. Could they drum up a million militiamen and train them and begin to take it back in a non-military environment, but in a civil law-enforcement environment using that manpower on a rotating basis? Every month you go for a weekend, you go for three days to Chicago. You're going to be scheduled to work with certain police units to secure certain neighborhoods and do this and that. Yeah. Chicago and Illinois can solve its own problem."

Sherwood does not see anything peculiar in the idea of military troops being deployed against citizens; indeed, with a worldview that appears to revolve around the concept of a coming civil war, much of his mental energy seems to be expended working out the mundane logistics of an apocalyptic future.

His 1992 book, *The Little Republics,* is mostly a blueprint for a post-Armageddon society—which Sherwood writes will emerge after a bloody war erupts in which "no state will survive" and the nation "shall not endure." Part of the scenario includes the appearance of a wormwood star that will destroy a third of the planet. At the end of the tribulations, Jesus Christ will appear and establish a theocratic government, giving homosexuals, abortionists and any criminal seven years to reform their ways, at the end of which time they will be put to death. The theocracy he envisions has a distinctly Mormonesque appearance.

"What I have said on numerous occasions," he tells me when I ask him about the death penalty for homosexuals, "is within a theocratic government—if we look forward to Christ coming and establishing a theocratic government, then you would be able to solve the homosexual problem in that manner, because it provided for the death penalty for homosexuals in the theocratic government of Israel, which they had for 435 years . . .

"Now, if you want to have a theocratic government, you can solve homosexuality that way. All in favor, please say 'aye.' Now, are we all going to agree upon just who is the savior when he comes? And when and where and who is going to be in charge of that theocratic government, because it's a religious government?

"So just which of the religions is going to be in charge? And is it the Mormons? If you're Mormon, you think you're gonna be in charge. If you're a Baptist, you think you're gonna be in charge. If you're a Catholic, you think you're gonna be . . .

"In other words, this is gonna be a theocratic-type religious reformation of when Christ will set his kingdom straight. And I think you'll find in the Bible here along the lines of 'my kingdom is not of this world.' So just what are we going to have politically as a civil government after Christ comes? The Baptists will tell you it's gonna be a theocratic kingdom. Well, OK, if you want that. The Catholics tell you it's gonna be a theocratic one, the Mormons tell you it's going to be a religion ruled by Christ and governmentally it's gonna be under the Constitution, which allows all men to worship who, where, what they may, or none at all—accepting, not accepting. Well, I'll buy down on that. I like that one. That's a good version. Because it maintains freedom, justice, equality, liberty for all. That's a good concept, I like that concept."

It is easy to follow Sherwood's line of thinking, and easy to see how, following it, he has climbed out onto such a bizarre, long tree limb. It is all so logical, so thoroughly worked out, that Sherwood exudes the certainty of someone assured of his own reasonableness, blind to certain holes in his own logic and how far he is treading from reality. Indeed, he is adamant that his views are mainstream. And, compared to other manifestations of the Patriot movement, it's probably true. Sherwood is clearly not an Identity believer; like most Mormons, he places Jews in a special category and is extremely disinclined to any prejudice toward them; he even applied for Israeli citizenship once. And, he takes great pains to shoot down black-helicopter sightings and the usual paranoid trappings of Patriot beliefs.

For that matter, he sees himself as a moderating influence on other leaders in the Patriot movement. "What I'm trying to do is be the voice of reality and sanity that says—that does not cede the field to the John Trochmanns and the Koernkes and Gritzes and et cetera, all by themselves. If they become the sole voice then the principle will become distorted," he tells me as we wrap up the interview.

"As long as I am willing to be outspoken, I can hold onto the principle and keep the principle in the proper position where it's supposed to be. And that keeps them off in the radical area. The moment I leave the ground, they're going to be able to adopt the principle of the militia, and they'll remake it, they'll be the spin masters of history and remake it in anything they want."

However, within the year, Sherwood and the U.S. Militia Association would be out of business.

★★★

The crusty old farmer who was my great-grandfather, David Neiwert, was alienated not only from my grandfather Alex, but from one of his younger daughters—Dolly, his twelfth child, a lively, brown-haired girl who fell in love with a man nine years her senior, Parney Pendrey, in 1931, when she was 17. The old man absolutely disapproved of the match: Parney was a mere carpenter and he sure as hell wasn't even German, let alone Pentacostalist (he was English!). So the two eloped, and David Neiwert, the man who had once commanded a cannon brigade but found he could not command his own children, disowned Dolly and did not speak with her again for many years.

Perhaps this is why Dolly and Parney were among the few relatives on Alex's side of the family I ever met when I was growing up: they too were familial outcasts of sorts. However, I suspect that the matter of proximity had more to do with it. Dolly and Parney lived in Rexburg, which is a mere 45 minutes' drive from my hometown of Idaho Falls. It was easy to drop in and see them, and they to see us. Sometimes we just had barbecues in the backyard, other times we went on picnicking trips. I don't think I ever knew anyone with as naturally sweet and unassuming, but firmly down-to-earth, a personality as my great-aunt Dolly. Parney was a prize human being too—quiet and modest but well-grounded, not to mention a terrific carpenter.

The Pendreys lived in one of the first pink houses I can remember seeing—a little one-story place just a block or so off Rexburg's main thoroughfare. Parney bought it in 1950 when it was a cheap little dump of a house, gutted it, restructured its foundation, and spent the next year rebuilding it just to Dolly's specifications, including all the cabinetry and the basement storage areas and even a cedar-lined upstairs closet. It contained some of the finest wood craftsmanship I ever saw—all tongued and grooved and perfectly fitted. Out back was the big long garage Parney had built himself, which doubled as Parney's woodworking shop. It was full of tools, the shapes and varieties of which I had never seen before. I always thought it was peculiar that the two of them chose to live in Rexburg, the home of LDS-run Ricks College, where the population is literally more than 90 percent Mormon, the Pendreys falling into the other 10 (more like 5) percent. They always said they didn't mind the

Mormons much, because they generally made good neighbors. And, the Pendreys were more or less used to sticking to themselves, though I think it must have been rough for their son and only child, Charlie, to grow up in an environment where, as I knew all too well, Mormon children could be especially cruel in the way of excluding and tormenting their "Gentile" playmates.

As I grew older it seemed we saw less of Dolly and Parney, though that was probably a product of my teenage pursuits, which hardly were ever directed toward Rexburg. By 1976, I had gone off north to Moscow to attend college, but still returned to Idaho Falls to spend the summer at home with my parents while I worked summer jobs for my tuition. My first week home, I got a welder's job at Mel Brown Company, putting together farm machinery.

Shortly thereafter Mom, my sister Becky and I drove up to Rexburg to visit Dolly and Parney. Dolly had fallen ill that spring with an enlarged heart and was confined to her bed. The doctors told Parney she probably would not live much longer, but she was a strong woman and we all held out hope for her. Still, it was a little shocking, seeing her in bed that afternoon, a mere shadow of the woman I remembered, a solid woman with a healthy build: now she was scarecrow-thin, scarcely recognizable. But she still had that famous smile that could light up a room, even if it was a little pale and wan. We spent an hour or so with her until it became plain we had tired her out. It was the last time I would see her alive.

She died—was killed, really—a couple of weeks later. June 5 was a Saturday, a sunny day off, and I remember that I had spent the morning making plans to put together a house-painting business, as I had done the summer before, so I could earn money on weekends and whatever off time I could put together. Dad was at work at the Idaho Falls tower. He called shortly after noon, and my mom answered.

"The Teton Dam has broken," he told her.

"You're kidding," she said.

"No. It broke about fifteen minutes ago. We're getting the emergency broadcasts right now."

The Teton was Idaho's most recently built dam—in fact, it had just been finished and was being filled for the first time. It was an earth-fill structure located in a narrow canyon on the Teton River, just above Rexburg, where it flowed into the Snake River. Farmers and ranchers in the surrounding valleys had been begging for it to be built for several years, because about every seven to 10 years, the Teton River flowed over its banks and flooded out everyone who lived in its path. So, in the finest tradition of pork-barrel politics, Idaho's congressional delegation as early as 1964 had approved funds for its construction, and the contract went to Idaho's largest employer, construction giant Morrison-Knudsen. However, it quickly became embroiled in controversy; fishermen claimed the dam would destroy one of the nation's best trout streams and set out through the courts to stop it. They only succeeded in delaying it; by 1974, construction was under way, and it was finished in the fall of 1975.

The dam reservoir that June day in 1976 was still just eight months into what was to have been a two-year process of filling for the first time, yet it had already reached the three-quarters mark on an accelerated schedule. On June 3, workers noticed "wet spots" midway down the 307-foot-high earthen wall—signs of water leaks on the canyon wall, though they were not considered unusual at first. On the morning of June 5, though, workers checking on them grew deeply concerned; they called back to their bosses and let them know the dam had sprung some major leaks, which were forming sinkholes in the dam wall. The men managed to fill two of the holes by shoveling dirt into them. But a third, much larger one suddenly appeared near the dam's right abutment.

One of the workmen drove a bulldozer down the dam's face and began pushing riprap material into the hole. But everything failed; suddenly, a whirlpool appeared in the upstream side of the dam, directly opposite the leak. More bulldozers atop the dam began pushing material into the whirlpool itself, in hopes that it would plug the hole, while the bulldozer on the dam's face kept shoving more dirt into the hole. The hole kept growing, and soon the bulldozer teetered on its edge. The operator jumped down and the men scrambled up the dam's face as the giant machine too was devoured by the hole. The hole became a pit, then a bank of crumbling dirt, a maw that now reached to the dam's crest. Suddenly, it all gave way, and with a roar the 288,250 acre-feet of water behind it came pouring forth with a vengeance, throwing first a cascade of dust high into the air before it, and then churning out a brown cauldron into the valley below. The dam had become a canyon wall, a gap through which flowed a gigantic, destructive torrent.

All any of us in Idaho Falls knew at the time was that the dam had broken. Idaho Falls wasn't in the immediate path of the floodwaters, but it was obvious that the Snake would flood over with that much water added to its steady flow, and the river passed through the city's heart. Our home was well away from the river, so we were in no danger. Our immediate concern was for Dolly and Parney: Rexburg lay directly in the flood's path, and their home, located in the flat river plain of the city's downtown district, was certain to be hit hard.

Dolly and Parney's son, Charlie, pulled in sometime that afternoon. He had driven up from Pocatello, where he now lived, but hadn't been allowed to get through to Rexburg. We decided to make our home a base of sorts; Charlie would stay with us until it was possible to get to Rexburg. We hoped Parney would call us if he was able to get to safety. The local TV stations began steady news broadcasts, keeping us updated as the flood moved down the valley and into Rexburg.

Some cameras were stationed on the hill above the town on the Ricks College campus, and from the rooftops of a dormitory relayed the pictures we all dreaded seeing. First came a wall of water about six feet high and as wide across as you could see of the town. Soon the entire downtown was underwater. Houses began floating away. One big, white two-story structure began floating down main street, twisting slowly in the current, until it struck another building and lodged itself there. Trees were everywhere in the water, their limbs and roots sticking out above the surface, and you could see cattle trying to swim through the torrent too. We watched the images coming across our screens with amazement and horror, and prayed that Parney and Dolly had gotten to safety.

Late that afternoon Parney called. Yes, he said, they had reached high ground in plenty of time. He had loaded Dolly into the back of their pickup hurriedly and driven up the hill to a friend's home. We all were relieved. Mom began making arrangements to drive up to Rexburg the next day and retrieve them, obtaining permits from the sheriff's office and making a bed in the back of our Travelall for Dolly. Dad, as a federal emergency employee, would have to go to work while Charlie, Mom and I drove up to Rexburg.

The next morning we were on the highway early. There was a roadblock about 10 miles outside of Rexburg, where our permits let us through. A mile or so later, we suddenly came upon the flood's path: the pavement was covered with mud, as was everything in sight. Water stood in the barrow pits, practically up to the road's edge. The elevated railroad bed next to the road was washed away in large chunks, leaving skeletal rails suspended in the air over mudholes and puddles.

And everywhere, cows. Dead cows, randomly scattered across the farmlands, in barrow pits and wherever the flood deemed fit to deposit them, legs splayed straight out, often straight into the sky. A few of them were already beginning to bloat and swell in the southern Idaho sun.

Rexburg looked like a scene from one of those end-of-the-world movies: houses knocked askew, some twisted sideways into the middle of the street. Trees that had floated downstream with the flood had rammed into a few of them, and I remember one house in particular had a tree driven through it like an arrow. Midway through town, the nose of a school bus was perched up in a tree, stuck there by the flood. The signboard that had been a town landmark—a drive-in joint's big neon sign that announced: "Home of the Famous Rexburgers"—had collapsed in a heap. A muddy waterline that marked the flood's crest—about six feet high—was on every building, except those that had been destroyed.

Sure enough, Parney's sturdily built home was still standing when we pulled up, and Parney's pickup was in the driveway. Parney was standing there, leaning on a shovel and talking to a neighbor. Charlie jumped out to meet him. We were all glad to see him.

"How's Mom?" Charlie asked. Parney hung his head.

"She died last night," he said quietly. He and Charlie walked away together and talked quietly. We all felt tears starting to rise. We had all seen it coming, but it did not make the moment any easier. Later, he told us what had happened: Dolly had awakened in the middle of the night and asked for help going to the bathroom. Finished, she stood up and put her arms around Parney, and then collapsed. By the time the ambulance arrived, she had no pulse.

We simply looked about at the scene confronting us, and the madness of it flowed over the rest of our emotions like a second flood and swept them away. A cow lay bloating in the schoolyard across the street. Midway down the road, a huge house that had been swept off its foundations lay in the middle of the street, awash in the now-caking mud. A few doors down were houses that had been turned into kindling when logs from a nearby sawmill crashed into them en masse.

Inside Parney's house, the same chaos reigned. Everything was covered with wet mud—about a foot's worth of silt covered all the floors. Pieces of straw and grass hung from the cabinet handles and the doorhandles. The furniture in the living room was a jumbled mess, although the TV, surprisingly, was OK: Parney had had the foresight to toss it onto the couch as he fled the house, and the couch had simply floated up with the floodwaters, circled a few times and come down with the TV still resting atop it. He also had thrown Dolly's stereo on top of the bed, and it too had survived intact in similar fashion.

Not much else in the house had. Mud was inside every cabinet; a couple of them gushed out little mudflows when we opened them. Then there was the basement; it was simply full of muddy reeking water that reached the top step of the stairwell. Not far from Parney's house and in line with the floodpath was a stockyard that was home to a large number of pigs, and the water in the basement had the distinct smell of having arrived there via their pen.

What all this meant, of course, was work, and lots of it, a job so big it was hard to know where to start. In some ways, it was a relief, for Parney especially, because it meant there was something to do, to throw ourselves into, that let us feel like we had to shelve our sorrow. And so, for the next few days, that is what we did.

In truth, we didn't know then whether the house would even be salvageable. Many of the houses in the neighborhood had been utterly destroyed—some swept off their foundations, others shattered by the water or the trees it swept along—and federal disaster relief funds were already being quickly promised for the victims. But we started to dig in and clear the place out, because it seemed likely the old house would pass muster when the federal inspectors came around to pass judgment on it (an assessment that eventually proved correct). First came the silt on the upstairs level: a thick, clayey goo that came up in heavy clumps. All the furniture, most of it ruined, went out on the front lawn. Then there were the cabinets in the kitchen; the top shelves were untouched, but everything beneath them was a muddy jumble of broken glass and warped boxes. They, too, reeked of pig excrement.

The basement, of course, was the worst and biggest project. The muddy water subsided only about a stair's worth before it became obvious it would never drain, and we were told that no pumps were available that could handle this kind of goo. So we started hauling it out bucket by bucket, dumping it into wheelbarrows that we then hauled out and dumped into the street, from which we were told bulldozers would eventually come by and sweep the mud away. This process took several days. At the end, I was certain my arms were going to fall off from hauling too many buckets of mud up too many flights of stairs.

From Rexburg, the floodwaters had continued down the riverbed like a gigantic teardrop, bearing a five-foot-high wall of water down the Snake River and sending its normally even-keeled levels well above the banks. In Idaho Falls, sandbaggers who had gone to work with plenty of warning managed to keep the flood away from the businesses that lined the river, though they had to excavate a giant canal at one end of the city's main bridge across the river on Broadway, in order to save the bridge itself from being washed away in the torrent. In Shelley and Blackfoot to the south, the floodwaters took out a few more homes and farmhouses and flooded a business district before it finally petered out when reaching the vast open plains of the American Falls Reservoir.

In the end, the flood had caused about $400 million in property damage and caused the loss of 14 lives. One of those was Dolly Pendrey. Others included a couple of fishermen who had been just downstream of the dam when it collapsed, though one such angler survived by hanging onto a tree and riding it downstream. One of the victims was a suicide: a farmer who shot himself in the head after walking around his devastated farm and seeing his entire family acreage transformed from fine arable soil, famous for growing marvelous potatoes, into a vast plain of untillable river silt.

Most people, though, chose simply to go to work to reclaim their lives. Certainly, that was the case at Parney's house: Dolly's funeral was Wednesday, and we took time out to say our farewells. But then it was back to work. Charlie and Parney stayed with us, and made the drive each day to Rexburg to work on the home. That next weekend, I finally met one of Alex's brothers. August Neiwert, who still lived on the family farm in Burley, drove up with his son Gary and pitched in to help us clean out the basement. By Sunday we had reduced the mud down to knee level, which enabled Charlie to find the drain. We cleared it out, put a screen around it to hold back the heavy sediment, and cleared off more of the mud in a few hours than we had in a week. Now all we were left with was a foot-thick layer of heavy silt. That took another couple of days to clear out.

We also found ourselves with a small army of other helpers: Mormon teenagers. They had been organized by the Church, pulling in members from Utah congregations and elsewhere in Idaho, then busing them out to Rexburg and everywhere the flood had struck. They were cheerful helpers and hard workers, and we appreciated them. If we ever harbored any resentment of Mormons in our hearts over the years—and most of us did—it vanished on that day. Not only did they manage to clear out all the silt from the yard, but they also hauled out the majority of the mud from Parney's garage/workshop, carefully sifting his tools from the silt as they went.

We did, in fact, rely on the generosity of Parney's Mormon neighbors a great deal. We ate most of our lunches at the Ricks College cafeteria, where another army of volunteers kept a cafeteria going steadily to feed flood victims. Occasionally we ate dinners there as well. It was easy to feel fortunate in these circumstances. All you had to do was look around at the faces at other tables: pain, misery and despair were written on the faces of people who had literally lost everything. Some were preoccupied with their large Mormon families of five or six squealing children, all wearing the same clothes they'd had on for two weeks. Others were simply mud-caked, dog-tired and downtrodden. And through all this gathering, there smoldered a quiet, rising anger at the culprit for this tragedy: the government. Not just the Bureau of Reclamation, which had built the dam, but the whole damned—in Rexburg, darned—system.

There was no small irony in this, of course, considering that these same people were the folks who had applied the political pressure that had built the dam. They knew that, too, but it only deepened their anger. After all, they had trusted the government, believed in it, had no qualms about whether the job would be done right. They had been tragically betrayed. Most of them would find it hard to ever trust a government official again.

During the tedious hours we spent cleaning Parney's house, I contemplated those faces at the cafeteria and the feelings that lurked behind them, and came to understand these feelings well. That summer, I too had come to hate the Government: not any specific agency, but simply the concept of it, the fact of its massive bureaucratic existence. I hated it for its venal stupidity—the incompetence that feeds its arrogance and vice versa, like a stupid frantic dog chasing its tail. I learned to hate its obsession with blind adherence to the status quo and adherence to its rules, the way its minions assumed the mantle of power as something outside the communities they are supposed to serve, so that they are somehow above those communities and their well-being. It is a stupidity that, through a blinkered, one-size-fits-all approach, thrusts disasters large and small on its victims, from collapsing dams to monolithic wetlands regulations, with little regard for the consequences. It does not surprise me that, eventually, some of these victims come to regard the stupidity as evil, and from there launch themselves into the abyss.

Parney, however, never did that. Within a few weeks we had managed to strip out all the mud and even most of the smell. All the sheetrock in the house had to be ripped out and replaced, and some of the flooring too, so we stripped it down and then let the house sit open and bare for a week or so in the summer heat. Eventually it was in good enough shape that Parney was able to move back in. Our lives gradually returned to a semblance of normalcy. I went back to college that fall. Parney settled back into his quiet life in Rexburg, made even quieter now by his solitude. Everywhere in Madison County, people put their lives back together, helped especially by the mass infusion of federal funds to help them get back on their feet.

Despite the aid, the bitterness and smoldering anger that I witnessed those afternoons in the relief-center cafeteria lingered on, especially after a congressional investigation of the dam's failure that fall and the subsequent hearings during the summer of 1977. The conclusion: Teton Dam failed because it was not built properly for its circumstances. It was situated on a canyon wall that featured porous rock, which meant the water backing up behind it would actually flow through the rock and around the dam itself, which of course posed a danger to any earthen structure that could erode easily. This was not an unusual situation; most such dams feature a "key trench" at the point of contact with these porous walls which actually seals the water out and away from the dam's central structure. Unfortunately, these canyon walls were so steep that, when combined with the rapid filling process, they created stress fractures in the key trench which allowed the water to leak through. The fracturing phenomenon had already been observed in the failure of a dam in France and was well known among engineers who stayed abreast of state-of-the-art developments and techniques. The Bureau of Reclamation's engineers, however, were of an old-fashioned school that scoffed at such advances and ignored concerns about the canyon's steepness. Their bureaucratic incompetence, in essence, cost 14 people their lives and created a flood of human misery.[25]

For all this, I never heard Parney express any bitterness over what had happened to him; that would have poisoned his life, I think, and made his remaining years shorter. He collected a hefty sum from the government for Dolly's death, but he never talked about it and I don't think he pushed too hard on the amount, because to him it reeked of death, and besides, was something of an insult to the memory of his beloved Dolly. As it was, he stayed healthy, fit and alert for another 20 years. He died in December 1995 at the age of 90, after a brief three-day illness when his respiratory system gave out. Charlie said he was the same old Parney, sharp and witty, right up until the end, and he died quietly in his sleep.

I couldn't make it to his funeral, but I stopped through Rexburg a couple of months later, the afternoon after I interviewed Samuel Sherwood. The house was still pink, and showed no signs of once having suffered a flood's ravages. I chatted for awhile with Parney's next-door neighbors, a couple my own age who had a young son they told me befriended Parney when they moved in a few years back. Parney was still an expert wood craftsman and made things for people he was close to, which he did for his young pal. I was glad to hear he still was making friends, as he always had, in his last years.

About a block and a half away from Parney's house, the county's historical society has put together a museum dedicated to the Teton Dam disaster. It's filled with memorabilia and photographs from the flood, and they show a film about the tragedy once an hour or so. It's kind of peculiar to have a whole museum dedicated to such an event, but then, the damaged lives and hard feelings it generated have remained here, just under the surface of polite Mormon society, and the museum is one way they find expression.

There are other expressions of this anger. They are not quite so constructive.

★★★

Greg Moffat was working for a Rexburg construction company in 1976 when the Teton Dam broke. He was out of work for a week or so, and his house was a mess. "I was here during the flood," he says. "We lived on South Fifth West, just up the street from where I live now. Yeah, I was here. And there were hard feelings about that. There were a lot of feelings against the federal government because of that."

Moffat is the sheriff of Madison County these days, having climbed the ranks from volunteer reserve to full-time deputy to a hugely popular sheriff, re-elected last time with 97 percent of the vote. He's fond of his community and supports it in every respect, but he also knows that there was a flip side to the Teton Dam disaster's effect on the community—namely, the willingness of some people, not necessarily even victims, to soak the flood funds for everything they could.

"The thing I saw most was people going in and taking advantage of the government after the fact," Moffat says. "Payments, so on and so forth. You know, the standing joke was that a few people went up and kicked a hole in the dam that were having trouble financially, and that's what solved all their problems. Even 20 years later, that's still kind of a standing joke. They wish they could build a dam back and kick another hole in it."

Even in a community as obsessively normal as Rexburg—in fact, it is not an exaggeration to say that fully 75 percent of Rexburg is white, Mormon, middle- or working-class, and conservative—there are a few odd apples. Sometimes they are the hidden ones, the people who feign normalcy and scrupulousness but are really dishonest or even malignant, like the people who bellied up to the federal disaster-aid trough for little real cause, or the town's well-known gynecologist who made a practice of molesting his female patients and wasn't caught or charged until he decided to retire.[26] Then there are the people who are more outspoken in their non-conformity, the most vocal of which are the people who hate the government and refuse to pay their taxes. Often, in Madison County, their tirades earn sympathetic nods.

Greg Moffat's biggest headaches happen to be some of the people who, ever since 1976, have been trying to ride the tide of anti-government feeling that flooded Madison County back then. In fact, the most vocal of them all, Detsel Parkinson, was making the same kind of noises long before the flood—but afterward, he found he had a bigger audience. Parkinson's activities date back to some of the earliest Posse Comitatus organizing in the nation, in the early 1970s,[27] and he helped organize Samuel Sherwood's Constitutional Militia Association in 1991 in Madison County. However, Sherwood soon departed, implying that the group was infested with radicals.

"Detsel has been in this for years and years," Moffat says. "He's a sage in this movement, especially compared to some of the folks who have come into it recently."

Moffat has known Detsel for years, dating back to his own days as a construction worker. He also is familiar with Parkinson's ideology, including the early Posse values. "Posse Comitatus, in and of itself, is nothing more than the power of the people given to the people, through the sheriff, from the county," Moffat says. "By law, that's basically what it says. But a Posse Comitatus cannot operate independent of a sheriff's office. That's why they put so much stock in the sheriff himself as being the chief law-enforcement officer, and probably the only law-enforcement officer in Detsel's case that he recognizes.

"So what a blow to him when we fulfilled the orders of the court, and that was specifically to put him in jail. I don't know how he feels about the sheriff's office now. I know how he probably feels about me as an individual, as a person, and I used to do a lot of work with Detsel, and his son actually contributed to my campaign in 1992. They didn't in '96, but that's another matter."

Moffat jailed Parkinson twice in late 1995—the first time in November, for failing to carry a driver's license, and then in December on a contempt-of-court citation after a judge ordered Parkinson to file a series of state income tax returns and he refused to do so. A follower, Gail Mason, was also jailed on similar charges. Within days, they and their compatriots in the common-law courts, including Gail Mason's father, Emerson Mason, had filed their "felony complaint" papers against Moffat, Lawrence Wasden, the judges and prosecutors in their cases and just about everyone else peripherally associated with the matter. The papers followed Gary DeMott's formulas—and were, in fact, simply DeMott's forms filled out with local names. All threatened to try their subjects in common-law courts, and for the judge, sheriff and Wasden, the death penalty applied.[28]

Moffat promptly announced he would take these threats seriously, and began tightening up security at the courthouse. The county prosecutor looked into charging Parkinson and Mason for making the threats, but decided the fight wasn't worth it.

At the same time, the Patriots' activities began to quiet down. Parkinson and Mason did their jail time and returned to their respective homes. Parkinson's home, repossessed by the IRS, was sold at an auction, but his children turned around and bought it back. "The kids, Detsel's family, came in and bought the house back, mostly to see that their mother had a roof over her head," Moffat says. "They moved back into the house, Detsel and Earlene did. But I understand Detsel's mad about his children doing that, and he's going to sell the house and move out of it because he doesn't want to live in that house now. So he's still stirring it a little bit.

"But most of what he's doing now seems to be legal. I mean, he's got a driver's license, he's driving legal. I don't know where he is on his tax debt, because none of the time they spent in jail—him or Gail Mason—was the result of tax fines or tax evasion."

Amid the jailings, the accusations flew. Moffat was called a traitor and similar names in letters to the editor of the local paper. Finally, local citizens decided they'd had their fill. A group of 1,200 of them, including some of the town's best-known citizens, church leaders, businessmen and doctors, put their signatures to a petition announcing their complete support of their local government generally and law enforcement in particular, and ran it as a full-page ad in the weekly Rexburg *Standard-Journal*.

"People here are conservative, but they are also a fairly logical-thinking group of people. It finally got to the point where enough was enough," Moffat said. "So much was being said in the paper derogatory about law enforcement, about me personally, about others who supported us, that finally people just took a stand and said, 'Look, we want it the way it is.' That probably took a lot of the soup out of them. Things really started to die off after that." If there was any doubt about where the sheriff stood in the community, it disappeared after his landslide victory in the 1996 election.

Indeed, as 1996 wore on, it became abundantly clear that the Patriot movement had played out its hand in southern Idaho, for the time being at least. Not merely in Madison County, but throughout the region, militias and common-law courts gradually melted back into the woodwork as it became obvious that, while average citizens might actually sympathize with them, they weren't interested in joining the Patriots' revolt—and many, in fact, were adamantly opposed to it.

Some of the decline, however, was a matter of the organizers losing credibility within their own ranks. That is what happened to Samuel Sherwood.

★★★

All along, there was the frequently voiced suspicion that Sherwood was a carpetbagger come to sell some snake oil to Idaho folks. "My theory on this thing is they were looking to make big bucks," says Sheriff Moffat. "And if the plan had gone together the way they wanted it to, and everybody paid their dues, we were talking about millions of dollars. And where does it go? Nobody really answered that question. I rather suspect they were looking at feathering their own nest. Not only him, but those people he had listed as liaisons, as trainers."

Sherwood's biggest problem was a reporter for the Twin Falls *Times-News* named Frank Lockwood, who was disinclined to take Sherwood's claims at face value. He too was curious about Sherwood's finances and enrollment figures. If the U.S. Militia Association really had 5,000 members, as Sherwood claimed to the media in the summer of 1995, then their $10 monthly dues would have made Sherwood a rich man. Instead, it was well known, both in the town of Blackfoot and in militia circles, that Sherwood hardly could feed his family. Furthermore, Sherwood did not file any tax returns throughout his tenure in Idaho, claiming he had no income, which of course caught the attention of the Internal Revenue Service, who called Lockwood for further details.[29]

This revelation sparked a sharp rebuke from a Republican legislator from Boise named Milt Erhart, who wrote a letter to the *Idaho Statesman* ripping into the USMA leader, saying the only reason he didn't pay any taxes was that he couldn't hold a job. "Sherwood is either a liar or a freeloader," Erhart wrote. "It's time for Mr. Sherwood to get a job and provide for his family."[30]

Lockwood also was skeptical of Sherwood's membership figures. He checked into it and found that the U.S. Militia Association's ranks actually were shrinking, and everyone previously associated with it was running from it as fast as they could, especially in the wake of the Oklahoma City bombing. Only in Washington state could Lockwood find evidence that the USMA chapter's rolls were growing. Everyone else—in Nevada, North Carolina, Utah and elsewhere—either said their groups had disbanded or they personally had quit.[31]

The clincher came that fall, when Lockwood looked into Sherwood's military record and found the reality was at something of a disparity with the militia leader's claims. First, he found that Sherwood's given name was Mason Stanley Sherwood, which he changed in 1993, just as the USMA was firing up. While Sherwood liked to depict himself as having an extensive military background, Lockwood found that yes, Sherwood had three separate flirtations with military service—but none of them ever advanced beyond the training stage. He avoided the Vietnam War draft—where he had a number much higher than Bill Clinton's—by enrolling on an LDS mission. He was inducted into Navy Officer Candidate School in 1981, but was discharged four months later for undisclosed reasons. Lockwood also found a number of other peculiar smudges in Sherwood's image: his onetime efforts to obtain Israeli citizenship, a bizarre episode in which he even listed himself as Jewish on government documents; and his personal non-possession of firearms (until 1994, at his son's urging) in stark contrast to his views on gun ownership.[32]

In the ranks of the Patriot movement, military veterans are common—in fact, they rank as probably the largest internal faction in militia organizations. A man's service record is held in almost sacred esteem. People who inflate their records, who make themselves out to be more than they are, are dismissed with contempt if they are discovered. Internally, that is what appears to have happened to Sherwood's following.

By that winter, hardly anyone was organizing USMA-led meetings anymore in the state of Idaho.

Sherwood tried to defuse Lockwood's charges. "I was able to completely and totally disprove everything that he said," Sherwood told me, "and local CBS channel KID had a half-an-hour program and showed the documents on television, and then following that had a half-an-hour program where I sat there and took live, on the air, no holds barred, any question answered, and completely refuted everything that Mr. Lockwood said."

He backs down now on some of his service claims. "I've never said it's anything more than that I was in Army ROTC and went TDY—temporary duty for training—at Fort Knox, Kentucky, as every good ROTC student does. And then after completing ROTC got a grift from the services after the Vietnam War reduction in forces. They grifted all butterball second lieutenants. And that's the only service I did with the Army. And then went into the Navy for active duty for training for OCS with the Navy. And having three children under three years old and a lot of complications in delivery, wanted a hardship out so that I could take care of my wife and family. And that's all I've ever said. I was in the Navy and I was in the Army. I'm a veteran of both and have an honorable discharge from both. I have the paperwork to show it."[33]

Sherwood's final foray into politics became his swan song. He and officials of the Idaho Citizens Alliance announced in the summer of 1995 that they would form a cooperative effort to gain approval for three major ballot initiatives: a measure to provide the death penalty for performing abortions, another to legalize job discrimination against homosexuals, and the third to institute prayer in the schools.

The ICA is the Idaho version of the Oregon Citizens Coalition, which has tried several times to pass anti-homosexual initiatives in Oregon. Kelly Walton, the ICA's director, first got his start in public activism in the late 1980s, when he raised a large public scare in the Burley-Rupert area by claiming that a satanic cult was operating in the vicinity and was conducting rituals of child sacrifice in the community's backyard. By 1992, he and the OCC's Lon Mabon had hooked up through fundamentalist Christian circles and formed the ICA, which made its first foray at passing a bill that would outlaw "special rights" for homosexuals in the 1994 election. It failed that fall, but the ICA kept going.

By the late summer of 1995, though, ICA officers discovered their agenda had become unpopular, and their new association with the militias may have worsened their image. They tried to set up a booth at the Eastern Idaho State Fair in Blackfoot, a huge affair that draws farmers and city folks alike. Volunteers at the booth were mercilessly harassed; some were even spat upon. One woman told an ICA organizer to go to hell, adding: "These people are like unpopped kernels of popcorn—they're greasy, oily, hard as rocks, and no one wants anything to do with them because they're completely useless." Ultimately, they closed the booth and reduced their presence to passing out anti-homosexual fliers.[34]

A week later, Walton and Sherwood announced their divorce. Sherwood said he didn't want anything to do with the ICA anymore because he had reviewed their proposals and found that "they violated the Declaration of Independence." For his part, Walton said he had consulted with Idaho Congresswoman Helen Chenoweth, who told him that she "regards Sherwood as a loose cannon." And he doubted Sherwood's denials that he ever told people to prepare themselves to shoot off their legislators' faces: "I'm not going to deal with a group that can't shoot straight, and I'm talking about telling the truth."[35]

As late as the spring of 1996, Sherwood was telling reporters the USMA was going strong. Evidence suggested otherwise. In Twin Falls, reporter Karen Tolkkinen observed that the group's newsletter was no longer being published monthly, that Sherwood's political-action chairman had quit, and his plans to put together a petition to legalize militia training had died on the vine.

Quietly, on September 1, Sherwood officially folded the U.S. Militia Association. Interviewed by the *South Idaho Press,* Sherwood explained why: "The whole movement is being distorted on one side by the press and the media and taken over by the nuts and the crazies on the other."

He said the group decided to disband in late June, as the Freemen's standoff in Montana was resolving itself: "We were trying to create a separation between what the Freemen were doing and what the militia movement was doing, but failed. Bit by bit, people became more and more disillusioned and disenfranchised."

At least he found a job. He told the reporter he had moved back to Utah with his family, where he had work as a computer analyst. As for further militia organizing: "We'll see what comes, but I am pretty much done," he said.[36]

★★★

Even Gary DeMott's Idaho Sovereignty Association eventually lowered its profile—after a final burst of threatening behavior. On September 11, a week and a half after Sherwood threw in the towel, DeMott appeared on the steps of the Idaho statehouse to announce that his followers intended to arrest an Ada County magistrate, and possibly a whole array of county officials across the state.

The magistrate who had incurred their wrath was Patricia Flanagan, who had the misfortune to preside over the case of a 67-year-old widow named Shirley Minton, an Alzheimer's disease victim. County officials assigned a guardian to care for Minton and her estate, and her family protested, calling it a case of unwarranted government intrusion. DeMott, on the Statehouse steps, accused Flanagan of stealing Minton's constitutional rights, for which charge she would face arrest.

Further, he called on all county officials—clerks, commissioners, sheriffs, treasurers—to retake their oaths of office, this time including the phrase "So help me God." That phrase was necessary, he claimed, in order for officials to be held accountable for perjury should they break their oaths of office. He said he had mailed out 391 notices to various county officials around the state.

ISA supporters around the state would appear on the steps of their respective county courthouses as "town criers" on September 28, DeMott said, to read the names of all county officials who had failed to comply. After that, they would be subject to arrest by "sovereign" citizens working with the help of county sheriff's deputies.

Flanagan was firm in the face of the threat. "I could dismiss the case right now if I wanted to pacify them, but I'm not going to do that," she said. "If they kill me, I guess someone else would step in." At the attorney general's office, deputy Lawrence Wasden was slightly amused, calling DeMott's documents "hilarious," and laughed as he read copies of them. "The basis of his so-called charge of grand theft is absurd and his group is without any authority to issue such documents anyway," he told reporters.[37]

Greg Moffat figured that Madison County officials would be on the list of those who failed to comply with DeMott's edict. When September 28 came around, he and his deputies kept an eye out for any town crier to show up on the courthouse steps and read the names of the offending officials, but no one ever did. No other county officials elsewhere in the state reported hearing from the common-law believers that day, either.

Wasden believes the Patriots ultimately self-immolate when ordinary people with common sense figure out what they're up to. "Most people that I talk to, they see this Patriot movement—militias, common-law courts—as some kind of a monolithic bloc of people and thinking, and it isn't that," he says. "It's sort of this seething, teeming, whacky ideas that fluctuate from day to day, and the people fluctuate from day to day, although there's the hard-core center that's always there.

"That's why I can't adhere to the 'we're in the middle of a civil war' kind of thing, because they're not unified enough to really do much. The day they get someone who unifies them, that's when they'll become dangerous."

The core of the believers, he says, will always be with us—the hard-nosed right-wingers who were John Birch Society members in the 1960s and are signing up as common-law jurors and sovereign citizens now. They are comprised of two tiers: the leaders, the idea people who spread the gospel and devise the organizational strategies; and their immediate followers, the people who are devoted Patriot believers and follow most of their conspiratorial beliefs and pseudo-legal systems.

What changes, he says, is a third tier of followers, comprising their largest numbers—the people who are disenfranchised and seeking answers to their problems, and think they may have found an answer. These are ordinary tax-paying citizens when they enter the movement, and they either spin off and away when the beliefs edge inevitably into radicalism, or they plunge ahead into the movement. These people, he says, can be reached and dissuaded, if they're handled properly.

"We have the greatest ability of affecting their behavior by responsible actions," Wasden says. "You stand up to them, but you don't be so aggressive that they can say that you're bad. From a government perspective, enforcement to the point where all you do is turn people against you is counterproductive. But appropriate, consistent, rational, respectful enforcement, that is how you will affect that third ring."

As for the first and second tiers, Wasden is pessimistic about changing their views. "DeMott's probably going to be around for a long time—doing the same things in one way or another," Wasden says. "He kinda wears out one group, and then he'll start up another one with the same ideas and concepts. He has to keep himself in the public eye somehow."

Tragically, in the case of Twin Falls common-law court organizers Bill and Helen Trowbridge, the steadfastness of these core believers extended even to imprisonment and death. Locked up in a federal prison in Oregon on tax-evasion charges, Bill Trowbridge died of a heart attack on October 13, 1997.

His common-law compatriots, not surprisingly, accused federal officials of murdering him. "We know they're giving them arsenic," said the Trowbridges' friend and fellow common-law juror, Linda Smith of Wendell. But she said his martyrdom would only inspire the people he left behind. "For those of us who understand, we will probably work harder," she said. "If we don't, they will start killing more of us."

For their part, prison officials said they don't make poisoning inmates a practice. They said an autopsy would be performed.

Helen remained incommunicado at her Texas prison, speaking only with family members. Her son, Lee Wagstaff of Twin Falls, says both his parents had faced the prospect of prison in good spirits, though Bill's death may not have been part of what they envisioned. "My mom said if they had to go, it would be an adventure for them," he said.

Wagstaff suggested he sympathized with his parents' views, but wasn't ready to take that final step. "I haven't got the stamina that Mom and Bill had," he said. "A lot of people, they have to go out and do it. I just don't. I'm just the quiet type."

As for his mother, he expected her to keep on fighting, even if stuck in a federal prison.

"It's probably something that will go on as long as my mom is alive," he predicted.[38]

Chapter 9 / Bitterroot

THE BLACK HELICOPTER spooked Calvin Greenup's elk. Calvin Greenup, too.

It came in low, under 200 feet, well under the restricted 500 feet, buzzing the treetops of his heavily forested ranch, which sat on a bench above Montana's Bitterroot River. The elk scattered in the pasture, and Calvin Greenup went running for his gun.

In his mind, Greenup knew what the visit meant: the feds were moving in now. He had been engaged in a one-man standoff with authorities for nearly a year now, by hiding out on his ranch and threatening to shoot any law officer who tried to take him in. Now, he thought, they are getting ready to make their move.

Greenup got on the phone with his fellow Patriots in the nearby town of Darby. Get the men together, he told them. A black helicopter just buzzed the place.

Within an hour, 30 or so armed men were on Greenup's ranch, ammo loaded, awaiting the assault. If the helicopter appeared again, Greenup told them, shoot it out of the sky. He told them where the fuel tank was, and how to aim for it.

"Yes, I was planning on shooting the sucker," Greenup says now. "Number one, he's not supposed to be below five hundred feet over my property. If he's below two hundred feet, which he was, then he's up to no good, and I'm going to shoot the bastard down. That's what he is, a bastard, because anybody who doesn't know God the Father is a bastard. And that's what those kind of people are."

Greenup says the men got word through the Patriot information network that the same chopper had been at Ruby Ridge. "We found out that that same helicopter was part of the same bunch that was over Randy Weaver's place, and so we knew then that they were up to no good," he says. "As I'm sitting here right now, I'm the first American that has made the statement that I would shoot the next one that comes over my house, I'll shoot him down.

"I know where to hit 'em. I could've got him down. And that helicopter has never come back. And I'm the only American that they didn't at least come back for the second time that I know of."

The armed group stayed on the ranch until nightfall, and some even stayed into the evening. No assault ever took place. Greenup figured it might have been because the feds decided they didn't want to deal with a group of armed civilians.

Greenup sent out a general nationwide alarm, staying on the phone well after midnight with militia members from around the country. Still, nothing happened. Everyone retired to their homes after awhile, but that nervous edge lingered for several more days. Some of the men had phoned Darby's town marshal, Larry Rose, and demanded to know what was going on. The marshal's office was confused. No, they said, they didn't know of any planned actions by the feds. Yes, they said, we'll promise to check it out.

The flyover, it turned out, was an AH64 Apache National Guard chopper returning to its Boise base from Great Falls. Apparently the pilot had deviated from his normal flight pattern at least partly out of boredom, perhaps even to get a look at Greenup's elk. Ravalli County Sheriff Jay Printz told reporters the helicopter had been practicing "low-flying maneuvers."

If Greenup already was inclined to believe the worst, his disposition was not aided at all by the behind-covering mode that National Guard officials immediately reverted to when confronted about the flyover. "See, when I called the National Guard in Boise, Idaho, the same unit that helicopter come out of, he said, 'Well, our officers said they maintained above five hundred feet.' I said, 'Tell your officers and those pilots they are dirty rotten liars, because over a hundred people seen them in this valley and had them under two hundred feet on any given time. So you tell your officers they're liars.'"

To Greenup, the incident simply underscored all of his dealings with government officials, who, he had long since decided, were ineluctably corrupt. "I know what they say," Greenup says. "I know exactly what they say. I also knew what they said when we went into Vietnam, too. I also know what they said when they murdered John F. Kennedy. I also know what they said at Randy Weaver's trial. I also know what Janet Reno said about Waco, Texas, too, that murdering scumbucket.

"They lie. They're not going to tell the truth about it. That helicopter was there for the sole purpose of to get a computer readout on the approach to Cal Greenup's house so they could destroy me and my family. There's no question about it. And until they prove me otherwise, that's the way it is."

It took another four months—four months in which the Bitterroot Valley became a cauldron that nearly boiled over into violence—before Calvin Greenup could be talked down from his ranch.

★★★

When he was a boy, Calvin Greenup would play with the elk that lived in the woods surrounding his family's Montana ranch. The Bitterroot Valley, tucked on the Montana border next to the vast north Idaho wilderness, is as green and fertile as any land in the Northwest, and home to large herds of deer and elk that find shelter and food in the deep woods. Calvin would creep through the underbrush and play hide-and-seek with the creatures, who apparently did not feel threatened by a human as small as Calvin was.

It was then that Greenup established a connection with the great regal beasts—with their great racks of antlers and graceful bearing and majestic power, and most of all, their will for freedom. Something clicked. As he grew older, Greenup developed some of the same traits as the elk—including an easily antagonized suspiciousness, and a willingness to plow over anyone who posed a threat to his freedom.

"I was setting this all up from the time I was eight or ten years old," he says now. His father, who had been a sheep rancher in the Bitterroot country since the age of 15, had taught Calvin how to handle and care for animals. In his mind, Calvin decided to take what he learned from his father to the next step—to raise elk on a ranch, just as other people had cows and sheep. And he began laying his plans to do just that.

Calvin also received an early political education. The John Birch Society was active in the Bitterroot Valley, where it was widely and readily believed that the government had been infiltrated by Communist conspirators, and that belief was reflected in the local schools. "That was going in this valley when I was in school," Greenup says. "My sixth-grade teacher, as a matter of fact, was a John Bircher. And she's the one that started me on the path of teaching me the Bill of Rights and the Constitution. John Birchers were strong then. Underground, but strong."

Young Calvin was on the smallish side and skinny, but he still went out for the football team. "When I was a freshman in high school I only weighed a hundred and one pounds," he says. "You had to weigh a hundred pounds to play football. And I was playing against guys that weighed 185, 190 pounds. And I was successful." However, he was not so successful at academics, which he says he hated.

Once freed from school in 1960, where Greenup always chafed at being pent up for hours on end, he decided to escape this small-town life and see some of the world, so he joined the Navy. "I served all over the Pacific. I was in the Philippines for awhile, and then the ship that I was on hit basically every port in the Pacific.

"When I left Montana to join the Navy, that was probably one of the worst cultural shocks that a young farm boy could ever go through. It was horrible, because when I got off the train in San Diego—I had never been to any large cities in my life, and when I got off that train in San Diego, I was scared to death. I was petrified.

"At that time, I said, 'Man, I'm in the wrong place at the wrong time.' But I was always one, when I vowed to do something, I was going to get it done. So I took the oath, I said I'm going to serve my time in the military, and I did so." He stayed in the service until 1964, and in those four years, he kept thinking about his elk, dreaming about them. "All the time I was in the Navy, it was always on my mind, even in the Philippines, I couldn't wait to finish my tour of duty, so that I could get home and get back on the ranch, 'cuz when I was a young boy, I wanted to raise elk. I wanted to raise elk in the worst way. So in my mind and in my heart, I never did really leave."

He was on leave one summer when he met a cute, dark-haired girl who worked for her folks at the local restaurant in Darby. She had grown up in California, but her parents moved to Montana in 1962, entranced after a summer-vacation visit a couple of years before. Her name was Lynda, and she thought she had been forced to take up residence in the country's biggest backwater, but she sure did like the farmboy who visited his folks when he got a leave from the Navy.

"She told people that she had a lot of respect for me, even though I was a sailor, that I treated her more like a gentleman than any of the other guys she ever went with," Greenup says. The pair dated seriously by the summer of 1963, and were married in May 1964 shortly after Calvin left the Navy and returned home to his folks' ranch south of Darby. Their first child, a boy named Scott, was born a few years later.

About the only work a young man could find in Ravalli County in those days was logging or mill work, neither of which appealed to Calvin Greenup, who saw his classmates and their parents trapped in a state of permanent semi-poverty by the kind of wages and hours that were part of that life. He dreamed of elk and bigger things.

"I knew that working on the ranch, and the lumber mills, was not going to get me in the position to do what I wanted to do in my mind," Greenup says. "So I took a correspondence course to work for the airlines. And I left the valley then in August of 1965, and I took on the job of working for Ozark Airlines for the next fourteen and a half years all over the Midwest."

The job took him to places like St. Louis, Denver and Sioux Falls, South Dakota. Even more than had been the case in the Navy, the corporate work put him in touch with other races—people whose otherness had initially shocked him when he left Montana, and around whom he didn't always feel comfortable now. His redneck Montana attitudes, for that matter, remained pretty much intact.

"If a black man stepped on my toes wrongfully, I told him, 'You back up, back up, you stinkin' nigger.' Oh, man, I was right at him. And one of them come to me, and he says, 'Listen, white honky,' and I said, 'Well, let's get it on.' I said, 'We either get along, or we're gonna get it on.' And we got along. That guy had a lot of respect for me.

"As a matter of fact, I wasn't at work one day, and he said, 'You know, the only white man I know of that's been honest in his stand is Cal Greenup. And right now, if I need him to help me on anything, he'd come and help me.' And he was right. As long as he was right, I would support him."

The Greenups were deeply conservative, although they had no religious inclinations back then. "Matter of fact, I hated church," Calvin says. "I hated Bible. I hated anything to do with churches or anything, because most of the people I seen going to church were hypocritical, they were a lyin' bunch of jackasses, and I didn't like 'em."

When the Greenups moved to Denver in 1975, however, they found their deeply conservative values at odds with the Denver school system. Lynda and Calvin both decided that their boys weren't getting a decent education in basic matters. And they found refuge at a local church.

"We had two of our boys in the public school system there," Greenup says. "When she [Lynda] went down and found out—my oldest son, they were not teaching him anything; they weren't teaching him math, reading, writing, arithmetic, any of that kind of stuff. And so she got mad, and then I checked into it a little, then I got mad. And I realized what they was." In Greenup's mind, these people were in cahoots with the same Communist conspirators he believed were trying to destroy the country.

"So we pulled our kids out. And the government says, you can't pull your kids out—we'll come and take them away from you. And I said, 'You do that. You try and come to take my kids away from me.' And that's when I first threatened the government, to leave my kids alone: 'They belong to me. I'll teach my boys. You people are not teaching them anything.'"

A next-door neighbor put them in touch with a church school run by the fundamentalist congregation where he was a member. The Greenups found it to their liking, despite the religious tone: "I thought, 'Well, they got to get an education, so they can throw the other stuff over their shoulder.' So I went down and checked with that preacher, and he said, 'I know you're having trouble with the government come threatening to come take your kids and everything.' He said, 'Don't talk to them no more. Let me handle it. I'll handle it. And I'll take care of your kids. You give me a chance to teach your boys.'

"And I said, 'What's this gonna cost me?' And he said, 'I am not gonna charge you nothin', Mister Greenup. You're concerned about your kids and your education, so am I. And as a preacher of the Gospel,' he says, 'I got a responsibility to help you with your children.'"

Greenup wound up attending the church, almost out of obligation, since his children were in school there and his neighbor invited him, but his feelings about it were tense, partly because Lynda became a believer. "I got to where I hated that preacher, because he'd stand up in the pulpit and pointed his finger at me and this and that and the other, and tell me I was going to hell if I didn't receive Christ as my savior and all this other stuff. And I thought, 'Well, puke on you.'

"In them days, I was fixin' to poke his lights out. And then one day, he give an invitation after the message, and everything—see, I thought him and my wife were talking to each other, and I thought she was telling him my background, and he was hammerin' on me too stinking much. And so that particular day, I thought, 'Well, you better not reach out and shake my hand today buddy, because I'm going to poke you in the gut.' So on the way out the door, I was trying to figure out a way where I didn't have to go by him.

"When I got to the door there, he was standing there, he reached out and he says, 'Is there something you want to talk to me about, Mr. Greenup?' And I says, 'Yeah. I'm going to hell, and I don't know what to do about it.' And he says, 'You want to come to the side room and talk to me about it?' And I said, 'Yeah, let's go.'

"So we went back over there, and he went over the Scriptures with me, and showed me where I was lost and undone without Christ, and I was hellbound if I didn't receive Christ as my savior. And so I received Christ as my savior that day, and I've been saved ever since."

The conversion to fundamentalist Christianity also deepened Greenup's conservatism, to the point that he decided he couldn't stand to have his children growing up in an urban environment anymore. In the fall of 1978, he packed up Lynda and the boys and moved them back to the family ranch near Darby, while he remained in Denver to work for Ozark Airlines. The next summer, they started building their home on the chunk of the family acreage that had been designated as Calvin's land, and Cal quit the airlines that fall and moved back to Darby for good.

Cal drove a truck and worked around the ranch, and helped his father run the local landfill. Ken Greenup had started the operation in 1972, opening up a portion of Cal's property to serve as the Darby dump when town fathers decided they needed to move the landfill away from the river. The contract, in exchange for upkeep on the road and the dump, provided steady money for the Greenup family—in fact, over the eighteen years they ran the landfill, the Ravalli County Garbage District alone paid out some $400,000 to the Greenups[1]—although Cal says his father "didn't get rich, because he never would charge the people what he really needed to to make a profit. But that's my dad, and that's the way he operated."

As the 1980s wore on and the population began rising steadily in the Bitterroot Valley, local officials grew increasingly concerned about the water supply, which lay just a few feet under the surface of the ground and was easily polluted. Landfills like the Greenups', which was only a half-mile or so from the Bitterroot River, started facing increasingly serious restrictions in order to keep the pollution that seeped out of them from leaching to the groundwater—and thus, everyone's tapwater. Many of the changes were mandated by state and federal regulations. Ken Greenup got mailings on the coming changes, but he didn't have the kind of money it would take to cope with them. Moreover, the license for his dump, and thus the responsibility for keeping it up to regulations, was in the hands of the Ravalli County Garbage District, whose board in the Greenups' view was trying to shift the costs to them.

"I knew something serious was happening," Greenup says. "I could see the buildup, because I started reading the paperwork in '86. I was reading the stuff that Dad was getting in the mail from the health folks, the environmental stuff, and he was starting to get upset, and they was putting the pressure on him to do certain things, and I said, 'Well, Dad, I don't know what we're going to do about it. They have the right to pass these regulations on these landfills.' But I said, 'One of the things of this business is, you are not responsible for people's garbage.' And he says, 'No, and I sure blankety-blank ain't.'

"Then in '87, I said, 'Dad, run the landfill, do anything you want to with it, but sign everything over in my name.' I said, 'They're after your ranch, Dad, and they're going to get it.' He said, 'How in the hell they going to get my ranch?' And I laid it down to him on how they was going to take his ranch. I said, 'Dad, understand what I'm telling you, I'm your son, and I've looked at this stuff now for two years. They're after your ranch. And they're going to get it.'

"So then, when things started foreclosing then, in '87 . . . November, December, he says, 'Son, you're right. I think you're right. They're after the ranch.' And I said, 'That's exactly what they're after. It's not a matter of right and wrong, Dad, they're going to try and hang you with that landfill.'

"So then in January he set down with me and the committee, the landfill committee and the county commissioners, and he said, 'I want to sign this over to Calvin.' He says, 'You go ahead and keep the profits . . . I don't need it anymore. You help your butt off for me and help me with this, just take the landfill and make the best of it you can, finish up the contract and do whatever you gotta do.' So in February of '88 he signed it all over to me.

"And it wasn't any moment too soon, because by July or August of '88, they were already coming down with such stringent rules and regulations for the landfill, you wouldn't believe. Plastic liners, test holes, the tests are $2,500 a year for a hole, and these kinds of flamboyant figures and all this crap."

Cal started attending garbage-board and county-commission meetings, urging them to shoulder the burden for making the improvements to the landfill, and steadfastly refusing to take on the job himself. The commissioners listened and politely refused. Greenup told them he couldn't possibly perform the upgrades they wanted, so the county commissioners decided simply to close down the dump. In the autumn of 1990, they did so.

It was not, however, such a simple matter as closing the gates and covering it over with dirt. State water-quality officials made out a list of specifications Greenup would have to meet for closing the landfill. Greenup says he took the matter to a contractor, who quoted a figure in excess of $150,000 to do the job. At that point, Greenup punted the whole matter to the county—who, he argued, ultimately bore the responsibility for closing the facility, since the license for it was in their name.

The county took quite another view, considering that it had in fact paid Greenup some $23,000, using funds reserved from their fees to pay for the closure costs at the time the landfill officially closed its gates. Greenup—claiming this was simply money that had been improperly withheld from him in the first place—went out and bought a new pickup with the cash, county officials say. The state came up with a closure plan they said would cost only $18,000, but Greenup kept claiming the costs belonged to the county.

"When they come and told me, and I says, 'Well, now, who do you expect to come up with the funds to do all this stuff that you want done with the landfill and the closures and all this?' And they said, 'You.'

"I told 'em, 'Go ahead, but pack a lunch, because you're going to be awhile if you come to get my property.' Well, when they said that, my father-in-law says, 'They mean that, and they're going to get it.' And my dad says, 'Yeah, they're after you.' And I said, 'Yeah, they're going to try to take everything I got.'"

The state attorney general's office in 1991 threatened to take both Cal Greenup and Ravalli County to court over the matter. Once the state stepped in, the county scrambled to work out a deal to close the dump under slightly looser restrictions—at a cost of about $4,000, which the county then paid, if only to get the whole mess out of their hair. In Calvin Greenup's mind, this was proof positive that government officials of all stripes were part of a cozy conspiracy to strip regular citizens of their property and their rights—which he'd been hearing about since sixth grade.

"The people that the One World Government is about is the elite, the money people of the world," is how Greenup describes his views on the matter. "The Gettys, the Rothschilds, the Bilderburgers, all of them. They're the ones that's causing the mess . . . They used the banking system, and then they used the IRS as a crooked, so-called tax-collect agency, to keep the Federal Reserve people satisfied until the government gets our guns away from us, so they can move in and take over the country. And then it's all over."

Despite losing his chief income source—ironically, a government monopoly he and his family had enjoyed for nearly a generation—Greenup was not left out in the cold completely by the dump's closure. All along, he had been preparing for it by following through on his longtime dream: building an elk farm.

"Through the '80s, there was two or three occasions where I had a chance to buy elk," he says. "And when I went to buy 'em, they sold 'em out from under me. So my last chance came in '88. Calf prices was high, so I sold all the cows I had—I don't recall how many there was—and I said, I'm going to get however many elk I can and get started. So in July of '88, I bought five elk."

It took another nine months before the elk calves' owners turned them over to him, during which time an anxious Cal Greenup made regular, nervous visits to the ranch where they were being kept, half-expectant to see them gone again. Finally, he got the call to come pick up his animals.

"So April Fools Day of 1989, I was over there early that morning. My mom and dad went with me—and Dad, he was against it, he didn't like it. And I said, 'Well, I just need somebody to go with me, in case if I break down, somebody won't let 'em go.' And so he went.

"And they were skinny, they were peeled up, they were bad-looking animals. So we got them down and got them loaded up. They did look bad to me, but I knew what I could do with them. That wasn't worrying me. I knew my bloodlines, I had a good bloodline."

Ken Greenup, who had been handling livestock all his life, was not impressed. "He says, 'I hope you know what you're doin', son, but I wouldn't give you ten cents for the whole bunch of 'em.' I told him, 'Well, Dad, just one time, let me do this, let me do this one thing. If I fall on my face, so what? But then again I might do all right. So just give me a chance and don't pick on it. If you just watch, within a month or six weeks, you won't even know they're the same elk.'"

Cal was as good as his word. "In three weeks, I had one of them eating out my hand, and in a month, I had all of them coming over smelling me. In six weeks, I had them all eating out of my hand.

"My dad seen that, he come to me, and big tears come down his cheeks, and he says, 'Well, I fulfilled my job. I trained one boy to understand and respect and do right by animals.' And he says, 'There probably isn't no one in this world that can handle elk like Calvin Greenup.' That was a compliment from my dad.

"Then I started building up, and one thing led to the other. I said I want to build up a bloodline as I recall seeing in them when I was kid. So I started on those lines. In 1994, I had a four-year-old bull that was seven-by-eight, had a huge rack on him. And I knew that I was well under way to do what it was that I wanted to do. And people were coming by and taking pictures of them from all over the country. I took them to the fair down there. I had one little female that was halter-broke. I could lead her into the brakes, and I could milk her. And that's what I wanted to do.

"Instead, I got into this trouble with the government and the fights. I was in the process of fighting with the government when I lost my first elk."

★★★

It was during his quarrel with the county over the landfill that Greenup also met his chief ally in battling the government, a Darby constitutionalist named Al Hamilton. Hamilton, who made a living as a backhoe operator and had many friends because of his generous nature, had similar views on government and the Communist conspiracy. "He jumped on my side, and he says, 'Those dirty rotten bums,' he says, 'I'm on your side. If they want to get a war on, let's get it on. I'm gonna support you,'" Greenup recalls. "And when they found out he was supporting me and standing beside me and voicing his opinions on what happened with the landfill at public meetings and stuff like this, well, right away, he became the enemy."

The year after the landfill closed, Greenup decided to take a stand against the government. He stopped paying taxes, on the grounds the government had no right to collect them. With Al Hamilton and other friends—people like Loran Herbert, a longtime local constitutionalist, and his son Lex, as well as Al's son-in-law, Pete Miller—he started spreading the gospel of Patriot beliefs and became even more deeply involved in organizing resistance to what he saw as an onslaught of oppression, embodied in his mind by the events at Ruby Ridge and Waco. The Weaver case especially rang bells of recognition for Greenup, and he began to wonder how long it would be before they came to do the same thing to him.

In 1993, he got in touch with a constitutionalist in Booneville, Indiana, named Joe Holland. Holland had been involved in Posse Comitatus activity in the 1980s and had lost his pig farm after deciding to stop paying taxes. Afterward, he kept himself afloat by organizing a couple of "patriotic" fund-raising outfits called the Freedom Council and the Bill of Rights Enforcement Center, most of them peddling Freeman-style phony money orders and offering advice on how to avoid paying taxes. But in the spring of 1993, inspired by the call to arms made at Pete Peters' Estes Park gathering, he set up a group called the North American Volunteer Militia.[2]

Cal Greenup read some of Holland's material and phoned him, and the two began forming a long-distance partnership. "He was putting to work stuff that I had already studied and got," Greenup says. "He says, 'I'm willing to help you.' So he helped me with my paperwork, and that's when we started putting it out about the Federal Reserve and the War Powers Act, and we started exposing all that stuff. And the more I put in there, the madder these people over here at this courthouse got, because they knew that I was onto something and they didn't want me to expose it."

Greenup announced he was forming the Ravalli County chapter of Holland's NAVM that fall. He also filed papers in the Ravalli County Courthouse declaring his own "American National Status"—and cosigned by more than a dozen of his relatives and neighbors, including Al Hamilton and Pete Miller. They published the notice in the September 28, 1993, edition of the weekly *Ravalli Republic*, which declared they wanted nothing more to do with the "Democracy" of the District of Columbia: "Any and all, past and present political ties implied by operation of law or otherwise in trust with said democracy are hereby dissolved. By this emancipation

I return to an estate of primary sovereignty and freedom that pre-exists all government(s)." The next year, he stopped buying a license to run his elk farm, too.

The Bitterroot constitutionalists started gaining a substantial crowd of sympathizers who shared their concerns. When Roy Schwasinger's "We the People" organization (which mostly specialized in providing a lien scheme based on the supposed suspension of the Constitution) came through Hamilton that spring, the gathering was billed as a meeting about gun control and the then-proposed Brady Bill; well over a hundred attended. Greenup and his friends were finding a lot of people were receptive to Patriot beliefs, and they became further emboldened. Most of his immediate circle, after filing for their "sovereign citizenship," removed the license plates from their cars.

Lex Herbert, driving a car with no plates, was pulled over in September 1993 by a state highway patrolman and charged with a seat-belt violation, failure to display a license, and obstructing an officer. He refused to identify himself, and eventually was released on $1,100 bail after serving four days in jail.[3] At his court hearings were a clutch of local sovereign citizens, including Cal Greenup. It was the first time Greenup encountered the man who would become his nemesis: George Corn.

Corn is a former Army Ranger who served in Vietnam, though you would not guess so from his appearance: small and slender with owlish wire-rim glasses, a little bit bookish but athletic too. He grew up in Shelby, North Carolina, and even after 16 years in Hamilton has not shed his gentle Southern drawl. He was elected Ravalli County Attorney in 1990, and shortly thereafter found himself besieged by Patriots in the courtroom. He came to know Cal Greenup very well.

In fact, they used to talk rather regularly. "It was cordial through September (1994)," Corn says, "because I remember he told me there were 300,000 U.N. troops in Florida, and another 300,000 off the coast, and I was going, 'God, ya know, Cal, I was at Edmonds Air Force Base when I was in Ranger school, and I don't remember—that's a big base, but I don't think you could put 300,000 people down there,' and so forth, but he was insistent I was just deluded. At any rate, we were still talking that summer."

Tensions began to build in the fall of 1993 when IRS agents raided the home of a Patriot couple, Marc and Cheryl Andra, in nearby Florence on November 13. Marc Andra was an insurance salesman and fundamentalist who became involved in a Schwasinger-style tax-avoidance scheme, and the feds, intent on breaking up his operation, busted down his door, and with guns drawn, handcuffed them both. Cheryl Andra claimed she suffered a miscarriage as a result of the trauma.

"The IRS conducted that raid with a much heavier hand than it needed to be," says George Corn. "That had people outraged. One of the county commissioners, Steve Powell, just hit it perfectly—you're going to give [a platform to] somebody like Marc Andra, who basically had this scheme that you didn't have to pay taxes if you sent in two boxtop labels and turned around three times and put your index finger on your nose. And he was perfectly harmless that way. Then the IRS conducted this heavy-handed raid and gave him a platform. Folks on Main Street were outraged at the way they conducted that.

"I think a lot of government agencies, particularly the federal agencies, they just don't act as if they were part of the local community, or part of any sort of community. And that's what concerns people."

The Andras, with the backing of Greenup and others, attempted to have the IRS agents arrested that spring for having caused Cheryl's miscarriage. On April 13, 1994, they forced a court hearing on their request to have Sheriff Jay Printz take the agents into custody.

"They came down here and tried to force the suit against Jay to get him to go arrest the federal agents," says Corn. "They tried to get a writ of mandamus. We ended up in a pretty big to-do in [District Court Judge Jeffrey] Langton's court in April. I know they were yelling at him. He gave them a lot of latitude, but it was a pretty exciting hearing."

The law had started catching up with Greenup in late 1993, when the IRS lodged tax-evasion charges for his failure to file a return in 1991. When Cal's February 1994 court date in Helena came and went with Greenup nowhere in sight except at his ranch, a warrant eventually was sworn out for his arrest in August, and he officially became a fugitive. However, the warrant was sworn out of Lewis and Clark County and didn't even come to Jay Printz's attention until later that fall. About the same time, the local press—alerted probably by Greenup or his followers—began reporting on the situation.

Problem was, no one wanted to drive up to Greenup's place in Darby and arrest him. He had announced to everyone in town and to local reporters as well that he'd defend himself if anyone came to arrest him. He posted a sign on the edge of his property:

"Notice: To All 'Public Servants!' You are hereby put on notice that this is 'private property,' as such, all rights guaranteed by the Constitution (which you've taken an oath to uphold and defend) are hereby reserved and demanded! Please Notice! No claims or demands of any kind will be recognized without full DUE PROCESS OF LAW . . ."

The sign, similar in appearance and language to the one erected by Rodney Skurdal at the Freemen's ranch in Roundup, cited U.S. Code regarding the penalty for denying someone their civil rights. It concluded with a postscript: "To all 'officers of the law,' if you've come to 'protect us,' you are welcome BUT if you've come to 'harass us,' . . . KEEP OFF—NO TRESPASSING! SURVIVORS WILL BE PROSECUTED!"

Although Sheriff Jay Printz was reluctant to serve the warrant, he vowed he'd bring in Greenup—but without any violence, and in his own time. "I'm not inclined to go up to his home," said Printz. "I don't want to have to kill the man for something this minor, and I don't want any of our people hurt."

Printz instinctively understood that both sides in the confrontation were being affected by what had happened two years before at Ruby Ridge. "The fact that people have backed off since Weaver has really emboldened some of these fugitives," he said. "But I still intend to get my man. I just don't want to create a situation where I have to kill someone."[4]

Cal Greenup, on the other hand, was all too happy to oblige. "I've told the sheriff what I'll do," he told an Associated Press reporter. "I would turn my back and he could put a bullet in my head. But I wouldn't be hauled to jail alive. I've told him personally, you've got the first shot. Don't wound me. Kill me."[5]

Greenup began appearing on talk-radio programs that Joe Holland helped him hook into, mostly Christian fundamentalist, Patriot or right-wing talk shows. Reporters from around the country started picking up on his story. "Do the political officials want this state to blow or do they want to get it back and hear our pleas?" Greenup asked one. "In my opinion, looking at it militarily, it is obvious that this state is a test state to bring people under slavery, under United Nations control—New World Order. We are fighting back, and we're not going to quit. We want our freedom and our country back . . . There cannot be cleansing without the shedding of blood."[6]

Joe Holland, who that fall had been the subject of a massive IRS raid in which all of his files and records were confiscated, joined in on the fiery rhetoric from his home in Indiana. He fired off a letter simultaneously to a variety of public officials around Montana, including Judge Jeffrey Langton, the Montana Revenue Department, and Attorney General Joe Mazurek. It took off the kid gloves:

"You have taken an Oath to uphold the Constitution of the United States. The Oath is your contract with the people. When you violate your Oath of office you become renegade to the Constitution and guilty of treason. I am sure you know what the penalty is for treason.

". . . We would prefer that you take a good hard look at what you and your agencies are doing and amend your ways immediately. We are prepared, however, to defend, with our life, our Rights to Life, Liberty, and the Pursuit of Happiness. We number in the thousands in your area and everywhere else. How many of your agents will be sent home in body bags before you hear the pleas of the people? Proceed at your own peril!"

Holland sent the letter on December 30, 1994; as New Year's greetings go, it left something to be desired. But then, there was no happy new year ahead for anyone involved—not the public officials who received the greeting. Not Joe Holland. And certainly not Calvin Greenup.

★★★

Martha Bethel is not a lawyer, and is rather proud of the fact. She's a judge, but her only legal background includes a couple of years of pre-law courses and work in legal research. Before she was a judge, she worked for a hairdresser and in a dental office (where she was fired) and then as a secretary for a local attorney.

Bethel is a stocky, firm-jawed city court judge of indeterminate age—someone who handles traffic complaints and minor citations for the city of Hamilton. Everyone knows her as Marty, not Martha. She's one of 130 or so "limited jurisdiction" judges the state of Montana certifies and maintains to handle low-level violations and legal matters, thereby freeing up the regular courts for more serious matters.

Officials in nearby Darby needed a city judge too, but couldn't find one locally who was qualified, so they hired Bethel to handle their cases once a week.

It was in Darby that Bethel met Pete Miller, Al Hamilton's son-in-law and one of Cal Greenup's "sovereign citizenship" co-signees. "January of '95 is when Pete Miller appeared in my driving court for no insurance, no drivers license, and expired registration," Bethel recalls. "He appeared with an entourage of people, including Calvin Greenup, and basically said, 'I'm not appearing because my NTA [Notice To Appear] orders me to appear, I'm appearing here as a special visitation under duress.' And my thought was, 'From what planet? What is he talking about?'"

Actually, Bethel had an idea. On one of her first few days in court nine years before, she had encountered a Posse Comitatus follower who contested his traffic ticket. "One of the first initial appearances and arraignments I conducted, after the appointment was certified, was a Posse Comitatus-type guy. The old judge was still there training me when this happened. And this guy, the first words out of his mouth, interrupting me, blatantly, were like, 'I challenge the jurisdiction of this court.' And I went, 'Soooo, that means . . . ' I didn't know what to do."

The judge who was training her suggested they reconvene the next day. "She sat down and had a talk with me, and the city attorney, and we went over all this common law, Posse Comitatus material. And the next day, he came in, and we reconvened, and I basically didn't let him bulldoze me, and dealt with him very fairly, but not without taking a stand about his blustering."

She hardly ever saw such cases, though, in the ensuing years, although she had read about the Greenup clan's growing agitation in the papers. She was unprepared for Miller's verbal assault on the court that day. "He basically just interrupted me, and interrupted me, and in my mind, I thought, 'Oh, God, here we go,' because I had been totally blind to what had gone on with district court and justice court. Justice court was dealing with these same people on the county level, but on the same criminal level that I do, two years before this happened.

"Well, when Pete Miller came in, things happened very fast. Shortly after he entered his not-guilty plea, the stuff with Calvin Greenup was smoldering and flailing. In fact, the day that he appeared on his ticket, when Mr. Greenup appeared with him, there was a valid warrant for Mr. Greenup's arrest, and the marshal refused to arrest him. Afterward, I asked him why, because I think it would have defused a lot of this going on, but he basically just said that the sheriff had called him off. Now in retrospect, it makes a lot more sense. There was no bloodshed, it didn't bring on a fight. Waiting it out was maybe the smart thing to do. That's their contention anyway."

Bethel reverted back to her previous tactic: She postponed the hearing for another date. Within a few days, though, she was handed a stack of Patriot papers, signed by Pete Miller and Calvin Greenup, and notarized by Rodney Skurdal. It was the usual set of pseudo-legalisms: the "Common Law Affidavit of Mistake" which refused the court's papers and jurisdiction, and other Freeman-produced documents warning the judge she would be found guilty of treason if she continued with the hearings against Miller.

"So in rapid succession, these things began to happen," Bethel says. "And in fact, in these papers, they demand dismissal of the charges against their Freemen—or else. And the 'or else' is, you'll be tried, civilly and criminally, and later through kind of innuendo they informed us we'd be tried for treason, and you know what the penalty for treason is."

The threats began to pick up. "For two and a half months there, I was followed home forty miles to my driveway by [Pete Miller] and another guy, and I was getting phone calls from informants who were attending militia meetings and calling and telling me what they were planning to do, which included Molotov cocktail-burning my home, riddling it with gunfire, kidnapping me from my car on the way to work or the way home.

"And I took these things seriously, because they did in fact pull one of our county commissioners right off the road on his way in from Darby one morning and demanded his support for what they were trying to do. So I knew they were that brazen."

Bethel learned to rely on a woman who appeared to be involved with the Patriots but was calling Bethel secretly to keep her informed of what was being said. "I got a call in February: 'There's gonna be a demonstration in court tonight, you really should have backup.' So I called the sheriff and said, 'You know, I'm hearing—and I have this on tape—I'm hearing there's going to be a demonstration by Pete Miller and Calvin Greenup, that whole crew from down there tonight.' And I'm thinking—it's a two-room city hall court building, and it has fish-bowl windows all around, no drapes, no blinds. I'm thinking, it's going to be dark and I'd like someone milling around outside to make sure we don't have a problem.

"Well, the sheriff provided two officers who sat outside, drove around, walked around. I could see them out in the floodlights, way before court adjourned, going, 'Where are they? We're out of here.' And they left." That night, Bethel says, Miller and a friend followed Bethel all the way home in their pickup—more than 40 miles up the highway to the town of Stevensville, where she lives with her three children.

"They got a message to me later about what my address was. This person who was informing . . . says, 'Well, they just want you to know they know where you live.' And I said, 'Tell them I don't care if they know where I live. Just tell them if they ever come on my property . . .'

"Shortly thereafter, within the next three weeks, twice I came home from my regularly scheduled Wednesday night court, where I take my kids to my ex-husband's, and I go to Darby court, and I'm home alone, I came home to find my doors wide open. Twice. And I live way out in the boonies, and we lock our doors. Nothing touched in the house. Walked through my house.

"I walked through my house with a handgun and my dog. I'm in tears, just pissed. I just felt like, 'God, this is insane. Who would have such hatred for me?'"

Phone calls became frequent—the kind where no one speaks on the other end, and then a click as the phone is hung up. Sometimes the caller would scream into the receiver before hanging up. Bethel says she began logging the calls just to keep track of how frequent they were. On some weekends they numbered well over a hundred.

Finally, she went to work to end the harassment—and made the chilling discovery that someone inside the halls of officialdom was leaking information to the Patriots. "We put a trap on my phone, and the day I put the trap on—law enforcement signed for it, that's the way it works in Montana—the calls stopped. And the day the trap went back off, they started again."

Bethel was more angry than frightened. "I was just really ticked that these people were messing with me. And then the next session of court was like a week or two later, and the night of that session, the morning of the same day, a woman called and said, 'Don't come to Darby tonight or you won't be leaving.' And this was after I'd received these papers. And I was like, 'What are you talking about?' . . .

"I called the sheriff and asked for backup. And he said, 'No, I can't babysit you. You're a Darby judge, let Darby protect you.' I said, 'I'm a citizen of this county, my home is in the county, I work in the city but I drive the county roads to get to my job in Darby, and I think it is your job to protect me.' And he didn't like that very well.

"Anyway, he did not provide security. I dismissed court that night, and had everybody start coming here to Hamilton. I just decided to hold court where I want to—I'm not about to die over a frickin' driver's license. For two and a half months, we held court here, including the Pete Miller trial, at which two of the militia members showed up. He was convicted in about three minutes."

Bethel laughs when she recalls how most people in Darby felt about the Patriots and their protests. "I had to dismiss three or four, maybe five jurors before the trial ever convened because they came in and said, 'Any son of a bitch that flies his flag upside down is guilty.' And I just had to say, 'You just won't do, then, will you?' Because they couldn't be objective. These people were furious over what was going on in their community.

"I had to pull jurors from the city of Darby, which is a very small pool—it's like 600 people. And most of them had no patience whatsoever with this defiance of law enforcement that was going on.

"Anyway, he was convicted, and I issued a warrant for him. In the time between the pretrial being held and the trial being held he was cited again for the same things, and was given the tickets at the City Hall in Darby, and he left them on a seat in the courtroom. So I had to issue another warrant for failure to appear on those.

"When I sent his paperwork to him, I told him, 'If you walk in here on your own and deal with this, I will not put you in jail. I promise you I will not put you in jail. Please see the writing on the wall. The way you're going about this is the wrong way. You've got to take this through the same civil process available to me and to my sister and my next-door neighbor—you can't just like, if you don't like the law, shoot the legislator. That's not the way this thing works.'

"He never responded."

As the tensions worsened on the Greenup ranch and in Darby generally, the underground rumblings about grabbing a judge—Bethel being the favored target—grew to a fever pitch. At that point, some other local lawmen stepped in.

"One of the Stevensville police, and one of the county deputies who worked for Printz, visited me," Bethel says, "and they walked the perimeter of my place, and they decided which room they'd expect us to be in if the house came under fire if these yahoos decided to come in and make a point.

"They showed the kids how to get under the house, in the crawl space, where in the woods they expected us to run to on the ten acres of very thick Ponderosa adjacent to me, and I was given a police radio, and told what to pack in a duffle and put it by the back door . . . That's when I went, 'Oh my God.' It's like, they'll still help you out, but you're on your own. And now I realize it really is not sensible to expect law enforcement to be my babysitter. That's not what it's about. They're response-oriented, and if I had a problem they'd be there as fast as they could. But frankly, we're at an hour and a half to forty-five minutes for response time, realistically."

About ten days later she heard from the Stevensville police chief. "He visited me with one of his deputies, and he said, 'You need to get the kids and get out of town this weekend.' I said, 'It's Easter, my sister's coming here, and I'm not going anywhere, I'm not leaving my home.' And he goes, 'No, you need to get the kids and get out of town this weekend, because this is the weekend where they're going to take you into custody and make an example out of you.'

"The words he used were, 'Small fish are easier to catch. They're not going to mess with Judge Langton, they're not going to mess with Judge Sperry or Sabo—they're too visible. They know where you are, you're out in the sticks.' He says, 'I don't mean go to Missoula, I mean go to Seattle and see Mom or go to Bozeman. Get OUT of town.'"

Bethel's own instincts, though, were to stand firm. "I said, 'The hell I will.' And I slept with a Mini-.14 by my bed for the next three nights. And my kids were sent off.

"Nothing happened, and I wasn't buffaloed. And I felt good about that."

★★★

The harassment of public officials was widespread that spring. Judge Jeff Langton received so many threats he bought himself a gun. George Corn's deputy, Mike Reardon, was the brunt of a variety of threats: "Last week I was threatened with burning, hanging, being shot in the back and being backed over with a pickup truck," he told Bill Morlin in early March. Corn himself was followed home one evening when he took the back road to Hamilton, after watching his daughter play in a volleyball game in Darby.

And the threats against Jay Printz's deputies became so common and widespread that the sheriff issued a memo advising them to remain cool in hostile confrontations with the Patriots. Most of the harassment was subtle in nature—nothing you could arrest someone for, but in the unspoken language of the Bitterroot community, as loud as can be.

"There had been these vague threats, starting in January or February, of, 'You people patrol the roads by yourself,' stuff like that," George Corn says. "Talk on the radio. There was a lot of stress going on among the deputies because of comments that had been made like that—not direct threats. Lots of sly glances. Two or three of these guys and one deputy would meet and there'd be that sort of smile and wave, but it'd be with a real intimidating grin.

"It was of a lot of concern to Jay, because he was so afraid that somebody would get forced into the position where they felt that they had to pull a gun, which he felt is what the other side was hoping to do. There was a lot of concern."

The harassment did not go unnoticed by the non-Patriot citizenry. In mid-January, a group of them put together an ad to run in the *Ravalli Republic,* signed by several hundred prominent residents. "We the undersigned express support for our local, state and nationally elected officials and public employees in their endeavors to do their respective duties," it read. "We abhor and speak out against threats of violence by any persons or organizations against these public servants."[7]

Around Hamilton, merchants began hanging up orange signs with the words: "We Support Our Public Officials." A few were hung, to no one's surprise, in the county courthouse and at City Hall. But a city councilman tore the latter one down, apparently out of fear of taking part in anything so controversial.

Greenup's local support eroded quickly in these weeks in no small part because of who he aligned himself with. F. Joe Holland was from Indiana; Judge Langton, on the other hand, was as local as you could get. "Jeff is a real popular guy," says George Corn. "He was elected handily. He's written a local history, grew up in Victor, went to school in Stevensville. He's well thought-of, and that's created a big backlash, no matter what people might have felt, just the fact that he's our first district court judge—which the county had been struggling to get for the last 12 years—and he's been in office a year and he has to put up with a threat like this. Particularly coming from F. Joe Holland, the out-of-stater, that threat was a bad move diplomatically. That carried over to Cal right through that."

Greenup began to feel increasingly isolated and paranoid, edgy like an elk in hunting season. First there was that black helicopter sighting on Greenup's ranch February 5. National Guard officials scurried to make sure no one else performed any further low-level maneuvers in the Darby area. Everyone slept with their guns for awhile on the Greenup ranch.

In March, someone cut down the cellular-phone transmission tower that was near the Greenups' ranch, taking a chainsaw to its base in the middle of the night. The sheriff's deputies rely on cellular phones for communication, since radio doesn't work well in the mountainous Bitterroot country. Taking out the tower meant that any lawmen trying to do anything at the Greenup ranch would be out of contact. The tower, however, was not severely damaged, and was put back up a few days later.

Up to that point, Greenup's two sons had managed to stay clear of any brushes with the law. But the eldest, 28-year-old Scott, finally had a run-in with sheriff's deputies on February 15. It turned ugly.

Cal Greenup's frequent predictions that the government was out to take everything they owned had not fallen on deaf ears. "My boys watched me through this whole thing and they could see where there just isn't justice in the court," Greenup says. "I mean, which way do you turn? So they knew that they were after their dad, because they said so. They said, 'We're gonna come after you and get anything and everything you got.' And so when the government agents and agencies make those kinds of statements, you just constantly look over your shoulder, and say, 'Well, how are they gonna come after me? When are they gonna come after me?' So, if they'd have approached Scott in any way other than what they did, the outcome wouldn't have been the same. But they went at him—well, they attacked him.

"He was down here [in Hamilton] buying materials—he was helping work on houses and stuff. When he started heading home, he saw the cop pull in behind him, and he thought, 'Oh boy, what's gonna happen next?' Another one pulled in, they turned the lights on. Then he knew—in the back of his mind, he said, 'Oh, boy, they're after my dad, and now they're after me for whatever reason.'"

The deputy, Sterling Moss, was someone the Greenups knew, but he was short and abrupt. "That pickup's ours now," is all Scott says he heard him say.

"And right away, my son says, 'No it's not.' Then one thing went to another, and instead of Sterling saying, 'We're confiscating the truck'—he didn't say anything about that until after the handcuffs were on. So that was another piece of stupidity on the police's part."

Scott started wrestling with police as they put on the handcuffs, and one officer wound up on the ground with him. "Their claim was that he was assaulting an officer or something, and he was protecting himself," Greenup says. "They were the ones that made the assault. They surrounded him, and he ended up on the ground. They accused him of being on drugs . . .

"It just killed my wife and I—and then to stand up in court and say he was—they entered that he was on drugs, and a bunch of crap."

In fact, Scott was charged with assaulting an officer and resisting arrest. He was freed on a $5,000 bond, and the court date was set for two weeks later. The Greenups didn't show up. They had been in Roundup, visiting some people Calvin had become acquainted with: LeRoy Schweitzer and Rodney Skurdal.

"I had had a couple of conversations over the phone with them," Greenup says. "And then when we went over there, a lot of it came together. Because in all the stuff at the court library—the law library and et cetera—there was stuff that kept popping out: the common law. Even in the Montana Code annotated, common law pops out in there. The very first time, the very first page, the common law is there. And yet these people say the common law is archaic. The common law is not archaic. It's the only just kind of law."

Greenup came back from his nine-day visit to Roundup freshly armed with a stack of new documents and forms. He tried paying his taxes with a check signed by LeRoy Schweitzer. He also had the standard "common law venue" papers, complete with Skurdal's signature as notary. There were papers for both Scott Greenup and Pete Miller to use in contesting their respective court cases. Miller's dealt only with his traffic citations in Martha Bethel's court, but Scott's case was more serious, and it was before the same judge who was handling Calvin's tax case.

Al Hamilton showed up at the courthouse on the date scheduled for Scott's appearance and handed court officials the papers, including a demand that they respond within 10 days, or else an arrest warrant would be issued. Judge Langton responded by issuing an arrest warrant for Scott, and set his bond at $50,000. Then, a week later, George Corn filed charges against Cal Greenup for violating state game statutes by raising his herd without a license.

Cal Greenup had an answer for them: the common-law court. He told bail bondsman Ben Bernatz in late March that the court had met and decided to hang Judge Langton and to shoot Sheriff Printz, George Corn and Mike Reardon. The level of fear in the county courthouse was raised another couple of notches. Word was getting around of Patriot outsiders coming in with loads of weaponry to help back up the Greenups. A 22-year-old believer who had just moved to Hamilton named Ben Schneider was flashing his gun around to others and telling them he was part of Calvin's secret army; the sheriff and the prosecutor heard about that, too.

"And we didn't know Ben Schneider at that point," Corn says. "We were real concerned about people I referred to as 'wild cards'—do we have any wild cards in here, folks that we just don't know? And we know that there's some in the Bitterroot because we had tried to capture Scott before in the north end of the county, and we didn't have scrambled radios and the deputies could hear people talking behind them, and there were houses they had stayed at, or they had to be pulling out from, and we didn't have enough proof. So there were people we knew in the county were assisting them that we didn't know, and we were afraid there might be some people from the outside we didn't know as well."

Fellow tax protesters Marc and Cheryl Andra, meanwhile, had also become full-time fugitives. After the initial raid, they refused to appear for subsequent court dates on their tax charges. When IRS agents pulled Marc over on February 10 and tried to arrest him, he ran off into the woods and eluded them. The couple stayed on the move, but only within the Bitterroot country. They rented an apartment for awhile, and they stayed with various friends, including the Greenups. They left their car at the Greenups' place and told them they could drive it.

Problem was, federal agents were looking for that car. On March 1, it was spotted on the road out of Darby, and town marshal Larry Rose radioed its location to waiting federal agents. This time, though, it was being driven by Karen Hamilton, Al's wife; Lynne Miller, their daughter (and Pete Miller's wife), was the only passenger.

"South of Hamilton here, the police turned around and put the lights on 'em," Cal Greenup recalls. "Well, they didn't think they were doing anything wrong. They weren't even sure why they was putting the lights on. So they were going slow and they pulled in down here at the stockyard, just south of town out here. And there was eight or ten, pulled their guns out, pulled the hammers, pointed their guns at them, told them to get out, you're under arrest."

The two women refused to identify themselves. The IRS agents running the arrest identified Lynne Miller as Cheryl Andra and took them down to the county jail. The women remained there overnight while county officials tried to figure out who they were.

The next day, the Hamilton city police received a call warning them that a procession of vehicles was on the way from Darby and the occupants intended to take over the county courthouse. Deputies went on alert, and George Corn watched from an office window above. Six cars arrived in a row and slowly pulled around the courthouse with their headlights on and horns blaring. Some of the occupants rolled down their windows and shouted. Then they parked, and a cluster of Patriots emerged and entered the courthouse, past a row of deputies, and proceeded to the jail to fetch Karen Hamilton and Lynne Miller.

Among them was Cal Greenup. "I had a warrant for my arrest—looked the undersheriff in the face, and deputies, and said, 'You dirty rotten lyin' scumbuckets,' I said. 'The people you should be arrestin' right now are those IRS agents down there at that motel room, and you ain't doin' it. And you ain't going to do it. Because you ain't got the guts.'

"But I said, 'You're holding two women here illegally.' And I went through a scenario. And I just lit on them for thirty minutes. I sat right there and told them what they was. And Al Hamilton was with me. So then we knew then that the government agents in this valley were corrupt. It was obvious they were trying to push us into a confrontation. No doubt about it. So they could bring in troops, or whatever. I don't know what their scenario was, it don't matter. But it was obvious to me they were pushing the confrontation. I mean, you just don't do those kinds of things."

As it turned out, after all the yelling and shouting was done, there was no attempt to take over the courthouse. The Patriots were able to leave with Karen Hamilton and Lynne Miller after Larry Rose arrived and identified them.

Greenup lit into Rose. "He finally showed up down here to identify those women and to tell them who they were, and he come out smiling. And I looked him right in the eye, and I said, 'You really think it's funny, don't you?' He said, 'If it wasn't so bizarre, it would be funny.' And I said, 'Larry, there's nothing humorous about it. You lyin' bastards, you lyin' scumbuckets has caused some damage, some more heartache, to people wrongfully, and it's got to stop.'

"And he started into his thing, and I said, 'Larry, why don't you just shut up, because every time you flap your lips open, you lie. You need to learn to shut your mouth.'"

Rose is a Darby boy, a onetime town hellraiser who got religion (he and Greenup attended the same church once) and became a lawman. In some circles—not just the Patriots, but with other lawmen too—his old-style, strong-armed, somewhat bullying method of law enforcement is viewed dimly, but Darby city fathers have apparently been happy with his methods over the years. After the March 1 incident, Rose decided he'd had enough of the Darby constitutionalists' threats.

One Sunday afternoon, April 2, he spotted Lynne Miller driving the family car—with, of course, no license plates, a mode the Darby Patriots had adopted some months before. He flipped on the lights and tried to pull her over. She refused, and proceeded instead to the home of her father, Al Hamilton.

"Well, she was scared—she was arrested once, wrongfully, and she had her little kids with her," is how Cal Greenup describes it. "So she run to Al's house for protection. She knew that Larry Rose was after her, and there is nothing beyond what he will do." Al Hamilton, however, was not home.

"We got a phone call that day from Al's youngest son, Lance, who said, 'My sister's in trouble, we need help,'" Greenup says. "Al wasn't home, and I was home and Shad was home. So we bailed in [Lynda's] car and run down there to give assistance. And when somebody calls for help, I'll go. Especially with this corruption as bad as it is. And I went because I figured if I could keep somebody from getting shot, I'm gonna go."

Rose had pulled his patrol car up to the culdesac where the Hamiltons' house stood, and was pondering his next move when the armed Patriots arrived. Shad Greenup, Cal's 21-year-old son, and Pete Miller popped out of their cars and brandished guns. Suddenly, Rose found himself in the middle of a bunch of angry men with guns. He backed up a couple of blocks and radioed for assistance.

Soon there were about 15 Patriots, some toting assault-style weapons. Pete Miller stood on the stoop and held a rifle above his head, shouting: "C'mon! Kill the pigs! C'mon! Let's get it on!" Al Hamilton showed up, packing a pistol and milling with the men.

The men stationed themselves behind their cars. The cops—Larry Rose and Deputy Sterling Moss and a couple of Montana Highway Patrolmen—decided the matter wasn't worth endangering anyone's life over, especially since the showdown was occurring in a residential neighborhood. They retreated to the Darby City Hall, where they decided to return later and get witness descriptions of the encounter to file away for later prosecution, and to shore up their weaponry in the meantime in case the Patriots decided to attack them. As the two state patrolmen were removing their high-powered shotguns from their back seats, Al Hamilton drove by with an assault-style weapon and yelled at them from his car and then drove away.

A few hours later, Larry Rose was back in the neighborhood, collecting witness accounts, when Al Hamilton and Pete Miller spotted him and confronted him again. Hamilton threatened Rose that he would "hunt him to the ends of the earth." He stood a distance away and screamed obscenities, demanding that Rose "come and get me."

Rose said nothing and continued his work. Two days later, when everything had returned to normal, deputies arrested Al Hamilton quietly at his home and took him to jail, charged with felony intimidation.

★★★

The standoff was reaching a boiling point. Greenup and his compatriots became increasingly certain the feds would be making their move soon. Joe Holland sent out a press release on April 8 asking militia members from around the nation to come to Montana to help defend Greenup.

The call to arms garnered only a mild response, however. Two days after it came out, a man in Helena who identified himself as a Patriot and militia member called Greenup and said he was ready to lend a hand. What, he wondered, should he bring? Cal told him to bring guns that would "shoot a pretty good distance straight to start off with, and then some of you will have to bring some, ah, close-quartered stuff, ya know, for close encounters."

What would they be doing? the caller asked. Greenup told him they would be arresting and overpowering local officials. He said they would seize bulletproof vests and handcuffs from the sheriff's office and use them against the lawmen.

The caller was not, however, a real Patriot, but an undercover detective for the Montana Criminal Investigation Bureau named Ward J. McKay, who had been alerted by Joe Holland's call to arms and warning that violence might be imminent in the Bitterroot Valley. He recorded the whole conversation, and showed up April 12 with another agent in tow at Greenup's ranch. He half-expected a near-army of recruits called up by Joe Holland's fax to be gathered there; instead, it seemed, he and his colleague were the only non-Bitterroot people who came to defend Cal Greenup.

Greenup says now that he was immediately suspicious. "Nobody from the militia or the Patriot movement ever called me and made those kind of questions. Matter of fact, all the Patriots that ever called me and talked to me says, 'We don't want to fire the first shot. We don't want to be the persons that kills somebody.' Well, when these people called, they said, 'Well, what kind of guns should we bring?' That was never asked by anybody else. So I just played along with their game."

The rest of the group, Greenup says, shared his suspicions. "We talked, we discussed it with the other people that was there. So when he came that afternoon—see, I told him we had an empty barn they could stay in. So when I was discussing with these other people the possibility that they was undercover agents, I says, 'Well, I'm gonna play their game with them.' So when they came, I had them come up my folks' driveway, which is across the field from my house, and I would meet them over there, face to face.

"Well, another fellow went with me, and I did meet them face to face. And as soon as they got out of their vehicles—they just didn't have the mannerisms that a person who was coming in support of you would have. They just—they were too phony."

One of them, Greenup says, was a nervous wreck. He decided against letting them stay in the barn. Instead, he sent them down to the fishing access outside Darby, where he told them to stay on guard and to flash their headlights if they saw any police approaching. The agents say he told them to wait until they heard shooting and increased police activity, then shoot to kill any uniformed or plainclothes lawmen they saw.

"Probably the mistake I did make," Greenup reflects now, "is I wanted them to play their hands one more time, and that was when I had them up to the house the night we left. And I wished I had left them down at the fishing access. We've all said that since then."

Pete Miller was on guard when the two agents returned that evening, carrying an SKS assault weapon with a 30-round magazine. More guns lay about the interior of the house, and even gas masks were visible. Greenup says they all were convinced the feds were going to move on them that night, or the next morning, because a group of Patriots calling themselves Montanans for Due Process had arranged for a public gathering the next night in nearby Corvallis, which Greenup said "was going to expose the corruption in the courts and the bar association." Government officials and the media, he believed, were trying to portray their meeting as a "militia" gathering, and a raid on Greenup's place the night before would further discredit their efforts. He told the agents as much, and then launched into one of his lectures on the court system.

"I had said, 'Anytime a government official violates their oath of office and violates the Constitution where somebody's been injured, what is that an act of?' And [McKay] said, 'Well, that's an act of treason.' And I said, 'Well, if it's an act of treason, shouldn't they be taken before a court of law, and if convicted, what's the penalty?' And he says, 'Well, death by hanging.' And yet they posed it that I was going to arrest public officials, try them in a common-law court and hang them.

"Well, I have always said that if they violate their oath of office, violate the Constitution—and I'm stating that right now—they need to be tried in a justifiable court of law, and if convicted, they need to have their sentence carried out. And I'm not going to change that."

The agents later suggested there was a plan discussed to take over the courthouse; Greenup vehemently denies that. "We never, ever discussed taking over the courthouse. We did discuss going into the courthouse to prove to the people that there was no justice in these courts—and there's not—and prove to them how the public servants that was elected in office was really the ones violating the laws. And we did do that."

One of their friends from the countryside around Darby, Dennis Stucker, showed up a little after 10:30 that night in his pickup. It was time to get Calvin and Lynda out of there, it had been decided, and arrangements had been made to sneak them over the Idaho border.

"We had reports that I was a dead man—they was going to kill me," Greenup says. "They were setting snipers on the hill above my house. And people had seen them."

Greenup argued with them as they loaded up guns, ammo, gas masks and various weapons into Stucker's pickup. "I was going to stay behind to take the bullets. I told everybody—I said, one more American must die. And they don't have anything on me. I've been a good American, I've been a good patriot to this nation, I've been faithful to this country. And I said, it's probably going to require one more of us die so that the rest of the people can really wake up and see what crooked, corrupt government is all about.

"My oldest son and my wife says no. They refused to let me stay behind. My oldest son throwed me in the pickup. He says, 'No, Dad, you know too much, you got too much knowledge of what's going on, and no one here's got the guts that you got to keep telling your story. You can come back. You're gonna get out of here tonight, and now.'"

A four-vehicle procession headed south up Lost Trail Pass that night with Cal and Lynda Greenup. A couple of passenger cars met them at the top, where they proceeded down the steep, windy road into Idaho's Salmon River country.[8] There they remained in hiding for several more weeks.

The two MCIB agents contacted Sheriff Printz the next day and informed him the Greenups were gone. That evening, as Montanans for Due Process held their common-law court gathering in Corvallis' Grange Hall without incident, Printz and state Fish, Wildlife and Parks Department officials arrived quietly at the Greenup ranch, rounded up Calvin's 10 elk, and hauled them off to their own facility. Three of them died before the state auctioned the surviving seven off for $9,051—well below market value.

The deaths of the elk angered some of Greenup's supporters. One of them called County Commissioner Devon "Smut" Warren, who had already been warned that he "wasn't living up to the Constitution." Warren dresses up each year as Santa Claus and tours the town with his pet burro, made up like a reindeer. The little donkey, named Rudy, is widely beloved in Hamilton. But the anonymous callers threatened to shoot Rudy as retaliation. "How would you like this, after Calvin's elk got killed?" they asked. Warren's wife suffered a heart attack that spring, and he blames it on the phone calls.[9]

Even though Greenup was gone, the tensions in the Bitterroot Valley grew worse. Someone phoned in a death threat to the county planning office on Friday, April 15. The next Monday, a bomb threat was phoned into the courthouse, and the building was evacuated for an hour. Everyone was fearful that something would happen on April 19, since the date held so much significance for the Patriots.

A bomb did go off that day—half a continent away, in Oklahoma City. And while the rest of the nation wondered about Arab terrorists, people in the Bitterroot Valley had an instinctive dread that the Patriots were involved as they watched the horrible images play across their televisions. When Timothy McVeigh was arrested two days later, and the cause of the disaster became more evident, the weight of sentiment that had been building against the Patriots in Hamilton exploded in an outpouring of anger and grief.

"I really think the bombing was one reason that Cal was cowed—the outpouring even in this part of the country, the sentiment was so overwhelmingly that this was a gross, terrible thing to have happened, irrespective of politics, irrespective of how you thought about the way the government had reacted in Waco and Ruby Ridge," says George Corn.

Sentiment coalesced, finally and irrevocably, behind the people who ran local government. "I got so many calls saying, 'George, what you're doing is the right thing, this is not right, if you need any help, if you need me to come sit with your family while you're gone somewhere . . .'" Corn says. "What faced Calvin and his group down was the community. I can't say that enough. That's really what happened."

Printz, George Corn and everyone else assumed Greenup would stay in hiding for awhile. Greenup, however, says that he returned only a few days after leaving in the nighttime caravan.

"I was only gone for just a few nights," he says. "We kept on the move. George don't know it, but we was sitting down here right here in this valley watching most of the stuff that was going on. He said I was gone for six weeks. At any given time, I coulda plinked Corn, could have plugged him in the head, and he'd have been dead today. Patrick Henry would have."

★★★

John Smith had read about Calvin Greenup in the newspapers, but hadn't paid close attention to the case. Smith had plenty to occupy himself with—i.e., a robust Missoula criminal-defense practice, built on several years' work as a public defender in the Missoula County court system. Greenup's far-right crusade in the Bitterroot Valley just to the south had only peripherally interested Smith, who describes himself as a "liberal to mainstream Democrat."

But on April 24, with Greenup's whereabouts still officially unknown, Smith received a phone call from another local lawyer who asked if he'd be willing to represent Greenup. Smith was reluctant, considering the violence that seemed to surround the situation, and the wide gap in their political views. But Smith, who had been involved with some high-profile criminal cases, said he'd listen to anyone who needed a good defense lawyer, even if it wasn't a popular thing to do.

"Someone will be contacting you, then," the lawyer said. Within a few hours, Smith received another call—this time, from Dennis Stucker, who asked Smith if he would take on the work of negotiating Cal Greenup's surrender and handling his defense in court. Stucker promised Smith he would be paid for his work through a family friend of the Greenups' who had made a fortune from timber. Smith still was leery, but agreed to come down to the Bitterroot Valley and talk it over with Greenup himself.

"Knowing that there was a possibility that I wouldn't even get paid on the deal—because I knew Cal didn't have any money, really—I agreed to go meet with him," Smith says. "Not knowing what I was getting into, because I really only had the media background up to that point, which wasn't too much."

Smith stipulated that he be able to bring someone along. "I asked a private investigator friend of mine, who does some PI work for me, to do it. Actually, we drove his truck. And he was well-armed. He's that kind of a guy. You know, he's into guns, and he's a cowboy. He kind of went along as a bodyguard." Smith himself is a burly man of modestly imposing size and a bushy dark mustache, but more important to these negotiations, he is a genial fellow with a disarmingly folksy and straightforward demeanor.

They were directed to Ken and Sylvia Greenup's place adjacent to Cal's ranch. "We drove up about half-a-mile dirt driveway, and were met outside by, it turns out now to be Dennis Stucker and Scott Greenup, who had a pretty good set of pistols and shoulder holsters. They were kind of dressed in black. They reminded me of commandos, or something. But they didn't really pose an intimidating presence, except that they looked like commandos. They didn't, in their faces, in their eyes, they didn't look scary. They looked kind of scared, if you want to know the truth.

"I just walked up and held my arms up and out, and they searched me, and we walked in a little front room, I kicked off my boots, and pretty soon we were in Sylvia's kitchen, which is a typical ranch kitchen, and we sat for about three, three and half hours having coffee and talking. Cal and Lynda were there, and Shad, the youngest son, Scott, of course, Dennis Stucker, and Sylvia—me and Jeff Patterson, the PI I took with me. We were all sitting in the kitchen."

Everybody pitched in their two cents' worth as they explained to Smith their situation, and their beliefs. Smith tried to keep the discussion to the pertinent aspects of the case, but it often wandered into ideological lectures, not all of them necessary. Ken Greenup, Smith says, "would just go off on these tangents about how he just couldn't understand what the world was coming to, and how the whole thing just really boils down to that Bill Clinton's really a homosexual, and that's why we have all the problems that we have. That was the bottom line for Kenny, is that we've got a homosexual in the White House.

"So, I was patient. I didn't really want this case. I didn't have anything to lose. It was kind of interesting. I like to meet interesting people in interesting places, and this certainly fit that bill. Scott cried, and said that he wanted only to be reunited with his wife and small baby, who was about eight months old at the time. Wanted a return to some kind of normalcy in his life.

"In my estimation at the time, and still, this whole thing snowballed way out of proportion and out of control for what Scott thought he was getting into—he had no idea, he had no clue. He was no longer acting at that point, he was reacting. It was scaring the shit out of him. And he just cried—broke down and cried, sobbed.

"Shad, the youngest, was far more belligerent and rebellious and militant, and said he'd stand by his dad until the end, and take the bullet with his dad. He wasn't gonna—he was sort of the opposite of Scott, at least in attitude. He put on a very brave face. He wasn't backin' down."

Smith never doubted Greenup's dedication to his cause—or for that matter, his willingness, even apparent desire, to become a martyr in its name. The two men first had to come to an understanding. Even though Greenup officially viewed people like himself as "prostitutes," Smith would be willing to represent him, but only if Greenup did what was asked of him. "I said, 'Look, I'm a lawyer, I exist within the system, I work within the system. I can't represent you, nor am I willing to represent you, and jump up on a soapbox and just spout, you know, "The government's corrupt, the courts have no jurisdiction over my clients, etc. etc." I'm not going to play this line at all. If you want me to represent you, then we're going to do it by the rules as they exist, by the laws as they exist, and I'll do what I can for you. I don't know what kind of case they have against you, and what kind of case they don't. I can probably save you from prison, knowing what I know about you. You don't belong in prison and I can probably avoid that for you. But other than that, I don't know. But that's the bottom line, take it or leave it. If you want me, those are the terms under which you are going to get me. Otherwise, you don't want me, because that's who I am and what I'll do.'"

At the end of the day, Smith drove away not sure if the Greenups would take him up on his offer. "I let them mull that over for a few days, and then I met with them again. And Scott definitely wanted me—Scott never wanted to fight this thing, at least by that time. He's about two months into this fugitive lifestyle, and he's not liking it one bit. His wife's threatening to divorce him, and she's scared, and he can't see his baby, and I mean he's bummed out.

"And in reality, I think Cal is very worried too, though he's trying not to show it at that point. But they're all pretty concerned and they're not liking this. And they want their lives back, and they just want to go on with their lives. I explained to them, 'Well, you've dug yourselves into a little bit of a hole here, and we're going to have to work ourselves back out. You cooperate with me and do everything I tell you to do, we'll be able to do that. It's not the end of the world, this isn't the end of your road, unless you choose it to be.'

"I tried to give them some hope, because they were looking and feeling and talking pretty hopeless. Their whole world's gone to shit, nothing we can do about it, and we're powerless anyway.

"He obviously wasn't getting anywhere. I mean, he's losing his ranch for not paying his mortgage and he has a warrant out for him for not filing his taxes, and he's a wanted man for harboring fugitives. It was creating a situation where he was more powerless and less powerful. And I kept telling him that."

Some of Smith's message got through to Greenup, who nonetheless refused to budge from his Patriot beliefs. "I've had a lot of arguments with John," Greenup says. "The very first thing that I told John— 'We're going to get one thing straight— you are not a licensed attorney, don't give me that crap, that's more of your fraud. I just said, you get home and you call me on the phone and tell me what your so-called license says. And he called me on the phone, and he says, 'It says right here, on the license.' And I said, read it to me. And he says, 'I'm certified to be licensed by the bar association of Montana.' . . . There's no such thing as a licensed attorney in the United States. It ain't there. That's a misnomer." Satisfied that he had scored his points, Smith proceeded to negotiate over how Cal Greenup would go about surrendering.

It took Smith a couple more meetings with Greenup before he contacted George Corn in early May and told him Cal was going to turn himself in. Complicating matters was a new set of felony charges Corn had filed the same week against Greenup and Joe Holland, as well as Dennis Stucker and Ben Schneider, who had been part of the entourage taking Greenup over Lost Trail Pass on April 12. Corn charged them with "criminal syndicalism" for threatening public officials—the same law Garfield County Prosecutor Nick Murnion had used the year before to put Bill Stanton away for 10 years. Most of the charges revolved around Holland's December 30 and April 8 faxes, and the wild events of April 12. The two MCIB agents' testimony formed the basis for several of the charges, especially those against Stucker and Schneider. Ravalli County deputies arrested Schneider, and then Stucker a few days later.

Joe Holland, arrested at his home in Indiana, tried fighting extradition for a few weeks. On May 16, he sent a mass mailing to all of the registered voters of Ravalli County attacking Judge Langton—informing readers he had investigated Langton and found he was guilty of judicial misconduct. The mailing, affecting as it did the entire jury pool for his own upcoming trial, constituted jury tampering, and George Corn had another charge to slap on the militia leader.

Meanwhile, talks between Smith and Corn continued apace. "It took six weeks of negotiating with the county attorney, with the sheriff involved, going to the judge, getting in place the lien against Ken and Sylvia's ranch to cover the bond," Smith says. "Their ranch is worth upward of three hundred thousand dollars, and they had a hundred thousand dollar bond on Cal, and I think fifty on Scott and twenty-five on Shad, I think. All protected by the lien on Ken and Sylvia's."

On June 1, Cal Greenup surrendered at the county courthouse with John Smith at his side. As part of the deal, he agreed to give up his guns, and conceded the authority of the court, promising to behave himself. He and his sons brought in all their guns, and then Cal and Lynda accompanied Corn and Printz back out to the ranch—already repossessed by the bank for non-payment—where the lawmen conducted a room-by-room search of the place.[10]

Smith notes that the weaponry fell far short of the myth that had grown around Greenup's supposed armament. "The whole thing had been blown completely out of proportion as to what kind of weaponry they had. It was mostly just hunting rifles—they did have an AK-47, semi-automatic. It had not been converted. Everything was legal, all the weapons were legal."

Greenup's first case before the court was on the game-farm charges after his refusal to buy a $25 elk-farm permit. He pleaded guilty in August to the charges, but after he was sentenced to 10 days in jail, he decided to appeal. He claimed the elk were pets, enjoying the same status as livestock and not game, and thus not subject to the state's laws regulating game farms. He lost that appeal, of course, and on December 4, he got a stiffer sentence than before—30 days in jail.

The next day, Joe Holland's trial opened, ushering in a flurry of Patriot trials that month. Holland's attorney, a constitutionalist from Nebraska named John DeCamp, tried to argue from the beginning that the courts had no jurisdiction over his client. He claimed the threats against public officials were protected by free speech. He neglected to object to Jay Printz's hearsay testimony about conversations he had with Greenup, after Greenup himself had testified that Holland's faxes were transmissions of Greenup's own ideas—crucial testimony in linking Holland, situated in Indiana, to the actual threat to public officials posed by Greenup's activities on April 12.

After only two days of trial, Holland decided to plead guilty, saying he would appeal on a higher level of jurisdiction. DeCamp tried to cast the plea in a positive light for his supporters, saying the trial was going so well they decided to take advantage of a clause in Montana law that allows defendants to plead guilty while reserving the right to appeal rulings made in the pretrial phase. Holland said they'd appeal the constitutionality of the criminal syndicalism laws.

On the other hand, there may have been other motives. Most of the jurors polled afterward indicated they would have voted to convict Holland in any case.[11]

A week later, Dennis Stucker—who had been convicted on November 11 for helping Greenup flee when he was a federal fugitive—appeared in court to be sentenced. Stucker still maintained his innocence. "A severe travesty of justice has occurred here," he told District Judge John Larsen. "This is totally unjust and unfair." Larsen seemed unmoved. He ignored a favorable probation report and handed down a six-year deferred sentence, with 90 consecutive days in jail to be served in the coming year.

The same day, Shad Greenup—who "watched Stucker get convicted and saw the handwriting on the wall," attorney John Smith told reporters—decided to cop a guilty plea to the felony intimidation charges Corn slapped him with after the incident at Al Hamilton's house. His sentence comprised a six-year deferred term and a few fines—and as part of the deal, he had to agree to testify against his father and others still facing trial.[12]

Al Hamilton's trial, starting the next Monday, only took three days. The jury deliberated five hours before deciding he was guilty of felony intimidation and an accompanying accountability charge. Two days later, Judge Langton sentenced him to 10 years in prison, suspending all but the time he had already spent in jail since his April arrest. Hamilton was a free man, but it only lasted a few months. He refused to cooperate with the court order to pay his back taxes and to perform community service, so Langton reinstituted the rest of his sentence in May 1996 and packed him off to the Montana State Prison in Deer Lodge.

Cal Greenup did his four weeks' jail time on the elk charges that January 1996. He also finally paid his 1991 state income taxes in exchange for having the charges dropped. With Cal still facing more serious felony syndicalism charges, John Smith worked out a plea agreement that would allow Cal to serve no prison time, while in return he would remain on probation for 15 years and would not be allowed to possess any guns during that time. Greenup entered his guilty plea to two felony counts of obstruction of justice in February, and was given the sentence on April 2, exactly a year after things got out of hand in Darby.

★★★

Greenup is defiant in court—inspired, perhaps, by his friends in Jordan who began their standoff with the FBI just the week before. Calvin wears a white ribbon on his sweater with the word "Freeman" inscribed on it with a magic marker. Lynda and Shad are both there with him, and they wear similar ribbons.

Before the judge announces the sentence, Greenup gets up and has his say, waving a big black Bible at the court. "This, your honor, is the ultimate law book," he says in a brittle, preacherly voice. "When man deviates from this law book, he deviates from the precious Godhead, and when you do that, you lower yourself from the kind of decency where husbands can lay the foundations of what is lawful . . .

"We have to be accountable to the Lord. In that respect, I have never injured anyone, never done anything. I believe that everyone, including government officials, have to be accountable for their acts. I have seen the last several years where government is violating the constitution in so many aspects, and they're violating them as institutions. Because the people of this country are sovereign under God—because that's the way the country was set up. We have a constitutional republic. We have receded from that so rapidly I fear this nation, and every land that I see, has fell from this book, has fell from decency on this planet."

The judge, John Larson, duly notes the lecture and proceeds to read the sentence.

Afterward, Greenup holds forth outside on the soggy brown lawn with a small cluster of newspaper and television reporters, where he expands on his courtroom lecture by explaining that the Constitution has been suspended and is being violated by phony government officials. He tells them that, despite being barred from possessing guns for the next 15 years, he plans to do battle with the New World Order when its minions invade the country.

Asked if, looking back on the past year, there is anything he would do differently, Greenup has a succinct response.

"Yes, I would change one drastic thing," he says. "I would never have hired an attorney and went into these courts."

What would you have done instead? the reporter asks.

"I would have done whatever I had to do to try and make people realize there's no redress of grievance and there's no justice in this country . . . When you take and destroy a man because of his trying to prove to people that there's no justice, and try to prove to people that public officials that are violating the Constitution don't get punished—yes, I was punished for my political views."

George Corn watches these proceedings and shakes his head. He's still not so sure Cal Greenup will return to being a good citizen, and talk of that nature just feeds his uneasiness. "You just don't know where this thing's going to go yet," he says.

"John's an excellent lawyer. He did a real good job, I think. He did a good job for his client, and a good job for society, I think. I really do. His client feels otherwise, but he doesn't know how lucky he is to have John represent him."

John Smith, however, lets Greenup's rhetoric roll off his back, despite its implications. That afternoon, he and Calvin, Lynda and Shad drink coffee at a Hamilton diner and talk over what their next move will be. Smith tries to stress the importance of staying on the straight and narrow, especially since staying out of jail has been one of Greenup's priorities.

Shorn of his Old Testament-style beard, Cal Greenup seems less regal and more like the skinny little hothead who roamed Darby as a teenager. He still appears edgy, ready to bolt, like an elk. Getting him to open up isn't easy, though he's all too glad to start lecturing any listener on the details of his constitutionalist beliefs. This is the lens through which he views all of his life, past, present and future.

In his own mind, he has been the reasonable part through all of this: "No violence ever came of my actions. I am one of the few people in this community who done everything I could to keep somebody from getting shot. It was Cal Greenup who stood up, and said, 'No folks, we're not going to shoot.'"

Still, it is plain he almost seems to long for the kind of celebrity martyrdom the Freemen in Jordan are currently enjoying. The white ribbons are symbols of that longing, symbols Greenup refuses to explain. "I don't agree with everything that goes on in the country as far as the Freemen, but the opposite of free man is slave—and I don't want to be a slave," he says.

He takes pains to explain his differences with the Jordan group. "We don't see eye to eye on the Scriptures," he says. "See, if you were a black man, sitting here, I would sit here and talk to you just like it doesn't make any difference to me. They wouldn't.

"I don't believe that way. I believe the Bible is very plain—it said, 'Whosoever shall come—whosoever shall call upon the name of the Lord shall be saved.' It doesn't say anything about color. It says whosoever. So if I am a whosoever, so is a black man.

"By the way, when I was in St. Louis, I worked with some real nice black people. Clean, nice black people. I don't have no problems with the black folks. I don't want to live with any of them—I don't think that's wrong. But I don't have no problem working with them, dealing with them, I'll go to church with them."

Greenup doesn't bat an eye at the apparent contradiction between claiming he's not a racist and simultaneously believing in racial separation. Nor does his belief in a conspiracy of Jewish bankers sound even slightly anti-Semitic to his own ears. By his own reckoning, he's unusually even-handed. After all, he says, he's more critical of his own family members than some Jews and blacks he knows.

"I'm a pretty broad-minded person," he says. "And the thing of it is, with my relatives, I flat tell them, I don't pull no punches with them. If they're a jackass, I believe in telling them so."

That's the thing about Cal Greenup; like many people, he's so certain he's on the side of Good that everyone arrayed against him is Evil by necessity. This is what enables him to ignore other brazen contradictions in his version of his life story, like living off the fat of a government contract for years, and then castigating the government as evil when that enrichment finally comes to an end. Greenup, as George Corn puts it, "gradually ended up with $400,000 for sitting there on his rear end, letting people come up there and throw stuff off a pickup truck. The irony was, the guy who is railing against the government couldn't make his living without the government monopoly and got mad about it and started waving a gun in people's faces."

Greenup believes he's been made a martyr for telling the truth. His home has been foreclosed on and he must come up with $93,000 to get it back, and he has no idea where it will come from. A month later, the courts will award Greenup $24,000 compensation for the loss of his elk, but even that won't be enough. He's starting to feel a little desperate. And the old anger is still there.

"I'll be honest with you, at this point in time, I don't know where our next buck is going to come from," he says. "We just took the last few pennies we had yesterday and went and got groceries, and that's it. We're done."

Greenup, for now, simply feeds on the belief that eventually the tables will turn on his tormenters.

"They're gonna be sorry someday," he says, "and I'm going to live to see the day that they're sorry for what they done to me."

Chapter 10 / High Noon

W HEN HE ENGAGED in an armed standoff with law-enforcement officials, Calvin Greenup was simply taking part in a storied tradition of the radical right in the Northwest: a ritual dance of death in which the heroes and martyrs of the movement, as well as its villains, are made. The most famous legends of the Patriot movement—Robert Mathews, Randy Weaver, the Freemen—were fashioned by gun-clacking confrontations with often fatal consequences.

A North Dakota farmer named Gordon Kahl was the model for all of these martyrs. A 63-year-old grandfather who had won a Purple Heart as a bomber turret gunner during World War II, Kahl worked as a recruiter for the Posse Comitatus during the farm-foreclosure crisis of the late 1970s and early 1980s. Kahl stopped paying taxes in 1967, about the same time he became a devout Identity follower and Posse activist, and served eight months in prison in 1979 for tax evasion. That did not deter him from publicly pronouncing his views afterward, working the crowds at farm foreclosures, telling anyone who would listen that the farmers were victims of a massive Jewish conspiracy, and urging them to refuse to pay their taxes, just as he did.

Ultimately, federal marshals came to get Kahl, who refused to show up at court hearings for his numerous probation violations and told everyone he'd shoot any law-enforcement officers who tried to arrest him. He was convinced a friend in the Posse Comitatus who died of a heart attack in prison had been poisoned by the feds, and he feared a similar fate awaited him were he sent back. He became a fugitive, moving around the Dakotas, Missouri and Arkansas, living with various friends.

Finally, on February 13, 1983, a sunny winter Sunday, the law caught up with Kahl near Medina, North Dakota—and the law lost. Kahl was just leaving town, where he had been attending a Posse meeting, when three federal marshals and two local lawmen surrounded him on a county road in a two-car caravan with his son Yorie, his wife and three fellow Posse members. Yorie Kahl opened fire on one of the marshals, critically wounding him, and the bullets started flying. When it was all over, two marshals lay dead, and the other three officers were wounded. Gordon Kahl had finished off the marshal Yorie wounded by walking up to him as he lay in the cab of the truck bleeding and blasting his head off with a shotgun.

Yorie was wounded in the battle and was arrested at the local hospital. David Broer and Scott Faul, the two Posse believers who had joined them in the gun battle, were captured within a few days. Gordon went on the run, the object of a nationwide manhunt that lasted nearly four months. The FBI finally caught up with him on June 3 in rural Arkansas, where he had taken refuge with friends. Again, Kahl killed a lawman: the local sheriff who had entered the house to try to arrest him peacefully. Again, bullets began flying. This time, Kahl was outnumbered. FBI agents purposely set the house ablaze, and Kahl refused to leave. His blackened corpse was found amid the ashes later that evening.[1]

Kahl's martyrdom spurred people on the radical right around the country to a new level of action. For the first time, all the talk about being willing to die for the cause had become a reality. In northern Idaho, Kahl's death inspired Robert Mathews to declare war on the government and begin forming The Order. A year and a half later, Mathews died in an almost identical fashion in a rural cabin on a Puget Sound island at the opposite corner of the country, defiantly consumed in the flames.

And just as Mathews was the heir to Gordon Kahl, so were Randy and Vicky Weaver perceived as the descendants of Mathews' The Order. Mathews' activities and those of similar right-wing fanatics operating out of the Aryan Nations compound in Hayden Lake brought an intense law-enforcement crackdown over the illegal acts inspired by Identity believers in northern Idaho. This ensnared Randy Weaver in the weapons-violation case that ultimately brought the marshals to his Ruby Ridge home. This time, though, the victims were not the subject of the manhunt itself, but the wife and son he had used as shields. And this time, public sentiment swung in the other direction. People wondered aloud why a heavy-handed, SWAT-team type response that kills women and children who happen to be in the way is necessary to bring someone in for sawing off a shotgun.

The questioning reached a culmination in the September 1995 hearings before a Senate Judiciary subcommittee on terrorism, called by U.S. Senator Larry Craig, an Idaho Republican, to inquire about the events at Ruby Ridge. Weaver himself tearfully testified, demanding justice for his dead wife. Much of the rest of the testimony, though, concentrated on the fact that Randy Weaver escalated the conflict with law enforcement at every step. Ultimately, as with House hearings a few months before on the 1993 deaths of 76 people at the Branch Davidian compound in Waco, Texas, the Ruby Ridge hearings were inconclusive. The final report, issued in December 1995, criticized the FBI for its handling of events at Ruby Ridge, especially the issuing of special rules of engagement that allowed agents to shoot at any adult at will.

The barrage of criticism from these hearings directed at the FBI and the Bureau of Alcohol, Tobacco and Firearms—for both agencies' roles in the two fatal standoffs—shook morale deeply within the agencies. Not only did agents feel they were being criticized for performing work required of them as public servants, but they felt as if they had been transformed into some kind of demons—especially by the rhetoric emanating from the likes of G. Gordon Liddy (who recommended "Head shots!" in dealing with agents) and the NRA, which likened them to "jack-booted thugs."

An ATF agent I interviewed put it this way: "You just go home and try to enjoy your family, because you don't know if you dare show your face in public or tell people what it is you do for a living. It's getting depressing. I know things are even worse back in Washington.

"People think we're hard-nosed killers. And we're just doing our jobs protecting them."

For awhile in 1995, there was even talk of dismantling the ATF. There was internal strife; a misconduct incident brought to light by a couple of Detroit whistleblowers within the agency brought out latent tension within the bureaucracy, and there were claims of racist behavior at an informal gathering of agents called the "Good Ol' Boys Roundup" in rural Tennessee. Though the ATF was criticized for its alleged entrapment of Randy Weaver on the Ruby Ridge weapons charge, the Waco episode weighed most heavily on the agency. There was a widespread feeling within the ATF that the original raid in which their people were involved would have succeeded had Koresh not been tipped off by a reporter who called the compound prior to the agents' arrival, and that they had been tainted by association with the FBI actions that resulted in the fiery deaths of everyone inside.[2]

The FBI was its own special basket case. The special orders given at Ruby Ridge especially came back to haunt the officials who issued them. At first they denied that the orders had ever been given, and one official, E. Michael Kahoe, destroyed documents during an internal investigation of the matter. Ultimately, FBI Director Louis Freeh's right-hand man, Larry Potts, was demoted in the rippling scandal.

The somber mood ultimately inspired some long-overdue reflection on the part of the people within the agencies on how to handle such cases. The war on drugs in the 1980s had drastically altered the face of law enforcement. It seemed as though every sizeable police department, let alone the federal agencies, had developed specially trained tactical teams for performing often dramatic raids on drug dealers and other lawbreakers. In many cases this was funded with the assistance of generous federal anti-drug moneys. Most everyone who had a job in law enforcement was trained in academies that focused on arrest techniques, but did little to teach officers how to become part of the communities in which they worked. The shift in emphasis to this style of enforcement led to a general estrangement of law officers from the public at large, especially when innocent civilians were injured or killed in heavy-handed raids.

Virtually everyone in law enforcement was geared to dealing with criminal lawbreakers, and this engendered a significant blind spot when it came to handling people who weren't ordinary criminals, especially political or religious zealots whose beliefs transcended civil law in their own minds. One ATF agent I know had begun his career busting crack dealers in the poor neighborhoods of Tacoma, Washington, and was accustomed to fairly standard responses from the criminals he arrested. If they were armed and they thought they could shoot their way out of the arrest, there was a slight chance that the dealer might try to open fire; but otherwise, once the jig was up, most criminals would relax, succumb to the arrest, and pose no further threat. "In a lot of cases these were guys we had met before, maybe arrested before, and we'd exchange jokes and friendly talk," he said. "With most criminals, they know they're breaking the law, and it's like a game to them; every once in a while they lose and have to go to court and usually jail. They expect that. It's part of the game to them."

But when he began dealing with Patriots, he instinctively understood it was a completely different ballgame. "With these folks, when you come to arrest them, they see it as Satan himself coming to take them away, and they're going to defend against that with their lives," he said. "That's what happened at Waco. Ruby Ridge. And as an agency, we haven't been prepared to deal with that. To us, a criminal was just a criminal. But that's starting to change. We're learning."

The FBI was heeding the same lessons, and began figuring out how to make them work, out on the plains near Jordan, Montana.

★★★

When warrants for the Montana Freemen—Emmett and Richard Clark, LeRoy Schweitzer, Dan Petersen and Rodney Skurdal—were issued in May 1995 for threatening local and federal officials, law enforcement at all levels was still in a state of extreme cautiousness due to the public criticism, eventually dubbed "Weaver fever" by field officers who felt their superiors were sitting on their hands.

An extreme case of this skittishness actually occurred just as the Weaver standoff was brewing. On June 27, 1992, a sawmill operator and constitutionalist named Gordon Sellner who lived in the woods near Seeley Lake, Montana, shot a Missoula County sheriff's deputy in the chest when Sellner was pulled over for driving without license plates on his car. The deputy was wearing a bulletproof vest at the time and escaped with a deep bruise. Sellner retreated to his cabin with his wife and children and refused to come out. The Lakes County sheriff, who had jurisdiction in the case, decided to wait him out instead of going in and getting him. It was a long wait.

The standoff, such as it was, lasted three years, and finally ended on July 18, 1995, when Sellner was caught by sheriff's deputies who set up an ambush on the perimeter of his property. Sellner spotted them and opened fire, and the deputies returned shots. This time, it was Sellner who was hit, shot in the leg, and then arrested along with his wife and two sons-in-law. When his place was searched, authorities found 30 firearms, a pipe bomb and a tube of dynamite gel.

The following September, with Joe Holland's attorney, Nebraska constitutionalist John DeCamp, as his lawyer, Sellner was found guilty by a Missoula jury of attempted deliberate homicide in the 1992 shooting. The judge sentenced him to life in prison.[3]

Despite the length of time it took to arrest Sellner, there were other signs that law-enforcement officials were learning how to deal with the Patriots. Most notably, the peaceful end to Calvin Greenup's standoff in Darby in June 1995 signaled that it was possible to bring resisters in without any gunfire. The lessons from that standoff clearly came into play with the Freemen in eastern Montana.[4]

For months after the Freemen's indictments were handed down by a grand jury in 1995, FBI agents watched and waited for the right moment to make their move. The Freemen then were still split into two locations: the Clark ranch at Brusett, and

Skurdal's place near Roundup, a two-hour drive to the south. Garfield County Sheriff Charlie Phipps and prosecutor Nick Murnion were told to back off and let the feds handle the Clarks' arrest, and the lawmen in Roundup were told the same. Musselshell County Sheriff Paul Smith says he could have arrested Rodney Skurdal on any of the many evenings he spent at the Branding Iron saloon on the road into Roundup, because Smith liked to drink there too. But he held off because he was afraid he would screw up whatever operation the FBI was planning—and he was not privy to the feds' plans, though he was aware of all the surveillance they were conducting.

The FBI circled Skurdal's cabin at the crest of a ridge on Johnny's Coal Road near Roundup and gradually tightened the noose. The place certainly was not problematic in terms of mounting an assault; it was surrounded by trees and sat just below the ridge's crest, so an armed force could easily come up from the other side of the ridge without detection. However, it was not exactly isolated. Five or six other homes were within a stone's throw, and their occupants might have been in harm's way if gunfire erupted. So the FBI tapped the phones, tracking who called in and out, and sent a couple of agents to live in one of the nearby homes, pretending to be new neighbors. Surveillance plane flyovers became frequent.

All this activity, though, apparently did not go undetected, because when the Freemen pulled out of Skurdal's cabin on September 28, 1995, it was because they had seen too many signs that the FBI was closing in. The move caught the FBI by surprise, perhaps because their agents were themselves on the verge of taking action. Rather than execute a hastily prepared arrest plan under the new circumstances, they simply stood by and watched as the caravan of three vehicles made the two-hour drive to the Clarks' ranch, where the Freemen's numbers were now almost doubled.

Nick Murnion fumed, because the Freemen in his county had just turned into an insurmountable army, at least for Charlie Phipps' three-man sheriff's department. Moreover, the new location not only was bigger and had more space for the Freemen to conduct their "Constitutional law" classes, but it was much easier to defend. It was approachable only from the south. Its entire northern edge was protected by a steep gully, and any southern assault could be seen coming for nearly a mile away.

The Clark ranchhouse itself sat in the middle of a depression of land near the gully, and Ralph Clark had built a miniature reservoir where his property bordered his brother Emmett's adjacent land. Next to the creek that filled the reservoir, Ralph Clark had built a trio of small hunter's cabins which he had once intended to rent to visiting outdoorsmen, but which instead became residences for the Freemen. Behind the cabins was the "schoolhouse"—actually a residence, but its flat, long structure gave it something of an institutional appearance, and from the day they arrived, it was anointed the building where Schweitzer, Petersen and Skurdal held their classes.

The most important feature of the Clark ranch, though, was the high arcing ridge to its south that bordered the property. The road in to the ranch lay on the other side of this ridge, and the driveway in from that road jutted northward at the low point of the arc; as a result, it was a simple matter for the Freemen to place sentries atop the hill, which allowed them to observe people approaching the driveway well in advance of when they turned into it. And if anyone drove by, the Freemen could simply drive down the little path they had built from the ridgetop down to the main road and come in behind them. This was how the various newsmen who had stumbled up to the property had been so easily ambushed.

Initially, the sentries simply sat in a van atop the ridge. But after awhile, they took an old travel trailer from the ranchyard and pulled it up atop the ridge so they could stand watch in a little more comfort. One night, a brutal prairie windstorm toppled the little trailer end over end down the hillside toward the ranch like a tumbleweed, scattering tin, wood and fiberglass insulation in its path. A few days later, the Freemen toted another trailer up there. This time, they bolted it down using large beams they drove into the ground vertically and then topped it with similarly large horizontal beams.

The FBI continued to circle and watch and wait. In the following six months, agents allowed a steady stream of the Freemen's proteges from around the country to pour in and out of the ranch—among them their own undercover agents. Finally, with local anger over the situation reaching a near-boil, the FBI made its move on March 25, 1996, capturing Schweitzer and Petersen with the radio-antenna ruse and setting off the armed standoff.

As the FBI set up surveillance posts on the ranch's perimeter, the remaining Freemen sharply stepped up their armed patrols on the ridge above the ranch. The sentries erected a flagpole, and flew the American flag upside-down from it—the signal for distress. And they built a gun stand in front of the trailer—a wooden shelter where they could kneel and shoot with some measure of protection. They installed a turret in it for a machine gun.

When the national media began arriving and parking mobile-broadcast trucks on the little turnout they soon dubbed "Media Hill"—visible to the Freemen guards but at a considerable distance—the Patriot sentries took a signboard up to the hilltop with them. They figured the TV cameras would pan in on it, which they did: "Grand Jury. It's The Law. Why Not? Who Fears The Evidence?" the sign read.

The FBI was not eager to conduct an assault for other reasons in addition to "Weaver fever." Besides the difficulties of approaching the Freemen's compound without being detected, the Patriots inside were dispersed so broadly about that any attack would be hard to coordinate. Ralph's ranch house was the central residence, but there were Freemen living inside each of the hunting cabins and some inside the schoolhouse. Edwin and Emmett continued staying at their respective homes on the adjoining property. An assault not only would have to be executed quickly, it would involve assaults at a number of points with no guarantee of success at any of them.

With agents staked out at their respective positions, the FBI moved fast to establish communications, in the hope of setting up negotiations. Both the Weaver and Greenup standoffs had ended with the help of third parties, though with wholly different negotiators: John Smith was nearly as far removed from Bo Gritz, in terms of both politics and motivation, as one could get. The FBI first wanted to try mainstream negotiators. FBI specialists were the first to talk to the Freemen by phone, and they received from them a list of possible negotiators, including a state legislator they actually seemed to trust: House Representative Karl Ohs, a Republican rancher from the Tobacco Root Mountains area in southwest Montana. The FBI called up Ohs and asked if he'd like to help.

Karl Ohs is not a dyed-in-the-wool conservative—indeed, he has been accused of liberalism at times by his Republican colleagues. He had built a reputation for trustworthiness as an activist for ranchers' rights who worked to keep people from losing their places through foreclosure, acting as a "peer counselor" in some instances to help stave off the wolves while ranchers got back on their feet. He also was a close friend of Val Stanton, the wife of Freeman Ebert Stanton—the son of the imprisoned Freeman "constable" Bill Stanton. Val's father, Butch Anderson, was foreman on Ohs' ranch, and Val had grown up with Ohs' own children. Val and Ebert were inside the compound, and Butch wanted someone to go in and talk the two of them out. When the FBI called, Ohs readily agreed.

Ohs says he already had an inkling he would be involved from the very day that the FBI arrested Schweitzer. "On March 25, that night," he recalls, "I got a call from somebody I didn't recognize, and they said, 'Do you know what's going on in Jordan?' And I'd just barely heard about it, so I said, 'Yes, but I certainly don't know much.'

"And he said, 'Are you going to come up for this meeting?' And I said, 'What meeting is that?' And he said, 'Well, I understand some of you guys are going to come up for a meeting.' He says, 'We want to call off the dogs.' And I said, 'You know, there's really nothing I can do.' I was trying to distance myself from them. The thought went through my mind, 'What the heck's going on? How would anybody get my name?'

"Well then, a couple of days later, the FBI called. And Butch and I in the meantime had discussed going up there just to see Val, to see if he couldn't get her out, talk her into coming out of there. And the FBI called, and there had been a list of names thrown out, of legislators that these people wanted to talk to, and evidently that was in reference to that first phone call I'd gotten. My name was on the list with a group of legislators who are the most conservative of the group up here."

Ohs, whose reputation as a Republican in Helena ran from moderate to liberal, was a little surprised to be included in such company. "So my thought was, 'Well, how did I get there?' And then I thought, 'Oh, it's Val.' They were looking for people they felt they could trust, and Val put my name on the list. From that point on, the FBI, once they found out that I was on the list, they were interested in talking to me. I was a state legislator—had a quasi-official position and maybe was a little more middle of the road, and they became very interested in talking to us further."

Ohs says he and Butch Anderson drove together to Billings that Thursday, and went to Jordan the next morning. "We drove up and met with the FBI, and the FBI was apprehensive about sending me in alone, or with Butch," he recalls, "and so Butch went in one afternoon, came back, and I went in with him the next morning, spent all day in there, got a list of demands of the things they wanted."

Ralph Clark set the early tone for the talks. "We were all tense going in there," Ohs says. "We were going to go out the back way so the media wouldn't see us.

Ralph was going to take us out. And he gets out to the car, and he says, 'Oops, I forgot my gun.' So he goes trudging back in with his little derby, he's trudging the whole way, straps his gun on his back, goes waddling back out to the car—'Oops, I gotta go relieve myself.' So he just stands right there at the car, stands there taking a leak.

"And I look at Butch and I say, 'Gosh darn, you know, these are really pretty high-level negotiations.'"

Ohs did manage to come out with a list of demands. "There were some things they were talking about, about this grand jury sort of thing, and that's when we came up with the idea of getting other legislators involved, in case there was some way we could handle this within the legislative process."

Ohs assembled a group of three other legislators, two Republicans and a Democrat, who traveled the following week to Jordan to meet with the Freemen inside the ranch. They offered an olive branch: the chance to have the Freemen's grievances and beliefs aired in a public forum, possibly before the state legislature. The offer seemed to go over well initially, but eventually the Freemen refused.

Nonetheless, Ohs succeeded in his initial mission: Val Stanton left the ranch with her two children on April 5, and a week later, Ebert and his mother Agnes surrendered as well. But by then, the Freemen had fallen silent, and the talks appeared to be at a standstill.

So when Bo Gritz flew in with Randy Weaver three weeks after the Freemen standoff began, officials figured it was worth a shot; after all, Gritz had ended the Weaver affair. Weaver was not allowed in to the ranch, perhaps out of fear he'd be too volatile of an element in the negotiations. Instead, Jack McLamb, who had been at Gritz's side at Ruby Ridge, played the role of the ex-Green Beret's sidekick once again.

The Gritz talks were not successful, but they broke the ice. For three days, the Freemen used Gritz as their public mouthpiece. Through him, the world heard the Freemen declare they'd surrender if federal authorities could prove the Freemen's legal claims wrong—something that had already been done numerous times through legitimate channels, including by the Montana Supreme Court. Even if officials agreed to the condition, they already knew the Freemen were impervious to any such proof, so they chose simply to decline. The next day, the Freemen reiterated their demand for a hearing in the Montana legislature, and Gritz again relayed the demand somewhat sympathetically.

Conversely, the Freemen refused to concede any matters from their side. The talks had rapidly deteriorated from a negotiation to a series of prolonged lectures from the Freemen. Gritz eventually exploded in frustration, denouncing the Freemen as frauds and departing the standoff in a huff on May 1. John Connor, a deputy in the Montana attorney general's office, met with the Freemen that same afternoon, and obtained the same result. "We've met with them four times and presented to them the most reasonable offer we can come up with," he said. "They have rejected that offer."

For another two and a half weeks, the standoff would be frozen in stasis.

★★★

The afternoon Gritz departed, as Connor was debriefing the press, the FBI had a bit of a scare. A caravan of five cars was spotted heading toward the ranch at a high rate of speed. Agents moved to intercept them in case they were Patriot supporters intending to run the roadblock or perhaps even attempt a rescue, converging at the "four corners" area where lawmen had established their main checkpoint.

It was a false alarm: the caravan consisted of five cars driven by Ford Motor Company employees out to test the vehicles. They simply had chosen the wrong road and were stunned to be suddenly surrounded by FBI agents and flashing police lights. The situation was cleared up in a few moments, and the cars turned back down the road toward Jordan.

A little laughter rippled through the assembled agents and the press, breaking the tension. But it took awhile for everyone's pulses to return to normal.

The incident underscored the biggest concern at the standoff, especially as negotiations fell silent and the long waiting game resumed: namely, that the most significant threat of violence came not from the people inside the compound, but from Patriots arriving from elsewhere to try to make something happen. No one wanted to talk about it, for fear of giving the Freemen's sympathizers ideas, but the concern had already sparked one gathering of locals out at the community hall. The FBI's watchful eye on everyone who came and went at the standoff was part of an unspoken effort to prevent any such violence from blossoming.

Norm Olson of the Michigan Militia had already threatened to bring men out to defend the Freemen, but Olson apparently had no credibility within the movement because his call was almost completely ignored. Other efforts to raise support met similar fates.

The Freemen Patriots of Kamiah, Idaho, who had organized that winter at Bo Gritz's "covenant community," issued a call for other Patriots to gather at a campground at Lewistown, 130 miles west of Jordan. When April 3 arrived, a total of seven militiamen gathered at the campground—along with about 13 media people, most of whom had grown tired of waiting around in Jordan. Two of Gritz's followers, Ed LeStage and Michael Cain, hogged the microphones for the day. They told the press that more militia people would be arriving in the coming days, but none ever did. Most of those who showed up that Monday eventually trickled out. A week later, the last of the Freemen Patriots picked up their stakes and pulled out, vowing to return if events warranted. The *Missoulian* dubbed the affair the "Seven Man March."

Another militia group, this time from LaGrande, Oregon, also warned of retaliation—only in this case, against military targets. "If they do another Waco situation, period, it's a declaration of war," said Eastern Oregon Militia leader Walt Hassey. "If they storm in there in Jordan and slaughter those people, there will be retribution." Hassey did not indicate which military bases would come under attack, but considering that his group's meetings usually numbered between five and twenty in attendance, the threat did not seem to be particularly ominous.

Every now and then someone else would trickle in—supporters from Oregon, some from Bozeman, fundamentalists from Texas and Arizona who came to hang their signs at the roadblock. They all made noise, but attempts at moving beyond the rhetoric into action were minimal. Agents found arms and other supplies in one would-be roadblock-runner's van; the visiting Patriots were simply turned back.

A militia "war warning" circulated on the Internet—eventually earning a Bill Morlin write-up in the *Spokesman-Review*—suggesting a scenario in which FBI agents would be shot in retaliation for any deaths at Jordan. Law-enforcement officials dismissed it as mere fantasizing. Militia members denounced it, saying they wouldn't go to war over the Freemen. Some read even deeper conspiracies into it. Since this "war plan" had been leaked to the press, they believed, the whole thing was a setup; the scheme was actually a plant by government agent provocateurs who wanted to have an excuse to crack down on the militias.

After awhile, though, it became almost embarrassing how little support the Freemen enjoyed—from other Patriots, from their neighbors and relatives, from other Montanans. There was some buzz of support on the Internet for the Freemen for the first month or so, but after Gritz pronounced them "scam artists" and urged other Patriots to withdraw their support, that talk was relegated to a distinct minority. Even John Trochmann—who had been among the Freemen's biggest supporters and closest allies until they issued an "arrest warrant" for him in January 1996—urged militia members to refrain from going to Jordan . . . for the time being.

"I don't think the public has risen up and embraced them," Nick Murnion said. "Most people look at it as a bunch of damn gibberish."

Especially in Garfield County, where people had been listening to Ralph Clark spew for years. "That's what they've failed to recognize," Murnion said. "This county has absolutely rejected it 100 percent."

If this rejection disheartened the Freemen, as most of the people close to the negotiations believed it did, it did not initially buckle their resolve. As they told Bo Gritz, they simply believed Yahweh had placed an invisible protective barrier around the ranch, so it didn't matter what the public thought.

Nor, for that matter, did the public disapproval embolden the FBI. The chief problem for them was logistical and tactical. There were now 21 people inside the compound—three of them children, essentially innocents whose presence most gave the FBI pause. The bulk of the adults were federal fugitives of some sort or another—some from other states: Russell Landers and Dana Dudley, wanted on Colorado securities-fraud charges; Stephen Hance, wanted on fraud charges in North Carolina; and Gloria Ward, wanted on Utah custodial-interference charges. Gloria's daughters Courtnie Jo Gunn and Jaylynn Mangum, ages ten and eight respectively, were two of the children inside the compound. The third was Dana Dudley's daughter, 16-year-old Amanda Michele Kendricks.

It had become obvious that, just as Randy Weaver had done, the Freemen were using the three children as shields. Bo Gritz was outspoken on the subject, noting Edwin Clark's fear that a violent fate awaited them if the children left. Gritz also observed a growing rift among the Freemen. Edwin and Ralph Clark, the proprietors of the ranch, seemed to be less convinced the standoff was going the way it ought to. A cadre of hard-core Freemen were running the show: Rodney Skurdal, Dale Jacobi, Russell Landers and Dana Dudley. And they appeared to be shouting down anyone else who questioned their decisions. Dudley in particular had become a bully in dealing with the others.

"Every time Ralph Clark tried to say something," Gritz wrote, "she ordered him to 'shut up and sit down!'"

Dudley had a similar hand in keeping the children on the ranch. When Gloria Ward's sister came to Jordan during Gritz's talks and attempted to bring the two Ward children out with a promise from Utah officials to drop the custody charges, Dudley stepped in and shouted her down, Gritz said, berating the sister as a "prostitute" of the state and intimidating her into leaving.

When Gloria Ward said she wanted to leave with her two girls, the ideologues bullied them into staying. Gritz said: "Before she could say another word, the gang of four was around her, pelting her with words critical of any thought of leaving. It was plain to see that the women and children were insulation."

It may have been a sleazy tactic, but it worked. A frontal assault with tear gas and rubber bullets might have been a higher option on the FBI's list if not for the continued presence of the children. As they had learned at Ruby Ridge and Waco, true believers like the Freemen had no compunction about sacrificing children for their own protection. And the repercussions from those fiascoes had knocked some perspective into performing such assaults: namely, that lives, especially the innocent lives, were not worth putting on the line for largely paper and money crimes like the Freemen's. They were content to wait the Freemen out.

Karl Ohs kept at the negotiations in his low-key way. After more than a week of silence, he returned to the Clark ranch on May 8 and kept the conversation going. Ohs was circumspect when he left. "It went well," is all he would tell reporters.

Inside, Ohs observed the same split among the Freemen that Gritz had seen, between the Clark family and the ideologues. Most of his conversations at the negotiating table were with Edwin Clark, "although Rodney was doing a fair amount of talking and Landers was doing a lot of posturing. Dale was always kind of in the background, not saying a lot, but he always seemed to be very rigid."

Despite the apparent rift, Ohs said, the Freemen always attempted to present a united front. Edwin denied that he was disenchanted with the other Freemen. "From the posturing that he was doing, you know, he was trying to let on that he wasn't, that they were all together. But you know, if you've lived on a ranch, it was pretty easy to see.

"You had all these outsiders and all these people, and you had the Clark family that had lived in this place for years. And they were all moved in on them. It was bound to cause some problems. That's just the way it is. Agricultural people have different sets of values. If you're from Jordan and Brusett, your values are a whole lot different from somebody from South Carolina."

At the same time, Ohs said, his hopes in negotiating an end to the standoff lay with Edwin Clark, a big, mustachioed bear of a man. "Edwin by far and away was always trying to find a middle ground," Ohs says. "And then when we'd leave he'd get overruled. But Edwin was really trying hard to get things over."

Ohs says the key to the negotiations lay in keeping things simple and rational, which was not an easy proposition when dealing with the Freemen. "You know, I'd see Ralph talk about losing the place, and some of the other personal stuff, and he'd cry, and I'd see Edwin talk, and he'd get tears. I mean, there was so much emotion, so much venting had to go on. And Rodney flying through the law books—I mean just on and on. And I'd try to understand, trying to see what was going on, and none of it really is making a lot of sense. Like I told 'em, I'm like a first-grader trying to get A plus B, and you guys are running algebraic equations at me. I just can't gather that.

"Which was great, because whenever it got thick, I would just plead ignorance, because it was just a safe place to go. But I'd come back, and my brain was just totally shot, because I was trying to listen, trying to make sense of what they were saying, but really understood very little.

"As time went on, I began to understand a little bit more and a little bit more, but you know, they'd give you verse, letter, chapter and page of the Uniform Commercial Code, and on and on, and jump from one thing to the next. It was just impossible for me, not ever having dealt with these issues at all, to try and put it together. I just tried to put together broad generalities that I could bring out and see if there was something we could work on.

"If there was trickery on my part, I never let them on that I couldn't understand. It was just too much to understand."

Ohs managed to keep the Freemen talking, and eventually they told him they would accept another mediator: Colorado State Senator Charles Duke, an avowed Patriot. So on Sunday, May 13, as the standoff reached its 51st day—the length of the Waco affair—the FBI contacted Duke and asked him if he'd be willing to participate. Duke quickly agreed.

Charles Duke is a balding, bespectacled 53-year-old with a mild middle-aged paunch who could pass for your neighborhood Amway salesman (or Kenneth Starr's brother). In Colorado, he had built his name as a constitutionalist who trumpeted the common-law courts' cause in the state legislature, as well as proposing a "10th Amendment resolution" meant to underscore states' rights. He held an impromptu press conference in Billings on Wednesday, briefly stopping over before flying on to Harrison to pick up Karl Ohs, and then returning to Jordan that afternoon.

His jacket slung over his shoulder, Duke seemed to relish the attention, especially since he was seeking the Republican nomination for the open U.S. senate seat in Colorado. But he remained low-key. "I may strike out too," he said. "I don't want to kid you."

The next day, Duke walked into the compound with Karl Ohs and two FBI agents at his side. They met the Freemen at a little rise on the edge of the ranch, next to the driveway. The FBI brought three folding chairs, but the four Freemen—Skurdal, Jacobi, Landers and Edwin Clark—declined to sit. They talked for an hour and forty minutes, then went home. There were handshakes at the end.

The next day, Duke and the agents brought a card table and seven folding chairs. This time, everyone sat and talked. At one point, Edwin Clark stood up and turned away from the table, but did not leave. Afterward, Duke told the assembled reporters that "we're not close enough that I can see the end yet." The talks, he said, were "horribly complex," involving "probably thirty or forty major issues."

At one point, Edwin Clark explained to Duke his chief fear about surrendering: If the Freemen gave up, he feared, they would be killed by being injected with cancer-causing toxins. He told an anecdote apparently relayed to them by LeRoy Schweitzer from prison, referring to Schweitzer's brief hunger strike when he spent a few days at a Missouri facility. "When he went to Missouri, a man, a doctor from New York City come in and told LeRoy, he says, 'You'll never see the light of day.' And he says, 'I'll guarantee you before you leave here I'm gonna inject you with a deadly, uh, dose of cancer."

Clark alleged there were other jailhouse druggings of Patriots. "I know two of them, one of them at least, he was as healthy as a fucking horse when he went in there, and he came back . . . there was another, I can't remember his name, they, they gave him a lethal dose of 'no brains' when he come back."

Russell Landers, Duke's onetime acolyte, was even more belligerent. "I can tell you right now I'm not the kind of damn fool that's going to lay over," he told Duke. "We're not here in this logistically defendable position as fools. We're guerrilla warfare, and I'm sorry, Charlie, but I feel very strongly about this, but they can take their fucking warrants and shove 'em right up their asses where that thirty-aught-six of mine is gonna drill 'em."[5]

After three days of negotiations, Duke announced a breakthrough on a "major issue" that he thought could bring about a surrender. As he described it, the Freemen had finally put something on the table on their own, a break from the talks' one-sidedness.

"It's their proposal, that's what makes it positive," Duke said. "In the past I've seen the FBI put something on the table, give a little, give a little, give a little. They've actually been very creative in the items they've placed on the table. Up until today we've had very little in the way of response. But that changed today."

The FBI was more circumspect, only emphasizing that no agreement had been reached. They already had seen how reliable the Freemen's word was. In the meantime, they erected a canopy at the roadside meeting site. The sun was out, and the Montana spring already was getting warm.

The first break in the talks came on the fourth day of Duke's negotiations, when Gloria and Elwin Ward brought Gloria's two daughters to the canopy to talk about getting out. Risking the wrath of the hard-core faction, they asked if the Utah officials' earlier offer to drop the custody charges was still good. The FBI said they would ask. Russell Landers stood off to one side with the girls and Duke, while Gloria Ward and the agents talked.

Apparently, the threat of losing the protection of the little girls made the Freemen pull in their horns. The next day, only Edwin Clark and Landers came out to meet with the negotiators, and they arrived 15 minutes late. The agents handed them a sheaf of papers and after only 40 minutes, they returned inside.

The next day, May 21, it all blew up. Only Rodney Skurdal came out to meet the agents, and he only came out to announce that the deals were off. Duke exploded at him, as Skurdal crept back inside a waiting vehicle. "You aren't man enough to come face me! Get out of that car!" the beet-red Duke shouted.

At Media Hill, Duke was still crimson-faced. "I told him, 'I'm going to go out of here and I'm going to tell the American people what you're doing here. You will not get support from the Patriot community, you will not get support from the militia community and if you die, nobody's going to avenge you.'

"Only a handful of the Freemen inside believed in the cause," he said, and "the rest are nothing but criminals trying to escape prosecution." Duke was especially indignant about their continuing grip on the fate of the three children inside. "One can only conclude that the adults inside care only for their safety and care not one whit for the safety of their children, because they're willing to sacrifice them and use them as a shield," he said. Duke flew back to Colorado that afternoon.

The Freemen rattled their sabers with the collapse of the negotiations, sending out six or seven men with rifles and sidearms on walking patrols along the compound's perimeter, then taking up positions at various strategic locations. They clearly anticipated an all-out assault—or at least had whipped up everyone inside into thinking one was imminent. None ever came, and they eventually crept back inside as night fell. The time for talking had ended once again. Now, the FBI began putting on the clamps.

★★★

From the very start of the standoff, Nick Murnion told anyone who would listen that he wanted the FBI to force the Freemen to immediately fall back on their own resources—namely, by cutting off their electrical power supply. The Freemen had plenty of food and their own water source, and they owned generators, but their gas supply probably was limited. The sooner the FBI forced them to rely on their generators to get by, the sooner the Freemen would run out of resources.

However, the FBI was not listening, at least not at first. Cutting off the power might be a provocative move, and the government negotiators worked hard to build the Freemen's trust. Maintaining complete honesty with the people inside the compound was the first working principle in the negotiations, according to Karl Ohs.

"We talked about that anytime I went in with anybody," he recalls, "and anytime anybody new was on the scene. It was: 'No lies, no promises we can't back up, no trickery. Be straightforward and honest. We can't get caught up in falsities here. We want them to understand we will honor their word, and they need to honor ours.' Trying to build that trust right from the very beginning."

When the Duke talks collapsed, though, the option to cut the Freemen's power moved up on the list. And even then, the FBI attempted to give the Freemen full warning. "I think I went in with a couple of messages that way," Ohs recalls, "and I know other family members and other people that were going in and out, they were using them all as messengers telling them this was going to happen."

There was one hitch in the logistics: the Freemen's three dozen or so neighbors, who mostly remained in their homes, were on the same electrical line, and cutting it would leave them without power. That meant the FBI had to bring in power generators to keep the neighbors' homes going once the lines into the Clark ranch were cut. The process of bringing those generators in began in mid-May, but was slowed considerably by a steady rain that turned all of the roads into a nearly impassable morass of mud.

The negotiators, meanwhile, were similarly spinning their wheels in getting the Freemen back to the table. "They wouldn't even pick up the phone, there was no communication," Ohs says. "Just none at all. And I tried calling, and I tried different things, and nothing. They flew me out there, and they said, 'Well, we're going to have you go in and just see if we can't get some dialogue going again.' We knew something was going on. We weren't sure what had happened to Edwin, because he had just kind of disappeared."

It came to a head on May 23. The steady rain had refused to relent, forcing Ohs and the negotiators to stay put at FBI headquarters in Jordan. "I flew back there and sat there for about three days, and it just rained and rained," Ohs recalls. "Of course, under that tension, I got kinda—'Either I gotta get home or do something, I don't want to just sit here for another week.' I don't know where the suggestion come from, but somebody said, 'Well, he oughta ride a horse in.' And I said, 'I'll sure do that.'

"So the FBI guys by that time are getting bored and tired, and they thought that was just a hell of an idea. So once that idea got thrown out, it was, 'Yeah, we gotta do that.'"

Donning a yellow slicker and a cowboy hat, Ohs cut a striking figure as he rode through the mud and rain into the ranch astride a brown horse. And what he found at the ranch left him concerned and discouraged.

"Actually that day, that was the first day that I ever saw that Edwin didn't show up," Ohs says. "It was only about a 45-minute meeting, a very short meeting, and it was because Russell was there, they were really pounding their chests at this time. And by this time the split between the Clarks and the rest of them had definitely taken place. It was just a lot of posturing. And I knew without Edwin there, talking wasn't much use to me.

"And when I came back, I felt, 'It's over.' I remember going to the FBI guy and saying, 'You know, we're screwed, this is over—it's done. Edwin wasn't even there.'"

The media, which had recorded Ohs' rainy ride in and out of the ranch and would broadcast it that evening across the nation, surrounded Ohs at the checkpoint, but all he could tell them was that no further talks were in sight. In the meantime, the FBI finished moving the generators into place. But they held off on snipping the lines for the time being.

Once again, the standoff went into a deep freeze for two weeks. Almost contrarily, the Montana countryside was finally starting to emerge from its winter crust.

Late May is the time of year when the prairie, drab brown or flat white the rest of the year, becomes a vibrant green—an expanse of grasslands and hayfields that looks like a vast, rolling carpet. People who live in these parts are always grateful for the change. After a winter of being cooped up inside, nearly everyone anticipates the chance to get out and get back to work.

One who couldn't, however, was Dean Clark, a 39-year-old farmer with a wife and two kids who just happened to be Richard Clark's son and Emmett Clark's grandson. Dean Clark does not approve of the Freemen—he disagreed with his father's gradually deepening constitutionalist beliefs, and he was dismayed when Richard talked Emmett Clark into joining the Freemen in the Patriots' alternative universe. When Emmett lost his farmland to foreclosure in late 1994, Dean stepped in at the public auction and purchased it, just to keep it in the family, in the hope that someday his grandfather—who until joining the Freemen had been one of the most down-to-earth, no-nonsense members of the community—might come back to his senses. In the meantime, Dean took up the chore of tilling the land, and he obtained a full harvest from it in 1995. Unfortunately, it directly abutted a long portion of Ralph and Edwin's property, putting him in a direct shooting line from the ranch.

When he went to check on a grain-supply bin on the land that winter, he was confronted by some of the armed Freemen. They called him a traitor to his own family for buying the land. Then his own father, Richard, came out and waved a shotgun at him and told him to get out. Richard told him they'd shoot him if he came back up to the property. Dean left without a word. The 14,000 bushels of grain he owned remained untouched in the bins.

When springtime rolled around and the standoff seemed destined to linger on interminably, and the land was still untilled, Dean Clark was beginning to become desperate. Like most people who make their living from the land, he lived on that edge where a certain amount of production was needed each year from the property, or else he wouldn't be able to keep up with his payments on the land itself (not to mention payments for crops or cattle feed). If he couldn't till the field near where the Freemen were holed up and likely to take a shot at him, he'd be in trouble with the bank and probably lose the property. He couldn't even sell all the wheat he owned because he couldn't get to the bins.

As May drew to a close and June arrived, Clark knew he had a serious problem. The short window of time he had to plant spring wheat would mean the difference between staying afloat and going under. "I've got bills I need to pay," he told an Associated Press reporter. "I could have made it work. But if I can't get an income out of the land this year, I'll be broke."[6]

Everyone began to act testy. The Freemen tried to circumvent the FBI by communicating directly with media people on the perimeter of the ranch. Most of the media that remained were pool cameramen. The Billings *Gazette*'s indefatigable Clair Johnson, however, spent most of the winter in a trailer next to Cecil and Ada Weeding's place. All of the media were by now seasoned veterans at watching through a lens from a distance, and most tried to be cooperative with the FBI. However, there were always the exceptions, especially the tabloid-oriented reporters. A

Fox News crew broke protocol by wandering close to the perimeter, and two Freemen came out to talk to them. The reporter, Rita Crosby, was handed a written invitation to return for an interview. She showed the note to the FBI, but the agents told her the crew wouldn't be allowed back in.

Moreover, because of the incident, the FBI decided it was time to move the media even further back. As it was, only the most powerful lenses could pick up wavy pictures of the negotiations from the vantage point of Media Hill, and being moved farther back would leave them with hardly anything to photograph. Everyone at the hill muttered about the relocation to the four corners checkpoint, and a few protested, to no avail. Reporters left two hours later to another location, this time on a hill owned by a local rancher who didn't mind the intrusion. The hill wasn't as close, but the Clark ranch was still visible. The media remained there through the end of the standoff.

Now all the reporters were sore—not just at the Fox crew, but at the FBI for overreacting. And the eviction didn't end without incident. The Freemen, observing what was transpiring and evidently watching news reports about it on TV, walked out to the end of the second driveway and stuck some news releases in a mailbox. Reporters walked up and began examining the releases, but FBI agents intervened, grabbing the papers out of reporters' hands. A few made it back to Media Hill anyway, especially after the Freemen walked back out and delivered another batch of notes. Ironically, the Freemen were coming to the defense of the so-called Jewish-controlled media.

"The press has been courteous and maintained a safe distance throughout the entire time of the FBI trespass upon the men and women of Justus Township," the release read, and went on to quote the 1st Amendment in urging reporters to stick up for their rights. "If you cannot occupy the county road near Justus Township, Montana state, united States of America, you cannot go anywhere without the permission of your masters."

The Freemen had success getting their views out through another form of the media as well. On May 23, they called the ultra-conservative "John Bryant Show," a radio talk program broadcast out of Johnstown, Colorado. Russell Landers, who had taken the role as ideological leader for the Freemen, phoned into the program and indicated where he was calling from. He was immediately patched through to Bryant, the host, who was so tickled to have the Freemen on the air he basically relegated his guest (the author of *Operation: Mind Control*, a conspiracy-theory tome) to the sidelines and interviewed Landers for the next hour.

Landers defended the Freemen's handling of the negotiations. "Well, first of all," he said, "there's never been any problem with them, with the exception with the fact that they are not negotiations. They are talks to resolve the matter lawfully. . . And the problem that we're facing here is the FBI and anyone that has come in to talk, first of all don't understand the law and second of all, have no intention of living by the law. And, for example, the FBI, in order to deal with any issue in good faith would have to present a written delegation of authority signed by the president."

Landers went on to cite a few obscure statutes as proof of his argument. And he said the Freemen never reneged on their word. "Absolutely not. On the contrary, the demands that were made were outside of the law. And they used the negotiating skills that they had to manipulate a couple of us at the gate. And they almost got us to act outside of the law."

Landers and Bryant bantered about points of the law according to their shared beliefs. Then Landers brought Rodney Skurdal onto the air to further illuminate the subject, explaining in detail how "sovereign citizens" could form a common-law jury. Skurdal rolled the citations out from memory over the air, explaining that the Constitution was directly descended from Scripture. "Basically anything you cite out of the Constitution, you can take it back to the Bible," Skurdal said. "It's not something that we just thought of, it's already been established by the word of Almighty God."

Finally, Bryant got down to the real question: "Are you guys a threat to the system?"

"Basically yeah," Skurdal answered. "The nation's in debt to me right now. I'm one of the largest bankers in the nation right now . . . based on law . . . and I can take it right back into Biblical law . . . because even though we talk about gold and silver . . . God also said we throw the gold and silver into the streets right? So, what's left? That's credit. It's all civilly correct and constitutionally correct."

Finally, as the interview drew to a close, Skurdal revealed the Freemen's negotiating position. They were demanding that the FBI set up a common-law grand jury of "sovereign citizens," then allow them complete freedom to prepare their court cases; in other words, for the FBI to walk away and everyone to return to their homes, and in return the Freemen would show up for their common-law court dates.

"What we want is full immunity for everyone to and from the Grand Jury where we can testify and present our own evidence and everything to show that these statutes not only don't apply to us, but have never applied to anyone," Skurdal said. "Immunity . . . full immunity with the release of the people who've been kidnapped already so that they can also prepare their evidence . . . and the thing is, a Grand Jury would have to be involved."[7]

It was not a very promising stance, as far as the FBI was concerned, because their negotiators knew full well what comprised the Freemen's idea of a grand jury: a collection of like-minded "sovereign citizens." In other words, the Freemen were demanding a rigged system outside the law, something the FBI could never accede to. Trying to pursue demands along these lines, the FBI negotiators knew, was fruitless. Instead, the FBI began to focus on more practical avenues.

On Saturday, June 1, the FBI brought in some of their firepower—armored vehicles with gun turrets, painted with the big white letters: "FBI." The three vehicles sat atop a truck bed on the edge of the ranch. Agents rolled back the tarps just to let the Freemen get a good look at them. Two days later, they moved the armored cars in closer. A helicopter was flown in, but it remained at the staging area at the Jordan fairgrounds.

Finally, on Monday, they pulled the plug. Power to the compound was cut off. The FBI called it "another effort to persuade the Freemen to resume negotiations for a peaceful settlement."

It turned out to be just what the doctor ordered.

★★★

The loss of electricity to the ranch was the final straw for Gloria Ward, who several times had been on the verge of leaving the compound with her two girls. She had become alienated from the "gang of four," especially Dana Dudley, for the bullying way they insisted on using her daughters as shields for the Freemen. But she and her husband, Elwin, also had a good relationship with Edwin Clark, who had stood up for them when Dudley or Russell Landers behaved badly. And Clark had pleaded with them to stay for his and his family's sake, so the Wards had remained.

When the lines were cut, though, and the FBI moved in more big equipment—a second chopper was flown in to one of the FBI positions the day after the shutdown—Gloria Ward decided enough was enough. It was obvious the waiting period was coming to a close, and she was not willing to risk her daughters' lives for the Freemen's cause. She asked Edwin to help them leave the Clark ranch, and he quietly agreed. Clark communicated with the FBI through an exchange of notes at the mailbox on the compound's edge. In the notes, he told the negotiators that Gloria and Elwin Ward and the two girls were willing to come out if Utah officials stuck to their earlier offer to drop the custodial-interference charges against Gloria. Justice Department officials responded with a somewhat similar deal: Gloria could leave the compound, but she would still have to go through a court hearing in Utah on her case. In exchange, though, the government promised that her two girls would be placed with her sister, Lynn Nielsen of Salt Lake City.

On Thursday, June 6, the Ward family—Gloria, Elwin, Courtnie Jo Gunn, and Jaylynn Mangum—walked out of the Freemen compound, escorted by two FBI agents. The Wards were taken to Jordan and then transported to Miles City, where the children were treated to ice-cream cones before the family was put on a plane to Utah. It was the first significant break in the standoff in the 74 days since it had begun. Now, two of the three children who had been the Freemen's shields against an assault were gone. The FBI's options were growing, and the Freemen's were shrinking.

"Now they can do what they have to do," said Joe Quilici, a legislator from Butte who had been part of Karl Ohs' negotiating team. "I think you should see things start moving now."

However, the negotiators tried to keep expectations to a minimum. "Tactical action is not imminent now that the girls are out," Karl Ohs said. "There are other considerations." Attorney General Joe Mazurek echoed Ohs' caution. "People should keep in mind the objective is to arrest these people, not to create an armed confrontation," Mazurek said.[8]

Edwin Clark's wife, Janet, had been making regular trips inside the compound, bringing in medication for their 21-year-old son, Casey, which was needed to treat a kidney condition. She remained with friends in Jordan. The visits at first had given the FBI the chance to send messages to warn Edwin and the others that the electrical power was about to be shut off. And then, when the crackdown came, she convinced Edwin to resume the talks.

"I think if there's a hero here, it might be Edwin's wife," says Karl Ohs. "You know, she started making regular visits to Edwin, and started to talk to the FBI just a little bit. She just had enough reality—she had a lot of questions about what was happening too, but she had just enough reality that eventually she got to Edwin."

Her talks with Edwin convinced him to finally bring the standoff to a close, Ohs says: "I think Edwin just decided this thing had to end—people didn't have to die, and that he was going to do it."

What brought Clark to that point, Ohs says, was "the whole process of the standoff: the emotions of everybody living there, the Clark family having all these outsiders moving in on them and them not having a lot in common other than their common-law things; that whole process of just wearing them down—they were doing the same thing we were doing, getting their hopes up and being dashed—the whole process, and then finally with the FBI moving in . . . About that time, Edwin was ready to face some reality. And that's when Janet moved in, and I think really convinced him that he should go out and visit with the FBI negotiator, which he did."

The FBI turned its attention now to removing the last non-Freeman—16-year-old Amanda Kendricks, Dana Dudley's daughter. The Wards' departure convinced the Freemen it was time to return to the talks. The next day, they met with FBI negotiators at the roadside card table for the first time in two weeks. And the main item on the government's table was getting Amanda off the ranch.

Edwin Clark was at the table, and this time around, it was clear he was in charge of the give-and-take. He told the FBI that if Amanda came out of the compound, he wanted their assurances an armed siege would not immediately follow. He was assured the agents were only considering an assault as a last resort, if negotiations completely disintegrated. Clark told them he'd talk it over with the people inside.

The negotiations continued for another week, led by Edwin Clark with either Landers or Skurdal in tow. The talks looked like they might be derailed, unexpectedly, by Gloria Ward, who upon her return to Utah was promptly ordered into court—where the judge placed her children temporarily with Courtnie's father, Robert Gunn. Ward complained that the government had reneged on its promise—and that bore ill for the situation in Jordan.

"Before today, I would have thought maybe things would end peacefully. But not anymore, not after today," she told reporters. "They (the Freemen) see me get screwed and they know they're going to get screwed and that the law won't be provided to any of them either."[9]

Three days later, Utah officials announced they were backing off on charges against Ward—for the time being. Though they said they wanted to reserve the right to refile the charges later, the Utah attorney general clearly did not want to be accused of monkey-wrenching the negotiations.

The talks in Jordan continued apace. The final piece of the puzzle came on June 9 when the FBI flew in Kirk Lyons, director of a North Carolina legal organization called the CAUSE Foundation, and two of his colleagues. The group (whose initials ostensibly stand for Canada, Australia, United States and Europe—everywhere that white people are established) describes itself as a defender of unpopular causes and the powerless. "I will always support the rights of radicals," Lyons is fond of saying. "The more radical they are, the more they need to be supported for their rights. If you take away their rights, we're all losers."

Actually, Lyons himself is a white separatist who sneers at the current American system. "Democracy in America is a farce and a failure," he once wrote. "It has led us to the brink of a police state."[10] He attended Pete Peters' 1992 gathering at Estes Park, Colorado, that is widely credited with giving birth to the militia movement. At the session, he led discussions on how to establish common-law courts throughout the country.[11]

Lyons first made a name for himself by successfully defending Ku Klux Klan Grand Dragon Louis Beam in his 1988 post-Order sedition trial in Arkansas. Lyons attempted to represent David Koresh during the standoff at Waco, filing for a restraining order against the FBI that a judge abruptly refused. After the siege ended in disaster, Lyons took up the cause of the surviving Davidians in their lawsuit against the government.

The Freemen indicated to the FBI that they trusted Lyons to handle some of the legal negotiations. Lyons had previously contacted the FBI in March and told them he'd be willing to act as a mediator. On June 9, the FBI called him and said: "You have been elevated to a viable option." Lyons and his colleagues caught a flight out the next day and arrived at the Clark ranch on June 10.

Lyons assured the Freemen they would be able to present their cases in court, as he had done in Arkansas. According to Karl Ohs, "Edwin was saying, 'Well, I'm gonna leave.' And the CAUSE people were then able to talk to the other four and convince them. Because if Edwin was going to leave, they knew they had to leave too. So they convinced them that there was some sort of legal documents that they could file—it gave them a glimmer of hope, even though everybody probably knew it was false hope, at least they could say that it wasn't, and have some dignifying grace."

Central to the Freemen's willingness to come out lay in the FBI guaranteeing to protect the Freemen's documents, law books and computer files that they had stored up over the years, so that they could easily access them in preparing their defense. Lyons negotiated an agreement to load the documents into a Ryder truck and turn the documents over to Karl Ohs, who promised to protect them from being mishandled by the FBI.

All of the elements were in place, except for one: Edwin Clark wanted to have a final consultation with LeRoy Schweitzer, who was locked up at the Yellowstone County jail in Billings. The Freemen wouldn't come out, they said, unless LeRoy gave the deal his blessing.

Lyons went to the FBI with a proposal: Let him accompany Edwin Clark in a plane flown by the FBI to Billings, so Clark could present the surrender package to Schweitzer and see if it passed legal muster in the Freeman's eyes—that is, that they wouldn't be signing their rights away by surrendering. Only Schweitzer, it seemed, could make the final ruling on that for them.

The FBI agent, according to Lyons, responded: "Let me get this straight. You want us to take a man who is technically under arrest, fly him in an FBI plane to a jail we hope to see him incarcerated in, bring him home and then put him under the siege again? Is that what you're asking?"

Yes, Lyons replied.

The negotiators checked in with FBI Director Louis B. Freeh back in Washington. Freeh personally approved the plan.[12]

On Tuesday, June 11, Edwin Clark walked out of the compound, where he met Lyons and two FBI agents. They piled into a Suburban and drove to the Jordan airport, and then flew to Billings. They arrived in Billings at about 2 p.m., and returned to the Jordan airport by 7 p.m. The FBI kept mum on whether or not Schweitzer had given his blessing to the plan, but the mood among the agents seemed decidedly optimistic.[13]

The next day, Dana Dudley's daughter, Amanda Michele Kendricks—or Ashley Taylor, as she sometimes called herself—walked out of the ranch with a female FBI agent and promptly asked for a cigarette. FBI agents did not mind letting the teenager smoke in front of them. They were just glad she was out. She was the last of the "innocents" to leave the Clark ranch.

At that point, though, an assault was the last thing on everyone's mind. It was clear the Freemen were about to surrender. The FBI took down the canopy where the negotiations had been held. Karl Ohs arrived with the Ryder truck and pulled up to the front door of the schoolhouse, and the Freemen spent the afternoon loading all their "evidence" in the back of the vehicle. "When we drove that Ryder truck in the day of the surrender, goddang, they just kept bringing stuff and bringing stuff," says Ohs. "And I kept going, 'Oh, no'—it became apparent to me what I had gotten myself into here. The thing was just practically full."

Dean Clark almost blew the whole thing apart that morning, however. Frustrated and uncertain whether he'd be able to plant his 2,300 then-fallow acres, and armed with a court order allowing him to work the land, he took his big tractor, hooked up a tiller, drove it out to the property and began digging up the soil. He figured his father wouldn't shoot him for doing a little plowing, not when they were about to give up anyway. But upon seeing the tractors, Skurdal and Landers flew into a paranoid frenzy, brandishing their guns, demanding to know what was going on, suspecting an ambush in the making. The agents walked out and talked to Dean, asking him if he'd mind just waiting a day and a half. Clark agreed, and shut down—and told them he'd be back the next afternoon.

Thursday morning, June 13, the Freemen at the guard post took down the upside-down flag that had flown over the ranch throughout the standoff. The Freemen each made their personal preparations to surrender. Karl Ohs sat out on the porch of Edwin's house waiting and talking with the Clark family.

"It was really tough, especially with the Clark family," he says. "The day was so full of tension anyway, getting that truck loaded, and on and on. And I was just totally tense. So we got the truck loaded, and we went back up to Edwin's place, and we're waiting for Russell and Dana to get their stuff together in that motor home. Sitting around with Ralph's wife, and Janet was there, and we were sitting in the shade just talking, just like you would talking about anything—talking about the weather, and talking about what was going to happen. There were a lot of tears, and Casey was just scared to death. And I'd spent enough time with these people and identified enough with them that—you know, they were just doggone good people that had gotten themselves in a bad way.

"Here we were—they were all ready to go, showered up and clean, ready to go, and here we were waiting on these other people. That division, it was there again. I felt a lot of—I mean, if you'd been a rancher, lived in eastern Montana, I understood that those people, who were third or fourth generation, were probably going to leave that place and never see it again. A place that was *their* place—it was not only the place where they lived, it was their place in life. And that means a lot of things when you say, 'Lose your place.'

"I could just really identify with what they had to be feeling—and it was just a lot of emotion, a lot of sadness."

The most relieved and happy people at the compound that day, Ohs says, were the FBI's negotiators. For the first time in such a standoff, they had been given the primary initiative in bringing about its conclusion. The agency's internal restructuring in the wake of Ruby Ridge—which gave birth to an integrated response team, one that empowered the negotiators ahead of the FBI's tactical units—had worked. "The negotiating team had probably more leverage than anybody else, because they were trying to do it different, and they wanted the negotiating team to handle it," Ohs says. "And there was a lot of pressure, I think, on the negotiating team, to prove that they could do it. Because I think in the other cases, they wanted to keep negotiating but they were overruled by the tacticals.

"And I think in this case, being as they had the opportunity, there was a lot of pressure on them to make sure that they could perform, that they could negotiate their way out of this, that it didn't have to be a tactical thing. So I think they had way more pressure, and probably more leverage, and they were worried they were going to lose that leverage if it didn't work out well."

The Ryder truck—filled, closed, and now locked up—was driven a short distance from the schoolhouse and parked near the main road. Late that afternoon, the Freemen began filing out of the schoolhouse, two by two. Each pair was escorted by Edwin Clark. The first 11, including Skurdal and Jacobi, were placed inside a large white van. Edwin shook hands with his son, Casey, then turned and went to get his father and his uncle.

Emmett and Ralph Clark were the last to come out. They were already elderly men who had led hard lives in a tough land, and the winter had been unkind to them. They looked pale and walked slowly. They were reluctant to leave. The ranch had been in their family since their grandfather had set stakes down in it before the turn of the century. And this time, they knew they would not be coming back.

Edwin Clark escorted them to a second van, which they could have all to themselves for the long ride to Billings. Edwin turned to an FBI agent as they climbed in, and said: "It's been a hell of a siege." The two men clasped hands. Some of the agents and lawyers around them had tears in their eyes. "You deserve the Nobel Peace Prize," the agent told Edwin.[14] The two vans drove off together, followed shortly by the Ryder truck, driven by Karl Ohs. True to his word, he was taking it to his ranch in Harrison to keep it under his supervision.

Dust rose from the road as the Freemen rode off into the sunset to the Yellowstone jail. Across the plains of eastern Montana, everyone else—the families and neighbors who had been held hostage to the fear, the public officials who had felt the weight of the Freemen's threats, the federal authorities who had hoped not to sacrifice more lives, or face more criticism, or create more martyrs for the Patriot movement—all these people sat back and breathed a great sigh of relief. At long blessed last, life could get back to normal.

Then again, they also sensed that it would never quite be normal again.

Chapter 11 / End of the Universe

I T TURNS OUT that getting out of handcuffs without a key is quite a trick indeed. Just ask the Washington State Militia.

By July 1996, mere months after their big meeting in Mount Vernon, the WSM's members had come a long way from talking about forming a big friendly neighborhood-watchdog group and manning the sandbags during floods. Now they were building bombs.

The militiamen had bought a warehouse space for stashing supplies and holding training sessions. Those sessions had quickly turned to a favorite topic: pipe bombs. By the middle of that summer, they were building the devices. Indeed, they seemed obsessed with them; it was all they talked about, just about everything they trained for.

There was one important change, though. On July 27 when the class had finished learning new ways to build pipe bombs, they turned their attention to learning how to get out of handcuffs.

It was a hot summer day, and the converted warehouse was still warm and stuffy during the late-afternoon gathering. But the eight participants were all dutifully gathered to hear more about bomb-building techniques from the group's instructor, John Kirk.

Kirk was not merely a member of the militia. He called himself a Freeman. He had filed "sovereign citizen" papers and had served as a juror when a group of Seattle Patriots organized its own common-law court. The leader of his Seattle-based Freemen group, William Smith, was a longtime friend of LeRoy Schweitzer and, like the Montanan, was considered a guru of "constitutional law" among Patriots throughout the Northwest. Smith was one of the participants this afternoon. They and two other Freemen had driven up together from Seattle to Bellingham for the class. There was the usual small talk, and then Kirk dove right in, spending the better part of a half-hour outlining techniques for building a short, squat pipe bomb comprised mostly of cap ends.

There was a kind of excitement that ran through the group that afternoon, a product of the danger inherent in what they were learning. It was all preparation for the eventuality of the United Nations invasion, the conflict they all were certain was coming.

When Kirk was done, "Rock" spoke up. Everyone knew Rock as the young, bearded ex-skinhead who was in the military-surplus business and was providing the money for the bombs being made. He was kind of quiet-spoken, but everyone trusted him, and some were hoping he'd move up as a leader for the group—something the militiamen had been lacking lately.

Rock, excited like the rest of the group, said it was his turn now to show the group his own special skill: how to get out of handcuffs without a key. The militiamen's eyes lit up. Now, that was a skill worth having.

Rock pulled out a boxful of handcuffs and handed a pair out to everybody. When everyone had one cuff clipped onto one arm, Rock went around the room and clipped the second one behind each of the students' backs.

Then he stepped to the front of the class and gave the group its final lesson—namely, that they'd been had.

"You are all under arrest," Rock announced, holding up his FBI badge. He walked over to the warehouse's single door and opened it, and in walked a cluster of FBI agents, some with guns drawn. The militiamen were all too stunned to resist. Classtime, once again, was over.

In that single swoop, the Washington State Militia's existence came to a sudden close. And, simultaneously, a marvelous window on the previously hidden world of militias—the secret organizing and training, the increasingly violent rhetoric, the paranoiac beliefs as they spiraled out of control—came open for everyone to see.

★★★

At about the same time his compatriots were clicking on their handcuffs, John Pitner answered the door to his home. A nice young couple was coming to look at the place, which he was trying to sell. They rang the bell, and he greeted them and let them in.

Suddenly, they had him in an armlock. The nice woman had a gun on him, and the husband had him pinned against the wall.

"You're under arrest," they told him. Pitner did not resist. In a matter of moments, he too was slapped into handcuffs and escorted out to a waiting car for transport to jail.

Pitner, the leader of the Washington State Militia since its founding in 1993, hadn't been around for the bomb-making class—in fact, he hadn't even been told about it. But arresting Pitner had been as important to the FBI as nabbing the bomb builders. They had a mountain of evidence that Pitner was involved in much more than merely organizing a well-armed Block Watch, the image of the WSM he had promoted to the public at January's big meeting in Mount Vernon.

The arrests were the culmination of a 13-month FBI investigation into the activities of Pitner's group. For most of the first few months that the FBI had kept an eye on them, the militias did exactly as they advertised: preparing for the United Nations invasion through education and training, and gathering followers through peaceful persuasion. But eventually the group started preparations to attack public facilities and then began building bombs. At that point, the FBI put them under close surveillance—tape-recording their meetings and strategic conversations, positioning undercover agents to move quickly in the event something was about to go off. Then, when they had enough evidence—and fearful that perhaps the militiamen were indeed on the verge of setting off a pipe bomb or committing some other act of violence—they struck.

Caught up in the sweep were Fred Fisher, a 61-year-old landscaper from rural Whatcom County; an employee of Fisher's, a burly 23-year-old with a close-shaved head named Marlin Mack; a former master mechanic named Gary Kuehnoel, who was a 48-year-old living off disability checks with his father in Bellingham; and the four Seattle Freemen: an out-of-work appliance repairman named John Kirk, 55, and his wife, Judy, a Boeing data technician, both of whom lived in the southern Seattle suburb of Tukwila; Richard Burton, a Boeing quality-control inspector who lived in West Seattle with his wife and two children; and most notably, William Smith, the 55-year-old guru of Seattle's Freemen, a man cited by LeRoy Schweitzer himself in one of the Montana Freemen's instructional tapes as a leading expert in the law, but who was mostly indigent, moving around from place to place and living off the generosity of his friends.

Smith, whose most notable feature is his long, flowing white beard, created a bit of a stir among the Seattle media the week he was arraigned, because of his resemblance to the similarly white-bearded character who drove the van for the Phineas Priests in Spokane—as it turned out, a groundless connection. Smith did, however, create a real stir in the courtroom that first week. Initially, he refused to accept a court-appointed lawyer, and when it came his turn to speak, he stood up and asked the judge to display a United States flag in the courtroom. The judge, a little baffled, looked behind himself at the large flag hanging there—complete with a gold fringe—and said there was already such a flag on display. Smith objected, saying the fringe made it a maritime flag of war and thus made the court an Admiralty court. The judge overruled the objection and proceeded to enter a not-guilty plea for Smith.

The rest of the militiamen all accepted court-appointed lawyers, who immediately went to work setting the stage for what clearly would be their defense: the FBI made them do it. Pitner hired James Lobsenz, a respected Seattle defense attorney, and Lobsenz and his colleagues all indicated they would be trying to establish that their clients were entrapped. "Is this really a conspiracy?" Lobsenz asked rhetorically, while arguing—fruitlessly, for the time being—for Pitner's release on bail.

Lobsenz also wanted immediate disclosure from the prosecution on whether or not the FBI had obtained its information through a confidential informant. And Marlin Mack's lawyer wanted to know if the informant was a man named Edward Mauerer.

It was indeed.

★★★

John Pitner had served in the Army in the 1960s, an experience that provided him with a vaunted military background when he was organizing the Washington State Militia. Pitner would tell his recruits that during his service in Panama, he had been part of an ultra-secret group of demolition operatives, training by night and learning a variety of special techniques of destruction. He said the group was so secret, his training with them did not even show up on his military record.

And it is true that no special-forces training shows up on Pitner's Army record—nor is there any hint of such training. It does note that he received automatic-weapons training, as well as standard orientation and ambush training in boot camp, but there is nothing to suggest Pitner ever was involved in secret operations.

What the record does show—and what Pitner almost certainly never revealed to his militia followers, because it would have destroyed his credibility—is that shortly after joining the Army in June 1968 and being stationed in Panama, he was court-martialed for stealing a 12-pack of soda pop, a machete, an aluminum folding chair, some cans of food and a hammock from several of his barracksmates, all of which apparently was discovered after Pitner jumped into a green MGB belonging to a major at the base and went for a joyride. Pitner also was charged with two counts of going AWOL. He was sentenced to a month of hard labor in the brig and forfeiture of $73 a month out of his pay for six months. Pitner lingered in the Army for another year, finally receiving a neutral discharge in February 1971.[1]

After that, Pitner stayed clear of any trouble with the law. He met his wife, Deborah, when he was 21 and she was only 14. They were married a few years later, and went on to raise a seemingly happy family of two daughters. They lived in a cute home out in the woods near Deming, due east of Bellingham. Pitner made a sporadic living as a house painter and handyman while Deborah, a registered nurse, provided the family with a steady income. During the 1970s John had made a good living in the painting business, but as the 1980s wore on, he seemed to find less and less work. By the 1990s, it seemed, he was only picking up the occasional job.

It was on his birthday in 1993—April 19—that things began to change for John Pitner. Already upset over the events at Ruby Ridge, he watched, shocked and angry, at the events unfolding in Waco, Texas, that day. What should have been a day of celebration for him was transformed into a stomach-churning, televised nightmare. It made him decide he had to do something.

An out-of-work gunsmith he had met at a tavern, Gary Kuenoehl, told him about a group that was meeting monthly at Bellingham's Harbor Center calling itself Citizens For Liberty, ostensibly to deal with government abuses like Ruby Ridge. When Pitner and Kuehnoel ran into each other that week, they decided to go to that Friday's meeting.

Citizens For Liberty was run by a Bellingham retiree named Ben Hinkle, who had originally set up the organization as a local recruiting arm of the Populist Party of Washington. Hinkle pulled CFL out of the Populist Party in 1993 when it became clear that its leadership, particularly Kim Badynski, had no compunction about associating with neo-Nazis and the Ku Klux Klan and engaging in racist talk. About that time, Hinkle appears to have shifted his alliances eastward to Idaho, where he hooked up with John Trochmann's post-Ruby Ridge group, United Citizens for Justice.

At the CFL meeting, Pitner and Kuehnoel first heard the idea of forming militias as a way to defend against jackbooted government thugs. Besides Hinkle, they also met a Bellingham contractor named Fred Fisher. And two weeks after attending their first CFL session, they held the little four-person gathering that Pitner would later call the first meeting of the Washington State Militia. It was held in his living room in Deming. "That was about three weeks after Waco," he recalls. "There were four of us."

If it was an organization beyond Pitner's own self-described cell, though, it remained hidden from view for the next two years. The whole idea of forming militias was being suggested in the growing circle of Patriots, but they didn't gather much impetus on the local scene because the need for one seemed remote. After all, Ruby Ridge and Waco were long distances removed, and the immediate importance of defending against a specific government plot in western Washington seemed remote.

The Patriots needed a local angle, and in the spring of 1994, they finally came up with one. It came in the form of a massive conspiracy to transform the North Cascades National Park into a United Nations enclave stocked with concentration camps, high-tech surveillance equipment and New World Order ground troops.

That, at least, was what some people living in the vicinity of the park believed. Already, residents of the Cascades region had lived through cutbacks and curtailments for extractive industries wrought by the creation in 1968 of the park, which abuts Washington's northern border with Canada and contains about 505,000 acres of pristine alpine wilderness. To the park's north lies Canada's Manning Provincial Park, and to the south are the Glacier Peak Wilderness and the Lake Chelan Recreation Area—each administered under totally separate bureaucracies. And now a group of scientists and environmentalists, weary of the frequent border conflicts in managing the ecosystem, had proposed creating a single Cascade International Park that would unify policy decisions and allow the vast swath of virgin land to be managed consistently.

To some people, that was going too far—particularly for the growing army of anti-environmentalist activists who had taken up the banner of the conservative "Wise Use" movement headquartered at Bellevue's Center for the Defense of Free Enterprise. Chuck Cushman, a Wise Use leader from the southwestern Washington town of Battle Ground, toured the state warning gatherings of blue-collar listeners that the proposed "United Nations takeover" of the land would cause thousands of timber and mining workers to lose their jobs. The seizure, he suggested, would be forcible, and local homes would be destroyed in the process.

One of these meetings was in March 1994 in Whatcom County, which borders on Canada. At the little Rome Grange about 10 miles outside of Bellingham, Cushman delivered what by then had become a stock stemwinder of a speech that lasted about an hour to a packed house of over a hundred. Cushman implied there was a hidden agenda to the environmentalists' proposal.

"Was the spotted owl about saving the owl?" thundered Cushman.

"No!" the crowd shouted.

"It was about stopping logging, wasn't it?"

"Yeaaah!"[2]

Ben Hinkle was a speaker too, and he delved even further into the hidden agenda. Hinkle rambled on about what he called the "Ultimatum Resolution," which was the second shoe of the U.N. conspiracy—not only would the "Peace Park" throw people out of work, it would be home to sophisticated surveillance devices and a series of concentration camps, where gun owners and other dissidents would be rounded up and transported after the U.N. completed its takeover of the country. The source material that he circulated at the session appeared to be reproductions of Militia of Montana propaganda, with his own group's name appearing where MOM's appeared on the original.

The Patriot community in western Washington continued to revolve around the Cascades conspiracy for awhile. In Snohomish County, just to the north of Seattle, similar meetings throughout April were organized to discuss the Cascades "conspiracy." New figures stepped forward—Don Kehoe, a Monroe landscaper, and Homer Bakker, a former Snohomish County sheriff's deputy—to trumpet the threat. They distributed Linda Thompson's conspiracy videotape, "Waco: The Big Lie," and the landscaper even played it for a group of fellow professionals at one of their monthly meetings.

That fall, Kehoe and the others launched a veritable tour of Cascades towns, bringing their vision of blue-helmeted stormtroopers amid their verdant mountains to communities like Arlington and Mount Vernon. Patriots like Ben Sams and David Montgomery, both Everett Constitutionalists, joined the speaking appearances by Bakker and Kehoe. So did Robert Crittenden, a conspiracy theorist who blamed declining salmon runs on Indian treaty rights—always a popular topic with Washington's right wing.

At the October 22 meeting at the Laurel Grange in Bellingham, a man came up to the mike during the question-and-answer session for Kehoe and told the crowd that he was helping to organize militia cells in response to this threat, and that if they wanted to know more, they should talk to him after the meeting. Some witnesses later said the man fit the description of John Pitner.

The paranoia seeped to the other side of the mountains as well, where the communities were even more resource-dependent, and likewise were more prone to believing the worst about the federal government. The Cascades conspiracy promoters, Cushman especially, made their way to those towns, too—Okanogan and Wenatchee, Chelan and Omak.

Soon, the rhetoric had grown to intimidation and harassment. Department of Ecology field workers had car windows broken and shot out. The state's DOE director was harassed and intimidated at a public hearing on agricultural issues in Chelan. When a local environmentalist tried to get time before the Okanogan County Commission to explain the park proposal, she found the meeting room was filled with shouting Wise-Users who harassed her during her presentation. In fact, she didn't get to make a presentation; she spent two hours instead fielding her neighbors' questions.

The woman, who has lived in Okanogan County for 20 years, knows who stirred them up: the Cascade conspiracy theorists. "They know how to make people afraid, and this was clearly a room full of very frightened people," she said. "They are afraid they'll lose everything."

Other conservationists were similarly threatened. At one public meeting, an anonymous audience member suggested that there would be a way of dealing with park advocates: "We're going to randomly take them out." Locals blocked them from meeting in public buildings. One of them was warned, "Better watch your lug nuts," and when he checked his vehicle's wheels, discovered the lug nuts had indeed been loosened.[3]

Even on the wet side of the mountains, "greens" were being harassed. When Ellen Gray, an activist with the Pilchuck Audubon Society, appeared at a Snohomish County Planning meeting, a man approached her with a noose in his hand and held it up for her to see. He didn't say anything, but then, he didn't have to.

The paranoia reached its apex on Labor Day 1994, when some local Patriots in northern Okanogan County observed some suspicious behavior—a large encampment of people near the Canadian border, all of them wearing new clothes, with all-new equipment and out-of-state plates, all of them males with clean shaves. Could it be a United Nations strike force?

Actually, it was a Border Patrol exercise—a secret operation along the boundary to deter smuggling and illegal crossings. It involved bringing in U.S. Army soldiers and dressing them as typical outdoorsmen. Little did they know the fear their little ruse would inspire.

Someone driving along the Similkameen River spotted the encampment and rushed into town to tell friends about the activity. Soon, phone calls began flooding into Sheriff Jim Weed's office, claiming that U.N. troops had landed at the border and were sweeping southward, confiscating people's guns wherever they went. And, the callers said, the locals were planning to mount an armed resistance. In fact, a force of men was ready right then to drive northward to meet the invaders.

The sheriff urged the callers to sit tight, then quickly got on the phone with the regional Border Patrol director and warned him that violence was imminent. "I finally said, 'Look, Ed, I've got a bunch of guys who want to go up and meet your guys with their guns, and somebody is going to get hurt. If you've got something going on, you need to let me know, because your super-secret sting is up,'" Weed recalled later.

The Border Patrol promptly broke up the encampment, but spread it out to a number of different locations so it would not appear so intimidating. The operation continued without incident for another couple of weeks.

The leader of the new Lake Chelan Citizen's Militia, however, was not exactly convinced that it was not an invasion. "We have photographs," said Bill Shoenmaker, a Chelan-area resident. Fortunately, the threat of militia action worked, in Shoenmaker's view: "They were getting ready to run a house-to-house search up there, which apparently they gave up because it was exposed before it happened."[4]

Indeed, the militia appears to have scared off the conspirators permanently. No other United Nations troops have been spotted in the area since.

★★★

Fears of a Cascade conspiracy gradually subsided that winter of 1994, but the western Washington Patriots who had developed some momentum from that debate kept going with a new cause—namely, the tax-protest case of a Whatcom County veterinarian, Donald Ellwanger.

Ellwanger was a friend of Ben Hinkle, the Citizens For Liberty organizer. He and Hinkle shared similar beliefs—including the notion that the Internal Revenue Service is an illegal entity and that paying your taxes is strictly voluntary. Ellwanger decorated the property of his animal-care clinic with signs reading "Stop Unlawful Evictions" and "Land Patent Contract, Private Property: No Trespass." He had stopped paying his taxes in the mid- or late-1980s and, by 1991, owed $130,000 in back taxes, by the IRS's calculation. The agency seized Ellwanger's property in 1994 and auctioned it off that fall. He was ordered to be off the property by New Year's Day, 1995.

Of course, he wasn't. A week before, on Christmas Day, he issued "Ellwanger's Call to Patriots," which declared that he'd discovered, through years of research, the existence of: "a 'Foreign Private Corporation,' international cartel known as the world bank/Federal Reserve Bank, who contract with the IRS to rob people like Dr. Ellwanger of the fruits of their labor and property." He said the IRS was actually a collection agency that had no power over private citizens. One of his faxes reached Theressa Sundstrom, a Seattle woman who ran The Liaison Group, an urban Patriot outfit.

Sundstrom called out to the militias, sending a fax of her own on the American Patriot Network. "There are fears this will escalate into another Waco or Weaver," it read. "Therefore, the militias of Montana, Idaho and Oregon have been alerted, as well as 'Bo' Gritz, who is advising them how to conduct themselves."[5]

The eviction notice was scheduled to be served by sheriff's deputies on Tuesday, January 3. When the day arrived, some 30 or so of the Patriots, wearing everything from camouflage gear to cowboy hats to suits and ties, showed up at Ellwanger's clinic, many making the drive from Seattle and Everett to take part. Nobody displayed any weapons. But the sheriff's deputies, smelling trouble and clearly outnumbered, circled the Ellwanger place a few times and decided to wait for reinforcements. Over the next couple of days, the militia members all trickled back home, convinced nothing was going to happen.

On Thursday, when the militia members all had gone home, the sheriff moved in and served the notice, then carted all of Ellwanger's belongings off the property. And that was the end of Don Ellwanger's bid for Patriot martyrdom.

★★★

Most of the Patriot groups in western Washington through that spring of 1995 had managed to avoid using the militia label. Besides Citizens For Liberty and The Liaison Group, they used titles like Citizens for Constitutional Law, the Everett Freedom Forum, and the Olympic Sportsman's Alliance. Only in Kitsap County, where a group calling itself the Kitsap County chapter of the National Association of Militia Educators held meetings and an occasional training session in the woods, did the name "militia" pop up.

Still, the first months of 1995 saw the highest level of activity by Patriots yet in the region. John Trochmann's Militia of Montana stayed particularly busy, holding meetings in places like Maltby and Port Orchard—small, blue-collar towns where disenfranchisement ran deep. A couple of Arizona Patriots, ex-cops Richard Mack and Jack McLamb, came out for a Patriot conference in Bellevue that February.

So when the bomb went off that April 19 in Oklahoma City, a reporter for the *Herald* in Bellingham, Leo Mullen, talked to Ben Hinkle to get a local angle on the bombing, and wrote a story observing that the same Patriot beliefs which seemingly had inspired Timothy McVeigh had found a home in Whatcom and Island counties. Hinkle ducked hard for cover, saying Citizens For Liberty had no members—it was, he said, a public group with an anonymous membership.[6] One of Hinkle's associates, Harry Nagel of Bellingham, wrote a letter to the editor of the *Herald* protesting the story as "false and sensationalist reporting" full of "dangerous misinformation, sowing fear and distrust, tearing the fabric of our community."[7]

Indeed, the Patriot grapevine was abuzz with rumors of an impending crackdown on militias in the wake of Oklahoma City. There was talk of raids on people's homes, massive gun confiscations, and mass imprisonment of Patriots. The members of Citizens For Liberty wanted to know what was going on, and whether their own sheriff would be party to such perfidies. So they invited him to their May 19 meeting at Bellingham's Harbor Center.

Dale Brandland had been Whatcom County Sheriff for seven years, and he had always heard people muttering about the federal government. After all, he himself had been first elected in 1989 with the strong support of the Christian Coalition, which in the ensuing years proved a steady source of his constituency. But he wasn't quite prepared for the Citizens For Liberty. He showed up as the "featured speaker," and gave a quick rundown on everyone's right to meet and talk about the government and urged them all to stay within the law, but it was clearly only an impromptu session for the sheriff.

Hinkle and his cohorts, on the other hand, had their end planned out very well, even going so far as to print up a brochure of questions for Brandland, most of them reflecting their belief that the sheriff is the supreme law of the land, with authority superseding the federal and state government: "Why is the office of sheriff an elected position? What do you consider to be your responsibilities to the voters of Whatcom County? What authority do federal law enforcement agencies such as DEA, FBI and BATF have over the Sheriff's Department?"[8]

As the session went along, Brandland found himself deluged with baffling questions and even more bewildering responses from his audience. Someone asked him if he thought militias were a threat. Brandland thought a minute. "The only time I would see a militia posing a threat in Whatcom County is if they are going to take some action and take the law into their own hands," he said. "If the militias are going to start taking the law into their own hands then, yeah, I have a problem with that."

John Pitner stepped up to the microphone. "Sheriff Brandland," he said, "You're aware of the Second Amendment, right?

"Yup," the sheriff answered.

"OK, to keep and bear arms," continued Pitner. "Now, what happens if the federal government, through some heinous activity or eleventh-hour legislation or through executive order decides that a United States citizen cannot keep or bear arms anymore? Do you instruct your deputies, here in this county, to go door to door and help the authorities collect our guns?"

Brandland didn't know how to respond. "Boy . . ." he said, and paused.

"That's pretty cut and dried," Pitner said.

"Pretty cut and dried," Brandland said, "but the likelihood of that happening is pretty remote."

"It's happening all the time."

The audience began chiming in with Pitner. "It's happening all the time in America, yeah. It already has," they said.

Pitner kept it up. "See, I think what the main fear here is, is that we're very afraid of the federal government. And we need somebody here in this county to tell us and soothe our fears—and let us know that these buggers are not going to come in and busting our doors down, collecting our weapons and things of this nature."

The crowd was getting behind Pitner now. "And I think that this is a large part of why the militias have been established. Just because people were afraid. Not because they are lurking around; wanting to shoot somebody or take the law into their own hands. Just because we are afraid of our own federal government. And when the federal government fears the people, it's time to get rid of the federal government.

"So I would just like to know, would you instruct your deputies to assist these people in going door-to-door and confiscating private citizens' weapons?"

Brandland went for the safe answer: "I was elected to enforce the law." The sheriff went to work to get the muttering crowd back on his side. "I was elected to enforce the law," he reiterated. "I don't interpret the law. We have a lot of laws that are not constitutional that we put in place and they are found to be unconstitutional and nobody enforces them."

Pitner stayed on the attack. "We're talking about a very serious issue here, sir."

"Yes, we are."

"And, uh, you swore to the Constitution when you took your office."

"Uh huh."

"To support that Constitution."

"I did."

"And, and, and that order, if you were to assist these federal authorities to take away our weapons, you would be in direct violation of the Constitution, therefore jeopardizing yourself."

Brandland didn't understand this as the disguised threat it was—that the "jeopardy" to which Pitner was referring was the charge of treason that Patriots believed all sheriffs who failed their oaths were guilty of, and the punishment for which is hanging. He kept trying to ride with the crowd.

By now, Pitner had launched into a laundry list of Patriot conspiracies. "From what I have seen," he told the sheriff, "from the advent of 666, HR 97 and all this other legislation, GATT and NAFTA and everything else—I don't think that anybody in here tonight has any faith in our federal government any longer.

"That's why we need you to make your statements to let us know how you're going to protect us. Whether you are going to protect us or not. So that we can go home tonight feeling semi-secure, knowing that our sheriff is going to protect us. And that's why you're in office right now. Not to protect the federal government, but to protect us."

Brandland was baffled by all this talk, and he kept repeating his mantra: "I'm here to enforce the law."

Pitner was finished. "Thank you," he said, and sat down.[9]

Having gotten a taste of public speaking, and even more important, public approbation, Pitner decided to move the whole business of organizing militias into the public sphere. In June, with the help of his wife, Deborah, he published the first photocopied issues of "Sighting In: The Militiaman's Newsletter," a publication of the Washington State Militia. No one had ever heard of the group before.

Pitner's closest partner in forming the group was Fred Fisher, a fiftysomething contractor he had met at the CFL meetings. They began culling prime recruits from Citizens For Liberty meetings, people they thought could prove useful to the Washington State Militia. A young employee of Fisher's, Marlin Mack, was one of their most enthusiastic followers and, since he was a strapping young man with a taste for woodsmanship and survivalist tactics, an ideal recruit. Mack, Fisher and Pitner would all make trips together into the woods that summer to bury their caches—sealed plastic containers stuffed with supplies like Army meals, soap and clean socks, and a little bit of ammunition too.

Brian Smith also came to the CFL meetings that spring, and he fully believed everything Hinkle and the others told him about their real intent—that there was no anti-Semitism or racism or violent plans lurking behind their agenda. An athletic young banker in his thirties, Smith was attracted to Citizens For Liberty because he was an avid outdoorsman, and he was particularly sensitive to the matter of gun rights. He had moved to Washington from California a few years before because of what he saw as a terrible erosion of gun owners' rights in that state, and he was concerned about it occurring on a massive scale.

Smith was also a skilled spelunker, a talent that intrigued the cache-obsessed militiamen, since finding a good cave to hole up and store their goods in fell well within their needs when the New World Order attacked. So Pitner invited Smith to join the militia that summer, and he readily agreed. Smith attended two meetings at Pitner's home and heard talk about learning how to reconnect electrical wires in the event of a disaster, the dangers of water fluoridation, the protection of property rights, and a discussion of how to cache properly. But it was at the third meeting that summer that he came in for a shock.

When Smith arrived at Pitner's home, he saw spread out on the living-room table a veritable arsenal—guns, powder, liquids and rags, mousetraps and wires, and propane bottles. Marlin Mack was there too, and he later described the scene: "We got in there and John's got his whole fuckin' coffee table spread out with all kinds of insurgency shit. Molotov cocktails . . . mouse traps rigged up, the whole, uh, shotgun shell with the . . . all that shit, you know. All kinds of different little things."[10]

Pitner proceeded to describe how to build a bomb out of propane bottles by filling them with black powder. The group learned how to set up tripwires on forested trails to set off bombs that could take out enemy invaders. They also discussed what they would need to do to disable three power substations and knock out electricity to the entire county. "My previous impression of the Washington State Militia was that it was generally a political-style group," Smith would later say from the witness stand. "The 'training meeting' . . . in my view was a preparation for terrorism."

The militia leaders started pressing Smith for help in locating good caves for caches and maybe even hiding. Smith told them he'd show them what he could, but left that night's meeting vowing never to go back. Fred Fisher called him 12 times over the next month or two trying to talk him into showing them the caves. He finally conceded, and drove out one afternoon with Marlin Mack to show him a cave that he knew wouldn't work for them—not only was it too small, it would be inaccessible in the winter.

"I figured that would get them off my back," Smith said. He was right; they didn't bother him again.[11]

For every Brian Smith scared away by the bombs, though, there were others to take his place. Guys like Ed Mauerer.

★★★

Like other members of the Washington State Militia, Ed Mauerer had been in numerous brushes with the law over his 40 years. There had been a couple of bad-check and forgery convictions, mostly dating to the breakup of his marriage. He stayed afloat by working as a mechanic at a gas station a little north of Bellingham, but he mostly lived hand-to-mouth, trying to pay off his debts in the wake of the convictions.

While serving some of the jail time for the forgery conviction in the Whatcom County Jail in 1994, Mauerer heard other inmates talking about a case that had been in the local headlines: That August, someone had burned a cross in front of a migrant-labor camp in Lynden, a conservative, nearly all-white town about 20 miles north of Bellingham. The FBI had been called in and were looking for clues, and Mauerer passed along what he knew to Special Agent Ramon Garcia, who was investigating. However, while Garcia was close to arresting two local men, it shortly became evident Bellingham police officials had mishandled the evidence in the case, ruining the chances of a successful prosecution. So no arrests ever were made in the cross-burning.

That in turn seemingly emboldened the perpetrators, and that October, the migrant camp again was attacked. This time, someone drove by and fired a couple of blasts from a shotgun into the side of the housing and through the windshield of someone's pickup. No one was injured, but it kept Garcia busy looking into whoever was harassing the migrant workers. He stayed in touch with Ed Mauerer, who also had information about another potential criminal case involving a series of burglaries and car thefts by a man named Ike Lantis.

In the meantime, Ed Mauerer expanded his contacts into the local right-wing scene as well. Don Ellwanger liked to frequent the gas station where Mauerer worked, partly because Mauerer was an excellent mechanic who did reliable work on Ellwanger's old vehicles. Ellwanger started telling Mauerer about Citizens For Liberty and the militias, and he persuaded Ed to attend some CFL meetings that spring of 1995. By summer, Mauerer had won their confidence enough that John Pitner and Fred Fisher invited him to join the Washington State Militia. The first meeting he attended was in June at John Pitner's house.

The militia brought Mauerer along slowly through that summer. In the fall, when the weather turned cold, the members decided to build an indoor training facility, so they set about creating one in a rural Whatcom County barn belonging to the mother of Judie Ellwanger, Don's wife. They went to the Lummi Indian Reservation for shooting practice, taking aim at targets with the profile of federal agents on them. Mary Ann Fisher, Fred's wife, turned out to be one of the best shots.

Mauerer also learned how to cache and store food and weapons, and finally went on a caching trip in early October with Marlin Mack, Don Ellwanger and another recruit named Dan Knight. That seemed to finally win the militia leaders' confidence. A week and a half later, at a meeting at John Pitner's house, Pitner first described in Mauerer's presence how to engage in counter-insurgency against invading New World Order troops—building bombs out of propane bottles, and setting tripwires on the trails to their mountain retreats.

Mauerer was intrigued with the night-vision goggles Pitner possessed, and Pitner offered to get goggles for him too. On November 1, Mauerer later testified, he went to Pitner's house in Deming and paid Pitner $500 for a pair of good goggles. They went to Pitner's garage, Mauerer says, and looked over a minor arsenal Pitner said he was going to cache soon. Mauerer says he saw plastic buckets filled with grenades, dynamite and guns. "Pitner picked one up and said they were real," Mauerer testified. "But I could see it wasn't. It had a hole in it, a hole in the bottom." Mauerer said Pitner never did get the goggles to him, nor did he ever see his $500 again.

At about the same time, Pitner had decided to introduce the Washington State Militia to the public. Its first announced meeting was November 11, 1995, at the Rome Grange located between Deming and Bellingham. Speakers included Fred Fisher and Sharon Pietila, a local Christian fundamentalist whose activism in political causes included opposition to Outcome Based Education and support of a movement among rural Whatcom County dwellers to secede and form their own, new "Pioneer County." About 40 people attended.

Little did Pitner suspect that the FBI was already circling. Mauerer had stayed in touch with Ramon Garcia the whole time, reporting on the militia's activities. Garcia initially was skeptical about any threat posed by Pitner's group; he told Mauerer to keep an eye out, but he was more interested in whatever information Mauerer could dig up on Ike Lantis' activities and the 1994 cross-burning. But when

Mauerer reported back about the October 11 meeting where bombs were discussed, Garcia began paying attention. Privately, he began talking to his superiors about expanding their surveillance of the Washington State Militia. By the November tête-à-tête in Pitner's garage, Garcia had decided to hit the switch and open a full-fledged investigation into the activities of John Pitner and his group.

Garcia, a burly third-generation Hispanic with a no-nonsense demeanor, believed he might have enough information to potentially charge Pitner with pipe-bomb violations, based on what Mauerer had told him, but he wasn't sure if he raided the militiaman's home whether the materiel Mauerer had seen would still be there. So, to keep the information coming, he began paying Mauerer on a monthly basis for his reports, which now came in almost daily. By early December, he had arranged for Mauerer to wear a body microphone during his meetings with the militia folks to record their conversations.

The first of these tapes was recorded on December 9, during a Washington State Militia meeting at Goldie's Restaurant in Bellingham. Most of the discussion centered around the New World Order's plans to round up gun owners and Patriots, and incarcerate them in large detention centers. According to one report, the new detention center being built in the SeaTac area south of Seattle was one such facility. They also discussed anti-terrorism legislation proposed by President Clinton, which the militiamen believed would be used as a pretext to round up Patriots. Pitner, who told his followers he was being fed inside information by a half-brother who happened to be the director of the FBI for the West Coast, told the group that if the legislation were passed, the feds would simply move in and throw them all in jail and keep them locked up at SeaTac without benefit of a trial.

The group began developing a strategy for the expected apocalypse. Pitner told them they'd need to damage the infrastructure—like taking out a microwave repeater station up in the hills near Deming, which enabled police to communicate in the county's hilly terrain.

Marlin Mack, the impressionable young hod carrier who seemed to look to Fred Fisher as a father figure, wanted more details. "If something goes down, where's the first place to hit?" he asked Pitner. "Is that one of them?"

"No," Pitner said. "The first option to do is get the fuck out of Dodge and regroup."

"Oh yeah," Mack said. "Mm-hmm."

"Then wait for your orders. Your orders will come."

"Yep," Mack said. He knew this part of the drill.

"Also," Pitner said, "I have two sealed documents that are placed in various places. Like the orders I've already seen. Our primary function is to catch and—and break people out of the detention camps. The next one is to fuck with the occupying personnel that are in here that are doing things to us, like fucking up their vehicles, like fucking up their power systems, generally just fucking with them, OK?"

Pitner was animated now, and everyone was laughing. "And then the third primary is the hit-and-run tactic we'll use. The real tactic is to kill 'em—to kill the sons-of-bitches."

Ed Mauerer tried finding out more about Pitner's supposed source inside the FBI. "But your brother's gonna get out, right?" he asked Pitner.

"Yeah," Pitner answered. "Oh yeah. He's got his provisions."

Mauerer kept probing. "Well, what if someone doesn't know he's your brother, just that he's a fed and kill him?"

"Well," Pitner answered, "he's in the line and he knows. But he won't be a fed anymore. He'll be out. He'll be out. He'll be wearing camos just like us."

"But you're lucky that you got him in there," Mauerer said.

"Yeah," Pitner said. "I got a lot more than just him in there."

"But he totally supports what we're doing, though," chimed in Marlin Mack.

"Oh yeah," Pitner said. "To a T."

"Fuck yeah," Mack said, "I'm sure there's a few people here and there that do."

"Oh yeah," Pitner said.

"But the majority are goobers," Mack said.

As the meeting wore on, the topic turned to weaponry. Most of the militiamen seemed taken with automatic weaponry and assault rifles. Mauerer grew keenly interested.

"I've got a fully automatic Uzi," Pitner boasted.

"For how much?" Mauerer asked.

"Fifteen hundred."

"Oh man, I love automatics," Mauerer said. "Fifteen hundred bucks?"

"Because it costs about eighteen."

"With a selector?"

"Selector. Full automatic, semi. The real thing."[12]

Mauerer told him he'd try to get the money together. Within the next two weeks, Mauerer did in fact buy an Uzi—but he got it from Gary Kuehnoel, who brought it over and sold it to him for the $1,500, ostensibly through Pitner.

After the meeting at Goldie's broke up and the tape on his recorder had run out, Mauerer says he and Pitner went for a drive on the Chuckanut Road south of town. The route follows the single north-south railroad line that connects Seattle to Vancouver, and at a particularly scenic point in the road, the rail line runs through a long tunnel. Pitner drove Mauerer to the tunnel and pointed it out. If they could close that tunnel with some well-placed dynamite, he said, they could seal off all the rail lines into Whatcom County and keep the U.N. forces from bringing in any equipment or troops via rail.

Mauerer says Pitner charged him with the assignment of taking out the police-communications tower near Bellingham in the event of an invasion, and said he wanted Marlin Mack to help him with the job. And he gave Mauerer a card. It read:

"One shot/one kill

"The bearer of this card is well-armed and prepared for self defense against the minions of a tyrannical government. Any and all agents of such a government who try to run away will only die tired. When executing such vermin the bearer will only feel the recoil of his rifle."

Mauerer turned over his tapes and notes to Ramon Garcia the next day. When he heard and read what was there, Garcia knew with certainty he was on the right track—if Pitner didn't blow up the tunnel first.

★★★

The Washington State Militia finally hit the big time in January 1996. First, on the 13th, Pitner made his debut before a large crowd, speaking to about a hundred potential recruits in Port Townsend. The next day, the 14th, was the real big time. Pitner brought in John Trochmann and the Militia of Montana, and became a public figure in the process.

On that Sunday afternoon in Mount Vernon, the Washington State Militia not only attracted a crowd estimated at between three and four hundred, but the TV cameras and newspaper reporters were there as well.

"We're a defensive organization trying to educate the public on what we feel are the major concerns of the nation these days," Pitner told the reporters. "A lot of heinous legislation, unconstitutional legislation coming—a lot of scary things happening in this nation."

John Trochmann was the star attraction, but John Pitner was the man of the hour. First he got the crowd bubbling by holding up a copy of the *Bellingham Herald*, which had run an unflattering portrait of the WSM prior to the big gathering, crumpling and throwing it at the feet of the reporter who wrote the story, Cathy Logg. Then he went out and chatted face-to-face to the cluster of 70 or so protesters who had gathered outside the meeting hall.

Some of his followers watched admiringly from the door. When he went back inside, one said to him: "That's more than I woulda done, John."

"Yeah, well, somebody's gotta set those people straight," Pitner said. It was a performance worthy of Bo Gritz.

This was precisely what Pitner had hoped for. As he envisioned the Washington State Militia, it would become a kind of umbrella organization for the many tiny little groups of Patriots throughout the state—all of the Citizens For Libertys and Freedom Forums and Sportsmen's Alliances would finally have a coordinating structure so they could "educate" people throughout the state on a consistent basis. Of course, Pitner's idea seemed to run counter to the spirit of "leaderless resistance" he was simultaneously promoting, but the grandness of it all was more appealing than thinking too much about such philosophical quibbles.

Afterward, he fielded the bulk of the press questions, which helped give John Trochmann some cover from the usual questions about his connections to Aryan Nations and Christian Identity. Pitner was able to look the cameras in the eye and deny his organization would ever engage in violent actions or racist behavior. "We're going to weed out the bad ones," he said. He also announced that the Washington State Militia would meet monthly at the Rome Grange north of Bellingham.

The militia had one last show in public. A month and a half later, on March 10, Pitner organized a similar gathering in Fife, a blue-collar suburb on the northern edge of Tacoma. It received less press than the earlier gathering, and the crowd was a little smaller, somewhere in the 200-300 range. But it helped draw potential members from what Pitner figured would be a prime recruiting area—namely, the Fort Lewis Army Base, just a few miles to the south. Again, Pitner was adamant that there were no hidden agendas in his group.

In between, Pitner and the gang all showed up for a February gathering in the town of Snohomish, a little east of Everett, to hear Eugene Schroder speak. Schroder, the revered Constitutionalist figure (and sometime associate of LeRoy Schweitzer's), had a pet conspiracy theory that President Franklin Roosevelt suspended the Constitution in 1939 under the War Powers Act and the "corporate" federal government had never relinquished the reins since. Only 60 or so true believers showed up—but then, there was a $15 "donation" at the door. Almost all of Pitner's troops were there.

This, as prosecutors would later suggest as they wrapped up their case against John Pitner and his fellow Patriots, was the public face the Washington State Militia liked to present—holding public meetings, talking about the government, gathering followers. But, as prosecutors also would suggest, there was a private face to the militia, too—one that only came out when they thought others weren't looking or listening.

It was clear not everyone was buying Pitner's story. Two days after the big January 14 gathering in Mount Vernon, officials of the Rome Grange announced they'd no longer rent their hall to the Washington State Militia. "We will take a stand on a legislative issue, but we're not going to get involved in the debate with the militia and the government," said a grange spokesman.

Pitner was furious, protesting that the militia had been unfairly smeared as a pack of radical revolutionaries. "We're not anti-government, we're anti-bad politicians," he said. "We feel it's time to change the way government does things."

He argued that all citizens are members of the militia under the law. "We're volunteering ourselves beforehand," he told Cathy Logg. "We're just painters, carpenters, bricklayers. We're trying to help our communities. We were out sandbagging in the floods and helping save livestock in Lynden. We're directing traffic at accident scenes. We serve when we're called to serve. We have Christmas programs for children. We're community-oriented people."

Pitner issued a plea for understanding: "Don't judge us by what we say—judge us by what we do."[13]

★★★

The Patriots' growing problems—the protesters, the bad press, the rejections—clearly disturbed the Patriots. Ben Hinkle announced in a January 18 *Herald* story that he was canceling the next night's meeting of Citizens For Liberty. But at their customary meeting place at Bellingham's Harbor Center the following evening, the CFL's 30 or so Patriots—including John Pitner and Fred Fisher—gathered as always.

Hinkle announced at the start that the meeting was canceled, so they would just be talking that night. Still, he set up his usual table and hawked his constitutionalist wares and Militia of Montana materials. And everyone talked that night at length.

Four days later, the Washington State Militia turned out in public again—only this time, it was to face down their opposition. News accounts of the Patriot movement had depended heavily on quotes from human-rights groups in the Seattle area. They presented the other side of the story, pointing out that the source of most of the movement's ideas was the old racist right. Two of these people, Devin Burghart of the Coalition for Human Dignity and Bill Wassmuth of the Northwest Coalition Against Malicious Harassment, were invited to address the Snohomish County Democratic Party on January 23 in Everett about the threat posed by the militias.

When they started speaking, though, they found their presentations interrupted by 30 or so militiamen who had invaded the meeting and vocally attacked them. Wassmuth says Pitner was among the leaders. Burghart, who thought he was walking into a private meeting with a few Democratic officials, says he and Wassmuth became concerned for their well-being when it became clear that the Patriots in the crowd intended to intimidate them. Fred Fisher and Marlin Mack began videotaping and taking photographs of Burghart and Wassmuth.

"At least a third of the seventy or so people there were from the militia," Burghart says. "It started from the very beginning. There were the obvious attempts to intimidate the presenters by videotaping them even without permission, by taking pictures. From that point, the presentation I did in particular was continually interrupted with accusations, boos, hisses, questions—the questions mainly focused around Patriot ideology stuff."

Burghart says no one in the crowd of Democrats stood up in his defense. "They just sat there," he says. "I think they were pretty intimidated themselves."

Certainly, both Burghart and Wassmuth felt threatened. "There was not even any security until halfway through the meeting, when the Everett PD sent over two bike cops," Burghart recalls. "I didn't feel secure—I'm in a room with thirty Patriots, and I've got two bike cops." The meeting ended peacefully, though. The two policemen cleared the room and Burghart and Wassmuth both returned to Seattle without incident.

This kind of intimidation hinted, as the prosecutors would later suggest, at another side to the smiling civic face of the Washington State Militia—one that fully emerged when they met in private. Barely a month after telling every reporter in sight there was no desire in his group to build bombs, Pitner was helping lead a session in making bombs at his home in Deming.

The meeting took place February 27. Fred Fisher, Marlin Mack and several new recruits were there. So was Ed Mauerer, wearing a body mike. Pitner had invited one of the recruits, a Bellingham native named Ted Carter, to make a presentation on his area of expertise: building sparkler bombs. This is a usually minor explosive device many kids know how to make, concocted from the most "safe and sane" fireworks money can buy.

As Carter explained to the group, it's a fairly simple process. You take a pile of sparklers, wrap them in a wad of strapping tape, leave one of the sparklers extending out part-way, light it and run like hell. It makes a big bang and can blow a nice little hole in the ground, as well as send a few shards of gleaming hot, sparkler wire flying through the air. The red sparklers, Carter explained, seemed to work the best.

Some of the militiamen wanted to know if it could be used as an anti-personnel device. Yeah, Carter explained, especially if, on top of the usual wrapping of tape, you added the nasty stuff that could really hurt someone. "Whatever is handy, you know," Carter said. "If you're desperate, hey, sheetrock screws, nails, finishing nails, anything, you know."

The students chimed in with other objects that could be used to magnify the impact: bird shot, glass marbles ("cuz they shatter, you know"), safety glass, and objects dipped in various kinds of infective substances. "Dip them in shit," Carter said. "You could dip them in poison, rat poison, whatever, you know. 'Cuz once they go, they get into your system that you're, you're gonna get sick or a hell of an infection or something."

Carter also showed the group how to make little anti-personnel bombs with pill bottles, filling them with gunpowder and wrapping them up with tape. Then the militiamen came up with strategies for using the homemade bombs. If they could lob them into groups of pursuing feds or U.N. troops, they figured, they could take out enough of the enemy and create enough chaos to run in and grab their weapons from the dead and maimed. Someone suggested obtaining an extremely cold refrigerant to lob onto the enemy tanks, which would enable the militiamen to easily knock out holes in the machines' sides for tossing grenades through.

Pitner told the group these kinds of training sessions would occur weekly. "That's why it's so important for us to get together and train all the new ones," he said. "The more we know how to make the more dangerous we are. The more dangerous we are the more heat we can bring on with the U.N. crowd when they decide to do their thing. That's exactly why we're taking the time to do this. This is exactly why we didn't do this right after Oklahoma."

When the class was over and they had put together a few sparkler bombs, the students took them outside to a spot alongside the Nooksack River to test their handiwork. First, they set off one of the sparkler bombs, and it made a loud blast and caused an impressive amount of damage to the surrounding foliage. The gathered militiamen were amazed, especially those who were skeptical about the idea of making a real bomb out of kids' fireworks.

"That is flat out impressive," one said.

"You want to be near that when it blows up?" crowed Carter.

"Jesus Christ, that was loud," Marlin Mack said.

"That was somethin' else, I'm here to tell you," said another recruit.

The militiamen were nervous about attracting attention by setting off more of their bombs, but they did it anyway. They tried another sparkler bomb and obtained similar results, then finished the evening off with one of the pill-bottle bombs. It too made a loud blast and dug a small crater in the dirt. Satisfied and excited, the militiamen got in their cars and went home.[14]

Fending off invading troops wasn't the only item on some of the militiamen's minds, though. They still burned at the public criticism they had endured in January at the hands of Bill Wassmuth and Vernon Johnson, a black Western Washington University professor who had been outspoken in opposing the Washington State Militia's activities and ideology, and they blamed the *Herald*'s Cathy Logg for putting their opponents' words into her stories. The militiamen dreamed of striking back.

Fred Fisher had an idea for drumming up public support: don police gear and pretend to be ATF agents or sheriff's deputies, bust down some innocent citizens' doors and take their guns away by force. That, he figured, would help convince people the threat was real and it would send more people over to their side. He talked the idea over with Marlin Mack and Ed Mauerer.

"We'd confiscate 'em all," Fisher told his troops. "Well, I'll get my uniform and go down the road and knock on the door and just say, we've been sent here by the sheriff's department to confiscate your weapons. So bring 'em out."

"I still like your idea with the ATF and . . ." Mauerer began.

"Yeah," Fisher said.

"Oh yeah," Marlin Mack said, "go to Cathy Logg's house."

"Oh yeah," Fisher said.

Mack was worked up now and everyone was laughing. "Go to Bill Wassmuth's house and Vernon Johnson's house. I guess I'll hit 'em all at one time," he said.

"Right, yeah," Fisher said. "Wouldn't that be somethin'?"[15]

★★★

They called it Justus County, but this one had a completely different look to it.

In the spectrum of things in the Pacific Northwest, Seattle and Jordan are about as far removed as you can get. Where one is the center of commerce and culture for the region, a bustling hive of diverse humanity, the other is isolated, depressed, sparsely populated.

But when the Seattle Freemen announced the King County version of Justus Township in December 1995, it highlighted just how similar the believers in such disparate places could be. Their ideologies were virtually indistinguishable, revolving around the concept of "sovereign citizenship" and common-law courts comprised of the like-minded—a bizarre melange of pre-American civil law and obscure Uniform Commercial Code citations. They even filed similar liens, and some attempted passing bogus checks and money orders.

This was not entirely a coincidence; indeed, there were some personal connections. The chief organizer of the Seattle Freemen, John Kirk, had attended sessions in Jordan under LeRoy Schweitzer's tutelage. The ideological leader of the group—William Smith, the white-bearded transient whose real name is Tracey Lee Brown, though occasionally he has used Bill Stanton's name—was friends with Schweitzer and regularly traded information with the Montana Freemen leader. And one of the participants in Smith's "Justus Township of King County" was Bill Hardisty, LeRoy's brother-in-law (and Tammy Schnitzer's ex-husband) who had moved to Bellevue from Billings in the 1980s.

Smith, as he now prefers to be called, is something of a mysterious figure, partly because he has gone by various names over the course of his life. He appears to have been born in Washington but lived in Alaska for awhile, where he first ran into trouble with the law. Sometime in the 1980s, he stopped paying his taxes, and was called before a judge who demanded he file his tax returns. When Smith refused, claiming the courts had no jurisdiction over him, he was slapped with a contempt-of-court citation. Smith went into hiding, and appears to have moved back to Washington shortly thereafter. He moved around from place to place, staying with friends until his welcome ran out. He mowed lawns for a living. His friends seem unsure (or won't say) how long he had been living in Seattle when he started appearing at constitutionalist gatherings, but he made an immediate impact with his knowledge of Patriot-style legal arcania—not to mention his striking, Old Testament-style visage.

Gene Goosman, a West Seattle Patriot who says he's known Smith for several years, remembers the first time he saw the white-bearded fugitive. Smith had shown up to a meeting on constitutional law dressed in a dark suit and bowtie, and sat quietly through most of the evening's presentation. Finally, he raised his hand and asked to speak.

"He came to the blackboard and gave us a first-class lesson on civics," Goosman said. "He said the Constitution will always be the supreme law of the land until it drowns in blood."[16]

The Patriot community in Seattle viewed Smith almost as a religious figure. He appeared on local cable-access television, discussing his views on the Bible and the Constitution. As with LeRoy Schweitzer, these clearly were rooted in two-seed Christian Identity.

David Newman, a Seattle free-lance writer who was tracking the militiamen's case, twice interviewed Smith in his jail cell after his July 1996 arrest—first in August, and again in November. Smith was a difficult interview subject from the outset, demanding to see Newman's business license. Newman explained that he didn't have such a document himself, though the weekly paper he was writing for might have a business license.

"If they do," Smith said, "they work for the Jews, whether you know it or not."

Settling into the interview, Smith voiced his pessimism that he would ever see justice in the American court system. "They can't allow the truth in court," he said. "If I am right and I come to court, if the truth is dared to be mentioned in court, they will see the prosecutor, the city attorney, the FBI, and all the lawyers are traitors."

Smith was not very forthcoming about his past, but he explained how he came by his legal knowledge. "I did all my learning outside formal schooling," he said. "Formalized schooling is socialism. Just like formalized religion is socialism.

"I've been at this for thirty-five years and my personal library goes back three hundred years. The oldest book I have is *Rules of Order and Rules of Peace* by De Grotius, and *Of the Law of Nature and Nations* by Baron Von Ruendorff, from 1703, the first English translation by a major general in the King's Army in England."

Smith returned frequently to the Bible as the guide for his legal beliefs. "I did enough reading and reached my own conclusions," he said. "You just have to learn to read that code." However, he evaded most of Newman's questions about Christian Identity. "I'll just say the Founding Fathers knew who they were," he replied to a direct probe in this regard. "Most people in this country don't even know they are living in a war zone. The Antichrist, the moneychangers in the temple, they already own the world." Further, these "moneychangers who own America run it from Europe," he said.

"In your opinion," Newman asked, "who are the people who are the true Israelites?"

Again, Smith deflected the question. "If this country was run the right way it would mean big changes," was all he would say. "Ninety-nine percent of all Americans would have to change their lifestyle completely. They would have to change their social clubs, and who they associated with."

For all his personal pessimism, Smith was nonetheless optimistic about the prospect of such a day dawning in America. "It already has returned to common law," he proclaimed. "Because there is no doubt of this nation's calling, the Patriots will win."

While Smith was the man with the ideas, it was John Kirk who made them reality. Kirk, who had pleaded guilty in 1980 to molesting his daughters, met Smith through the same gatherings as Gene Goosman. This community was the remnant of the old McCarthyite anti-communist groups of the 1950s and 1960s that had floated about Seattle's fringes. Goosman had been an official of Homer Brand's old Duck Club, the Seattle constitutionalist group whose paranoid style had convinced David Rice in 1986 that the entire Goldmark family was comprised of Communist conspirators, which in turn inspired Rice to hideously murder David and Annie Goldmark and their two children in their Queen Anne home on Christmas Eve of that year.[17] After that incident, the radical right in Seattle kept an extremely low profile, and appeared to have drifted into virtual non-existence—until, that is, John Kirk and the Freemen came along.

Kirk, who told his friends he had been in the Special Forces in the Army, used to work as a television repairman for J.C. Penney but had been out of a job since the 1980s. The couple got by on Judy's income from her job at Boeing as a data technician. John had taken to wearing a beard under his chin and talking about the big government conspiracy, and had become an active member in Goosman's community of Christian Patriots.

Kirk first made a splash as the co-founder of a Justus Township in the town of Sultan in rural Snohomish County. With Bill Hardisty and another Patriot named Clayton McFarlan, they filed papers in Snohomish County declaring themselves "sovereign citizens" and establishing their township. The trio also turned up at a common-law court training session in Boise on December 14, 1995, convened by Gary DeMott's Idaho Sovereignty Association. Kirk told the gathering he intended to announce the court's formation the old-fashioned way—by having a crier announce it from the steps of the post office.[18] If such a crier actually did so, his appearance went unreported.

As Bill Hardisty later explained it, the "Justus Township" they had created was meant to encompass the entire "Washington republic," with all of that title's implications for the court system as well. He described it as "a geographical and political township that covers Washington state and a hell of a lot more." Evidently, the township also incorporated a common-law court.[19]

Two weeks later, Kirk—who actually lived with his wife, Judy, in the southern Seattle suburb of Tukwila—presided as the "Referee/Magistrate" of the first recorded session of "our one supreme court Common Law, Washington republic." According to the document itself, the court was convened on Mercer Island at the home of James Gutschmidt, a Patriot who was attempting to stave off foreclosure on his property. Gutschmidt claimed in the document he was "not a Fourteenth Amendment citizen or subject . . . not a resident, but a Citizen as described in the Holy Bible and in the Constitution prior to the Fourteenth Amendment."

Sitting in as "jurors" for the case was a virtual "who's who" of the Patriot community in the central Puget Sound area:

—Ben Sams, the Snohomish County "sovereign citizen" who organized the Militia of Montana appearance in Maltby in February 1995.

—Thomas Naumann, an Everett resident and onetime member of the mainstream conservative think tank, Washington Watch, who later organized the February 1996 appearance by Eugene Schroder in Snohomish.

—Mark Sunde, a devotee of Homer Brand's philosophy and active in constitutionalist circles. Sunde is a large man who was later designated the "constable" of the common-law court.

—Ross Tylor, a 68-year-old Lynnwood-area man who changed his name in 1991 (he was born Maynard Vernon Hill in Kansas) for "philosophical and religious reasons." It couldn't have hurt that the Internal Revenue Service also was pursuing him then for non-payment of taxes.

—Curtis Lee Sawken, a regular at Puyallup constitutionalist John Prukop's "law" classes at the Pierce County Annex. Sawken also attended Identity minister Pete Peters' brief appearance at a Seattle prayer group session in January 1996.

—Glenn Stoll, a longtime associate of Don Ellwanger's who was present during the standoff at Ellwanger's veterinary clinic. Stoll was designated "Clerk of the Court."

Gutschmidt himself was a figure of no minor importance on the constitutionalist scene in the Seattle area. Since 1979, he had been involved in more than 30 civil cases, 13 of which involved collections and five filings over tax matters by the state Department of Revenue.[20] As early as 1993, he began filing documents against Mercer Island city officials and regional growth-management authorities over what he claimed were unconstitutional restrictions on his plans to improve his property. Gutschmidt, a contractor himself, had proceeded with construction work on his home after Mercer Island city officials issued a stop-work order, and was slapped with a fine for the violation. In turn, he filed a "criminal complaint" against Mercer Island city officials as well as regional planning authorities, and in October 1994 declared himself a "sovereign citizen" and posted a so-called "Allodial title" claim on his property. Gutschmidt's complaint was dismissed in December of that year, but not before he filed a phony lien against the planning officials based on his complaint. Using that lien as collateral, he tried making a $170,000 payment on his home with a Freeman-style bogus money order. In response, the bank foreclosed on his home, at which point he began filing documents registered to the Kingdom of the Lord Ecclesiastical Common Law Court, including a lien against the bank and the city attorney.

It was for this action which the renamed "our one supreme court Common Law, Washington republic," now an adjunct of John Kirk's "Justus Township," had convened to consider in its first public appearance in December 1995, with Kirk as "Referee/Magistrate." The hearing appeared to be a last-gasp attempt to stave off the foreclosure, but in January 1996 a process server arrived to remove Gutschmidt from the property anyway. Gutschmidt allegedly assaulted the server before leaving and officially became a fugitive when Mercer Island officials issued a warrant for his arrest in the assault. He remains at large.

Right up to the eviction, Gutschmidt's common-law court remained active in another case. Veryl Edward Knowles, a Tacoma man, was charged with several counts of buying automobiles from Kitsap County dealerships with phony "LeRoy checks," and to worsen matters, when he filed phony liens against Kitsap officials in the case, they responded by charging Knowles with intimidating public officials, barratry—the offense of stirring up quarrels and lawsuits—and the unauthorized practice of the law. The Mercer Island common-law court filed documents in Knowles' defense, but to no avail. In April 1996, a jury found him guilty of all counts, and he was sentenced to five years in prison.[21]

When Gutschmidt was evicted and became a fugitive, John Kirk took charge as the organizational leader of the common-law court. Meetings were held at his house in Tukwila, as well as at Gene Goosman's West Seattle home, discussing the court's next steps in confronting "unconstitutional" authorities. Richard Burton, a 37-year-old Boeing inspector, was one of Kirk's followers, and he too hosted several of the meetings at his West Seattle home. Gene Goosman said Burton was renowned for whipping up terrific feasts of roast turkey and stuffing. "He's a damn good cook," Goosman told one reporter.[22]

William Smith mostly worked behind the scene, although he stayed in touch with LeRoy Schweitzer. Kirk, as well, boasted at various times that he was among the acolytes who made the pilgrimage to Jordan in the months when the Freemen held classes unimpeded at the Clark ranch prior to Schweitzer's arrest.

It was the March 25 sweep in Jordan, initiating the Freemen standoff, that spurred the Seattle Freemen to make contact with the Washington State Militia. Until then, they had mostly disdained the militias, in part because the WSM seemed to lack the religious component that was such an essential aspect of the Freemen's worldview. But when Schweitzer and Dan Petersen were arrested and the FBI surrounded the Clark ranch, Kirk decided it was time to contact whatever allies they could muster if the situation turned violent. He called John Pitner on March 26 and arranged a meeting with the militia the next day.

On Wednesday, March 27, John Kirk, William Smith, Richard Burton and Smith's roommate, Don Rice, drove up to Mount Vernon to meet with Pitner and several of the militiamen—including Ed Mauerer—at a Howard Johnson's restaurant. Mauerer later recalled that the Freemen struck everyone in the militia as "very religious—they talked about scripture a lot."

The main topic of conversation was the Montana standoff and whether or not the Washington militiamen would respond to a call to arms in Montana. Pitner and the others agreed that if the federal agents brought in the SWAT teams and launched a bloody assault, the militia would organize a squad to travel to Jordan to attempt a defense of the Montana Freemen. Until then, they would train and wait for the callout. The Seattle Freemen agreed to join forces in providing and participating in the training, especially in insurgency tactics that might be needed in Montana.

That week, John Pitner also spoke to Cathy Logg about the Freemen standoff, and offered a solution. "It could be totally resolved in a matter of hours if the federal government would allow the Freemen to be tried in a common-law court by a jury of their peers," he said. Of course, Pitner observed, such a court would never convict the Freemen; it would follow the Constitution, he said, and not the "Admiralty law" that prevails in government courts.[23]

The following week, the training for the Seattle Freemen began in earnest. Six of them—Kirk, Smith, Burton, Rice, Ross Tylor and another man who was never identified—drove up from Seattle to meet Marlin Mack and Ed Mauerer for some target practice. They arrived an hour late; Smith was apologetic, explaining that it was his fault.

"We've been saying we appreciate you fellows sincerely, all of us," Smith said, and then babbled: "We, you know, I'm not as prepared as I should be because it's a lot of people if they don't see, so I spent the time out lecturing and do much of that, which is a necessity, because of, you know, the right people . . ."

Mauerer cut to the chase and asked if the Freemen had any more "intel" on the situation in Jordan. Kirk said he hadn't anything new. Smith indicated he was in close touch with the Freemen's allies in Montana. "The guy I talk to is pretty well in connection back there, is that, just information on LeRoy, but as far as . . . negotiations, I really don't know," Smith said. "They may . . . it's hard to tell. Who knows? They may or may not come in, you know, sit down and go to the bargaining table and come in."

The group drove out to a gun range and set up targets. Marlin Mack and Mauerer started explaining weaponry and how to use it—which types of guns were most effective, and the conditions for using pistols as opposed to rifles or shotguns. Then they began firing away at human silhouette targets with the letters "ATF" printed on them. After awhile, Mauerer pulled down one of the chewed-up targets and joked about it with the Freeman who wouldn't give his name.

"That poor ATF guy's already dead a couple of times," he laughed. "Been hit in the head, the nuts, the gut."

The Freeman had a better idea: "Should bring a couple of real ones and hang 'em up there."[24]

Two days later, Pitner called another meeting of the militiamen to discuss the situation in Jordan. He told them they had been in contact with 15 other militia leaders from around the nation, and they were all in agreement that if the government used military troops to invade the Freemen compound, there would be only one possible recourse:

"We go to war," Pitner said.[25]

★★★

April 1996 was a bad month for John Pitner.

Just when it seemed he was on top of the world—Pitner was something of a media figure now, and his Washington State Militia was gearing up for its first real action in Montana—it all started falling apart for him. By mid-summer, things would become so bad, his own men would begin planning how to kill him.

The first crack in Pitner's facade came in early April, when Cathy Logg interviewed him at his home for a story on the militias, which the *Bellingham Herald* planned to run as part of a package on the anniversary of the Oklahoma City bombing. The interview seemed to proceed normally, until Logg dropped a surprise in his lap—Fred Fisher's secret, dirty past.

Fisher, Pitner's second-in-command from the start, was also a convicted child molester, just like John Kirk. Logg had discovered court records which showed that in 1982, Fisher pleaded guilty to a charge of incest for molesting his then-16-year-old stepdaughter. Logg found more papers revealing the stepdaughter told police that Fisher had abused her sexually since she was seven years old. So Logg asked Pitner what he knew about the case.

Pitner, she says, did not appear surprised at the story itself—rather, he was more upset that a reporter had discovered the truth about Fred. "How did you find that out?" he demanded to know.

"John," she answered, "that's my job. I have to check all of you out that way. It's my job to search the records for your backgrounds. I've done the same with you, too."

This seemed to especially upset Pitner. "He just grew kind of silent and said nothing," Logg recalls. "His jaw clenched tight and he just looked intently at me for a minute. He wanted to know if that was legal, and I assured him it was. These were all public records." Logg says she simply continued the interview. Pitner denied he knew anything about the Fisher case, and in short order had concluded the conversation and escorted her to his door.

At the time, Logg had not yet uncovered the fact of Pitner's 1968 court-martial for theft (she found it while doing further research during Pitner's trial in 1997). In retrospect, Logg suspects the fear of that fact being uncovered was what scared Pitner the most, because he had built up an ever-expanding myth around his own military record with his followers, one clearly at odds with the truth. If the facts had emerged, Pitner's career as a leader of militiamen may have been over.

A few days later, Pitner called a meeting of the Washington State Militia at his home. With the Freemen standoff in Montana foremost in everyone's minds, Pitner warned them that they too were under attack. Without mentioning the specifics of Fisher's case, which had not yet been printed, he implied that Cathy Logg was in cahoots with the New World Order forces trying to destroy them.

"Other situations are escalating with individual attacks beginning with us in the Washington State Militia," he told the group. "There's certain individuals that are starting to formulate here in order to do us the utmost damage they can. We had the paper, we had private citizens checking us out, our criminal records. Some of us are on hit lists as far as who to round up, and there's several individuals in this unit that are to be rounded up in the event things start escalating here."[26]

But not even a paranoid theory could explain away Fred Fisher's child-molestation record. Pitner knew Fisher could no longer remain his right-hand man, if only because such a crime is viewed with such deep horror by the bulk of Christians who filled his militia's ranks. By the time Logg's story appeared on April 14—the Fisher case was only briefly mentioned—Fisher apparently had been removed as second in command in the Washington State Militia, and even from leadership of his own cell. Gary Kuehnoel was named new platoon leader for Fisher's cell, which included Ed Mauerer and Marlin Mack. It may have been the right thing to do, but the move also turned Fred Fisher into John Pitner's worst enemy.

This, however, turned out to be the least of John Pitner's worries. There was trouble at home, too. His wife of over 20 years, Deborah, had grown tired of supporting the household virtually on her own, especially since John had started up the militia. He had not worked in months, and all of his energy and time was being devoted to Patriot work. On April 20, the day after his birthday, she packed her bags and moved out. She closed their joint accounts and took whatever money they had left with her.

Pitner was devastated. Ten days later, he called a meeting of the militia to let the troops know he'd be forced to back off on his role with them. "I've been through some trials and tribulations lately, so I haven't been getting much work done," he said. "My old lady left me, cleaned out my account too. So, I'm really kind of screwed up right about this point in time, so this is going to be the last meeting that I hold for the next two weeks, until I get my shit together . . . I'm going to see what I can do and I might have to give up the directorship. 'Cause I'll have to go back to work."

It was clear who Pitner blamed for the mess: his wife. "I'm getting really tired of hearing about all these women cutting their own men's balls off," he said. "I really am. I know I'm not the only one. This has been happening in other squads and it's been happening to other would-be company commanders. It's just the women can't seem to handle this. I don't know why. I mean, it's not like we created the scenario, but by golly, we're gonna do something about it."

Pitner was in his mainstream Militia mode this evening. He warned his troops to stay on the straight and narrow when it came to using their weapons. "Now remember," he said, "our job is to protect the infrastructure, not destroy it. Remember that. I want you guys always to remember that. If I get taken out and somebody advocates taking out a power station or something like that, you tell 'em—you know,

'That's not it.' I'm not kiddin' you. We're here to protect our families and our infrastructure."

Marlin Mack, who had driven to Pitner's house with Ed Mauerer, had listened the whole time to Pitner's talk, but he had other notions. On the ride back home, he made it clear he had no intention of focusing on good citizenship if "the button's pushed."

In a hyped-up voice he told Mauerer and a passenger, "I'm taking command." "Fucking, saving people, my ass. We're gonna go on a killing spree starting with Ed's old lady . . . Then we'll go kill Cathy Logg and Dale Brandland."[27]

Within John Pitner's purview, the world was crumbling—his wife had left him and he was destitute—and unknown to him, the troops were growing out of control. His biggest problem, though, was similarly falling into place and without his knowledge: the FBI's investigation.

Also that April, Pitner met "Rock." It was Ed Mauerer who, at a meeting in his home on the 17th, introduced the new recruit to the men in his cell. His name was Kevin Jackson, he said, though everybody had called him "Rock" since he was a kid. Mauerer told the group he'd known the new man since they were boys.

"Rock" was a youngish, athletic, good-looking "Aryan" man, with blue eyes and blond hair and beard, and smart as a whip. He told the militiamen he was a former Skinhead from California who had gotten into the military-surplus business and could provide the troops with all kinds of gear. And, he said, some of his old connections back in California could provide them with things they could only get on the black market.

The militiamen were interested. Some already had a shopping list in mind. They welcomed "Rock" to their cell, and said they looked forward to working with him.

"Rock" told them he was looking forward to it too.

★★★

Special Agent Michael German had been specially trained in undercover work by the FBI. After he graduated from college—he attended Northwestern and Wake Forest—and the FBI Academy, he underwent an intensive week-long course in the art of making criminals believe you're one of them. He learned how to assume and maintain an identity, how to keep yourself safe and how to prevent the suspects you have under surveillance from committing any overt acts before you can arrest them. He also learned how to avoid entrapping a suspect.

German originally was called into the Bellingham district to work undercover on the Ike Lantis case, arriving in February and immediately setting up shop as the military-surplus dealer known as "Rock." It was "Rock" who, when Lantis and some friends burglarized a local sporting-goods store, acted as the "front" who would buy the stolen goods from Lantis.

But Ramon Garcia had grown concerned about what might happen to his informant if he were found out. Garcia decided to use German in both investigations, with a growing emphasis on the militia group, which he feared was becoming volatile to the point of real violence. It took until April to obtain clearance, which in turn led to the introduction of "Rock" to the troops.

It didn't take long for German to work his way through the entire group. By mid-May, it seemed, everyone in the Washington State Militia knew him, as did the Seattle Freemen. And it didn't take long for German to realize the biggest potential problem the group had was Marlin Mack.

The first time they talked, May 11, Mack asked German if he could get him a silencer for his .22-caliber pistol. "I'm talking for assassination, man," Mack said. "I'm talkin' go up, knock on the door and when they answer the door, boom, boom, boom, walk away."

"To who?" asked Ed Mauerer, who had tagged along.

"Whoever I want to do it to," Mack answered, laughing. "You know?"

"I ain't opening the door for you no more," Mauerer said.

"No, you know," Mack said, "local people that you decide it's time to take 'em out, you know? Send a message to these people, you know?"[28]

Mack was like a puppy around a big dog when he was with "Rock." German later testified that it appeared Mack was always trying to impress him with talk about increasingly dangerous activities. A week after talking about the silencer, the conversation shifted to sawed-off shotguns and pipe bombs. When German suggested that he could sell pipe bombs on the black market if someone could make them, Mack's eyes lit up. He told German he had come up with a way to mass-produce the bombs.[29]

The next day, Mack got together with German and discussed it some more. German said he could come up with $150 for each bomb. The idea of making a big profit off a few dollars' worth of materials was especially enticing to Mack. "I just really want to start making some fucking pipe bombs, if we can get, sell 'em, you know," he said.

That afternoon, German, Mack and Mauerer got together with William Smith and John Kirk, who had indicated he could obtain the raw materials, especially the powder. They placed their order. Kirk suggested getting several different types of powder for mixing and matching, and said he could even get ahold of some plastique. They agreed to get together in a few weeks, at which time Kirk would show them how to make the devices.

This was the first time the Freemen had met "Rock," though they had heard all about him and how he could get black-market military goods for them. Kirk wanted to know if German could get some small munitions. German skirted around the idea, saying his source was skittish about those things.

"They're not necessary, but a couple of frags would be real good," Kirk said.

Smith started quizzing German about his source's ideology, obviously an important subject to him. "Rock," he said, "does he understand what's really going on? To speak of? Or is it just a . . ."

"I don't think he cares, you know?" German answered. "He's more, uh, just, what's in it for me."

"Just a financial aspect."

"You know," German said, "if everything does go to hell, he's the type of guy that can survive anyway because all he cares about is, you know"—pointing his finger at himself—"and those types of people survive, you know?"

"Well," Smith said, "there's only two philosophies of murder."

"Yeah?" German said.

"Me first," Smith said, "and others first."[30]

The Freemen stayed in touch with the militiamen over the next few weeks, working out details on where to buy materials and how to make the explosives. As Marlin Mack talked about his plans to manufacture pipe bombs, German and Mauerer coordinated all the activity artfully, and managed never to be pushy or coercive. In fact, German went out of his way one day to give Marlin a chance to back out. Mack adamantly stuck to his plan for making bombs.

Finally, on June 14, all the pieces fell into place. It was a sunny day. Mauerer and German had agreed to rendezvous with the Freemen at a gas station on the edge of town, ostensibly to go up to test out some "toys" Kirk said he had for them. The Freemen were late, as usual, which gave Mauerer a chance to create some cover. When Kirk and Richard Burton arrived an hour after the appointed hour, Mauerer went to a phone and pretended to call the owner on whose land they were going to conduct the practice. He went back to the group and said they couldn't go up there now, because the owner's disapproving wife had returned from a shopping trip. Instead, Mauerer invited them over to his house.

When they arrived there, a birthday party for Mauerer's young daughter was under way in the back yard. The four men went to Mauerer's garage, where he had a workbench, to take a look at the "surprises" Kirk had for them in his bag. When they closed the door, Kirk set the bag down on the bench and pulled out pipe bombs.

There were two completed pipe bombs, constructed of short, wide pieces of pipe with end caps and a fuse. Kirk also had the components to build another one, and the makings of a couple of pill-bottle bombs. When Kirk pulled them out, German instinctively walked to the garage window to place himself between the bombs and the girls playing outside, whose squeals and laughter could be heard through the thin pane of glass. He stayed there during most of the demonstration.

Kirk himself scarcely blinked an eye. He proceeded to go through the steps of putting a bomb together, from selecting the right amount of powder, to tamping it down properly, to placing the detonator squarely, to ensuring that no powder remained on the threads. If they weren't properly brushed out, Kirk warned the men, then even tiny amounts of powder could ignite in tiny flashes as the caps were being screwed on and set off the explosive. "You're holding a bomb," Kirk said, "and believe me, it'll take your head clean off." German shifted his position nearer the window.

It was clear Kirk expected one of the two "students" to learn bomb-making in a hands-on way. He asked the men which of them was going to do it. German was palpably reluctant—"Ummmmmm . . . ," he said—and Mauerer was less than eager, but the informant quickly realized that German couldn't put be in the position of building a bomb, so Mauerer stepped forward. He brushed out the threads some more and screwed the cap on slowly. The sound of the girls' laughter continued to filter through the window. When he was done, Mauerer let out a gasp and set the bomb down.

When the lesson was over, they packed the bombs into a box. The four men went back in the house and talked further. Kirk told German he had another bomb at home just like the one they had made, and he could get that to them as well. German said he could come down the next morning and pick it up.

Kirk said, "I'm not going to be there, but my wife is."

"Okay."

"So I'll tell her you're coming and I'll put this in a bag."

The next morning, German and Mauerer made the two-hour drive south to Tukwila. On the way down, German called Mack and told him he had a buyer. They made arrangements to meet that night.

When the two men arrived at the Kirks', no one answered the door, but it was open. They walked around to the back yard and found Judy with a couple of her grandchildren, who were playing in the yard on a broken-down playset. "Rock" introduced himself and they exchanged pleasantries. Judy Kirk went over to the barbecue grill, opened it, and pulled out a brown paper sack with the bomb inside.

"This was to keep little hands off it," Judy said, pointing to the grill and to the nearby children.

German tried to find out if Judy Kirk knew she was delivering a bomb. She looked inside the sack and didn't seem surprised at what was inside, he later testified. It became clear she knew what the device was. "He just said don't drop it," she told German. "I asked him about the heat and everything being in there, and no, just don't drop it. I says, oookay."[31]

The two men drove away and a few miles down the road, pulled the car over. The FBI's bomb squad rendezvoused there with them, and took the bomb away after disarming it, as they had done for the other pipe bombs the afternoon before.

Later that day, John Kirk called up Ed Mauerer to inquire if they had been able to test any of the devices. Mauerer told him they had set one of them off and videotaped the results, promising to show the tape to Kirk later so they could decide what mix of powder worked best.[32]

That evening, Marlin Mack rode over on his mountain bike to an agreed-upon meeting place wearing a backpack containing two pipe bombs almost identical to the ones Kirk had made in Mauerer's garage the day before. He placed them in a box and rode off, and a few minutes later, German retrieved them and handed them over to the bomb squad.

An hour or so later, German and Mack met up. German told Mack the sale was a success and that Mack had done a good job. "I was thinking, shit, you know, hope they look good, 'cause, you know, at a hundred fifty bucks a pop, I'm thinking, man . . . if they don't look good, he's gonna shit," German said. "But he was so happy. I mean, he just fuckin' gave me the money. He thought he was getting away with it."

Mack told German to be sure to tell the buyer not to tamper with the bomb, but said he wasn't too concerned about the devices' general safety. "I'm pretty confident," he told German. "I mean, I rode across town with them in my backpack, so I don't think they're gonna go off."

When FBI agents examined the bombs Mack and Kirk had made, their experts decided the militiamen had been extremely lucky. All the bombs had traces of powder in the threads; all could have gone off in their makers' hands, or even as they were being transferred. Twice, children had been nearby when the bombs were exchanged by the militia.

★ ★ ★

John Pitner's personal troubles had forced him to retire from his intensive organizing activities. He put his home up for sale, and ceased having meetings there. He did attend other cell gatherings, though, often playing the role of mentor to the newer militiamen.

Pitner was at a small gathering of militia recruits on May 29, with Marlin Mack, Ed Mauerer and "Rock" observing at the end of the table. Pitner and Mack lectured two new militiamen, Josh Leibrandt and Mike O'Laire, about what it meant to be in the militia.

The militiamen explained their code to the recruits. "Whatever's said in this room stays in this room," Mack said.

"That's right," said Pitner. "You don't cross-talk even if another guy and you've seen his face before and he's on a different squad and you know he's in the militia and he's a good guy."

"You don't say anything to him," Mack said.

"Don't cross-talk," Pitner said. "You can get stuck on the hot seat. And boy, do we like sticking people on the hot seat. That's fun."

"Not for you, though," Mauerer said.

"We don't want egos or braggarts either," Mack said. "We don't want you goin' around, 'I'm in the militia. Don't fuck with me or my fuckin' friends will come and kick your ass and shit like that. We don't need that."

"If you're in the militia," Pitner said, "you've gotta carry yourself above the norm, you've gotta be beyond reproach here . . . The way you treat people, the way you act, is reflective on the whole unit. So it's very important that if . . . you become part of the militia, you've gotta be a good person.

"You've gotta be an ambassador of good will, basically. Until they fuck with you. Then you gotta be ambassador of dead will. And that's the way it goes."

Pitner's words of wisdom, however, were heard less as his appearances became more infrequent in the following weeks. In his absence, the Washington State Militia drifted in Marlin Mack's direction, though no one in the group conceived of Mack as the leader. No one else, however, seemed to be willing to take the reins. Certainly, Fred Fisher had already been disqualified, and Gary Kuehnoel's bad back kept him from being very active as well—although it did not prevent him from helping German convert a semi-automatic gun into a fully automatic one.

German and Mauerer had explicitly told the group they wished to avoid leadership positions because of their situations, though the pair had arranged for a new, centralized meeting place—a warehouse space in Bellingham with an outer meeting room and an inner sanctum stocked with some weapons caches, a table and a pair of well-hidden video cameras. German told the group he'd paid for it with the proceeds from the pipe-bomb sales. The militia kept meeting there without Pitner, but Fred Fisher started returning to the fold. The Freemen showed up for more talks about obtaining chemicals, and they informed German they'd obtained a source in Seattle for some of their needs.[33]

But it was Marlin Mack's crazy energy that was driving the militia now. This became plain May 30, when he conducted a bomb-making class in the warehouse for some of the new recruits—namely, Mike O'Laire and Josh Leibrandt. Fred Fisher showed up too—as did German and Mauerer.

They started out talking about *The New American,* a John Birch Society publication, which in its July issue included a special report on the new federal detention centers being built in locations around the country and the role it was believed they would play in the New World Order's crackdown on Patriots and gun owners. One of the centers listed by the magazine was the new facility being built at SeaTac, south of Seattle.

"It's pretty scary," Marlin Mack said. "I mean, that gets your blood pumping when you start reading stuff like that."

The talk turned to black helicopters—the men discussed the kind and frequency, where they were traveling to and from. Fred Fisher figured there was some kind of secret base just over the Canadian border, from watching the patterns of their flights, which he said came right over his house.

"Yeah," Fisher said, "the son of a bitch come down pretty low over my house and just went right straight through. I told my wife, I oughta shoot that son of a bitch down, take a picture of it, give it to the *Herald* and say, 'Here. It's a black helicopter there's not supposed to be any of.'"

"Yeah, and that's the thing about the black helicopters," Mack said, "is that, you know, you can't see a number on 'em, so you can't call to confirm, so basically, they don't exist. That's the whole thing. But keep going back, so what? Who cares about a black helicopter? they don't think about it, you know? You're just paranoid, you know. Which I am. But . . ."

"You're not paranoid if they're really out to get you," observed German, without a trace of irony.

"Yeah," Mack said.

German had been looking over the copy of *The New American* with its back-page graphic on the detention centers.

"Well, what do you think about that little back page?" Fisher asked him.

"That is interesting," German replied.

"It's interesting, isn't it?"

"Yeah."

"Makes you kinda get your blood pumping," Fisher said.

"Yeah, no kidding."

"Makes you want to go out and shoot some son of a bitch, before they come knocking on your door," Fisher said.

With their paranoia worked up to a froth, the militiamen turned to Marlin's lesson on bomb-building. The session took about another half-hour, and then devolved into more conversation. This time, the talk turned to John Pitner.

At issue was the vast store of supplies Pitner had told the group he had purchased with the money collected for the Washington State Militia at its meetings. Pitner said he had bought grenades, guns and powder with the money, and then had cached the items in locations known only to him. He had told some of the troops that Fred Fisher knew the locations of the caches, but when the men asked Fisher, he denied knowing anything. Pitner spun other stories about the caches as well. He told Mauerer and Mack that the only other people who knew their location were members of an ultra-secretive group of Vietnam veterans, all Patriots with Special Forces training, who called themselves the "Daiwee." The "Daiwee," he told the men, would contact them with important coordinating information at the time the U.N. invasion started, including the caches' locations, in the event Pitner was taken captive.

By now some of his onetime followers—Fisher especially—had become skeptical. Some of them had talked about putting Pitner "in the chair"—setting him in front of the group and forcing him to suffer interrogation. The plan was to do it that Friday. Mauerer asked Fisher what he thought of the plan.

"That works," Fisher said.

"What do you think?" Mauerer asked.

"I'd sure like to get some things settled," Fisher replied. "I surely would."

Fisher related a story of a recruiting trip to the Olympic Peninsula that he took with Pitner to attend a militia-organizing session. He said Pitner "just lied something terrible to those guys over there," apparently over the inflated enrollment numbers Pitner liked to roll out (he typically told reporters that the Washington State Militia had 6,000 members, but the only membership list ever found had only about 60 names on it).

"And I asked him about it on the way back," Fisher said, "and I said, 'Why do you have to lie to those people like that?' 'Well, I gotta get 'em all pumped up, you know, I gotta make 'em think we got a big group up here and we got all the equipment so they'll all, you know, be with us.' I said, 'That's not the way to be.' "[34]

"We're into quality over quantity," Mack pronounced. "We don't care how many people we got. I mean, as far as I'm concerned, the people in this room right now, we could cause holy living hell in Bellingham right now. Take out power. Blow shit up. Kill every fucking cop in town. I mean the cops, they're just targets."

The men's mistrust of Pitner was so complete that they all agreed not to tell him about the existence of the new meeting place. And it stayed that way until they put him in "the chair." The session finally took place on July 14 at Mauerer's home. Pitner arrived, thinking it was just another meeting, and went to the garage with the rest of the men. But it quickly became obvious that he was to be the object of an interrogation by the group.

Pitner put up a spirited defense. He claimed he was restrained from revealing the location of the caches, and that everyone in the platoon had all the information they needed. "You don't even know you know," Pitner told them. If the time came, he said, they'd receive a call, from the "Daiwee," which would reveal everything to them.

None of the men were satisfied, but Mauerer tried later that evening to mend fences with Pitner. He called him up and talked with him for a half-hour, telling him about the new training warehouse. They agreed to meet there the next day. When Pitner arrived, Mauerer showed him around, and tried to convince him that he should come clean and at least show the group a few of the things Mauerer himself had seen in Pitner's garage that night in November. Pitner said he'd think about it.

Five days later, Mauerer called Pitner again and tried convincing him one last time to come clean with information about the caches. Pitner refused.

"As far as I'm concerned, they, Fred and Marlin, are a big fuckin' problem," Pitner said. "And I don't need to fuckin' prove anything to 'em, Ed, because everything that's ever been bought has been bought with my own fuckin' money. It's my stuff, you know what I mean?"

Pitner was especially riled at Fisher. "Fuckin' Fred has got a fuckin' royal beetle bug up his fuckin' ass and he thinks I'm responsible for him losing the assistant directorship," he told Mauerer. "And he's allowed this to get out of hand. Rather than come forward and be a fuckin' man, and to realize that, hey, no matter what the personal differences are here, the unit is of the utmost importance."

For Fisher, the feelings were reciprocal and growing worse. A week later, Fisher got together with Marlin Mack, Ed Mauerer and "Rock" before another bomb-building session, and again, the topic was John Pitner.

"What are we going to do about him?" German asked.

"Well, I would like to take him out in the bush and make him talk," Fisher said. "That's what I'd like to do. I'd like to see what he knows, if anything."

"Wire his teeth," Mack suggested.

"Oh, I ain't got nothin' to wire his teeth to," Fisher said, laughing, "but I got a damn good axe and a huntin' knife."

"Yeah," German said.

"That's all it takes," Fisher said. "I wouldn't want anyone choppin' on me."

"Wonder what, how could we get him out there?" German asked. "Out somewhere, I mean, you think he'd meet with us?"

"No," Mack said. "He'd cancel. He'd say, 'Yeah. I'll see you out there.' 'Oh, I couldn't make it.'"

"Hell," Fisher said, "when you get someone like John, who to me is a traitor, he needs to be eliminated. That's my philosophy, period."

"Yeah," German said.

"And I want to know what he's got before we eliminate him," Fisher said. "Like I say, I'd like to take him and work him over a little bit."

"Yeah."

"And then, ah, well, you have to kill him afterwards," Fisher said.[35]

The men dropped the talk as the rest of the class arrived. John Kirk, William Smith and Richard Burton arrived from the Freemen group. Kirk led the lesson, mostly talking about mixing chemicals for the bombs. It seemed like just another lesson for the members of the Washington State Militia.

Then the men learned the trick of getting out of handcuffs without a key. And what the inside of a jail cell looks like. It was July 27.

★★★

The trial, when it finally began in January 1997, seemed as though it would last forever. For six weeks, jurors, lawyers, defendants and spectators in U.S. District Judge John C. Coughenour's court strained over hours and hours of audio and video tapes that were being introduced as evidence, and then they waded through the tangle of multiple charges, arguments from attorneys, and the many legal intricacies of a large conspiracy case.

Most of these hours turned into interminable drones, but there were moments of high drama too, particularly when the tapes were played revealing Fred Fisher's discussions to kill John Pitner, and Pitner's obscenity-laced denunciations of Fisher. The two men were seated at the defendants' table, separated only by Pitner's lawyer. When Fisher's "hit" tape was played, he smiled and laughed as though it were all just a joke.

The defense lawyers provided their moments of entertainment as well. Marlin Mack's attorney, James Roe, tried on the "my client is too stupid to have actually been dangerous" defense. "This Washington State Militia, folks, they're not very bright," he said. "You heard it here first." He recited some of Pitner's nonsensical discussion of explosives and weapons, noting precisely that Pitner "clearly didn't know what the hell he was talking about."

"These are all Walter Mittys," Roe said. "That's the level of this."

Roe went on to suggest there was some reason for the men's behavior: "We all think the government has gone a little bit whacko, don't we?" And he suggested that anti-government talk like theirs is a common thing: "I hate the FBI, I hate the ATF—it's a little like saying you hate liberals."

The best entertainment in the courtroom, however, could be found in the gallery, where family members and Patriot supporters came out to root for the defendants. It was a veritable who's who of the old radical right in Seattle—Gene Goosman was there almost daily, and Homer Brand made frequent appearances as well, along with fellow common-law jurors like Mark Sunde and Ross Tylor.

Another longtime Seattle right-winger, Doyal Gudgel, introduced himself to reporters as "Ralph Johnson." He urged them to go to his Web site (http// www.eskimo.com/~ralphj/) and check out his daily reports, which he said were an attempt to keep an eye on the media through the whole trial. And sure enough, on the Web page were daily reports from Gudgel's viewpoint—which, of course, hewed closely to the defense's party line. What Gudgel did not mention to reporters is the fact that he is an avid Holocaust revisionist; the remainder of his Website is devoted to destroying the "myth" of the Holocaust, and it contains several written articles and art pieces devoted to Hitler worship as well. Gudgel's criticism of the press provided reporters with some good laughs during recesses.

The Patriot frolic took a serious turn when William Smith's attorney, Robert Leen, attempted to have the "Citizens Rule Book" made available to the jury, claiming it was part of the defendants' belief system and should be admitted as evidence. The pamphlet to which he referred is probably the most popular item available at militia meetings, since it only costs $1.25. It claims to prove the concept of "jury nullification," the Patriot notion that jurors are the law unto themselves—that they can actually sit in judgment on the justness of a law and, moreover, they can ignore the instructions of the judge to the jury. Coughenour, the embodiment of the no-nonsense judge, turned Leen's request down.

However, this outraged the Patriots in the gallery. Gene Goosman filed a Patriot "Affidavit" against Coughenour, demanding that he uphold his oath of office. Hartford Van Dyke, a Patriot from the southwestern Washington town of Battle Ground, filed a lien of $1.7 billion against Coughenour as well as U.S. deputy attorneys Gene Porter and Susan Dohrmann, who were prosecuting the case.

When the case finally went to the jury for a verdict, the complexity of it all ensured that several days would pass before anything emerged from the jury. When a week had passed, however, concern started to grow on both sides of the aisle, especially when it became clear, through communications to the judge, that a single juror appeared to be slowing down the process. The jury foreman asked if that person could be replaced, and the judge said no.

Finally, eight days after the final arguments, the judge called the jury into the court room to make an inquiry on their progress. He asked if they had reached verdicts on any of the counts, and they answered yes. He then asked if any of the jurors felt that further deliberation would be pointless, and a single man—the only minority member of the jury—held up his hand. In short order, the judge asked them to provide him with the verdicts they had reached a decision on, and they did so.

John Pitner was found guilty of possessing and transferring an unregistered machine gun. Marlin Mack was found guilty of seven counts of bomb possession. John Kirk was found guilty of one count of bomb possession. And Gary Kuehnoel was found guilty of one count of illegally possessing a machine gun, but was found not guilty on three other counts.

But on the major charges, especially the main conspiracy charge, Coughenour was forced to declare a mistrial. The defense attorneys celebrated as though this were some kind of victory, but Gene Porter promised he'd refile charges again soon. Only Judy Kirk and Fred Fisher walked out of the courtroom free. William Smith was detained before he could leave; marshals had in hand the warrant for his old contempt-of-court charge in Alaska, and so the bearded guru of the Freemen remained in jail.

One juror, interviewed afterward, explained that conspiracy laws are so demanding that the panel would have had "a very difficult time" finding all the defendants guilty on that count. Because the FBI moved in and arrested the militiamen before they had formulated a concrete plan for battling the government, they found that the only conspiracy they could attach to the defendants was that of building pipe bombs—and even then, they weren't all conspiring to build the same pipe bombs, which is a requirement of conspiracy laws. And, the juror explained, the lone holdout on several of the other counts—including John and Judy Kirk's bomb-making charge, which the other jurors were prepared to enter a guilty verdict on—made it almost certain there would be no agreement on the major conspiracy counts.

Ultimately, prosecutors settled down for the long process of a retrial. They had obtained some key convictions, particularly of Marlin Mack and John Pitner, and William Smith was still behind bars. But the conspiracy charge was important to the prosecution team; it formed the heart of what they hoped to prove about the Washington State Militia. As Gene Porter later put it: "I think it's important to protect the public, and that's what we intend to do in this case."

Still, its inconclusive ending seemed strangely appropriate for a case that was never what it seemed. It seemed as though the story never would end neatly. Back in Bellingham, the Patriots in Citizens For Liberty continued holding their meetings as though nothing had happened. And more secretively, Cathy Logg discovered, militia cells continued meeting, forced underground now by what to them appeared to be obvious persecution.

However, with the trial over, her editors at the *Herald* were cutting back on their coverage of the militias, believing that with Pitner's organization defunct, the story would go away. "They think the head's been cut off the snake," she said with a sigh.

That, however, was not the assessment of Burdena Passenelli, the FBI's agent in charge of the Seattle office, who has overseen both the Phineas Priesthood and the Washington State Militia cases. In her view, her agents in either instance had not cut off the head of the snake—merely its rattle.

"I do not believe that we have seen the end of this type of activity in the West," she said. "I believe we're going to continue to see this for awhile. They're a continuing risk to public safety—that's what makes them so dangerous. And in the investigations we've had just in this state, we've simply been blessed that no one has been killed."

Chapter 12 / Home of the Brave

B Y THE FOURTH OF JULY, 1996, it seems, life is returning to normal in Jordan. The high school held its annual reunion the weekend before and graduates came from all over. Many of them still lived in Garfield County but others farther removed from their hometown filled the two motels in town, which had suddenly emptied in mid-May when the Freemen standoff whimpered to an end. The proprietors were happy to put out the "No Vacancy" signs again—though in truth, the rising tide of returning fishermen plying the waters of the Fort Peck Reservoir always gave them plenty of business this time of year anyway.

At the big reunion dance on Saturday, most of the talk was about the normal things—cattle prices, tractor repairs, the weather. No one really wanted to discuss the standoff, but it still hung in the air. It was bad taste to talk about it, but conversations took on new shadings because of it. And hugs and greetings took on deeper meaning as well. The only references to the standoff were anecdotes about the media or the FBI, never about the local participants. You never knew when you might be talking about somebody's relative. It's that kind of town.

On the face of it, really, Jordan is not much of a town. It almost has a Third World appearance: all of the streets are dirt roads that turn into black mud in the winter, spring and fall—and on occasion, when there's been a big downpour, in the summer. The buildings are generally a little old and run-down in appearance. Even the high school looks worn out. Children play in the short web of narrow residential lanes surrounding the downtown core. Only the two-lane Highway 200 that splits the town is paved.

A lot of the reporters who spent time in Jordan during the standoff, people accustomed to New York City and Los Angeles, remarked on this aspect of the town's personality in condescending tones. And it is true that Jordan's outward appearance is neither very clean nor very much like the well-scrubbed, golden-toned West of popular myth. Jordan's reality is stark and harsh—the flat, open landscape, and the cruel wind.

Some of this is a reflection of the larger picture in rural America today, where disenfranchisement is like an inextricable feature of the landscape, where out-of-the-way towns like Jordan can scarcely afford to keep a three-man sheriff's department, let alone to pay for improvements in their high schools. Life here has been a matter of quiet desperation for so many years that it's hard to even think about the future.

But anyone who spends time in Jordan can discern something deeper there. If you get to know a little about the people who live, work and raise families in Garfield County, a different picture emerges: one of a community with a remarkably resilient, well-woven fabric. A community capable, it seems, of facing up to people like the Freemen.

Part of this is its smallness and its hugeness. Everyone knows everyone else— either they're related to them, or they've done business with them. That's what happens when the entire population of a county the size of New Jersey hovers at around 1,400, and the economy is bad and all the young people move away constantly; the ones who stay are the children of others who have stayed, and they marry the children of still others like their parents.

The life to which they are the heirs is not just any life. It is the last remnant of the Old West—the West of Charles Russell and Zane Grey, where cowboys drove horses across the plains and branded the calves in a makeshift corral. People who survived the harsh landscape in this way were fiercely independent and hard-working, yet innately interdependent; none of them could hope to make it without the help and goodwill of their neighbors.

You can still glimpse this life in the scrapbooks and family albums of the people who live out here. If they are kind enough to show them to you, you'll see photographs of their parents, standing proudly outside their new sod home on the prairie with children in their arms, or hauling their year's harvest into town by a horse-drawn wagon with wooden wheels. Or pictures of their brothers and sisters and themselves astride horses—riding into town, or just working the roundups, or even breaking a bronc or two. Rodeos, it seems, were a chance to get duded up with a white shirt and string tie. Even funeral processions, especially those for the old pioneer parents, were conducted with horse-drawn wagons and attendants on horseback.

When you see this side of Jordan you come to view the town with new eyes—as perhaps the last, barely disguised remnant of a dying way of life, where hardship forged iron-willed communities. That internal strength even carries over to the way townsfolk handle invasions of outsiders, people about whom they might feel some insecurity. No one, after all, likes to be thought of as a buffoon. And the invasion of media folks from around the world, all of them brimming with hoary clichés about life in the West, in the winter and spring of 1996 provided plenty of opportunities for tensions of this kind.

Instead, the town displayed a remarkable kind of steely self-assuredness during the standoff. Reporters, even famous ones, received the same even-handed friendliness as anyone else new in town. After awhile, the long-term reporters, like Clair Johnson of the *Billings Gazette* and a few of the TV pool cameramen, became like family members. So did several of the FBI team members.

When the standoff ended, there were even a few people who were sorry to see everyone go. The co-owner of the town's main-street dry-goods store, is one of them. "Yes, I was almost sorry to see it end. It sure was good for business," she says.

Over at the Hell Creek Bar, the young bartender—a fresh-faced kid, barely of legal age—feels the same way. He was saving up his money to catch a plane from Billings to Los Angeles, so he could see his girlfriend, who moved there the year before to find work. He was kind of counting on the big tips he got during the standoff. Now that the standoff was over, he was having to put in more hours to make up the difference.

"Yeah, they coulda kept going for another 81 days and I'd have been happy," he says, grinning.

His bosses, Joe and Charlotte Herbold, shoot him a look from the other side of the bar, where they are mingling with the customers. They know he's only kidding. To them, the Freemen standoff was no joke.

Charlotte Herbold had been doubling as the county clerk and recorder during the days when Ralph Clark and Dan Petersen started filing their documents establishing a common-law court, and had been one of the people who refused to accept them. She and Joe both had been slapped with the Freemen's liens.

Still, their little tavern became one of the chief beneficiaries of the standoff that winter. Instead of the typically semi-vacant barroom the Hell Creek becomes when the freeze sets in, it bustled that winter with FBI agents and media types bellying up for pitchers of beer and even a shot or two.

The Hell Creek is one of the great bars of the world, truth be told. It reeks of stale beer and roundups, range talk and cigarette-stained fingers. The main bar is an ornate cherrywood piece that was brought up the Missouri to Fort Peck in the 1880s and transferred to Jordan in the 1920s. The mirrored insets are racked with the usual broad range of liquor, and an assortment of T-shirts and bumper stickers adorn various parts of the woodwork. The main room of the tavern has an old ornate tin ceiling. The heads of several trophy animals adorn the walls, both in the main room and the newer, adjoining pool-table area. Of course, there are also the obligatory poker and keno machines.

Charlotte has added a whole new section of decorations on the wall at the end of the main room—baseball caps and T-shirts and jackets, all adorned with various logos belonging to the FBI, ATF, Marshals Service and the State Patrol.

"We exchanged them for Hell Creek hats and T-shirts," says Charlotte proudly.

Joe, to be honest, is grateful for all the business the standoff brought him—as well as what he calls "the pleasure" of ejecting Randy Weaver from his bar. But he has no regrets that it's over.

"I definitely benefited from it all," he says. "But I don't think anybody would have wanted to trade places with us, for what we went through. It was hard. I was very glad to see it end."

Joe Herbold is a little disappointed in how the townsfolk initially responded to the Freemen's threats. "Unless you were one of the people being threatened, no one wanted to hear about it," he says. "And I wanted to know: When will we take a stand? If not us, who will stand up to these guys?

"But eventually we couldn't ignore it anymore. And we did stand up to them. And I think it made the difference. I think we can be proud of that. And I hope other people around the rest of the country who have to deal with these people and their beliefs can learn from us, from what we went through."

It was especially hard for Charlotte. Bill Stanton, the first Freeman arrested for placing bounties on public officials back in 1994, is her uncle. She grew up with him, and her father was extremely close to Bill—until he became involved with the Freemen ideology. Now, she shakes her head at the thought of what he has become.

A couple of weeks ago, her aunt received a letter from Bill, still imprisoned at the state penitentiary at Deer Lodge, stating flatly that he intended to be out of jail soon, and when he was out, he was going to "take care" of everyone who turned on him. Charlotte has to wonder if that includes her. After all, she knows Bill thinks she betrayed him.

"He told me so," she says. And she shudders a little. She knows that Bill Stanton does what he says he'll do.

"Now that it's all over, everyone says to forgive and forget," says Charlotte. "Well, I'm not sure I can. Not after all the grief they put our families through."

Charlotte is not alone. The hard feelings, nearly everyone in Jordan says, may never go away. The people who backed the Freemen—a small minority of the town—will continue to live alongside the rest of them. History is always part of a person's reputation, and in a town like Jordan, your reputation determines how well everyone else treats you. The Freemen's reputation in Jordan is worse than dirt.

However, not even the people who led the way in standing up to the Freemen escape the public judgment unscathed. Nearly everyone respects what Cecil and Ada Weeding did in organizing local ranchers against the Patriots: Cecil wasn't running for anything anymore, even though he was a former legislator, and Ada was the sister of two Freemen, so it wasn't as though they had anything to gain from the situation—except the lives of their family members. But folks are a little skeptical about Nick Murnion's motives. At least, they are unsure of them.

Murnion, after all, is still the county prosecutor and is clearly going to run for re-election in 1998. By now, he'd been on "Nightline" with Ted Koppel and a dozen other TV programs. He'd been traveling the countryside, even going to other states, to give talks about the Freemen. The state county prosecutor's association honored him as the year's top prosecutor. Some of the townsfolk began to wonder if he wasn't getting a little big for his britches. "Nick *has* pumped himself up a lot in all this," is how one Hell Creek patron put it.

Murnion himself has heard the talk. He knows there isn't much he can do about it. He is, after all, the only attorney in the entire county. If he wasn't going to stand up to them, who would? It's not as though he particularly relished the role.

Murnion is a stocky, balding man—a real homegrown product. There are a bunch of Murnions in Garfield County, and he's related to a number of other families through marriage. His folks owned a ranch outside of town, and the only time Murnion has been away was when he went to Bozeman and Missoula for college. He'd barely returned home in 1978 when he was elected the new county attorney, and he's held the job since. He's lost a few hairs and gained a few pounds, but his bluff Irish personality has always been the same, folks in town say.

Murnion is not an intense man, but he does look you directly in the eye—not interrogatingly, but rather just interested. He has his opinions, and he's not afraid to voice them. He rarely flies off the handle, but you wouldn't want to make him mad. And when he speaks, it has the resonance of common sense. If some people in town want to think he did it to make himself famous, all he can do is smile a little and shake his head.

"Well, everybody's entitled to their opinion about what I've done," he says with that slight drawl only eastern Montanans genuinely possess. "But I had an opportunity to speak up and I thought it was important that somebody do it."

★★★

Nick Murnion is glad just to have something to smile about. For the past two and a half years, he has borne the toll of being the man most directly in the Freemen's line of fire. The smiles have been few and far between.

Murnion won't say it, but through the entire ordeal, he has been right. He was right when, in the beginning, he recognized that the Freemen's claims to legitimacy had to be countered with the law of the land, and that it was his job to protect the public from their threats. Murnion raised more than a few eyebrows in the legal community when, in 1994, he filed charges against the Freemen who had taken over the county courthouse, citing the state's criminal syndicalism statute, a law that hadn't been used since the days of the wildcat strikes of the 1930s. But within the coming months, other prosecutors dealing with Patriot threats (notably, George Corn in Ravalli County) followed Murnion's lead in using the same law against the rebels. And Murnion was proven right in February 1995 when he obtained Bill Stanton's conviction on the charges.

Murnion also was right when he argued that federal agencies needed to move swiftly and serve the arrest warrants while the Freemen were still split into two camps. And he was right when he argued, once the Freemen had been allowed to combine their forces, that the only way to bring them out would be a show of force and to cut their power.

While events were unfolding in Jordan, these were the actions Murnion was trying to persuade his fellow law-enforcement officials to take to resolve the situation. And while he is pleased that the standoff ended with no violence, he is still dismayed at the way the drama unfolded and its unusual length, and especially with the scars it has left not just on his community, but everywhere the Freemen's influence can be felt.

Particularly, Murnion is haunted by the four months in 1995 that law enforcement sat on its hands while LeRoy Schweitzer, Rodney Skurdal and Dan Petersen were holed up in the cabin on Johnny's Coal Road near Roundup. Had the Freemen been arrested shortly after the May 1995 warrants had been issued, as Murnion had been quietly urging the FBI, the situation in Jordan could have been quickly defused. Instead, not only were the Freemen allowed by the delay in action to combine their forces and position themselves in a strategically difficult place, but they were then able to bring literally hundreds of students out on Jordan's dusty roads to learn the Freemen Gospel and return home, thereby spreading the liens, phony checks and threats to nearly every other state in the nation.

"That's my frustration—more that than the actual move, because, in the middle of the night, they did catch them off guard," Murnion says. "I don't know if you know much about the feds—I didn't know much about it, but it looks like everything is prepared and planned to the Nth degree before they can do anything. Certainly, they didn't have near enough plan developed at that point."

Murnion had relatively good working relations with the federal agents during the standoff, but it had its limits. "They were fairly forthcoming with information," Murnion says. "But really, what the feds do, in my opinion, is they want to control the whole thing, and they want to manage you. So you're kind of like a commodity out here that has to be managed while they take their time and ride things out. So they kind of pat you on the head and send you on your way. That's the feeling I kept getting.

"After you've been patted on the head six or eight or ten times, you start to figure out that they're not listening to you. They're doing it for whatever reasons—political reasons or whatever. So finally you get to the point where you say to hell with them. And that seems to be the point at which things happen. When they realize they can't manipulate you any longer."

More than anything, Murnion felt the federal authorities were playing with fire by making his isolated county the staging ground for a standoff. He shudders when he thinks of possibilities had Jordan been closer to some center of population; had that been the case, he believes the little town would have drawn a contingent of like-minded Patriots.

But Murnion is willing to give credit to the feds where it is due. "They did fine in this situation for two reasons: For 81 days, the world got to see what a bunch of kooks this movement is about, and that might have helped some people out there that might have been thinking this was an option. Maybe they'll reconsider now.

"They did discredit the Patriot movement a little bit, I think. And then we didn't end up with a martyr, so we won't be up in the ranks of this movement. We don't have a martyr for these guys to rally around and beat up on the government.

"But they could have done that just as easily at Day 41 as they did at Day 81. The question is, why did it take so long to shut the power off? That's the thing that still bothers me."

Murnion's conflict with the Freemen went on for so long that he admits it took him some time to even believe the standoff was over when they departed for Billings in the FBI's vans. "I didn't believe it for a day or two," he says. "I was still waiting to see if they were all out of there. Of course, I was one of the ones that said I'd just believe it when I saw it. I never believed they were going to come out of there that easily."

For that matter, Murnion believes the hard feelings and the turmoil will never go away. "I'm certainly not over it, by any stretch of the imagination, until they all go through their trials and find out what kind of punishment they get," he says. "There will be some concern from all these different neighbors that have been affected to the point that if any of these guys get out of jail, people up there will be concerned about it. They are such a threatening group, and they're so vindictive.

"I just figure it will be hanging over my head for the rest of my life. I don't think I'll ever be free of those threats." In the back of his mind, the memories—that map in Dale Jacobi's truck giving directions to his house, Bill Stanton's vow to hang him from a bridge, LeRoy Schweitzer's threat to bring in an army of Patriots to string him up—are lingering reminders that the threats were real.

Murnion, who has a wife and children, still takes this talk seriously. And a little personally. "I guess the real thing that bothers you is you look back on everything you've done, and you ask, what did you ever do to deserve those kinds of threats? I can't see it—I stood up to them, is what I did. And they're going to point at me for going to, probably, the federal pen. Because I was the one who stood up to them."

Murnion has no illusions about where the blame lies. "The tragedy is that you have these groups that go around and build the government into such a scapegoat figure that you don't have to acknowledge your own personal failings anymore," he says. "That's kind of what went on here. I mean, that's human nature, to find someone to blame other than yourself. That these groups can go around conning people into believing their gibberish is the real tragedy."

★★★

Even from the time when they were little kids, Ada Weeding says, her brother Ralph was a little on the "rangy-tang" side.

Ada was the baby of the Clark family. Ralph, born in 1931, was three years older than Ada. In between was Earl, born in 1932. They were the three youngest kids of the family. The three of them grew up playing together on the Clark ranch that one day would gain some kind of fame as the Freemen's compound.

Todd and Ethel Clark were homesteaders in the Missouri Breaks, about 20 miles to the west of the Brusett area; Todd had proved up the claim after first arriving in 1909, spent two years in the Army during the Great War, then returned to the homestead, married Ethel and started raising family. Eventually, they purchased a farm closer to Jordan and moved there. It was at this second home that Ralph and Ada grew up together, and where Ralph would eventually engage federal agents in an armed standoff. In the 1930s, however, it was an isolated childhood. The only other children they had contact with were their cousins at the neighboring Loomis ranches. Only the parents went into town much. Even farms as close as five miles away were out of reach for social purposes for the kids. Todd and Ethel Clark's four older children—Nellie, Marie, Emmett and Alven—were enough distant in years that they mostly served as sitters and authority figures, not playmates. So the three youngest grew up with each other's company, and for the time, it made them close— at least, until they grew into teenagers.

"We didn't travel much back then," says Ada. "It was very isolated. No phones, no electricity. See, there wasn't even any girls in my neighborhood, so I was a tomboy. I did everything the boys did—fished, hunted, rode horseback, mostly, and worked on the farm—until high school, anyway.

"Earl went to high school and that paved the way for me. Well, my older sisters had tried to go to high school, and it was pretty difficult. They had never been away from the farm, and they—because it was cheaper to go, they started at the high school down in Cohagen. It was cheaper to go there than it was in Jordan, I think because of the dormitory—you had to stay in the dormitory. So of course, since we were pinching pennies, they went down there. And didn't know anyone."

Her sisters, Ada says, grew homesick quickly in Cohagen, which was another 24 miles east of Jordan. "And of course, they got picked on, too, because they were bashful. But anyway, they didn't go very long. Maybe six weeks."

Neither of the two older boys, Emmett or Alven, made it to high school. And Ralph dropped out early in the game. "Ralph didn't do so great," Ada recalls. "He didn't get along in school. He dropped out, I think fourth or fifth grade. It didn't seem so bad because at that time I don't think we had any state law requiring him to stay in school. Or if we did, well, he just dropped out and didn't go to school. He had never learned to read. He hid it."

When Earl's turn to attend high school came along, it wasn't easy to convince Todd and Ethel it was the right thing. "He had to talk the folks into letting him go to high school," Ada says. "Because it just wasn't the thing people, at least in that community, did. And then I got to go. I was in the eighth grade in town when Earl was in high school. So I got to stay in the dormitory. Normally, grade-school kids couldn't stay in the dorms. But if you had an older brother or sister there, you could. So I got to stay in the dorms for a few months to finish my eighth grade.

"And then my folks moved to town—they bought a house and moved to town. And that's about the time they turned things over to Alven and Emmett. They both were in there and bought the place."

It was at the high school that she first met Cecil Weeding, a classmate of her brother's. The Weeding ranch was only about 12 miles from the Clark place, but the two had never crossed paths before. They fell in love and, when Ada graduated from high school in 1952, married.

While all of his siblings and family members were getting schooled and finding work, Ralph chose to enjoy the freedom of his youth—and he paid a price for it. From early on, Ralph was not considered a reliable young man. "Ralph was probably more of a funny boy," Ada says. "He liked to make people laugh. Goofy. Always goofing off.

"He was always doing things like—him and two other boys, they would take off on horseback, the three of them, and they'd ride down to Wyoming and maybe work down there or something, I'm not sure.

"They weren't going to school. So they'd ride off, or they'd ride over to Ortman. It was a mining town, or just a cowboy town, little old town. They'd ride over there and goof around for a week or so. And maybe they gambled, I don't know what they did—and they probably did—penny-ante poker or whatever. They were always taking off and doing stuff like that."

As the years rolled on, though, Ralph's horseback buddies peeled away as they grew up and, like his siblings, became responsible members of the community.

When Ralph finally married Kay Nordell at age 18, he had no visible means of support at the time. Instead, with his father's help, he promptly built a house at the ranch directly adjacent to his parents' home. He made a living of sorts by doing odd jobs—shearing sheep, branding cattle, fixing trucks—while his tight-fisted father doled out a few pennies at a time for Ralph and Kay to buy groceries with. Ralph didn't seem inclined to do steady work; he told people he figured he'd get through life by talking.

"He was always telling stories about something that happened or whatever," Ada says. "I don't know—maybe some of it was enlarged. Built up. Earl tells me that Ralph said he was going to get through life by talking. Being able to talk his way through life."

When Ralph finally began making a steady living in the 1960s by operating a Caterpillar and setting up his sheep-shearing business, he finally had some pocket money for the first time in his adult life. But that introduced another problem: alcohol.

"He began spending too much time in town, spending quite a little of his new wealth on liquor and partying," recalls Cecil Weeding. "He wasn't a town drunk at all, but he nevertheless was developing this tendency to become addicted to things."

Ada says Ralph's propensity for finger-pointing began then too. "Anytime he was drinking or thinking about drinking, it was somebody else's fault," she recalls. "It was his family's fault. I know that he blamed Dad for things he should have outgrown someday. And I imagine he blamed his immediate family for things as he got older."

Cecil says the view of Ralph as unreliable was shared throughout the family and probably the community as well—which didn't always sit well with a family that had built a reputation for hard work. "Ralph was the only 'rangy-tang'—you know, nobody took him very seriously. He was always off on a tangent. The rest of them were pretty solid."

Ralph, he says, was as much an object of pity as of scorn. "Yeah, he'd lie to himself and you too," Cecil says. "But everybody took Ralph with a grain of salt. It was just Ralph. Hell, you didn't think much about it. Why, you know—basically, he was a good guy. He'd give you the shirt right off his back. Except he generally didn't have one. But when he had a shirt, he'd give it. I mean, he was *always* broke. Always desperate about something.

"I can remember him hiding out from car payments. And a refrigerator payment. He borrowed dibs and dabs of money, and he'd never pay it back. That was just his nature.

"He always said, 'Well, I can't read, but I can figure.' Well I don't think he knew the difference between a thousand dollars and a million dollars. I don't really believe he did."

As for Cecil and Ada, they took over his parents' place between Brusett and Jordan and began making a modest but steady living from the land. Earl picked up a parcel of land adjacent to theirs and farmed it for a couple of years before packing his bag and moving south to Broadus. Emmett and Ralph picked up his parcel and began farming it.

"We were kind of partners here at that time," Cecil says. "And Ralph would come by every day and bitch and bellyache and talk about how tough it was, how hard up he was.

"Finally, one day I said—I couldn't stand to listen to him all the time—I said, 'Ralph, you want a job?'

"'What ya payin'?'

"'I don't know, oh, twenty-five dollars a day.'

"Oh! . . . Hell, he wouldn't work for that!" Cecil laughs at the recollection. "'I have that place and the money I owe,' he said, 'I couldn't work for that.'

"'Well, that's the going wages.'

"'Well, I ain't going to work for $25 a day,' he says. 'I have to have 50.'

"I said, 'Well, I'm not going to pay you 50.'

"So he didn't work at all. He never did."

Cecil was on the other end of the personality spectrum from Ralph. For 40 years now, he has made a steady living at his family's farm and has become a pillar of the community. He was elected Garfield County's representative in the State House of Representatives in 1970, but lost the seat two years later. He then served 11 years on the state's Board of Natural Resources, ran for the House seat again in 1984 and lost. But he was appointed to the state Senate in 1985 to fill a retiring Democrat's term and was elected to the post in 1986, and re-elected in 1990, before he finally decided to retire after the 1994 session, preferring to spend time with his grandchildren. He and Ada still run the farm, even in their sixties, but they're thinking of handing it over to their grown sons now.

Part of Ralph's problem, Cecil believes, is that his mercurial temperament was poorly suited to the steady, plodding kind of work ethic required for success in farming. "Something like guiding and shearing, that was his thing," Cecil says. "He spent a lot of time guiding. And Ralph's fault was that every client was his friend. Whether he ever knew him before or not, why, you were an instant friend of Ralph. You knew him 12 hours, and then he wouldn't take your money. Well, hell, people would come out and spend two, three weeks with him, and he'd chase all over the country guiding, put 'em up and board 'em, and—oh, they'd lend him a hundred dollars, but he'd never charge."

Ralph's generosity, Cecil figures, was part of his charm, but not the only part. There was something else about him that, for some people, especially his closest family members, kept them in thrall—even as their attempts in the 1970s and 1980s at making a go at farming began to founder. "Charisma doesn't come with education," Cecil says. "He has baffled me for years up there—he's the most simple one of the whole family, and his own family as well. His kids went to high school, his wife went to high school. His daughter-in-law is an RN. Edwin was in the service. All of them had a lot more experience in the world around them. But he led them around by the nose.

"If he told them that they were gonna do everything backwards today, why, we'd do everything backwards. And you know, they seemed just as happy to do it, never argued with Ralph. Why, he came up with some of the goofiest schemes and they'd buy right into it. My gawd, he might believe this, but why did the rest of them go off with this?

"I don't know—he never convinced me of anything."

As Ralph Clark's farm debts began to mount and foreclosure became a stark reality, Cecil says, he began hearing Ralph spout conspiracy theories and, eventually, Posse Comitatus-style beliefs. "He talked about the Federal Reserve and the gold standard towards the end," Cecil says. "For the most part, it was this contrivance of the farm credit system to take his farm away. And then it finally got, you know, that they want to take all of our farms away. You know, he figured this out, and he couldn't understand why everybody else couldn't either. That we should jump right in with him.

"Even to the end, you know, they were still confounded why people didn't join with them."

Ralph spent many hours trying to persuade his little sister he was right. "The thing of it is, Ralph could come and sit, and he could talk for hours and hours and hours," Ada says. "And most of it just slid off me—I didn't pay any attention."

Ultimately, though, even Ada's patience with Ralph's rantings wore out. She found she couldn't talk to him. The last time she saw him, the summer before the Roundup faction moved onto Ralph's ranch and the standoff began, the day started out like old times—rounding up cattle together, enjoying the sunshine.

"We kinda had a good time together, it was like when we were kids," she says. "We were in cattle—we had a place we rented from Cecil's sister. The Seven Blackfoot runs between us and Ralph. Well, we run our cattle up there to get down in this horrible Blackfoot Canyon, which is BLM land. We have part of our own land, and then it goes into the BLM land, and then it crosses the creek to Ralph's—he didn't have any BLM land.

"The cows would cross the creek and they'd get clear up to Ralph's house. So, me being the cowgirl, I go after them, because everyone else was busy. They're farming and harvesting. I go up there, and this one time Kay was gone—her mother was in the hospital in Miles City, I guess. Ralph got on his horse and we went and took these cows. And he wanted to show me maybe a better trail, or at least help me get the cows across the creek.

"My horse trailer was at his place, and we go back up, and he showed me how to get up what we call Whitehorse—it's a canyon. But you know, it was all talk about the dinosaur hunters, the bone hunters, and different things. And we get all the way back to the house."

That, she says, is when Ralph launched into another wild conspiracy theory—some unreported sightings of a group of slain federal judges in body bags. Ada couldn't make head or tail of the story. She left the house shaking her head, and sorrowful over the strange chasm between her brother and herself that just a few hours before seemed to have vanished.

However, it was older brother Emmett's conversion to Ralph's beliefs that still most confounds Cecil and Ada, and most other residents of the community as well.

Emmett had always made a solid living off the land, had always paid his taxes and followed the letter of the law. And he had always ignored Ralph's rantings.

"Them guys, if I hadn't seen it with my own eyes I'd have never believed it," Cecil says. "Emmett in particular, but all of them."

"It used to be that Emmett wouldn't listen to Ralph when Ralph would be talking his talk," Ada says. "Emmett would just walk away."

Of all the broken relationships wrought by the Freemen in his family, the one with Emmett still bothers Cecil the most. "Emmett was the one that I was really a friend with," he says. "Emmett farmed here, Emmett helped us build this house. Emmett helped me one summer when I was having a very difficult time with my farming. We weren't together very much, but he stopped by regularly, coming and going at the farm. He'd come in and use my shop, stop and have dinner, stop and visit.

"Their mother stayed with us quite a bit, and he'd stop in to see his mother, stop and visit Ada. He didn't have a big circle of friends, most all he did was work. All the friends he had were just relatives—close neighbors, at least. Certainly, he was a friend.

"And you know, I don't think he got out of the eighth grade either, but he wasn't illiterate. Ralph couldn't read, Emmett could. But Emmett had good sense. He was somebody that people would go get advice from occasionally—you know, on farming and things like that. He just had good common sense.

"Why, we talked many, many times about Ralph. And he would think just like I did, that Ralph had a screw loose, and he was just wild, and Ralph was never going to get anywhere, because Ralph was going to blow everything he ever had. And that Ralph's problems were his own making. He thought just the same as all the rest of us did about Ralph and his problems."

The change came when Emmett's son, Richard, came under Ralph's sway, at about the same time that Richard left his wife of 20 years. "Richard's divorce is what set that whole thing in motion," Cecil says. "And Richard was the bigger part of that."

Ada says she's pretty sure that the trauma of the divorce, especially Richard's ridiculous claim that Gloria was going to take the whole ranch away, is what pulled Emmett into the Patriot world. "That's what most everybody figures," she says. "Richard drug him into it, and then, why Ralph showed him the light."

The culminative event for Emmett, she says, came when he traveled with Ralph to Billings on November 16, 1992, to hear Roy Schwasinger present his "We The People" lien scheme that became an integral part of the Freemen's fraudulent money system, brushing shoulders for the first time with LeRoy Schweitzer and Dan Petersen. "Roy Schwasinger—that was the biggest one," Ada says. "I know they both went to meetings with Roy Schwasinger. Emmett swears he never gave him any money, but I'll bet you Ralph paid money to him, or Richard did or somebody. Emmett said, 'I never paid him any $300.'

"If Emmett didn't go to the meetings, at least he watched the tapes. And they brought me a tape. And then after that, Ralph would bring Emmett over and try to get me to believe in this stuff."

Ada and Cecil watched helplessly as the quagmire of Patriot beliefs pulled Emmett further in—first, he stopped paying taxes and was slapped with a tax-evasion charge and threatened with foreclosure, then Nick Murnion named him among the Freemen charged with criminal syndicalism in February 1995. The Weedings tried to help in whatever ways they could; that winter, after he was charged and an arrest warrant issued, they almost convinced Emmett to surrender.

"In fact, he asked to come out," Ada says. "He wanted his bail reduced—it was just a misdemeanor, it was the very first charge. We worked it out with Nick and the justice of the peace. The JP was the one they were using at Hamilton—he was off in California somewhere for schooling. By the time he got back, two or three days before—well then, we're calling Emmett back and forth and we're calling Nick and we're going through all this red tape.

"And then Emmett wanted everybody's bail reduced—everybody up there. Now I don't know who all, but the locals. And then when they wouldn't go for that, it was all over. He changed his mind. 'Just forget it. Don't send anything else,' he said."

When the authorities foreclosed on Emmett's property that summer of 1995, Ada and Cecil tried one last time to help. They considered buying the land at the sheriff's auction with the idea of getting it back to Emmett eventually—but above all, to keep it in the family.

"We called, and couldn't talk to Emmett—he was up in Roundup, I guess—but we talked to his wife, Rosalie, and she was hostile," Ada says. "She said, 'Well, you wouldn't help before.' And we were trying to say, 'We'll do this.' 'Oh, no, it's all paid for. It's all paid off.' Well, they sent one of Skurdal's checks in to the sheriff's sale.

"But she told us to go to hell, and hung up the phone on us. So we didn't try very hard to purchase it. We didn't want into it anyway. We've got our kids and our grandkids—they didn't really feel like they wanted everybody mixed up in this. Where you were going to be threatened to be shot. And, it just really hurt." Fortunately, Richard's son Dean bought the property instead—and was run off at gunpoint by his own father that September for his pains.

"We took my mother out there," Ada says. "There wasn't anything wrong with my mother's mind. Not up until the day she died. We took her out there to try to get him convinced that they should go in, face the charges they had—a year ago last May. They told her no, no way. She didn't understand it all—we didn't tell her our view of it. But she didn't think much of it.

"And it's so hard to even explain or even figure out or accept. And really, Kay is one of my favorite people. And I don't know where we stand today. I don't know when I talk to her whether she's going to turn on me."

The personal toll of standing up to what her brothers were doing made Ada reluctant to do it—even though she was appalled and horrified both by their beliefs and by their actions. "I did want to stand up against what they were doing, but I didn't want to lose the relationship with them," she says. "But now I realize there can't be any anyway. Because if I don't say, 'I'll just get behind you a hundred percent,' there's nothing there anyway."

Ada and Cecil both eventually came to that conclusion. Cecil finally decided to make a stand when Ralph and Emmett invited him to the schoolhouse to attend a LeRoy Schweitzer lecture.

"I called Emmett up and said to him, 'I'm not going to dignify your school with my presence.' And we talked for probably an hour. Oh, they hadn't done anything wrong and they whined that everybody was pickin' on them. Something came up about these checks and it was, 'Oh, we have money.'

"And I said, 'Where did you guys get any money?'

"'Well, we just won a big lawsuit. Tax refund judgment.'

"And I said, 'Oh, is that right? Whadja get?'

"'Seventy million.'

"'Oh, that's a pretty good chunk of money,' I said. 'I never heard about it in the papers or anything.'

"'Oh, it was there.'

"I said, 'Well, you know, if there'd been a 70 million dollar suit against a U.S. judge, that would have to be the biggest news in the country. I don't think you've got anything. I didn't know Judge Hatfield had that kind of money anyway.' I kind of started to call him on it.

" 'Oh,' he said, 'his family does. They're rich, they got lots of money. The 70 million's there all right.'

"I said, 'You're dreaming. You didn't get 70 million dollars from Judge Hatfield. You can't tell me that.'

Taking a stand has a momentum all it own; once Cecil stood up to the Freemen, he suddenly found himself in the fore of community leaders taking a public position urging their arrest. He knew a group of local ranchers started talking about getting a posse together to back up Dean Clark when he tried to collect his grain, and he knew that a petition was drawn up urging the FBI to arrest the Freemen before the community members found themselves in armed conflict with them. He didn't step forward then; he suspected the time might come when he would be needed as a negotiator, and thought it best to keep his name off the petition. But when the FBI shortly thereafter acted and arrested Schweitzer and Dan Petersen, and the threat that his wife's brothers might be killed over the Freemen ideology became very real, things changed.

The day after the arrests, members of a Bozeman militia group were on TV saying they'd be up in Jordan to "monitor" the situation. "I thought, 'Bull-*shit*, we'll monitor it all right. Don't need you sons-of-bitches down here monitoring things. We can do that ourselves.'

"I was just mad when I heard that them bastards were coming. I'm going to be over there, and if they're going to sound off, I'm going to sound off. I'm going to tell them sons of bitches that we live here, and those are our relatives up here. And we don't need them down here monitoring a damned thing. We don't want people killed either, but by God, we're sick and tired of them. Something's gotta be done. We don't need a buncha militia out of Bozeman down there looking things over."

So Weeding called the town meeting that frigid, windblown morning, and most of the ranchers he called to the Fairview Hall to organize a response to the outsiders showed up. The militias, however, failed to arrive as advertised—probably because Steve McNeil, one of their leaders, had been arrested in that cloakroom the afternoon before while attending LeRoy's and Dan's arraignment in Billings.

"They didn't show, but the media showed," Weeding says a little ruefully. "I don't know how word got around so well." Next thing he knew, he had become the chief spokesman for the community opposition to the Freemen. Cecil is plain-spoken and makes a great quote, so many journalists called him up over the course of the long standoff whenever they needed the community's general view of things. Cecil probably never thought he'd be quoted in the *New York Times* or the *Washington Post*, but he was.

Cecil admits he was kind of swept up by events, but taking a public stand against the Freemen ultimately became a conscious decision on his part. "It was not an easy decision to make," he says. "It was just so—such a repulsive philosophy they had. You know, I knew they were on a course of ruination, before, for several years. And they got this anti-Jewish thing, anti-black, you know, that whole northern European thing—that was . . . just so repugnant and repulsive to me. And I thought, 'Why not?'

"One thing I thought, is that the public needs to know what these guys are really about. Anybody who thinks this is a bunch of Robin Hoods out here or something, they better have another look at it. They're not a nice little bunch of do-gooders.

"As it turned out, with the length of the thing, they got pretty well exposed. Had that thing been over in a week—I don't know if there would have been people like me that spoke out and told people and the world what it was about."

★★★

Even after they surrendered on May 13 and took up residence at the Yellowstone County Jail in Billings, the Freemen continued to act like Freemen. First, they refused en masse to be fingerprinted or photographed for booking purposes. In their court hearings, they created a ruckus; Dale Jacobi was booted from his arraignment and sent to a holding cell after he chided Magistrate Richard Anderson for "wearing a black wedding dress. I hope your mother is proud of you."

Following in LeRoy Schweitzer's footsteps, the Freemen also refused court-appointed counsel—except for Ralph Clark, who meekly accepted the offer. Not even Edwin Clark, who was complimented by Anderson for helping to end the standoff, would take anyone other than his fellow Freemen for counsel. His 21-year-old son Casey, facing charges out of Garfield County and possible transport to the Miles City jail to await trial, pleaded to remain in the Billings jail. "I don't trust Nick Murnion," he told the magistrate. "I ain't going nowhere."[1]

Stephen Hance, a Freeman acolyte from North Carolina, was even nastier than Dale Jacobi. "You're going down, son," he told Anderson at his arraignment, pointing his finger at the judge. "No venue. No jurisdiction. I'm not a party to your proceedings. This is not a court. I think this is an inferior tribunal."[2]

When the FBI obtained permission to search the "evidence" stored in the Ryder truck at Karl Ohs' ranch, the Freemen hit the roof. They told their contacts on the outside they were certain the information they needed for their defense was being destroyed. Kamala Webb of the Bozeman chapter of the Militia of Montana issued a warning that the FBI had confiscated the evidence.

Actually, Karl Ohs, as protector of the materials, had reached an agreement with the feds for the court to hire a neutral third-party observer, and he suggested they contact John Smith, Calvin Greenup's Missoula-based attorney, and ask him to sit in on the search as the FBI conducted it. Smith agreed; the inventory took place over a four-day period inside the sweltering truck under the July sun on Ohs' ranch near Harrison. Smith said it was hot and unpleasant, but he was impressed with the FBI's professionalism. "That was a real eye-opener," he said.

In the search, the FBI found more than the expected pile of documents contained in rows of file cabinets, law books, computer equipment and CD-ROM discs. There was also a minor arsenal: nearly a hundred rifles, pistols and shotguns, including SKS assault-style guns. When they were done with the inventory, the FBI closed it back up and left Karl Ohs' ranch.

Back in court, the Freemen appeared at a couple of preliminary hearings with U.S. District Judge James M. Burns, an unpretentious World War II veteran assigned to the case out of his usual jurisdiction in Oregon. Burns favors bow ties and occasionally appears without benefit of a robe, and he did so in his first sessions with the Freemen. It created something of a stir among them, as though he had ordered the fringe removed from the flag.

LeRoy Schweitzer, who by now had grown a bushy white beard, tried to convert the sessions into common-law court hearings, as he did at all his court appearances, by swearing his fellow defendants in as they entered the courtroom, raising his manacled hands and conducting a brief ceremony with them. "All rise for the King's Bench," he said when Burns entered the room.

"Could you please wait?" Burns asked.

"OK, I'll wait," Schweitzer said.

And from there, the hearings proceeded politely. Burns indicated he had researched the Freemen's legal claims and would deal with them where it was appropriate. The Freemen seemed pleased—almost ecstatic.

That evening, the Patriot World Wide Web site devoted to monitoring events in Billings posted the big announcement:

"Proclamation: Greetings to We the People of the United States of America.

"LeRoy Schweitzer, Chief Justice of Justus Township, held a Common Law Grand Jury today in the Federal Building in Billings, Montana state. He was taken there with 6-8 other freemen today, not knowing what was about to happen.

"Judge Burns was there WITHOUT A ROBE!!!!!!!!

"History was made today. We have WON!!!! They have WON!!!!!!!

"Details to come tomorrow and in the following days. Documents are being transcribed [memorandum of law, and others from LeRoy Schweitzer]. Check my homepage as the text will be too long for e-mail.

"Court transcription request in - will post as soon as is made available if it is not squashed or sealed.

"God does answer prayers!

"I pledge allegiance to the flag of the United States of America, and to the Republic for which it stands, one Nation, under God, indivisible, with liberty and justice for all.

"God Bless!"

The next day, the *Billings Gazette* was flooded with calls from people around the country—California, Florida, Texas, you name it—who had heard that the Freemen had been exonerated in court and were about to be freed. Clair Johnson, the reporter who had been in Burns' court that day, checked with the sheriff and the U.S. Attorney's Office to make sure she hadn't missed anything. She hadn't. The Freemen remained in jail.[3]

Schweitzer filed a legal demand for the Freemen to be released, referring to Judge Burns' "good behavior."[4] It did no good. Quickly, the euphoria faded. Burns continued to hold preliminary hearings with no indication the Freemen were about to go free. A month or so later, Burns destroyed their hopes when he rejected Schweitzer's documents as "legal bunkum" and warned that "any further attempt by him to repeat this conduct may very well produce a citation for contempt of court."[5]

Cecil Weeding drove down to Billings to visit Emmett in early July, and found all of the Freemen confident they'd be out soon. "He likes it there, actually," Weeding says. "He told me they treat him well. He says, 'I've got a pretty good notion'—the tone of the conversation was that he believed they were going to win this thing yet. And regardless of whatever side they were going to be on, that they were catering to them there—pretty nice. And they knew why, boy.

"Well, too, he was bitching. I asked him how his health was. Well, they lied to him—he was supposed to get to see a doctor. I said, 'Well, if you behaved yourself in court a little better, you might have a little better luck getting to see the doctor and things like that. You guys haven't been behaving very nice around here. Pretty hard to expect any favors, even if they've promised them something.'

"So that pushed him a little bit, because we'd heard for a year or two that he's got prostate cancer. Well, I didn't ask him that, but I said, 'I understand you've got a little prostate problem.' 'Yeah, well, that ain't the worst.' Never did figure what the rest of it was, either."

Emmett was also angry at the FBI's search of the truck. "Well, they'd been lied to," Cecil recalls with a smile. "They stole all their evidence out of that truck. I said, 'Well, I don't think they stole it, I think they looked at it and got a search warrant and went in there and looked at it. I don't think you were gonna get to stick all your secret evidence in that truck and nobody could get to see it. It was just guaranteed that it was gonna stay there, is all.'

"'It's gone,' he says. 'Why, they just stole it.' They was worried about it up there, you know. They said, 'The FBI will destroy all of our evidence.'

"I said, 'You been back in court?'

"'Yep. We was holding court yesterday,' he says.

"And I said, 'How'd it go?'

"'OK.'

"I said, 'Get arraigned?'

"'Yep.'

"'Trial date set?'

"'No.'

"'When's that gonna be?'

"'Oh, I don't know,' he says. 'I don't think there's gonna be a trial. We've about got this all quashed down anyway. I doubt there will be a trial.'

"I said, 'Emmett, I don't think the FBI spent 81 days out there unless they had a case against you guys.' I was talking back. I said, 'Have you got a lawyer?'

"'No, can't afford it.'

"I said, 'Well, hell, they'll give you one.'

"'Naw, they're all crooks.'"

Weeding says he was tempted to rib Emmett about the $70 million he had supposedly won from the judge, but decided better of it. "He was hostile, he was really mean," Weeding says. After all, the Freemen still viewed him as a traitor.

"When we walked in there, he had a funny look on his face. I never saw Emmett look like that. He's always been such a docile—you know, he'd talk a little, but I've never seen him that aggressive, ever, in my life. The first thing he said, he says, 'I don't know if I'm going to talk to you or not.' He says, 'You shoulda kept that there mouth shut—running off your mouth all the time.'

"I said, 'Yeah, I talked a little bit.'

" 'Emmett,' I said, 'you guys were the newsmakers. Them people didn't come all the way out here to talk to me. You guys are what the damned media is all out here about, not me. Nobody had ever chased me around before.'

"He didn't say much about that. You know, 'You shoulda just kept your damned mouth shut.' As if somehow this wouldn't have happened or something, I don't know."

Though he felt compelled to try, Weeding knew it was probably futile trying to do any good by visiting his wife's brother and lifetime friend, because he and all the other Freemen were given completely over to the idea that if people weren't with them, they were against them. And the July visit was no different, Cecil says.

"Emmett, he lamented to me a time or so: 'You're our own people—come help us!' In January, one of the things he said: 'When are them guys in Jordan gonna wake up and get with us here? We gotta have some help.' I said, 'I don't think you're gonna get any help from Jordan.' He just couldn't believe it. He said, 'My God, you know, we're not doing this for ourselves. Why, this is for everybody. Why, we're saving the country. You guys sit back there and won't do a thing.' The other day, he says, 'The family's let me down. The family's betrayed me.'

"All I said was, 'You know, Emmett, you're the one that changed.' I said, 'The rest of us are just like we always were. Why, we haven't done anything different. We're just like we were five years ago. You're the one that's different.'"

Weeding holds his head down, thinking about his old friend. "Ahh, I don't know," he mutters.

Ada says she can't bring herself to make the drive down there.

"Cecil was upset when he got home that night. He visited Emmett, and then he came home. And it was probably 10 o'clock by the time he got home from Billings. And he was telling me about it, that he wished he had never went. He said, 'The next ones to go will have to be you guys.' Meaning Alven and I. Well, I don't know that it has to be any of us."

Ada Weeding has a dread of meeting her estranged brothers now. She wants to see them and know how they're doing, but she fears they will abuse her—not a groundless fear. And she doubts that anything she does now would make any more difference with them than it has in the past. "You know, all the time they were up here," Ada says, "I kept saying, 'Well, I should go up and see them.' The FBI would have let me, I think. I just didn't feel that I could do any good."

She looks out the window of her kitchen and swipes a finger under her eyes a little, trying to hide the dampness there.

★★★

On the Fourth of July, life returned to normal in Jordan. At the Clark ranch, a solitary plume of dust rose into the summer air behind Dean Clark's tractor. He was at peace now, able to mow his hay and sow his wheat. It looked like he was going to have a bad harvest, he told his neighbors, but help was on the way. Montana's two U.S. senators, Max Baucus and Conrad Burns, were working jointly on a bill to provide Clark with some emergency congressional funds to compensate him for his lost income.

The Clark ranch itself where the Freemen had holed up for 81 days was quiet under the vast eastern Montana sky. Two security guards hired by the Farm Credit Association, which now had possession of the ranch until it went up for auction, patrolled the premises and kept the curious away. They took up position at the trailer the Freemen themselves had used from atop the ridge overlooking the ranch.

Gone from the hilltop was the upside-down American flag the Freemen had flown during the standoff. FBI agents had climbed the hill on the evening of May 13 as the Freemen were carried off in vans and had taken down the flag.

Dan and June Loomis had watched it all from their living-room window. Loomis, long retired from farming, is Ralph Clark's uncle. He and his wife had remained in their home directly adjacent to the Freemen compound during the whole drama. They didn't speak to the media much, although they did allow the journalists to take up a position on a piece of their property that came to be dubbed "Media Hill."

Loomis is just grateful now that it's all over. "Life is pretty much back to normal now," he says.

Dan Loomis served under General George Patton in World War II. A tank crewman, he had survived the Battle of the Bulge unscathed. The American flag carries special meaning for him. "A lot of boys gave their lives for that flag," he says.

And it had burned at him deep down inside to look out his front window for 81 days and see it flying upside-down. To Dan Loomis, it was a sacrilege. "It didn't seem to me they were very patriotic," he says. "Not at all."

On the Fourth of July, the security guards at the Clark ranch decided to celebrate in their own quiet way. They hoisted an American flag up the Freemen's flagpole early that morning, right-side up. They flew it all day, and took it down that evening.

The sight warmed Dan Loomis' heart.

"Yeah, I watched it go up," he says. "It sure looked good to me."

Afterword / Ash on the Sills

I REMEMBER A STORY a German professor of mine once told, on one of those sunny spring days all professors dread after a long gray winter. On this afternoon, the professor (who I think was rather fond of the curmudgeon's role) scanned the sun-drenched room, which remained sullenly silent in the face of his attempts to spur a discussion, saw us all slouching at our desks, and stopped. He set down his chalk and book and looked at his feet. After a few moments' more silence, he looked up at us and launched into a short history lesson.

When he was a young man, he told us, he served in the U.S. Army as part of the occupation forces in Germany after World War II. He was put to work gathering information for the military tribunal preparing to prosecute Nazi war criminals at Nuremberg. His job was to spend time in the villages adjacent to one concentration camp and talk to the residents about what they knew.

The villagers, he said, knew about the camp, and watched daily as thousands of prisoners would arrive by rail car, herded like cattle into the camps. And they knew that none ever left, even though the camp never could have held the vast numbers of prisoners who were brought in. They also knew that the smokestack of the camp's crematorium belched a near-steady stream of smoke and ash. Yet the villagers chose to remain ignorant about what went on inside the camp. No one inquired, because no one wanted to know.

"But every day," he said, "these people, in their neat Germanic way, would get out their feather dusters and go outside. And, never thinking about what it meant, they would sweep off the layer of ash that would settle on their windowsills overnight. Then they would return to their neat, clean lives and pretend not to notice what was happening next door.

"When the camps were liberated and their contents were revealed, they all expressed surprise and horror at what had gone on inside," he said. "But they all had ash in their feather dusters."

The professor looked out over the class, which now was more stunned than bored into silence. "We all like to think that what happened in Nazi Germany was something that occurred far away to people different from us, that it couldn't possibly happen here," he said. "But you're wrong. The German people are very much like us. If you don't believe me, all you have to do is look at yourselves now."

Silence fell over the class. Some of the students wore looks of disbelief, and a few shook their heads. The professor sighed, picked his book back up, and returned to his explanation of conjugation of verbs. When the lesson was over, I heard my class-mates exiting the room complain about Professor Reed's history lesson. Why did he waste our time with that story? one wondered. That's not what he's paid to do, said another. Who gives a damn about his opinion anyway? What a joke, comparing us to Nazi Germany.

I listened briefly and walked on my own way. The students may not have got-ten the professor's point, I thought, but they certainly were living proof of it.[1] Most of my classmates had steadfastly refused to participate in the learning process over the course of the semester, preferring instead their frat-boy gossip and sullen resent-ment of all things pedantic. There may have been a qualitative difference between the complacency and willful ignorance of the German villagers and these Idaho stu-dents, but its wellsprings were the same—and the fruits, perhaps, not far removed.

I think about those students when I deal with the phenomenon of the Patriot movement in America, especially when I consider its significance and its sources. Americans today are like my 1980s college classmates—and their German counter-parts—when confronted with the hard reality and the immediate challenge the Pa-triots represent: They choose denial. As the ashes of Oklahoma City, and the many other smoldering acts of violence the movement inspires, settle on our windowsills, we opt merely to sweep them off with our feather dusters and pretend it's nothing. In so doing, we only ensure that more ashes will fall.

We don't want to know about Patriots, militias and common-law courts be-cause we can't be bothered with the rantings of right-wing ideologues. We don't think what they are doing is important—until, that is, a bomb goes off somewhere and people are killed, or someone gets into an armed standoff with federal agents. Then we send out the media and they report on that day's event and wonder how it could happen. Before anyone can answer, though, they move on to the next day's di-saster, feather-dusting yet another windowsill. No one makes the connections be-tween the arsons of Southern black churches and an armed standoff in Montana, between a pipe bomb at the Olympics and those used by bank robbers in Spokane.

Americans choose not to believe that what happened in Germany could happen to them because it seems too horrible to contemplate, yet they underestimate the power of their own complacency, the desire and willingness to turn a blind eye to the violence that is growing within their own communities. It was this same trait that provided the fertile ground for Nazism in Germany, and now has allowed the poli-tics of fear embodied by the Patriots to flourish in America's rural areas.

However, the Patriots are not Nazis, nor even neo-Nazis. Rather, they are at least the seedbed, if not the realization, of a uniquely American kind of fascism. This is an overused term, its potency diluted by overstatement. However, there can be little mistaking the nature of the Patriot movement as essentially fascist in the purest sense of the word. The beliefs it embodies fit, with startling clarity, the definition of fascism as it has come to be understood by historians and sociologists: a political movement based in populist ultranationalism and focused on a core mythic ideal of phoenix-like societal rebirth, attained through a return to "traditional values."

As with previous forms of fascism, its affective power is based on irrational drives and mythical assumptions; its followers find in it an outlet for idealism and self-sacrifice; yet on close inspection, much of its support actually derives from an array of personal material and psychological motivations.[2] It is not merely an accident, either, that the movement and its belief systems are directly descended from earlier manifestations of overt fascism in the Northwest—notably the Ku Klux Klan, the Silvershirts, the Posse Comitatus and the Aryan Nations. Like all of these uniquely American fascist groups, the Patriots share a commingling of fundamentalist Christianity with their ethnic and political agendas, driven by a desire to shape America into a "Christian nation."[3]

Patriot beliefs embody perfectly many of the characteristics of fascism as we have known it historically:[4]

—The goal of creating a new nationalist state based on traditional principles or models.

—The goal of a radical change in the nation's relationship with other powers.

—An idealist, voluntarist creed involving the attempt to realize a new form of modern, self-determined culture.

—Its negations: antiliberalism, anticommunism, anticonservatism.

—Attempted mass mobilization with militarization of political relationships and style, with the goal of a mass party militia.

—The willingness to use violence.

—An extreme stress on masculine principles.

—The cult of tradition.

—The rejection of modernism.

—The belief in action for action's sake while simultaneously viewing the intellectual world with distrust.

—The view of disagreement as treason.

—The fear of difference.

—The appeal to a frustrated middle class.

—The obsession with an international conspiracy.

—The feeling of humiliation at the ostentatious wealth of their enemies.

—The belief that life itself is warfare, coupled with a rejection of pacifism.

—The contempt for the weak.

—The glorification of heroism, with its inherent dynamic of creating an enemy.[5]

—A rejection of "rotten" parliamentary governments coupled with a selective populism.

—And the use of Orwellian Newspeak to obfuscate their agenda and provide code words to the like-minded.[6]

It can be argued that the Patriot movement lacks certain key elements that have historically defined fascism. Mark Pitcavage, the historian who oversees The Militia Watchdog—an organization that monitors militias and assorted Patriots, and posts the results on its Web site (www.militia-watchdog.org)—notes that "though it definitely has nationalistic and *volkische* elements," the Patriot movement does not meet "the key standard: a corporatist-statist authoritarianism. Indeed, it often seems antithetically opposed to such arrangements (and often believes that this is the arrangement the U.S. government has).["7] This view, however, overlooks the historical fact that Italian, German and Spanish fascism all lacked any corporatist-statist leanings in their developmental stages as well—and indeed could have been described as antithetically opposed to authoritarianism.[8]

Another missing characteristic might be more telling: leadership under a central, authoritarian figure. The lack of such a personage is what leads Chip Berlet to define the Patriot movement as "proto-fascist." Berlet, an analyst at the Cambridge, Massachusetts, think tank Political Research Associates, says: "This is a kind of right-wing populism, which historically has been the seedbed for fascist movements. In other words, if you see fascism as a particularly virulent form of right-wing populism, it makes a lot more sense. It's missing a couple of things that are necessary for a fascist movement. One is a strong leader. It doesn't mean they couldn't get one. But until they get one it isn't fascism."

Berlet takes little comfort in the difference in terms. "This is one trigger event away from being a fascist movement," he says. "There's no guarantee it'll go that way. You would need a very charismatic leader to step forward. But it could happen at any time."[9]

Moreover, the Patriots' nominal normalcy, particularly the recruitment-phase focus on political issues that often cross into mainstream conservatism, has enabled them to enlist people otherwise disinclined (or forthrightly opposed) to the racist or violent behavior typically associated with fascism. Once recruited, these followers are drawn into a kind of alternate universe populated by evil government conspirators and sheeplike citizen/slaves—plus a handful, naturally, of heroic Christian Patriots. The Patriots' revolution, after all, is essentially a belief system rather than a system of organizations. And these beliefs also have a tendency to eventually spin out of control, as once-normal citizens begin engaging in activities ranging from armed standoffs with federal authorities to constructing pipe bombs in their basements.[10]

The Patriots' beliefs grow in a vacuum of public awareness. When their outlandish claims—United Nations troop movements, charges that the President is a murderer and a traitor engaged in a massive conspiracy to destroy our freedoms, suggestions that there is no separation of church and state, or that the income tax is unconstitutional—are dismissed out of hand and ignored by the community at large (and especially by the media), they also go unchallenged. The Patriots tell their recruits that this silence is proof they are actually right, and the result is an increase in the number of ordinary people who begin to believe that government is indeed conspiring to enslave the world.

The bias that creates this vacuum is not simply a matter of East Coast media failing to understand a threat emanating from obscure Pacific Northwest states, but a reflection of a larger bias inherent in the media generally: an urban one. As in politics, the larger numbers of people in urban areas translate into greater attention given to America's population centers in the news, and moreover, relatively few media types are genuinely familiar with rural lifestyles and values. They, like many urbanites, often joke and engage in caricatures of rural dwellers that, if used to depict an ethnic group or a religious minority, would be considered serious social gaffes. Indeed, some of the most vicious stereotypes of rural people I have heard have come out of the mouths of the same people who on another occasion might leap on a hapless victim insensitive enough to refer to Native Americans as "Indians."

This is as true in Seattle as it is in New York City. The desire and ability to adequately comprehend and report on rural phenomena is limited or nonexistent at the major media outlets possessing the resources to pursue such journalism, and the media in rural areas—small weeklies, tiny AM stations—who might have reporters in close contact with these issues are usually too underfunded to effectively attempt it.

What this urban bias has prevented the media from comprehending (let alone reporting), and what the Patriots understand innately and exploit to the fullest, is just how widespread the feeling of disenfranchisement is in rural America—how removed the nation's farmers, ranchers, loggers and miners feel from the mainstream political discourse. The bias of political power toward urban areas has particularly fed this feeling. Rural dwellers often fear that their fates rest in the hands of people who dismiss them as irrelevant and disposable, particularly in matters of land policy and economics.

I wonder if the nation can adequately comprehend the words of Gilles Stockton, a Montana rancher who counts Freemen as neighbors and has incurred their wrath by standing up to them:

> My neighbors and I may not understand how the Freemen got where they are, but I think we do understand their anger. Because we too, are angry: about an economic system where each generation of farmers and ranchers must buy the land again; where more money leaves the farm to pay interest than ever stays; a system where any disaster, a sick child, a blizzard, a flood, or a hailstorm can tip the balance towards foreclosure.
>
> So the Freemen come from a society that has turned its back on its rural roots; where agricultural policy is designed by and for investment bankers, stockbrokers and corporate lawyers of Westchester County, New York—not for the farmers and ranchers of Garfield County, Montana; where the North American Free Trade Agreement and the globalization of the U.S. economy affirm that rural America is just a colony. We natives happen to speak English and the toilets flush, but like all colonies, rural America supplies raw materials at a net loss to its inhabitants and to the land.
>
> . . . Now we have the "Freedom to Farm Act", which is just politicalese for the "stick it to the farmer act." Hypocritical politicians say we have the freedom to grow any crop we wish, but whether we plant wheat, corn, beans, or Belgian endive, we can't make a living. And all the while, a demented Greek chorus of economists advises us to "plant for the market." But there is no market. An interlocking web of monopolistic corporations controls all the distribution channels.
>
> It is awfully strange that we are intent on converting the world's most efficient agricultural system into one that is centrally controlled and planned—the Stalinization of American agriculture—that's what it is. Why would anyone expect that the corporate apparatchuk will be better than their communist counterparts?

The corporations steal my labor, my produce, and my land. Society at large insults me as being obsolete and ignorant. Every day there are fewer and fewer farmers. But we are not obsolete, and it is society at large that is ignorant. The cheap food will not last because corporations control the worldwide distribution of food. The name of the game is money and power.

. . . I make no apology for the "Freemen." We don't need more racism, threats of violence and extremist rhetoric. But there is a sickness when the people who work the land are abandoned and abused.[11]

Society at large may have failed to recognize this sickness, but the political opportunists of the radical right have not. By the 1970s they had already identified the Pacific Northwest as the future home of the Aryan Nations, at least partly because they recognized that the fertile ground of discontent was everywhere to be found in its vast landscape. And in the 1980s they seized the opportunity presented by the Farm Crisis as the means of burrowing into the rural culture itself, by presenting themselves as an entity willing to lend a sympathetic ear and offer a concrete solution.

Though the depth of the movement has not been great, its breadth has been remarkable. Once the Patriot movement took root and blossomed in the Northwest, its tendrils quickly spread to the rest of the nation. Militia units now can be found in upstate Pennsylvania and New York, in the Florida swamps, the plains of Oklahoma and Nebraska, the oilfields of Texas and the farm country of California. Patriots likewise began declaring themselves sovereign citizens and forming common-law courts in virtually every state.

But if the Northwest has been a testing ground for the Patriot movement, it also has provided plenty of examples of what is most likely to work when confronting the Patriot movement's challenges. Amid the widespread disenfranchisement, the Northwest's rural areas are nonetheless largely populated by great numbers of people of good common sense and generousness. Most of them understand that the cure offered by the Patriot movement is plain snake venom bound to only poison their communities. They understand that the only way to meet the challenge the Patriots represent—to counter the fraying of the social fabric these beliefs cause—is not to attempt to suppress or intimidate or censor them. Rather, it is simply to stand up to them: to say no, you're wrong. Respectfully, but firmly: We will not succumb to your wild fantasies and your anger. We live in the real world. And we dare you to do the same.

The people who have had the courage to stand up to the Patriots have defused the movement in their communities by meeting it head-on, refuting its false logic and distortions of the truth, and banding together the rest of the community in a show of solidarity for the institutions of democracy that the Patriots oppose. When the movement's followers come to understand that they have raced out onto one of life's long tree limbs, and that no one else—not their friends, not their families, not their neighbors—will ever join them out there, there is at least a chance that they will come back of their own accord.

Just as the Northwest has a long history of radical-right activity, so too it has a tradition of local citizens standing up to its manifestations in their communities and effectively facing them down. It dates back to the 1920s, when the Ku Klux Klan arose as a political power in Oregon and Washington and was faced down by local citizens who challenged the organization's wild slanders against the Catholic Church.[12] Even today, this tradition can be found in the work of Coeur d'Alene's Kootenai County Human Rights Task Force, which has effectively raised awareness of the threat posed to the community by the activities of the Aryan Nations.

It is embodied in the paper menorahs the residents of Billings posted in their front windows as a show of solidarity with a local Jewish family whose window was shattered by a brick and their home sprayed with anti-Semitic graffiti. Its living practitioners are the residents of Jordan, Montana, who organized their community to oppose the Freemen, many of whom were their own family members and longtime neighbors. Most striking are close relatives like Cecil and Ada Weeding, who not only refused to condone what the Freemen were doing but spearheaded the community-wide effort to stand up against the threats and violent rhetoric that emanated from both the Freemen and the Patriots from elsewhere who hovered near the scene.

The human-rights activists who have shouldered the burden of monitoring and opposing the Patriot movement are part of this tradition, too. Bill Wassmuth, who heads the Northwest Coalition Against Malicious Harassment in Seattle, is an Idaho native who grew up in a small Camas Prairie town. Ken Toole, director of the Montana Human Rights Network, is the son of a much-beloved Montana historian, with family ties dating back to the state's origins (Montana's first governor was a Toole). The Portland-based Coalition for Human Dignity is staffed primarily with Northwest natives. Local organizations like the Montana Association of Churches that have been in the front of the fray likewise draw on their long and deep ties to the mainstream communities to counter the radical revolutionarism of the Patriots.

All these people, however, are only a bulwark against the rising tide of the movement. Until the conditions that make America's rural landscape such fertile ground for these beliefs are eliminated or at least mitigated, the Patriots will continue to fester and grow, tearing families and communities apart, destroying our sense of security as their most violent followers wreak havoc through threats, bombings, robberies and murders. Changing those conditions is a task that befalls all Americans.

The most important (and perhaps most difficult) step entails healing the huge rift between urban and rural America. Globalization has meant a spurt of high-technology employment for urban dwellers, but it has brought little but misery to people who make their living from the land. It has hit them hard on two fronts: by enhancing the growth of massive corporate operations at the expense of small family farms; and secondly, by expanding the scope of their market. Now, instead of having to compete simply with fellow countrymen who produce the same commodities—grain, beef, wood products, minerals and other essentials of life—they're up against Argentine farmers and Indonesian loggers who can produce the same goods at a fraction of the labor and cost. Though the rate of farm foreclosure is no longer steeply climbing, it has remained high since the 1980s. So has the rate of rural suicide.

The process of globalization, by reducing local economies to rubble, has transformed thousands of rural communities from the golden-hued repository of upstanding American values they once were into hard-scrabble, increasingly mean-spirited and hollowed-out shells, scarcely able to afford schools and libraries, more resembling Third World villages than American hometowns. Urbanites inclined to dismiss such radical shifts in the social landscape as the inevitable product of merciless economics should stop to consider the high social cost that comes with such offhandedness. A keen observer need look no farther than Oklahoma City to know what the price is.

Indeed, until rural society is healed—through steps to save the broad, intricate system of family farms, ranches, and small logging and mining operations that comprise much of their economic base, alongside efforts to give the rural point of view a greater voice in the national debate—the toll will continue to rise. As long as the Patriot movement continues to attract believers ready to take action against a decadent society, the Tim McVeighs and Robert Mathewses will continue to emerge from the other end of its funnel.

Along with the healing, it will be important to confront the direct challenges to the American community that the Patriot movement poses. The work begins at the political level, in the arena of national and state politics, where Patriot-inspired fearmongering has spread even to the halls of Congress and the state legislatures. The need to confront such rhetoric, to counter its distortions with facts and hard reality, should be self-evident, but in the course of political debate it is often neglected. Politicians who play to Patriots' sensibilities by feeding their fear of government should be held accountable for their irresponsibility, yet they rarely are.

The more deafening silence, though, has emanated from the nation's media—newspapers and television, both on the national and local scenes. Reportage on the Patriots and their beliefs in general has been sporadic at best, confined to a few sensational events like Oklahoma City, the Ruby Ridge hearings, and the standoff at Jordan. Numerous local media outlets have done a generally sound job of reporting on the movement's growing influence, though they often lack the investigative resources to check the factual grounding of the Patriots' claims or to examine their sources. The urban-oriented media, though, have largely failed to disseminate this information to the general population. And when they do report on the movement, they almost invariably engage in shallow stereotyping of the movement's followers, dismissing their sometimes legitimate (though inelegantly voiced) concerns as the products of hopelessly backwards buffoons. The image of the movement fed to the nation—the lunatic rantings of an insignificant smattering of yahoos in the distant woods—is dangerously shallow. The reality—that the Patriot movement is widespread, though not yet particularly deep, throughout most of rural America—thus escapes the attention of most Americans.

Finally, there's the hard work of confronting the Patriot movement in our homes and neighborhoods. When our friends darkly suggest the government is conspiring to implant the "Mark of the Beast" on every person, or when our grandfathers proclaim that the whole system is set up by and for Jewish bankers, it's important to let them know you stand opposed to such beliefs. The inflammatory nature of such talk usually inspires one of two responses from non-Patriots: an equally heated counterargument, or stony silence, neither of which is effective in the least.

There is a third course, as the citizens who have stood up to the Patriots in their communities have demonstrated: to respond with respect and courtesy, but firmly, with facts and reality. Point out that there is a legitimate, perfectly rational explanation for literally every piece of evidence the Patriots can produce for their theories that the government is part of a grand conspiracy to destroy the nation. Explain that the legal arguments they present for their constitutionalist beliefs have long been answered by real court rulings, many dating back to the Civil War, and that the web of pseudo-legal theory the Patriots espouse is a sham with no recognizable legitimacy, especially not in the body of law as practiced in America today. If they have fallen into the snare of Christian Identity and begin claiming that white people are the true children of Israel, discuss with them the fact that such beliefs have been regarded by Christian leaders and theologians, since as far back as the third century, to constitute an egregious heresy, a blasphemy that runs counter to the spirit of Christianity itself.

The spirit of respect has been notably absent from most discussions about the Patriots, in large part because the Patriots themselves are so openly contemptuous of everything outside their belief system that it is difficult not to respond in kind. The movement challenges so many everyday American assumptions about the core foundations of our society that it is often difficult to even begin to respond. But that response ultimately, to be effective, must reflect the very values the Patriots' beliefs most deeply corrode: a public discourse based on mutual respect; a sense of fair play and decency; an appreciation of the value of community and cooperative action.

These are the same values that people in rural areas see as integral to their everyday lives, in contrast to the ragged social fabric that often passes for urban life. These are the values that they most fear are being destroyed in the tide of urban dominance over American culture. Their view of the depths of this decay is reflected in the growth of the Patriot movement, because it means they have come to believe the urban sickness can only be cured by destroying it.

The attraction of fascism always has been that it promises to destroy the old in order to build the new. The Patriots flourish in the land of the disenfranchised, among those who most have a reason to tear down the status quo, and as that class grows—not just in rural areas, but spreading as well to the millions of dislocated workers chewed up and spit out in modern, downsized corporate America—the movement will continue to rain ashes adrift on the winds of violence it engenders.

And feather dusters, it appears, will continue to rise in demand.

Postscript

P ROSECUTING THE MONTANA FREEMEN for their many crimes was a daunting task, one that ultimately required three trials before laying the episode to rest. The first trial, in March 1998, involved the six men charged with some of the lesser crimes, and brought swift convictions. Kansan Jon Nelson and North Carolinian Stephen Hance, along with his twentysomething sons, James and John, were convicted of accessory charges, and Elwin Ward was convicted for paying taxes with a LeRoy check. However, the man who brought the standoff to an end—Edwin Clark—was acquitted of all charges and walked out of the courtroom a free man.

The remaining Freemen—12 in all—were generally not so fortunate in the second trial, which began in late May 1998 and ended with the jury in deliberation on July 4. As in other trials involving Patriots and their web of criminal behavior, the jury had difficulty wading through the complex case that the prosecutors presented. The jury deliberated for over a week, issuing a cluster of verdicts early, and then deliberated some more, ultimately delivering mixed verdicts: convictions on a wide range of charges, a few outright acquittals, and a hung jury on nearly half of the 126 total charges. The government promptly refiled its case and went back to trial in October 1998 making the conspiracy and robbery charges more succinct, and was rewarded with a fresh round of convictions in November. When all was said and done, the results looked like this:

LeRoy Schweitzer—Convicted on a total of 25 counts, including armed robbery, conspiracy, bank, mail and wire fraud, threatening a federal judge, false claims to the IRS, illegal possession of firearms and interstate transportation of stolen property.

Daniel Petersen—Convicted on 19 counts, including armed robbery, bank fraud, conspiracy, bank and mail fraud, false claims to the IRS, interstate transportation of stolen property and threatening a federal judge.

Rodney Skurdal—Convicted on 5 counts, including bank fraud, armed robbery and threatening a federal judge.

Dale Jacobi—Convicted on 13 counts, including armed robbery, conspiracy, bank fraud, false claims to the IRS and being an illegal alien in possession of firearms and ammunition.

Russell Landers—Convicted on 4 counts: conspiracy, bank fraud, threatening a judge and being a fugitive in possession of a firearm. Landers had been convicted and sentenced to a 30-year term earlier in a separate trial in his home state of North Carolina for using Freemen checks to buy vehicles.

Richard Clark—Convicted of 5 counts, including robbery, bank fraud and threatening a judge.

A handful of Freemen associates and spouses—Dan Petersen's wife, Cherlyn; the previously convicted Bill Stanton and his wife, Agnes; and Californian John McGuire—were convicted on a range of related charges, including bank fraud and firearms charges. Cornelius "Casey" Veldhuizen of Minnesota was acquitted of two robbery counts. Earlier, Ebert Stanton had pleaded guilty to bank-fraud and accessory charges.

The Clark brothers—Emmett and Ralph—left the courtroom for their homes with the 20 or so months they served in jail sufficing for punishment. Emmett pleaded guilty at the start of the first trial to three charges of making threats, and was sentenced to time served. Federal prosecutors decided not to refile charges against Ralph Clark after the first trial ended in a hung jury, and handed his case over to state prosecutors. As 1999 dawned, those charges had been filed but the trial had not yet been scheduled.

Other recent developments concerning people described in this book include: Charlie Phipps, sheriff of Garfield County, Montana, was defeated in the 1998 elections, as was Sheriff Paul Smith of Musselshell County, Montana.

Cecil Weeding, after sitting out of public service for a couple of years, got the itch to return and filed to run for a seat on the Montana Public Service Commission. He began making regular flights in his single-engine Cessna to Helena and wherever else he needed to make campaign appearances. In early April 1998 Cecil's plane did not come back as scheduled from a flight to Havre. Ada and her sons, assisted by search-and-rescue teams, spent the next week scouring the countryside for him, and finally found the Cessna's wreckage in the Little Rocky Mountains. Cecil's body was inside. He was 64.

Bo Gritz recovered fully from his self-inflicted gunshot wound, but did not reconcile with his wife, Claudia. Instead he retreated to his old property in Nevada to spend the winter, recovering further.

Helen Trowbridge was released from prison to attend the funeral of her husband, Bill, who died while serving his tax-evasion sentence. Helen eventually served out her sentence for the same crime. She was released for good from jail in August 1998 and returned to her home in Twin Falls.

Alex Neiwert, my grandfather, died of leukemia in August 1998. He was 85.

Endnotes

Foreword / Notes of a Native Son

1. See "Oklahoma Bombing Suspect: Unraveling of One Man's Frayed Life," by John Kifner, New York Times News Service, Dec. 30, 1995, for a complete portrait of McVeigh's descent into the world of militias. Another excellent discussion of McVeigh's and Nichols' radicalization appears in Kenneth S. Stern, *A Force Upon the Plain: The American Militia Movement and the Politics of Hate* (New York: Simon and Schuster, 1996), pp. 187-199.
2. See James A. Aho, *The Politics of Righteousness: Idaho Christian Patriotism* (Seattle: University of Washington Press, 1990), esp. pp. 68-82.
3. See James A. Aho, *This Thing of Darkness: A Sociology of the Enemy* (Seattle: University of Washington Press, 1994), pp. 100-104, for an enlightening examination of the symbiotic nature of the enemy mentality.

Chapter 1 / Land of the Freemen

1. See "Edict" issued Oct. 24, 1994, by Rodney Skurdal in Musselshell County, Montana.
2. See James A. Aho, *The Politics of Righteousness: Idaho Christian Patriotism* (Seattle: University of Washington Press, 1990), pp. 164-184.
3. See James Brooke, "Freeman depended on government subsidies," *New York Times*, April 30, 1996. Brooke describes the thousands of dollars Ralph Clark took from government agencies for years, beginning in the 1960s and continuing well into the 1990s. At the time he was being foreclosed on in 1994, he was still receiving $48,000 annually from a grant to preserve grasslands and prevent erosion, grants locals call "paying farmers to grow nothing."

Chapter 2 / Parallel Universe

1. An interesting inclusion, considering that Ford was an anti-Semite of some renown; he reputedly authored the conspiracy-theory opus *The International Jew*, and was awarded the Iron Cross by Hitler, who was quoted saying at the award ceremony, "We look to Heinrich Ford as the leader of the fascist movement in America." See Norman Cohn, *Warrant for Genocide: The Myth of the Jewish World-Conspiracy and the Protocols of the Elders of Zion* (New York: Oxford University Press, 1967), p. 162.
2. Kevin Flynn and Gary Gerhardt, *The Silent Brotherhood: Inside America's Racist Underground* (New York: Free Press, 1989), pp. 93, 332.
3. Robert Pummer, *The Road Back to America* (Water Valley, Ky.: privately printed, 1994), p. 209.
4. This was true enough at the time, though the Trochmanns since then have developed a couple of World Wide Web sites: one for the Militia of Montana (http://www.nidlink.com/~bobhard/mom.html) and another for the American Patriot Internet Classified Service (http://logoplex.com/classifieds/view.html) that are popular in Patriot circles.
5. "Yahweh" is the appellation for God preferred by believers in Christian Identity, the racist religion which holds that white people are the true Israelites, Jews are the children of Satan and blacks are "mud people"; see James Aho's *The Politics of Righteousness: Idaho Christian Patriotism* (Seattle: University of Washington Press, 1990), pp. 83-113. Hearing it at a militia meeting is not uncommon, and does not necessarily denote that the speaker is an Identity follower, but the frequency of its use is not likely to be a mere coincidence, either.
6. Also, personal interview with Trochmann, Nov. 15, 1994.
7. A survey of "Enemies: Foreign and Domestic" by the author found that of the 191 pages contained in the package (and explained at times in the accompanying videotape), 141 were comprised of information from mainstream sources with legitimate underlying explanations (or being in fact, legitimate explanations themselves); 47 were material provided by other conspiracy theorists, comprised of a synthesis of legitimate fact and unsupported innuendo; and 2 were inexplicable,

primarily because their contents and source were both unidentified. Among the second type, some 16 were "evidence" of conspiratorial activity—military-equipment movements, equipment with United Nations or foreign-army insignias, or repainting jobs with same—which are unaccompanied by any information regarding where they were sighted or what the equipment actually consists of. Some of these have been tracked to the sources and are, again, instances of legitimate activity. (An instance of the latter is the military equipment depicted on pp. 151-152, which carry Russian Army insignias and are on U.S. soil. These photographs were taken near a facility in Louisiana which specializes in refurbishing used military equipment and counts numerous foreign military forces among its customers, including Russia. The equipment in the photos, according to officials at the facility, was simply worn out and was in the process of being rebuilt, and eventually was shipped back to customers in Russia.) The two inexplicable instances (pp. 116 and 155) are photographs of military installations or equipment which appear to be legitimate but which cannot be properly identified from the photo contained in *Enemies* and are otherwise unexplained by Trochmann on the video tape.

8. See "A Season of Discontent: Militias, Constitutionalists and the Far Right in Montana," Montana Human Rights Network, 1994, p. 8.
9. Indeed, Mack is one of the chief contact points between the NRA and the militias. He's received $25,000 backing from the group in his lawsuit against the federal government over the Brady law (see "NRA becomes militias' beacon," by Charles M. Sennott, Boston *Globe*, Aug. 16, 1995).
10. See "Guns and Gavels: Common Law Courts, Militias and White Supremacy," Coalition for Human Dignity, Portland, Ore., January 1996, pp. 13-15.
11. Author's telephone interview with Liberty, February 1996.
12. See "Park conspiracy aficionados hear familiar story at meeting," by Michelle Partridge, *Wenatchee Daily World*, Oct. 31, 1994, and "Group Proposes U.S.-Canadian Park in North Cascades," Associated Press, June 14, 1995,
13. Personal interview with Trochmann, Nov. 15, 1994.
14. See "Infighting rips Militia of Montana," by Ron Selden, *Missoula Independent*, Feb. 29, 1996.
15. These beliefs are outlined in a couple of pamphlets: "Our One Supreme Common Law Court of the Sovereign People," published by Schroder's United Sovereigns of America, and "On Common Law Procedure," by John William and Joe Allen, available from DeMott's Idaho Sovereignty Association. See also CHD's "Guns and Gavels," op. cit. Further discussion of the common-law courts appears in chapters 7, 8 and 9.
16. The Second Amendment has been traditionally interpreted by the U.S. Supreme Court as pertaining only to the formation of militias, which the courts say are embodied in the U.S. National Guard; the precedent was established in *The United States v. Miller* 307U.S.174,178 (1939), when the court unanimously held that laws affecting guns do not offend the Second Amendment. Subsequent rulings have sustained the precedent. See "NRA has a warped view of the Second Amendment," by Roger Tatarian, McClatchy News Service op-ed writer, June 19, 1995. A further discussion of the gun-control question appears in Chapter 11.
17. See further discussion in Chapter 9.
18. From a speech by Richard Mack before Citizens for Constitutional Law and Law Enforcement, a Patriot organization, on March 30, 1996, in Bellevue, Washington, recorded by the author.

Chapter 3 / God's Country

1. See the speech given by John Birch Society founder Robert Welch on Sept. 17, 1961, in Chicago, "Republics and Democracies."
2. See James A. Aho, *The Politics of Righteousness: Idaho Christian Patriots* (Seattle: University of Washington Press, 1990), pp. 56-57.
3. See Lawrence J. Saalfield, *Forces of Prejudice in Oregon, 1920-25* (Portland, Ore.: University of Portland Press/Archdiocesan Historical Commission, 1984), pp. 2-4.
4. See James Ridgeway, *Blood in the Face: The Ku Klux Klan, Aryan Nations, Nazi Skinheads, and the Rise of a New White Culture* (New York: Thunder's Mouth Press, 1995), pp. 52-62.
5. See David M. Chalmers, *Hooded Americanism: The First Century of the Ku Klux Klan* (New York: Doubleday, 1965), pp. 72-90.
6. See Malcolm Clark, Jr., "The Bigot Disclosed: 90 Years of Nativism," *Oregon Historical Quarterly*, June 1974, p. 178.

7. Saalfield, op. cit., pp. 3-5.
8. See Clark, op. cit., pp. 164-165.
9. Ibid., pp. 27-37.
10. Ibid., pp. 16-18.
11. See Chalmers, op. cit., pp. 217-219. See also J. Kingston Pierce, "Issaquah's Night of the Klan," *Eastsideweek*, July 24, 1991, pp. 6-7.
12. Chalmers, op. cit., p. 219. See also Pierce, op. cit., pp. 1, 9.
13. Saalfield, op. cit., pp. 56-58.
14. Ibid., pp. 58-60.
15. See Karen E. Hoppes, "An Investigation of the Nazi-Fascist Spectrum in the Pacific Northwest: 1924-1941," Master's Thesis, Western Oregon State College, 1983, particularly pp. 2-14. On p. 5, Hoppes charts the growth of fascist groups in the Northwest, and observes that they grew dramatically in the years 1933-38.
16. Ibid., pp. 58-62.
17. Ibid., pp. 66-68.
18. See Karen E. Hoppes, "William Dudley Pelley and the Silvershirt Legion: A Case Study of the Legion in Washington State, 1933-1942," Ph.D. Dissertation, CUNY, 1992, esp. pp. 174-181. See also Ridgeway, op. cit., pp. 62-64.
19. Hoppes, "William Dudley Pelley," p. 177.
20. Ibid., pp. 179-182.
21. Ibid., pp. 137-140.
22. Ibid., pp. 182-206.
23. Ibid., pp. 117-118.
24. See *Life* magazine, "Fascism in America: A Cell in Chehalis" and "Seattle Hears a Silver Shirt 'Isms' Lecture," March 6, 1939, pp. 62-63. Also included in the "Fascism in America" articles was a sidebar titled, "These Are Men to Watch," which included a strikingly posed silhouette portrait of Frank W. Clark of Tacoma, "a house painter by trade, [who] helped organize the Bonus March on Washington. As William Dudley Pelley's right-hand man, he organized Silver Shirts, headed Pelley's Christian Party. He now pursues his hatred of 'Communist Capitalistic Jews,' the C.I.O. and the Federal Reserve as head of his own National Liberty Party."
25. Hoppes, "William Dudley Pelley," pp. 207-255.
26. Ibid., pp. 85-102.
27. See Page Smith, *Democracy on Trial: The Japanese American Evacuation and Relocation in World War II* (New York: Simon and Schuster, 1995), pp. 410-412, and David A. Neiwert, "Eastsiders: The Rise and Fall of a Japanese-American Community," unpublished manuscript, 1997, pp. 210-216.
28. See Melvin Rader, *False Witness* (Seattle: University of Washington Press, 1969), esp. pp. 156-165.
29. See William L. Dwyer, *The Goldmark Case: An American Libel Trial* (Seattle: University of Washington Press, 1984).
30. For a discussion of Rice's motivations, see James A. Aho, *This Thing of Darkness: A Sociology of the Enemy* (Seattle: University of Washington Press, 1994), pp. 35-47. See also Ronald K. Fitten, "In plea deal, Rice finally gets life for '85 slayings," *Seattle Times*, May 28, 1998.
31. See Benjamin R. Epstein and Arnold Forster, *The Radical Right: Report on the John Birch Society and Its Allies* (New York: Vintage Books, 1967), pp. 73-90.
32. Ibid., pp. 199-200.
33. See Charles Jeffrey Kraft, "A Preliminary Socio-Economic and State Demographic Profile of the John Birch Society," Political Research Associates, Somerville, Mass., April 10, 1992.
34. See Epstein and Forster, op. cit., p. 201.
35. See the *Salt Lake Tribune*, March 21, 1963.
36. See Aho, *The Politics of Righteousness*, p. 115.
37. See Brigham Young's remarks about the Constitution in *Journal of Discourses* 2:182.
38. It is probably worth observing that British Israelism emerged from the same socio-religious milieu that gave birth to Mormonism. An early Victorian fascination with divining the fate of the "Lost Tribes of Israel" produced several competing theories, one of which formed the basis for British Israelism. Mormon church founder Joseph Smith seems to have been drawn to the theory that American Indians were actually the descendants of the Lost Tribes, a theory he appears to have drawn primarily from a text written by a Vermont preacher, *View of the Hebrews; or the Ten Tribes*

of Israel in America, published in 1823. See Fawn M. Brodie, *No Man Knows My History* (New York: Alfred A. Knopf, 1945), pp. 45-49.

39. See The Book of Mormon, especially the books of Alma and Helaman.

40. See Robert Welch, *The Politician* (Belmont, Mass.: John Birch Society, 1959).

41. See Aho, *The Politics of Righteousness*, pp. 123-27.

42. Despite all this—or perhaps because of it—Hansen still was a top candidate for the Populist Party vice-presidential spot in 1988 alongside former Klansman David Duke, but he was beaten out for the job by none other than Colonel James "Bo" Gritz, who would soon assume his own presence on the Idaho landscape. For more on Hansen's connections to Moon, see Rick Shaughnessy, "George Hansen develops ties to Rev. Moon's church," *Twin Falls Times-News*, Sept. 16, 1984, p. A1.

43. A review of the *Daily Bee* archives during the author's tenure as editor there revealed no appearance of Mathews' letters, which were the object of some discussion among the various editors of the small local newspaper chain then owned by publisher Pete Thompson of Sandpoint. The editor of the *Priest River Times*, Thompson's weekly in the logging town of Priest River, received even more of Mathews' letters than I did, and he occasionally ran them, as did the editor of the *Times'* cross-river competitor, the *Newport Miner*.

44. See Dick Cockle, "Founder of Posse Comitatus decries radicals, lives quietly," *Oregonian* (Portland), June 23, 1985, p. B1.

45. See Henry L. Beach, *The Blue Book,* 1972. See also the Posse Comitatus pamphlet, "Our One Supreme Court of the sovereign people/Common Law Court/united states of America," published by United Sovereigns of America, Del City, Okla.

46. See Devin Burghart and Robert Crawford, "Guns and Gavels: Common Law Courts, Militias and White Supremacy," Coalition for Human Dignity, Portland, Ore., 1996, pp. 2-3.

47. See Ridgeway, op. cit., pp. 129-133.

48. See Aho, *The Politics of Righteousness*, p. 57.

49. See J. Harry Jones, *The Minutemen* (New York: Doubleday, 1969), pp. 129-130.

50. See "Suspected Plot Leader, Minuteman Spoke Here," *Seattle Post-Intelligencer*, Jan. 27, 1968, p. B1.

51. See J. Harry Jones, op. cit., pp. 252-256, 280-283.

52. See Jack Jarvis, "Bomb Gang vs. FBI: No Contest," and "Plotter 'Not Minuteman,'" *Seattle Post-Intelligencer*, Jan. 27, 1968, pp. A1, B1.

53. See J. Harry Jones, op. cit., pp. 398-404.

54. See Kevin Flynn and Gary Gerhardt, *The Silent Brotherhood: Inside America's Racist Underground* (New York: Free Press, 1989), p. 23, and Kenneth S. Stern, *A Force Upon the Plain: The American Militia Movement and the Politics of Hate* (New York: Simon and Schuster, 1996), p. 49.

55. See Aho, *The Politics of Righteousness,* p. 57.

56. Ibid., especially footnote 68 (Chapter 2), p. 273.

57. See Flynn and Gerhardt, op. cit., p. 63.

58. Ibid., pp. 29-37.

59. See James Coates, *Armed and Dangerous: The Rise of the Survivalist Right* (New York: Hill and Wang, 1987), pp. 44-48.

60. See Flynn and Gerhardt, op. cit., p. 41.

61. See Chapter 10 for a more detailed account of the Kahl case.

62. Ibid., p. 89.

63. See Coates, op. cit., pp. 110-118.

64. Flynn and Gerhardt, op. cit., p. 98. See also the court testimony of Charles Ostrout, one of the eight, during the trial of The Order members in 1985: *Oregonian*, Oct. 30, 1985.

65. Ibid., pp. 100-102.

66. See court testimony, *Seattle Times*, Oct. 25, 1985.

67. See Flynn and Gerhardt, op. cit., pp. 217-272.

68. See "Aryan band linked to million-dollar robberies," *Seattle Times*, Dec. 11, 1984.

69. Interview, *San Francisco Examiner*, Dec. 16, 1984.

70. Interview, *Seattle Times*, Dec. 11, 1984.

71. See Joni Balter, "Family members don't fault FBI in Mathews death," *Seattle Times*, Dec. 10, 1984, p. A10.

72. See "Human Rights Violation," Idaho Human Rights Commission, July 28, 1982, filed by Alleconda Fort.

73. A catalogue of these events appears in a report by the U.S. Department of Justice, "Bigotry and Violence in Idaho," Government Printing Office, Washington, D.C., 1986, pp. 3-4. The 1980 "Nigger" letters are from the author's personal recollections and are mentioned in Flynn and Gerhardt, op. cit., p. 63.

74. The rise of the Kootenai County Human Rights Task Force has been documented several times elsewhere, perhaps most thoroughly and thoughtfully in Chapter 10 of James Aho's *This Thing of Darkness*, "A Community With Heart," pp. 152-175. Aho makes a strong case for KCHRTF as a model response to the activity of hate groups, and his analysis is generally correct. The author notes, however, some disagreement with Aho's assertion that: "There is nothing in the political culture of northern Idaho permitting us to have predicted that its population would favor liberalism over a right-wing agenda" (p. 171). To the contrary, the author believes the progressive current in northern Idaho until the 1980s was pronounced and far stronger than the conservative undertow that appears to dominate the scene there now; this progressive current remains a major force in northern Idaho's politics and culture.

75. See "No leads in bombing of priest's home," by Theresa Goffredo and D.F. Oliveria, *Spokesman-Review* (Spokane), Sept. 17, 1986, p. A1.

76. Author's interviews with Bill Wassmuth, September 1996.

77. See "Bombs jolt Coeur d'Alene," by David Newman, *Spokesman-Review*, Sept. 30, 1986, p. A1.

78. See "Agents converge on home," by Theresa Goffredo and David Newman, *Spokesman-Review*, Oct. 2, 1986, p. A1; "Similar powder used in five bombs," by Bill Morlin and David Newman, *Spokesman-Review*, Oct. 4, 1986, p. A1; "Judge told of FBI tracking Aryans," by Bill Morlin, *Spokesman-Review*, Feb. 3, 1987, p. A1; "Judge hears claim Aryan was a killer," by Bill Morlin, *Spokesman-Review*, Feb. 4, 1996, p. A1; "Trial ends abruptly when Idaho couple plead guilty," by Bill Morlin, and "Alleged bomber charged with Clark Fork killing," by Dean Miller, *Spokesman-Review*, Feb. 5, 1987, pp. A1, A9.

79. See Jess Walter, *Every Knee Shall Bow: The Truth and Tragedy of Ruby Ridge and the Randy Weaver Family* (New York: Regan Books, 1995), pp. 108-109.

80. See court testimony, and *Seattle Times*, "Neo-Nazi plot aimed at gay bar, FBI says," May 15, 1990, p. A1, and "3 convicted in Capitol Hill disco plot," Oct. 19, 1990, p. E3.

81. See Walter, op. cit., pp. 74-87.

82. Ibid., pp. 48-50.

83. Ibid., pp. 74-80.

84. This was a key point in Randy Weaver's eventual trial. Weaver claims Fadeley approached him about providing the guns. Fadeley claims the contrary. The jury believed Weaver, but there is evidence in their later taped conversations—the first meeting where the subject arose was not taped—that Fadeley's version is correct. See court testimony, *United States v. Randy Weaver and Kevin Harris*, U.S. District Court, Boise, Idaho, 1993.

85. See Dean S. Miller, "Boundary Sheriff Candidate Opposed to Mixed Marriages," *Spokesman-Review*, May 12, 1988, p. B3.

86. John and Randy Trochmann vehemently deny they or David Trochmann were involved in any gun-running activity (author's interview, February 1996). The Trochmanns were never charged in the investigation.

87. See especially Bill Morlin's definitive early account of the Weaver case, "Feds have fugitive 'under our nose,'" *Spokesman-Review*, March 8, 1989.

88. From the author's interviews with ATF agents.

89. The question of who fired first remains a controversy. At the trial, Harris claimed the marshals fired first. The marshals claimed Sammy fired first. Evidence introduced in the trial suggested the first shot fired was the one that killed the dog, followed by Sammy Weaver's shot directed at one of the marshals.

90. The story of the Weaver standoff has been told many times. Factually accurate accounts can be found in Aho, *This Thing of Darkness*, pp. 50-67, which also offers a strong sociological analysis of the affair; in Stern, op. cit., pp. 19-34; and in Morris Dees' *Gathering Storm: America's Militia Threat* (New York: HarperCollins, 1996), pp. 9-27. The most thorough and complete account is Jess Walter's *Every Knee Shall Bow*. Several newspapers provided daily coverage of the standoff, as did the Associated Press; the most authoritative and complete coverage can be found in the *Spokesman-Review*, Aug. 22-Sept. 3, and Walter's analysis, "Warning Shot: The Lessons of Ruby Ridge," *Spokesman-Review*, Nov. 19, 1992.

91. See the interview with Sara Weaver by Jess Walter, "Sara feared for father," *Spokesman-Review*, Sept. 1, 1992.
92. See Christopher Hanson, "Weaver's shot killed son, marshals say," *Seattle Post-Intelligencer*, Sept. 16, 1995, p. A1.

Chapter 4 / MOM and Apple Pie

1. See the court documents filed in Sanders County under Trochmann's name: a felony warrant from Wright County detailing Trochmann's alleged role in hiding his daughter, Brandi Trochmann, from the girl's mother, Janis Henning, filed Jan. 24, 1992; and Trochmann's own "Affidavit of Facts" in the case, filed Feb. 24, 1992, plus another affidavit from Trochmann regarding his complaints over his arrest, filed Feb. 7, 1992.
2. Author's interviews with Janis Henning.
3. See "Public Notice: Positive Identification of John Ernest Trochmann," filed Jan. 27, 1992, in Sanders County, Montana.

Chapter 5 / Roundup

1. See Bill Morlin, "Tax woes launched freeman leader's militancy," *Spokesman-Review* (Spokane), March 28, 1996, p. A7.
2. *Lewiston Morning Tribune.*
3. See Bill Morlin, op. cit.
4. Ibid.
5. See Joe Kolman, "Reputation grew in '80s," *Billings Gazette*, March 28, 1996, pp. 1C-3C.
6. Ibid.
7. The filing of liens and other court documents is an old Posse Comitatus tactic. See Devin Burghart and Robert Crawford, "Guns and Gavels: Common Law Courts, Militias and White Supremacy," Coalition for Human Dignity, Portland, Ore., 1996, pp. 1-7. See also Mark Pitcavage's account of Posse filings in "Every Man a King: The Rise and Fall of the Montana Freemen," a document on the Ohio historian's "Militia Watchdog" World Wide Web page (http://www.militia-watchdog.org/freemen.htm) and ostensibly a chapter in a forthcoming book on the Patriot movement.
8. See "Skurdal's behavior tied to Wyoming accident," *Casper Star-Tribune*, April 2, 1996.
9. See Pitcavage's "Every Man a King," p. 4.
10. Ibid. Corroborated by author's interviews.
11. See J. Todd Foster, "Provider becomes protester," *Spokesman-Review*, March 26, 1996, p. A7.
12. Ibid.
13. Author's interview with Keven Entzel, Dan Petersen's stepson (though not the stepson whose property was confiscated), Yellowstone County Courthouse, March 28, 1996. See also Ibid.
14. The best discussion of the dynamics of heroism in this area is in James A. Aho's *This Thing of Darkness: A Sociology of the Enemy* (Seattle: University of Washington Press, 1994), pp. 23-34.
15. See Skurdal's "Our de jure county government pursuant to the Word of Almighty God," an "affidavit" dated Jan. 8, 1995.
16. Interview with Murnion. See also the "Timeline" by Murnion detailing the dates of his confrontations with the Freemen.
17. Interview with Paul G. Smith, Musselshell County Sheriff, Feb. 13, 1996.
18. Interview with Charlie Phipps, Garfield County Sheriff. This threat is consistent with Posse Comitatus' prescription for sheriffs who fail to uphold the "supreme law": "He shall be removed by the Posse to the most populated intersection of streets in the township and at high noon be hung by the neck, the body remaining until sundown as an example to those who would subvert the law."
19. See Clair Johnson, "After their own brush with the law, couple stays out of the Justus Township clash," *Billings Gazette*, April 14, 1996, p. A1.

Chapter 6 / A Destroying Wind

1. This account is drawn from the author's conversations with FBI officials and from news accounts of the attacks. See especially the reporting in the *Spokesman-Review* (Spokane), "Robbers bomb Valley offices," p. A1 (a staff report); "S-R employee saw pair plant bomb, leave in van," by Gita

Sitaramiah, April 2, 1996, p. A6; "Bomb note suggests Aryan ties," by Bill Morlin, "Bombers failed to destroy van after robbery," by Adam Lynn, p. A1, and " 'Phineas Priests take name from Bible," by Jeanette White and Bill Morlin, p. A7, April 3, 1996; and "Valley bank robbers shouted slogans about freemen, FBI says," by Bill Morlin, April 24, 1996, p. B1. See also local television news accounts of the robberies, especially KHQ-TV's footage and interviews.

2. Flyer distributed by The Ekklesia of the King Christian Assembly in Jacksonville, Florida.

3. See accounts of the trial and the conviction in the Jackson, Miss., *Clarion-Ledger*, October-November 1991, and the *Atlanta Constitution*, "A Beginning: Racist killings reopened," by Peter Scott and Andy Miller, Nov. 3, 1991.

4. See James Ridgeway's account of the Phineas Priesthood in "Arms and the Men: Are Far Right Militia Cells Using Robbery to Fund Their Cause?" *The Village Voice*, May 9, 1995.

5. See David Fallis, "Robberies tied to supremacists," *Tulsa Tribune*, Jan. 28, 1992.

6. See *The Jubilee*, July/August 1994 issue.

7. For a more complete discussion of the links between white supremacists and anti-abortionists, see Loretta J. Ross's reports on the subjects: "Using the Bible to justify killing," *Baltimore Sun*, Aug. 8, 1994, p. 7A; and "Anti-abortionists and white supremacists make common cause," *The Progressive*, October 1994, cover story.

8. See the photograph appearing in the July 1995 issue of *Ms.*, accompanying a story on anti-abortion activists.

9. See "The Northwest Imperative: Documenting a Decade of Hate," Coalition for Human Dignity, Portland, Ore., 1994, p. 2.25.

10. Ibid., p. 3.14.

11. See Richard Kelly Hoskins, *Vigilantes of Christendom* (Lynchburg, Va.: Virginia Publishing, 1990), pp. 54-55, 58, 60-66, 230-233, 240-248.

12. Ibid., pp. 326-330, 337, 352-356.

13. Hoskins is clearly a Christian Identity believer. Not only is his theory of Jewish predation consistent with Identity beliefs, he also endorses the concept that white people are the true children of Israel; see esp. the footnote on p. 435 of *Vigilantes*.

14. Ibid., p. 433.

15. Ibid., pp. 417-442.

16. Ibid., pp. 409-410.

17. Ibid., pp. 361-364, 444, 416-417.

18. Ibid., pp. 407-409.

19. Author's interview with undercover informant, August 1998.

20. See the *Atlanta Constitution*, op. cit.

21. Ibid.

22. *Tulsa Tribune*, op. cit.

23. See the *Columbus Dispatch* coverage of the Aryan Republican Army, Jan. 12-20, 1996, and Morlin's "Bomb note has Aryan ties," *Spokesman-Review*, April 3, 1996.

24. See "Suicide rocks white supremacist probe; death: body of admitted member of right-wing group of bank robbers is found in jail cell," *Los Angeles Times*, July 13, 1996.

25. See Ridgeway, op. cit.

26. See Morlin's and Jeanette White's *Spokesman-Review* piece, " 'Phineas Priests take name from Bible," April 3, 1996, p. A7. Morlin also described his interview with Lindholm to the author.

27. See Bill Morlin, "On the move with the militia," *Spokesman-Review*, Dec. 3, 1995, p. H1.

28. See Bill Morlin, "A common bond," *Spokesman-Review*, Dec. 3, 1995, p. H4.

29. See the report, "AntiGay/Lesbian Violence, Victimization and Harassment in 1995," National Gay and Lesbian Task Force Policy Institute, Washington, D.C.

30. See Sharon Lem, " 'Perfect life' ended: N.Y. abortion MD first fatality of Remembrance Day sniper," *Ottawa Sun*, Oct. 25, 1998. Also see Carolyn Thompson, "Sniper Kills N.Y. Abortion Provider," Associated Press, Oct. 24, 1998.

31. See Martha Irvine, "Shannon warns fellow abortion foes in letters," Associated Press, June 16, 1995 (Portland dateline).

32. See the report, "AntiGay/Lesbian Violence, Victimization and Harassment in 1995," National Gay and Lesbian Task Force Policy Institute, Washington, D.C. See also the NGLTF press release of Jan. 9, 1998, "NGLTF urges greater federal action to curb hate crimes."

33. Nothing in the Phineas Priesthood's literature—either in Hoskins' book or in other pamphlets and flyers—explicitly suggests that burning down black churches would be an appropriate way of enforcing God's law. *Vigilantes* does, however, condemn the mainstream churches, calling them Judeo-Christianity, a corruption of true Christianity. Hoskins refers to a church that committed three "capital crimes," including allowing "strangers" to teach from its pulpit and allowing interracial marriage ceremonies in its sanctuary. Hoskins does not elaborate on what the appropriate punishment to be administered by Phineas Priests would be, but considering their designation as crimes befitting a death sentence, it is not hard to envision a violent outcome. A mere arson attack might well be, in the mind of a Phineas Priest, an appropriate way to gently discourage what Hoskins calls "anti-Christian" activity—and black churches, beyond fitting the description of "Judeo-Christianity," are widely regarded in Christian Identity circles as hotbeds of civil-rights work (or "race-mixing") and a home for welfare "parasites."

34. The Coalition for Human Dignity's reports refer to a person's inclusion in the Phineas Priesthood as an "honorary status."

35. This analysis is based in large part on the description of the methods of "proving your place" that occurs within the militant segments of the radical right given to the author by a former member of the Covenant of the Sword and the Arm of the Lord.

36. See Andrew Ross' interview with Reynolds, "Fire in the House of God," SALON Online Magazine (http://salon1999.com), June 10, 1996. Reynolds reiterated the connection with Beam's strategy in a later interview with the author.

37. See Brian Coddington, Bill Morlin and Mike Prager, "Bombers strike again," *Spokesman-Review*, July 13, 1996, p. A1.

38. See Ward Sanderson, "Witness had seen it all before," *Spokesman-Review*, July 13, 1996.

39. See Kim Barker, "Bomb, notes make clinic operators wary," *Spokesman-Review*, Dec. 31, 1996, p. A4.

40. See Bill Morlin, "Informers add detail to bombings," *Spokesman-Review*, Dec. 21, 1996.

41. See Bill Morlin and Jeannette White, "Bombing suspects arrested," *Spokesman-Review*, Oct. 9, 1996, and Kim Barker, "Suspects drew parade of agents," *Spokesman-Review*, Oct. 16, 1996.

42. See Jeannette White, "Raid livens things up in Union Gap," *Spokesman-Review*, Oct. 10, 1996.

43. See Nickolas K. Geranios, "Three Idaho men charged in bombings, robberies," Associated Press report, and Bill Morlin, "Three charged with bombings and robberies," *Spokesman-Review*, Oct. 10, 1996.

44. See Kevin Keating, "Detonators, bomb gear confiscated," *Spokesman-Review*, Oct. 11, 1996.

45. See Bill Morlin, "Terror suspect a nuclear expert," *Spokesman-Review*, Oct. 27, 1996.

46. See Kim Barker, "Bombing suspects held without bail," *Spokesman-Review*, Oct. 17, 1996.

47. Ibid.

48. See Craig Welch, "Witness discounts revolutionary motives," March 12, 1997; "Differences in robbery MOs debated," March 14, 1997; "FBI tries to tie suspect to bomb notes," March 18, 1997, *Spokesman-Review*.

49. See Craig Welch, "Suspect denies bombings, robberies," *Spokesman-Review*, March 26, 1997.

50. See Kelly McBride and Kim Barker, "Juror ready for deadlock from start," *Spokesman-Review*, April 3, 1997.

51. See Patrick Heald and KPBX-AM radio news staff, "Inland Journal" news report, May 8, 1997. See also Bill Morlin, "FBI lacks evidence, says Barbee," *Spokesman-Review*, May 9, 1997.

52. See Bill Morlin, "FBI arrests fourth bombing suspect," *Spokesman-Review*, March 14, 1997.

53. See Bill Morlin, "Fourth suspect hid out in Stevens County," *Spokesman-Review*, March 18, 1997.

54. See Craig Welch, "Three guilty in Valley bombings," July 24, 1997; and Bill Morlin, "Bombing trial jurors say it was hard to convict," July 25, 1997, *Spokesman-Review*.

55. See Bill Morlin, "Bomber sounds warning before 55-year sentence," *Spokesman-Review*, Dec. 3, 1997.

Chapter 7 / Almost Heaven

1. See news accounts of Gritz's appearance in Jordan, especially Clair Johnson's and Matt Bender's reporting for the *Billings Gazette*, April 23–May 2, 1996, James Brooke's reporting for the *New York Times*, and NBC television coverage of Gritz's news conferences. Other information for this section

was compiled from interviews with residents of Jordan (notably Joe and Charlotte Herbold, owners of the Hell Creek Bar) and others who were present during Gritz's stay.

2. Center for Action Newsletter, May 1996.

3. See Gritz's autobiographical book, *Called to Serve*.

4. See the text of Gritz's speech in The Monitor, the newsletter of the Center for Democratic Renewal, December 1991. It is worth observing that even though this text comes from a tape recording of Gritz's talk, Gritz later tried to claim he knew nothing about Identity Christianity when he attended Peters' gatherings. In an interview with David Johnson of the *Lewiston Morning Tribune* published June 12, 1995, Gritz said of his trips to Peters' gatherings with his wife, Claudia: "Neither one of us knew anything about Pete Peters. Neither one of us had ever heard about Identity Christians in our lives. We had no idea of this concept of mud people and that kind of crap."

5. Author's interview with Gritz, Nov. 10, 1994. All quotes from Gritz in this section, except where noted, are from this interview.

6. *The Jubilee*, April/March 1992.

7. Center for Action Newsletter, vol. 3, no. 8 (March 1994), p. 2.

8. Gritz is mistaken. Joseph uttered those words while surrendering near the U.S.-Canada border in north-central Montana. Joseph and other chiefs had led the rebelling faction of the Nez Perce tribe through the Clearwater country shortly after defeating the U.S. Cavalry at White Bird Hill at the beginning of the Nez Perce War, and it is the Nez Perce tribe which chiefly occupies the Indian reservation in the Kamiah area. However, Joseph's band primarily inhabited the area now known as the Wallowas in northeastern Oregon.

9. It is worth observing that the aquifer to which Gritz's friend probably was referring was the massive southern Idaho aquifer, which fits the description. No such massive aquifer exists in the region where Almost Heaven is situated, although the region receives so much annual precipitation that the water tables lying beneath Gritz's land probably will never run dry.

10. See ABC's 20/20 report of March 1995.

11. See David Johnson, "Discontent arises in Bo Gritz's camp," *Lewiston Morning Tribune*, Feb. 5, 1996.

12. See David Johnson, "Covenant Community," *Lewiston Morning Tribune*, June 11, 1995, p. A1.

13. See Bo Gritz, "Turnabout: I give options, not recommendations," *Lewiston Morning Tribune*, July 5, 1995.

14. See David Johnson, "Bo's found his home," *Lewiston Morning Tribune*, July 15, 1996.

15. There are several news accounts of the Connecticut arrest. For a definitive account, see Jonathan Rabinovitz, "A Militia Leader's New Battle With Authority," *New York Times*, Oct. 2, 1996. See also Gritz's press releases through the Center for Action dated Oct. 1 and 9, 1996, outlining his involvement and participation. David Johnson also wrote a localized update on the case for the *Lewiston Morning Tribune*, Oct. 30, 1996, titled "Bo Gritz proclaims his, son's innocence."

16. See "Gritz can be a substitute teacher after criminal charge is resolved," *Lewiston Morning Tribune*, Nov. 23, 1996.

17. See Kevin Sack, "Bomb Suspect's Whereabouts and Possible Motives Are Mysteries," *New York Times*, Feb. 28, 1998.

18. See Chapter 9 for more on Holland's case, while Chapter 10 includes details of Sellner's case.

Chapter 8 / A Hard Land

1. See Tim Woodward, "Old West sheriff hanging up his star," *Idaho Statesman* (Boise), Feb. 11, 1996, pp. 1A-10A.

2. Ibid.

3. See Jack Olsen's true-crime version of the Claude Dallas story, *Give a Boy a Gun: A True Story of Law and Disorder in the American West* (New York: Dell Publishing, 1985), pp. 24-54. Olsen's account, while written for a general audience, is factually quite accurate. The same information can be found in coverage of the saga in the *Idaho Statesman*, and in other accounts as well—in *Time* and *Rolling Stone* magazine, for instance. The author was involved as an editor in coverage of the case while working at the *Lewiston Morning Tribune* and the *Twin Falls Times-News*.

4. Ibid., pp. 170-186.

5. See "Affidavit of Default," filed Nov. 21, 1995, in Owyhee County, Idaho, by David Dean Hawks.

6.   See "Asservation of Invalid Citation," filed Nov. 28, 1995, in Owyhee County, Idaho, by David Dean Hawks.

7.   See "Non-Statutory Abatement," filed Nov. 28, 1995, in Owyhee County, Idaho, by David Dean Hawks.

8.   See "Courts of Justice: Common Law Venue—Supreme Court," legal notice published Monday, Dec. 4, 1995, in the *Idaho Press Tribune*, p. 6B.

9.   See Jim Lynch, "We Are the Law," *Spokesman-Review* (Spokane), Sunday, Dec. 3, 1995, p. H9.

10. Ibid.

11. See Michelle Cole, "'Courts of Justice' spring up across state," *Idaho Statesman*, Dec. 14, 1995, p. 1A-12A.

12. See "On Common Law Procedure: Part One, The Abatement," by John William and Joe Allen, and "Book Two: Why Call a Constitutional Common Law Jury," by Velma R. Griggs.

13. Ibid., p. 43.

14. See Michelle Cole, op. cit.

15. See "Entry of Default, State of the Forum," in the *Idaho Statesman*, Sept. 15, 22, and 29, 1995.

16. Author's interviews with Wasden, November 1996.

17. See Associated Press, "Madison sheriff beefs up security," Dec. 2, 1995; published on that date in the *Idaho Statesman*, p. 3B.

18. See David Foster and Arlene Levinson, "Beyond the Bombing: Militias, Government, and the Politics of Frustration," Associated Press, Friday, May 19, 1995.

19. Ibid.

20. See Liz Wright, "Activists take on court system," *Twin Falls Times-News*, Feb. 11, 1996, p. 1A.

21. See Associated Press report, "Man arrested after trying to 'arrest' reporter, manager," April 15, 1996; published in the *Idaho Statesman*, April 16, 1996, p. 2B.

22. See Karen Tolkkinen, "Tax refusal brings prison sentence," *Twin Falls Times-News*, May 21, 1996, p. 1A.

23. See Frank E. Lockwood, "Since bombing, militiaman softens words," *Twin Falls Times-News*, July 1995, p. A1. Lockwood, who has done the most thorough examination of Sherwood in the press, cites a report in the *London Sunday Telegraph*, Feb. 19, 1995, as the source of this quote.

24. From March 2, 1995, Associated Press report on Boise militia meeting with Otter.

25. There are two official federal reports on the Teton Dam case: "Report to U.S. Department of the Interior and State of Idaho on Failure of Teton Dam," by the Independent Panel to Review Cause of Teton Dam Failure, published December 1976 by the U.S. Government Printing Office; and "Teton Dam Failure," a report of the Subcommittee on Energy Research and Development of the Committee on Energy and Natural Resources, United States Senate, published June 1977 by the U.S. Government Printing Office. I have summarized their findings; though these reports do not say pointedly that the bureaucrats in charge of the project are directly to blame for the dam's failure, I believe this is a fair assessment of the substance of their findings. See also the author's series of newspaper articles, "Teton Dam: Five Years Later," published in the *Blackfoot Morning News*, June 5-10, 1981.

26. See Barry Siegel's examination of the small-town culture of Rexburg through the lens of the case of Dr. LaVar Withers, a well-known gynecologist and LDS Church member in good standing who was charged with a range of molestation crimes resulting from claims made by various former patients during his 30-year practice in Rexburg, but which did not emerge publicly until after he announced his retirement. "Everyone knew; no one talked: Doctor fondled patients for three decades," *Los Angeles Times*, Dec. 1, 1996.

27. See James Aho's description of the Madison County Posse Comitatus activity in *The Politics of Righteousness: Idaho Christian Patriotism* (Seattle: University of Washington Press, 1990), pp. 44-47.

28. See, for instance, the "Notice of Felony" filed by Gail Mason on Nov. 30, 1995, and the "Courts of Justice, Common Law Venue, Supreme Court" document filed by Emerson J. Mason on Nov. 9, 1995.

29. See Lockwood's *Twin Falls Times-News* column of July 1995, "Militia membership shrinks under IRS gaze," p. C1.

30. See Erhart's letter, Aug. 1, 1995, in the *Idaho Statesman*.

31. See Frank Lockwood, "Ranks of USMA—Growing or shrinking?" *Twin Falls Times-News*, August 1995, p. B1.

32. See Frank Lockwood, "Sherwood: Militiaman of many names," *Twin Falls Times-News*, Sept. 1995, p. A1.

33. On the contrary, according to Lockwood, Sherwood told a television station, for instance, that he had been assigned to air artillery in the Army and was a Surface Warfare Officer ship driver in the Navy. Navy officials, Lockwood reports, say his only assignment at Newport was in Officer Candidate School.

34. See Dan Yurman, "Predicting the Future at the Blackfoot Fair," *Western Lands Gopher Service*, Sept. 9, 1995.

35. See Dan Yurman, "Militia Men Don't Ride These Rails No More," *Western Lands Gopher Service*, Sept. 10, 1995.

36. From "Militia Association Quietly Folds," Associated Press, Sept. 11, 1996.

37. See "Common Law Group Threatens to Arrest Officials," Associated Press, Sept. 11, 1996, Boise dateline.

38. See Liz Wright, "Tax protester dies, some believe from poison in prison," *Twin Falls Times-News*, Oct. 18, 1996, p. 1A.

Chapter 9 / Bitterroot

1. Interview with George Corn, Ravalli County Prosecutor, Dec. 29, 1996.

2. See Mark Pitcavage, "Joe Holland, Calvin Greenup, and the Anti-Tax Militia," The Militia Watchdog (World Wide Web site: http://www.militia-watchdog.org/holland.htm), March 28, 1996.

3. *Ravalli Republic*, Sept. 22, 1993. Cited in "The Northwest Imperative: Documenting a Decade of Hate," Coalition for Human Dignity, Portland, Ore., 1995, p. 2.9.

4. See "Sheriff not ready to go after fugitives," *Columbian* (Vancouver), March 9, 1995.

5. See David Foster, "Confrontations Spread as Gun-Packing Militias Flourish in Montana," Associated Press, May 24, 1995.

6. See Kenneth S. Stern, *A Force Upon the Plain: The American Militia Movement and the Politics of Hate* (New York: Simon and Schuster, 1996), p. 87.

7. "Proclamation" published as paid advertisement, *Ravalli Republic*, Jan. 20, 1995.

8. For a thorough recounting of the events of April 12, see Patricia Sullivan, "Rebels face felony charges: Court papers say Greenup and others were plotting to execute Ravalli County officials," *Missoulian*, May 5, 1995.

9. See Michael Downs, "Angry Callers Threaten Commissioner's Pet Burro," *Missoulian*, April 27, 1995.

10. See John Stromnes, "Greenup gives up his guns," *Missoulian*, June 2, 1995.

11. See Michael Moore, "Militia leader thinks it over, pleads guilty," *Missoulian*, Dec. 8, 1995.

12. See Justin Smith, "Rebel justice: Judge hands defiant extremist a stiffer sentence," *Missoulian*, Dec. 15, 1995.

Chapter 10 / High Noon

1. There have been several accounts of Gordon Kahl's martyrdom, but the most detailed and exhaustive is James Corcoran's *Bitter Harvest: Gordon Kahl and the Posse Comitatus-Murder in the Heartland* (New York: Penguin Books, 1990). See also Kevin Flynn and Gary Gerhardt, *The Silent Brotherhood: Inside America's Racist Underground* (New York: Free Press, 1989), pp. 87-88, and James Ridgeway, *Blood in the Face: The Ku Klux Klan, Aryan Nations, Nazi Skinheads, and the Rise of a New White Culture* (New York: Thunder's Mouth Press, 1995), pp. 138-143.

2. For a discussion of the pressures that the ATF faced after Waco, see Erik Larson, "ATF Under Siege," *Time*, July 24, 1995.

3. See John Stromnes, "Sellner given life in prison," *Missoulian*, Oct. 17, 1996, p. A1.

4. For an assessment of law-enforcement techniques in handling the Patriots in western Montana, see Erik Cushman, "Showdown versus slowdown: Montana law enforcement struggles to decide how to take on the armed right wing," *Missoula Independent*, March 23, 1995.

5. See "Freemen had fears of deadly injections," Associated Press, June 16, 1996. A portion of the tapes, recorded by Duke, were played as part of a Dateline NBC report on the same date.

6. See "Freeman standoff leaves young farmer unable to plant," Associated Press, May 27, 1996.

7. See transcript, "The John Bryant Show," American Freedom Network, May 23, 1996.

8. See "Four people leave ranch as FBI tightens screws," Associated Press, June 6, 1996.

9. See "Mom says Freemen will see that the law has betrayed her," Associated Press, June 6, 1996.

10. See the Usenet exchange between Lyons and Alabama militia leader Mike Vanderboegh of Wednesday, Aug. 21, 1996 (address: UnreConfed@aol.com, sent to dyurman@world.std.com). Vanderboegh is a militia leader vehemently opposed to the presence of neo-Nazis within the movement, and his fiery exchanges with Lyons accused him of being in cahoots with Nazis in the government who actually set off the Oklahoma City bomb.

11. See Morris Dees, *Gathering Storm: America's Militia Threat* (New York: HarperCollins, 1996), pp. 64-65.

12. See Louis Sahagun and Richard A. Serrano, "FBI found rightists key to ending Montana standoff," *Los Angeles Times*, June 16, 1996.

13. See Clair Johnson, "Clark visits jail, returns to the ranch," *Billings Gazette*, June 12, 1996.

14. This account appears in Kirk Lyons' recounting of the surrender to a *Tulsa Tribune* reporter, but was corroborated by others present at the end. See Julie DelCour, "Freemen negotiator aids the underdog," *Tulsa World*, June 23, 1996.

Chapter 11 / End of the Universe

1. Information obtained from U.S. Department of Defense records.

2. See Paul deArmond and Jim Halpin, "Steal This State," *Eastsideweek*, June 24, 1994, which discusses the broad overlaps between western Washington's anti-urban "county-secessionist" movement, the Wise Use movement and the Christian Patriots. DeArmond attended and videotaped the meeting, which was sponsored by the Coalition for Land Use Education, a property-rights group. CLUE's leader, Skip Richards, was the Republican candidate for the Washington State Senate from the 40th District in 1996, but lost after his advocacy of Patriot leaders was publicized.

3. See Kathie Durbin, "The Battle for Okanogan County," *Seattle Weekly*, Jan. 11, 1995.

4. See "Sheriff recalls Labor Day 'invasion,'" Associated Press, Feb. 10, 1995.

5. See "The Dignity Report," Coalition for Human Dignity newsletter, winter 1995.

6. See Leo Mullen, *Bellingham Herald*, April 26, 1995.

7. See "For community, we must have truth," letter to the editor, *Bellingham Herald*, May 3, 1995.

8. See "Welcome To Ask the Sheriff: Questions for Dale Brandland," brochure distributed at Whatcom County Citizens for Liberty meeting, May 19, 1995.

9. See Paul deArmond, "To Soothe Their Fears," a Public Good report containing a transcript of the May 19 meeting. Public Good is a World Wide Web site operated by deArmond, a Bellingham political researcher, located at the address http://nwcitizen.com/publicgood/.

10. From a transcript of a taped conversation between Marlin Mack and confidential witness Ed Mauerer, see Tape No. 10 introduced as evidence in *United States v. John Pitner et al.*, pp. 17-18.

11. See testimony of Brian Smith, Feb. 17, 1996, in *United States v. John Pitner et al.*

12. See transcript of Tape No. 1, presented as evidence in U.S. District Court during the 1997 trial in *United States v. John Pitner et al.*, pp. 74-77, 100, 118.

13. See Cathy Logg, "Granges say no to militia group," *Bellingham Herald*, Jan. 17, 1996.

14. See transcript of Tape No. 3, presented as evidence in U.S. District Court during the 1997 trial in *United States v. John Pitner et al.*, pp. 50-98.

15. See transcript of Tape No. 4, presented as evidence in U.S. District Court during the 1997 trial in *United States v. John Pitner et al.*, pp. 41-42.

16. See Susan Byrnes, "Local bomb suspects had shared ideas," *Seattle Times*, Aug. 2, 1996.

17. See Chapter 4.

18. See Devin Burghart and Robert Crawford, "Guns and Gavels: Common Law Courts, Militias and White Supremacy," Coalition for Human Dignity, Portland, Ore., 1996.

19. See Nina Shapiro, "The Militia Bust," *Eastsideweek*, Aug. 7, 1996, p. 22.

20. See Jim Christie, "A Movement Spreading," *Washington Journal*, April 18, 1996, p. 11.

21. See Jim Christie, "Kitsap County Case Links Defendants To Mercer Island 'Common Law Court,'" *Washington Journal*, April 11, 1996.

22. See Susan Byrnes, op. cit.

23. See Cathy Logg, "Whatcom nearly had militant showdown, leader says," *Bellingham Herald*, April 4, 1996.

24. See transcript of Tape No. 12, presented as evidence in U.S. District Court during the 1997 trial in *United States v. John Pitner et al.*, p. 70.

25. See transcript of Tape No. 13, presented as evidence in U.S. District Court during the 1997 trial in *United States v. John Pitner et al.*, p. 10.

26. Ibid.

27. See transcript of Tape No. 58, presented as evidence in U.S. District Court during the 1997 trial in *United States v. John Pitner et al.*, p. 88.

28. See transcript of Tape No. 51, presented as evidence in U.S. District Court during the 1997 trial in *United States v. John Pitner et al.*, pp. 36-38.

29. See transcript of Tape No. 54, presented as evidence in U.S. District Court during the 1997 trial in *United States v. John Pitner et al.*, p. 3.

30. See transcript of Tape No. 55, presented as evidence in U.S. District Court during the 1997 trial in *United States v. John Pitner et al.*, pp. 47-49.

31. See transcript of Tape No. 81B, presented as evidence in U.S. District Court during the 1997 trial in *United States v. John Pitner et al.*, pp. 3-5.

32. See transcript of Tape No. 94, presented as evidence in U.S. District Court during the 1997 trial in *United States v. John Pitner et al.*, pp. 3-6.

33. See transcript of Tape No. 101A, presented as evidence in U.S. District Court during the 1997 trial in *United States v. John Pitner et al.*, pp. 153-194.

34. See transcript of Tape No. 102, presented as evidence in U.S. District Court during the 1997 trial in *United States v. John Pitner et al.*, pp. 121-126.

35. See transcript of Tape No. 182, presented as evidence in U.S. District Court during the 1997 trial in *United States v. John Pitner et al.*, pp. 29-32.

Chapter 12 / Home of the Brave

1. See Clair Johnson, "Judge boots loud Jacobi out of court," *Billings Gazette*, June 21, 1996.

2. See Clair Johnson, "Freeman threatens magistrate in court," *Billings Gazette*, June 26, 1996.

3. See Clair Johnson, "Not true! Freemen rumors fly," *Billings Gazette*, July 24, 1996.

4. See "Affidavit: Protective Order of Release," filed by LeRoy Schweitzer at the Yellowstone County jail, July 17, 1996.

5. See Clair Johnson, "Judges reject 'bunkum' by Freemen backers," *Billings Gazette*, Aug. 13, 1996.

Afterword / Ash on the Sills

1. The professor was the late Dr. Eugene Reed, who taught German at the University of Idaho for over 20 years before retiring in 1986. None of Reed's former colleagues recall him retelling this anecdote, but his service time in the U.S. Army—1944-46—is consistent with the story.

2. See Roger Griffin, *The Nature of Fascism* (London: Routledge, 1991), pp. 26-27. Griffin, an Oxford historian, is widely credited as one of academia's foremost experts on fascism, and this text is the definitive examination of its sources. In Chapter 2, "A New Ideal Type of Generic Fascism," Griffin appears almost to be describing the Patriot movement two years before it arose, particularly in his description (on pp. 36-37) of populist ultra-nationalism, which he says "repudiates both 'traditional' and 'legal/rational' forms of politics in favour of prevalently 'charismatic' ones in which the cohesion and dynamics of movements depends almost exclusively on the capacity of their leaders to inspire loyalty and action . . . It tends to be associated with a concept of the nation as a 'higher' racial, historical, spiritual or organic reality which embraces all the members of its ethical community who belong to it."

3. Particularly noteworthy is Karen E. Hoppes, "An Investigation of the Nazi-Fascist Spectrum in the Pacific Northwest: 1924-1941," a 1983 Master's Thesis at Western Oregon State College. Writes Hoppes (pp. 10-12): "Finally, the link with fundamental Christianity establishes the uniqueness of American fascism. The majority of fascist groups justified their existence by their desire to change the United States into a Christian society . . . The relationship between the religious identity of these groups and their political demands can be shown by a careful survey of their rhetoric. The Christian fascist does not distinguish between the application of the terms anti-Christ, Jew and Communist. Neither does he distinguish between Gentile and Christian." Hoppes particularly notes Silvershirts leader William Dudley Pelley's sermons arguing that "Christians of the

United States must put the issue of conniving Jewry above all other issues and treat with it drastically. This means a pogrom . . . of colossal proportions." Observes Hoppes: "For the Christian fascist, this up-and-coming war against the Jew would result in the founding of a new moral community—a Christian America. This community would tie itself to Christian ethics and Christian structure, as interpreted by these Christian fascists. Thus, the link with Christianity provided a unifying element for the membership in American fascist organizations. Members not only prayed with their comrades, but fought the 'Christian' battle against the anti-Christ Jew. This gave them a surpassing sense of righteousness. Most of the membership came from the evangelical styled churches, with each Christian fascist group claiming to be under the umbrella of Christian thought and action."

4. See Stanley G. Payne, *Fascism: Comparison and Definition* (Madison: University of Wisconsin Press, 1980), pp. 5-21. However, it should be noted that Payne concludes (pp. 161-176) that fascism is almost purely a European phenomenon and thus it is "doubtful that a typology derived from European fascism can be applied to non-European movements or regimes with any specificity." Others, including Ernst Nolte and Renzo de Felice, insist on fascism's European nature, and even Walter Laqueur, in *Fascism: Past and Present* (Oxford: Oxford University Press, 1996) treats fascism as purely European in nature. All of these, however, overlook the substantial body of work establishing the existence of fascist movements outside of Europe, particularly in North America. As Griffin, op. cit., observes: "First and foremost, fascism is not intrinsically a European phenomenon, nor did 'the fascist era' conveniently end in 1945 . . . Palingenetic ultra-nationalism as we have ideal-typically defined it can draw on any number of raw ingredients, local or imported, religious or secular." (p. 147).

5. See especially James A. Aho, *This Thing of Darkness: A Sociology of the Enemy* (Seattle: University of Washington Press, 1994), whose thesis explores the dynamic of hero-vs.-enemy as central to the radical right and the Patriot movement.

6. See also Umberto Eco, "Eternal Fascism," *New York Review of Books*, June 22, 1995. Eco is an artist/philosopher with personal experience regarding fascism. While he is considered one of Europe's leading intellects, he is not technically an expert on the subject, but his summary of traits accurately reflects the same traits discussed by sociologists and historians, and it is useful for our descriptive purposes here.

7. Author's correspondence with Pitcavage. See endnote 4 above for a brief discussion of other theories of fascism.

8. See Griffin, op. cit., pp. 56-66, 85-101. Griffin also notes that fascism by its nature as a political ideology predictively becomes a travesty of its original ideals when it attains power (pp. 26-27).

9. Author's interview with Berlet, September 1998.

10. Two recent instances will illustrate this propensity. Emmett Clark, one of the Montana Freemen engaged in an armed standoff in Jordan for 81 days, was by all accounts of his neighbors a no-nonsense, taxpaying citizen who ran a financially sound ranch for years and was esteemed by his neighbors and family as hard-working and down-to-earth. He was persuaded to join the Freemen by his son, Richard, at which point his family observed a dramatic change in his personality and behavior, culminating with his arrest on a range of federal charges. Another recent instance occurred in Washington state, when eight Patriots were arrested by the FBI on a range of weapons charges, notably constructing pipe bombs. Among those arrested was John Pitner, president of the Washington State Militia, who had been adamant in all his public appearances and interviews that his organization was strictly "defensive" in nature and was designed more as a regional Block Watch. Pitner, too, had up until his involvement with the Patriots been an apparently normal citizen, and his organization emphasized recruitment of followers from the mainstream. But in the wake of the arrests, the author through interviews with former participants discovered that the group had begun secretly engaging in paramilitary training exercises in addition to the bomb-building sessions. One member specialized in converting semi-automatic guns into illegal fully automatic weapons.

11. Gilles Stockton, "Where did the Freemen come from?" broadcast commentary, High Plains News Service, for the Northern Plains Resource Council, May 10, 1996.

12. See Lawrence J. Saalfield, *Forces of Prejudice in Oregon, 1920-1925* (Portland, Ore.: University of Portland Press/Archdiocesan Historical Commission, 1984), pp. 17-18.

Index